BECOMING ARAB

Becoming Arab

THE FORMATION OF ARAB IDENTITY IN THE MEDIEVAL MIDDLE EAST

YOSSEF RAPOPORT

PRINCETON UNIVERSITY PRESS
PRINCETON & OXFORD

Published by Princeton University Press

41 William Street, Princeton, New Jersey 08540
99 Banbury Road, Oxford OX2 6JX

press.princeton.edu

GPSR Authorized Representative: Easy Access System Europe - Mustamäe tee 50, 10621 Tallinn, Estonia, gpsr.requests@easproject.com

Library of Congress Cataloging-in-Publication Data

Names: Rapoport, Yossef, 1968– author.
Title: Becoming Arab: the formation of Arab identity in
the Medieval Middle East / Yossef Rapoport.
Description: Princeton: Princeton University Press, 2025 |
Includes bibliographical references and index.
Identifiers: LCCN 2024054614 (print) | LCCN 2024054615 (ebook) |
ISBN 9780691210636 (hardback) | ISBN 9780691276311 (ebook)
Subjects: LCSH: Arabs—Middle East—Ethnic identity. | Clans—Middle
East—History. | Villages—Middle East—History. | Middle East—History. |
BISAC: HISTORY / Middle East / Arabian Peninsula | SOCIAL SCIENCE
/ Ethnic Studies / Middle Eastern Studies
Classification: LCC DS38.3 .R36 2025 (print) | LCC DS38.3 (ebook) |
DDC 956/.004927—dc23/eng/20241213
LC record available at https://lccn.loc.gov/2024054614
LC ebook record available at https://lccn.loc.gov/2024054615

British Library Cataloging-in-Publication Data is available

Editorial: Fred Appel, James Collier, and Tara Dugan
Production Editorial: Theresa Liu
Production: Erin Suydam
Publicity: William Pagdatoon and Charlotte Coyne
Copyeditor: Leah Caldwell

Jacket image: © Bodleian Libraries, University of Oxford

This book has been composed in Minion Pro

Printed in the United States of America

10 9 8 7 6 5 4 3 2 1

In Memory of Mohammed Abuqamar

(July 2002, Gaza—December 2023, London)

CONTENTS

ILLUSTRATIONS

Figures

Maps

Table

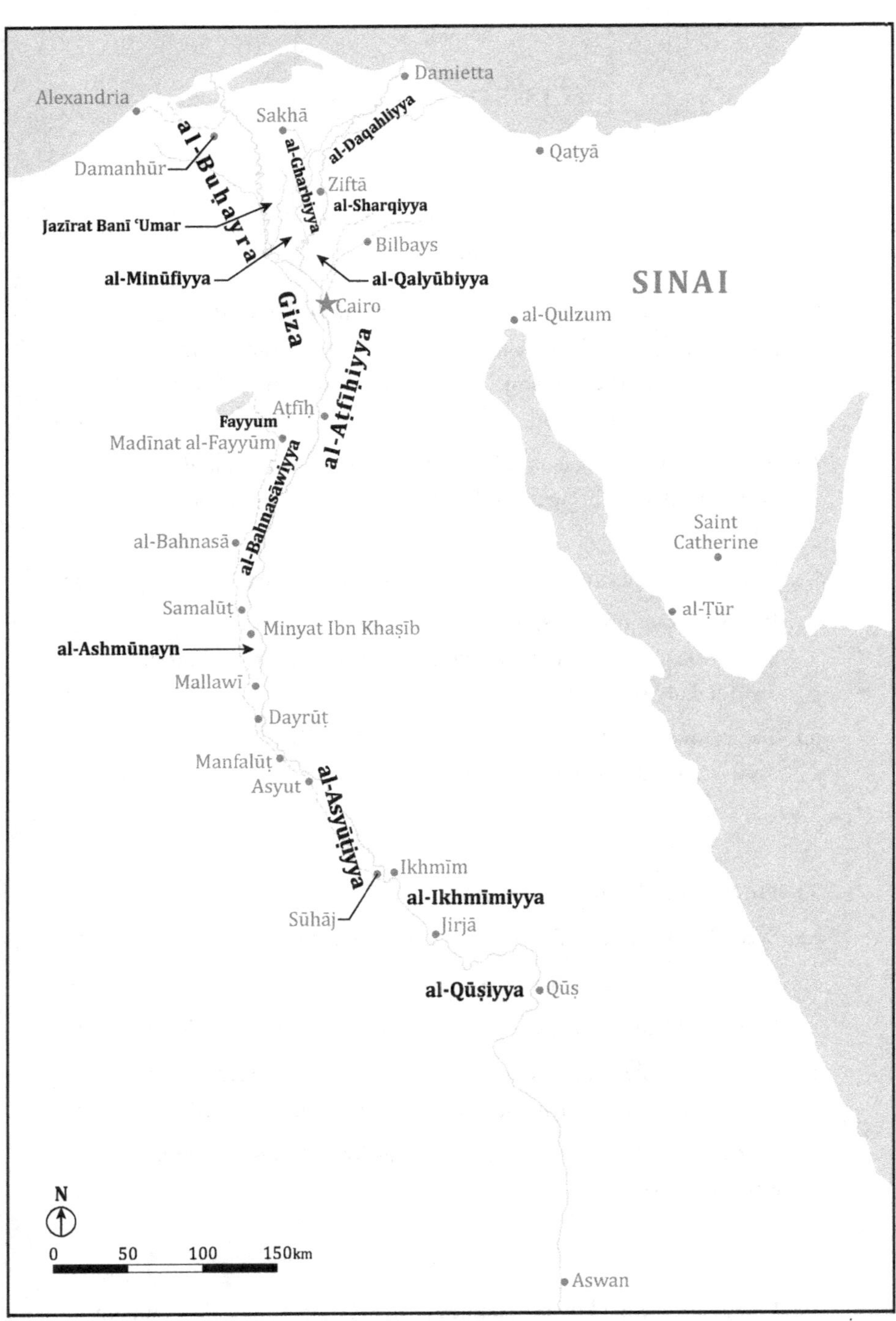

MAP 0.1. Provinces of Egypt circa 750/1350.

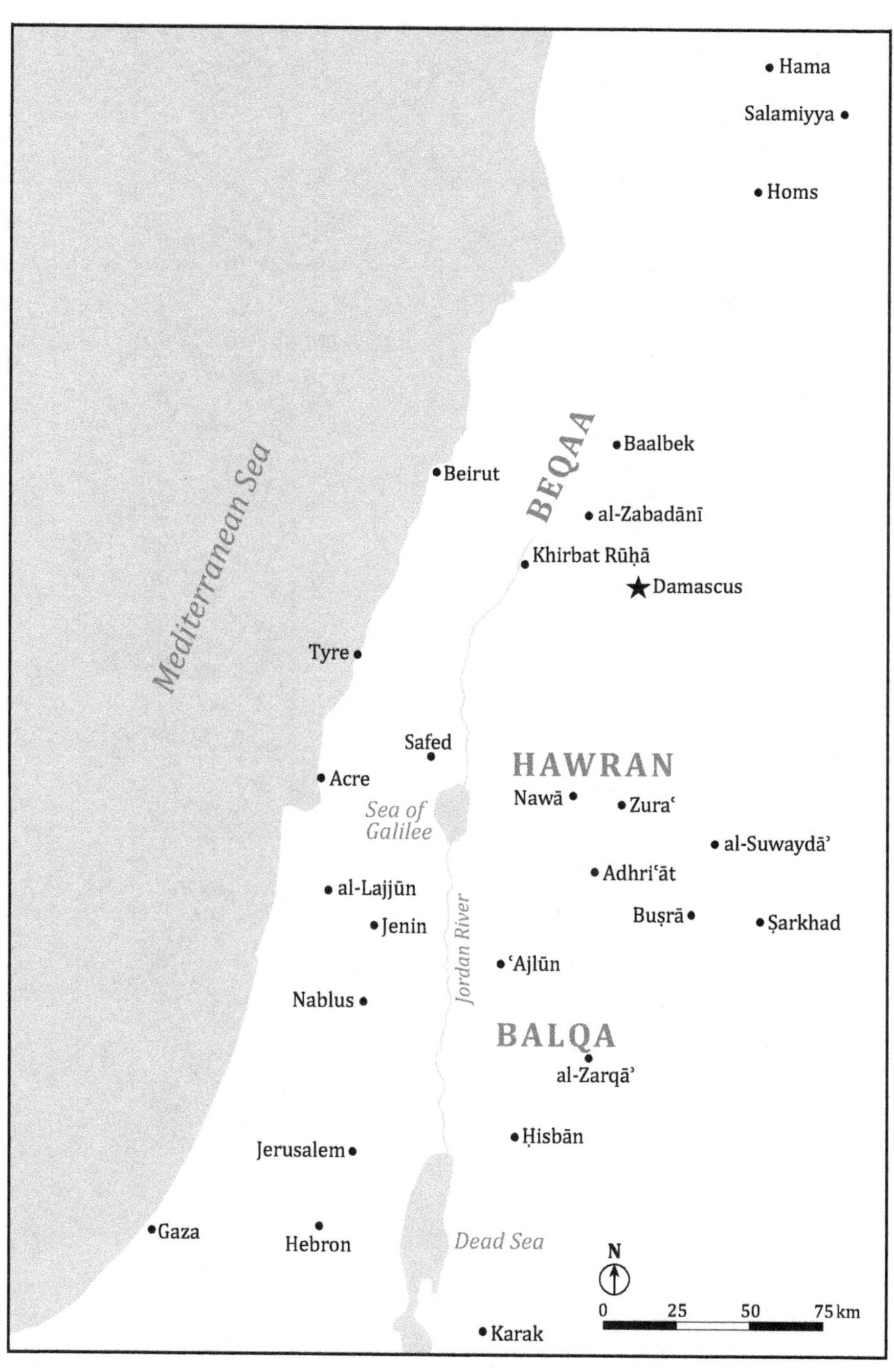

MAP 0.2. Syria, Palestine, and Transjordan circa 750/1350.

BECOMING ARAB

Introduction

OVER THE COURSE of the later Middle Ages, from the eleventh to the fifteenth centuries, the villagers of Egypt, Palestine, and Greater Syria turned Arab. This does not mean they began to speak Arabic, a linguistic change that had mostly taken place already by the end of the ninth century, three centuries after the Arab Conquest. Rather, men and women of Middle Eastern villages came to see themselves as members of village clans and as descendants of tribal migrations from the Arabian Peninsula. They adopted manners of speech and dress they considered distinctly Arab, told each other epic stories about the great Arab heroes of pre-Islamic and early Islamic Arabia, and began eating with a new type of pottery utensils. They revolted against the government and the tax collectors under the banner of Arab solidarity, and they fought neighboring villagers in the name of multi-clan tribal confederacies such as Qays and Yaman. This was a transformation not limited to rural elites or to marginal areas on the edge of the desert. In Upper and Lower Egypt, in Palestine, Transjordan, and the Beqaa, Muslim villagers invariably came to view themselves as members of clans and confederacies that harked back to the Arabian Peninsula and to the dawn of the Islam. This formation of Arab village clans throughout Egypt and Greater Syria was the most important development in the history of the Middle Eastern countryside in the Islamic period, and the process left its mark on what we recognize as Arab and Bedouin cultures and identities today.

The shift toward Arab village clans began by the late tenth or early eleventh century and took about two centuries to complete. Our first evidence of this change comes from villages of southern Fayyum in Middle Egypt, where documents dated 1015 to 1070 show the swift rise of new village elites who carried Arab clan names and acted as official protectors of Christian Coptic villages and monasteries. This local phenomenon in the Fayyum coincided with the sudden emergence of Arab dynasties in cities of the Jazīra, Palestine, and Greater Syria, most of them lasting until the 1060s. This early phase of Arab village elites and Arab dynasties ended with the major economic and agricultural crisis of the late eleventh century, which led to mass desertion of village sites in the 1060s and 1070s.

During the twelfth century, Arab identities took root further down village societies, with Arab village clans coalescing around the nuclei of the Arab elites who emerged in the eleventh century. The most visible expression of this filtering down of Arab identities is the appearance of the term *ʿurbān*, a novel and nonclassical derivative of the name *ʿarab*. The ʿurbān was the collective name for the armed elements of the now widespread Arab village clans, and they became the dominant force in the Egyptian countryside during the late Fatimid period. In twelfth-century Palestine, held at that time by the crusader Latin Kingdom, we do not find ʿurbān but rather a new class of poor and mobile Muslim peasantry called *beduini*. From 1150 onward, Latin charters refer to the recruitment of *beduini* for work on rural estates, and they even provide a detailed account of a named clan of these *beduini* inhabiting a village near Nablus.

By the end of the twelfth century, following the demise of both the Fatimid empire and the Latin Kingdom, Arab clans had been formed in most villages of Egypt, Palestine, and Greater Syria. This is borne out by fiscal, administrative, and legal sources from the Ayyubid (1187–1250) and Mamluk (1250–1517) eras. In al-Nābulusī's cadastral survey of the Fayyum, composed in the 1240s, nearly all villages and hamlets were identified with either an Arab or a Berber clan, usually one clan per village. A set of documents from the Islamic court of Jerusalem dated to the first decade of the fourteenth century similarly shows Arab clans inhabiting all the Muslim-majority Palestinian villages represented in the sample. In both Ayyubid Fayyum and Mamluk Palestine, the village clans were led by a new class of headmen, who acted as co-guarantors for the payment of the collective land-tax and were responsible for law and order in their own villages and in the surrounding area. Beyond these two well-documented examples, further evidence of the spread of Arab villages clans comes from a series of genealogical treatises composed by Mamluk-era bureaucrats, who mapped clans and tribal confederacies throughout the agricultural regions of Egypt and Greater Syria, with the authors explicitly identifying Arab clansmen as sedentary villagers. In fact, from the thirteenth century onward, whenever administrative and legal sources allow us to zoom in on a Muslim-majority village with any level of detail, we find it inhabited by an Arab clan.

Arab village clans were not merely administrative rubrics imposed from above. Rather, these identities were enthusiastically endorsed by members of village communities. Biographical dictionaries from the twelfth century onward contain dozens of notices for rural scholars who boasted of Arab lineages. Shihāb al-Dīn Aḥmad al-Qalqashandī, the well-known Mamluk bureaucrat who was born in 1355 in the village of Qalqashanda (present-day Qarqashanda) in al-Qalyūbiyya, proudly recounts that his native village was solely inhabited by the Banū Badr clan of the Fazāra confederacy. The autobiography composed by the jurist and theologian Burhān al-Dīn al-Biqāʿī, born 1406, states that the inhabitants of his native village of Khirbat Rūḥā in the Beqaa belonged to the Banū Ḥasan clan and claimed descent from the Prophet's Companion Saʿd b. Abī Waqqāṣ.

The localized village clans formed wider territorial confederacies, and these became a vehicle for political and military mobilization. Throughout the Fatimid, Ayyubid, and Mamluk eras, confederacies of village clans were part of provincial administration and were expected to contribute a set number of cavalry for royal campaigns. These tribal confederacies then came to be the backbone of a series of major Arab uprisings in Upper Egypt, beginning with the rebellion of the Sharīf Ḥiṣn al-Dīn Ibn Thaʿlab in the 1250s and culminating with al-Aḥdab's rebellion of the 1350s. Multivillage confederacies could also be used for the violent resolution of disputes among the peasantry. In fourteenth-century Syria and Transjordan, rural people, partly nomadic but mostly sedentary, organized themselves into Qays and Yaman coalitions that regularly fought each other over land and resources. By the end of the fourteenth century, the Qays and Yaman came to ally themselves with opposing factions of the Mamluk ruling elite.

Late medieval Arab identity was expressed by a novel set of cultural markers: Arab speech, Arab dress, and Arab historical memory. From the twelfth century onward, Arab speech was identified by the /g/ vocalization of the letter *qāf*, a feature still retained in many dialects known today as "Bedouin." This distinctive vocalization is not attested as a distinctive marker of Arab identity in the Umayyad or Abbasid periods, and the cultural significance attached to it from the twelfth century onward coincided with the spread of the Arab village clans. Another novel cultural marker was Arab headgear; from the twelfth century onward, one dressed like an Arab by tucking the loose ends of the turban under the beard or chin or drawing them over the face and mouth as *lithām* face-veil. This manner of tying the turban under one's chin was uniformly used to identify Arab types in book illustrations of this period. Finally, Arab history and Arab values found their expression in the new genre of popular epics (*siyar*), most famously those of ʿAntar, Banū Hilāl and Dhāt al-Himma. The earliest of the genre, Sīrat ʿAntar, is first attested in twelfth-century Iraq, but it became extremely popular in Ayyubid and Mamluk Egypt and Syria, carried by popular storytellers who frequented both town and village. It is in this period that the heroic deeds of these Arab pre-Islamic or early Islamic heroes became a staple of village culture, so much so that the Mamluk bureaucrat al-Qalqashandī drew on his intimate knowledge of the ʿAntar epic to augment the status of his own village clan. Like the cultural significance attached to the Arab pronunciation of *qāf* and to the Arab headgear, popular epics dealing with Arab history appeared around the twelfth century as means of expressing and consolidating the new Arab identities of peasant communities.

The depth of the transformation of Middle Eastern villages is tangibly demonstrated by the material remains found in archaeological excavations and surveys. Starting from the 1100s, handmade geometrically painted wares appeared in great numbers in villages of Greater Syria and Palestine. This process accelerated in the thirteenth century, so that distinctly decorated handmade wares dominate nearly all village assemblages of Greater Syria and Palestine in the Ayyubid and Mamluk periods, and they became the main tableware of villagers for the rest of the Middle Ages. These handmade wares, known as HMGP, unexpectedly supplanted a long tradition of fine-bodied, wheel-thrown wares found in the same villages throughout the early Islamic and pre-Islamic periods. This shift in pottery went under the radar of the narrative sources and is known to us only from the archaeological record of excavations in Greater Syria. Archaeology of Mamluk-era village sites in Egypt is practically nonexistent, but extensive finds of brittle and coarse wares from Mamluk Cairo suggest the possibility of similar ceramic shifts in the Egyptian countryside. Given the absence of any textual reference, we do not know that Syrian HMGP wares were viewed as "Arab." Nonetheless, the dramatic shift in rural pottery in Greater Syria is concrete evidence of the break between the earlier Islamic centuries and the late medieval period. The material culture of village societies was fundamentally transformed in the space of a couple of centuries, precisely coinciding with formation of Arab village clans.

The shift to Arab village clans in late medieval Egypt and Syria was driven by two main factors. First, following mass rural conversions to Islam in the eleventh and twelfth centuries, Muslim villagers adopted Arab identity and the prestige associated with it to enhance their social status. A wide range of documentary, narrative, and material evidence shows that the agricultural countryside of Egypt and Syria remained mostly Christian—and non-Arab—at least until 1000 CE. Coptic names dominate in the abundant papyri that have come to us from Abbasid and early Fatimid Middle Egypt, and churches and monasteries were still very common in the countryside of tenth-century Palestine. Muslims became a majority in the Egyptian countryside only by the end of the twelfth century, as shown by quantitative analysis of demographic datasets from the time of the Arab Conquest up to the middle of the nineteenth century.[1] Greater Syria witnessed similar processes of Islamization following the defeat of the Latin Kingdom of Jerusalem in 1187. Claiming Arab lineage was a byproduct of this momentous rural conversion to Islam. As Tamer el-Leithy has shown for late medieval Egypt, new Coptic converts were subject to suspicion by existing Muslim elites and were therefore forced to erase the traces of their conversion.[2] For peasants of Egypt and Syria, a claim to Arab lineage concealed the recent Christian past of their communities and replaced it with the merits accorded to the Arabs by the Islamic tradition: the nation of the Prophet and the native speakers of the language of revelation.

Peasants also used claims to Arab lineage as means of distinguishing themselves from the urban-based Turkic military elites who dominated Egypt and Syria since the middle of the thirteenth century. By 1260, following their victory over the Mongol army in ʿAyn Jalut in Palestine, the *mamlūk* military corps unified Egypt and Syria under the reign of Sultan Baybars, the founder the Mamluk sultanate. The ruling elite of the Mamluk sultanate was mostly composed of former military slaves recruited in Central Asia and the Caucasus, and contemporary Arab authors called the regime the "Dynasty of the Turks." Fifteenth-century observers, both European and local, reported that the Arabs of the countryside saw themselves as superior in lineage and in Islam to the Turkish-speaking elites of former military slaves who ruled over them. They also reported that this sense of Arab superiority mobilized and justified the earlier major rural rebellions that rocked Upper Egypt between 1250 and 1350. Peasant use of Arab lineage as a claim for status was therefore not restricted to the new converts, but it possessed currency long after the rural landscape has been comprehensively Islamized.

The second major reason for the spread of village clans was the twelfth-century introduction of the *iqṭāʿ* landholding regime, which transformed the peasantry from landowners into tenants. In earlier Islamic centuries, private ownership of land was common, as is attested by many preserved Egyptian land-sale documents up to the middle of the eleventh century.[3] By the beginning of the twelfth century, however, more and more land fell under the iqṭāʿ regime, whereby the state asserted ownership over arable land and then awarded military officers rights to collect taxes from the villages assigned to them, rights known as iqṭāʿ grants. The use of iqṭāʿ grants in Egypt and Syria began under the later Fatimids but was then extended and systematized by Saladin, and it became the hallmark feature of the political economy of the Ayyubid and Mamluk sultanates, at least until the end of the fourteenth century. With the consolidation of the iqṭāʿ system, the peasantry of Egypt and Syria were transformed into tenants, known as *fallāḥūn*, who cultivated state-owned lands under collective leases. The collective annual leases were contracted by groups of headmen, who acted as co-guarantors for the cultivation of the land and the payment of taxation.[4] In response to this dramatic change of the landholding regime, peasants formed pervasive clan structures, coalescing around the village headmen and ensuring that access to tenancy rights was open only to members of the community. Deprived of any long-term right over the arable lands they were cultivating, and always at risk of being uprooted at the end of their leases, peasants came to be defined not by the land they cultivated but by the lineage to which they belonged.

Thus, like the term *fallāḥ* itself, Arab village clans were born out of the iqṭāʿ regime. The fallāḥūn and the Arab village clans were two facets of the same social and legal framework of landless tenancy. The term fallāḥ indicated the fiscal status of all tenant cultivators who were due to pay land-tax. It appears in administrative and fiscal contexts and refers to the collective of cultivators in a given village under the leadership of headmen, whether Muslim or Christian, Arab or non-Arab. The term indicated submission and the burden of taxation. But once a Muslim fallāḥ rode a horse, carried arms and dressed like an Arab, he became part of the ʿurbān; conversely, captive Arab rebels were identified as fallāḥūn of individual holders of iqṭāʿ. The ʿurbān are regularly presented as the champions and defenders of the fallāḥūn, and the two groups are often mentioned together. Not every fallāḥ was a member of the armed ʿurbān, but any Muslim fallāḥ could become one. And practically all grain-producing Muslim fallāḥ cultivators appear to have turned Arab, through the clans formed around their village headmen and through their claims to Arab lineage. Being a fallāḥ was at this time devoid of cultural significance; the near absence of representations of fallāḥūn in late medieval Arabic literature is remarkable, and the term is also missing from medieval European accounts. In late medieval literary representations, the fallāḥ was overshadowed by his Arab identity, empowered by clan-based social organization and by the cultural currency of Arab-ness.

The pervasive formation of Arab village clans was a result of the major religious, economic, and political changes that took place around the twelfth century: mass rural conversion, domination by Turkic military elites, and the consolidation of the iqṭāʿ landholding regime. It is unlikely, on other hand, that the omnipresence of Arab village clans in Egypt and Syria was down to the settling down of nomadic tribal groups. A full-scale population replacement, by which nomadic groups pushed out the existing non-Arab and mostly Christian peasantry, is neither plausible nor backed by sufficient textual and material evidence. Admittedly, there are narrative reports of mass movements of tribal groups during the tenth and eleventh centuries, and there is archaeological evidence for settlement expansion in Egypt and Syria during the thirteenth century. But most village sites throughout Egypt and Greater Syria remained in the same locations as they had been in previous centuries, and village names have also remained largely unchanged. Only a minority of villages took on names of the Arab clans who inhabited them, and that usually occurred only by the fourteenth century. Moreover, the preliminary results of pioneering ancient DNA analysis have yet to pick up any significant changes in the ethnic composition of Egypt and Syria in the medieval period.[5] Rather, the assumption that Arab village clans emerged from the migration and settling down of nomads is based on a dogmatic association of tribes and clans with nomadic societies, as well as on the stories villagers were telling about themselves. As peasant communities reordered themselves as Arab clans, a memory of migration became a constituent component of their identity; claims to Arab lineage required an origin story of settlement on the site of the current village.[6]

A Feudal Economy

The society of the late medieval Middle East was agrarian, and its economy was primarily based on the extraction of surplus from subsistence cultivators. In that, it was one variant of a world system of feudal economies that characterized medieval societies from Britain to China, as recently described by Chris Wickham.[7] Moreover, the consolidation of the iqṭāʿ landholding regime in the twelfth century meant a shift away from the centralized state taxation that characterized the Abbasid empire in the earlier Islamic centuries. The central conflict that permeated rural society in late medieval Egypt and Syria revolved around the extraction of agricultural surplus by lords—i.e., officers of the military ruling elite—who were awarded the rights to collect taxes and rents from the villages assigned to them. As in all feudal economies, lords needed to justify their rights to take that surplus through moral and legal claims that presupposed some form of shared values with the peasantry, and this always required some collaboration from local village elites. A feudal economy, in the sense ascribed to it by Wickham, serves here the fundamental analytical framework for explaining the rise of Arab village clans in late medieval Egypt and Syria.

This broad model needs to be adjusted to the specific historical and geographical conditions of the Middle East. Under the iqṭāʿ regime, *military* officers were assigned rights of tax collection from villages, but they did not reside locally and were not usually involved in the provision of justice and public order in the countryside. As a result, villagers were required to develop their own modes of internal political organization and customary legal systems to regulate most aspects of communal life. Moreover, the loose control of lords over the villages assigned to them, compounded with the relative scarcity of water in Middle Eastern contexts, meant that rural groups constantly competed for limited resources. While this was true elsewhere, and nowhere were peasants ever free of internal conflict,[8] the relative absence of direct intervention by either state or lords led to structural and endemic violence among Egyptian and Syrian cultivators, as reported by nearly all late medieval observers.

Village clans emerged in this context of vertical struggle against extraction by lords, as well as horizontal competition against other rural groups, both sedentary and nomadic. Clans provided internal political organization in the absence of state presence, protection against other rural groups, and a platform for resistance against taxation. Village clans are known from extensive ethnographic fieldwork from Morocco to the Arabian Peninsula.[9] A particularly rich example comes from ethnographic studies of the peasantry of modern Yemen, where most of the settled villagers self-identify as members of village clans and regional tribal confederacies. In Yemen, the village clan involves protection of shared territory, mobilization of labor for communal projects, and adherence to shared mechanisms of conflict resolution and to a set of cultural values. Village clans are bound together by cooperative activities, proximity, and selective kinship, which assimilates daily life relations into affective bonds. There is ample evidence that Yemen has been dominated by such tribal structures for over a millennium. The idiom of common descent fulfills essential social functions among the settled peasantry and is not a remnant of some distant migration.[10]

Ayyubid and Mamluk clans and tribal confederacies were also administrative categories, borne out of the interaction of state and rural societies and in response to the need of lords for local collaboration. In Morton Fried's conceptualization, tribal confederacies—"secondary tribes"—emerge as tools of provincial administration and control but often transmute into a nexus of resistance.[11] This is especially true of regional, multi-clan confederacies, which are often a product of contact with state power.[12] In a well-documented study of Ottoman Transjordan in the late nineteenth century, Nora Barakat demonstrated that the officially appointed headmen actively employed and maintained the tribe as a power field through which to contest taxation and resource distribution; it was through their position that the tribe became a foundational category of rural administration.[13] In the Ayyubid and Mamluk contexts, the key figures in this process were the village headmen appointed by local iqṭāʿ holders and the leaders of the territorial confederacies who were routinely selected by the state bureaucracy. Clans and tribes were thus embedded in the administration of the countryside. As in other historical contexts, late medieval Egypt and Syria territorial confederacies were bound with the Fatimid, Ayyubid, and Mamluk states, whether as provincial troops, tax-collecting elites, or the platforms for armed uprisings.

Becoming Arab combines Fried's model of bureaucratic tribes with Frederik Barth's social constructionist approach, where awareness of common ancestry is a consequence of shared interests, not their cause. In this model, genealogy belongs to a derivative category of "cultural stuff"—together with language, food, and dress—developed in order to maintain the boundaries of the group against outsiders.[14] As ethnography demonstrated, village clan genealogies were not a record of actual historical events: "A society that appears to be constrained by the past . . . is in fact generating the very genealogy through which it explains the present."[15] This approach has been widely applied to modern Middle Eastern kinship groups, where genealogy is malleable and routinely manipulated.[16] In Islamic societies, Arab ancestry has a special value, and a claim for Arab ancestry is a common mechanism of integration by many ethnic groups in the contemporary Islamic world, from Africa to Southeast Asia.[17]

Historians of medieval Islam have extended this insight into a critical reading of genealogical literature. In his *Roots of Arabic Genealogy*, Zoltán Szombathy argued that the genealogical tradition was a product of the early Islamic period and served as a skeleton onto which all later manufactured family pedigrees could easily be attached.[18] In *Imagining the Arabs*, Peter Webb contended that books of genealogy, such as the foundational genealogical text by Ibn al-Kalbī (d. 204/819), were vehicles to produce an Arab collective identity among the urban elites of the Abbasid empire. According to Webb, these genealogical texts imagined a pre-Islamic Arab ethnic nation that had never existed.[19] Webb's analysis is focused on literary texts and offers a top-down model of ethnogenesis. *Becoming Arab*, on the other hand, examines the elaboration of an Arab identity at the village level—from the bottom up—when groups of peasants were not creating a new ethnic group but rather negotiating their way into an existing one.

The clearest example of the power of Arabic genealogical science to generate new identities is that of the Berbers of Islamic North Africa. As pointed out by Ramzi Rouighi in his *Inventing the Berbers*, "No one was a Berber in northwest Africa before the seventh century."[20] It was only after the Arab-Muslim conquest that Arabic authors imposed the category Berber to collectively describe the culturally and linguistically diverse populations that the conquerors found in North

Africa. This was, without doubt, an external imposition of a collective identity on a population that did not have one before the conquest. However, it was then quickly adopted by these subordinate groups as a mark of pride and distinction, and attached to claims of lineage. Genealogical chains that traced the origins of the Berbers to the Ḥimyarī Arabs of Yemen emerged within two centuries of the conquest.[21] Thus, the genealogical literature was not a record of any real migration from Yemen to North Africa, but rather a tool to cement the creation of a new Berber identity within a shared world of Islamic values.

In the late medieval Middle East, village clans chose lineage claims that most suited local conditions and social hierarchies—claims that made sense to them and which were constructed out of the building blocks of historical memory. As expected, many villagers opted to claim descent from the Prophetic line, and the more successful acquired the status of *ashrāf*. Others had to settle for less venerable lineages, from those of Companions of the Prophet or simply those of well-known pre-Islamic Arab tribes. The hierarchical relations between rural groups were projected back onto a pre-Islamic or early Islamic past and were usually expressed through chains of patronage that went back to the formative days of Islam. In western and Upper Egypt, on the other hand, some rural groups chose to claim Berber lineage. There is no evidence that any of these groups spoke a Berber language, but they may have opted for a Berber identity because of the prestige North African Berber groups acquired under Fatimid rule in the tenth and eleventh centuries. In Syria, non-Arabic speakers attached themselves to non-Arab Kurdish and Turcoman genealogies, even if some Turkish-speaking groups could also claim Arab descent. Boris James's study of Kurdish groups during the Mamluk period parallels many of the findings of *Becoming Arab*: Kurdish clansmen were sedentary cultivators yet were also seen as rebellious and prone to infighting; Kurdish tribal organization was reinforced by state bureaucracy; and the Kurdish genealogical tree evolved to reflect a set of group identities and social hierarchies.[22]

Becoming Arab proceeds from the framework of a feudal economy based on the extraction of surplus from subsistence cultivators, combined here with social constructionist and bureaucratic models of clan and tribe formation. The insights of Barth and Fried allow us to imagine the appointment of headmen as embedding the village clans in state administration, thus creating a nucleus for internal political organization and a platform for resistance. The solidarity of the village clan was reinforced by an appeal to common ancestry and by the adoption of shared cultural markers of dialect, dress, material culture, and popular epics. Muslim, Arabic-speaking villagers developed lineage claims and cultural markers that drew on broader Islamic tradition and distant pre-Islamic and early Islamic history, using the language of Islam to cement internal cohesion, compete against rival rural groups over limited resources, enhance their social status, and resist taxation.

The Desert and the Sown

In focusing on the extraction of agricultural surplus, *Becoming Arab* departs from previous scholarship on the history of Arab rural groups in late medieval Egypt and Greater Syria, where the main analytical framework is that of conflict between sedentary villagers and nomadic groups. Moreover, current scholarship's use of the term Bedouin, which in the modern period primarily designates tent-dwelling communities, imputes the Arab clansmen with a nomadic identity that is not present in the medieval sources. It relies on a dichotomy of *badw* and *ḥaḍar* adapted from Ibn Khaldūn (d. 1405), as refracted through articulations of Bedouin identity in the colonial and modern periods. When historians did acknowledge the spread of Arab clans throughout the late medieval countryside, this phenomenon is usually explained through the prism of opposition between farmers and nomads.

The prevailing assumption in modern scholarship is that Arab clans were pastoralists who migrated from the Arabian Peninsula and were distinct from the local peasants of Egypt and Greater Syria. In an influential article, Jean-Claude Garcin explained the evident mass peasant participation in Arab uprisings as a temporary alliance of two distinct groups, the politically active Bedouin and the docile and passive farmers.[23] Stuart Borsch explained the increased visibility of Arab groups in the fifteenth century through nomadic usurpation of good agricultural land.[24] Sarah Büssow-Schmitz's monograph on the "Bedouin" of the Mamluks in fourteenth-century Egypt offers a comprehensive survey of the narrative sources and devotes much space to the variety of economic activities of Arab groups.[25] The evident prevalence of Arab farmers is still explained away through a recent settlement of nomads who adapted a "semi-sedentary" lifestyle.[26] Usāma Jumayl's study of the economic activities of Arab tribes in Mamluk Egypt demonstrates that the Arabs of late medieval Egypt lived in settled communities integral to a wider economy and society, specifically highlighting their engagement in agriculture. This conclusion notwithstanding, Jumayl still asserts that the Arab tribes were a distinct ethnic group and argues that the Arabs had become acculturated to sedentary life and gradually lost their disdain for agricultural labor.[27] An alternative view of acculturation, offered by Frank Stewart in his broad survey of premodern Arab tribes, is that village communities adapted the social organization and cultural values of the surrounding, politically dominant nomads. In Stewart's interpretation Arab identity is no longer biologically determined, but it still arose from an interaction between the desert and the sown.[28]

This emphasis on the conflict between nomads and villagers is compounded by the obfuscation of terminology. When historians writing in European languages discuss the Arab clans and tribes of late medieval Egypt and Syria, they invariably choose to speak of the subjects of their inquiry as "Bedouin," even though the term *badw* is only irregularly used in late medieval Arabic narrative and documentary sources.[29] In these medieval sources, the *badw* rarely appear on their own; rather, they are often coupled with *ḥaḍar* (or *ḥāḍira*), or sometimes with the fallāḥūn tenants, to form an idiomatic compound designating the entire population of a certain region. Individual *badw* men and women are common in love poetry or romantic tales, less so in chronicles. When a person was named al-Badawī, as in the case of the famous thirteenth-century Sufi saint of the delta town of Tanta, it was a way of highlighting his outsider status and cultural identity, not to indicate he was a nomad. And in Arabic documentary sources the term *badw* is almost entirely absent.

When using the term Bedouin to describe the rural Arabs of the medieval Middle East, modern historians evoke Ibn Khaldūn's dichotomy of *badw* and *ḥaḍar* to project a conflict between the desert and the sown as their main framework of analysis. Ibn Khaldūn's cyclical philosophy of history assumes an eternal struggle between the *badw*, who possess a strong group solidarity produced by life in the harsh conditions of the desert, and the *ḥaḍar*, the urban elites accustomed to a life of luxury. Yet Ibn Khaldūn himself used the term *badw* in ways that go beyond the modern sense of Bedouin as tent-dwelling nomads. At the beginning of the *Muqaddima*, he defines the *badw* as all rural people who live either by tilling the land or by animal husbandry. This is reflected in recent translations of Ibn Khaldūn, where *bādiya* is rendered as "rural" while *ḥaḍāra* is rendered as areas under state control."[30] For Ibn Khaldūn, the peasants were part of the *badw*, not of the *ḥaḍar*. This was also true of the Ayyubid tax collector al-Nābulusī, for whom the *badw-ḥaḍar* dichotomy captured not the competition between the desert and the sown, but the distinction between grain-producing rural communities and the orchardists, merchants, and officials of market villages and towns.[31]

Moreover, Ibn Khaldūn eschewed a biological, ethnic definition of Arab identity and was perceptively aware of the malleability of genealogy, which he viewed as reflecting claims to status and as a means of cementing group solidarity.[32] He emphasized dynamic elements of identity, where subjugated or weak groups imitate the elites in dress, language, and social custom to acquire higher social status.[33] His attitude to the Banū Hilāl epic shows his appreciation for the social power of myths: the historian Ibn Khaldūn denies the events described in the epic, but as a social observer he comments on the importance of the epic for creating a collective identity and group solidarity among the Banū Hilāl. Moreover, Ibn Khaldūn argues that the Arabs of his own time have turned non-Arab (*al-ʿarab al-mustaʿjama*) as they lost the purity of the Arabic language.[34] Nor were they the descendants of the Arabs who took part in the original conquests, as the descendants of these tribes all but disappeared.[35] Many of them lived the life of sedentary farmers, such as the Berber tribes in the western delta,[36] the Banū Hilāl and Banū Kilāb in Upper Egypt,[37] and the mercantile Banū Jaʿfar between Qūṣ and Aswan.[38] Ibn Khaldūn perceived a lack of continuity between pre-Islamic Arabs and the Arabs of his own time—in genealogy, language, and lifestyle. This Khaldunian rupture between the Arabs of his own time and the Arabs of old undermines any ethnic definition of Arab identity or its simple association with pastoralism.

The distinction between mobile Bedouin and sedentary *fallāḥūn* is not a medieval distinction—it is not found in Ibn Khaldūn or in the medieval documentary and narrative sources. Rather, it is a product of Ottoman and colonial administrative practices. As shown by Nora Barakat, Ottoman administration created a bifurcation between the inhabitants of villages (*ahālī*), as in the province of Nablus in Palestine, and the "tent-dwelling" clans of the Balqa in Transjordan, who were also called *ʿarab* and invariably belonged to a clan (*ʿāshira*). As we know from Ottoman court records, the tent dwellers of the Balqa cultivated land as well as livestock, moving seasonally to the lower lands of the Jordan Valley. In court, the Balqa clansmen were not identified by their village of residence, only by their tribal unit. This dichotomy between sedentary village *ahālī* and the tent-dwelling Arab clansmen was a late Ottoman administrative practice connected with attempts to force "unruly" tent dwellers to settle down.[39] It built on a longer Ottoman tradition, probably, of distinguishing settled village communities from ethnically defined communities of Arabs, Kurds, and Turcomans, as already evidenced in the sixteenth-century cadastral surveys of Greater Syria.[40]

The Ottoman distinctions between sedentary villagers and mobile "Arabs" must have reflected some realities on the ground. Nonetheless, these Ottoman distinctions are not known to us from medieval, pre-Ottoman administrations. There is no evidence that Fatimid, Ayyubid, and Mamluk bureaucrats formally divided the rural population into the categories of peasants and nomads, even if some commented that only a minority of Arabs had a nomadic lifestyle. We also have no evidence that such distinctions between nomads and peasants were as significant to Arab rural groups as they are today. The same was true of medieval Kurdistan. As Boris James recently argued, the modern caste-like distinction between a tribal armed Kurdish elite (*'ashiret*) and a subject nontribal Kurdish peasantry (*guran*), as known from modern ethnography, is not found in medieval narrative sources. James concluded that medieval peasants were not excluded from membership in Kurdish tribes.[41]

While the Ottomans distinguished Arab clansmen from the rest of the rural population, the full elaboration of a "Bedouin" identity is the product of colonial and nationalist practices, as European explorers and ethnographers insisted on describing the Bedouin as a race of foreign conquerors, separate and isolated from the settled peasantry.[42] In the racial classifications that dominated nineteenth-century social sciences, the Bedouin were not just another race, but a unique race singled out for their avoidance of any intermarriage with other groups, and therefore of pure lineage. This over-racialization of the Bedouin led to intense interest in collecting "Bedouin" skulls and, in the twentieth century, in collecting "Bedouin" blood.[43] Another colonial legacy is the view of the Bedouin as the "barbarians at the gate" and the destroyers of agriculture. In her study of French scientific knowledge produced during the colonial era, Diana K. Davis demonstrated the way French authors consistently depicted nomadic societies as destructive races opposed to state power and civilization.[44] Colonial administrators, followed by postcolonial nation-states, drew on Ibn Khaldūn to develop a view of the Bedouin as remnants of pre-Islamic ignorance and a threat to progress and modernity.[45] It is important that our historical inquiry of the Arab rural groups is free from such racialized assumptions. The Arab clans at the heart of this book were not a biological race, nor were they inherently opposed to economic prosperity.

Ultimately, this book is about sedentary villagers, not nomads. There were certainly nomadic Arab groups in late medieval Egypt and Syria, and the leadership of the nomadic Arab tribes of the Syrian desert has already received a good amount of scholarly attention.[46] But the countryside of late medieval Egypt and Syria was dotted with several thousand village communities of cultivators—surely the majority of the population and the mainstay of the economy—whose history has yet to be told. As elsewhere in the medieval world, these villages relied for their subsistence on a mixed economy of cereals and livestock, including herds of small cattle, poultry, riding animals for transport, and oxen for ploughing. A few groups practiced semi-sedentary cultivation with seasonal migration, but this was the case only in a few marginal environments. We need to resist the temptation to see a nomad hiding behind every sheep, or even a camel. The documentary and administrative records emanating from these village communities revolve around their relations with state bureaucrats and military lords and show little trace of interaction with mobile communities of pastoralists. The dichotomy of the desert and the sown, the Bedouin and the *fallāḥ*, is not only a misleading projection of modern identities, but it fails to capture the key features of the available historical evidence.

Centering Documentary and Material Sources

A fresh history of the Arabs of the late medieval Middle East requires a novel approach to the historical sources at our disposal. Previous scholarship relied almost exclusively on Mamluk-era chronicles written in Cairo and Damascus; among these chroniclers, al-Maqrīzī in particular stands out for his interest in the Arab tribes, and his narrative of the rebellions and insubordination of Egyptian Arabs against the Mamluk state is so rich and unique as to overshadow all other sources.[47] Yet, ultimately, for all his brilliance, al-Maqrīzī was a member of the Cairene urban elite writing for other members of this elite, removed in space and often in time from the rural societies that he described.[48] The same is also true of the rich accounts of late medieval European pilgrims, who passed through rural landscapes but only encountered the menacing armed elements of rural societies, without direct experience of village life. Al-Maqrīzī, the European travelers, and other chroniclers are indispensable, but they should come at the end of the conversation, after the sources that offer a truly rural perspective have taken center stage.

Becoming Arab moves from the bottom up, and therefore foregrounds documentary, administrative, and material sources that more closely emanate from the countryside. First in importance are the documents found in rural contexts. Even if state archives were lost, the documentary trail at our disposal is very rich.[49] For Islamic Egypt we have thousands of extant documents, of which hundreds have been published. They contain dozens of references to Arab groups, either as the object of state administration and policing, or as expressions of self-identity. A major portion of the relevant documents comes from sites of eleventh-century Fayyumi villages abandoned in the environmental and political crisis of 1068–74.[50] These are complemented by a sparser trail of Egyptian rural documents in the following centuries and occasional rural correspondence of Jewish merchants represented in the Cairo Geniza. A second major documentary corpus is that of the Monastery of St. Catherine in Sinai. It contains over a thousand decrees, petitions, and legal documents from the late Fatimid, Ayyubid, and Mamluk periods. Most of the edited documents deal with the triangular relations between the monks of St. Catherine, state authorities in Cairo (or their local representatives), and local armed groups, mostly Arab clansmen.[51] For Palestine, the crusader charters preserved by the Hospitaller Order of St. John contain a surprising number of references to people called *beduini*. For the fourteenth century, the Haram al-Sharif collection from the *qāḍī* court of Jerusalem consists of about a thousand deeds, including a subset of twenty-seven documents, all dating from the 1300s, concerned with villages endowed for the benefit of the Haram al-Sharif in Jerusalem or the Tomb of the Patriarchs in Hebron.[52]

We also have at our disposal a wide range of administrative, genealogical, and literary texts that deal with the Arabs of the Egyptian and Syrian countrysides, some of them composed in the countryside or by men with rural roots. This corpus is utilized here much more than in earlier scholarship. It includes fiscal registers such as al-Nābulusī's thirteenth-century *Villages of the Fayyum* and the genealogical treatises of the bureaucrats al-Ḥamdānī, al-ʿUmarī (d. 749/1349) and al-Qalqashandī. Biographical dictionaries are a huge mine of information concerning men born in the countryside and their careers and families. Those produced by provincial men, such as *al-Ṭāliʿ al-Saʿīd* by al-Udfūwī (d. 748/1347) or the chronicle of Ibn Ḥijjī (d. 816/1413), hold particular interest. Works of philology sometimes talk about "Arab" pronunciation, and the illustrations of the *maqāmāt* show representations of "Arab" men identified by their attire. The earliest manuscripts of Sīrat ʿAntar, dating to the fifteenth century, are our best evidence of the dissemination and popular reception of epic narratives of Arab origins.

Beyond texts, *Becoming Arab* also seeks to integrate extensive fieldwork conducted in Ayyubid and Mamluk rural sites of Greater Syria with significant progress taking place since the 1990s in Palestine-Israel, Jordan, and Syria (up to the civil war).[53] The most extensive excavations of Mamluk-era villages were undertaken in Jordan, with work led by Bethany Walker at Tall Hisban allowing reconstruction of local architecture and material culture. The mixed economy of these village communities is now far better understood, aided by archaeobotanical analysis for the crops grown and bone analysis for animal husbandry. The increase in the number of excavations also led to a refinement of ceramic chronology.[54] Most relevant to the topic of this book, the sudden visibility of handmade geometrically painted wares in Ayyubid and Mamluk village contexts was brought to the attention of historians by Jeremy Johns in the 1990s.[55] The rural landscape has changed in other ways, too: dozens of abandoned sites were reoccupied by repurposing the existing ruins, while Christian monuments were transformed into Islamic shrines. While the archaeological record is far from complete and many results remain unpublished, excavations have already shown us a rural society that was turned upside down within a couple of centuries. The material culture tells a narrative of dynamic transformation that is completely missing from the chronicles and is therefore not reflected in current historiography of the late medieval countryside.

Terminology: Arab and ʿUrbān, Clans and Tribes

As noted above, the term *badw* is rare in Arabic documentary and narrative sources concerning the late medieval countryside. Rather than *badw*, the term most often used to designate late medieval Arabs is ʿurbān, a neologism current from the twelfth century onward. The coining of a new term reflected the new meanings of Arab identity in this period. It was derived from the collective name *ʿarab*, but its use emphasized the evident difference between the Arabs of old and the present ones. As such, the term ʿurbān parallels the neologism *turkmān* (Turcoman), derived from the name *turk* around the same time and first attested in Anatolia.[56] Initially, the ʿurbān were the Arab provincial troops in the service of the late Fatimids and the Ayyubids. In Mamluk Egypt, from the thirteenth century onward, the meaning of the term extended to include all Arab armed groups, especially Arab rebels against the Mamluk state. In Mamluk Syria, the officially mandated ʿurbān were distinct from the *ʿashīr* (sometimes *ʿashāʾir* or *ʿushrān*), a term that indicated armed villagers who were not considered part of the provincial troops. The term ʿurbān is also commonly used in the Arab popular epics, denoting the collective might of the Arab tribes. These semantic distinctions are germane to the arguments of this book, and the use of the terms ʿurbān and *ʿushrān* will be indicated throughout.

While the term ʿurbān implied military power and political independence, the term *ʿarab* was used to indicate cultural and ethnic identity. Thus, village clans were *ʿarab* while the armed men they contributed to the state auxiliary forces were ʿurbān. Cultural identity was *ʿarab*, whether Arab dress (*libās al-ʿarab*), Arab poetry (*ʿalā ṭarīq al-ʿarab*), or distinctive Arab pronunciation (*qāf al-ʿArab*). Such cultural identity could also be expressed by the term *badawī*, which in the context of dress and speech appears to be interchangeable with *ʿarabī*. Occasionally, the meanings of this *ʿarab* identity are spelled out. For al-Qalqashandī, for example, the *ʿarab* were defined by their eloquent Arabic speech and by a lineage that went back to Arabian Peninsula. His genealogical treatise also included a section on the lore of the Battle Days of the Arabs in pre-Islamic times, the *ayyām al-ʿarab*, incorporating historical memory as part of Arab identity.[57] The word

ʿarab will be routinely translated in this book as "Arab" or "Arabs," since the modern sense of Arab identity carries similar cultural, linguistic, and genealogical connotations.

The terms *ʿarab* and ʿurbān encompassed both sedentary and mobile groups. When medieval authors wished to single out Arab nomadic groups, they referred to *bādiyat al-ʿarab*, translated here as "the Arabs of the steppe," or utilized the Qur'anic term *aʿrāb*. Ibn Taymiyya, for example, explains that the *aʿrāb* are the steppe people among the Arabs, distinguished from sedentary or settled Arabs.[58] The terms *aʿrāb* and the singular *aʿrābī* are also relatively rare in late medieval documents and chronicles. In literature, the *aʿrābī* is the stock character for Arab cultural stereotypes: a source of deep wisdom and hospitality and a simple-minded object of ridicule. As with ʿurbān, I will consistently indicate the use of the term *aʿrāb* and its derivatives.

The use of the term *badw*, with its complicated relationship to the modern Bedouin, will be indicated in transliteration alongside the translation as "Bedouin." As noted above, the Arabic *badw* is relatively rare in Arabic documentary sources and in the Arabic chronicles of the period. On the other hand, the term *beduini* appears quite often in medieval Latin accounts of the Middle East. Specifically, it is the term used by twelfth-century crusader-era Latin charters to refer to rural Arab clansmen employed as agricultural labor (see chapter 2). In Latin travel accounts and chronicles, the term *beduini* also appears quite often alongside the collective "Arabs," indicating that for the European authors—unlike for the indigenous Arabic ones—the two terms were indeed interchangeable. In discussing Latin sources, the *beduini* will be regularly translated as "Bedouin," since it seems that European authors intended to convey an image of a nomadic people and way of life. I will also use the term in reference to modern dialects that are conventionally named "Bedouin" by sociolinguists, and to other aspects of modern Bedouin identity.

Modern historians, my own earlier work included, also tend to add the labels "tribesmen" and "tribal" to their discussion of the Arabs of the medieval Middle East. But we must acknowledge that these are potentially misleading categories. The use of the category of "tribesmen" evokes associations of unlimited autonomy, cohesion, and primordial identity—qualities that late medieval peasants aspired to but did not necessarily possess. Current anthropological literature largely avoids the term tribe because of its association with social evolutionary theories and with European colonialism. In the context of early modern European expansion, the concept of tribe was used to describe "earlier" forms of human development and peoples considered "inferior" and therefore suitable as subjects of colonial domination. David Sneath has further argued that even in the medieval context of the Mongol empire, tribal units were merely administrative categories and that the term tribe distorts our understanding of Mongol society.[59] Pace Sneath, the term "tribe" should be banished from historical scholarship altogether.[60] But, as Najwa Adra argues in the context of Yemeni ethnography, avoidance of the term "tribe" has its own pitfalls, since members of rural communities do speak about themselves as members of clans and tribes.[61] Similarly, the villagers of late medieval Egypt and Greater Syria used the idiom of descent as a form of social organization and cultural capital and employed a range of terms to express these social realities. One should be careful not to superimpose modern articulations of tribal identities, but it would be disingenuous to avoid the vocabulary of clan and tribe altogether.

It is therefore astute to closely examine the terminology used by medieval Arabic chroniclers, who employ the Qur'anic term *qabīla*—the closest term to the English "tribe"—to refer to large provincial confederacies, such as that of Sinbis and Lawātha, or the notional confederacies of Qays and Yaman. The narrative sources also use the collective *qabā'il al-'urbān*, "the tribes of the Arabs," when they wanted to highlight the segmentation of Arab society. Most of the time, however, late medieval narrative and documentary sources flatten out the distinctions between tribes, clans, subclans, and all levels of descent groups. The kinship terms *baṭn* and *fakhidh* are the most common, and they are indiscriminately used both for village clans and for groupings of several village clans. Most commonly, social units of common descent are not placed in any hierarchical order and are simply called Banū X (Sons of X). When a group is called "the Sons of," it is a generic designation that could mean any social group below the level of a territorial confederacy.

In light of the nomenclature of the medieval Arabic sources, I use here the term "clan" to describe the lineage-based social organization of Arab village communities, in which a cluster of households claimed descent from a common ancestor and assumed collective tenancy leases. Following the nomenclature of the administrative texts of the period, I use the term "clan" for individual village communities as well as for claims of common descent that united several adjacent villages; it broadly corresponds to the Arabic terms *baṭn* and *fakhidh*. The village clan, in the sense used in this book, is different from the elite Arab and Berber families or "houses" that assumed leadership roles in provincial administration, especially in the fifteenth century. The terms "ruling families," "elite families," and "houses" broadly correspond to the Arabic terms *awlād* and *bayt*. The ruling families discussed in this book usually held positions of leadership over regional or provincial coalitions of clansmen; these broader coalitions are called here "confederacies." The term "lineage" is used here to indicate a claim of ancestry and descent, equivalent to the Arabic *nasab* (so the term "lineage" is not used to indicate a kinship unit). I will reserve the term "tribe" to translations of the Arabic classical *qabīla* and its plural forms.

Chapter Outline

Becoming Arab proceeds chronologically from the Fatimid era to the Mamluk era, and from the documentary to the narrative. Part I, consisting of two chapters, examines the emergence of Arab village elites and ʿurbān armed groups under the Fatimids and the Latin Kingdom of Jerusalem, during the eleventh and twelfth centuries. Chapter 1 deals with the emergence of Arab village protectors in eleventh-century Fayyum against the backdrop of the rise of Arab dynasties in Syria and Palestine. Chapter 2 tracks the emergence of ʿurbān provincial troops in Egypt and Sinai in the twelfth century, alongside the appearance of the *beduini* mobile peasantry in Crusader Palestine. Part II presents the documentary and administrative evidence for the proliferation of Arab village clans in the thirteenth and fourteenth centuries. Chapter 3 is focused on the Arab villages of al-Nābulusī's thirteenth-century Fayyum, followed by chapter 4 on the Arab villages of fourteenth-century Palestine. Chapter 5 considers the genealogical treatises composed by Mamluk administrators as well as the Arab identities expressed in Mamluk-era biographical dictionaries and autobiographies.

The second half of *Becoming Arab* is devoted to cultural and political manifestations of Arab clan identities. Part III looks at the historical development of Arab cultural makers. Chapter 6 is devoted to the emergence of distinctive Arab pronunciation and Arab dress, as well as the shift to handmade wares in Syrian and Palestinian villages. Chapter 7 focuses on the growing popularity of the Arab popular epics as reflected in narrative and literary sources from the twelfth century onward. Part IV then takes up the Arab village clans as historical actors. Chapter 8 highlights the salience of Qays and Yaman alliances during the fourteenth century and their increasing importance in the politics of Mamluk Syria. Chapter 9 shifts the discussion to Egypt and goes back to the thirteenth century. It offers a reinterpretation of the major Arab uprisings in Upper Egypt during the first century of Mamluk rule, from 1250 to the 1350s. Chapter 10 takes up the narrative of Egyptian Arab clans into the fifteenth century, when the provincial authority and tax collection were delegated to leading Arab houses, causing a rift between these elites and the peasantry.

This book covers five centuries of the history of the countryside of Egypt and Greater Syria, from the beginning of the eleventh century up to the early sixteenth century. Caveats are unavoidable. Dictated by the availability of sources, the geographical focus of this book is the agricultural provinces of Egypt and Palestine, with some excursions into Transjordan, the Hawran, and the Beqaa. Syria north of Damascus receives little attention, and neither do the mountain villages of present-day Lebanon, which have fortunately been the subject of a superb study by Wissam Halawi.[62] Halawi's work also sheds light on the emergence of rural customary law in the Druze context. It is likely that rural customary laws played an important role in the political and ideological cohesion of Arab village clans in Egypt and other parts of Greater Syria, but the evidence is limited, and a sustained examination of Islamic legal sources was not feasible during the preparation of this monograph.[63] Finally, this book ends with the Ottoman conquest of Egypt and Syria in 1517, which represented a major watershed both in terms of fiscal administration and in terms of rural identities. The trajectory of the Arab village clans under Ottoman rule and into the modern period goes beyond the scope of this book, but key features of Ottoman-era transformations are discussed in the book's conclusion.

At its heart, this book tells the story of the late medieval Middle Eastern peasantry, the story of the social group that constituted an overwhelming majority of the population. Unlike previous histories of the Middle East that focused on cities or on nomads, this book views the villagers of Egypt and Syria as proactive agents who interacted with economic, political, and cultural changes in inventive, dynamic, and sometimes ruthless ways. Their voices, this book hopes to show, were much more nuanced than that of the victim of oppression or of the Spartacus-type rebel. The rural Islam that emerged in this late medieval period was very much their own creation, a product of conversion and amalgamation of Muslim and non-Muslim traditions that had roots in pre-Islamic periods. This was a dialectical process of distinguishing rural Muslims from non-Muslims by setting cultural boundaries of dress, speech, and material culture.

This is a book about medieval history, and it should be read as such, with academic and temporal detachment. Nonetheless, most readers will inevitably make comparisons with Arab and Bedouin identities that are familiar to them from their own experience. These modern Arab and Bedouin identities, like the village clans of late medieval Islam, are ideological constructions. Tribes and clans are not primordial; in the Middle Eastern societies studied here, they come and go in response to interactions with bureaucratic states and to the needs of rural communities. The current constructions of the Bedouin and their place within the wider Arab nation are especially elusive, and this book may help decipher some of the pre-history of the modern Bedouin. It unequivocally argues for upholding the rights of modern Bedouin communities over the lands they inhabit and cultivate. But, moving beyond those who see themselves today as Bedouin, this book seeks to offer a fresh historical perspective on what it means to be Arab: on the space Arabs (and those who claim Arab lineage) occupy within the wider Muslim world, on the fraught relationship between the people of the Arabian Peninsula and the Arabs of the surrounding lands, and on the centrality of Islam within the modern constructions of Arab national identities.

PART I

Arab Protector Elites, 1000–1200

1

Protection, Tax Collection, and Rural Elites, 960–1070

IN 461/1069, in the village of Uqlūl in southern Fayyum, the amir Qirwāsh b. Ḥumayd of the Banū Kalb married ʿAzīza daughter of Ḥudayj, whose guardian in marriage was Abū al-Khayr b. Qashshāsh of the Banū ʿĀmir. Both bride and groom were identified as protectors (*khufarāʾ*) of the village of Uqlūl. The marriage was extravagant, beyond anything previously known to us from Islamic Fayyum. The groom promised eight hundred dinars, half to be paid on the spot; this sum is fifty times higher than any marriage gift in an ordinary marriage contract from the village in the same period. The groom also acknowledged that he owes his bride a silk tent, fine robes, curtains and pillow, a golden basin, a necklace, and a female slave.[1] While marriage contracts tended to inflate the value of matrimonial gifts, the mere claims for opulence in this remote corner of southern Fayyum are astonishing. As protectors of the local village, both groom and bride belonged to a new type of rural elite that had sprung up very rapidly in the villages of southern Fayyum over the course of the eleventh century and which identified itself through the idiom of the Arab clan.

The marriage of Qirwāsh and ʿAzīza took place a century after the Fatimid Ismaʿili-Shiʿa caliphs took over Egypt and Syria and founded their new capital in Cairo, some one hundred kilometers north of Uqlūl. During this century, the Fatimid caliphs delegated provincial security to Arab and Berber groups throughout Egypt and Palestine, allowing clans such as the Banū ʿĀmir and Banū Kalb to dominate rural provinces. Moreover, this lavish marriage came at the end of the so-called Bedouin century, in which Arab rural elites expanded their power in many other areas of the Middle East. From about 960 to 1060, Arab dynasties mushroomed in cities of the Jazīra, Palestine, and Syria. In North Africa, the Banū Hilāl invasion took place circa 1050, imposing Arab rural elites over much of the countryside of what is today Tunisia. The Arab protectors of southern Fayyum were part of this wider process, hence the importance of the documentary trail they left behind. While other manifestations of the Arab ascendancy of the eleventh century are known to us only from urban-based narrative sources, the exceptionally rich documentary evidence from the Fayyum, before and after the Fatimid conquest, allows us to grasp what this transformation meant on the ground and at the level of the village community.

From 1015 to 1070, individual men with Arab clan affiliations assumed a formal role as protectors of villages and monasteries in southern Fayyum. The Arab protection (*khafāra*) appeared in the Fayyum several decades after the Fatimid takeover of Egypt in 969 and was sanctioned, and probably even encouraged, by the Fatimid state. The extant papers of the Arab protectors and other documents from these villages show that they formed an elite minority among a majority Christian Coptic peasant population. Their new wealth and patronage allowed them to supplant the Coptic village elites of previous centuries, which used to act as intermediaries in the collection of agricultural taxes. After 1070, Arab protection disappears from our sources as abruptly as it appeared. The great economic crisis that engulfed Egypt in 1068–74 led to the desertion of Uqlūl and several other villages in southern Fayyum, and the local protectors left their caches of documents behind. These represent our first documentary evidence for resident Arab village elites in the Egyptian countryside and a key starting point for the long-term emergence of Arab village clans.

The appearance of an Arab protector class has already been recognized as a key turning point in the history of the province.[2] But the precise meaning of the institution of protection, its causes, and its impact have not been fully explored. This chapter argues that *khafāra* protection was primarily a tax guarantee: men and women of financial resources and social status took it upon themselves to guarantee the delivery of the taxes of Christian villages or monastic institutions, in return for monetary compensation. Arab protection in eleventh-century Fayyum was a formalized and routine fiscal institution, one that directly affected cultivation and landownership. It was not ad hoc extortion and appears to have been state sanctioned. The documents clearly show that the right of protection was treated as an alienable right and was bought, sold, and transferred. Moreover, the term *khafāra* was also applied to the fiscal status of individual plots of land. The spread of Arab protection should be seen in the context of other fiscal innovations of the eleventh century, such as the *ḍamān* tax guarantee and the iqṭāʿ award of tax collection rights, which appeared at around the same time.

The processes visible to us through the unique documentary evidence of the villages of southern Fayyum were taking place throughout tenth- and eleventh-century Egypt and Syria. The institution of rural protection, called either *khafāra* or *ḥimāya*, is first attested in Iraq and the Jazīra in the tenth century, where it is described as a delegation of provincial security and local taxes to Arab or Kurdish local elites. As in the Fayyum, the rise of rural protection was intertwined with decentralization of state power and with erosion of private landownership. More directly, the rise of the Arab village protectors in the Fayyum should be seen as a result of a wider Fatimid reliance on Arab elites in other Egyptian provinces and in Palestine. The Fatimids, following the Buyids in Iraq and the Jazīra, introduced new fiscal instruments, including early instances of iqṭāʿ grants, in order to avoid payments for standing garrisons. In Egypt, this policy resulted in the decline of the class of Christian officials that mediated earlier forms of tax collection, and the imposition of Arab and Berber dominance.

This chapter proceeds from the bottom up, from the documentary and microhistory of the Fayyum to the narrative sources that pertain to the wider Egyptian, and then the Syrian, countryside. The first section examines in detail the papers of the Arab protectors of southern Fayyum and their swift amassing of wealth and power. The second section looks at the wider Egyptian countryside and follows the Fatimid introduction of Arab provincial security forces as a cheaper alternative to the hiring of a standing army. The best documented example is the Banū Qurra, who extracted protection payments both at sea and on land, and who were awarded the province of al-Buḥayra as iqṭāʿ by the middle of the eleventh century. The third section follows the rise of Arab dynasties in the Jazīra and Greater Syria from the middle of the tenth century. This section will highlight the institutional practices of protection, called either *khafāra* or *ḥimāya*, associated with Arab or Kurdish clans in this region. It then zooms in on the clan of Āl Jarrāḥ that dominated Palestine in the first half of the eleventh century. The conclusion discusses the collapse of the Arab dynasties in Syria in the 1050s and 1060s and the disappearance of the Arab protection in the Fayyum after 1070, coinciding with a series of major agricultural breakdowns.

The Arab Protectors of Southern Fayyum

When the Fatimid armies conquered Egypt in 969, a century before the lavish marriage of Qirwāsh and ʿAzīza, there were no Arab protectors in southern Fayyum. In the abundant documentary evidence from Umayyad and Abbasid Fayyum, men with Arab *nisba*s are visible only as administrators and military commanders and rarely (if ever) as cultivators or even permanent residents. The presence of Arab groups in ninth-century Fayyum is mentioned in narrative sources, as we find a rebel with an Arab name, Jābir b. al-Walīd al-Mudlijī, fighting *a'rāb*—the common name for Arab nomadic groups—in western Fayyum in 867.[3] Mostly, however, pre-Fatimid sedentary Arab or Berber groups were only found on the eastern and western frontiers of the Nile Delta. Ibn Ḥawqal notes Berber presence in al-Buḥayra, where the Zanāta and Mamjāna sowed their lands with water from the Alexandria Canal.[4] A Mudlij clan settled in the village of Kharibtā in the western delta.[5] A Qays group from Syria settled as cultivators around Bilbays in the eastern delta under the Umayyads.[6] Overall, however, the presence of Arab clans in the pre-Fatimid Egyptian countryside was limited; biographical dictionaries have few entries for rural Egyptians who claimed Arab lineage before the end of the tenth century.[7] The term *khafāra*, in the sense of protection rights over the peasantry, was also unknown in the Fayyum before the Fatimid period. When pre-Fatimid Coptic peasants required protection from the authorities and from tax collectors, they had access to other institutions. In the seventh and eighth centuries, for example, Coptic letters of protection were issued by village officials or monastic leaders to grant tax exemption or immunity to individuals, usually as an incentive for fugitives to return.[8]

Most of what we know of the eleventh-century Arab protectors of southern Fayyum comes from the archives of the protectors themselves, including deeds of sale, partnership, and marriage. The most prolific clusters are of Qashshāsh b. Shabīb al-'Āmirī, resident of Uqlūl, whose papers were preserved together with those of his son Abū al-Khayr; of 'Uqayl b. Ḥudayj, also of the Banū 'Āmir, one of the protectors of the village of Ṭuṭūn; and of Abū al-Dīn Ramaḍān of the Banū Rabī'a, identified as a resident of the village of Qūs Narmuda (Narmouthis) and as the protector of the Monastery of Qalamūn. Protectors also come up in the papers of Jirja b. Bifām, a landowning Copt who served as the tax official of his village of Damūya. Jirja was responsible for contact with the fiscal administration and for collecting the poll tax from other Christian villagers. His surviving archive, dated from circa 990 to 1024, contains three letters sent to him from individuals who demand their annual protection fees. Individuals of the Arab clans of Banū 'Āmir and Banū Rabī'a appear not only as protectors, but also as witnesses, guardians, or legal patrons, although never as scribes or religious functionaries.

The *khafāra* protection that propelled Arab men and women into positions of power in the villages of the Fayyum was a collective tax guarantee, by which the protector guaranteed to pay the taxes of a village or of a monastic institution in return for routine and formalized modest payments, collectively levied on a

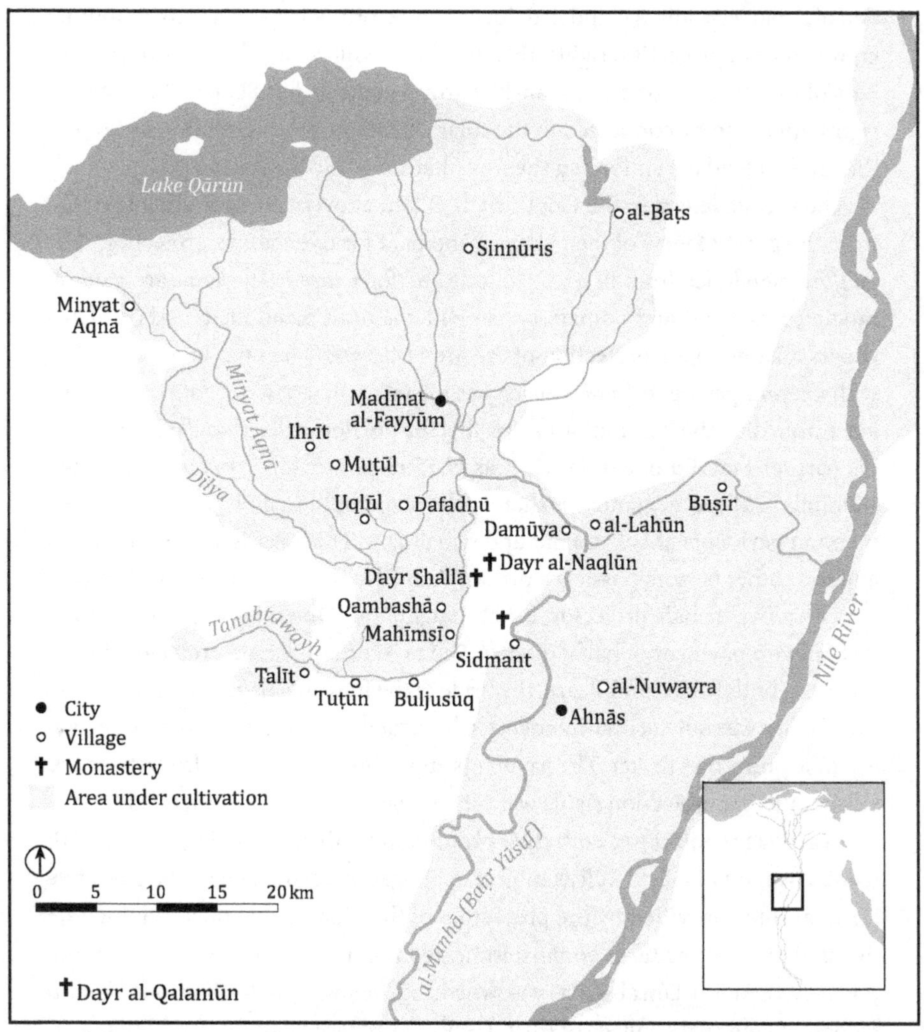

MAP 1.1. The Fayyum in the 5th/11th century.

village or a monastery and often shared between several stakeholders. The right to these payments could be bought and sold, as is shown in the papers of Abū al-Dīn al-Rabaʿī. On three separate occasions, Abū al-Dīn purchased shares in the annual "protection" rights of the Monastery of Qalamūn located in the deserts south of the Fayyum depression.[9] He bought annual protection rights of 1 dinar or ¼ dinar, for which he paid sums of 4.5 dinars, 1 dinar, and ¾ of a dinar. Another document records the transfer of a protection right worth ¼ dinar in lieu of a marriage gift. An undated document records what appears to be another conveyance of protection rights, this time in the village of Ṭalīt, involving members of the Banū ʿĀmir and a clan-like group identified as Shāfiʿīs.[10] Protection rights appear to be connected to the solar calendar of the agricultural year, not the lunar calendar, reinforcing the fiscal nature of the institution.[11]

The private letters of the Copt Jirja b. Bifām allow us to view the institution from the point of view of the villagers who paid for the *khafāra* protection. The *khafāra* demanded from Jirja was routine and formalized. The sums are modest, ranging between ½ and 2 dinars, on par with the sums mentioned in Abū al-Dīn's papers relating to the protection of the Monastery of Qalamūn. Jirja had to deal with *khafāra* payments in his capacity as the village tax official (*dalīl*). A friendly letter from one Abū Ṭāhir informs Jirja that the previous village *dalīl* paid him and his partner Marzūq one dinar each as *khafāra* protection.[12] In a second letter, Murāmir b. Miṣbāʿ demands his share of the *khafāra*; the legible parts of the letter mention payments of half a dinar and two dinars. The letter is addressed to Jirja and to another person, possibly a priest.[13] A third letter, in a more menacing tone, is written by a female protector, Falfala daughter of Duwayk, who demands her due *khafāra* payment of half a dinar.[14] The presence of female protectors in our records—both Falfala and ʿAzīza, the bride of the 1069 marriage contract—shows the *khafāra* was not necessarily collected by armed men and that it was more than a simple protection racket. The payments appear to be demanded from the entire village, and the protection rights were shared between several individuals.

In a village subject to a collective *khafāra*, individual plots of land were both owned by individuals as well as subject to obligations generated by the collective tax guarantee provided by the protectors of the village. Several surviving sale deeds show that the term *khafāra* indicated the fiscal status of the land being transferred. Abū al-Dīn al-Rabaʿī co-owned, together with his brother, one *khafāra* feddan of land in the village of Ihrīt. He also purchased two feddans designated as *khafārat mulk*, which seems to mean "ownership subject to protection rights."[15] *Khafāra* plots of land could also be passed on to non-Arab owners. In 456/1064, ʿUqayl b. Ḥudayj sold three *khafāra* feddans of arable land to two brothers, Marqūra and Buṭrus, sons of a former Coptic tax official of Ṭuṭūn. One of the three feddans was said to be "at the hands of" Bandalūs son of Helva, most likely the Christian tenant working the land. The price of four dinars per feddan was the standard for any sale of arable land in eleventh-century Fayyum, and the sale must have involved transfer of title to the land, not merely rights to collect protection payments.[16] The labeling of plots of land as *khafāra* feddans means that the land was subject to some form of "protection" rights. It seems to carry the same meaning as arable land designated as *mulk fī ḍamān*—"private land subject to a tax-guarantee"—bought by one of the Arab protectors.[17]

The *khafāra* was essentially a fiscal instrument, and its appearance should be seen against the backdrop of fiscal changes introduced by the Fatimids in the first decades of their rule. As shown by Lorenzo Bondioli, the early eleventh century saw the disappearance of the *qabāla*, the main fiscal institution in rural Egypt in the ninth and tenth centuries. Up to the Fatimid period, the *qabāla* was the mechanism by which members of the local elites contracted to pay the taxes on state land. The last known *qabāla* contract comes from the archive of Jirja b. Bifām, who in 1023 partnered with an associate to pay fifty dinars as annual land-tax in return for a lease of land. After that, the *qabāla* died out, no longer mentioned either in documentary or literary sources. Arab protection crowded out and replaced the *qabāla*, as is illustrated in an undated fragment of a petition by a local cultivator, either from Fatimid Fayyum or from elsewhere in rural Egypt. The petitioner explains that a local official handed him a *qabāla* contract for the cultivation of a vineyard, which he worked hard to make productive. However, the officials now informed him that the *bādiya*—here meaning "steppe Arabs"—require him to pay also an annual *khafāra*, and he cannot afford this extra cost.[18] This local cultivator contracted a *qabāla*, meaning a lease of land for a fixed sum, but was now charged with a supplementary *khafāra* payment and could not afford to pay both. We can surmise that with time the introduction of an additional layer of *khafāra* obviated the need for *qabāla* contracts, since these were two parallel methods of guaranteeing tax payments by individual peasants.

The *khafāra* protection was one of several new fiscal institutions that appeared in early-eleventh-century Fayyum, in what appears to be a period of transition and experimentation. The rich documentary corpus of the village of Buljusūq, also in southern Fayyum, shows no evidence of either Arab tribesmen or *khafāra* protection, suggesting variation even at the local level. Instead, land in Buljusūq was registered to individual tenants through annual land leases, with a standard price of four dinars per feddan per annum.[19] The lessor in the transactions of Buljusūq remains unnamed and was probably a state official. In addition, three *ḍāmin* tax guarantors (two Copts and a Muslim) were responsible for the entire payments of the village in 454/1062–63.[20] In the village of Dhāt al-Ṣafā in northern Fayyum, a *ḍāmin* tax guarantor by the name of Abū al-Ḥasan b. Wahb left us dozens of tax receipts for the years 1012–15.[21] This variation notwithstanding, it is noticeable that all three models—*khafāra* protection, the *ḍamān* tax guarantee, and the leasing of land in Buljusūq—imposed an obligation toward a superior who mediated between the peasant and the tax collector.

Thus, an important side effect of these new fiscal institutions was the erosion of private land ownership. Chris Wickham has used the archive of Jirja b. Bifām and other papyrological evidence from Middle Egypt to argue that private landownership was the norm throughout the Umayyad and Abbasid periods. Wickham contends that the shift to state ownership occurred only in the Fatimid period, leading up to the full appropriation of arable lands required by the Ayyubid and Mamluk iqṭāʿ regimes in the twelfth and thirteenth centuries. Wickham's position has been challenged by Bondioli, who highlights the importance of *qabāla* leases of state land, existing alongside the exchange of privately owned fields.[22] While scholarship has yet to determine the precise balance between private and public ownership in the centuries leading up to the Fatimid period, *khafāra* protection and other forms of tax guarantees clearly limited free use and alienation of land and were instrumental in the process of transforming landowning peasants into tenants.

In those villages subject to the new institution of *khafāra* protection, the change of the social landscape was dramatic, as the Arab protectors replaced the Coptic tax official (*dalīl*) as the village elite mediating between the state and the peasant cultivators. Jirja b. Bifām is the last *dalīl* known to us from the documentary corpus, with his papers dating no later than 1024. In Buljusūq, the last *dalīl* to be mentioned is Theodore b. Isaac in 369/ 980.[23] Over the next few decades, until the trail of our documents goes cold in 1069, the Arab protectors grew wealthy very quickly. We can follow the swift rise of Qashshāsh's family from his documents: in the early decades of the eleventh century he bought shares of houses and an adjacent courtyard.[24] Five decades later, his son Abū al-Khayr co-owned with his nephews a palm grove on the outskirts of Uqlūl and a female slave.[25] The same Abū al-Khayr was also guardian of ʿAzīza, the bride in the lavish marriage of two tribal protectors discussed at the beginning of this chapter.

While these new Arab elites replaced the Christian *dalīl*s of previous centuries, the population of the villages in southern Fayyum and elsewhere in Egypt likely retained a Christian majority. In Egyptian documents from Fatimid Fayyum and other sites in Middle Egypt, most of the named peasants had distinctively Coptic names.[26] A list of poll-tax payments from Buljusūq for 454/1062–63 suggests that this modest village had at least fifty Christian men subject to the poll tax.[27] The resilience of the local Coptic elites up to the early eleventh century is also attested in material culture. Dozens of religious texts found all over Upper Egypt are signed by scribes working in the southern Fayyumi village of Ṭuṭūn (Tebtynis), at least up to 940.[28] In the Naqlūn Monastery, new churches were built in the ninth century and then renovated and repainted as late as the 1030s, as attested by foundation inscriptions.[29] Christianity was still the majority religion, not only in the Fayyum, but in Egypt generally. Ibn Ḥawqal, writing in the second half of the tenth century, states that the population of Egypt is Coptic, even if many churches are in ruin.[30]

Yet the Arab protectors were instrumental in changing this demography. In the villages in which the Arab protectors were installed, they established ties of legal and economic patronage vis-à-vis local villagers, whether Copts, Muslims, or recent converts. In 411/1021, the Muslim preacher of Uqlūl sold a courtyard to Coptic man called Barūs, who confirmed that he ratified the purchase with Qashshāsh b. Shabīb, the Arab protector of the village. Barūs required Qashshāsh's consent because the Arab protector held some kind of guardianship over him, perhaps like a protégé or client.[31] In a sale of land around 461/1069, both seller and buyer are identified as protégés (*mawlā*) of Arab men of the Rabīʿa. The buyer, Yūsuf ibn Khayyāṭ, was the protégé of Jarād ibn Ghaylān al-Rabaʿī, while the seller, Ziyād ibn Muslim ibn Qaṭrān, was the protégé of Rāfiʿ ibn ʿAbdallāh al-Rabaʿī. These two villagers bearing Muslim names, clients of Arab men, may have been converts to Islam or sons of converts.[32] In a court document from Ṭalīt dated 404/1013–14, ʿAlī al-Muslimānī is identified as the *ghulām*, servant or slave, of the Arab ʿAbdallāh b. Furayj al-Rawḥī. This appears to be the earliest documentary attestation of the term *muslimānī*, commonly used in later centuries for a convert to Islam. Significantly, it is used here for a convert in the service of an Arab superior, who may have also been a village protector.[33]

Alongside formal and legal patronage, Arab protectors also assumed the role of local creditors through advance purchase of the harvest. In January 1054, the protector Abū al-Dīn al-Rabaʿī bought 1¹¹⁄₂₄ irdabb of wheat and 1½ irdabb of beans from Jarrāḥ b. Ziyād, who promised to deliver them during the harvest season of the Coptic month of Ba'ūna (June–July). In 1065–66, Sulaymān b. Jabāra acknowledged a debt of one dinar to Abū al-Dīn, to be paid again in the harvest month. This advance payment made by Abū al-Dīn for future delivery of grains, not made explicit because of the Islamic legal prohibition on speculative sales, shows that he acted as the creditor of local peasant cultivators.[34] The peasant cultivators indebted to Abū al-Dīn al-Rabaʿī had Muslim names but no Arab *nisbas*. In general, Arab men and women appear in eleventh-century villages as members of an elite class of protectors and almost never as cultivators.

A Fatimid-era account book discovered on the grounds of the Naqlūn Monastery, currently being studied by Naïm Vanthieghem and Lev Weitz, appears to shed more light on the role of Arab protectors in relation to the bulk of the peasant cultivators.[35] It includes two accounts of deliveries of grains (wheat, barley, and broad beans) by half a dozen men with Arab Muslim names, such as Ḥasan b. Ghurayb and Ḥusayn b. Ramaḍān, and by Arab kinship groups named as Banū 'Abbās and Banū Ḥanẓala. The individuals and kinship groups were interchangeable, as Banū 'Abbās (perhaps Banū 'Ibāda) in one list corresponds to 'Abbās b. 'Ibāda on the other. The grain deliveries are dated to the time of the harvest (the Coptic month of Ba'ūna/Paoni) and amount to over 2,100 irdabb, representing the annual payments, either land-tax or rent, on the arable land of the Naqlūn Monastery. At least four of the named individuals and kinship groups delivered hundreds of irdabbs of grains each, so they must have been acting on behalf of clusters of peasant cultivators.[36] Another register from the same account book has each of these four individuals and kinship groups leading a group of up to six men with mostly Coptic names, who appear to be under their charge. Although not named as such, these Arab Muslim men and kinship groups were probably acting as official protectors and were delivering the grain payments on behalf of a mostly Coptic peasantry.

Protection rights were formal, alienable, and monetized, and the Arab clansmen and clanswomen must have acted with the sanction of the Fatimid state. Like all those involved in tax collection, their role must have carried an implicit threat of violence: we know that Abū al-Dīn Ramaḍān was armed, as one document has him involved in a dispute over the ownership of a sword.[37] But the protectors were primarily acting with an authority invested in them by their official position as protectors of a village or monastery. They provided a guarantee for the delivery of the taxes of villages and monastic institutions, a service for which they were paid by collecting *khafāra* payments. That made them closely involved in village life: the "protection" they offered was attached to plots of land in the village, whether owned by them or not, and transfers of land among villagers required their approval. Their protection replaced the *qabāla* land leases that were practiced in the Fayyum in previous centuries and that were usually held by Christian village elites. Less than a century after the Fatimid conquest, village societies in southern Fayyum were transformed; money and power shifted from the well-to-do Christian peasants to a thin layer of men and women of the Banū Rabī'a, Banū 'Āmir, and Banū Kalb.

Fatimid Arab Policy in Egypt, 969–1068

The sudden emergence of Arab protectors in southern Fayyum should be viewed as part of broader Fatimid policies of decentralization of provincial administration. The Fatimid army incorporated tribal military units since its inception in

North Africa, most prominently Kutāma Berbers. The power of the Kutāma gradually waned following the conquest of Egypt in 969, and for a few decades the Fatimids came to rely on slave troops.[38] Then, in the first decades of the eleventh century, Arab and Berber tribal groups began to provide security on behalf of the Fatimid state in several Egyptian provinces. The turning point was the major anti-Fatimid revolt of Abū Rakwa in 1005–7, a rebellion that enjoyed the support of the Berber Zanāta and the Arab Banū Qurra in the western frontier of Egypt. Abū Rakwa was defeated in the Fayyum by a Fatimid army that was bolstered by local Arab Kilāb troops as well as the Palestinian Arab clan of Āl Jarrāḥ. The Rabīʿa leader who captured the fleeing Abū Rakwa was rewarded with the hereditary title of Kanz al-Dawla and authority over Aswan.[39] Thus, the pacification of the countryside in the aftermath of the Abū Rakwa revolt, itself supported by Arab and Berber clans, involved the delegation of provincial powers to these same social groups.

During the early decades of the eleventh century, new Arab troops acquired a visible role in the administration of several Egyptian provinces, as is evident in the extant portion of the chronicle of al-Musabbiḥī, a rare eleventh-century eyewitness account. A royal procession of 414/1022 included contingents of the Ṭayy confederacy—both the Āl Jarrāḥ clan from Palestine and the Ṭayy clans of the steppe (*bādiyat Ṭayy*)—as well as Banū Qurra and Banū Kilāb.[40] In Upper Egypt, Arabs of the Hilāl, Kilāb, Qurra, and Juhayna rebelled, and African and North African troops were ordered to quell the uprising.[41] A combined force of black African troops and Arabs raided the provinces of al-Ashmūnayn and of the Fayyum, taking with them thousands of heads of cattle.[42] The Fatimids reacted to this raid by awarding the entire province to the protection (*ḥimāya*) of a senior Fatimid official.[43] Despite this reported lawlessness, Arab groups clearly enjoyed official Fatimid support and were acting within the framework of Fatimid legitimacy. An edict, also dated 414/1022, deals with outlaws who evade the authority of local governors, and it orders officially sponsored tribes not to accept "anyone who claims to belong to them and who submits himself to them (*li'l-iḥtimāʾ bi-him wa'l-iltijāʾ ilayhim*), but is not listed in the registers (*jarāʾid*) and does not receive a pay through the established grants . . . they should shun the claims of these men with regard to lineage, rights, or blood relations."[44] The edict shows that the Fatimids were paying wages to members of allied tribes, and it attempted to regulate access to their ranks.

The Banū Qurra, known to us from a rich variety of sources, exemplify provincial Arab troops at the service of the Fatimids. The Banū Qurra were first employed by the Fatimids in a failed attempt to capture Tripoli in 1002. They then supported the Abū Rakwa anti-Fatimid uprising of 1005–7 but quickly returned to the Fatimid fold. By 1014, their leader Mukhtār managed to take over the port of Barqa west of Egypt and use it as a base for extracting protection money, called *ghifāra*, from commercial boats traveling between Egypt and North Africa. As Geniza letters show, the Barqa amirs of the Banū Qurra also owned ships that could be hired by merchants. They acted with the blessing of the Fatimids in Cairo.[45] Like their Arab contemporaries in the villages of the Fayyum, the Banū Qurra amirs made their wealth from exacting formalized and routine protection payments—not from peasants, but from ships.

Alongside their revenues from maritime trade, the Banū Qurra were also active in the Egyptian countryside, coming into conflict with other provincial elites. In 414/1022, a group of thirty men of the Banū Qurra raided the province of Giza and killed the *qāḍī* of Saft Giza and its *dalīl* tax official. The Arabs also took hundreds of riding animals belonging to high-ranking state officials and thousands of heads of small cattle. The conflict erupted, says al-Musabbiḥī, because the *qāḍī* and the *dalīl* were stingy with the provisions due to the Banū Qurra.[46] These were not marauding nomads coming out of the desert, but unruly soldiers demanding better pay. Their murder of the *dalīl* of Saft Giza replicates the way the Arab protectors of the Fayyum pushed aside the local Coptic *dalīl*s from the top of village hierarchies.

Groups of the Banū Qurra became dominant in the western delta, where they constituted a regional security force. In 403/1012–13, during al-Ḥākim's anti-Christian campaign, the Banū Qurra and the Banū Kilāb intervened to protect the monastery of Ibn Maqqār in the western delta, from which they were deriving some income.[47] The *Book of Curiosities*, a Fatimid geographical treatise composed in the first half of the eleventh century, reports that large throngs of the Banū Qurra inhabited low coastal lands near Alexandria, an area reclaimed from the Lake of Alexandria two centuries earlier.[48] Al-Maqrīzī states that by the middle of the eleventh century, the entire province of al-Buḥayra was the iqṭāʿ of the Banū Qurra, who "owned it and saw to the cultivation of its villages (*malakū-hā wa-ʿammarū ḍiyāʿa-hā*)."[49] Whether the cultivators saw themselves as Banū Qurra is unclear from this report. The control of the Banū Qurra in al-Buḥayra may have been similar to that exerted by the Berber Lawāta in the western Oases (*al-wāḥāt*), farther to the west in the Egyptian desert. According to Ibn Ḥawqal's account from the second half of the tenth century, the Oases were dominated by the Āl ʿAbdūn of the Lawāta, who lived in forts among the peasants, raising taxes from local grains, orchards, and palms. The Copts residing in the Oases were clients of the Āl ʿAbdūn, their status like that of manumitted slaves (*walāʾ Āl ʿAbdūn ʿatāqatan*).[50]

The dominance of the Banū Qurra in the western delta came to an end in 443/1052, and they were replaced by the Sinbis, another Arab group brought over from Palestine. According to al-Maqrīzī's account (based on a lost contemporary work by Ibn al-Ṣayrafī), the Banū Qurra held the province of al-Buḥayra as iqṭāʿ and were entitled to its tax revenues, so they were not paid in cash. But when a clan affiliated with the Banū Qurra demanded three thousand dinars in wages promised by the Fatimid governor of Alexandria, the Banū Qurra supported the demand of their client clan. They were defeated and fled westward to Barqa, leaving no trace in al-Buḥayra.[51]

Since the Banū Qurra were the local security force, their banishment required the Fatimid authorities to find an alternative:

> Once the Banū Qurra fled, the vizier [al-Yāzūrī] realized that placing a standing garrison in the province of al-Buḥayra will be very expensive. He therefore sent for Banū Sinbis, who at the time lived in the region of Dārūm in southern Palestine, where they grew in numbers and posed a danger to the local governor. He proceeded to hand over to the Sinbis the former territories (*diyār*) of the Banū Qurra and gave them their lands as iqṭāʿ. After that, the Sinbis expanded their power in al-Buḥayra.[52]

The settlement of the Sinbis Arabs is viewed here as an alternative to a paid, standing army. Instead of paying in cash, the government granted the Sinbis a provincial iqṭāʿ—the one previously held by the Banū Qurra—and they were installed as a provincial security force. It is unclear from al-Maqrīzī's account whether the Sinbis cultivated the lands of al-Buḥayra themselves or derived income from peasant communities put under their charge, in the same way the Arab protectors derived income from villages in southern Fayyum. The report also highlights how rising Arab power in Palestine contributed to the installment of tribal groups in Egypt. Since the Sinbis had come to dominate in southern Palestine, their relocation to the western delta killed two birds with one stone.[53]

The settlement of the Sinbis as a local security force was part of a wider Fatimid policy of settling Arab tribal groups in Egyptian provinces. The caliph al-ʿAzīz (r. 975–96) settled the Banū Hilāl and the Sulaym, previously part of the armies of the Qarāmiṭa, on the eastern banks of the Nile in Upper Egypt. The intention was to provide local security, although al-Maqrīzī states they caused harm to the region.[54] Al-Maqrīzī also reports how the Fatimid army helped to uproot the Juhayna confederacy from the province of al-Ashmūnayn, eventually handing the province over to a Quraysh group. The Juhayna, together with their Baliyy neighbors, withdrew southward and settled in the areas north and south of Ikhmīm.[55]

None of these groups—the Hilāl, Kilāb, Qurra, Sinbis, or Juhayna—are mentioned as residing in the Egyptian countryside prior to the Fatimid conquest.

Another manifestation of the Arab policy of the Fatimids was the migration of the Banū Hilāl to Ifrīqiya in 1048–52.[56] We know little of the Banū Hilāl in Egypt before that date. Ibn Ḥawqal mentions them as camping in the western Oases during the summer months, and in the early eleventh century they are mentioned as participating in a rebellion in Upper Egypt. The events leading to the Hilālī migration began in 1048–49, when the Riyāḥ clan of the Banū Hilāl allied themselves with the Zirid ruler of Ifrīqiya, Muʿizz b. Bādis, in return for a territory between Gabes and Tripoli. They then turned against him and defeated him in Ḥaydarān, south of Qayrawan, in 1052. As the narrative goes—and, as we shall see, this narrative was subject to much later elaboration—the chiefs of Banū Hilāl then became the lords of the countryside, "policemen of the plain and its surroundings."[57] As with the Banū Qurra, the Banū Hilāl's capture of North Africa was part of a Fatimid de-centralization of the administration of the countryside, where provincial security was devolved to armed Arab and Berber groups.

What was the effect of this devolution of provincial security on life in the villages? The eleventh-century papers of the Cairo Geniza suggest that urbanite Jews saw the Arabs as a class of murderers and thieves who had taken control of rural society. In a letter sent from Aleppo, one Jewish man grieves for his brother murdered in a village in the Egyptian countryside by people identified as *al-bādiya* (*qawm yuqalūn* [sic] *al-bādiya*).[58] A rural agent reports that cultivators complain about damage to crops caused by the camels belonging to amirs, owners of the presses, and to the Arabs (*al-ʿarab*), all involved in the transport of produce.[59] Finally, the author of a long letter complains about a useless provincial governor, saying that "on Saturday Arabs (*ʿarab*) came to the village (*kūm*), stole a cow, and left." The governor's lack of authority, says the sender, led the protectors (*khufarāʾ*) to be emboldened against him (*ṭamaʿū fīhi*).[60] This letter has Arabs stealing cattle, while the local protectors disobey the local governor and are themselves a potential threat to law and order.

The sudden appearance of the Arab men and women as the protectors of Fayyumi villages and monasteries, beginning in the 1010s and the 1020s, precisely overlaps with a Fatimid policy of delegating Egyptian provinces to Arab and Berber groups, who received access to tax revenues in return. This access to local tax revenues could take the form of *khafāra* protection or iqṭāʿ, fiscal instruments used to recompense these provincial forces without resorting to cash payments. The precise operation of the *khafāra* and its relationship to other fiscal instruments remains obscure. But the effects on village societies appear clear enough, and the documentary corpus of southern Fayyum provides us with the perspective of the Arab protectors themselves as seen through their own archives. In the Fayyum and elsewhere in eleventh-century Egypt, the local Christian elites of *dalīl* tax officials were pushed aside, to be replaced by a dominant class of powerful and increasingly wealthy Arab and Berber clansmen, who extended patronage to all classes of rural society.

The Arab Dynasties of Greater Syria and Palestine, 960–1070

The growing power and visibility of Arab groups in the Egyptian countryside overlapped with a century of Arab domination of the Jazīra, Greater Syria, and Palestine. From 935, dynasties that traced themselves to Arab clans took control of most of the urban centers in the Jazīra, starting with the Banū Ḥamdān in Mosul. By the 960s, Arab houses established independent states in Raqqa, Ḥarrān, and Aleppo. These Arab dynasties had their origins in Abbasid or Buyid provincial elites, as illustrated by the Banū Ḥamdān, descendants of a family who held the governorship of Mosul in the ninth century, and commanders of Taghlibī troops fighting for the Abbasid army.[61] They and other dynasties, such as the ʿUqayl in Mosul and the Kilābī Midrās clan in Aleppo, acted in the manner of sedentary states in collecting taxes, minting coins, and raising heavy cavalry.[62] The Fatimid conquest of Syria in the 970s did not halt this process but rather led to the extension of Arab power westward. The peak of Arab power was in the 1020s, when a coalition of Arab local rulers took over much of Syria and Palestine. They were ultimately defeated by a Fatimid army near Tiberias in 1029, and in the following decades the Arab dynasties of the Jazīra and Aleppo succumbed to the advancing Seljuks in the 1050s and 1060s, bringing the century of Arab dominance to an abrupt end.

This period has been frequently discussed in modern scholarship, which dubbed it the "Bedouin century."[63] By necessity, the historiography has had to follow a top-down approach focused on a set of narrative sources and urban centers. As acknowledged by Kurt Franz in his comprehensive study, the effect of the rise of Arab dynasties on the countryside, and even the precise nature of the groups described as Arab in the narrative sources, remains quite obscure.[64] A comparison with the documentary evidence for the rise of Arab protector elites in the Fayyum can help to fill this gap and conversely place the evidence from the Fayyum within a far wider context of a tenth- and eleventh-century ascendancy of rural elites all over the Islamic Middle East. Viewed against the background of the appearance of Arab protectors at the village level, the rise of Arab dynasties in Greater Syria and Palestine shares some of the same features: the sudden appearance of an institution of rural protection, called either *khafāra* or *ḥimāya*; decentralization of tax collection; and erosion of private ownership of land.

In the Jazīra, as in the Fayyum, *khafāra* protection was an important aspect of the rise of Arab or other kinship-based groups. According to Ibn Ḥawqal, groups of Rabīʿa and Muḍar Arabs had been pasturing in the Jazīra since pre-Islamic times and then attached themselves to non-Arab villages by providing them with protection (*khafāra*). Eventually their way of life had become that of *bādiya ḥāḍira*, a term by which Ibn Ḥawqal seems to mean settled communities with an Arab cultural identity.[65] Then, again according to Ibn Ḥawqal, clans and tribes originating from northern Arabia, including the Qushayr, ʿUqayl, Numayr, and the Kilāb, took hold in the Jazīra in the first half of the tenth century, replacing the Rabīʿa and Muḍar as the protectors of sedentary population.[66] These new Arab groups came to control the protection and resources of settled communities (*yataḥakkamūna fī khafāʾiri-hā wa-marāfiqihā*) in the Euphrates Valley.[67] On the outskirts of al-Khābūr and ʿArabān, the clans controlled agricultural revenues, both grains and cattle, as the weak defenses of these towns forced the inhabitants to resort to Arab protectors.[68] According to Ibn Ḥawqal, the *khafāra* in the Jazīra of the tenth century referred to a system of political domination that affected the use of agricultural resources. He sometimes describes the Jazīra Arabs themselves as agricultural cultivators, whether in the villages northwest of Sinjār,[69] or in Barqaʿīd, with its abundant fields of wheat and barley, inhabited by the Banū Ḥabīb.[70]

Under the Buyid rulers of Baghdad (945–1055), the protection offered or extracted by provincial clansmen was usually called *ḥimāya*. As shown by Jürgen Paul, Buyid *ḥimāya* was primarily a fiscal institution, a grant of taxation rights by the central government with the aim of integrating tribal groups into provincial administration.[71] Paul highlights the official and public nature of tenth-century Buyid *ḥimāya*, exemplified by an official "Protection Bureau" (Dīwān al-Ḥimāya) alongside the land-tax bureau. Appointment decrees for Kurdish leaders in the Jibāl and for Arab leaders in southern Iraq grant them responsibilities for all aspects of local security. For example, a late-tenth-century decree issued in favor of the Banū Thimāl granted them *ḥimāya* in the vicinity of Kufa: protection of roads and caravans, of settled peasantry, and of grazing flocks. The term *khafāra* was specifically reserved for the protection offered to sedentary villages, as is shown in a Buyid decree that lists *ḥimāya* over roads, *ḥirāsa* over travelers and *khafāra* over agricultural properties.[72] These protection rights were awarded to resident provincial elites who relied on their local networks. Paul argues that Buyid *ḥimāya* was central to the emergence of the Arab political entities in tenth-century Greater Syria: these were hybrid provincial states, both nomadic and sedentary, with their independence qualified by the Buyid overarching administrative framework.[73]

A second similarity with Arab protection in the Fayyum villages is an erosion of the rights of private land ownership. In Naṣībīn, Ibn Ḥawqal's hometown, the Arab Ḥamdānī ruler Nāṣir al-Dawla (r. 936–67) confiscated properties of those who fled the city and bought the rural properties of others. He went on to replace orchards with cereals and leased the fields to sharecroppers.[74] Nāṣir al-Dawla followed a similar policy after taking Mosul, confiscating much of the landed property in Mosul, here forcing a shift toward vineyards and palm plantations.[75] This trend was not limited to the Arab principalities, as Buyid policies in Iraq led landowners (*tunnāʾ*) to surrendering their land to Turkish holders of iqṭāʿ.[76] Overall, tenancy appears to have replaced private land ownership under both the Ḥamdānids and Buyids.[77]

In Syria, we first hear of *khafāra* protection over the agricultural lands just before the Fatimid conquest of 970. Ibn al-Qalānisī reports that *khafāra* was imposed in the villages of the Ghuta hinterland of Damascus, and that the authorities attempted to stop the practice and prevent anyone from carrying weapons.[78] This occurred when Damascus fell into the hands of Qassām al-Ḥārithī, himself a villager from Talfīta, to the north of the city. His name shows that he, too, claimed an Arab lineage.[79] Qassām's allies among the urban militia (*ʿayyārūn*) and the peasantry imposed *khafāra* on rural areas and, according to al-Maqrīzī, those collecting *khafāra* on the villages became very wealthy, traveling with horses and servants.[80]

The Fatimid conquest of Palestine and Greater Syria in the 970s led to increased visibility of rural Arab groups and of institutions of protection.[81] The Āl Jarrāḥ of Palestine offer a close parallel with the Banū Qurra of Egypt, both groups thriving under Fatimid policies of provincial decentralization. The Āl Jarrāḥ of the Banū Ṭayy are first mentioned in 973, when the Fatimid army attempted to buy them off to facilitate control over Palestine. A large force of the "Arabs of Greater Syria" defeated the Fatimids in central Palestine in 976 or 977.[82] The Āl Jarrāḥ are then mentioned as allies of the Byzantines in northern Syria.[83] By 1011 they were back in Palestine, heading a full-scale revolt against Fatimid rule. Once Āl Jarrāḥ took Ramla, reports the contemporary al-Anṭākī, "the Arabs (*al-ʿarab*) were the masters of the country (*istaḥwadhat*) and dominated all its regions, from al-Faramā to Tiberias. They even besieged the citadels along the coast for a considerable time but did not succeed in taking any of them."[84] Ḥassān b. Jarrāḥ returned to the Fatimid fold in 1014 and is then mentioned as holding the region of Bayt Jibrīn as iqṭāʿ, a new form of landholding introduced to Palestine in the early eleventh century.[85] Al-Musabbiḥī reports correspondence between Ḥassān b. Jarrāḥ in Ramla and the Banū Qurra in the western delta, demonstrating a regional network of Arab elites.[86]

Arab domination in Greater Syria and Palestine reached its apogee in 1021–29, when Āl Jarrāḥ again captured Ramla, the Kalb advanced on Damascus, and the Kilāb took Aleppo. The aim of these unprecedented coordinated attacks was to push the Fatimids out of Syria and, probably, to replace them with Arab-led principalities of the type that was already present in the Jazīra for nearly a century.[87] Arab clansmen led by the Banū Kalb laid siege on Damascus, reportedly cutting trees and killing peasants (*fallāḥīn*) in the villages around the city, but they were eventually repelled by an armed militia of townsmen (*ʿayyār*).[88] The Fatimids then defeated the joint forces of the Arab clans at the battle of Uqḥuwāna, near Lake Tiberias, in 1029.

Jewish eyewitnesses perceived the Arabs who came to dominate Palestine and Syria in the eleventh century as a distinct, less civilized group of Muslims. A fragment of a letter sent from Palestine in the spring of 1025 recounts the Arab sacking of Ramla: "The Arabs gathered, and with them the sons of Qedar [black Africans] who live with the Ishmaelites, and they came like locusts," killing everyone who opposed them and taking women and property. The black component in the Arab troops clearly attracted the attention of the Jewish author.[89] A letter of complaint from the Jewish community in Damascus, circa 1050, opens with "The hand of the Arabs has become strong," leading to harsh measures against the Jewish community. The use of the term "Arabs" (Heb. *ʿArviyim*) is unusual and serves to distinguish them from the rest of the Muslim population.[90]

In eleventh-century Palestine, the Āl Jarrāḥ of Ramla dominated a rural society that still had a significant Christian population, and in which few peasants identified as Arab. Al-Muqaddasī, a native of Jerusalem writing in the 970s, suggests that peasants are mostly Christian. He does not mention any Arab clans as residing in Palestine, and he specifically comments that local Muslims are not as "Arab" as the people of the Jazīra.[91] Admittedly, both the Iraqi al-Yaʿqūbī (d. ca. 292/905) and the Yemeni al-Hamdānī (d. 334/945) note the presence of several Arab tribes in Abbasid Palestine—for example, the Judhām in Bayt Jibrīn and the Ashʿar in Tiberias—but their reports are too brief and geographically removed to be conclusive.[92] The penetration of Islam in rural areas was limited, as confirmed by biographical dictionaries for pre-crusader Palestine: men with

Arab tribal names lived in Palestinian cities and towns, but it is hard to find any Arab born or raised in a local village.[93]

Recent assessments of the material evidence also point out that the central areas of the Palestinian countryside remained predominantly Christian for several centuries after the Islamic conquest. Before the ninth century, Muslims are rarely visible in archaeological contexts of rural Palestine, while churches and village monasteries continued to function almost without interruption.[94] There is no material evidence of massive penetration and settlement of nomadic populations.[95] In the hills around Bayt Jibrīn (which al-Yaʿqūbī claimed was inhabited by the Judhām), regional surveys show continuity of settlement, with churches and monasteries the common religious structures in the pre-crusader period.[96] In some sites, there is evidence for religious change around the ninth century. The elaborate Byzantine church of Khirbet Beth Loya was in use for two centuries after the Arab Conquest but was repurposed as the settlement's cemetery sometime in the Abbasid period, when a small mosque was built nearby.[97] In the ninth century, a large settlement was built in Nebi Zecharia, also in the Judean hills. There is currently no conclusive evidence regarding the religious identity of the inhabitants of this Islamic-era settlement, built over a Christian Byzantine site.[98]

Viewed against the background of a persistent Christian peasantry, the rise of the Āl Jarrāḥ in Palestine has much in common with the Arab protectors of the Fayyum and other Arab groups employed as provincial security by the Fatimids. Like the Banū Qurra of Egypt, Āl Jarrāḥ only emerge in the sources after the Fatimid takeover—often as rivals, but also, commonly, as allies. Āl Jarrāḥ were also recipients of a Fatimid provincial iqṭāʿ, a novel fiscal institution in Palestine; their iqṭāʿ covered the hills west of Hebron, which were at the time still dotted with churches and monasteries, as we know from archaeological evidence. No account of the Āl Jarrāḥ mentions the term "protection," but our sources for rural Palestine are not as granular as the sources for the Arab protectors of the Fayyum. Given the overall pattern of Arab power in the tenth and eleventh centuries, it is likely that in Palestine, too, institutions of fiscal tax guarantees and rural patronage were similarly at work.

Arab Village Protectors and Arab Dynasties

All over the Middle East, Arab groups, and sometimes Kurdish or Berber groups, emerged as new provincial elites exerting military, economic, and political authority over the peasantry. The Arab protectors of the Fayyum appear to us as localized individuals, their names marking them as members of the Banū Rabīʿa and the Banū ʿĀmir. The Arab dynasties in Palestine, Syria, and the Jazīra, such as the Ḥamdānids, the Kalbids, and the Āl Jarrāḥ, are presented in the narrative sources as corporate units that held independent power over large regions. Yet these differences are partly down to the uneven coverage of our sources. The microhistorical evidence from the Fayyum translates the narrative reports by the chroniclers into relations of power between new rural elites and the inhabitants of the villages they were tasked with protecting.

The institution of protection in Fatimid Fayyum mirrors references to formal protection offered by Arab and Kurdish leaders in the Jazīra under Buyid rule. In both cases, the "protection" of peasant communities was a fiscal initiative directed from the capital, whereby provincial resident elites guaranteed the local collection of taxes in return for a share of the revenue. In both Egypt and the Jazīra, the devolution of provincial security and the decentralization of tax collection were alternatives to standing garrisons. The protection model, called either *khafāra* or *ḥimāya*, was first tested in the east then carried over to Fatimid lands—perhaps by way of imitation, as Marina Rustow suggested in relation to Fatimid scribal practices[99], or perhaps by way of similarity of political and economic challenges.

The rise of the new Arab elites contributed to an erosion in private property rights, whether through the confiscation policies of the Ḥamdānids around Naṣībīn and Mosul, or by the various restrictions placed on the free transfer of land between villagers in the Fayyum. The Fayyum documents suggest protectors had the right to certify sales of land in which they were not directly involved, and that privately held land was designated as subject to protection or guarantee. The deeds of the Arab protectors of the Fayyum demonstrate that they forged ties of legal and economic patronage vis-à-vis local villagers. These patron-client relations not only restricted the freedom of individual villagers to dispose of their land, but also accelerated conversion to Islam.

Protection was one of several novel fiscal institutions that made an appearance in the Middle East during the tenth and eleventh centuries. The other major novel fiscal institution was the iqṭāʿ, which at that time had the meaning of a temporary assignment of state land to high-ranking officials. The iqṭāʿ was well known in Buyid Iraq but first attested in Palestine in the late tenth century, and in Egypt only in 1031.[100] By the end of the eleventh century, however, the iqṭāʿ would come to eclipse the *khafāra* protection as the predominant fiscal arrangement in Egypt and Syria. The same process was noted by Cahen for Iraq and the Jazīra, where the increase in iqṭāʿ grants at the end of tenth century rendered earlier protection institutions redundant.[101]

The new Arab elites were often outsiders to the regions that they came to dominate. Narrative sources attribute the sudden rise in Arab power to the migration of nomadic tribes from the north of the Arabian Peninsula toward the Jazīra.[102] This migration may have been associated with the Qarmāṭī movement, an Isma'ili-inspired Arab revolt that established a state in eastern Arabia in 907.[103] Most of the Arab dynasties, and especially the Āl Jarrāḥ, displayed some aspects of peripatetic existence. There is some documentary indication that these new elites were attached to a mobile way of life. A marriage contract of a wealthy Kalbid couple from Damascus, probably from the eleventh century, includes an unusual reference to a head of cattle and five heads of small cattle as part of the marriage gift.[104] As we have seen in their letters, the Geniza Jewish observers viewed these new Arab clansmen as outsiders, sometimes called *bādiya*.

Yet not all the people who identified as Arab in the eleventh century came from the desert. Abbasid cities were full of people who saw themselves as Arabs. Marriage contracts from Fatimid Damascus have artisans and merchants with Arab tribal names but with no apparent link to the countryside.[105] Tenth-century Fustat and Mosul still had Arab clans and *khiṭaṭ* of Arabs, going back to the time of the conquest, even if such presence was clearly on the wane.[106] It is important to emphasize that the Arab protectors in southern Fayyum practiced what appears to be a sedentary lifestyle. They owned land and houses, and there is no mention of wealth held in cattle. The silk tent promised to 'Azīza in the 1069 marriage contract is the only indicator of a peripatetic lifestyle, but it might have been only a symbolic gesture.[107]

The marriage of Qirwāsh and 'Azīza in 1069 took place as the institution of Arab protection was nearing its end. The rise of Arab protectors in the Fayyum was followed by the Egyptian major economic and political crisis of 1068–74, which led to the desertion of villages in southern Fayyum and the inadvertent survival of the archival caches of these local Arab protectors. In Palestine, the Āl Jarrāḥ lost the decisive battle against the Fatimid army in 1029, then rapidly declined in importance by the 1030s. The Arab dynasties of the Jazīra and Aleppo succumbed to the advancing Seljuks in the 1050s and 1060s, and all but disappeared by end of the eleventh century. In these areas too, the end of the Arab century came on the heels of an eleventh-century wholesale desertion of sites, in what Ronnie Ellenblum called the "Collapse of the Eastern Mediterranean."[108]

The important legacy of the "Bedouin century," from 960 to 1070, was the ascendancy of rural groups who expressed an Arab clan identity harking back to the Arabian Peninsula. Even as their political power in the urban centers waned and the Arab dynasties all but disappeared, rural society was already transformed. At the village level, Arab protectors pushed aside the older Christian elites. The landscape and the people became markedly more Muslim. Private land ownership was increasingly curbed. The descendants of the eleventh century Arab elites were the nucleus around which Arab identity would spread to much of the peasantry in the twelfth century, turning the settled villagers into unsettled ʿurbān.

2

The Rural Arabs of the Twelfth Century

ʿURBĀN AND *BEDUINI*

THE ELEVENTH century—a century of Arab domination—ended with a widespread desertion of sites in the Egyptian and Syrian countrysides. In southern Fayyum the Arab protectors left their small archives behind. Over the next century, our sources for the Egyptian countryside are much more limited and sparse, and even the merchants of the Cairo Geniza did not venture into the Egyptian countryside as much as they used to. As the Arab dynasties lost power in Syria and Palestine, they were no longer at the center of the attention of the chroniclers. By 1099, the armies of the First Crusade took over much of Syria and Palestine, limiting the access of Arabic authors to the events of the countryside, while Latin authors showed a lack of interest in the Muslim cultivators of the lands they captured.

Nonetheless, despite the scarcity of sources, it is possible to trace two major and complementary developments associated with the spread of Arab village clans during the twelfth century. The first is the emergence of Arab auxiliary units called by the generic term ʿurbān, which became omnipresent in the Egyptian countryside and were paid through the now pervasive fiscal institution of iqṭāʿ. The second is the appearance of a class of landless and mobile cultivators in Crusader Palestine, known in Latin sources as *beduini*. Both phenomena suggest that Arab village clans had become widespread in both Egypt and Palestine by the end of the twelfth century. We have direct documentary evidence of a village near Nablus inhabited by an Arab clan in 1178, and anecdotal evidence for Arab cultivators from both Egypt and Palestine. Combining these two threads allows us to imagine the Arab village elites who emerged during the previous century being integrated into village communities; instead of the individual Arab protectors who had formed thin village elites, we start observing the spread of Arab village clans.

In the first half of the twelfth century, especially in Egypt, Arab or Berber tribal groups come to be known as ʿurbān, a novel term that is not mentioned in the Qur'an or in the early Islamic literature. While there are occasional references to ʿurbān in eleventh-century Syria, the term really comes into common usage at the beginning of the twelfth century, especially with regard to Egypt. By 1150 the ʿurbān appear to be the dominant force in the Egyptian countryside, eclipsing all other provincial rivals. The term itself reflected the integration of these Arab or Berber clans in provincial administration. The first appearance of the ʿurbān in the extant documentary corpus dates to the end of the Fatimid dynasty, circa 1170, and comes from the Monastery of St. Catherine in Sinai. At this point in the twelfth century, as is clear from the St. Catherine archive, the term ʿurbān meant provincial auxiliary military force at the service of the state.

Parallel processes were occurring in the Palestinian countryside under the control of the Latin Kingdom of Jerusalem. The Arabic narrative sources provide meager information on the rural areas that fell under crusader control, and the Latin narrative sources are tinted by the prejudices of outsiders. Fortunately, the voluminous corpus of charters of the Hospitaller Order of St. John contains several references to people called *beduini*, or Bedouin, who become visible in our records from 1150 and until the fall of Jerusalem to Saladin in 1187. One key set of documents, dated to 1178, detail the names of 103 "tents" or households of the clan of Benekarkas, who reside in the village of Seleth in the mountains of Nablus. The *beduini* of the Latin charters appear to be groups of landless agricultural laborers, attracted to Frankish estates by the availability of land and migrating over from Muslim-controlled Syria. While European chronicles and travel narratives describe the Arabs they met as nomads, the Hospitaller charters record the presence of Arab clans of agriculturalists that are associated with specific villages and estates.

The Rise of the ʿUrbān

In Egypt, the major crisis of 1068–74 was associated with a sharp and brief peak in Arab and Berber power. The most visible group was the Berber Lawāta, who, according to the *History of the Patriarchs*, numbered forty thousand horsemen and had taken over most of the Nile Delta, cultivating agricultural lands without paying tax. This Coptic source also reports that the Lawāta intentionally avoided the maintenance of irrigation works in order to drive up prices. They became the "masters of the countryside (*rīf*)" and prevented other communities from sowing the land. The report likely reflects the viewpoint of the Christian peasantry of the delta.[1] The Lawāta are not known to have operated in Egypt prior to this crisis, but only in North Africa. Given what we know of the Arab protectors of the Fayyum and the Banū Qurra in the western delta, it seems likely that the Lawāta were previously employed by the Fatimids as a provincial security force.

While the *History of the Patriarchs* focuses on the Lawāta in the Delta, other sources confirm that provincial power shifted toward Arab or Berber clans in other areas of Egypt. A Geniza letter from these troubled years reports that female slaves in Cairo fled to join the "Arabs," either the Berber Lawāta or other groups.[2] Arabic narrative sources report that the Juhayna, the Thaʿlab and Jaʿāfira dominated in Upper Egypt until the Fatimid restoration of the 1070s, when they were defeated by Badr al-Jamālī. Farther south, al-Jamālī also attempted to limit the autonomous rule of the Banū Kanz in Aswan; as mentioned above, Aswan was held by the Kanz since the early years of the eleventh century, in the wake of the Abū Rakwa rebellion.[3]

As a new Fatimid political order was established after the crisis, the disparate tribal groups in the Egyptian countryside came to be collectively known as ʿurbān. The term ʿurbān is a postclassical word and is not found in the Quran or in early Islamic literature up the end of the fourth/tenth century. There are no ʿurbān in the history of al-Ṭabarī (d. 310/923); in the tenth-century geographical text of Ibn Ḥawqal; in the genealogy of Ibn al-Kalbī (d. 204/819 or 206/821); or in the dictionary of al-Azharī (d. 370/980). Fifteenth-century chroniclers, especially al-Maqrīzī, use the term to describe Arab troops in eleventh-century Syria.[4] Ibn al-ʿAdīm (d. 660/1262) uses the term in relation to the Āl Jarrāḥ around the turn of the eleventh century.[5] Ibn Taghrī Birdī (d. 874/1470) records the title *muqaddam al-ʿarab* as employed by a Kalbid amir in the Hawran in 466/1073–74.[6] These references to eleventh-century ʿurbān come from later sources and are relatively infrequent. It is noticeable that the term is not mentioned in chronicles composed during the eleventh century, such as the one authored by Yaḥyā al-Anṭākī (d. 458/1066).

The term ʿurbān comes into common usage at the beginning of the twelfth century, when it is frequently mentioned in the chronicles of al-Maqrīzī, in the *History of the Patriarchs*, and in the memoirs of the contemporary eyewitness Usāma ibn Munqidh, especially for Egypt.[7] For the annals of 516/1122–23, al-Maqrīzī reports on the role played by *muqaddam al-ʿurbān* of the Judhām in Fatimid politics. The proximity of this *muqaddam* to the Fatimid authorities meant he was able to secure the release from jail of the future vizier Shāwar, who was of the Banū Sa'd of the Judhām and whose clan was resident in Minyat Ghamr in the eastern Delta.[8] The annals of the following year report the 'urbān routinely taking an annual share of the grain harvest and small cattle along the Mediterranean coast and in the western delta.[9]

The institutional role of Egyptian 'urbān as state-sponsored military units becomes evident during the reign of the Caliph al-Ḥāfiẓ (1132–49). A letter by the caliph, preserved in al-Qalqashandī's fifteenth-century encyclopedia, is jointly addressed to the army and to the tribes of the 'urbān (*qabā'il al-'urbān*).[10] In 1137, the governor of al-Gharbiyya, Riḍwān b. Walkhashī, gathered thirty thousand 'urbān around the town of Sakhā in the central delta. Two years later, he assembled 'urbān in the eastern delta, from among the tribes of Darmā', Judhām, and Zurayq.[11] The eyewitness Usāma ibn Munqidh reports that in 1149, under the new caliph al-Ẓāfir, Ibn Maṣāl recruited an army from among the African units, the Lawāta, and the 'urbān.[12] He was helped by *muqaddam al-'urbān*, a certain Badr b. Rāfi'.[13] Usāma was also present in Cairo five years later, during the civil war between 'Abbās and Ibn Ruzzīq. He witnessed 'Abbās summoning the *muqaddams* of the Arabs of Darmā', Zurayq, Judhām, Sinbis, Ṭalḥa, Ja'far as well as the Berber Lawāta, then forcing them to take an oath of loyalty on a copy of the Quran and on pain of divorce.[14] The author of the *History of the Patriarchs* uses the term 'urbān for the first time in 549/1154, again in relation to the activities of 'Abbās.[15]

The Lawāta, although nominally Berber through their lineage, were integral to the network of armed rural groups that dominated the Egyptian countryside in the final decades of the Fatimid caliphate. They resurfaced in Middle Egypt in 1123–24, when they killed a local governor. They were then defeated by Fatimid forces, and their cattle were taken as booty, but their leaders—called *mashāyikh*—reconciled with the authorities for a payment of thirty thousand dinars.[16] By 1146 Lawāta troops were sent by the Fatimids to quell a revolt in Upper Egypt. Two years later the Lawāta joined a rebellion in the name of a Fatimid pretender, but eventually their *muqaddams* turned over to the side of the caliph in return for iqṭā' grants.[17] This appears to mark their full incorporation into the Fatimid military elite. The Sicilian geographer al-Idrīsī, writing around that time, states that Arab and Berber tribes dominate and devastate the area of Dalāṣ in Middle Egypt.[18]

'Urbān control over the Egyptian countryside peaked in 1163, with the accession of Shāwar to the vizierate. Shāwar, identified as a member of the Judhām from al-Sharqiyya, gathered ten thousand Sinbis 'urbān in al-Gharbiyya. He gave the amirs of the 'urbān free reign to pillage the granaries, presses, and cattle found in the iqṭā' of his rival Ibn Ruzzīq. The latter was captured by an Arab *muqaddam* in Aṭfīḥ, in Upper Egypt. Shāwar's own Judhām did not necessarily side with him, as one Judhāmī amir in the eastern delta sheltered an opponent and delivered him safely to ʿAqaba. Al-Maqrīzī also comments on the growing wealth of the ʿurbān in those years. They controlled the grain revenues of the eastern delta and competed with the military iqṭāʿ holders.[19] The ʿurbān were then accused of bringing about the demise of the Fatimids by informing the invading general Shīrkūh of the alliance Shāwar had made with the Latin Kingdom of Jerusalem.[20]

Al-Maqrīzī reports that when Shīrkūh arrived in Egypt in the 1160s, he found in Egypt "the Arab [tribes of] Ṭalḥa, Jaʿfar, Baliyy, Juhayna, Lakhm, Judhām, Shaybān, ʿUdhar, ʿUdhra, Ṭayy, Sinbis, Ḥanīfa, and Makhzūm. Thousands of these Arabs were listed in the registers of the Fatimid state."[21] By 1171, three thousand Judhām tribesmen were on the payroll of the state, when that number had been over seven thousand in previous decades. In 1181, Saladin attempted to punish ʿurbān units accused of collaboration with the Franks. He ordered the disbanding of the Judhām and Thaʿlaba ʿurbān in the eastern Delta, claiming that they transported much of the harvest to the lands of the Franks over the Sinai Peninsula. He also ordered them to relocate to the western delta, although there is no later evidence of such a migration. By 1189–90, Arab auxiliary units were allotted resources equivalent to 235,000 dinars, 5 percent of the total budget of the Ayyubid state.[22]

ʿUrbān units were found in twelfth-century Syria too, where they were employed by Nūr al-Dīn Zengi (r. 1146–74). Al-Maqrīzī reports that Nūr al-Dīn gave the amirs of the ʿurbān responsibility of guarding (*ḥifẓ*) the pilgrimage route between Damascus and the Hijaz and remunerated them for this service with an iqṭāʿ.[23] According to the contemporary Ibn al-Qalānisī, Nūr al-Dīn received complaints from the people of the Hawran and from the ʿurbān about Frankish raids against the women and children of the peasantry, called here fallāḥīn. In this account, the ʿurbān appear as champions as the peasantry, a role that would become typical over the course of the Ayyubid and Mamluk periods.[24]

Amirs who claimed Arab lineage were also rewarded with an iqṭāʿ in Mount Lebanon, where Nūr al-Dīn appointed a member of the Banū Buḥtur clan as iqṭāʿ holder over the Gharb region in 556/1161. The appointment decree was reproduced by the local chronicler Ṣāliḥ Ibn Yaḥyā (d. 839/1436) and includes a reference to the descent of the Banū Buḥtur from the pre-Islamic Arab tribe of the Tanūkh. This is the earliest document relating to the iqṭāʿ holdings of the Banū Buḥtur, who continued to dominate the region until the fifteenth century. Their claim to Tanūkhī lineage is attested throughout this period, including in a 714/1314–15 inscription.[25]

The administrative manual of al-Makhzūmī, written circa 1170, just after the demise of the Fatimid caliphate, sets out the formal role of the ʿurbān as an auxiliary force. The iqṭāʿ grants for auxiliary ʿurbān, called here *iqṭāʿ al-iʿtidād*, were separate from iqṭāʿ grants for the regular army. According to al-Makhzūmī, the protocol of paying the Arab troops had become established in Fatimid times and began with the presentation of the registered (*al-mudawwanūn*) Arab riders. Each group was composed of a *muqaddam* and his followers (*atbāʿ*). They did not receive daily wages, but rather iqṭāʿ grants in the provinces. In return, each group undertook certain bespoke responsibilities of safeguarding roads and participating in royal campaigns, and these responsibilities were guaranteed by the *muqaddam*. This guarantee by the leader of the ʿurbān unit, which was primarily financial, was called *ḍamān* or *darak*.[26] The administrator Ibn al-Ṭuwayr adds that the iqṭāʿ of these ʿurbān was located in marginal areas. The nominal value of the iqṭāʿ grants of the Arabs was calculated on a different scale from standard iqṭāʿ allocations, making them less profitable.[27]

Payments to the ʿurbān were made through the iqṭāʿ institution, which became quite widespread in the Fatimid countryside in the twelfth century.[28] During the twelfth century, soldiers and state officials derived revenue from their iqṭāʿ by developing commercial infrastructure.[29] Whether the ʿurbān also invested in their iqṭāʿ is unknown. Alongside iqṭāʿ grants, other lands were subject to tax-farming *ḍamān* contracts handed out to private entrepreneurs; the few examples we have concern Jewish and Coptic tax farmers.[30] These tax-farming contracts were not handed out to the ʿurbān; in fact, a clause in a 1106 contract for the silk revenues in the town of Ibwān mentions the threat of the *bādiya*, presumably Arabs.[31]

What can we say about the social identity of the twelfth-century ʿurbān? The author of the *History of the Patriarchs* describes them as living in tents (*bayt shiʿr*).[32] On the other hand, it appears that each Arab unit had defined territorial boundaries and was located in a specified Egyptian province and responsible for its security. Following the great crisis of 1068–74, there are no further references to conflicts between the ʿurbān and the peasantry. Most remarkable are the numbers of Arab troops, given in the tens of thousands: ten thousand Sinbis ʿurbān in al-Gharbiyya; thirty thousand in the vicinity of Sakhā; three thousand or seven thousand Judhām riders on the payroll of the Fatimid state in its final decades. Such large fighting forces could not have been recruited solely from the few purely nomadic tribes of Egypt. It is evident that the ʿurbān were not marginal or minority groups but were inseparable from the mass body of the Egyptian peasantry.

A trickle of documents from the Egyptian countryside confirms that Arab clan identity was no longer the sole preserve of village elites. In 1102, a couple from Ibwān, near al-Ashmūnayn, came before the town's *qāḍī* to settle a dispute over ownership of cows and calves, as well as twenty-five heads of sheep. The husband is named as Durrī b. ʿAskar al-Qarīṭī, almost certainly an Arab clan name.[33] A set of eight documents from the small village of Buljusūq in southern Fayyum, dated 1132–33, records the allocation of seed advances in wheat to local cultivators by a state official, possibly an iqṭāʿ holder.[34] While most of the cultivators in this set have distinctly Coptic names, one was called Thābit b. Danīn (?) al-Ḥākimī of the Banū Rafʿ. Unlike the other peasants, he received his seed allocation from another cultivator (*muzāriʿ*), suggesting he was of a lower social status.[35] These are the earliest documents from Egypt where Arab individuals appear not as government officials or protectors, but rather as ordinary cultivators.

Egyptian rural men who carried names of Arab clans are also known to us from late-twelfth-century narrative texts. The most well-known was the aforementioned Shāwar (d. 1169) of the Banū Saʿd of Judhām from the eastern delta. His lineage, going back eleven generations, was compiled in the form of a genealogical tree by one of his grandchildren.[36] Three more Egyptian Arab villagers born around the middle of the twelfth century are mentioned in al-Dhahabī's biographical dictionary: the future vizier Ibn Shukr al-Shaybī, born in Dimayra in al-Daqahliyya[37]; as well as the scholars Abū al-Muhannad al-Judhāmī and al-Kamāl al-Hāshimī, from the villages of Safṭ and al-Muʿtamadiyya in Giza.[38]

To sum up, by the second half of the twelfth century, tribal groups were formally employed by both the Fatimids and Nūr al-Dīn as military units of ʿurbān led by *muqaddams*, receiving their revenues not in cash but in grants of iqṭāʿ land. They were present in Syria and throughout Egypt—in the western and eastern delta, and in several regions of Upper Egypt. The Arab tribes of the Darmāʾ, Zurayq, Judhām, Sinbis, Ṭalḥa, and Jaʿfar are mentioned alongside the Berber Lawāta and generic references to unnamed ʿurbān troops. The size and prevalence of the Egyptian ʿurbān units suggests that they were recruited from all sections of rural society, and this is confirmed by anecdotal evidence of ordinary cultivators identified by Arab clan names throughout the twelfth century.

The ʿurbān most probably developed out of the Arab protectors; like the Banū Qurra in the first half of the eleventh century, the ʿurbān were responsible for provincial security and were paid by way of iqṭāʿ grants of land. The term ʿurbān itself may have come into use during the eleventh century, but it was only by the second Fatimid century that the ʿurbān were systematically integrated into provincial administration and were employed throughout the Egyptian countryside.

If in the eleventh century tribal groups were only one of several provincial forces, including Turkish and black African troops, in the twelfth century the ʿurbān swallowed up the competition, growing in power as well as in numbers. The twelfth-century ʿurbān were also distinguished by their territorial stability. If the narrative accounts of the eleventh century are replete with tribal migrations and relocations, there is no record of mass migration in twelfth-century Egypt; they were now embedded in village communities.

The ʿurbān would go on to have a long life in Middle Eastern history, surviving until the late nineteenth century. The term has obvious parallels with the term *turkmān* (Turcoman), which gained popularity in Anatolia around the same time, and would also last until the modern era.[39] The Turcoman were rural peoples who claimed lineage from the nomadic Turkish tribes of central Asia but whose status and way of life were at odds with that identity. The ʿurbān appear to have had a similar relationship with the Arab tribes of pre-Islamic Arabia. The individual names of ʿurbān units referred to tribes of great pedigree, but the collective name ʿurbān indicated a gap and a divergence: they were not the same as the *ʿarab* of old.

The ʿĀʾidh *ʿUrbān* of Sinai

The documentary corpus of St. Catherine Monastery in Sinai provides us with a case study of one ʿurbān unit, the ʿĀʾidh section of the Judhām. The St. Catherine corpus contains several hundred decrees, petitions, and legal documents from the late Fatimid, Ayyubid, and Mamluk periods. Over one hundred were edited and published, mostly decrees and petitions, which predominantly deal with the relations between the monks, the state authorities in Cairo and provincial governors, and local armed groups of Arab clansmen.[40] One such petition written by the monks circa 1169–70, at the time of the Fatimid-Ayyubid transition, contains our earliest documentary reference to ʿurbān troops, and this document points to their employment by the state and their alliance with the local governor. Earlier petitions and decrees from the Fatimid period, while few in number, do not contain any mention of either the ʿĀʾidh or any other ʿurbān group, suggesting that the ʿĀʾidh ʿurbān of Sinai were primarily formed as an administrative and military unit in the wake of Saladin's takeover.

The earliest extant documents from St. Catherine are eight Fatimid decrees, from 1129 to 1158. None of them indicates any conflict with Arab clans, or even their presence. They are mostly addressed to the governor (*mutawallī al-ḥarb*) in al-Tūr, and they order him not to interfere with the grains, palms, and vines of the monks and not to burden them with extra taxes.[41] Special attention is given to the properties of the monks in Cairo and other Egyptian cities.[42] As for protecting the monks from attacks, the decrees only mention a generic protection from "settled and nomadic people" (*al-ḥāḍira* and *al-bādiya*). This coincides with a surprising rarity of references to Arab clans in Sinai before the twelfth century.[43] Christian authors reported that the guardians of St. Catherine Monastery converted to Islam and came to be known as the Banū Ṣāliḥ, presumably having a clan identity.[44] The eleventh-century Yaḥyā al-Anṭākī reports that when al-Ḥākim ordered all churches to be demolished, he awarded the St. Catherine Monastery as an iqṭāʿ to an "Arab" man (*rajul min al-ʿarab*).[45] The monastery must have had connections with Arab tribesmen, but we have little concrete information about the names of their clans or the precise type of relationship between the Arabs and the monastery before the end of the Fatimid period.

The earliest mention of an Arab threat to the monastery, as well as the term ʿurbān, is a document dated 564/1169, when the Fatimid caliphate was just about to give way to Saladin.[46] In this decree, addressed to governors in al-Sharqiyya and al-Ṭūr, the Caliph al-ʿĀḍid repeats earlier prohibitions against fiscal exactions by local officials and against interference with monks traveling to Egypt. He also adds a specific instruction to prevent the ʿurbān from entering monasteries and grabbing provisions. The first reference to ʿĀʾidh Arabs follows shortly thereafter, in an undated petition that is almost certainly addressed to Saladin, nominally acting as the vizier on behalf of the last Fatimid caliph.[47] As the petition sheds unique light on the identity and role of the ʿĀʾidh Arabs, and of the twelfth-century Egyptian ʿurbān more generally, it deserves to be quoted in full:

> The Slaves, the community of monks who dwell in the monastery of Mount Sinai in the Holy Valley.
>
> In the name of God, the Merciful, the Compassionate.
>
> May God Almighty perpetuate the dominion of the Exalted Seat, the most Excellent Lord, Commander of the Armies, Sword of Religion, the Defender, the Protector, the True Guide; and support religion through him and grant the Commander of the Faithful enjoyment of his long life and continue his power everlastingly and exalt his word.
>
> The slaves kiss the earth and report that they possess noble and gracious deeds containing order for their protection and respect for them, and warnings to the military governors and the ʿurbān against entering their monastery and seizing their possessions, which provide their own livelihood and that of pilgrims and travelers who come to them.

When the amir Ibn al-Faramāwī was appointed as governor of the forts at al-Tūr, the half-caste ʿurbān of the ʿĀʾidh—namely ʿUsaykir, ʿĀlī, Raḥim, Muraybiṭ (?), Ḥuwayr, and their cousins—met with him and urged him to enter the monastery and take up residence there.

If he carries this out, then he and the ʿurbān will plunder and destroy it. The usual practice is that the governor dwells where the Sultan's sources of revenue are (May God strengthen his triumphal power and perpetuate his reign and dominion), namely the coast, and that he should protect the produce brought in and guard it for the Sultan (may God perpetuate his dominion and reign).

The slaves [i.e., the monks] fear in their hearts the harm to them and to the monastery, for that will be a cause of its plunder and destruction. So they kiss the earth anew and beseech and beg him to take them by the hand for the sake of God Almighty, and to issue an exalted order (May God increase its efficacy and effectiveness) to the Officer of the Pure, Mighty Porte (May God perpetuate its honor) to summon the amir and the ʿurbān mentioned above and to obtain their signatures to a document comprising noble sworn declaration that they will not interfere with the monastery, nor take up residence there, nor come near it.

For when the bishop leaves the monastery, the monks block up its gates with stones and they have no way of opening it. If the governor will arrive requesting them to open it, and they cannot do that, this will end in mutual malice and spite. The slaves report this so that it would be known.

To the exalted opinions belong the superior . . . in this matter, God willing, Mighty and Glorious is He! Praise be to God alone and His blessings be upon Muhammad and his family, and His peace.

In this petition, the monks mention that they possess written guarantees prohibiting the governors and the ʿurbān from entering the monastery. The monks then report that the recently appointed governor of al-Tūr, the amir Ibn al-Faramāwī, was advised by the ʿĀʾidh clansmen to establish court within the monastery. The monks give the names of the leaders of the ʿĀʾidh, whom they describe as ʿurbān as well as *muwalladūn*, or half-caste. In Ayyubid and Mamluk documents the term *muwallad* always refers to slaves born into bondage, but here it likely means "people with no Arab lineage who adopt Arab identity," which is the meaning of *muwalladūn* widely attested in early Islamic Spain.[48] The monks warn that if the governor would indeed relocate to the premises of the monastery, both he and the ʿurbān will pillage and destroy the institution.

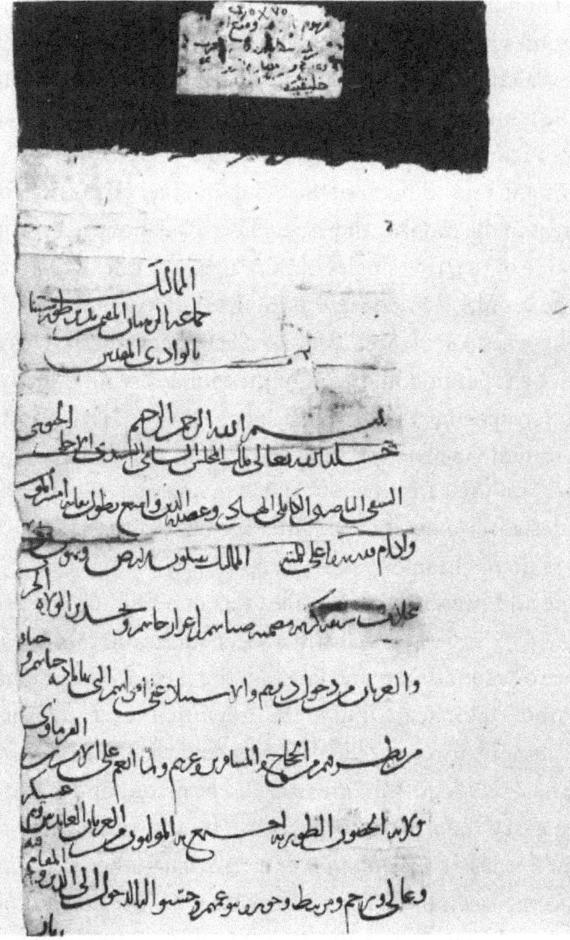

FIGURE 2.1. The top section of a petition from the monks of St. Catherine Monastery, probably to Saladin, circa 565/1170. P.AtiyaHandlist. 118. By permission of the Library of Congress.

From the very beginning, the ʿĀʾidh appear to us linked to state structures and the local governor. There are no earlier references to the Sinai ʿĀʾidh in any literary or documentary source, and there is no evidence of the social existence of the ʿĀʾidh outside of that institutional setting. The ʿĀʾidh's sudden emergence coincided with a focused Ayyubid attempt to control the Sinai desert and its routes. As shown by Jean-Michel Mouton, Saladin introduced to Sinai a new system of apportioning regional security to named Arab groups.[49] A tangible piece of evidence of Saladin's overhaul of military control over Sinai is the Fort of Ṣadr

(Qalʿat al-Guindi), which he built in the 1170s, as part of his major attempt to secure the routes between Egypt and crusader-held Palestine. Excavations from the fort revealed much about the everyday life in this desert outpost, even graffiti with the names of the soldiers in the local garrison; they had Arabic names, but no Arab names of clans and tribes.[50]

Following the installment of the ʿĀʾidh in Sinai circa 1170, they continued to pose a threat to the monks, and especially to the monastery's agricultural property. A decree of 592/1195 singles out the ʿurbān as one of the groups that seek to oppress the monks.[51] In 606/1209–10, the monks complained that a group of Arabs took possession of three feddans of fruit trees and started sowing in them.[52] In a subsequent petition, the head of the monastery identified the leader of the Arab group trespassing on the monastery's lands as Hajal al-ʿĀʾidhī. The monks complained that Hajal was forcing them to accept a sharecropping agreement (*mushāṭara*) on their fruit trees.[53] Hajal, the named leader of the ʿĀʾidh ʿurbān, sought to derive revenue from orchards and fields; he is not presented as a nomad and there is no mention of pastoralism.

The role and presence of ʿĀʾidh leaders as a regional security force is reaffirmed by a 637/1239 deed that still awaits publication. In the concluding part of a torn scroll, containing the date and the names of the signatories to a now lost legal undertaking, we find eight individuals carrying the tribal *nisba* al-ʿĀʾidhī.[54] Of these, three are identified as being the *muqaddam*s, or officers, of ʿĀʾidhī clans—two legible names are the Mazādīd and Banī Sulaymān. Two other men carry the *nisba* al-Sulaymānī, that is, of Banū Sulaymān, and one of these men is also a *muqaddam* of a clan. The other signatories are four officials from the town of al-Ṭūr and the local governor (*mutawallī*). Together, the signatories seem to include all the provincial state officials who have responsibility for the safety of the monastery. These were mostly ʿĀʾidh clansmen led by their *muqaddam*s, as well as state officials who were resident in the provincial capital.

The ʿĀʾidh's official role in central Sinai began toward the end of the twelfth century. As we have seen, ʿurbān power consolidated all over the Egyptian countryside during the twelfth century, and the introduction of the ʿĀʾidh to central and southern Sinai, circa 1170, was a manifestation of this wider process, which continued under the Ayyubid sultans. Al-Malik al-Kāmil (r. 1218–38), for example, delegated responsibility for the protection of merchants on the Sinai Road to al-Arish to a group of Arabs and held them accountable for stolen goods.[55] Pilgrims to Sinai had to be accompanied by Arab guides from the early thirteenth century onward. Thietmar hired his guides in Shawbak in the Transjordan, as they were the only ones who knew the road to St. Catherine through the *birrie* (*barriya*, desert).[56]

As with other 'urbān units of this period, we do not know how the 'Ā'idh were recruited, although the unique skills required for navigation in the Sinai desert would lead us to suppose that they were drawn from among the local population. Ibn al-Dawādārī, writing at the beginning of the fourteenth century, states that the 'Ā'idh not only watched over the inner desert road across Sinai, but they also acted as indispensable guides, expertly navigating the desert terrain through their familiarity with the landscape and by watching the stars.[57] And the power of the 'Ā'idh military officers didn't necessarily translate into local wealth. The North African traveler al-'Abdarī, who visited Sinai circa 1290, said that the Arabs there were wretched (*ṣa'ālīk*) pastoralists who subsist on plundering lonely travelers.[58] Nonetheless, the St. Catherine documents of the Ayyubid period make no reference to wealth in cattle; instead, the 'Ā'idh coveted the monastery's orchards and sowed the monastery's lands. Tellingly, the monks initially referred to the 'Ā'idh as half-bred *muwalladūn*, suggesting that their claim to an Arab lineage was not yet universally accepted.

The *Beduini* in the Latin Kingdom of Jerusalem

The establishment of the Latin Kingdom of Jerusalem in 1099, lasting until 1187, brought European crusaders and pilgrims into contact with the Syrian and Palestinian countryside. Most of the population who fell under Latin rule were peasants, either Muslims or Christians, and they were subject to a distinct version of European feudalism, significantly adapted to local conditions. Village units were granted as fiefs to military lords, who exercised ownership and were able to sell or donate their villages with the permission of the crown. The cultivators, on the other hand, were not of servile status and were never called serfs. We mostly hear of cultivators called *villani*, mostly Christian but occasionally Muslim, who were tied to the land and appear to have had the status of secure tenants. Much like peasants under Muslim rule, these peasants were not obliged to perform corvée labor and were in possession of their houses and personal belongings, which they were able to pass on to inheritors without requiring the lord's consent. On the other hand, named or unnamed peasants were often donated by the military aristocracy to support religious institutions, a phenomenon far more common in the Latin Kingdom than in contemporary Europe. The exact meaning of these widespread donations of persons is still a subject of debate; it may have been a way donate land without detailing the exact borders of the property. In the final decades of the Latin Kingdom, at least from the 1170s onward, villages were led by a headman called *raʾīs*, and some of the Christian headmen are known to have owned the lands of the village under their charge in the manner of a military lord.[59]

European authors in the Latin East have much to say about the people they called Arabs or Bedouin (*beduini*), names that for them were indeed interchangeable. The literary narratives routinely present the Arabs as the archetypal pastoral nomads. William of Tyre states that Turcomans and Arabs "habitually live in tents and sustain themselves from animal produce."[60] The anonymous author of the *Tractatus de locis et statu sancte terre ierosolimitane*, datable to 1168–87, presents them as people who have no homeland or house, live in tents (*tentoriis*), and who pasture at one time in Christian land and at another in Saracen land.[61] Thietmar, writing circa 1217, says that the Bedouin have "no land" and live in the open air, wandering from land to land with their flocks.[62]

Latin chroniclers also recorded Arab and Bedouin groups purchasing pasturage rights from Muslim or Christian lords. Albert of Aachen, describing the events of the spring of 1119, reports that Bedouins came out "of their land and region" to graze tens of thousands of camels, oxen, sheep, and goats in the pastures south of Damascus. The right to use this pasture was purchased from the Muslim ruler of Damascus, and the flocks were guarded by four thousand cavalry and infantry.[63] Thietmar and William of Tyre also note the seasonal pasture of flocks in the region of Banyas, south of Damascus, with the permission of local Muslim or Christian rulers.[64] In the 1180s, a group of "Arabs" came to pasture their flocks near the fort of Daron (present-day Deir al-Balah, south of Gaza) with the promise of protection from King Baldwin IV, but they were attacked by Guy de Lusignan, then Count of Jaffa.[65]

While European chroniclers and travelers generally viewed people they called Arabs or Bedouin as pastoral nomads, European writers of the twelfth and thirteenth centuries have remarkably little to say about Muslim peasants under Latin rule, even though we know for certain they existed. The term fallāḥ is rare in European sources of this period. Even when it is used, it is in conjunction with the Arab tribesmen: Thietmar, writing in 1217, warns his readers of the dangers of highway robbers in Sinai, "both fellahs and Bedouin."[66] A rare reference to Muslim peasants concerns the villagers of Bethnoble (Nūbā) between Jaffa and Jerusalem. The author notes that the vicinity of this Muslim village was prone to attacks by the "Bedouin."[67] As we shall see in chapter 4, by the 1300s the inhabitants of this village of Nūbā identified themselves as Arabs of the Banū ʿĀmir.

Latin documentary sources, too, talk more about the Bedouin than about any other group of rural Muslims. The *beduini* appear in a cluster of charters of the Hospitaller Order of St. John, all relating to the countryside of Palestine under the Latin Kingdom of Jerusalem. The original charters have now been lost, but they were edited and published by Delaville Le Roulx at the end of the nineteenth century. In these charters, the *beduini* appear as tent-dwelling and clan-based, yet they are associated with specific territories and are bought and sold like other villagers. From 1160 onward, we see the Hospitaller Order trying to recruit groups of these *beduini* to its estates, presumably as part of the repopulation patterns that typified the Latin Kingdom in its final decades. The increased visibility of the *beduini* in late-twelfth-century sources, where they are the main segment of the Muslim rural population visible to us, indicates the widespread adoption of Arab identities among the Muslim villagers of Palestine.

The most important set of documents regarding the *beduini* of the Latin Kingdom dates from November 1178. It concerns the sale of 103 named households of the clan of Benekarkas or Benicarguas (probably Banū Karkas, or perhaps Banū Karka, as suggested by H. E. Mayer). The Benekarkas clan was sold to the Hospitallers by Amalric, the viscount of Nablus. In the first document, Amalric describes the object of sale as "All my Bedouin (*omnes beduini meos*) that belong to the people (*genere*) of Benekarkas, and all of them who live in tents," whether in the Kingdom of Jerusalem or outside of it, including their families and heirs.[68] This sale is then confirmed by King Baldwin IV, and the price listed as 2,500 besants.[69] In a third deed, Amalric sells the village of Seleth, present-day Sīlat al-Dhahr north of Nablus, including all its land and the villagers (*rustici*) who inhabit it.[70]

The final and fourth document, dated November 17, 1178, contains the royal confirmation of the two sale contracts, here joined together: the sale of the village of Seleth and its villagers (*villani*), and the sale of the named members of the Benekarkas clan.[71] The joint price is again 2,500 besants.[72] Here we also find a list of the 103 households of the Benicarguas, surely the same as Benekarkas of the previous deeds. This is in fact our only extant census of the members of any clan from the Middle Islamic period, and one of the longest lists of Muslim subjects produced in the Kingdom of Jerusalem:

> Baldwin, sixth king of the Latins in the holy city of Jerusalem, confirms under seal the possession by Rogerius de Molinis, Master of the Holy House of the Hospitallers in Jerusalem, and his brothers, of a village (*casale*) called Sileta in the territory of Nablus with its *villani* and especially of all the Bedouin

(*Beduinos*) whose names are recorded and their heirs. These were possessed by Amalric, Count of Nablus, and his father Baldwin. They had been given them by Queen Melisende and they had owned them for a long time. Amalric, with the agreement of Queen Maria and Balian of Ibelin lord of Nablus, of Stephania, the wife of Amalric, of her father Baldwin lord of Ramatensis, of Ysabella the mother of Amalric and his brothers Renaldus, Iohannes, Raymond, Roger, and Balianus, and his sisters Milissendis, Gisla, and Agnes, had sold under seal the village and the Bedouin to the brothers of the Hospital of St. John of Jerusalem for 5,500 besants. King Baldwin confirms the Hospital's ownership of any of the heirs of these Bedouin who migrate from Muslim to Frankish territory.

The names of the Bedouin (*beduinorum*) are as follows, of the descendants [*de genere*] of Benicarguas:

Saraf, Hamet son of Homet, Turqui son of Nohel, Mahomot son of Homet, Hahata son of Caimem, Nede son of Haun, Geber son of Gerar, Semes son of Mefereh, Hataya, Cavam, Rumma—these are descendants of Benicelge, comprising 10 tents;

Ozia son of Holihan, Ozzi son of Hahazi, Salem son of Cahalin, Salmen son of Cahalin, Mensor son of Menaeb, Sacre son of Hyahys, Fehet son of Hassen, Bedre son of Haub, Heuz son of Hassen, Haneb son of Hassen, Hahanob son of Assen, Hassen son of Hous, Hataye son of Gemil, Gemma, Mensor son of Gemma, Solta son of Hassen, Zyede son of Haneb, Rahafe son of Sereta, Syble son of Hahassen, Hahata son of Gemil, Nahassen clan (*radix*)—these are descendants of Nahassen son of Mahan, comprising 21 tents;

Sarquam son of Rafa, Sahatlahabil, Hali son of Zet, Marahob, Haatem son of Sarquam—these are descendants of Marahob, comprising 5 tents;

Ziede son of Zyede, Hiessir son of Zyede, Zeyet, Mefereg son of Matar, Hali son of Lahantar, Salta son of Aloi, Meissor nephew of Bedre, Hahamer son of Secleb, Socre son of Mehelec, Bedre son of Cossa, Mobesser son of Zyede—these are descendants of Bedre son of Cossa, comprising 11 tents;

Nasser son of Haloen, Guatfel, Rodaem son of Cab, Tergem son of Maumet, Sebib—these are descendants of Sebib Lahagerse, comprising 7 tents;

Saleme son of Elforsie, Soar son of Senen, Sora son of Sohar, Fela son of Senen, Hahamer son of Mofatzar, Selmen son of Selin, Guadir son of Hahazis, Turqui son of Fazale, Gzace son of Olien, Bedre son of Habie, Haisse son of Bedre, Hermes, Fahazel brother of Belfadle—these are descendants of Beniflel of the clan of Beilfbzle, comprising 14 tents;

Cahnus son of Mahazer, Sem, Mathar son of Mothaer, Haris son of Mothaer, Sale son of Mothaer, Haamede son of Seair, Hali son of Mefareg, Selmen son of Hali, Targem son of Selmen, Sehel son of Sehem, Selim son of Messellem—these are descendants of Mothaer son of Mathar, comprising 12 tents;

Mere son of Hamt, Guahli son of Hamt, Savar son of Hamt, Sehebet son of Hamt, Sacra son of Gebil, Saraf son of Gemil, Mahumet son of Gemil, Hazem son of Socre, Solta son of Metcol, Rabia son of Zafar—these are descendants of Serif and of the Serif clan, comprising 11 tents;

Nasser son of Hennoine, Fazle son of Ali, Haloi son of Almen, Nahale son of Olien, Hoies, Olien, Merdes son of Sohea, Hahamer son of Ha, Obet son of Assaquer, Aloi son of Assaquer of the Solta clan, Gatfel son of Alaha. Sept son of Camis also belongs to this lineage. These are the descendants of Solta, comprising 12 tents.

Two others—Albi son of Cap and Nede son of Mahumet—are of the aforesaid descendants of Sebib Lahagerse.

The total of all these tents is 103.

In this extraordinary document, the Benekarkas are described as *genere* or "people," probably a translation of the Arabic term *qawm*. They are divided into ten named clans, called *genere*, and sometimes divided into subclans or *radix* (literally "root," perhaps *aṣl* or *baṭn*). For each named clan, the deed lists the names of the male heads of "tents," or households, that belonged to it. For example, the first section lists ten "tents" of the Benicelge, who are Saraf (Sharaf), Hamet (Ḥāmid) son of Homet (Muḥammad?), Turqui son of Nohel, and so on. The names, both of clans and of men, can be usually identified as Muslim, even if it is often impossible to retrace the correct Arabic form. As said above, the original documents have been lost, and we must rely on Delaville Le Roulx's readings. All in all, there are 103 named "tents," with seven to twenty-one households in each of the named subclans. If we assume that each tent corresponded to a nuclear family, the Benekarkas had a total population of about five hundred. The sale extended to all the descendants of the Benekarkas who might arrive from Muslim-ruled lands to the Kingdom of Jerusalem, implying hope that more men will come over to join the clan.

Previous historians were inclined to see these tent-dwelling Benekarkas as a pastoralist community. Prawer assumed that the sale of the Benekarkas concerned payment for pasturage. In a brief note at the end of his discussion of serfs and slaves, Prawer explains that the nomadic Bedouin were the king's property and owed him tribute for their grazing rights.[73] Yet the text of the charters does not explicitly refer to the king's unique authority, and Arab payments for pasturage are mentioned in narrative texts only. In any case, his interpretation poses several practical difficulties. First, the collection of grazing fees is more likely to be secured by control over the pastureland, not from authority over the shepherds. Second, if these 103 Benekarkas households relied exclusively on animal husbandry, they would require more than twenty thousand heads of small cattle to graze, assuming two hundred to three hundred cattle per household. Such large herds would mean that they would need to pasture their herds through the entire countryside of the Nablus region. Finally, the listing of the names and the clans of a truly transhumant community is an extraordinary feat of administrative control, especially given that we have practically no equivalent information for any community of sedentary Muslim villagers.

With these difficulties in mind, Ellenblum had to speculate that the Benekarkas had some sort of tribal territory bordering on the village of Seleth, and Sidelko suggested that beyond grazing rights, the Benekarkas perhaps also contributed transportation and military services.[74] Given the spread of armed ʿurbān units in Egypt and Sinai at the same time, it is not impossible that the Benekarkas were employed as an auxiliary force. Thietmar likens the Bedouin of his time to the *routiers*, the groups of itinerant mercenaries that operated in France in the twelfth century.[75] But the charter doesn't speak of any military obligations of the Benekarkas, and neither Latin nor Arabic sources refer to employment of Arab auxiliary forces in the crusader armies.

The plain sense of the document, however, is that the clan of Benekarkas resided in the village of Seleth. In the text of the charter, the village is sold with its Arab clan. The object of the sale is "of a village . . . with its *villani* and of all the *beduini* whose names are recorded and their heirs," noting that these people were possessed by Amalric, Count of Nablus, and were given to him long ago by Queen Melisende (d. 1161). Once we make the methodological shift of imagining the *beduini* as cultivators and not only herdsmen, it becomes clear that the Benekarkas were long-term inhabitants of the village, a class of cultivators that was somehow distinguished from the *villani* peasants yet part of the village community. They were organized into clans and identified by tents rather than households, but they were nonetheless the people of Seleth.

That should not really surprise us. By the late twelfth century, Arab village clans were already common in the mountain region of Nablus. Arabic biographical texts tell us that in the second half of the twelfth century, villagers in the vicinity of Nablus regularly boasted Arab tribal names. A Sufi saint, Ghānim b. ʿAlī al-Saʿdī, was born in the village of Būrīn in 1166 or 1167, with his family name suggesting he claimed lineage from the Banū Saʿd. The family of the Cairene jurist Muhalhal b. Badrān al-Ḥassānī, born 567/1171–72, was from the village of Jīt and claimed descent from Ḥassān b. Thābit.[76] Abū al-Ḥasan al-Ḥarīrī (d. 645/1247–48), a Sufi born in the Hawran in the late twelfth century, reported that he belonged to the tribe (*qabīla*) known as Banū Qarqar, of which another branch was found in the village of Mardā, southwest of Nablus.[77] The name Banū Qarqar is a possible scribal variation on the Benekarkas/Benicarguas mentioned in the Hospitaller charter of 1178.

That the Benekarkas were agricultural cultivators is strongly supported by two other Hospitaller deeds that deal with recruitment of a large number of *beduini* for agricultural work. In the first deed, dated 1160, Baldwin III gave the Hospitallers fifty "tents" of *beduini*, to be drawn from wherever they can find them. Baldwin only specifies that those recruited should not be from among those *beduini* who had been serving him.[78] In the second deed, dated 1180, Baldwin IV permitted the Hospitallers to recruit one hundred tents of *beduini* for their recently purchased estate in Belvoir in the Jordan Valley, including from Muslim-controlled lands beyond the river.[79] In both cases, it is hard to see why the Hospitallers would be in need of such large numbers of shepherds. These are almost certainly attempts to attract agricultural cultivators, including from beyond the borders of the Latin Kingdom, due to the chronic scarcity of manpower.[80] The *beduini* coming from lands beyond the River Jordan may have been attracted by the availability of good farming land in the Jordan Valley and the Nablus hills, where many villages were abandoned in the previous century.

While the Hospitallers were trying to recruit *beduini* to their estates, other Muslim peasants were fleeing from the Latin Kingdom to Syria. Thanks to a narrative composed by the Damascene Ḍiyā' al-Dīn al-Muqaddasī (1173–1245), we have a detailed account of the migration of about one hundred and fifty named villagers from the Nablus area, from the 1150s onward. According to Ḍiyā' al-Dīn, the villagers were relatives and followers of the Ḥanbalī preacher Aḥmad Ibn Qudāma and attended his Friday sermons in the village of Jammāʿīl. This attracted the attention of the local Frankish lord, who thought the sermons were negatively impacting his peasants' productivity. The same lord also increased the poll tax on the Muslim peasants from one dinar to four and brutally punished the Muslims who worked for him. Aḥmad fled to Damascus in 1156, and his disciples followed him over the next two decades, despite attempts by Frankish forces to stop the fugitives near the Jordan River.[81] While Talmon-Heller and Kedar tended to view this migration as representing the attitude of a "radical minority," the flight appears to have been motivated by the economic and legal conditions of the villagers and underlines the desire of Frankish lords to forcefully keep peasants on the land.[82]

The migrant Muslim villagers listed by Ḍiyā' al-Dīn did not form a clan, suggesting that not all Muslim villagers in the Latin Kingdom subscribed to an Arab clan identity—at least not yet. A deed of the 1150s includes a renunciation of royal claims over the lands of the village of Bethsuric (Bayt Sūrīk) and its twenty named Muslim *villani*.[83] This appears to be our only other reference to named Muslim peasants in the Latin documentary corpus.[84] Most donations and alienations of peasants refer to Oriental Christians, either urban craftsmen or peasants.[85] In the same series of deeds from the 1150s, the crown renounced its rights over named *suriani* (oriental Christians) in four villages north of Jerusalem, including twenty-seven inhabitants of Ramatha (present-day al-Rām).[86] Donations of anonymous individual *villani* peasants were especially common in the early decades of Latin rule. In 1110, for example, Baldwin confirmed the donation of eighteen unnamed *villani* from various localities.[87]

Overall, the *beduini* appear to have been a class of the peasantry, coexisting alongside the established *villani*. The earliest documentary reference to the term, in 1138, has the *beduinos* coupled with the *villanos* as part of the donation of four villages in the region of Jerusalem.[88] In a charter of 1161, Baldwin granted Transjordan to Phillip of Nablus and specified that the grant excludes the *beduini* that belong to the king, defined here as any of them born outside of the lands of Montreal (Transjordan). The grant also excludes *villani* who originated in Baldwin's own lands and caravans heading to Egypt.[89] Finally, a settlement of a dispute between the Hospitallers and the Templars in 1179 refers to "the Bedouin of the Templars," meaning that the Templars, like the Hospitallers and the king, also had their own dependent *beduini*—surely, cultivators rather than shepherds.[90]

The distinction between *beduini* and *villani* in the charters appears to be a distinction between two classes of villagers, not between the desert people and the sown. Instead of associating the *beduini* with pastoral economy, it makes better sense to compare them with the landless classes of contemporary European (specifically English) villages, who, unlike the *villani* serfs, were not bound to the land by tenure. In the Domesday Book of 1068, for example, villeins accounted for about 40 percent of peasant tenants while the remaining 60 percent were either slaves, or cottagers who worked for the lord or for the wealthier villeins.[91] Over the course of the twelfth century, the majority of the English peasantry still consisted of free and mobile tenants, either landless or with smallholdings, while the wealthier villeins would become unfree serfs.[92] A comparison with the divisions within the English peasantry allows us to view the *beduini* of Crusader Palestine through a similar opposition to the established landholding *villani*. The *beduini* Arabs were poorer, but mobile and free, not legally attached to the land they were cultivating—or at least this was how they were seen by their European landlords.

The Twelfth Century and the Disappearance of the Peasant

This chapter highlighted two key documents relating to Arab clans, both from the 1170s and separated from each other by only a few years. The first is an Arabic document from the Monastery of St. Catherine in Sinai dated to the final days of the Fatimid caliphate, probably around 1170. It contains a petition by the monks against an alliance between the governor of al-Ṭūr and the leaders of the ʿĀʾidh clan of ʿurbān. The second is a Latin deed of sale, dated November 1178, which transferred ownership of the village of Seleth near Nablus and the resident *beduini* clan of Benekarkas to the master of the Hospitaller order. As different as the two documents are—in language, legal formula, geography, and purpose—they complement each other to give us a view of the nature of Arab rural communities in the later twelfth century.

The petition from St. Catherine Monastery is the earliest documentary attestation of the term ʿurbān, following on the increasingly frequent use of this term in narrative sources earlier in the twelfth century. The coining of the neologism ʿurbān reflected new meanings of Arab identity and was used as a collective and generic name for armed provincial units at the service of the Fatimid, and then the Ayyubid, state. These clan-based units were led by officers called *muqaddams*, were paid by iqṭāʿ grants, and could comprise tens of thousands of men. Their sheer size and their omnipresence in the Egyptian countryside strongly suggest that they were recruited from among the wider peasantry, a proposition supported by fleeting references to Arab villagers in the limited papyrological corpus of the twelfth century.

The petition by the monks of the St. Catherine monastery against the ʿĀʾidh clansmen captures the ambivalence inherent in the term ʿurbān. The monks describe the ʿĀʾidh as half-caste, *muwalladūn*, casting doubt on their lineage and perhaps suggesting an original slave status or African descent. They are presented as both a threat and as allies of the local governor; Ayyubid and Mamluk sources confirm their sustained role as the security force in central Sinai, rewarded by state grants of iqṭāʿ. And yet they are known to us only through their administrative duties, not as a social group. We have no proof that they emerged from among the local inhabitants of Sinai, or even that they lived a nomadic lifestyle. In fact, early-thirteenth-century petitions show the ʿĀʾidh attempting to cultivate orchards on the monastery's lands.

In twelfth-century Egypt, we hear a lot about ʿurbān and very little about Muslim peasants. The same was true for twelfth-century Palestine, ruled by the Latin Kingdom of Jerusalem. Latin sources, both narrative and documentary, rarely mention Muslim *villani* cultivators, but they frequently refer to Arabs or to Bedouin (*beduini*). Pilgrims to Jerusalem distinguished between urban areas, inhabited by "Saracens," and the countryside, "the haunt of nomads."[93] This contrast in visibility is not a coincidence and suggests that many of the people Europeans called Arabs or Bedouin belonged to the Muslim peasantry. While the narrative sources of the crusader period consistently portray the Arabs as pastoralist nomads, the *beduini* of the Hospitaller charters were almost certainly agricultural cultivators. They are described as living in tents, but they were not primarily pastoralists.

In 1178, the *beduini* clan of Benekarkas, numbering just over one hundred households, were sold together with the village of Seleth in the mountains of Nablus. The deed strongly suggests that they occupied the village for some time and may have been its only inhabitants. Other groups of *beduini* were mobile, as the Hospitallers attempted to recruit groups of fifty or a hundred *beduini* to their estates in 1160 and 1180. In all these cases, the *beduini* appear to be the landless section of the peasantry, distinct from Muslim and Christian *villani* but living alongside them. During the final decades of the first Latin kingdom, at a time when some Muslim peasants were migrating away from the Latin Kingdom, the *beduini* became increasingly visible, overshadowing any other Muslim rural group.

By the end of the twelfth century, many village communities in Palestine claimed Arab lineages. Beyond the Benekarkas of Seleth, biographical dictionaries record men with Arab clan identities born in at least three other villages of the Nablus region in the second half of the twelfth century. After the fall of the first Latin Kingdom of Jerusalem in 1187, the spread of Arab clans in the countryside also began to make an impression on European travelers. If at the beginning of Latin rule William of Tyre talked of the Arabs as outsiders, living in the "Lands of the Arabs" beyond the Jordan River, thirteenth-century authors emphasized the omnipresence of the Bedouin, who "can be found in the kingdom of Egypt, in the kingdom of Jerusalem, and in all the other lands of the Saracens"[94] and who "fill the whole of Syria" on both sides of the River Jordan.[95]

The sources available for twelfth-century villages in Egypt and Greater Syria are particularly patchy. The Arabic documentary evidence is either very fragmentary or emanates from the marginal environment of Sinai, while the Latin charters of the crusader era are tantalizing but are doubly removed from the village societies to which they relate. And yet it seems that the twelfth century was a period of a major transformation, both in Fatimid Egypt and in Crusader Palestine. The 1068–74 *shidda* crisis in Egypt and the desertion of sites in eleventh-century Palestine occurred in a still largely Christian countryside of peasant landowners. By 1200, the countryside had become much more Muslim, with Christian peasants few and far between. The iqṭāʿ fiscal regime, still in an embryonic phase during the eleventh century, became widespread in a later period of Fatimid rule. The European version of feudalism similarly militated against peasant landownership in Palestine and Transjordan. Saladin's victory in 1187 ensured that the iqṭāʿ regime was extended to the entire countryside of Egypt and Greater Syria. As a result, when our sources for rural society become abundant again during the thirteenth and fourteenth centuries, we see the countryside of Egypt, Palestine, and Greater Syria covered with a blanket of Arab village clans.

PART II

Arab Village Clans, 1200–1450

3

Village Clans in the Fayyum, 1245

IN 643/1245, the bureaucrat Abū ʿUthmān al-Nābulusī was sent from Cairo to the Fayyum on the order of the Ayyubid sultan of Egypt, al-Malik al-Ṣāliḥ. Al-Nābulusī, who had been a top official in the administration of al-Ṣāliḥ's father, Sultan al-Kāmil, was now called out of retirement to report on the agricultural conditions in the province. He proceeded to survey the Fayyum by going from village to village, relying on local tax and irrigation officials and paying careful attention to minute details of agricultural production. The resulting account has survived in two manuscripts, and the treatise was first published by B. Moritz in 1898. It has now been reedited and translated into English as *The Villages of the Fayyum.*[1]

Al-Nābulusī's account is divided into nine introductory chapters dealing with the geography, climate, irrigation systems, and population of the province. These are followed by the main survey, with entries for more than one hundred villages. For each village, al-Nābulusī indicated the size of the village and the state of its habitation, its geographical location, the clan affiliation and religious identity of its inhabitants, its sources of water, and local mosques, churches, and monasteries. He also noted whether the village's tax revenues were paid to the sultan or to a religious endowment (*waqf*) or, more commonly, if they were allocated to army officers in return for military service (*iqṭāʿ*). This is followed by lists of taxes levied on each village that relate to the fiscal obligations of the villages, not to actual payments, and are based on the tax registers of a previous year, 641/1243. The lists are divided into in-kind taxes levied on grains, and cash taxes levied on other agricultural products, such as livestock and cash crops. The category of cash taxes also includes the poll tax levied on non-Muslims, recording with precision the number of non-Muslim men residing in each village.

For our purposes, the most striking aspect of the 1245 survey of the Fayyum is the omnipresence of Arab and Berber village clans. In nearly all villages of the

Fayyum, and practically in all villages that relied on field cultivation rather than plantations or orchards, al-Nābulusī identified the local inhabitants with a named Arab or Berber clan, usually one clan per village. Each village was led by a group of headmen (*mashāyikh*), sometimes joined by village guards (*khufarāʾ*), who were responsible for the payment of the collective land-tax imposed on their villages. The inhabitants of villages that lay along the same irrigation canal often belonged to the same clan, forming multivillage clans. The multivillage clans also provided a levy of riders for the Ayyubid ʿurbān auxiliary units and in turn were the constituent elements of larger territorial tribal confederacies, which between them carved the entire agricultural territory of the Fayyum.

The 1245 survey of the Fayyum offers a particularly useful point of comparison with the eleventh-century documentary corpus from the villages of southern Fayyum discussed in chapter 1. A close analysis of al-Nābulusī's text shows that the shift from an elite of Arab protectors to Arab village clans coincided with three major changes that took place in the Fayyum between the eleventh and thirteenth centuries. First, by 1245, the villages of the Fayyum were overwhelmingly Muslim, with Christians a relatively small minority concentrated in market and orchard villages. The data collected by al-Nābulusī shows few Christian men subject to the poll tax and few active churches, while Friday mosques were now found in nearly every village. The second major change was the spread of iqṭāʿ grants as the predominant form of landholding. Under the Ayyubid iqṭāʿ regime as practiced in the Fayyum at the time of al-Nābulusī's visit, all arable land was state property by default, and the field cultivators were transformed into fallāḥ tenants who collectively paid their taxes to iqṭāʿ holders. Finally, Ayyubid Fayyum witnessed a reoccupation of abandoned villages and rural migration, although very little interaction with nomadic populations. The spread of Arab village clans as the predominant form of social organization and identity in Ayyubid Fayyum was a combined result of these changes—and in particular the spread of the iqṭāʿ landholding regime and the mass Islamization of people and landscape.

Village Clans and Headmen

According to al-Nābulusī, nearly all villages and hamlets in the Fayyum were inhabited by Arab clans.[2] He describes the entire clan structure in the introductory chapters of the treatise and then repeats the information in the individual village entries, where the people of a village (the *ahl*) are always identified as belonging to a clan. Each village was normally identified with one clan only, and the clan

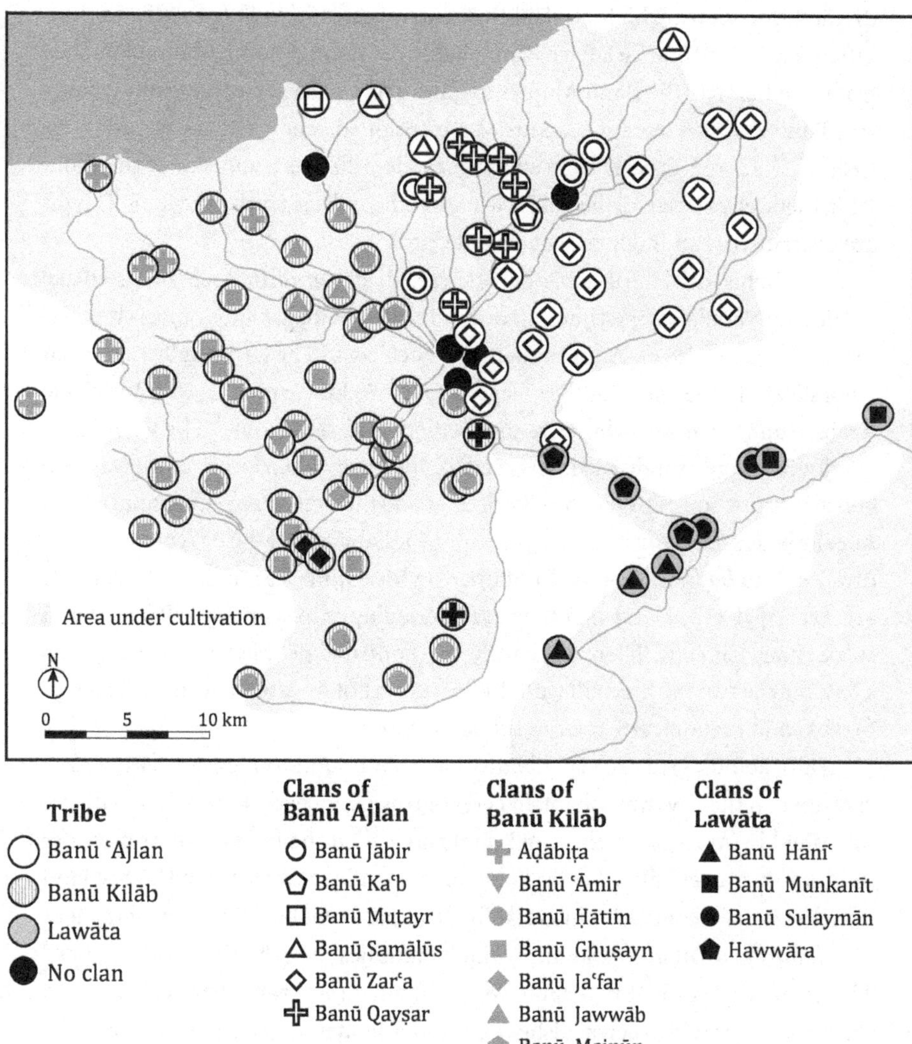

MAP 3.1. Clans and tribes of the Fayyum listed by al-Nābulusī, 643/1245.

identity defined the boundaries of the population of the village. The social system presented by al-Nābulusī was a simple segmentary model. At the top level were three confederacies (*aṣl* or *āl*), each inhabiting dozens of villages. First in importance were the Banū Kilāb, with as many as fifty villages, followed by the Banū ʿAjlān and the much smaller Lawāta, a Berber tribe. The Banū Kilāb dominated in the center, south, and west; the ʿAjlān in the east and the north, while the Lawāta dwelt in villages along the Lahun Gap. Each tribal confederacy was divided into clans, which al-Nābulusī usually calls *fakhidh* (pl., *afkhādh*) or, infrequently, *far'* (branch). Each clan inhabited a varying number of settlements, from one hamlet (the Banū Muṭayr in Sanhūr) to as many as nineteen villages (the Banū Zar'a). A few subclans are also mentioned, albeit with a degree of confusion. The Banū Qayṣar were sometimes identified as a subclan of the Banū Jābir, themselves a clan of the 'Ajlān, while in other village entries the Banū Qayṣar are described as an independent 'Ajlānī clan.[3]

Al-Nābulusī calls the inhabitants of these villages *'arab*, or Arab. In the village entries, al-Nābulusī sometimes identifies the local villagers not only as belonging to a clan but also as "Arab, of such-and-such clan." The term Arab is also used pejoratively. In the entry for the village al-Qubarā', for example, it was "the crude Arabs" (*ajlāf al-'arab*) who were disobedient and rebellious.[4] The term *badw* (Bedouin) is only rarely used, reserved for instances when al-Nābulusī wants to create a distinction between the village clans and the non-Arab population, whom he calls *ḥaḍar*. He dedicates a chapter to "the inhabitants of the Fayyum and their division into *badw* and *ḥaḍar*," but opens it by stating that "most of the people are Arabs [*al-'arab*], and that they are divided up into sections (*afkhādh*) and subsections (*shu'ūb*). There are hardly any nontribal people (*ḥaḍar*) in it, only a few, maybe two or three villages." In the context of Ayyubid Fayyum, the terms "Arabs" and *badw* clearly refer to the same people.

In al-Nābulusī's survey, clan identity had an economic dimension, as the Arab clansmen of the Fayyum inhabited cereal-growing villages. In nearly all villages inhabited by Arab clans, the inhabitants are called the *muzāri'ūn*, sometimes *mu'āmilūn*, the tenants who are liable to pay land tax as part of a lease of land from the state. A common phrase is "the land tax from the cultivation of the tenants (*kharāj zirā'at al-muzāri'īn*)," which identifies them by their fiscal duties.[5] The *muzāri'ūn* cultivator-tenants who inhabited the Arab villages also reared chickens and provided cereal dishes for the iqṭā' holders as part of their hospitality dues. In contrast, the few villages described as *ḥaḍar* or non-Arab were also the only villages in the Fayyum not to pay any taxes in grains. The non-Arab village of Bāja, for example, paid 292 dinars in land tax on long-term leases of land (*aḥkār*). Al-Nābulusī reports that it had "no field crops worthy of note, except for some sugarcane and green vegetables [irrigated] by waterwheels."[6] In this non-Arab village of Bāja, the absence of in-kind taxes, indicating no local cultivation of grains, perfectly overlapped with the absence of clan-based social structure. The opposition between Arab and *ḥaḍar* identities corresponded to the presence or absence of grain cultivation, and Arab clans inhabited all villages in which grain cultivation was the predominant economic activity.

Al-Nābulusī uses the term fallāḥūn for both Arabs and non-Arabs, and often pejoratively, with connotations of boorishness.[7] The inhabitants of the Arab villages of Babīj Unshū, Ṭubhār, and Qushūsh were fallāḥūn and thus obliged to provide hospitality dues. The inhabitants of the non-Arab Muslim village of Akhṣāṣ al-Ḥallāq were also fallāḥūn, mocked because they began wearing *ṭaylasān* shawls and calling themselves jurists. In Arab Minyat Aqnā, al-Nābulusī identifies the fallāḥūn and their "scoundrels" as those who destroyed the local bathhouse. Both the "uncouth Arabs" and the "fallāḥūn and their scoundrels" represented insubordination and lack of civilization.

The identification of Arab clans with settled village communities is unequivocal. Al-Nābulusī begins his exposé of the clan structure by noting that he only lists clans "according to their places of dwelling," specifically excluding "those who travel (*muntaji'ān*) to the province in times of drought, or put up their campsites in its open country in search of livelihood during the transport of the grain harvest."[8] His quantitative data regarding the alms tax levied on herds and flocks demonstrate that camels were found only in villages on the edges of the Fayyum and amounted to no more than a thousand heads for the province as a whole. He mentions the livestock of transhumant population as a separate, minor category, a tax recorded only in a handful of villages on the periphery of the province.[9]

The pervasive clan structure of cereal-growing villages was linked to collective taxation. The most important in-kind tax, the *munājaza* land tax, was collectively levied on villages' arable land.[10] Under the *munājaza* lease, common not only in the Fayyum but in other parts of Egypt, leases were granted to the villages' representatives, so officials did not have to bother with parceling land to individual tenants or listing the names of the individual cultivators. In this context, clan affiliation would appear to be the most effective way of defining who belonged to the privileged group of peasants entitled to the lease. This also explains how al-Nābulusī knew of the clan affiliation of village communities. Assuming lease contracts were indeed registered in the name of a clan, this information was then systematically passed on to the visiting bureaucrat from Cairo.

The village clans of the Fayyum were led by headmen called *mashāyikh*, a new village elite not previously attested in Islamic Egypt.[11] The headmen, always a group of men and never in the singular, held records of the village tax obligations, undertook the lease contracts of the village's arable lands on behalf of the community, and sold the village's surplus. Together with the village guards, from whom they were not clearly distinguishable, the headmen were also responsible for keeping the peace. For these services, the headmen and the guards were entitled to allowances (*rizaq*), minutely recorded by al-Nābulusī. These allowances were mostly granted as tax-free plots of arable land measured in feddans. These lands were exempt from the land tax, and their surplus therefore remained with the village headmen rather than delivered to the iqṭāʿ holder.[12]

The key role of village headmen in the fiscal system is illustrated right at the beginning of the treatise, when al-Nābulusī states that the headmen (*mashāyikh*) provided him with fiscal information in those villages in which the iqṭāʿ holders kept no clerks. The headmen gave witness to the total taxes owed by their village, and not just the in-kind taxes on arable lands.[13] Headmen also acted on behalf of the village by selling the village surplus. Al-Nābulusī notes that village headmen in Minyat Aqnā, alongside local iqṭāʿ-holding soldiers (*ajnād*), sold more than one thousand irdabbs of beans as fodder for the government's beasts of burden.[14] An anecdote told by al-Nābulusī in another administrative treatise shows that village headmen were also the recipients of the seed advances handed out to villages and were supposed to sign the receipts.[15]

The headmen shared some of their responsibilities with groups of village guards (*khufarāʾ*), a term that shows continuity with the Arab protectors of the eleventh century.[16] The two groups were not always clearly distinguishable from each other. In Abū Ksā, a village described as mostly non-Arab by al-Nābulusī, the headmen and the guardsmen were co-recipients of twelve feddans of tax-free allowances. In nine other villages allowances went either to headmen or to guards, but not to both, suggesting that the two groups were interchangeable. The register makes an occasional distinction between the guardsmen of a village (*khufarāʾ al-nāḥiya*) and the watchmen of roads and irrigation installations, who received much larger allowances. This suggests that the headmen and the village guards occupied the same rank in the village hierarchy and were different from the few armed men employed in guarding key installations and roads. In practice, law and order at the village level must have been the responsibility of headmen and guards, remunerated by tax-free allowances.[17]

A cluster of thirteenth- and fourteenth-century documents from al-Ashmūnayn in Middle Egypt sheds further light on the role of the *mashāyikh* headmen as the village officials responsible for law and order. As identified by Daisy Livingston, the relevant documents come principally from a dossier that belonged to the amir Jamāl al-Dīn al-Azkā, who was active in al-Ashmūnayn circa 1300, possibly as the provincial governor.[18] In the petitions addressed to Jamāl al-Dīn and in the decrees that he issued, village headmen appear frequently as the point of connection between provincial government and the village community. Typically, al-Azkā called upon the *mashāyikh* headmen or on the *nuwwāb wa'l-mashāyikh* (the agents of the iqṭāʿ holders and the headmen) to hand over villagers accused of crimes, such as unlawfully seizing property. In one case, the headmen of the village of Abū Qurqāṣ were called upon to explain the case of a fallāḥ tenant, evidently a Christian, who refused to pay his poll tax to the local iqṭāʿ holder. The complaint came from other villagers.[19] Jamāl al-Dīn al-Azkā and his sons were associated with the office of *majlis al-ḥarb* in the province, almost certainly meaning the court of the governor. They viewed the headmen in the villages of al-Ashmūnayn as their local representatives and called upon them to summon litigants and to report on local disputes. It is very likely that the headmen of the Arab villages of the Fayyum were fulfilling similar roles.

In al-Nābulusī's Fayyum, clusters of clan-based villages formed territorial groupings who in turn were the constituent parts of the three major tribal confederacies. These multivillage clans and confederacies had a major role in the regulation of the unique irrigation system of the Fayyum depression, where gravity-fed canals had the potential to cause friction between upstream and downstream village communities.[20] The irrigation system of the Fayyum had several mechanisms that aimed at efficient distribution of scarce water resources. One was an alternating schedule of low-level canals, which were closed for prolonged periods so that water was diverted to canals that lay on higher ground. Another mechanism was the allocation of rights over water—effectively, a maximum usage limit—to ensure that there was no excessive consumption.[21] In his survey, al-Nābulusī's focus was on identifying the feeder canal of each village and the water rights (*ḥuqūq*) of the community or individuals within it.

Like the village's arable lands, water rights were normally conceived as a collective right. Internal divisions of water quotas within a village are mentioned only in relation to lands excluded from the village's collective fiscal duties, such as sugarcane plantations or privately owned orchards.[22] In the register, water was awarded to the village as a unit in the same way taxes in grain were levied collectively. Non-Arab villages, such as the Christian or market villages of Minyat al-Usquf, Bāja, and Bamawayh, had no designated collective water rights. It therefore appears that collective water rights allocation was correlated with the presence of clan structure at the village level.

A close reading of al-Nābulusī's text points to a low level of state intervention in the management of irrigation. There were only minimal fees associated with local irrigation maintenance, and they supported simple irrigation administration and dredging tools. About half the villages along gravity-fed canals made small payments in kind to *khawlī al-baḥr* (canal overseer), a local official in charge of the schedule of the opening and closing of weirs. An additional irrigation tax, a "dredging fee" (*rasm al-jarārīf*), was paid by villages along gravity-fed canals. The total for 62 villages was 4,700 silver dirhams, about 115 gold dinars, less than 1 percent of the total cash taxes of the province.[23]

Given the low level of state intervention, it is likely that villages had much autonomy in the management and the upkeep of the canal system, with villages belonging to the same clan sorting out disputes without recourse to state officials. As shown in map 3.1, multivillage clans often united a string of settlements along an irrigation canal. Eight of ten villages along the Sinnūris Canal were inhabited by the Qayāṣira, or the Banū Qayṣar, of the ʿAjlān confederacy. The Banū Qayṣar inhabited no other villages in the Fayyum. All five villages lying along the al-Sharqiyya Canal, in the water-scarce area of the eastern Fayyum, were inhabited by the Banū Zarʿa clan of the ʿAjlān. The same pattern is found in the southern part of the province: of a total of sixteen villages along the Dilya Canal, eight were occupied by the Banū Ghuṣayn of the Kilāb, and five of nine villages along the Tanabṭawayh Canal were inhabited by the Banū Ḥātim, who also belonged to the Kilāb.

The match between clan structures and irrigation is even more apparent when we examine the larger confederacies. In the east, the clans of the Lawāta inhabited all villages irrigated by the Nile flood, and no Lawāta village was irrigated by the canal network of the depression. In the Fayyum itself, the two confederacies of the ʿAjlān and the Kilāb shared no branch-canals with each other. All the villages along the al-Sharqiyya, Dhāt al-Ṣafā', and Sinnūris canals were inhabited by the ʿAjlān; all the villages along the southern Tanabṭawayh, Dilya, and Minyat Aqnā canals were inhabited by the Kilāb. The ʿAjlān and the Kilāb occupied clearly demarcated territorial units. Remarkably, the territorial division between the ʿAjlān in the northeast and the Kilāb in the southwest replicated the administrative divisions of Roman Fayyum.[24] This is not to suggest any direct continuity between Roman administrative structure and Ayyubid tribal organization; rather, it suggests that the boundaries between the Kilāb and the ʿAjlān were carved by topography and reproduced the fissures of the irrigation network, unmistakable markers of territory and political power.

The *ʿUrbān* of the Fayyum

Al-Nābulusī's 1245 survey records with precision the levying of ʿurbān troops from among the village communities. It confirms beyond doubt that the ʿurbān auxiliary units were embedded in and drawn from the mass of the Muslim peasantry.[25] As we can see in al-Nābulusī's survey, the ʿurbān were recruited from among the peasants but were distinct from clanless, better-off orchardists, over whom they exercised protection. Multivillage clans also acted as protectors for non-Arab orchard villages, in what seems to be a leftover from the protection institution of the eleventh century. While Arab clan identities engulfed entire villages and were no longer the exclusive domain of village protector elites as they were in the eleventh century, village guards (*khufarā'*) were part of the village elites, alongside and almost indistinguishable from the village headmen.

Multivillage clans offered protection to clanless townsmen and orchardists in nearby villages. Thus, Bāja, whose inhabitants were *ḥaḍar* Christians, was under the protection of the Banū 'Āmir of the Kilāb, a clan that inhabited eight nearby villages. In Minyat al-Usquf, the Christian *ḥaḍar* inhabitants were under the protection of the Banū Rabī'a of the Kilāb, who lived in Dumūshiyya, just to the south.[26] We have seen that men and women of the Banū Rabī'a and the Banū 'Āmir acted as village protectors in the villages of southern Fayyum during the eleventh century. We can assume that over two centuries the Arab clans of the protector elites diffused among the broader village communities, so much so that entire villages now assumed Kilābī or 'Āmirī identities. These Arab village clans could then offer protection to the few remaining non-Arab villages, although the meaning of the protection institution must have transformed. While eleventh-century Arab protectors assumed the role of tax guarantors for the local cultivators, by the thirteenth century most of the villages had turned predominantly Arab and only a few non-Arab villages required protection.

In addition to their role as armed protectors of clanless people, the multivillage clans were also the building blocks from which the Arab auxiliary 'urbān were recruited. At the end of the treatise, al-Nābulusī gives an account of a levy of four hundred horsemen to be provided by the 'urbān clansmen of the villages of the Fayyum as auxiliary forces in the event of a royal military campaign. The term 'urbān does not appear anywhere else in the treatise and has, as we have seen in the twelfth century, a specific military connotation. The distribution of the established levy of riders is remarkably bureaucratized, and the account of this levy must have been taken from some central records. The register suggests that the troops were to be raised on demand, and not in return for any specific privilege.[27]

The total of four hundred 'urbān riders levied from the villages of the Fayyum was divided equally between the Banū Kilāb and the Banū 'Ajlān, with each required to provide two hundred riders. The Lawāta Berbers on the edge of the province were excluded, perhaps because they were attached to the main body of the Lawāta in the province of al-Bahnasāwiyya, farther to the south. The levy on the Banū Kilāb was subdivided among the constituent clans, with each clan having to contribute a share of the overall two hundred riders recruited from the Kilāb, such as a sixth or a third. The levy on the Banū ʿAjlān was divided between the clan of Banū Samālūs, required to raise one-sixth of the tribal total of two hundred, and all the other ʿAjlānī clans who were jointly responsible to raise the remaining five-sixths.[28] The shares of each clan were translated to a precise number of horsemen, including fractions: the one-sixth share of the Banū Samālūs meant they had to provide thirty-three horsemen and one-third of a horseman. The use of fractions in the calculation of the number of ʿurbān riders suggests that this list was only loosely related to the realities of units, or even that the levy was perhaps commuted into cash.

The ʿurbān were an integral part of village communities, the armed element of the omnipresent village clans. This comes across in other accounts of the relationship between the ʿurbān and wider rural society in this period. In another treatise, al-Nābulusī reports a warning by Sultan al-Malik al-Kāmil against alliances struck between the rustics (*ahl al-rīf*) and the officers of the *ʿurbān* units (*muqaddamī al-ʿurbān*), reinforcing the link between the ʿurbān and the peasantry.[29] In an Ayyubid-era anecdote from *The History of the Patriarchs*, an Arab group looted twenty-five villages in al-Gharbiyya. The troops sent by the sultan to chase them pillaged a set of nearby villages, claiming that these were the homes of the families of the Arab brigands. The local population denied the charge, but the troops assumed that the Arabs originated in settled communities.[30]

The History of the Patriarchs, which contains a rich section for the Ayyubid period, also confirms that Egyptian ʿurbān continued to function as auxiliary military units, as they had been in the twelfth century. While these ʿurbān troops were recruited from among the villagers, as we can clearly see in the 1245 Fayyum register, while on campaign they were mobile, living in tents (*buyūt shiʿr*) and riding on camels.[31] During the crusader siege of Damietta in 1218, an Arab force of three thousand men recruited from the Fayyum and Upper Egypt was defeated by the Franks.[32] In 1242/43, two years before al-Nābulusī's visit to the Fayyum, an ʿurbān force of two thousand men, led by Arab leaders (*ashrāf*), participated in the suppression of a rebellion by a Turkish garrison in Qūṣ in Upper Egypt. The Arab force moved along the western bank of the Nile, while the regular army moved along the eastern bank.[33] That the Arab confederacies continued to exercise substantial military power is not in doubt. In the 1230s, a feud between the Judhām and the Thaʿlaba in al-Sharqiyya led to them taking sides in infighting between the Egyptian and Syrian Ayyubid princes. Additional confederacies from nearby provinces were sucked into the conflict, which then paralyzed economic activity in the region.[34] After capturing Cairo in 1238, Sultan al-ʿĀdil summoned two thousand Arab riders to swear allegiance to him in the capital. Their presence was greatly feared by the author of the Coptic chronicle.[35]

Islamization and *Iqṭāʿ*

The village clans of thirteenth-century Fayyum were the culmination of a process that started in the eleventh century, when Arab protectors established themselves as the new village elites, performing fiscal duties previously undertaken by wealthy Coptic villagers. The shift from an elite of Arab protectors to village clans was simultaneous with three major changes in the history of the province. One was Islamization: thirteenth-century Fayyum was far more Muslim and far less Christian than it was two centuries earlier; most villages were Muslim, and most of the Muslim villages were also Arab. The second major change was the rise of iqṭāʿ grants as the predominant form of landholding, and the corollary shift to collective taxation of field cultivation. Finally, the Ayyubid-era reoccupation of villages abandoned in the late eleventh century, which must have involved some rural migration. The spread of village clans as the predominant form of social organization and identity in Ayyubid Fayyum was a combined result of these triple changes—demographic expansion, collective taxation, and mass Islamization of people and landscape.

Al-Nābulusī's 1245 survey demonstrates not only the spread of Arab village clans but also a concurrent Islamization, both of the population and the landscape. As we have seen, when Arab protectors first established themselves as the elites of the southern villages at the beginning of the eleventh century, most of the inhabitants were Copts—the majority of individuals who appear in the documentary evidence from the province had Christian names, and tenth-century geographers still referred to the Egyptian countryside as largely Coptic. By the middle of the thirteenth century, on the other hand, the Fayyum was an overwhelmingly Muslim province, where non-Muslims had become a minority. The records available to al-Nābulusī showed only 1,142 non-Muslim men registered as subject to the poll tax. A third of these non-Muslim men lived in the city of Madīnat al-Fayyūm, and the remainder in eighteen different villages across the province. Applying a multiplier to account for women and children, this represented a community of some five thousand non-Muslims, a small proportion of an overall rural population of about seventy-five thousand.[36]

The small size of the non-Muslim population is corroborated by the rarity of references to Christian villages and by the relatively few functioning churches.

Out of over one hundred villages, al-Nābulusī describes only two villages as predominantly Christian. These were two small suburban villages, Bāja and Minyat al-Usquf, which were also the only two settlements in the Fayyum where there were churches but no mosques. There were fifteen other active churches in the province, four of them in Madīnat al-Fayyūm.[37] Compared to the village churches, on the other hand, the monasteries of the Fayyum held on relatively well. The Fayyum had thirteen monasteries, all of them active, of which several were supported by allowances of tax-free land from Muslim-majority villages in their near vicinity.[38] Most of the monasteries mentioned by the Christian author Abū al-Makārim, who visited the province in the 1170s, were still standing by the end of the Ayyubid period, reinforcing the impression that these institutions held on better than the peasant communities around them.

Outside the main city of Madīnat al-Fayyūm, Christian communities were found in the market villages of Bamawayh and Sinnūris, each with over one hundred non-Muslim men. The two suburban villages of Bāja and Minyat al-Usquf, identified by al-Nābulusī as predominantly Christian, had non-Muslim communities of one hundred men and fifty men, respectively. Other clusters of over fifty Christian men lived in villages that served as nodes of the emerging sugarcane industry of the time (Dhāt al-Ṣafā, Fānū, and Dimashqīn al-Baṣal). Christian communities were closely associated with orchards and textile production. The two villages that al-Nābulusī identifies as predominantly Christian, Bāja and Minyat al-Usquf, paid all their taxes in cash, mainly on the cultivation of trees and gardens, which accounted for 50 percent of the taxes in Bāja and 60 percent in Minyat al-Usquf. The correspondence between Christian presence and textile production is evident in the distribution of taxes on pits of weavers (*ḥufar al-qazzāzīn*), mentioned in seven villages. The largest sums were paid in the predominantly Christian villages of Bāja and Minyat al-Usquf, nine dinars and six dinars, respectively. A tax of 4.8 dinars on the weavers in Ihrīt may be related to the presence of 25 non-Muslim men in this medium-sized village.[39]

The shift from Christianity to Islam is best illustrated by re-visiting villages mentioned in the documentary evidence of earlier centuries. In the eleventh century, most inhabitants in the village of Damūya were Copts, as known to us from the papers of Jirja b. Bifām. By the time of al-Nābulusī's register, the village was called Dimūh al-Lāhūn or Kūm Darī, and was an entirely Muslim community, with not a single Christian man subject to the poll-tax. The inhabitants, according to al-Nābulusī, all hailed from the Hawwāra branch of the Lawāta Berbers.[40] The southern villages of Tuṭūn and Buljusūq, now in new sites, were also predominantly Muslim. Tuṭūn, a center of Coptic learning up until the 950s, was now inhabited by the Banū Ḥātim, without a single resident Christian. The nearby village of Buljusūq, which had a substantial Coptic community as late as the 1130s, had in 1245 only nine non-Muslim men registered to pay the poll tax, of which only one was present in the village. The church of Buljusūq is described as deserted, and the only religious building standing was the village's Friday Mosque, serving the local clan of the Banū Ḥātim.

The disappearance of the Coptic peasantry is striking. By 1245, the Copts were concentrated in Madīnat al-Fayyūm and its nearest orchards, in market villages, or in centers for textile production, but they are rarely recorded in the cereal-growing villages. Outside centers of trade and artisanal production, Christians were few and far between. Non-Muslim minority communities of less than thirty men, sometimes only a handful of individuals, were found in some dozen predominantly Arab villages. These scattered groups, presumably all Copts, were generally unable to maintain a functioning local church and lived in overwhelmingly Muslim villages. The negative correlation between the presence of poll-tax-paying Copts and the cultivation of cereals suggests—with near certainty—that Ayyubid Fayyum had no Copts tending to arable land. Rather, the cultivation of wheat and barley appears to have become the exclusive domain of Muslim peasants.

As Christianity gave way in the villages, the peasant population and the architectural landscape turned Muslim as well as Arab. By the time of al-Nābulusī's visit, the province had at least seventy-eight mosques, of which fifty-one were found in forty-seven villages.[41] Nearly all medium- and large-sized villages in the Fayyum had a congregational Friday Mosque, and a few also had a smaller *masjid*, or a neighborhood mosque, at the edge of the village. The settlements that had no Friday Mosque were either small villages or even smaller hamlets. Al-Nābulusī further reports unregistered neighborhood mosques in seven small villages and hamlets.[42] Village mosques became a common sight in the Fayyum for the first time during the eleventh century; by the thirteenth century they had become ubiquitous.

As Islam replaced Christianity, whose traces were still visible, the same structures could acquire new Islamic meanings. The Sufi *zāwiya* built in the land of Iṭfīḥ Shallā stood where a monastic institution called Shallā existed as late as 947.[43] The site was just below the still functioning Monastery of Naqlūn and shows how Sufism could tap into pre-Islamic local traditions of sacred sites. In an aside, al-Nābulusī acknowledges the Coptic past: he tells us that the village of Sīla, where only seven Christian men are mentioned in his tax survey, was once a center of Coptic Christianity and home to forty churches.

The poll tax had a major role in the disappearance of the Coptic peasantry and in its conversion to Islam, as has been recently demonstrated empirically and theoretically by Mohamed Saleh. Saleh argues that the regressive flat-rate poll tax triggered a process of self-selection of converts since the beginning of Islamic rule in Egypt, leading to both the long-term decline in the proportion of Copts out of the overall population of Egypt and to the formation of interreligious socio-economic gaps between Copts and Muslims. Poor Copts had a much stronger incentive to convert to Islam, as the poll tax represented a larger share of their income. Nonconverts, on the other hand, were encouraged to invest more in human capital to prevent the conversion of their offspring. The Fayyum register of 1245 perfectly conforms to this model. The Coptic minority that remained in the Fayyum specialized in skilled professions, such as textile and bureaucracy, or in the more lucrative cultivation of orchards. The poorer peasantry, who had been majority Coptic in the first centuries of Islamic rule, have by now converted to Islam. Considering various Egyptian demographic datasets from the time of the Conquest to the middle of the nineteenth century, Saleh shows that a new equilibrium was achieved in Egypt circa 1200, independently matching the evidence from the Fayyum: a Muslim rural majority and a relatively skilled, highly urbanized Coptic minority.[44]

The proliferation of village clans was also cotemporaneous with a shift to iqṭāʿ grants as the central plank of the fiscal regime. As we have seen, iqṭāʿ grants were known in Fatimid Egypt alongside other fiscal instruments, such as the *khafāra* protection and *ḍamān* tax farming, but the Ayyubids made the iqṭāʿ the cornerstone of their political economy. The holders of the iqṭāʿ grants were members of the Ayyubid army who rarely resided in the countryside. In return for providing military service to the sultan, the iqṭāʿ holders received temporary rights to the fiscal revenue of the villages assigned to them, including the right to lease out the land to tenants. At the time of al-Nābulusī's visit, the vast majority of the villages in the Fayyum, over 90 percent, were assigned in this way, meaning that most fiscal revenue of the Fayyum—in grains and in cash, from agriculture and commerce—was channeled to the holders of iqṭāʿ grants. Only about half a dozen villages lay outside the overarching iqṭāʿ regime: three large villages that belonged to the private domain (*khāṣṣ*) of the sultan, where the sultan had a personal right to taxes, and three small villages and some individual orchards endowed as waqf for the benefit of religious institutions, both in Cairo and in Madīnat al-Fayyūm.[45]

The iqṭāʿ system was a complex political and economic model that has yet to receive sustained scholarly treatment. It could encompass a variety of landholding arrangements. At the beginning of the Ayyubid period, the entire province was awarded wholesale to a succession of Ayyubid princes, and in the 1220s it was handed to the high-ranking amir Fakhr al-Dīn ʿUthmān, who made extensive investments in irrigation and water supply. By the time of al-Nābulusī's visit, however, the Fayyum was parceled out into small iqṭāʿ units, each normally consisting of a single village. The complexity of the iqṭāʿ system comes primarily from the dynamic interaction of iqṭāʿ holders with other agents: the allocation of iqṭāʿ was decided by the central government, but local management was often at the hands of administrative agents, and the enforcement of the iqṭāʿ holders' rights depended on the troops of the local governor.

Most importantly, the shift to a regime of iqṭāʿ impacted the very fabric of peasant communities. As shown by Nicolas Michel, the iqṭāʿ regime necessarily turned most of the peasantry into fallāḥ tenants who had to lease the fields of the village from iqṭāʿ holders.[46] The lease contracts for the village lands were handed to the headmen, who were subsequently collectively responsible for the taxation levied on the village. The grant of collective tenancy leases to the village's representatives was fundamentally different than the collection of taxes from privately owned land. All forms of tax farming known from the Abbasid and Fatimid periods have by now disappeared. The 1245 survey of the Fayyum has no mention of *ḍāmin* or *dalīl* tax farmers and tax officials, only village headmen. By this time, taxes on villages' fields were levied collectively at the village level, as arable land formally and unambiguously belonged to the state under the pervasive iqṭāʿ regime.

The collective lease contracts over state lands were directly linked to the proliferation of village clans. In the 1245 survey, all villages that had to pay any in-kind taxes over arable land were inhabited by named clans. From the perspective of the iqṭāʿ holder, the social category of the clan was a way to identify the collective identity of the group carrying out the cultivation. From the cultivators' point of view, membership in a clan delineated the boundaries of the lease contract: one had to be a member of a clan to gain a share in the village's rights of cultivation. Conversely, the only clanless villages in the survey are those without any arable land. In villages where the entire land was used for privately owned orchards and plantations, state officials had no need to award lease contracts or to identify village clans.

Another byproduct of the iqṭāʿ regime was the forced potential mobility of the village community. Lease contracts could be terminated at the will of the iqṭāʿ holder and given over to another group of cultivators. When tenancy contracts were revoked, village clans might be forcibly removed from the land, and the rights of cultivation given to others. Al-Nābulusī relates that the Banū Kaʿb villagers of al-Qubarā' were driven out by the governor of the Fayyum due to their insubordination. Thereafter, the lease contracts for the arable land of the village were registered (*musajalla*) in the name of the tenants of the nearby village of Akhṣāṣ al-Ḥallāq.[47] Apart from destroying the houses of the original villagers, the governor is also said to cut off their *āthār*—referring to the traces of their cultivation from previous years and therefore, perhaps, also erasing their claim to receive the tenancy lease in the following one.[48] The protection of Akhṣāṣ al-Ḥallāq, previously at the hand of the Banū Ka'b, was now given to the Banū Qayṣar. One could say that the Banū Ka'b were now a community on the move, but this was because they *had* to become mobile—not because of any cultural predilection for peripatetic lifestyle, but rather because they were thrown out of their lands.

In addition to widespread Islamization and the rolling out of iqṭā' grants, al-Nābulusī's survey also attests to a significant reoccupation of sites. The village of Ṭalīt, which had been deserted in the late eleventh century, was reestablished thanks to a new canal dug in the 1220s. The new village was on lower grounds compared to the previous site, which was located higher up on the mountain. Tuṭūn and Buljusūq were similarly replaced by smaller settlements to the north of the older site. The reoccupation of sites was accompanied by significant investment from a major iqṭā' holder, the *ustādār* Fakhr al-Dīn 'Uthmān, aimed at increasing the water flow entering the Fayyum.[49] Al-Nābulusī noted that the lands of abandoned villages were at the time of his visit sown by peasants from nearby settlements and that many new villages were established toward the center of the Fayyum on lands reclaimed from the receding Lake Qārūn. Overall, he says, "it is possible that the majority of the current villages in the center of Fayyum are newly built after the retreat of the Fayyum's water from them, so they make up for all the deserted and derelict villages that we have mentioned."[50]

The newly reoccupied sites required additional workforce to cultivate them, necessarily involving some form of rural migration. Yet it is unlikely that the Arab village clans of Ayyubid Fayyum were nomads who settled down. First, al-Nābulusī noted that the people who reoccupied abandoned sites came from nearby villages, giving the impression that the migration was local in nature. Second, village clans were found not only in reoccupied sites or on the edges of the desert. In fact, the register shows that areas at the center of the Fayyum were as inhabited by Arab village clans as the more vulnerable margins. Third, the names of villages in the Fayyum showed remarkable continuity. Not even one of the ninety villages listed in the 1245 survey carries a name that reflects the clan identity of its inhabitants. Only thirteen carry unambiguously Arabic names; the rest had names that predated the Arabization of the province and in many cases can be traced back to settlements mentioned in Roman and Greek papyri.[51] Arabic names are common only in smaller hamlets.[52] Exclusively among the hamlets, only a couple are identified by the name of the dominant clan. Usually, hamlets are identified by reference to a family, such as Munsha'at Awlād 'Arafa, al-'Athāmina (those descended from 'Uthmān), or to a named individual, such as Ibn Kurdī or Abū 'Uṣayya.[53] Changes to the toponymy of the Fayyum took place only later, in the late Mamluk and early Ottoman period. The village of Uqlūl came to be known in Ottoman sources as al-Ja'āfira, after the name of a local clan.[54] The ancient village of Damūh came to be known as Hawwārat 'Adlān, referring to a clan of the Berber Hawwāra.[55]

The Omnipresent Arab Village Clans

Shortly after al-Nābulusī's visit to the Fayyum, Jean de Joinville accompanied Louis IX on his campaign in Egypt in 1249–50. Joinville speaks of the Egyptian Arabs with great authority and much detail, saying they do not live in villages or towns but set up tents each evening and live off the milk of their livestock. He adds that the Bedouin purchase "pasturage for their animals on the plains owned by rich men" and make large tribute payments each year.[56] Yet Joinville copied from earlier authors, with biblical references betraying an attempt to frame the realities of the thirteenth century within categories familiar to European audiences. His account is typical of the way the *'arab* identity was often idealized and reified, uprooted from its local contexts.

Joinville's account is surely outweighed by al-Nābulusī's 1245 register of the Fayyum. Al-Nābulusī—close to the ground, going village by village—describes the omnipresence of village clans of Muslim tenants, led by headmen who were responsible for the payment of the collective land-tax. Clans spread over several villages appear to have regulated disputes over access to water. They were subject to a provincial levy of riders for the 'urbān auxiliary units, recruited from among the village clans. There were *mashāyikh* headmen responsible for law and order in thirteenth-century al-Ashmūnayn, as is known to us from fragmentary documentary evidence. It is beyond doubt that the Arabs of the Fayyum were by and large the inhabitants of sedentary villages, not nomads.

The proliferation of Arab village clans in the Fayyum was cotemporaneous with demographic expansion, a shift to collective tenancy contracts, and mass Islamization. Reoccupation of abandoned sites and the expansion of cultivation changed the landscape of the Fayyum in the thirteenth century. Yet the continuity of village names suggests that the cultivators in these reoccupied sites mostly came from within the Fayyum and not from nomadic settlers. The key factors leading to the spread of village clans in Ayyubid Fayyum were not demographic, but fiscal and religious. The shift to an iqṭāʿ regime meant that the cultivators were considered tenants, while most rural administration was devolved to iqṭāʿ holders. This decentralization led to the emergence of autonomous clans, who collectively undertook leases for cultivation. The clans also regulated networks of water distribution and local security and were the building block of the ʿurbān auxiliary units. At the level of cultivation, membership in a clan meant access to arable land, which was leased to the headmen. One had to be a member of the clan to gain rights of cultivation; only villages without arable land were clanless.

The villagers of the Fayyum organized into Arab clans following their mass conversion to Islam. We can suppose that converts to Islam fashioned for themselves Arabian genealogies as symbols of status and a means of erasing their non-Muslim ancestry. Some may have been clients of the Arab protectors of the eleventh century, and their previous identities were gradually subsumed by the Arab village elites. One could be a member of a clan only if one were Muslim, and membership of a clan was a precondition for gaining a share in the village arable lands. The spread of the village clans reinforced conversion to Islam as the only means for poorer Christian peasants to stay on the land. Eventually, as in all groups arising in illiterate contexts, the memory of the actual formation of the clan was suppressed, to be replaced with nomadic myths of origins.

New Muslim identities in rural Fayyum were bound up with genealogy. In al-Nābulusī's register, there are hardly any non-Arab Muslim peasants; the villagers were either Arab Muslims or non-Arab Copts. This conflation of genealogy and religion was also reflected in texts produced by minority religious communities. From a Christian point of view, conversion was an act of ethnic transformation. In a Coptic martyrdom text set in thirteenth-century Upper Egypt, all the Muslims of Egypt are consistently called Arab.[57] Egyptian Jews, on the other hand, sought special status by claiming lineage from the Jews of Khaybar, based on a supposed bill of rights given by the Prophet Muhammad. The alleged bill of rights was first produced in the early Fatimid period and was then used in the following centuries by individual Jewish men who sought exemption from the poll tax by testifying to their Khaybarī ancestry.[58] In Ayyubid and Mamluk Egypt, one's religion and one's ancestry were seen as inseparable: in an anti-Coptic treatise composed by al-Nābulusī himself, the treacherous nature of Copts is due to their ethnic background and could never be washed away by conversion.[59]

In a seminal essay on the social function of genealogy in fifteenth-century Spain, David Nirenberg showed that genealogy was elevated to a primary form of communal identity following the mass conversions of Jews to Christianity between 1391 and 1415. As converts attempted to integrate into majority society, the dominant Christian reaction was to treat Jewish ancestry as inherently corrupt, thereby invoking an intense attempt by the *conversos* to purify their lineages.[60] Tamer el-Leithy had applied this model to Mamluk Egypt, showing how new Coptic converts to Islam were subject to suspicion by existing Muslim elites and were therefore forced to constantly engage in erasing the traces of their conversion.[61] Claiming Arab lineage was one of the routes to achieve this erasure—perhaps, as the 1245 survey of the Fayyum suggests, the most popular and effective route of turning former Coptic communities into good Muslims.

4

The Village Clans of the Palestinian Highlands

THE HARAM AL-SHARIF documents are the single largest surviving collection of Mamluk-era legal documents.[1] This documentary corpus was discovered by Amal Abou el-Hajj in the mid-1970s in the Islamic Museum, within the precinct of the Haram Sanctuary in Jerusalem. It consists of nine hundred documents, including estate inventories, contracts, procedural documents, accounts, decrees, and petitions. More than half the documents were produced in the court of the *qāḍī* of Jerusalem in the 1390s, and nearly all the rest were produced earlier in the fourteenth century. More than half the documents show some connection to Abū al-Rūḥ ʿĪsā Sharaf al-Dīn, who intermittently held the position of the Shāfiʿī *qāḍī* in Jerusalem from 793/1391 to 797/1395. As argued by Christian Müller, this corpus was probably assembled as part of an inquiry into corruption allegations made against Sharaf al-Dīn. The corruption case was abandoned because of Sharaf al-Dīn's untimely death, and the dossier of evidence was subsequently forgotten, somehow escaping the fate of all the other documents produced by the Mamluk court of the city.[2]

While most of the Haram corpus dates from the 1390s and is mostly concerned with residents of Jerusalem, a subset of twenty-seven documents, all dating from the first decade of the fourteenth century, is concerned with villages endowed for the benefit of the Haram Sanctuary in Jerusalem or the Tomb of the Patriarchs in Hebron.[3] This cluster of rural documents pre-dates Sharaf al-Dīn's tenure as *qāḍī* by ninety years and does not appear to have any direct relationship with the rest of the corpus. It originated from archive-like depositories of the two endowments in Jerusalem and Hebron, as is evident from short filing notes found on the verso of many of these documents.[4] Of the twenty-seven documents discussed here, fourteen were published by

D. S. Richards, Kāmil al-ʿAsalī, and Christian Müller, and the remainder are available on microfilm.[5]

The set of rural documents from the Haram collection mostly record obligations undertaken by the headmen of a village (*raʾīs*, pl. *ruʾasāʾ*) to cultivate the land of the village, to pay the village taxes, or to keep the peace. Invariably, the village headmen stand as guarantors for each other for the fulfillment of these commitments. In some cases, the headmen also take a *qasāma*, a sworn undertaking distinctive to Mamluk legal practice.[6] Breach of the *qasāma* entailed a significant penalty payment, ranging between five hundred and two thousand silver dirhams. Other documents in this rural subset have the headmen acknowledge receipt of payment for goods they delivered to the administrators of the endowment, and a blood-money settlement in the court of Jerusalem following a murder of one of the villagers.[7]

The Haram documents primarily deal with villages that were endowed at that time for the benefit of the holy shrines of Jerusalem and Hebron. One group of villages was in the highlands north of Jerusalem, mostly near Ramallah; Ramallah itself, at the time a modest village, was endowed for the benefit of the holy shrine of Hebron. The second cluster of villages was located on the western slopes of the Judean mountains, northwest of Hebron (see map 4.1).[8] All in all, there are references to individuals from twenty-one different villages, not only those that were part of the endowments but also several nearby villages where individuals were involved in keeping the peace. These villages are known to us from earlier and later sources. The systematic Ottoman cadastral surveys, and specifically the 1596 census published by Hütteroth and Abdulfattah, give demographic and fiscal data about most of the villages mentioned in the Haram documents.[9] These villages are a random sample of the settlements of the Palestinian highlands at the time: Muslim and Christian, on highlands and on the hills, producing grain and olives.

This chapter argues, based on this set of rural documents, that Arab village clans were as prevalent in early-fourteenth-century Palestine as they were in thirteenth-century Fayyum and that they were as closely linked with conversion to Islam and with the tenant status of the farmers. Each Muslim village in the sample was inhabited by a clan with a name taken from the Arab genealogical tree; only majority Christian villages were not inhabited by Arab clans. Arab clans were closely tied to the novel institution of village headmen who undertook collective fiscal obligations, acted as co-guarantors for each other and for other villagers, and oversaw the peace in their own village as well as in neighboring ones. While these villages were not subject to the predominant iqṭāʿ regime, the cultivators in these villages were nonetheless tenants whose headmen leased their lands from the administrators of the endowments. The village clan organization in fourteenth-century Palestine was linked to collective lease contracts and tax payments.

As in Ayyubid Fayyum, the spread of Arab village clans in the Palestinian highlands followed a mass wave of rural Islamization, communicated by village mosques, cemeteries, and saintly tombs. This was mainly a consequence of conversion: as village communities converted to Islam, they turned Arab to erase their Christian past. This chapter will also show that the spread of Arab clan identities was accompanied by an expansion of sedentary agriculture in Greater Syria during the twelfth and thirteenth centuries. This agricultural expansion was characterized by systematic reoccupation of sites abandoned in previous centuries and the reuse of building material from collapsed buildings. As in Ayyubid Fayyum depicted in the 1245 survey, the proliferation of village clans went hand in hand with reclamation of agricultural land, not with abandonment or desertification.

Village Headmen

The majority of rural documents from the Haram collection record collective fiscal obligations undertaken by groups of village headmen—never a single individual—who stood as guarantors for each other and for other villagers. These headmen are mostly identified by Arab clan names, one clan per village. The headmen were co-guarantors for the cultivation of the lands of the village, for the payment of the taxes, and for law and order. At least in one case, they also appear as the leaders of peasant groupings, with each grouping responsible for a share of the village lands. As in Ayyubid Fayyum, the headmen were also the recipients of the seed advances allotted to the village and in charge of the sale of surplus produce. Men identified by names of Arab clans, most probably headmen, also undertook responsibility for securing the peace in their own village and neighboring ones.

Bayt Ūniya, present-day Beitunia, today a suburb of Ramallah, is the village best represented in this rural corpus. Four documents, dated from August 1306 to August 1308, record undertakings by named village headmen to keep the peace and to pay the tax on the olive and grain harvests of the village. Another document concerning Bayt Ūniya is a lease of a shop to a Christian man who originated from another village. The four headmen of Bayt Ūniya—Sulaymān b. Yūsuf b. Ghazwān, ʿAlī b. Ḥamad b. Ḥammād, Mūsā b. Muḥammad b. Ḥamdān, and

ʿAlī b. Mannāʿ b. Sulṭān—are all identified by the clan's name of al-Ṣubāḥiyyīn (or al-Ṣabāḥiyyīn). The clan's name is mentioned in three of the four documents, and it is evident that the scribes thought it was an important aspect of the identity of the four headmen. The waqf administrators and the court of the *qāḍī* of Jerusalem identified the headmen not only by their social and political function in the village, but also by their clan affiliation.

The social and economic roles of the four headmen of Bayt Ūniya can be deduced in some detail. First, they stood as co-guarantors for the tax on the olive harvest of the village, a tax that was levied in the form of a future sale. In a document titled "Guarantee (*ḍamān*) of the olives in the village of Bayt Ūniya," the four men bought from the supervisor of the waqf all the olive harvest of the village for five thousand dirhams, with payment to take place in two installments, one in December 1306 and the remainder in March 1307. The four stood as guarantors for each other; although they are not specifically recognized as headmen, we know them as such from the other documents in the set.[10] This document takes the legal form of a sale, but it is in fact a record of the taxes on the olive harvest of the village that took place in the previous autumn months. This fiscal procedure for the taxation of olives is explained in al-Nuwayrī's administrative manual.[11]

The same four Ṣubāḥī headmen also stood as co-guarantors for the payment of the grain taxes in the village, as we know from a Ṣafar 708/August 1308 document.[12] The four men, here identified as headmen, acknowledged that they owe crops from last year's harvest, comprising $23^{14}/_{24}$ *ghirāras* of grains, about 500 liters, mostly in barley. Based on normal prices of grain in Syria in this period, the monetary value of this tax in grains was 2,000 to 2,500 dirhams, half the cash taxes on olives in the village.[13] Again, the four men stood as guarantors for each other with regard to the payment of these taxes. They also undertook to cultivate the land of the village, to plough and sow it, and not to leave it fallow. The last line is partly illegible and appears to contain the penalty for noncompliance.

In a third document, dated Rajab 706/January 1307, the headmen stood as co-guarantors for cultivation by one of the villagers, a certain Kāmil b. Ḥamad b. Manṣūr.[14] In the document, Kāmil is not identified by a clan name, but neither are the headmen, and this may be an oversight by the scribe. Kāmil testified that he would attend to all his lands and vines through farming (*filāḥa*) and by sowing summer and winter crops; if any lay fallow, it was his responsibility (*taḥta daraki-hi*). His commitment was backed up by a collective guarantee made by the four headmen, in the form of both *ḍamān* and *kafāla*, that Kāmil will reside and cultivate (*iqāma* and *ʿimāra*). Whenever the administrator of the waqf demand that he be summoned, they will present him; and if they cannot present him in person, they [text says: "he"] will do what was asked of him. While the headmen vouchsafed for Kāmil's behavior, the language of the document suggests that Kāmil had individual responsibility for his own lands and his vines. The headmen of Bayt Ūniya guaranteed the payment of collective taxes on the village's grains and olives, but these collective responsibilities still allowed for the assignment of lands to individuals within the village.

The collective obligations of the Ṣubāḥī headmen extended to keeping the peace outside the boundaries of Bayt Ūniya. In August 1306, three of the four headmen undertook a sworn *qasāma* oath not to disrupt the peace in Bayt Ūniya or to travel to the village of Yālū, located some fifteen kilometers to the southwest of their village, at the foot of the highlands.[15] The language of the document suggests an alliance of sorts between Bayt Ūniya and Yālū, which the authorities were keen to break up. After promising not to travel to Yālū, they also undertook to avoid corruption and people of evil deeds. If they did any of these things or helped the people of that village in illegal activities, they were liable to a penalty of two thousand dirhams, to be paid to the public treasury (*bayt al-māl*).

To sum up, the headmen of Bayt Ūniya in the highlands north of Jerusalem were all identified by the same clan's name. They stood as co-guarantors for taxes in olive and grains, for cultivation by individual villagers, and for law and order more broadly.[16] This was replicated in other villages visible to us in the Haram corpus. In Nūbā, three 'Āmirī (i.e., Banū 'Āmir) headmen acknowledged the annual taxes in grains owed to the waqf authorities. They also stood as guarantors for each other, in a format comparable to the acknowledgment of taxes in grain made by the headmen of Bayt Ūniya.[17] Two 'Āmirī men identified as shaykhs from the village of Zakariyā al-Biṭṭīkh, fifteen kilometers northwest of Nūbā, similarly undertook to cultivate the village lands.[18] In Ḥalḥūl, a village near Hebron, two 'Abbāsī headmen acknowledged receipt of seed advances of grains, presumably on behalf of the entire village.[19] Headmen were co-guarantors for taxes and cultivation, and it is only logical that they were also the designated recipients of the seed advances allotted to the village.

In addition, village headmen were also in charge of selling surplus local produce. In November 1306, two named villagers from 'Ayn Yabrūd, identified as *al-'Āmirayn* (that is, of the Banū 'Āmir), sold olive oil the to the endowment of the Haram al-Sharif compound.[20] The two sellers jointly received the sale price of 1,400 dirhams and acknowledged they would share the sum with a third villager, Mūsā b. Qāsim b. Isma'īl, so that the money would be split equally between the three of them. The first two villagers appear to be more senior and were at hand to accept the payment; they are also identified by the name of the clan, the Banū ʿĀmir, unlike the third partner. Another document from the same village shows that one of these two men was a headman and the second the father of another headman.[21] The sale deed discussed here suggests that the revenues accruing to villagers from the sale of the olive oil were pooled, mirroring the villages' collective fiscal responsibilities.[22]

Village headmen identified by clan names, or other indications of clan identity, are attested for thirteen Palestinian villages in the regions of Ramallah, Jerusalem, and Hebron that appear in the Haram corpus. A reference to the Turcoman clan of the Döger is attested in Ghāziya (present-day Ghaziyeh) near Sidon, a village that was endowed to the Prophet's Mosque in Medina.[23] The same individuals might appear without their clan name in some types of documents that regulated internal affairs within the village, such as a division of peasant groupings or deeds regulating the behavior of individuals. But, as can be seen in table 4.1, in those thirteen villages where headmen were identified by their Arab clans, scribes appended the name of the clan in almost all documents relating to taxation.

The headmen—clearly the central fiscal and political institution of Palestinian villages in this period—were a new phenomenon. They are not attested in the pre-crusader period and probably emerged only during the twelfth century. The first mention comes from William of Tyre, who reports a delegation of headmen (*ruʾasā*) from the hilly region around Nablus submitting to the Latins immediately after the conquest, in 1100.[24] But this is an outlier, written long after the events it describes. Christian headmen appear in the Latin charters from the 1170s onward, appearing to own the villages under their charge in the manner of a military lord.[25] A first account of a Muslim headman is by Ibn Jubayr in 1181, who was hosted in the elegant house of a village headman, or *raʾīs*, in the Galilee. His account suggests one headman in the village, chosen by the local landlord.[26] In Latin documents, references to headmen come in Zorzi's detailed report concerning Venetian-held villages in the regions of Tyre and Tripoli, dating from the 1240s. According to Zorzi, some villages had one headman while others had two or three. These headmen were entitled to a tax-free *carrucate*, a ploughing unit, probably similar to the Arabic *miḥrāth* mentioned in the register of the Fayyum as a prerogative of village officials.[27] By the 1250s, the Hospitallers awarded villages in the Galilee to one or more *rays*, i.e., *raʾīs* headman, who undertook to "hold, work, and guard" the land on their behalf.[28] A reference in an

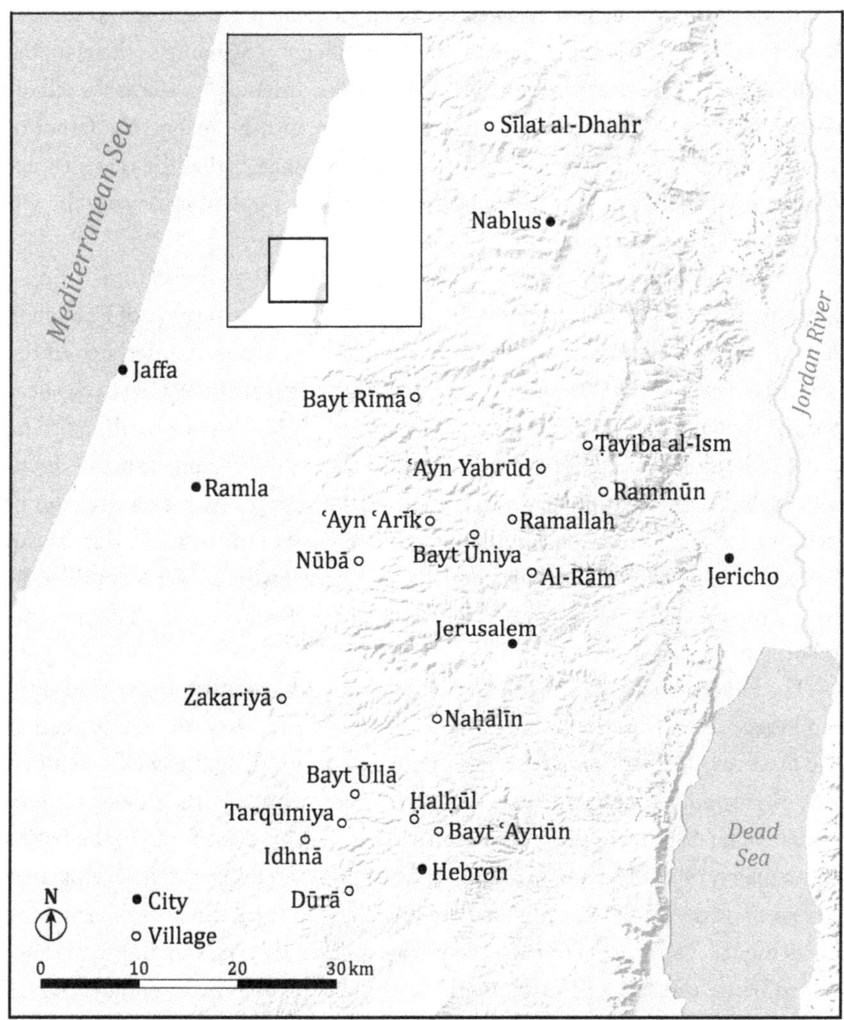

MAP 4.1. Villages of Palestinian Highlands mentioned in the documentary sources from the Mamluk court of Jerusalem, circa 700/1300.

Arabic narrative text to headmen from Kūfiyya near Gaza in the 1260s shows that the institution was adopted by the Mamluks.[29] The omnipresence of village headmen in the Haram documents of the first decade of the fourteenth century demonstrates the deep reach and quick spread of this institution. Within a couple of centuries, the headmen became a key feature of Palestinian rural society, inextricably linked with the formation of village clans.

TABLE 4.1. Villagers Identified by Clan Names in the Haram Documents, 1305–8

Village	Number of documents	Of which, clan name mentioned in:	Headmen (or shaykhs): With clan name	Headmen (or shaykhs): No clan name	Nonheadmen villagers: With clan name	Nonheadmen villagers: No clan name	Tribal *nisba*
Bayt Ūniya	5	3	X	X		X	al-Ṣubāḥī
ʿAyn Yabrūd	2	1	X	X		X	al-ʿĀmirī
Nūbā	3	2	X	X	X		al-ʿĀmirī
Zakariyā	1	1	X				al-ʿĀmirī
Ḥalḥūl	2	1	X		X		al-ʿAbbāsī
Bayt ʿAynūn	1	1			X	X	al-ʿAbbāsī
Tarqūmiya	1	1			X	X	al-Ghāzī
Dūrā	2	2			X		al-Rabaʿī
Khān al-Ifranj	1	1			X		al-Saʿdī
Rammūn	1	1	X				Banū Sālim
Miʿṣartā	1	1	X				Banū Sālim
Kafr Rʿaīl	1	1			X	X	al-Ḥārithī (?)
Idhnā	1	1				X	al-Ḥalāfī (?)
Bayt Ūllā	1	—				X	
Bayt Nāṣīf	1	—				X	
Ṭayiba al-Ism	1	—				X	
Bayt Rīmā	1	—				X	Christian
ʿAyn ʿArīk	3	—		X		X	
Naḥālīn	1	—				X	
Ramallah	1	—				X	
al-Ghāziya (Sidon)	2			X	X		al-Duʿārī

Village Clans

Village headmen appear to have derived their authority from leading peasant groupings, with each grouping responsible for a share of the village lands. Our evidence for that comes from a single key document concerning the village of ʿAyn Yabrūd, dated September 1307. The document records the names of twenty-five men, identified as "the headmen and the peasants (fallāḥīn) of ʿAyn Yabrūd." This collective of headmen and peasants undertook to reside in the village and to sow, turn, and cultivate the lands that belonged to the waqf, which comprised three-quarters of the total lands of the village.[30] They were divided into five groupings of unequal numbers, each headed by a village leader. These twenty-five men probably represented all cultivators in this small village, where twenty-four households were recorded in the Ottoman survey of the late sixteenth century.[31] The leaders of the five groups are identified as headmen, and each stood as guarantor to his companions and in surety for the other headmen. One of the five headmen co-sold the village's surplus olive oil in the previous year, and another headman is almost certainly the son of the other co-seller.[32]

Similar documents listing groupings of male peasants, each grouping led by a village headman, are well known from sixteenth-century Ottoman registers. In the Ottoman records of the highland villages around Jerusalem studied by Amy Singer, local peasants were also divided into groupings, generally called *jamāʿa*.[33] Each group of peasants had a designated leader standing as guarantor for the other members of their group; these men were sometimes identified as the village headmen (*ruʾasā*). They could be held responsible for paying the taxes of the village as a whole or paying a fixed share of the total.[34] Such lists are also known from the surviving Ottoman *dafātir al-tarbīʿ* for Egyptian villages.[35] In sixteenth-century delta provinces, each grouping of peasants was responsible for a *ḥiṣṣa*, a share, of the overall tax levy of the village, or for a specified number of feddans. The groupings of cultivators could be identified by a single name, by a list of individuals, or as the "sons of" (*awlād* X).[36] The leader of a *ḥiṣṣa* functioned as one of the village headmen, with each headman responsible for a share of the tax due on the village, divided up among the peasants.[37]

Early fourteenth-century ʿAyn Yabrūd clearly had the same method of dividing up the villagers into groupings, each responsible for a share of the village lands and led by a headman who acted as guarantor. In ʿAyn Yabrūd, this list of the peasant groupings has no mention of clan names or of kinship groups (save for two pairs of brothers). In the Ottoman registers, too, the division of the village peasants into work groups did not necessarily follow family lines. Nicolas Michel pointed to the association-based, rather than kinship-based, peasant groupings in the Ottoman records as proof that sixteenth-century Egyptian villagers did not adopt clan identities.[38] Nonetheless, we have seen that two of ʿAyn Yabrūd's headmen were identified with the Banū ʿĀmir when selling surplus olive oil; even though the peasant groupings were not kinship-based, the village headmen were members of the same clan. As far as we can see, the village of ʿAyn Yabrūd was identified with the Banū ʿĀmir, even if our sources do not show traces of internal subclan divisions.

While in most cases we only hear of the clan names of village headmen, there is fleeting evidence that Arab identity was shared by the other peasants in the village and was not an elite privilege. Our best indication for the spread of clan identities across the village community comes from a record of a blood-money settlement between three brothers from the village of Dūrā and two men from the nearby village of Idhnā, southwest of Hebron.[39] The three brothers, identified as al-Rabaʿiyyīn (of the Banū Rabīʿa) appeared before the *qāḍī* of Hebron to forfeit their right to retaliation from two Idhnā men who murdered a fourth brother called Mubārak. The two men from Idhnā are also identified by a clan name, al-Ḥalāfiyyīn or al-Jalāfiyyīn.[40] Thus, all involved in this murder case carried names that indicated their membership in a clan. There is no indication in the documents that any of those involved was a headman; if they were, one would have expected this fact to be noted by the court. The village of Dūrā had other men acting as headmen, as attested in another document that has three Rabaʿī headmen from Dūrā acknowledging taxes due from the sale of sumac.[41] All in all, six men in Dūrā were identified as Rabaʿī, in two different contexts. This suggests an inclusive clan identity: that every man of Dūrā could be ascribed membership of the Banū Rabīʿa. By extension, it is likely that everyone in Bayt Ūniya was a Ṣubāḥī, and everyone in ʿAyn Yabrūd was an ʿĀmirī.

This documentary evidence for the prevalence of village clans in the Palestinian highlands in the hinterland of Jerusalem, dating from the first decade of the fourteenth century, shows much continuity with the documentary evidence for Arab village clans from the final decades of the Latin Kingdom. As we have seen in chapter 2, a sale document of 1178 lists over one hundred households and subclans of the *beduini* clan of Benekarkas who resided in the village of Seleth in the mountains of Nablus. In the Hospitaller deeds of the late twelfth century, the *beduini* appear to be the landless section of the peasantry, distinct from Muslim and Christian *villani* but living alongside them. But by the early fourteenth century, some four generations later, Arab village clans appear to have become the dominant form of social structure in the Palestinian highlands, overshadowing any other Muslim rural group and marginalizing the minority of villagers who remained Christian.

Contemporary European pilgrims and travelers to Palestine came to be aware of the omnipresence of Arab village clans and Arab villagers, and the blurring of the line between the peasants and Arabs. The Jewish traveler Issac b. Joseph Chelo, who visited Palestine in 1334, reports that the people in the village of Djiba, biblical Geva, in the Jerusalem highlands, were Arab and that a mosque had replaced a church. He also reported that the village of Arad in the Negev is inhabited by poor Arabs and Jews, who mainly subsist on animal husbandry.[42] Burchard of Mt. Zion, writing in the 1280s, pointed out that in the Hawran the "children of Esau"—i.e, the Arabs—were practically indistinguishable from other Muslims.[43] While the stereotypical nomadic Bedouin are still prevalent in European accounts, the occasional acknowledgment of villages inhabited by Arabs confirms the overwhelming evidence for village clans in the Haram corpus during the first decade of the fourteenth century.

Village Clans and Regional Peacekeeping

The Haram corpus shows village headmen as guarantors of law and order in their own villages, similar to the roles of Egyptian village headmen as known to us from the al-Azkā cache of documents from al-Ashmūnayn, also dating from the 1300s, discussed in the previous chapter. A couple of other documents in the Haram corpus demonstrate that the headmen's responsibilities for law and order were integrated into a regional network of co-guarantors, representing several village communities. Here, the headmen acted as leaders of their clans, with territorial authority that extended over a cluster of villages.

The first example concerns a sworn undertaking by thirteen clan leaders and headmen from various localities to guarantee the internal peace in the village of Nūbā. In Dhū al-Ḥijja 705/July 1306 four named headmen and shaykhs (*mashāyikh*) of Nūbā swore to behave in a lawful manner, to cultivate the waqf land, and, in the key phrase of this document, not to fight with each other or draw arms against each other.[44] They did so at the behest of the governor of Jerusalem, and the filing note confirms that this record binds the four headmen of Nūbā against causing *fitna* or fighting each other. The unique feature of this document was that thirteen leaders from nearby villages reinforced this undertaking by offering personal surety for the conduct of the Nūbā headmen (*kafālat wajh wa-badan*). Four of the guarantors came from villages found within a very short distance to the south: Tarqūmiya, Bayt Ūllā (on the other side of the local wadi), and the satellite settlement of Bayt Nāṣīf.[45] Six other guarantors came from the villages of Bayt ʿAynūn (modern-day Beit Einun) and Ḥalḥūl, located some ten kilometers east of Nūbā; three of these six men are identified with the same Arab clan name, al-ʿAbbāsī.[46] Thus, the peace in the village of Nūbā was guaranteed by men representing two clusters of nearby villages that lay to the south and to the east. None is identified as a headman or a shaykh (one is given the honorific *ḥājj*). Five of the thirteen men are identified by a name of an Arab clan, but the text pays more attention to the geographical origin of the men than to their clan affiliation. It turned out that upholding the peace in the village of Nūbā was not a straightforward task. Another document drafted a year later orders three Nūbā villagers to avoid mischief and behave in a lawful manner. They are not identified as headmen, but they all belonged to the Banū ʿĀmir.[47]

The second example involved a certain Aḥmad b. Mūsā b. ʿAlam, a former resident of the village of Ṭayiba al-Ism (present-day Taybeh) east of Ramallah, who was ordered to reside in Jerusalem and not go back to his native village. In this case, eleven men were appointed to stand personal surety (*kafālat wajh wa-badan*) to his movements. All men were either from villages near his native village or from the suburbs of Jerusalem.[48] One of the men—a "shaykh" of the Banū Sālim clan—is identified as residing in Rammūn, some three kilometers from Ṭayiba. Another shaykh of the Banū Sālim resided in an unidentifiable village. The two men appear to have been leaders of the clan of the Banū Sālim, present in two adjacent villages. In addition, once Aḥmad had gone to Jerusalem, the policing of his movements was handed over to leaders of clans from the village suburbs of the city. Four guarantors who were identified by the clan name al-Saʿdī came from Khān al-Ifranj, on the outskirts of Jerusalem (*ẓāhir al-Quds*). Khān al-Ifranj was located a few hundred meters to the north of the city on the road to Nablus. Significantly, by the fifteenth century the village came to be known as Khān Banī Saʿd, acquiring the name of the clan that inhabited it since the early fourteenth century.[49] The four Saʿdī men from Khān al-Ifranj must have been called upon to police any attempt by Aḥmad to leave Jerusalem toward Nablus. Another group of guarantors included residents of Jerusalem identified by another tribal *nisba*, which could be read either as al-Khāzimī or al-Ḥārithī. Al-ʿUlaymī notes that the neighborhood of the Banū al-Ḥārith was outside the city, near the citadel.[50] That would have made them keepers of the western entrance to the city. Here, too, security was primarily devolved to territorial clans.

The Haram corpus consistently shows headmen and other men affiliated with Arab clans as responsible for regional security. Unlike in Ayyubid Fayyum, there are no traces of multivillage tribal confederacies covering large territories. Nūbā was affiliated with the Banū ʿĀmir, but the external guarantors appointed for maintaining peace and order in the villages were members of other clans, such as al-ʿAbbāsiyyūn or al-Ghāziyyūn, who inhabited nearby villages. Other Banū ʿĀmir villages, such as those in ʿAyn Yabrūd or Zakariyā, were not called upon to guarantee the peace in Nūbā, presumably because they were located farther away. Only pairs of adjacent villages, such as Ḥalḥūl and Bayt ʿAynūn, shared the same clan affiliation. While in Ayyubid Fayyum villages that lay along the same irrigation canal were joined together by idioms of clans and tribal confederacies, the villages of the Palestinian highlands seem to have maintained their clan identities without forming wider coalitions.

The fourteenth-century Haram corpus is silent about drawing peasants into ʿurbān auxiliary units. So far it has yielded only a single reference to ʿurbān, in a document concerning an amir of the ʿurbān of Karak in Transjordan who came to court to retrieve a lost camel identified by its brand marks.[51] The ʿurbān of Transjordan are frequently mentioned in narrative sources because of their role in securing the Syrian pilgrimage caravans (see also chapter 8).[52] In Palestine, the principal ʿurbān unit was that of the Jarm in the region of Gaza. The Jarm, which are not mentioned in sources from the Fatimid and crusader eras, were integrated into the Mamluk political and military system by Baybars in 1263.[53] Jarm amirs are then frequently mentioned in Mamluk administrative treatises, and by the late fifteenth century they held considerable autonomous power in the area between Gaza and Hebron.[54] The Jarm do not feature in the early-fourteenth-century documents of the Haram corpus, and we do not have evidence for recruitment of soldiers from among the village clans of the Palestinian highlands. This is maybe a result of the bias of the source base, as the Haram documents tend to focus on matters of taxation and local security, or it may reflect real differences between the way ʿurbān units were recruited in the Fayyum and in the highlands of Palestine.

Christian Villages and Arab Clans

Village clans are attested for most of the villages represented in the Haram corpus, but not in all of them. Most significantly, we have no evidence of the presence of clans in three villages—Ramallah, Naḥālīn, and ʿAyn ʿArīk—which had significant orchard cultivation and were most probably Christian at the time. The village of ʿAyn ʿArīk, seven kilometers west of Ramallah and Bayt Ūniya, is particularly well documented. In June 1307, three men from ʿAyn ʿArīk, named as Muḥammad b. Zikrī b. Mufliḥ, ʿAbdallāh b. Muḥammad b. Sulaymān, and Ismāʿīl b. Aḥmad b. ʿUmar, acknowledged that they owe the waqf of Jerusalem 950 dirhams from the sale of fruits such as figs, apricots, and apples.[55] A second document, issued a year or two later, has two of the men identified as the headmen of the village. Here they acknowledge a joint debt of 410 dirhams they owed to the waqf authorities, again from the sale of fruits.[56] A third document from ʿAyn ʿArīk has three other headmen, also with Muslim names, acknowledge the tax obligation and the seed advances in grains from the harvest of the preceding year.[57] None of the three documents from ʿAyn ʿArīk identifies the headmen by a name of a clan.

Similar fiscal documents originating in Ramallah and in Naḥālīn, a village north of Hebron, attest to collective obligations taken by men who are not identified by a clan name. In Naḥālīn, two men—Yūsuf b. Qāsim b. Sulaymān and ʿAbd al-Nāṣir b. Aḥmad b. Naṣṣār—acknowledged they owed six thousand dirhams to the waqf of the Tomb of the Patriarchs in Hebron.[58] In Ramallah, a group of twelve named men, collectively identified as the peasants (fallāḥīn) of the village, acknowledged a debt of 950 dirhams to the waqf in Hebron from the proceeds of their olives, apples, and cotton. The debt is divided equally among the twelve peasants and mutually guaranteed.[59] In examples of this type of document emanating from the neighboring villages of Bayt Ūniya and ʿAyn Yabrūd, the headmen were consistently identified by clan names; in ʿAyn ʿArīk, Ramallah, and Naḥālīn they were not.

ʿAyn ʿArīk, Ramallah, and Naḥālīn were different from other villages in the Palestinian highlands because they had expansive orchards of fruit trees. The fiscal documents from ʿAyn ʿArīk record taxes from the sale of grapes (or raisins), figs, apples, apricots, walnuts, and almonds. Similarly, the fiscal document from Ramallah records proceeds from apples. These two villages also produced grains (ʿAyn ʿArīk), olives, vetch, and cotton (Ramallah), but in no other village are there records of taxes on fruit trees. In thirteenth-century Fayyum, orchardist villagers were less likely to be members of a clan, and the same was probably true in early-fourteenth-century Palestine. Most fruit trees, other than olives and date palms, required higher levels of investment and therefore a greater degree of private ownership and lesser reliance on communal labor.

Equally importantly, Ramallah, Naḥālīn, and ʿAyn ʿArīk were all majority Christian villages, or at least had a substantial Christian population. We do not have direct evidence for this from the Mamluk period, but their religious composition is recorded in the Ottoman population surveys of the sixteenth century. In 1596, ʿAyn ʿArīk had fourteen Muslim households and ten Christian households; Naḥālīn had forty Muslim households and sixteen Christian households; while Ramallah had seventy-one Christian households and only nine Muslim households (it remained a predominantly Christian village up to the middle of the twentieth century).[60] In contrast, all the villages associated with Arab clans in the Haram corpus—Bayt Ūniya, ʿAyn Yabrūd, Nūbā, Dūrā, Tarqūmiya, Rammūn, Idhnā, Ḥalḥūl, and Zakariyā—were exclusively Muslim by the time of the Ottoman census. While there is a risk in reading back religious identity from the Ottoman records, it stands to reason that the proportion of Christian villagers declined between the early fourteenth century and the late sixteenth century. Therefore, villages with substantial Christian communities in the Ottoman records—such as Ramallah, Naḥālīn, and ʿAyn ʿArīk—were likely Christian-majority villages in the Mamluk period.

While we assume Naḥālīn and ʿAyn ʿArīk were majority Christian villages, their headmen carried Muslim names. As mentioned above, the headmen of ʿAyn ʿArīk are named as Muḥammad b. Zikrī b. Mufliḥ, ʿAbdallāh b. Muḥammad b. Sulaymān, and Ismāʿīl b. Aḥmad b. ʿUmar. Even the list of twelve peasants from Christian Ramallah included a certain Aḥmad b. ʿAbdallāh b. Khalīfa and his brother Muḥammad; only a couple of the other names on the list are distinctly Christian.[61] Naḥālīn, Ramallah, and ʿAyn ʿArīk had some Muslim presence, and perhaps specifically at the level of the village headmen. One could speculate that only Muslim men could act as headmen, even in majority Christian villages, because only Muslims were legally capable of providing the social and political guarantees required from headmen. Be that as it may, the documents do not identify these Muslim headmen of majority Christian villages by the names of Arab clans, perhaps because clan affiliation was meaningful only once it encompassed the entire village.

Nowhere in the Haram corpus are non-Muslim men identified by names of Arab clans. When a Christian man from the village of Bayt Rīmā, named Abū al-Waḥsh b. Yuḥannā, leased a dye shop in Bayt Ūniya in February 1307, he was identified not by a clan name but rather by his physical features—medium height, round beard, and structure of his eyebrows—as was common in Islamic legal documents involving non-Muslims known to us from the Cairo Geniza.[62] Multiple cleavages separated the resident villagers of Bayt Ūniya from Abū al-Waḥsh from Bayt Rīmā who rented the local dye shop: a Christian man in a Muslim village, a merchant or an artisan among farmers, a non-Arab individual in a clan of Ṣubāḥīs.

Islamization in Ayyubid and Mamluk Palestine

As in the Fayyum, the proliferation of Arab village clans in the highlands of Jerusalem and the Hebron hills followed a period of intense Islamization.[63] While the mountains around Nablus had probably become predominantly Muslim in the pre-crusader period, as shown by Milka Levy-Rubin and by Ronnie Ellenblum,[64] the hinterland of Jerusalem remained Christian up to the crusader period, and this Christian presence was sustained and supported by the Latin Kingdom. As we know from Latin charters, most villages north of Jerusalem were inhabited by an eastern Christian population well up to 1187. Lists of peasants from the villages of Qalandiyya, Ramatha (present al-Rām), and Bethlegel (Bayt Lijja), all in the vicinity of Ramallah, show a complete dominance of Greek or Semitic names that are likely to be Christian.[65] The Latin elite heavily invested in this area north of Jerusalem, and they promoted Frankish settlement.[66] Their material imprint, a construction on a scale not seen since the Umayyads, included an oil press in Bayt Ūniya.[67]

Saladin's victory changed that. Village mosques and Muslim cemeteries, rare up to the eleventh century, became common by the early thirteenth. Inscriptions on village mosques in ʿAjjul, south of Nablus and in Beit Hanun, near Gaza, show that they were built in 1176–77 and 1239, respectively.[68] In Transjordan, several rural mosques can be dated to the second half of the thirteenth century.[69] The northern church of Tall Hisban, abandoned since the eighth century, was repurposed in the early thirteenth century as the settlement's Muslim cemetery.[70] The excavated Mamluk-era mosque in Faḥl, in Transjordan, would have accommodated up to one hundred worshippers. Mamluk-era Faḥl also had an extensive cemetery, with distinctive Muslim burial practices but without external markers. Such rural Muslim cemeteries became common from the later Middle Ages and are dubbed "Bedouin" cemeteries by archaeologists.[71]

In Transjordan, where excavations of rural sites have been systematic, one finds also a marked Islamization of diet. Pig bones were found only in crusader settings and disappeared from the menu after the Muslim reconquest of the late twelfth century.[72] Another material indication of the retreat of Christianity in Transjordan is the decrease in the consumption of parrotfish, a species indigenous to the Red Sea that was traded within networks of Christian communities and is mentioned several times in the St. Catherine documents. Parrotfish were commonly consumed in villages of the Transjordan up to the end of the crusader period, but that consumption considerably decreased from the thirteenth century onward.[73]

The spread of rural mosques in Greater Syria was closely related to the proliferation of Sufism and the establishment of shrines. Muslim rural shrines that commemorated local saints spread rapidly over the twelfth and thirteenth centuries, often by replacing and reusing older monasteries.[74] The erection of Islamic shrines and mausolea in the countryside was accompanied by a new literary genre, that of the pilgrimage guide. The first surviving example comes from the pen of al-Harawī (d. 1215), whose work lists many rural Muslim shrines in Syria and Palestine. Most of these are not previously attested.[75] As argued by Dana Sajdi, the Ayyubid and Mamluk genre of shrine visitation (*ziyārāt*) replaced an earlier genre of books of monasteries (*diyārāt*), which disappeared in the eleventh century. In the *diyārāt* literature, which peaked in the tenth century under the patronage of Banū Ḥamdān, rural Christian monasteries appear as sites of Muslim subversive indulgence in wine, music, and love. In the *ziyārāt* literature of the Ayyubid and the Mamluk period, on the other hand, some of these same structures are converted into Islamic shrines, often commemorating events and people sacred to Muslims, Christians, and Jews.[76] As Josef Meri demonstrated in his study of popular religion in Ayyubid and Mamluk Syria, the deeper we penetrate the countryside, the more we find sanctity to be shared.[77]

As in the Fayyum, the spread of Arab village clans in the highlands of Palestine coincided with an expansion of agriculture characterized by systematic reoccupation of sites abandoned in previous centuries and the reuse of building material.[78] The reoccupation of marginal sites is evident in the Negev, where the Mamluk-era inhabitants of Horbat Ma'on reused Byzantine-era water systems and buildings, while adding new constructions. In Ein Gedi, a Mamluk village was built over Roman ruins.[79] New marginal sites were also reoccupied in Transjordan. As in earlier periods, these villages had mixed economies of crops and animal husbandry, but phytolith analysis has shown a relative dominance of barley, possibly as demands for fodder grew, or as a result of limited water supply.[80] Another change in the archaeological assemblage is an increase in goat remains, with the ratio of goats to sheep shifting from 0.75:1 in the pre-Ayyubid period to 1.5 goats per 1 sheep in the Mamluk era. The most likely explanation to this shift from sheep to goats is that grazing expanded into arid areas, accompanying the reoccupation of abandoned sites in less fertile areas.[81]

Nonetheless, it seems unlikely that the appearance of Arab village clans in the highlands of Palestine was a result of large-scale nomadic migrations. The Haram corpus's evidence for village clans concerns highland villages that had never been abandoned, such as Bayt Ūniya, continuously settled since pre-Islamic times.[82] 'Ayn Yabrūd was similarly a site of continuous habitation since the Hellenistic period and has the remains of a fourth-century Byzantine tomb.[83] By the early thirteenth century its extensive vineyards, olive groves, and sumac had been endowed as waqf, as reported by Yāqūt.[84] Most Syrian and Palestinian villages also kept their pre-Islamic names, with some village names going back several millennia.[85] Bayt Ūniya and 'Ayn Yabrūd carried non-Arab names, even if their headmen claimed Arab lineage.

Only a few rural localities acquired names that identified them with Arab clans, and this phenomenon is attested only from the fourteenth century onward. We have seen that Khān al-Ifranj, a name that appears in the Haram documents of the early 1300s, had come to be known as Khān Banī Sa'd in a fifteenth-century narrative source. The most famous "Arab" place-name in Palestine, Marj Banī 'Āmir or Ibn 'Āmir (Jezreel Valley), is first attested in the work by al-Ṣafadī (d. 764/1363).[86] This adoption of an Arab name occurred in the fourteenth century not because of a sudden migration of the Banū ʿĀmir, but because the villagers of the Jezreel Valley came to see themselves as descendants of the pre-Islamic Arab genealogical tree, and they began to couch their landscape in the idiom of the Arab clan. The toponymy of the rural landscape changed retrospectively, following several generations of local villagers boasting of their newly acquired Arab identity.

As there is no evidence of mass migration and displacement, it seems certain that the late medieval Islamization of the Palestinian countryside occurred through rural conversion. But the process of rural conversion was then completed and complemented by claims to Arab lineage, and the Haram corpus, with its sample of Muslim and Christian villages, sheds light on the process of religious and ethnic transformation. Thus, we find headmen with Muslim names in villages that were likely to be majority Christian, such as ʿAyn Yabrūd or Ramallah. These Muslim headmen of Christian villages were not identified by names of Arab clans, unlike the headmen in nearby Muslim villages, perhaps because the invocation of a clan identity was relevant only once the entire village had converted. It appears that the installation of Muslim elites as village headmen preceded the conversion of the village, a conversion later sealed by the adoption of a shared clan identity.

Claims of Arab lineage could also serve as an assertion of rights over land. The best documented example is the claim of the al-Dārī clan to the lands of the Palestinian village of Bayt ʿAynūn near Hebron. In the 1430s, a group of villagers who claimed descent from Tamīm al-Dārī approached the Cairene jurist Ibn Ḥajar al-ʿAsqalānī (d. 852/1449) and the historian al-Maqrīzī and asked them to confirm early Islamic reports that the Prophet granted Bayt ʿAynūn to the Companion Tamīm al-Dārī and his descendants.[87] The practical implication of the request is obvious—the local villagers argued that, by virtue of being descendants of Tamīm al-Dārī, their rights to the lands of Bayt ʿAynūn derive from the authority of the Prophet himself. In his response, however, al-Maqrīzī questioned the continuity of the Dārī line, given the crusader interruption. Since the arrival of the Franks meant that all Muslims in the region either fled or were killed, no Dārī from the pre-Frankish period could have remained in these lands. How, then, did the Dārī clansmen reclaim the lands of their forefathers after the reconquest? Al-Maqrīzī leaves the question unanswered.[88] As it happens, Bayt ʿAynūn also appears in the Haram documents, which show that in the 1300s it was inhabited by a village clan called the ʿAbbāsīs. A century later, on the other hand, local villagers actively sought scholarly confirmation of their descent from Tamīm al-Dārī, evidently to bolster their rights over the land of the village.

The inhabitants of Bayt ʿAynūn had good practical reasons to claim Tamīm al-Dārī as their ancestor. In most cases, however, we don't know why villagers chose a specific lineage. In the case of Bayt Ūniya, for example, what did the Ṣubāḥī affiliation of the villagers signify, socially or ideologically? In *al-Lubāb fī Tahdhīb al-Ansāb*, an encyclopedia of tribal names compiled in Iraq by Ibn al-Athīr (d. 1233), several Ṣubāḥī clans (*buṭūn*) are listed, each made famous by an early Islamic poet or narrator of Prophetic traditions. There were al-Ṣubāḥiyyīn from the Ḍabba and others from the Quḍāʿa, from the ʿAnza, and from the ʿAbd al-Qays.[89] Two centuries later, al-Qalqashandī (d. 1418) lists ʿAdnānī and Qaḥṭānī groups of Banū Ṣabāḥ.[90] Did the villagers of Bayt Ūniya read Ibn al-Athīr? Did the genealogical tree of the al-Ṣubāḥiyyīn remain stable over time and place? Perhaps it didn't matter. The Ṣubāḥī headmen could be Ḍabba or Quḍāʿa, Qaḥṭān or ʿAdnān, depending on local alliances and conditions. The exact name of the clan was less important than the Arabian lineage it entailed: by acquiring this Arab *nisba*, they gained a place along the branches of the Arab genealogical tree, whose roots lay in pre-Islamic and early Islamic Arabia, in the traditions of Arabic poetry, and in the age of the Prophet. The suspicion of non-Muslim, Christian ancestry was averted.

Arab Village Clans in Mamluk Palestine

The prevalence of Arab village clans in the highlands of Palestine is strongly indicated by the set of rural documents from the Haram corpus, which complements and enriches the evidence from al-Nābulusī's tax register. Despite the immense economic and environmental differences between the two regions, it appears that Muslim villagers in both regions adopted a clan social structure as well as the status claims of Arab lineage. In Muslim villages, headmen and—probably—ordinary peasants claimed for themselves a shared Arabian lineage, with each village inhabited by members of one clan. The Haram corpus, even more so than the 1245 survey of the Fayyum, highlights the role of the new institution of village headmen, attested in Palestine since the late twelfth century. Headmen undertook collective fiscal obligations and handled the sale of the village produce. Each headman was responsible for a group of peasants, and probably also for a share of the tax due from the village. The Palestinian and Egyptian headmen offer striking similarities with the village headmen widely attested in eastern Iran since the late twelfth century and who were similarly in charge of local security and defense, involved in tax assessment and collection, received tax exemptions, and offered hospitality to visitors.[91]

As far as we can tell, the village communities of early-fourteenth-century Palestine acted as collectives of tenants. The headmen received the village's seed advances, guaranteed the collectively levied taxes, and sold surplus produce on behalf of the village. But the lands belonged to the landowner, either the state or the waqf, not to individual cultivators. By chance of survival, the Haram documents that relate to the rural hinterland mainly concern villages endowed as waqf. But most villages in fourteenth-century Palestine were handed over to military iqṭāʿ holders, as was common in the landholding regime of Egypt and Greater Syria since the Ayyubid period. The cultivators in the villages that were endowed as waqf, like all other cereal-growing cultivators in Palestine under the iqṭāʿ regime, had the status of tenants whose rights to the land depended on collective leases handed out to their headmen.

Village clans spread in a countryside that was now predominantly Muslim, with rural mosques and Islamic burials. Shrines of saints now dotted the landscape, often taking the place of Christian holy sites. We know this through the visible material remains and inscriptions, as well as from a new genre of Muslim pilgrimage guides that emerged in the later twelfth and early thirteenth century, after Saladin's defeat of the Latin Kingdom. It seems likely that in Palestine, too, Arab lineage was used to erase the memory of conversion, and we know that in the case of the Dārīs the claim of descent from a Companion was used to assert rights over the lands of Bayt ʿAynūn near Hebron.

This chapter presented documentary evidence for the prevalence of Arab village clans in Muslim-majority villages of the hinterland of Jerusalem and Hebron. It has also shown that the appearance of village clans coincided with widespread rural Islamization of the landscape and reoccupation of sites. It confirmed the finding of the previous chapter, which put forward the evidence for the prevalence of village clans in Muslim villages in the Fayyum from al-Nābulusī's 1245 survey and placed it in a similar context of Islamization and land reclamation. The next chapter will go beyond these two case studies to document references to village clans as well as territorial confederacies throughout the Egyptian and Syrian countrysides in Ayyubid and Mamluk literary sources, focusing on the genres of genealogical literature and biographical dictionaries.

5

Administrative Categories and Self-Identity

THE PREVIOUS TWO CHAPTERS highlighted microhistorical evidence for Arab clans in Muslim villages in thirteenth-century Fayyum and in the hinterlands of fourteenth-century Jerusalem and Hebron, set against the expansion of agriculture, the transformation of peasants into tenants, and Islamization. This chapter zooms out from the local level and demonstrates the spread of village clans all over the Egyptian and Syrian countrysides, as reflected in two late medieval literary genres: genealogical treatises written by bureaucrats working for the Mamluk state, and biographical dictionaries recording the names and careers of contemporary Muslim scholars. Both genealogical treatises and biographical dictionaries attest that the Fayyum and the Palestinian highlands were no exceptions: Arab clan identities had become prevalent throughout the Egyptian and Syrian countrysides of the Ayyubid and Mamluk periods.

These genealogical writings of administrators and the biographical entries of men born in villages provide us with complementary perspectives on the meaning of Arab identity. First, a distinct new genre of genealogical treatises, written by Mamluk bureaucrats and closely intertwined with the practices of Mamluk bureaucracy, focused on locating tribes and clans within the territorial boundaries of the Mamluk empire. Its territorial focus differed from earlier treatises of Arab genealogy, which were generally organized through the hierarchy of the Arab genealogical tree. Moreover, these Mamluk-era genealogical treatises viewed clans and tribes primarily through the prism of the state and emphasized accounts of Arab tribal leaders who sought audience with the sultan. The earliest work of this genre, by the thirteenth-century al-Ḥamdānī, is a register of the Arab tribes in his time based on his experience as the official *mihmindār* of the late Ayyubid and early Mamluk states. Al-Ḥamdānī's work has been lost, but it was extensively used by the later bureaucrat authors Ibn Faḍl Allāh al-ʿUmarī (d. 1349) and al-Qalqashandī (d. 1418), as well as by the historian al-Maqrīzī. The first part of this chapter will focus on the works of al-Ḥamdānī, al-ʿUmarī, and al-Qalqashandī, exploring their bird's-eye view of the tribal confederacies and clans of the Mamluk countryside and their relations with the central government in Cairo.[1] Their collective oeuvre demonstrates the pervasive spread of Arab village clans; moreover, this Mamluk administrative-genealogical genre only makes sense as a response to the dominance of village clans and was a bureaucratized method of mapping relations of power in the countryside.

Biographical dictionaries, on the other hand, offer us the perspective of the individuals who belonged to these village clans. In the biographical entries, we see how rural people wanted to present themselves to a wider audience, and the entries reflect the way individuals understood, adopted, and expressed their own Arab and clan identity. Through the biographical dictionaries and the semi-autobiographical material preserved in them, we see clan names not just as administrative rubrics, but also as a key constituent of self-identity. A few preserved Egyptian documents from the period, including two lavish marriage contracts from Aswan, enrich our understanding of the appropriation of Arab lineage for self-representation. This material is capped by the well-crafted expression of clan identity found in the autobiographical notice of the fifteenth-century Burhān al-Dīn al-Biqāʿī, born to the Banū Ḥasan of the Khirbat Rūḥā village in the Beqaa. His account allows us to follow the formation of his village clan in the thirteenth and fourteenth century, followed by tentative claims to Arab lineage as articulated in al-Biqāʿī's own lifetime.

Administrative Genealogical Treatises

The genealogical literature of the Mamluk period was a product of its time and the concerns of its authors, not simply a record of biological descent groups. This observation is true for the entire Islamic genealogical tradition. The science of Arab genealogy emerged in the urban centers of Abbasid Iraq as an attempt to create an exclusive Arab identity vis-à-vis recent converts of Persian origins, and Abbasid-era scholars such as Ibn al-Kalbī sought to homogenize different lineages with Quranic and biblical figures, inventing a pan-Arab and universal genealogical framework.[2] The genre of Ṭālibid genealogies emerged in the tenth century in tandem with the new institution of the urban *naqīb al-ashrāf*, responsible for distributing pensions and endowment benefits to descendants of the Prophet's household.[3] The Rasulid al-Malik al-Ashraf (d. 696/1296) wrote a genealogical treatise on the Qaḥṭānī tribes of the Yemen, grafting his own ancestry onto local lineages while also mapping contemporary tribes and their armies.[4] The visualization of genealogical trees in the post-Mongol world has been linked to the rise of dynastic forms of political legitimation and with a universalist outlook that aimed to combine the entire known history of the world.[5]

The state-centered focus of Mamluk genealogical treatises had its origin in official production of genealogical material during the Ayyubid period. In the preceding Ayyubid period, the most prolific author of genealogical material was Muḥammad b. As'ad al-Jawwānī (d. 588/1192), a Cairene-born son of an immigrant from Mosul appointed by Saladin as *naqīb al-ashrāf* in Cairo. Al-Jawwānī produced many treatises on genealogy—he was so prolific that his earliest biographer, Ibn al-Qifṭī, mentions that he was widely suspected of fabrication.[6] Out of eighteen titles in the science of genealogy attributed to him in biographical dictionaries, only a couple survived, but his introduction to the science of Arab genealogy has been incorporated into al-Nuwayrī's fourteenth-century encyclopedia, and al-Maqrīzī cited him frequently on the settlement of different Arab groups in Fusṭāṭ. Al-Jawwānī's work, as far as it is known to us, was concerned with the establishment of genealogical rank among the urban classes. Nonetheless, this Ayyubid-era author was effectively a state-sponsored genealogist, showing an intertwining of genealogy and bureaucracy that will become very apparent in the genealogical treatises produced by Mamluk-era bureaucrats.

Another antecedent for the Mamluk genealogical genre and its administrative focus is found in the work of the Aleppine historian and diplomat Ibn al-'Adīm (d. 660/1262), who devoted a long chapter to the tribes of northern Syria as part of his geographical introduction to a biographical dictionary of people connected with Aleppo.[7] Ibn al-'Adīm listed tribes and clans according to their location, frequently associating clans with named rural settlements and integrating them into the landscape. These clans were evidently mostly sedentary, and his work reflects the spread of Arab village clans already achieved in the hinterland of Aleppo by the first part of the thirteenth century.

The distinct genre of Mamluk genealogical writing starts in earnest with Badr al-Dīn al-Ḥamdānī, who served several Ayyubid and Mamluk sultans as *mihmindār* in charge of receiving delegations of Arab tribal leaders, of providing them with accommodation, and of presenting them to the ruler. The office of a *mihmindār* was itself an Ayyubid innovation, possibly connected with Sultan al-'Ādil's appointment of the "amir of the Arabs" in the Syrian desert around the beginning of the thirteenth century. The position of the *mihmindār* was then adopted by the Mamluks and is attested up to the beginning of the fifteenth century.[8] Most of what we know of al-Ḥamdānī comes from his first-person accounts of hospitality extended to Arab amirs, some of them arriving from beyond the borders of the Ayyubid and Mamluk territories.[9] In biographical dictionaries, al-Ḥamdānī is known mainly for his poetry that dealt with "Arab" topics, as well as lines of praise for Sultan Baybars. He was born in 602/1205–6 and died toward the end of the thirteenth century.[10]

The purpose of al-Ḥamdānī's genealogical treatise was to map out the Arab tribes of Mamluk Egypt and, to a lesser extent, those of Mamluk Syria. According to a précis by al-ʿUmarī, al-Ḥamdānī began his treatise by listing the tribes that arrived in the wake of the Muslim conquest of Egypt, but this section has not survived. The preserved material begins with a section on the Arabs of Upper Egypt "in his own time," starting with Aswan and going up the Fayyum.[11] Each tribe and clan were given specific bounded territories, *diyār* or *bilād*, along the fertile areas of the Nile Valley. As an example of the strictly geographical sequence of al-Ḥamdānī's work, take the following account of the territories of the Lakhm, cited verbatim by the later authors al-ʿUmarī, al-Qalqashandī, and al-Maqrīzī:

> Al-Ḥamdānī said: a confederacy (*qawm*) of Lakhm are found in Upper Egypt, on the eastern bank of the Nile.
>
> They include the Banū Simāk, whose lands (*bilād*) are from Ṭārif Bibā (modern-day Biba) to the lower part of Dayr al-Jummayza and the Ṣawl Canal (*turʿa*). The [Banū Simāk] consist of the Banū Murr, Banū Malīḥ, Banū Nabhān, Banū ʿAbs, Banū Karīm, and Banū Bakr.
>
> They also include the Banū Ḥaddān. Their territories (*diyār*) are from Dayr al-Jummayza to the Ṣawl Canal. The Banū Ḥaddān consist of Banū Muḥammad, Banū ʿAlī, Banū Sālim, Banū Mudlij, and Banū ʿAbs.
>
> Also of the Lakhm are the Banū Rāshid, whose territories are from Masjid Mūsā to Askur and half of the lands of Aṭfīḥ. The Banū Rāshid consist of Banū Muʿammar, Banū Wāṣil, Banū Mirā, Banū Ḥibbān, Banū Maʿādh, Banū al-Fayḍ—also known as al-Fayāḍa—Banū Ḥajara, and Banū Ashtūh. Banū Fayḍ possess al-Ḥayy al-Ṣaghīr (literally, "the small encampment"), while Banū Ashtūh have the area from al-Sharīf canal to the press of Būsh. The Banū Ḥajara have half of Ṭurā.
>
> Also of the Lakhm are the Banū Jaʿda, whose territories are on the banks of Aṭfīḥ. They consist of the Banū Masʿūd, Banū Jarīr, Banū Zubayr, Banū Thimāl, and Banū Naṣṣār.
>
> Also of the Lakhm are the Banū ʿAdī. Their territories lie next to those mentioned above. They consist of the Banū Mūsā and Banū Maḥrib.

Also of the Lakhm are the Banū Baḥr, whose territories are in al-Ḥayy al-Kabīr (the large encampment). They consist of the Banū Sahl, Banū Miʿṭār, Banū Fahm—also known as al-Fahmiyyūn—Banū ʿAshīr, Banū Musnad, and Banū Sibāʿ.

Also of the Lakhm are the Banū Qasīs, whose dwellings are the lands of Askur.

Also of the Lakhm are the Banū ʿAmr, who territories are al-Rastaq and who have half of Ḥulwān (present-day Helwan). The other half of Ḥulwān belongs to the Banū Ḥajara, and half of Ṭurā.[12]

Al-Ḥamdānī's geographical account of the territories of the Lakhm proceeds from the south to the north along the Nile Valley, covering a one-hundred-kilometer-long stretch of agricultural land along the Nile, from present-day Biba in the south to Helwan in the north. The Lakhm confederacy is divided into nine sections, with each section controlling a fixed area along the banks of the Nile. Most sections are further divided into several subsections or clans, with a total of thirty-five clans spread over the Lakhm territories. According to Ibn Mammātī's late-twelfth-century cadastral survey of the Egyptian countryside, this stretch of the Nile Valley supported some seventy villages.[13] This gives us an average of two villages per clan, comparable to the average of five villages inhabited by each clan in Ayyubid Fayyum reported by al-Nābulusī.

According to al-Ḥamdānī, each major confederacy occupied a segment of the agricultural lands in Upper Egypt, which was their *masākin* (dwellings), *diyār* (territories), or *bilād* (lands, but also villages). Confederacies were sometimes defined by their locality and vice versa, so that the province of al-Ashmūnayn has become known as "the land of the Quraysh." The relationship between the tribal group and its territory was that of possession or ownership, a right that had to be negotiated with other tribes and with the authorities in Cairo. The Juhayna confederacy were forced by the Fatimid army from their previous territory in al-Ashmūnayn toward the more southern regions of Manfalūṭ and Asyut. The former Juhayna localities (*amākin*) were handed over (*udīlat*) to the Quraysh confederacy, "who came to possess them (*malakat*)."[14]

The localized clans that populated the Egyptian countryside in al-Ḥamdānī's time were settled. The Banū Zubayr of the Quraysh in al-Bahnasā are said to draw their livelihood from agriculture, sowing their fields, and raising small and large cattle (*dhā maʿāsh wa-ahl filāḥa wa-zarʿ wa-māshiya wa-ḍarʿ*).[15] Five different Saʿd groups of Judhām resided in the regions of Minyat Ghamr and Ziftā in

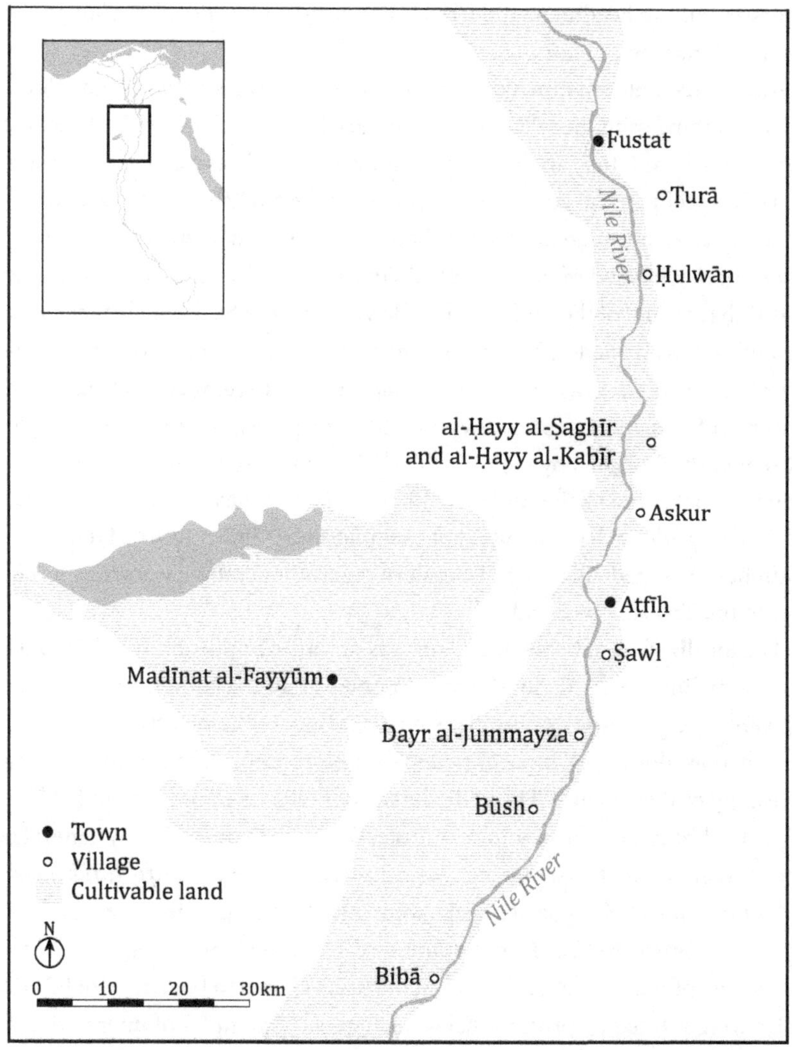

MAP 5.1. Territories of the Lakhm confederacy as listed by al-Ḥamdānī, circa 648/1250.

the eastern delta province of al-Sharqiyya. They lived in Tall Ṭanbūl and Nūb Ṭarīf and were the people (*ahl*) of the villages of Barhamtūsh, Taqdūs (present-day Daqados), and Damdīṭ. Al-Ḥamdānī is quoted as saying that the Banū Saʿd are "village headmen and guards (*mashāyikh al-bilād wa-khufarāʾuhā*) and own fields and victuals (*maʾākil*)." He adds that they cause much mischief (*fasād*), a rare negative comment.[16] The Banū Ḥarām were *qāḍīs*, jurists, professional witnesses, village headmen, and irrigation officials (*khawla*). This clan was unusual, as it had no territory (*dār*) of its own.[17]

Al-Ḥamdānī also mapped the military ranks and roles of the military ʿurbān units, emerging from the village clans and the tribal confederacies. In the extracts from al-Ḥamdānī, the rank of *muqaddam* is invariably associated with leadership of a specific tribal confederacy, following the twelfth-century examples of ʿurbān units led by *muqaddams* (see chapter 2). Al-Ḥamdānī mentions the *muqaddams* of the Suwayd of Judhām, of Kināna and of the Banū ʿAdī, of the Sinbis in al-Buḥayra, and of the Judhām in al-Ḥawf. The Banū Saʿd were led by *muqaddam* officers who lived in Minyat Ghamr and its hinterland.[18] Al-Ḥamdānī also recorded the granting of amiral titles of *būq wa-ʿalam* (Trumpet and Flag) to Arab officers in Syria and Egypt, an Ayyubid honorary designation of Seljuk origin subsequently abolished by the Mamluks.[19] The title was granted to *muqaddams* of the Thaʿlaba and of the Judhām.[20] The leaders of these tribal confederacies received agricultural lands as iqṭāʿ. For example, the Fatimids awarded the Judhām a number of named villages in the eastern delta as iqṭāʿ; these were later handed over to the Thaʿlaba by Saladin.[21]

The localization of tribes and clans was far more important for al-Ḥamdānī than their lineage. Al-Qalqashandī lamented that al-Ḥamdānī rarely traced "upward" the genealogy of the clans he discussed. Certain sections are merely described as allies or as *mawālī* (clients) of more important groups, lacking a genealogy of their own.[22] The confederacy of the Jarm in Syria included "their allies, neighbors, and those who seek protection with them."[23] The Syrian Āl Faḍl were mixed with the groupings who joined them (*yanḍāfu ilayhim wa-yadkhulu fīhim*).[24] Claims of lineage were often disputed or invented, and mixing of clans prevented clear-cut boundaries. There were opposing claims about the lineage of Judhayma, and Banū Makhzūm's claims to be from Khālid b. al-Walīd were refuted by professional genealogists.[25] Examples of intermixing are also common: Aslam of Judhām mixed with Judhayma; a motley group of Arabs joined the Kināna; Zabīd intermingled with Jarm; and all five Saʿd groups of the Judhām were so intermingled in the delta as to be indistinguishable.[26] Al-Ḥamdānī employed the terms *baṭn*, *fakhidh*, and *ʿashīra* for clans, while the term *awlād* is used for leading or amiral households.[27] Mostly, however, he only used the generic "Banū" or the indeterminate *qawm* (people, folk), leaving the group's place on the genealogical tree open to interpretation.

Despite his state-centered perspective, al-Ḥamdānī is usually sympathetic to the Arab tribes, and especially to the Arab amirs, who embodied stereotypical traits of generosity and courage. Ṭarīf b. Maknūn of the Judhām fed twelve thousand souls during the great Fatimid famine; Muhayyā b. ʿUlwān of the Halbā used his expensive textiles as fuel when guests came by.[28] Al-Ḥamdānī was especially keen to note the military qualities of the Arabs of Syria in the face of both Mongols and Franks. They were good warriors who were willing to act as vanguard forces, barely losing a battle: "They have won all the battles I witnessed, except the battle of Homs."[29] He admitted that the Thaʿlaba of Syria are known for collaborating with the crusaders, but in his personal experience they were brave raiders and holy warriors who inflicted heavy losses on the Franks.[30]

Overall, al-Ḥamdānī's treatise was a tribal register rather than a genealogical treatise, and it did not present to his readers a genealogical tree unifying all the different Arab clans he mentioned. His historical and geographical horizons were quite limited. The key periods of interest are the transitions from Fatimid to Ayyubid rule, and then from Ayyubid to Mamluk. His data mostly consist of a demographic mapping of the countryside ruled by the Mamluk empire and of an account of the relations of the Arab amirs with the authorities in Cairo. In this regard, his work has much in common with al-Nābulusī's survey of the Fayyum in 1245, which mapped the village clans and tribal confederacies as part of a fiscal register.[31] Both thirteenth-century bureaucrats—al-Nābulusī and al-Ḥamdānī—were trying to map the social groups of the countryside, showing how genealogy, administration, and tax collection had come to be closely intertwined.

In the following century, al-Ḥamdānī's work was adapted by Ibn Faḍl Allāh al-ʿUmarī, head of the royal chancery of the Mamluk sultanate and one of the most important bureaucrats and polymaths of the later medieval period. His encyclopedic *Masālik al-Abṣār fī Mamālik al-amṣār* is a mine of information on diplomatic, political, and administrative aspects of government in Egypt and Syria during the first half of the fourteenth century. Its substantial genealogical chapter is the most important text on Arab clans composed in the fourteenth century, interweaving sections from al-Ḥamdānī's treatise with al-ʿUmarī's personal observations based on his vast experience at the pinnacle of Mamluk administration. Like al-Ḥamdānī, al-ʿUmarī focused on the Arab tribes of his own age, and in particular on their relationship with the Mamluk state. His administrative manual, *al-Taʿrīf*, also deals with the hierarchy of Arab, Kurdish, and Turcoman amirs appointed by the Mamluk state and the proper ways of corresponding with them.[32]

The fourteenth-century context of al-ʿUmarī's interest in Arab affairs was different than that of his predecessor al-Ḥamdānī. Since the 1250s, Mongol invasions greatly increased the importance of Syrian Arab auxiliaries to the defense of Mamluk territories. They reached the apogee of their power and wealth during the third reign of Sultan al-Nāṣir Muḥammad (1310–41), and this is reflected in the praise heaped on them by al-ʿUmarī in the 1340s. This was also the heyday of the iqṭāʿ fiscal regime, where a central bureaucracy awarded Mamluk military officers rights to nearly all agricultural revenues in the Egyptian countryside, dispensing with the rural elites employed by the Fatimids and Ayyubids. A series of Arab revolts in the Nile Valley and the delta, starting in the 1250s, were met with an unprecedented repression of the Egyptian peasantry and their ʿurbān leaders (see chapter 9). Therefore, al-ʿUmarī's high praise for the Arabs of the Syrian desert is coupled with contempt for the subject Arab peasantry, especially in Egypt.

Al-ʿUmarī acknowledges al-Ḥamdānī as his main textual source for his account of the Arab tribes and follows him in arranging the discussion geographically rather than by lineage.[33] He opens with a historical prologue about the classical divisions of the Arab tribes—the Arabs of Yaman or Qaḥṭān and the Arabized (*mustaʿriba*) descendants of Ismaʿīl through the line of ʿAdnān.[34] But his main emphasis is an account of the Arab groupings (*ṭawāʾif*) found in his own day.[35] The section, titled "The Arabs found in our present time, and their locations," nominally covers Arab tribes from the Atlantic to Iraq, but the vast majority of the text is devoted to the Arab tribes that inhabited Egypt and Syria. He starts with the Arabs of Syria, to which he devotes a major part of the chapter, and then follows with shorter sections on the Arabs of Egypt and the Maghreb, mostly progressing in geographical sequence from province to province.

Unlike al-Ḥamdānī, al-ʿUmarī is keen to prominently display his own clan identity. He deliberately opens his section on the tribes of Egypt with an account of the Banū ʿUmar, and he reports that he himself is a descendant of Khalaf b. Naṣr Shams al-Dawla Abū ʿAlī, who arrived in Egypt under the Fatimid vizier Ṭalāʾiʿ ibn Ruzzīq in the middle of the twelfth century. This is "my lineage and my people," he boasts, and adds that he devoted a separate volume to the noble qualities of his tribe, a work he titled *Fawāḍil al-sumar fī faḍāʾil Āl ʿUmar* ("Valuable late-night conversations on the virtues of Āl ʿUmar").[36] This work, unfortunately, has not survived.[37]

Al-ʿUmarī also places even more emphasis than al-Ḥamdānī on the interactions of the Arab amirs with the Mamluk court. This is his stated reason for dealing with Arab tribal affairs: "Rulers are always well disposed toward their delegations, shower them with hefty gifts, and give them the most noble parts of the land as iqṭāʿ."[38] Al-ʿUmarī is especially interested in the amirs of the Āl Rabīʿa of the Syrian desert, whom he calls the "kings of the desert,"[39] as they participate in military campaigns and fight each other over herds of camels.[40] The account of the rather tumultuous relationship between the amirs of this confederacy and the Mamluk sultans takes up as much as a quarter of the entire chapter on the Arabs. As al-ʿUmarī tells us, this section was based on interviews he conducted with the professional genealogist of the Rabīʿa, a certain Maḥmūd b. ʿArrām, and conversations he held with the amirs Faḍl b. ʿĪsā and Mūsā b. Muhannā during their stays in Cairo.[41]

The Arab amirs were not only al-ʿUmarī's interlocutors, but also part of his audience, as he counseled them on framing genealogical claims in the most effective manner. Al-ʿUmarī—perhaps here reproducing al-Ḥamdānī—advises the Rabīʿa to avoid claiming lineage from the line of Abbasid-era Barmakid viziers and opt for an alternative lineage from a noble Ṭayy Arab man called Silsila b. ʿUnayn b. Salāmān. Al-ʿUmarī explains that it is better to claim a noble Arab lineage than to attach themselves to the non-Arab lineage of the Barmakids, despite the latter's power and prestige.[42] Similarly, al-ʿUmarī advises the Banū Khālid of Homs to drop their claim to be descendants of the great conqueror Khālid b. al-Walīd. This claim went against the consensus of the scholars of genealogy, who agreed that Khālid's line had been extinguished. It is sufficient for the Banū Khālid to take pride in their Qurashī origin.[43]

Finally, and most importantly for our purposes here, al-ʿUmarī projects a stark distinction between the "true" Arabs of the desert, camel-herding and mobile like the Āl Rabīʿa, and the sedentary tribes, who are Arabs in name only. In concluding the section on the Arabs of Syria, where he mostly dealt with the Āl Rabīʿa, al-ʿUmarī writes:

> In the lands of Syria there are various people of pure Arab stock (*min ṣalībat al-ʿarab*) who are no longer to be considered Arabs (*qad kharajū bi-hā ʿan ḥukm al-ʿarab*). The have become settled, sedentary people (*ahl ḥāḍira sākina*) who occupy fixed abodes (*ʿummār diyār qāṭina*). Banū Tamīm al-Dārī are in the cities of Gaza and Hebron. Groups of Banū Jaʿfar b. Abī Ṭālib and of Banū ʿUmar b. al-Khaṭṭāb are in Wādī Banī Zayd and in Jerusalem. In Nablus there are many Qaḥṭānīs and some of Muḍar b. Nizār. Folk of [Banū] Ḥāritha and [Banū] Bakr b. Wāʾil are in Jenin and its villages. In Jabal ʿĀmila one finds [Banū] ʿĀmila of pure stock. There is a motley of tribal clients in the Jordan Valley. A group of Banū ʿUmar b. al-Khaṭṭāb are in ʿAjlūn and in the Balqa region, where one finds also [Banū] Ghassān. [Banū] ʿĀmir b. Hilāl are in Ṣarkhad and its villages. They claim they are of Banū Jaʿfar b. Abī Ṭālib. Banū Asad are in ʿAthlīth and its environs. There are people of Taghlib and Azd in

> Zuraʿ and Buṣrā. In Adhriʿāt there are people of Banū Jamaḥ of Quraysh, and in some villages around Adhriʿāt there are people who claim they are of Banū Jaʿfar b. Abī Ṭālib. In the region of al-Yarmūk one finds people of Ghassān of pure stock. In Nawā there are people who claim they are of the Banū Mundhir b. Māʾ al-Samāʾ. There are people of Banū Umayya in al-Shaʿrāʾ, and in al-Lajjūn there are people who claim lineage from Kinda. There is a motley of Arab groups in the Marj of Damascus. People of Ghassān are in Homs, and in Hama there are folk of ʿAbd al-Dār, Juhayna, and Shaddād of the Anṣār. In Shayzar there are people of the Banū Kalb. In al-Maʿarra there are Tanūkhīs of pure stock. In Aleppo and its countryside, one finds the Banū Ḥusayn b. ʿAlī, Banū ʿAqīl, Banū Kilāb, Banū Kalb, Juhayna, and Banū Qurra. In Tadmur and al-Manāẓir there are men of Aslam and people of Banū Kalb. In al-Qaryatayn there are some Banū Taghlib. In al-Raḥba, known by the name of (its founder) Mālik b. Ṭawq,[44] there are people of Bakr b. Wāʾil and men of Muḍar and Rabīʿa. It is said that most of al-Raḥba's inhabitants are descended from Jews. I have mentioned this list by way of illustration, since it is impossible to verify it nor convey it in full here.[45]

Al-ʿUmarī provides here a long list of the sedentary Arab groups found in Syria and Palestine, starting with those who inhabit Gaza and Hebron. This list, which al-ʿUmarī describes as incomplete, covers nearly every cultivated region of Palestine and Greater Syria. Writing in the 1340s, his statements confirm the sample of Haram documents from the Mamluk court of Jerusalem, dated to the 1300s. By the early fourteenth century, many of the villages of the Palestinian and Syrian countryside were inhabited by people who considered themselves Arabs. Al-ʿUmarī viewed these settled communities with disdain, denying them the full Arabness he accorded to the amirs of the Syrian desert. At the same time, he also admitted they can still claim descent from the Arabian genealogical tree. This reality of sedentary Arabs did not fit his definition of what Arabs should be, and al-ʿUmarī therefore created a narrative of settling down, where the village clans were of Arab stock but had lost their Arabness by becoming sedentary.

When moving on to discuss the tribes of Egypt, al-ʿUmarī replicates the same distinction between "true" nomadic Arabs and sedentary Arab communities. He then links this distinction with his preoccupation with the state-tribe nexus. The vast majority of Egyptian Arabs, he explains in his administrative manual, are settled agriculturalists and are therefore not held in great esteem by the court:

> The Arabs in Upper and Lower Egypt belong to many groups, peoples, and tribes (*jamāʿāt, shuʿūb wa-qabāʾil*). However, despite their wealth and

> territorial extent, they are not held in high regard by the sultan, as they are sedentary people of the sown fields (*idh kānū ahl ḥaḍira wa-zar'*). None of them makes seasonal travels to Najd or Tihāma, Iraq or Syria (*lā yunjid wa-lā yatham, wa-lā yu'riqu wa-lā yash'am*), and they do not leave the boundaries of the fences.[46]

As the vast majority of the Egyptian Arab clans were not nomadic, the gap between al-'Umarī's idealized Arab way of life and the reality on the ground was particularly wide. The Arabs of Egypt are specifically identified as agriculturalists, people of the sown, and here al-'Umarī does not even impose a narrative of settling down of pastoralists. The village clans of Egypt lacked full Arab-ness, which meant that they did not have the same social respect and political clout accorded to the nomadic tribes who fulfilled al-'Umarī's Arab ideal.

Put together, the genealogical texts of al-Ḥamdānī and al-'Umarī confirm the spread of Arab village clans in Egypt and Syria in the thirteenth and fourteenth centuries. Al-'Umarī is quite explicit on this point, stating that nearly all the Arabs of Egypt are sedentary agriculturalists and that settled Arabs occupy most regions of Palestine and southern Syria. The same picture can be inferred from al-Ḥamdānī's earlier text, where tribes and clans are invariably located in defined and often limited geographical areas of agricultural cultivation. The sedentary Arabs of al-Ḥamdānī and al-'Umarī were, undoubtedly, the same people as the Arab villagers of the 1245 Fayyum register, or the villagers represented in the documents of the *qāḍī*'s court of Jerusalem in the first decade of the fourteenth century.

The fifteenth century witnessed a continued intense interest in genealogical knowledge, most evident through the works of the Mamluk bureaucrat Shihāb al-Dīn Aḥmad al-Qalqashandī (1355–1418), author of the famous administrative manual *Ṣubḥ al-A'shā*. The *Ṣubḥ*, completed in 814/1412, contains a long genealogical section derived from al-Ḥamdānī. Al-Qalqashandī then followed up with *Nihāyat al-arab fī ma'rifat ansāb al-'arab* (The Ultimate Ambition in the Knowledge of the Lineages of the Arabs), a genealogical treatise that holds over one thousand entries for Arab tribes and clans, arranged alphabetically. His final genealogical treatise, *Qalā'id al-jumān fī al-ta'rīf bi-qabā'il 'arab al-zamān* (The Abundant Necklaces regarding the Knowledge of the Arab Tribes of Our Time), was written in 819/1416. In all these works he mentioned his own rural origins in the village of Qalqashanda in al-Qalyūbiyya, and his village clan of the Banū Badr.[47]

Al-Qalqashandī's interest in Arab genealogy was not only personal. Since the beginning of the fifteenth century, Arab elite families acquired power and authority in most provinces of the Egyptian countryside, acting as officials of the Mamluk state. They were also the beneficiaries of an increased amount of iqṭāʿ grants (see chapter 10). Al-Qalqashandī was also witnessing a fundamental restructuring of the Mamluk sultanate, which came to increasingly rely on commercial revenues from the international spice trade that passed through Egypt and Syria to compensate for dwindling land-tax income. The shift from agricultural to commercial revenues was accompanied by the integration of civilian, non-*mamlūk* elites of Egyptian administrators and scholars, who often used their claims to Arab lineage as a source of social capital and legitimacy.

Nonetheless, al-Qalqashandī was following in the steps of al-Ḥamdānī and al-ʿUmarī in forging a genealogical tradition bound with the practices of the Mamluk state. The administrative purpose of genealogical writing is articulated in *Qalāʾid al-jumān*, his later treatise, which is presented as a handy manual for the secretary. Al-Qalqashandī is here entirely focused on contemporary tribes within the Mamluk realm with whom the secretary needs to correspond:

> The *kātib al-inshāʾ* is required to know in detail only those Arabs (ʿurbān) of this day and age who are within the realms of the kingdom of Egypt, and to whom royal correspondence is addressed. He also needs to know what concerns the more minor clans (*adhyāl*) that do not merit to be addressed, and those who are in alliance with them, or take pride in a relationship with that tribe (*qabīla*) for any reason.[48]

Here, the primary functional rationale for genealogy is epistolary. Al-Qalqashandī formalized the state-centered prism of genealogical writing: a scribe needs to know both how to write to tribal people who take pride in their lineage and how to know which tribal group is fitting of royal correspondence.

At the same time, al-Qalqashandī noticeably sought to expand the remit of genealogy to society at large. In a section on the benefits of the genealogical science, al-Qalqashandī emphasized the role of genealogy in establishing social hierarchies and political legitimacy. He opens with praising God for singling out the Arabs from the great multitude of nations and tribes, and pointing out that knowledge of the Prophetic lineage is part of Muslim belief.[49] Al-Qalqashandī then demonstrates the importance of genealogy for maintaining social order: knowledge of genealogy prevents false claims to lineage and therefore has legal implications for matters of inheritance, guardianship in marriage, the identification of beneficiaries of endowments, and the rules regarding the *ʿāqila*, or blood-money group. Another benefit is that knowledge of genealogy ensures that a prospective groom is equal in social status to the bride, under the legal principle of *kafāʾa*. Conversely, knowledge of genealogy also ensures the noble lineage of prospective brides, a matter not regulated in Islamic law. Finally, lineage determines the choice of the caliph, who, according to the Shāfiʿīs, should be a Qurashī.[50] Al-Qalqashandī's articulation of the purpose of genealogy is highly idealized. Mamluk-era collections of responses (*fatāwā*) rarely contain questions regarding equality in marriage or the *ʿāqila* blood-money group.[51] The choice of a caliph, largely a ceremonial office in the Mamluk sultanate, did not require genealogical knowledge.

Rather than taking these legal questions at face value, we should recognize al-Qalqashandī's broader vision: a society where every Muslim person, man or woman, belongs to an Arab lineage. By broadening the purpose of genealogy in this way, his audience is no longer merely chancery scribes, but parents who wish to marry off their children. The ability to distinguish a false lineage from a correct one should be, in this reformulation, key to social status in a Muslim society, whether urban or rural, sedentary or nomad. It is for this reason that al-Qalqashandī used his genealogical writings to highlight the clan affiliations of his contemporaries, family members, and patrons. The entry for the Berber Banū Ghumāra contains a biographical entry for his maternal grandfather, the companion of an itinerant Andalusi Sufi Shaykh.[52] The entry for the Banū Kināna is an occasion for mentioning al-Qalqashandī's link to the prominent jurist Abū Ḥafṣ Sirāj al-Dīn al-Bulqīnī (d. 1403), a native of the village of Bulqīna who traced his lineage back to the Kināna.[53] Al-Qalqashandī also specifically mentions the Kināna as second only to the Quraysh in their entitlement to community leadership. The entry for the Banū Mudlij includes a reference to al-Qalqashandī's commentary on the legal treatise of Kamāl al-Dīn al-Nashāʾī (d. 1356).[54]

On the question of who an Arab was, al-Qalqashandī advances two definitions of Arabness, one based on ethnic origin and one based on language. The first is taken from the philologist al-Jawharī (d. ca. 1010), who states that the Arabs are a people (*jīl min al-nās*) residing in garrison towns, while the *aʿrāb* are the people of the countryside. Al-Qalqashandī clarifies that the Arabs is the general name, and the *aʿrāb* are a category of Arabs.[55] The primordial abode of the Arabs was the Arabian Peninsula, but they had been migrating outside of it well before the advent of Islam. The Muslim conquests then allowed the Arabs to "fill the horizons," reaching Central Asia, the Atlantic, and the Sudan.[56] In a universal, post-deluge genealogy, the Arabs are descendants of Sām (Shem). Whether the Berbers are Arab or not is a matter of dispute.[57]

According to a second definition, taken from Ibn Khaldūn, who died in Cairo a decade earlier, the Arabs are those who speak articulate Arabic and among whom rhetoric and eloquence (*bayān* and *balāgha*) predominate. A person who does not speak good, clear Arabic (*lam yufṣiḥ*) is a non-Arab, an *ʿajamī*, even if they are an Arab by lineage.[58] This Khaldunian definition is not, however, followed through in the body of al-Qalqashandī's genealogical works, where poetry is sparse and proficiency in Arabic is not used as an actual criterion of Arabness. One glaring example are the Banū Kilāb of northern Syria; the fact that they speak Turkish, as reported by al-ʿUmarī, does not seem to disqualify them from being Arabs.[59]

Al-Qalqashandī's notion of Arabness is not based on pastoralism. Unlike al-ʿUmarī, who regarded the seasonal migration of nomads as the ultimate realization of Arab identity, al-Qalqashandī rarely mentions camels or tents.[60] He copies some of al-ʿUmarī's passages on the Āl Faḍl of the Syrian desert and their leaders, but he chooses not to reproduce al-ʿUmarī's passages on the distinctions between the true nomadic Arabs and the sedentary tribes who are no longer fully Arab. Al-Qalqashandī's primary definitions of Arabness explicitly blur any line between settled and nomadic existence, and he does not deem sedentary Arabs in lower esteem. He was himself, as mentioned above, a member of village clan from the delta.

Al-Qalqashandī does offer novel observations about different classes of Arabs within rural society, a phenomenon that may have become more important in the early fifteenth century (see also chapter 10). Commenting on the Lakhm clansmen of Middle Egypt described by al-Ḥamdānī (see map 5.1), al-Qalqashandī states that the Lakhm migrated from the eastern bank of the Nile to the western bank, retaining their identification with their tribes (*maʿa shuhratihim bi-qabāʾilihim*), while those who stayed were "people of plough and sowing." The Lakhm were then replaced by Arabs from the Halbā of Judhām, who adorn themselves in the accoutrements of the Arabs (*wa-hum mutaḥallūna hunāka bi-ḥilyat al-ʿarab*).[61] Al-Qalqashandī seems to describe here the replacement of one Arab elite with another. When the Lakhm Arab elites moved to the western bank, the peasants in the eastern bank came to be associated with the Halbā of Judhām. This Arab elite distinguished itself from ordinary peasants through dress or other trappings specifically associated with Arab culture.

Unlike al-Ḥamdānī and al-ʿUmarī, al-Qalqashandī also comments on the constant state of conflict between neighboring clans. In the delta, al-Qalqashandī reports that the Banū Saʿd were in a state of constant hostility with the Banū Wāʾil, and the fighting between the two groups involves a great number of men.[62] Ibn Khaldūn, writing toward the end of the fourteenth century, similarly commented on the endemic infighting among the agricultural Egyptian Arabs. According to

Ibn Khaldūn, the Banū Hilāl, Banū Kilāb, and Banū Rabī'a in Upper Egypt ride horses and carry weapons yet also cultivate the land and pay the land tax to the sultan (*yu'mirūna al-arḍ bi'l-filāḥa... wa-yaqūmūna bi'l-kharāj*). He then notes that the internal fighting among them is acute, worse than the internal fighting among the Arab clans of the desert.[63]

Al-Qalqashandī's work, written in the 1410s, allows us to follow how the place-names of rural Egypt gradually adapted to the spread of village clans, which by then had been commonplace for more than two centuries. As the claim for Arab or Berber descent had become entrenched, more rural settlements had come to be known by the names of the clans that inhabited them, shedding in the process older Coptic names. The Fawāṭiṭa, whom al-Ḥamdānī located in the region of al-Rashīd, were in al-Qalqashandī's days associated with a village (*balda*) near Alexandria named after them, Birkat al-Fawāṭiṭa.[64] Other Egyptian villages that became known after the names of tribal groups included Banū 'Alī and Banū Nizār in al-Bahnasāwiyya, and al-Fahmīn in al-Aṭfīḥiyya.[65]

Such changes to the toponymy of Egyptian villages can also be detected through comparison of cadastral surveys from across the Ayyubid and Mamluk eras. For example, Ibn Mammātī, writing circa 1200, lists only 11 percent Arabic village names in al-Minūfiyya and only 17 percent in al-Ashmūnayn. Only a handful of those referred to names of clans.[66] The cadastral surveys of Egypt by Ibn Duqmāq (1378) and Ibn al-Jī'ān (1480), on the other hand, show that the proportion of Arabic village names had doubled, from 11 percent to 25 percent in al-Minūfiyya and 17 percent to 34 percent in al-Ashmūnayn.[67] In al-Daqahliyya and in nearby al-Murtāḥiyya the surveys of the fourteenth and fifteenth centuries list eighteen Arab clan names, up from only four recorded by Ibn Mammātī in the late twelfth century. Quite a few of these new Arabic names reflected Arab or Berber clan identities, including the adding of clan suffixes to existing names. Thus, Barqā became Barqā Banī 'Imrān; Naqīda came to be known in the fourteenth century as Naqīdat Banī Fulays; and Dharwat Sarabām, present-day Dayrūṭ, became known as Darūṭ al-Sharīf, after the Ibn Tha'lab family. Overall, some Egyptian villages took over the names of the Arab clans who inhabited them, but they did so several generations *after* the process of becoming Arab had been complete and Arab identities have been well established.

To sum up our discussion of al-Ḥamdānī, al-'Umarī, and al-Qalqashandī, a distinct Mamluk genealogical genre emerged in the late thirteenth century following the proliferation of village clans across Egypt and Syria. The three authors discussed here were Mamluk officials, and the genealogical literature they produced was a distinct branch of Mamluk state administration. The most characteristic feature of this Mamluk genealogical literature was the geographical mapping of clans, with most groups located in the agricultural provinces of the Mamluk realm. While all three authors were sympathetic to the Arab clans and self-identified as Arabs themselves, the primary axis of these works is the relationship between the tribes and the state, and they advised chancery scribes on the correct titles and lineage to be used in correspondence with Arab amirs. Each author also advanced their own agenda, with al-ʿUmarī promoting an idealized distinction between the pastoral Arabs and the mass of agricultural village clans. Al-Qalqashandī, on the other hand, brushed aside al-ʿUmarī's distinction between the "true" Arabs of the desert and the Arabs of villages and towns; for him, writing after two centuries of entrenched Arab identities in the countryside, scholars, bureaucrats, amirs, village headmen, and irrigation officials were all equally Arab.

Biographical Dictionaries and Arab Self-Identity

Arab village clans were not merely an administrative category but were also a manner of fashioning the self. The Ayyubid and Mamluk periods saw the production of many volumes of biographical dictionaries, and the entries were often a space to individual self-representation, whether indirectly through reports concerning the subjects of the biography, or directly in the form of autobiographical notes. Entries for individuals with roots in the countryside clearly show that they often laid claim to an Arab lineage, to a nomadic past, and to membership in a clan. As village clans proliferated, such claims became very common—nearly universal—from the thirteenth century onward. Moreover, the entries allow us to see that these claims were propagated by the villagers themselves and not imposed from above. In Mamluk-era villages, everyone wanted to be seen as Arab, and practically nobody wanted to be remembered as a peasant.

A good vivid example of the prestige attached to Arab identity comes from the biography of the Mālikī jurist Shihāb al-Dīn al-Maghrāwī (d. 820/1417), a North African who migrated to Cairo. When debating a legal question with the older Egyptian Mālikī ʿAlam al-Dīn al-Busāṭī (d. 786/1384), the latter teased al-Maghrāwī by saying: "I have known that matter while you were still in al-Maghrāwa behind the cattle." Al-Maghrāwī didn't take the affront lightly, and replied: "You ignoramus shit-face (*walad al-kharā*)! There never was cattle in al-Maghrāwa. The people there are camel-herding Arabs (*ʿarab*), who are constantly on the go. It is me—by God—who has known this legal question while you were in Busāṭ herding cattle."[68] We have here two men of rural origins—one from a village in present-day

Algeria, the other from the village of Busāṭ in al-Daqahliyya—insulting each other by referring to the settled life of farmers who tend to cows. The riposte to the insult was the affirmation of origins in a camel-herding Arab milieu. Neither al-Maghrāwī nor al-Busāṭī went by an Arab clan name; their claims to Arab identity were not tethered to any specific lineage, but to an idealized way of life.[69]

It was usually not too difficult to claim an Arab heritage. When a fourteenth-century Mamluk bureaucrat dictated a long Sharifian lineage for himself, al-Ṣafadī quoted it in full, adding that "one has to take his word for it (*wa'l-ʿuhda ʿalayhi bi-dhālika*)."[70] Ibn Ḥajar al-ʿAsqalānī articulated this rule when assessing the lineage claims of the Tamīmīs of Hebron: "Lineage is acknowledged if it becomes common knowledge (*bi'l-istifāḍa*), unless there is evidence to the contrary."[71] Once a group was known by a certain lineage, any member of the group could claim that lineage, as well as testify for the lineage of another member. A critical approach to lineage claims does occasionally appear, but is generally uncommon. The *qāḍī* Taqī al-Dīn al-Zubayrī (d. 749/1348–49) reported his lineage going back fourteen ancestors until reaching the Companion Zubayr b. al-ʿAwām, but Ibn Ḥajar noted that in truth the family originated from the delta village of al-Zubayriyya near al-Maḥalla.[72] The state-appointed *naqīb al-ashrāf* was formally responsible for verifying claims of descent from the Prophet,[73] but there are no records of actual enforcement, and in any case most Arab lineage claims were non-Sharifian.

By the thirteenth century, Arab clan names had become a prevalent form of identification for Egyptian and Syrian scholars. Based on a study of seven major Mamluk-era biographical dictionaries, Koby Yosef has found that 30 to 40 percent of Shāfiʿī scholars were identified with Arab clan names, a rate consistent across the works examined.[74] The Shāfiʿī school was the dominant one in most rural and urban areas of Egypt and Syria, and a rate of 30 to 40 percent means that at least one in three men worthy of a biographical entry claimed an Arab lineage. As Yosef notes, these numbers are an underestimate, as the referencing of clan names was not systematic across parallel biographies of the same individual. Yosef also found that the ratio of Arab clan names among Shāfiʿīs is higher than among Ḥanafī and Ḥanbalī scholars, standing at about 10 to 15 percent. He argues the reason for this disparity lies in the value placed on Arab origins and the Arabic language in the Shāfiʿī school.[75] However, the pronounced Arab identity of Shāfiʿī scholars was probably due to the proliferation of Arab village clans in the Mamluk countryside. Ḥanafī scholars, on the other hand, were much more likely to be immigrants from the eastern Islamic world or from Anatolia, and this pattern better explains the lower rate of Arab clan names in this group.[76]

Claims to Arab lineage were made both in the city and in the countryside and could have different social meanings. Ibn Ḥajar al-ʿAsqalānī, born and bred in Cairo, claimed that he was from the Kināna. He learned of his lineage by reading a note left by his father, who claimed that his own ancestors came with the Ascalon Kināna troops, transferred to Egypt by Saladin.[77] Jamāl al-Dīn Ibn al-ʿAdīm (d. 787/1385), scion to a long-established scholarly dynasty of Aleppo, claimed a lineage that went back to Rabīʿa b. ʿĀmir b. Saʿsaʿa.[78] The Ibn al-Bārizī scholarly dynasty from Hama claimed to be from the Juhayna.[79] For these prominent urban men, the prestige of lineage was important, but it was not a focal point of their social identity. Ibn Ḥajar was a Kinānī but not a member of the Kināna: he didn't seek out bonds with other Kinānīs, nor did the Bārizīs appear to favor other Jahnīs.

Things were different in the countryside, where claims of Arab lineage often played a more central role in one's public persona. As seen in the anecdote above, rural men were often keen to avoid being identified as peasants; even if their peasant origins could not be concealed, their biographies included references to nomadic, camel-riding ancestors. Some played out their Arab identity by composing poetry in an Arab style, or they are noted for other aspects of "Arab" customs; much more will be said about the cultural expression of Arab identities in the following two chapters. For our purpose here, the biographical corpus indicates that clan membership was part and parcel of growing up in a Muslim village community—whether in Upper Egypt, the delta, Palestine, or the villages of Beqaa.

Arab clan identities in Upper Egypt are widely attested in the regional biographical dictionary composed by al-Udfūwī (d. 748/1347). Al-Udfūwī's aim was to celebrate the contribution of Upper Egypt to Islamic and Sunni history, and the timing of his writing reflects the ambitions of the newly formed Muslim and Sunni majority in the region.[80] There are over eighty individuals with Arab clan names in al-Udfūwī's dictionary, both villagers and townsmen.[81] When Arabs are mentioned in a village context, they are often identified as local elites. The saint of the village of al-Jurf near Edfu had a Kilābī lineage.[82] The bureaucrat and author al-Nuwayrī, whose family was from the village of Nuwayra near al-Bahnasā, had a Bakrī—Qurashī lineage.[83] The saint Mujallī b. Khalīfa (d. 690/1291–92) of Zarnīkh, near Esna, punished the insubordination of his slave (*mawlā*, perhaps a former slave) by humiliating him "in the manner of the Arabs"; he put a pack-saddle on his shoulders and led him on the public road.[84] Al-Udfūwī himself claimed lineage from the Banū Thaʿlab, and several of his family members are mentioned as engaged in agricultural cultivation.[85]

These Upper Egyptian Arabs were part of village communities. Al-Udfūwī uses the term *ahl al-bādiya* to refer to the inhabitants to the villages (*bilād* and *qurā*), so the term *bādiya* could denote in this period sedentary populations.[86] At the same time, and in keeping with other narrative sources of the period, al-Udfūwī rarely mentions fallāḥs, who are presented as either thieving or exceedingly stupid.[87] A *badawī* man is associated with trade of camels in the Hijaz.[88] But a love poem about a woman called Sitt al-ʿArab, from the village of Babūya, describes her as a "Bedouin woman" (*badawiyya*). The poem, said to have been composed by the *qāḍī* of Armant, begins with a dialogue between the author and the beloved, and it ends with his fear of reprisal by her itinerant kin, armed with swords and lances.[89] Sitt al-ʿArab, the idealized Bedouin beloved, lived in an Upper Egyptian village with the distinctly Coptic name of Babūya, protected by her virile and armed clan.

A smattering of Mamluk-era documents from Middle and Upper Egypt have been published, and they, too, contain references to villagers with Arab clan names. In an early-fourteenth-century petition from al-Ashmūnayn, a villager complains that a man called Riḍwān al-Labbān (the Milkman) of the Banī Jiyād clan of the Banū Rabīʿa, is using a co-owned animal without permission.[90] Here, Riḍwān the Milkman is identified by the name of his clan and of his tribe. The petition suggests that the Banū Jiyād were distinct from other groups in the village. The response of the local governor was to order the village headmen (*mashāyikh*) to bring Riḍwān to court, suggesting that he was a local resident. In another petition from the same early-fourteenth-century cluster, a man called Aḥmad b. Taghlab (or Thaʿlab), identified as one of the "slaves" (*ʿabīd*) of the Sharīf Ḥasan, is accused of beating his wife to death.[91] The name Taghlab (as well as Thaʿlab) was a typical "Arab" name. He is identified as a slave—perhaps a follower, a servant, or indeed unfree person—under the authority of a man of Prophetic descent.

An elaborate expression of elite Arab identity, as well as a rare female claim to lineage, comes from a cache of documents relating to a high-ranking woman, Umm al-Khayr bint Rukn al-Dīn Ḥusayn, of the Banū Kanz dynasty that ruled Aswan since the beginning of the eleventh century. The cache, dating from the 1330s and the 1340s, includes two lavish marriage contracts woven into a piece of green silk, plus another marriage contract relating to Umm al-Khayr's female slave.[92] In the contracts, clearly intended for public consumption, Umm al-Khayr is identified as an *amīra*, a rare use of the feminine form in either documentary or narrative sources. Most of the contract is taken up by Umm al-Khayr's long lineage, going all the way back to Maʿad b. ʿAdnān. The value of the property owned by Umm al-Khayr was staggering: in one marriage she was promised five hundred gold dinars, and in the second marriage two hundred dinars, which were paid thirty years later by the transfer of shares in two villages her husband owned in Giza as well as by a gift of a female slave and her child. Umm al-Khayr's elite marriages are suffused with genealogical claims. Her own lineage and that of her second husband went back to ʿAdnān; her first husband was a Kāhilī; her guardian in marriage was the *naqīb* (presumably *naqīb al-ashrāf*) of Aswan; and the *qāḍī* was a Qurashī from Esna. This cluster suggests that lineage mattered to women as much as it did to men. It also highlights the importance of slave ownership among the Arab elites of Upper Egypt, reinforcing a theme that comes across in al-Udfūwī's biographical dictionary.

Arab clan identity permeated the villages of the delta almost as much as it permeated Upper Egypt. The jurist and genealogist Nūr al-Dīn al-Khaḍarmawtī was born in Damrīṭ, a village in al-Sharqiyya, in 646/1248–49. He claimed to be of the Sīnānī clan of the Ḥimyar, and he composed poetry in the manner of the Arabs (*ʿalā ṭarīq al-ʿarab*).[93] His composition of "Arab" poetry and his expertise in matters of genealogy were significant cultural markers of identity. The potter and textile merchant ʿAbd al-Raḥmān b. al-Ḥasan, born in 668/1269–70 in the village of al-Qibāb near Damietta, was known as al-Lakhmī.[94] An early-fourteenth-century scholar from al-Fāqūs in al-Sharqiyya carried the *nisba* al-ʿĀmirī.[95] Kamāl al-Dīn al-Nishāʾī, born in 691/1292 in Nishā or Nashā in the central delta, was known as al-Mudlijī.[96] A more famous man was ʿAbd al-Kāfī b. ʿAlī al-Subkī (d. 735/1334–35), first in the line of the Subkī scholarly dynasty; he told his descendants that the clans (*maʿāshir*) of Subk in al-Minūfiyya were Anṣārīs.[97] This rather offhand claim to lineage suggests uncertainty about the place of the Subkīs' clan in the Arabian genealogical tree.

In Syria and Palestine, too, we find biographical entries for villagers who claimed Arab lineage. In the previous chapter we noted Abū al-Ḥasan al-Ḥarīrī (d. 645/1247–48), who claimed to belong to the Arab tribe (*qabīla*) of Banū Qarqar, with branches in the Hawran and in Nablus.[98] One could cite several other examples from the villages of thirteenth- and fourteenth-century Greater Syria. The famed Shāfiʿī jurist al-Nawawī, born in Nawā in the Hawran in 631/1233, reported that his great-great-grandfather, Ḥusayn b. Jumʿa al-Ḥizāmī, settled in Nawā "as Arabs do (*nazala . . . ʿalā ʿādat al-ʿarab*)," took residence there and had progeny until his descendants reached great numbers. Thus, a man who claimed Arab lineage settled down in the village of Nawā in the twelfth century, and after a few generations he became the genealogical focus of local identity. Interestingly, a further lineage chain provided by al-Nawawī's grandfather was contested.[99]

Similarly, the family of the historian Ibn Qāḍī Shuhba (born 1377), of the village of Shuhba in the Hawran, claimed lineage from the Banū Ghāḍira of the Banū Asad. Ibn Qāḍī Shuhba was not certain about the roots of his own family and copied the information from the books of al-Ṣafadī and Ibn Ḥabīb.[100]

Claiming Arab lineage was routine for rural Muslims in fourteenth-century Syria and Palestine, an almost indispensable part of their social status. Faraj al-Sāhilī (d. 751/1350–51) was of Arab lineage (*aṣlu-hu min al-ʿarab*); he was raised in villages around Safed and later moved to the village of Sāhiliyya near Tiberias.[101] Shaykh al-Islām Shihāb al-Dīn Ibn Arslān (or Raslān), born in Ramla or one of its villages circa 1355, also claimed Arab lineage. Whether he was from the Kināna or from the Nuʿayr was a matter of dispute.[102] The chief Ḥanafī qāḍī of Cairo, al-Dayrī al-ʿAbsī, was born in the village of al-Dayr near Nablus circa 1350.[103] The clan name ʿAbs referred to the Banū ʿAbs of the Hijaz, famed as the tribe of ʿAntara b. Shaddād. Another Ḥanafī, Burhān al-Dīn al-Asadī—from Asad Khuzayma—was born in Adhriʿāt in the Hawran in 644/1246–47.[104] Nāṣir al-Dīn al-Taghlibī (d. 728/1328) was the preacher of Zuraʿ, present-day Izraa.[105] The historian Shihāb al-Dīn Ibn Ḥijjī, born in Damascus in 715/1315 but with roots in rural Ḥisbān (present-day Hisban), claimed lineage from Banū Saʿd b. Bakr and signed his name as Aḥmad b. Hijjī b. Mūsā b. Aḥmad al-Saʿdī.[106] Arab clan names were common in the rural hinterland of Damascus throughout the Ayyubid and the Mamluk periods.[107]

The meaning that individuals ascribed to Arab clan identities is spelled out in the remarkable autobiographical self-reflections of Burhān al-Dīn al-Biqāʿī, one of the most controversial and extrovert scholars of fifteenth-century Cairo.[108] Al-Biqāʿī was born in the village of Khirbat Rūḥā (present-day Kherbet Rouha) in the Beqaa in 809/1406, but he was forced to leave the village at the age of twelve following the murder of his father and eight other relatives. After traveling to Damascus with his mother, he embarked on a path of scholarship that brought him to the circle of Ibn Ḥajar al-ʿAsqalānī in Cairo and from there to the vicinity of the royal court. In 841/1437, at the young age of thirty-two, he inserted an autobiographical note in the biographical dictionary he composed. He complemented it by biographical entries for his father and his uncle. As superbly discussed by Kenneth Goudie, this autobiography was intended to "underscore his transition from his peasant background to membership of the intellectual elite," as well as to make sense of the traumatic murder of his father that shaped his childhood. He was a young man painfully aware of his imperfect Arabic pronunciation and outsider status, out to show that his trials were part of a divine plan to lead him to greatness.[109]

Al-Biqāʿī opens his autobiography with a discussion of his clan identity, stating that he is from a people (*qawm*) called Banū Ḥasan, who inhabit his native village of Khirbat Rūḥā as well as other localities in Syria and Egypt.[110] Al-Biqāʿī states that there are at least five hundred men of the Banū Ḥasan in Khirbat Rūḥā; it is very likely that Banū Ḥasan was the only clan in the village. They originated in this village sometime in the distant past, perhaps seven generations before the generation of al-Biqāʿī (that would place the ancestor in the early thirteenth century). They were subdivided into three clans (*abṭun*): Banū Yūsuf (or Yūnis), Banū ʿAlī and Banū Makkī, after the three sons of the eponym. Al-Biqāʿī knew that he belonged to the Banū Makkī, although he was not certain about the precise lineage beyond his great-great-grandfather. As pointed out by Goudie, the limits of al-Biqāʿī's knowledge of genealogy match the memory of genealogies among modern tribal groups.[111] The social meaning of his Makkī identity is not evident from al-Biqāʿī's writings, as he mentions "paternal cousins" who belonged to the two other clans.[112]

From their base of Khirbat Rūḥā, other clans of the Banū Ḥasan had scattered across the Mamluk countryside: some were found in the villages of Aleppo, some in the village of Majdal Marʿash (?) in the northern Beqaa, some in the region of Karak and Shawbak, and a final group migrated (*nazaḥat*) to the region of Bilbays in al-Sharqiyya. Overall, al-Biqāʿī informs us that the villagers of Khirbat Rūḥā identified themselves as the Banū Ḥasan and that they were vaguely aware of other villages of the Banū Ḥasan near Aleppo, in the Balqa and in the eastern delta. They also had specific knowledge of another village of Banū Ḥasan in the same region of the Beqaa. They believed that all these groups originated from their own village. As might be expected, al-Biqāʿī boasts that wherever they are found, the men of the Banū Ḥasan are known as the bravest of all.

The Arabness of the villagers of Khirbat Rūḥā was bolstered by a vague claim that the Banū Ḥasan were descendants of the Companion Saʿd b. Abī Waqqāṣ. This claim was put forward to al-Biqāʿī by a man from the village and confirmed by relatives he met in Damascus in 836/1433.[113] Al-Biqāʿī asked these relatives for written evidence, which he calls a *nisba*, for this prestigious lineage, but to no avail. Al-Biqāʿī's attempt to validate these claims by written proofs is unprecedented, and even his use of the term *nisba* for such documents is unusual. Our earliest extant lineage document validated by *qāḍī* courts comes from late-fifteenth-century Damanhūr.[114] Al-Biqāʿī's interest in written proofs may be a reflection of his scholarly pursuits. Be that as it may, the process by which the Khirbat Rūḥā clan of the Banū Ḥasan attempted to "graft" itself onto the Arab genealogical tree follows a familiar pattern.[115]

Al-Biqāʿī's autobiography illustrates the process by which Muslim inhabitants of villages in Ayyubid and Mamluk Egypt and Syria assumed common ancestry and a clan social organization. The village identified with one clan, imagined around a figure of a shared Muslim ancestor. Then, at later stage, perhaps as a result of encounters with learned elites, the villagers sought a historical figure from early Islamic conquests to which they could attach their lineage. Al-Biqāʿī records no active memory of migration, and it is not entirely clear that al-Biqāʿī understood himself to be "Arab." An anecdote about his grandfather—dashingly handsome and incredibly valiant—has him fighting off sixty "Arabs" armed with lances at a nearby village.[116] The use of the term "Arabs" here seems to be negative, marking them as brutish outsiders, although the villagers of Khirbat Rūḥā themselves were organized into clans, claimed Arab lineage, and may well have been seen as Arabs by others. Becoming Arab was always a relative process.

Genealogy, Administration, Clan, and Self

It is worth commenting here on the name of al-Biqāʿī's village of origin, Khirbat Rūḥā. The prefix Khirba—literally, "ruins"—suggests that the village had been reoccupied after it had been deserted and is typical of the expansion of agriculture in the Ayyubid and Mamluk eras, as pointed out by Bethany Walker.[117] The communal memory in Khirbat Rūḥā, as recounted by al-Biqāʿī, was that the ancestor of the local clan was an Arab who settled in the village at the beginning of the thirteenth century. This fits with wider patterns of proliferation of village clans and reoccupation of sites in the Ayyubid period. It is also worth pointing out that the village didn't take the name of the resident Banū Ḥasan, so it is likely the clan of Banū Ḥasan came into being after the site had been reoccupied. The search for an Arab lineage that would tie the villagers to an early Islamic figure came much later, and it was still ongoing in the early fifteenth century.

The evidence from the Fayyum and from Jerusalem, from the genealogical texts and from the biographical dictionaries, all demonstrate that from the thirteenth century onward Muslim villagers commonly identified as Arab clansmen, both for fiscal purposes and as a form of self-representation. Each village typically identified with one clan and saw itself associated with other clans carrying the same name in other villages—sometimes nearby, sometimes in other provinces. The name of the clan was used in official papers concerning collective tax collection and tenancy rights but was also used by individuals as a form of social capital. An Arab clan name could imply a nomadic past and an Islamic pedigree, especially if one could claim a lineage going back to early Islam or even the pre-Islamic Arabs. The precise place of any given clan on the Arab genealogical tree was often a matter of confusion, and probably of lesser importance.

This chapter and the previous two—the second part of *Becoming Arab*—sought to highlight the overwhelming evidence for the proliferation of Arab village clans in the Ayyubid and Mamluk countryside. The next two chapters deal with the ways this Arab identity was expressed. Claims of Arab lineage involved a link to a nomadic past and to the Arabian Peninsula, and villagers in the Egyptian and Syrian countrysides had to reconcile claims to these Arabian pastoralist origins with their sedentary existence. They were always at risk of being accused of being Arabs in name only, as we have seen in al-ʿUmarī's derogatory remarks. How did villagers make the claim to Arab lineage and Arab identity? How did they become part of an overarching culture and ethnicity that went beyond their local community? As the next two chapters will show, the most common ways of becoming Arab were through adoption of distinct dialects, the wearing of distinct Arab dress, and the recounting of shared popular epics.

PART III

Markers of Arab Identity

6

Arab Speech, Arab Dress, and Handmade Wares

MUSLIM VILLAGERS in thirteenth- and fourteenth-century Egypt, Palestine, and Syria commonly identified themselves as members of Arab clans. State administrators routinely identified the inhabitants of villages as members of such named clans, and this name carried fiscal and security consequences: tenancy contracts were issued to village headmen who all belonged to the same clan, and ʿurbān auxiliary forces were recruited based on quotas levied from clusters of village clans. At the same time, the urge to adopt Arab clan names and identities also came from below. Individual villagers regularly and forcefully presented themselves as descendants of tribal nomads who migrated from the Arabian Peninsula. Taking an Arab clan name was a claim to a lineage and, therefore, to a history and a cultural tradition.

Yet taking on an Arab name was not enough. The prestige associated with Arab lineage had to be earned through a set of cultural symbols used to distinguish members of the group from outsiders, what Frederik Barth famously called "cultural stuff." In the late medieval countryside of Egypt and Syria, as in many other societies, the two primary markers of identity were dialect and clothes. One had to speak and dress like an Arab in order to pass as one. Given the wide geographical range of the communities and individuals who claimed Arabness, the performance of Arab speech and dress had to be reduced to simple symbolic gestures. This chapter argues that Arab speech was indicated by the /g/ vocalization of the letter *qāf*, a feature still retained in "Bedouin" dialects in the present day. Arab dress primarily took the form of tucking the loose ends of one's turban under beard or chin or drawing them over one's face and mouth as a *lithām* face-veil. Other aspects of what was considered Arab speech and dress varied, although, in the case of dress, the ʿurbān official auxiliary units wore distinctive uniforms. Overall, medieval authors understood the Arab vocalization of *qāf* and the manner of wearing the turban as shorthand for a man's cultural Arab identity.

The twin practices of Arab *qāf* vocalization and the wearing of the Arab *lithām* share important similarities. First, medieval sources make it clear that both speech and dress could be taken on and off, and they were willfully adopted by people who wanted to pass as Arabs. Arabs and non-Arabs had the same physical features, so crossing the line from one group to another was a matter of performance. Second, both the vocalization of *qāf* and the distinctive Arab *lithām* emerged as cultural symbols from the eleventh century onward, gaining popularity and currency in Mamluk Syria and Egypt. While both were found in the Arabian Peninsula in earlier centuries, neither practice was considered distinctively Arab before the later Middle Ages. The *qāf* vocalization and the *lithām* only acquired their cultural capital as markers of Arab identity among rural communities outside Arabia, during the spread of Arab village clans in the countryside of Greater Syria and Egypt. Villagers adopted these cultural markers based on their knowledge of what it meant to be Arab; this must have involved imitation of local elites and followed points of contact with the Arabian Peninsula and trajectories of cultural circulation that are not usually visible to us in the available sources. But, ultimately, the articulation of Arab identity among these predominantly peasant communities didn't simply replicate the linguistic and sartorial culture of the Arabian Peninsula. This is a crucial point for the argument of *Becoming Arab*: cultural markers of identity were not passed down in inheritance across generations—they were actively constructed by late medieval rural people, who chose to imbue these forms of speech and dress with the cultural capital of Arabness.

Alongside the explicitly Arab markers of speech and dress, archaeological excavations and surveys show a significant shift in the material culture of villages of Greater Syria and Palestine. Starting from the 1100s, handmade geometrically painted wares (known as HMGP), unexpectedly supplanted a long tradition of fine-bodied, wheel-thrown wares found in the same villages since pre-Islamic times. This process accelerated in the thirteenth century, so that distinctly decorated handmade wares dominate nearly all village assemblages of Greater Syria and Palestine in the Ayyubid and Mamluk periods, with the notable exception of rural administrative and military centers. This shift in pottery went under the radar of the narrative sources and is known to us only from the archaeological record. These handmade wares may have been an attempt to imitate the handmade pottery tradition indigenous to the Arabian Peninsula, and their sizes and shapes suggest a connection with practices of communal dining. Given the absence of any textual reference, the social meaning attached to these utensils can only be surmised, and we do not know that Syrian HMGP wares were viewed as distinctly Arab. Nonetheless, the dramatic shift in rural pottery in Greater Syria is concrete evidence of a watershed moment separating village life in the early Islamic period and in the later medieval centuries, coinciding with the formation of Arab village clans.

Qāf al-ʿArab: Voiced Vocalization of q* and Arab Identity

The pronunciation of the Arabic letter q* (ق) as /g/ is considered today as one of the three main indicators of what are known as the Bedouin dialects of modern Arabic, alongside the preservation of the interdental consonants (e.g., <u>th</u>) and the gender distinction in the plural of the verb. This typology has many exceptions, and linguists are in some disagreement about what constitutes a Bedouin dialect, and whether all instances of q* = /g/ fall under the definition of such a dialect. But, by and large, this pronunciation is often taken to be its most distinctive and easily discernible feature.[1]

Today, Bedouin and sedentary dialects exist throughout the central lands of the Arabic-speaking world, with the exception of the Arabian Peninsula itself, where the Bedouin dialect is prevalent in nearly all contexts. Again, the distinction between Bedouin and sedentary can be misleading, as dialects deemed Bedouin are not limited to nomadic groups, nor to people who regard themselves today as Bedouin. The q* = /g/ vocalization, as the most distinctive feature of Bedouin dialects, is similarly widely attested outside pastoralist communities.[2] In Egypt, for example, the /g/ articulation is the dominant one in the countryside. Even though it is commonly seen as part of the Ṣaʿīdī, or Upper Egyptian, dialect, it is found also in the western and eastern areas of the delta. The /g/ articulation is also dominant in much of the Iraqi countryside (known as *qilit* dialects), as well as among the Muslim population of Baghdad and in all rural areas of Jordan.

Modern linguists agree that the /g/ articulation, together with the other distinctive features of Bedouin speech, were part of a late medieval wave of "bedouinization" of dialects.[3] It is now widely accepted that features of the Bedouin dialects, such as the q* =/g/ pronunciation, spread from the eleventh century onward at the expense of regional Arabic dialects that developed in the earlier Islamic centuries. As a result, these early regional dialects became restricted to the urban centers and to the minority religious communities of Christians and Jews, while the Bedouin dialects became common in much of the countryside.

Some scholars view the Bedouin dialects as preserving an ancient layer of Arabic that was in circulation in the Arabian Peninsula before Islam, but recent research generally tends to view the Bedouin dialects of the wider Middle East as a new type of Arabic that emerged as part of a second wave of dialect formation.[4] As argued by Versteegh, the bedouinization of speech involved a "de-creolization" of rural dialects, i.e., a conscious attempt to take on a higher register of speech and rid the language of what were perceived to be foreign influences.[5] This was a process of the leveling up of Arabic to its imagined original form, which, in reality, was not the same as the Arabic of the early Islamic community. Even if the Bedouin dialects accrued features of earlier layers of Arabic, Versteegh—following Ibn Khaldūn—viewed them as a "New Arabic type," classicizing rather than classical.[6]

This late medieval bedouinization of dialects has been commonly explained through the migration of tribesmen from the Arabian Peninsula, including in Versteegh's more recent work.[7] The primary example given here is that of so-called Hilālī Bedouin dialects of North Africa, which are said to reflect the Banū Hilāl invasion of the eleventh century. This model assumes that dialects are tied to relatively fixed ethnic identities, with each tribal group retaining its distinctive dialect over a millennium. The present-day distribution of dialect groups is then taken as a reflection of the history of these migrations. Based on this assumption, historians of the Arabic language have mined medieval accounts of tribal migration, especially the fifteenth-century works of al-Maqrīzī, in an attempt to match current dialect distribution with medieval population movements.[8]

Late medieval references to the pronunciation of q* = g, which will be presented in this section, tell a different story.[9] Legal, philological, historical, and biographical sources from the later Middle Ages refer to this linguistic feature as *al-qāf al-maʿqūda* (literally, "tongue-tied" *qāf*) or, tellingly, *qāf al-ʿArab*, the qāf of the Arabs. These terms are first attested in the late eleventh century and then become widespread from the early thirteenth century. By the fifteenth century, this pronunciation is identified as the prevalent one in the agricultural regions of Upper Egypt and North Africa. Importantly, the q* = /g/ pronunciation was identified with a collective Arab identity that superseded tribal distinctions, and, at the same time, as one willfully adopted by individuals who wished to acquire an Arab social identity. Rather than an ethnic marker of nomadic migration, the q* = /g/ articulation emerges from medieval sources as a cultural marker that allowed rural people to claim for themselves the social prestige of Arabness.

Whether the q* =/g/ pronunciation was common in pre-Islamic Arabia is matter of debate, both today and in the medieval period.[10] Sībawayh (d. c. 180/796) classified *qāf* as a voiced phoneme, and this is taken to mean that in his time the normative pronunciation was /g/.[11] References to the *qāf* of Banū Tamīm, which may or may not be an antecedent of the /g/ vocalization, depict it as a nonnormative pronunciation. Pierre Larcher suggests that the Arabic of Tamīm was a philologist shorthand for spoken, non-Quranic Arabic.[12] Other variants are also reported, such as a mispronunciation of q* = /ṭ/, attributed to nonnative speakers of Arabic, such as the Persian Abū Muslim. The early jurist Makḥūl (d. 112/730–31) reportedly pronounced q* = /k/.[13]

While it is likely that the q* = /g/ articulation was a common one in the early Islamic centuries, Abbasid-era grammarians did not refer to any distinct Arab or Bedouin reflexion of the letter q*.[14] The Iraqi philologist Ibn Jinnī (d. 1002 CE) offers a brief discussion of differences between Arab and non-Arab (*ḥaḍar*) dialects, a discussion that underlines the ideological dimension of this distinction.[15] Ibn Jinnī states that non-Arab dialects tend to omit the case and mood endings (*iʿrāb*), but he then adds that in his own time—i.e., the late fourth/tenth century—no one among the pastoralist Arabs actually speaks "correct" (*faṣīḥ*) Arabic. This means, as insightfully argued by Larcher, that Ibn Jinnī viewed the Arab manner of speech as an ideological construct: it represented the ideal, Quranic form of Arabic and bore little relationship to actual speakers. By his time, the pure language of the Arabs, like their pure lineage, became an article of faith, not a sociolinguistic observation.[16] For our purpose here, it is remarkable that Ibn Jinnī states that Arab and non-Arab dialects do not differ on the matter of *ḥurūf*, i.e., on the articulation of letter sounds. Despite Abbasid scholars' fascination with the nomadic, camel-herding Arabs as preservers of the purest form of the Arabic language, Ibn Jinnī didn't point out the pronunciation of q* as a feature of Arab speech.

The earliest reference to the pronunciation of *qāf* as distinctive to the Arabs comes a century later, in the late eleventh century. It is found in the legal compendium of the Shāfiʿī scholar ʿAbd al-Wāḥid al-Rūyānī (d. 502/1108–9), who lived in Tabaristan. When dealing with the question of leadership in prayer, al-Rūyānī considers the permissibility of praying behind a man who pronounces ambiguous letters, giving the example of an Arab who vocalizes the *qāf* somewhere between *qāf* and *kāf*. He was surely referring to the sound /g/, for which there is no equivalent letter in Arabic. Al-Rūyānī viewed this typically Arab pronunciation as defective and compared it with the non-Arab (*ʿajamī*, probably Persian) who cannot pronounce *ḍ*, but says *ẓ* instead. Al-Rūyānī rules that it is reprehensible to pray behind such men, indicating that he considered both pronunciations to be nonnormative.[17] Later Shāfiʿī sources mention that the same question was also discussed by his contemporary, the Syrian jurist Naṣr al-Maqdisī (d. 490/1096–97).[18]

A second twelfth-century reference is found in the biography of the poet Shihāb al-Dīn Abū al-Fawāris Saʿd b. Muḥammad al-Tamīmī, nicknamed Ḥayṣa Bayṣa (492/1098–9 to 574/1179). Ḥayṣa Bayṣa lived in Baghdad, where he was an authority on language, poetry, and belles lettres, and specialized in panegyrics for Abbasid caliphs and Seljuk sultans. His biographers report that he was infatuated with Arab heritage, an interest reflected in the lexicon, themes, and motifs of his poetry, as well as in his appearance: he dressed like an Arab, rode purebred Arab horses, and carried two swords and a lance. He was fond of obsolete quaint vocabulary—he got his nickname from the expression *fī ḥayṣa bayṣa* "in straits and distress"—and addressed everyone in classical Arabic with all its grammatical niceties. Most relevant to our topic, he also affected "Bedouin" speech (*wa-yatabādā bi-lafẓihi*), pronouncing the *qāf* in a "tongue-tied manner" (*wa-yaʿqidu al-qāf*).[19] As we shall see, late medieval grammarians used the term "tongue-tied *qāf* (*al-qāf al-maʿqūda*)" to express the q* = /g/ pronunciation. Ḥayṣa Bayṣa understood the tongue-tied vocalization of *qāf* as a cultural marker of Arab identity and consciously adopted it in the same way he donned Arab swords and clothes.

By the beginning of the thirteenth century, biographical dictionaries contain a good number of entries for individuals who pronounced q* in the "Arab way," and this aspect of their speech was then associated with their public persona. The litterateur al-Mubārak b. al-Bakr Ibn al-Shaʿʿār (d. 654/1256) devotes a biography to an acquaintance by the name of Sulaymān b. Yaḥyā, a *badawī* (Bedouin) soldier who served in Baghdad. Sulaymān was born and raised in the steppe, claimed a long lineage that stretched back to ʿUqayl, and used to vocalize q* = /k/ in his entire speech—even when a shift to a higher register was expected.[20] Muʿīn al-Dīn Abū ʿAlī al-Taghlibī, the vizier of the amir of al-Ḥadītha in Iraq circa 600/1200, was "Bedouin in his speech" and tongue-tied his *qāf*.[21] Ibn al-Shaʿʿār also refers to the tongue-tied *qāf* of the poet Muwaffaq al-Dīn ʿAlī Ibn al-Muqarrab (d. 1234), of Baḥrayn in eastern Arabia.[22] The same was said about Abū al-Rabīʿ Sulaymān al-Makkī al-Tamīmī al-Dārī (d. ca. 1240), who lived in Irbil and Mosul.[23] Ibn al-ʿAdīm devoted a very revealing entry to a certain Zayd al-Ḥawrānī, a crippled black man who used to play with Ibn al-ʿAdīm and his boyhood friends in the streets of Aleppo. Zayd pronounced *daqīq* (Arabic for "wheat") with tongue-tied *qāf*, something that the urbane Ibn al-ʿAdīm found unusual or amusing. It was reflective of Zayd's lower social class and rural origins in the Hawran.[24]

Ibn al-ʿAdīm is one of the last authors to present the q* = /g/ pronunciation as a curiosity. From the thirteenth century onward, several prominent North African scholars discuss this Arab pronunciation and comment on its wide circulation. The first author to reflect on the religious and historical meanings of this phenomenon was the mystic Ibn al-ʿArabī in his *Futūḥāt*, a work that he began writing in Mecca in 1202. When discussing the esoteric meaning of the letters of the Arabic alphabet, Ibn al-ʿArabī notes that "all the Arabs we encountered, whose language has not been subject to change, such as the Banū Fahm, pronounce a tongue-tied *qāf* (*maʿqūda*). This is the case with all the Arabs."[25] The Banū Fahm were a tribal group resident in Mecca, and they presumably represented for Ibn al-ʿArabī a continuity with Arabic pronunciation at Islam's place of origin. Beyond the Banū Fahm, Ibn al-ʿArabī generalized this feature to all other Arabs. He then noted that in the Islamic West, meaning, North Africa and Muslim Spain, this pronunciation was considered defective, and Quran reciters insisted on pronouncing the *qāf* as non-*maʿqūda*, claiming this was the Prophetic pronunciation.[26] Thus, Ibn al-ʿArabī generalized the /g/ articulation to all contemporary Arabs, noting that Quran readers in North Africa insisted that this Arab pronunciation was nonnormative and diverged from the Prophetic origins.

The eminent philologist Abū Ḥayyān (d. 1344), an Andalusi scholar who spent most of his life in Egypt, took up the same sociolinguistic observation a century later. Like Ibn al-ʿArabī, Abū Ḥayyān also distinguished between the two pronunciations of q*, defining the ambiguous vocalization that falls between /q/ and /k/ as tongue-tied. He states that this ambiguous tongue-tied *qāf* was known to the tenth-century grammarian al-Sīrafī (d. 979), but only as an oddity. In "our own days," however—meaning in the early fourteenth century—this pronunciation had come to dominate the speech of nearly all the Arabs of the *bawādī*, meaning here either the steppe or the countryside more generally. He adds that the tongue-tied pronunciation doesn't conform to the unambiguous pronunciation of q* espoused in the books of grammarians and by Quran reciters.[27] Interestingly, Abū Ḥayyān himself spoke with a tongue-tied *qāf*, at least according to his student al-Ṣafadī, but he reverted to normative (*faṣīḥ*) *qāf* when reciting the Quran. This quirk was attributed by al-Ṣafadī to Abū Ḥayyān's Andalusi origins and was found in the speech of other Andalusis who migrated to Syria.[28]

The most elaborate and sophisticated discussion of the social and historical implications of the q* = /g/ pronunciation comes from the pen of Ibn Khaldūn.[29] Ibn Khaldūn not only conceptualized Arab tribal organization as the driving force of Islamic history but also understood language as a key component of this Arab identity. In a passage that has already attracted the attention of several modern linguists, he provides a thorough and detailed explanation of what he considered the Arab vocalization of q*. He then follows with a historical discussion regarding the original Prophetic vocalization, without reaching firm conclusions. Most importantly for our purposes, Ibn Khaldūn views this pronunciation as a cultural marker taken on by individuals and groups as a way of indicating and projecting an Arab identity. It is not an innate characteristic, nor a distinguishing mark of a certain tribe, but a form of speech that signals an attachment to broader ethnolinguistic ethos.

The passages by Ibn Khaldūn deserve to be cited in full:

> One of the phenomena that happen in the contemporary speech of these Arabs, wherever they dwell, is their special way of pronouncing the *qāf*. They do not pronounce it at the place of articulation of the urban people, as it is mentioned in the books on Arabic philology, namely between the back of the tongue and the opposite point of the upper palate. They do not pronounce it at the place of articulation of the *k*, either, which is somewhat lower than the place of the *qāf* on the tongue and the upper palate, but they pronounce it at a place that is somewhere in the middle between the *qāf* and the *kāf*.[30] . . . This is the case with all Arabs, wherever they are, in the West or the East. It has eventually become their distinguishing mark (*ʿalāma*) among the nations and races. It is a characteristic of theirs that no one shares with them. This goes so far that those who want to affiliate themselves (*al-intisāb*) to the Arabs and enter in their midst, imitate the Arab pronunciation of *qāf*. They consider the pronunciation of *qāf* the way to distinguish the eloquent (*ṣarīḥ*) Arab speaker from a sedentary (*ḥaḍarī*) and someone who entered Arabness (*ʿurūbiyya*) recently, for they consider this to be the precise language of Muḍar . . . But in our day, both Muḍar and Kahlān speak with this feature.[31]

According to Ibn Khaldūn, *qāf al-ʿArab* was understood to be a distinctive mark of being Arab, whether Qaysī Muḍar or Yamanī Kahlān, and distinguished them from non-Arab, nontribal individuals. The /g/ pronunciation became the shibboleth of Arabness regardless of individual tribal affiliation. At the same time, it functioned as mechanism of entry into Arab identity; those who wished to be identified as Arabs adopted it to gain prestige and to validate their newly discovered Arab social persona. In a related passage, Ibn Khaldūn states that the Hawwāra Berbers adopted the dress, lifestyle, and the eloquent Arabic of the Sulaym Arabs who lived next to them between Barqa and Alexandria, suppressing the coarse Berber accent (*raṭāna*) so that now it is no longer possible to distinguish between the Berber Hawwāra and the Arab Sulaym.[32] One is reminded of Ḥayṣa Bayṣa, the bedouinizing poet of twelfth-century Baghdad, who donned his /g/ alongside his Arab dress and sword. Ibn Khaldūn was able to transcend the chauvinism of claims by Arabs and non-Arabs, and, in the manner of modern sociolinguists, understood the agency of speakers to convey identity not only by what they say, but by how they say it.

Ibn Khaldūn remains agnostic regarding the roots of this difference between sedentary and Arab dialects. The main import of his chapters on the Arabic spoken in his time is that late medieval dialects, both those of the Arabs and of the town dwellers, are not defective variants of classical Arabic. Ibn Khaldūn thus breaks away from the enduring myth of the conservativism of the Arabic spoken by Arab clansmen. The traits of the Arab dialects—first and foremost the /g/ articulation, but also syntactic positioning of the subject and the distinctive use of declension—amount to a novel language with its own internal logic.[33] The /g/ pronunciation may or may not have been the Prophet's vocalization. But it does not represent a purer Arabic; both varieties of the vocalization of *qāf* are legally permissible and aesthetically pleasing.

When Ibn Khaldūn was making these observations at the end of the fourteenth century, the /g/ pronunciation had become dominant in much of the Egyptian countryside. The earliest indication is reported by Ibn al-Dawādārī (d. 1335) in his account of the suppression of an Arab rebellion in Middle and Upper Egypt circa 1300. According to Ibn al-Dawādārī, the /g/ pronunciation was a marker of Arab identity. He reports that whenever a group of rustics was captured by the Mamluk army, they were made to talk in order to determine whether they were Arabs or not. Anyone who pronounced *qāf maʿqūda* was executed while those who pronounced it in the proper way were released (*idhā umsika minhum jamāʿa istanṭaqahum fa-man ʿuqida fī kalāmi-hi al-qāf atlafa-hu wa-man qāla-hā mustaqīma aṭlaqa-hu*).[34] A century later al-Maqrīzī adds some literary flourish to this report, stating that when any of the rustics taken captive claimed to be a non-Arab *ḥaḍarī*, he was asked to pronounce the word *daqīq* (wheat), and "if he said this with the *qāf* of the Arabs he was killed."[35] This is surely a literary topos, referencing the biblical shibboleth. Realistically, one could probably switch pronunciations if one's life depended on it. Nonetheless, Ibn al-Dawādārī's account indicates that the /g/ pronunciation of q* had already become a distinctive marker of Arab identity in rural Egyptian provinces during the first half of the fourteenth century.

Two other examples of /g/ pronunciation occur in al-Sakhāwī's fifteenth-century biographical dictionary of contemporary scholars. Zuhayr b. Ḥasan, chief stableman in the Mamluk court and a member of al-Yasār tribe, was thwarted in his attempts to be accepted into the ranks of the *'ulamā'*, partly because he used to pronounce *qāf* in the manner of the Arabs. As countermeasure, he sought legal opinions in support of the permissibility of an Arab *qāf* in prayer.[36] Al-Sakhāwī also has a biography of a rural man called Abū al-Jūd, who was born in a village in al-Gharbiyya in 792/1390 and who died in Cairo in 863/1459. Once he moved to Cairo he was accepted as a scholar, even though he continued to pronounce the tongue-tied *qāf* in the way he was brought up.[37] In fifteenth-century Cairo, the /g/ was considered an inferior pronunciation, associated with Arabs and villagers.

Outside of Cairo, however, the /g/ became the default vocalization throughout Upper Egypt and North Africa, as witnessed by the development of Shāfi'ī legal writings on the permissibility of pronouncing *qāf al-'Arab* during prayer, a topic first raised in the late eleventh century. During the Mamluk era, the topic was discussed again by the jurists Ibn Rif'a (d. 710/1310–11) and al-Isnawī (d. 772/1370), and then by al-Suyūṭī (d. 911/1505) in reference to Arab pronunciation of a declaration of divorce (*ṭalāq*).[38] By the sixteenth century, however, the Shāfi'ī Ibn Ḥajar al-Haythamī (d. 974/1566) found that the terms of the discussion were no longer relevant to the realities of his time. On the matter of "someone who pronounces the *qāf* of the Arabs between *qāf* and *kāf*" (*aw naṭaqa bi-qāf al-'Arab al-mutaraddida baynaha wa-bayna al-kāf*), one must acknowledge the spread of Arab groups throughout the Islamic world. As a result, the /g/ pronunciation is common everywhere in Upper Egypt and North Africa: "The term 'Arabs' refers to different and innumerable groupings of Arab peoples; for this reason, some of our masters attributed the [*qāf al-'Arab*] to the people of the Islamic West and to Upper Egypt (*wa'l-murād bi'l-'arab al-mansūba ilayhim akhlāṭuhum alladhīna lā yu'taddu bi-him wa-lidhā nasaba-hā ba'ḍ al-a'imma li-ahl al-gharb wa-ṣa'īd Miṣr*)."[39] In this comment, al-Haythamī states that the /g/ articulation had by the sixteenth century spread to the entire population of Arabic speakers in Upper Egypt and North Africa and had become the normative articulation of *qāf* in these regions.[40]

To sum up the evidence, q* = /g/ as a distinctively Arab pronunciation is first mentioned in legal texts in the late eleventh century. It then crops up in biographies of Iraqi and Syrian men of rural origins in the twelfth century and becomes a topic of religious, social, and historical interest in the following two centuries. By the fifteenth century it had become common in the Egyptian countryside as well as in North Africa, anticipating the present-day distribution of "Bedouin" dialects. Its use crossed over tribal divisions and reflected a broader cultural identity, connecting Arab clansmen from all over the Middle East. Despite the prevalence of this vocalization in the Arabian Peninsula itself, urban Muslim scholars considered it nonnormative and disapproved of its use in Quranic recitation and in prayer. Individuals like Ḥayṣa Bayṣa and Abū Ḥayyān were able to switch from one vocalization to another depending on the social context, and Ibn Khaldūn regarded it as an acquired marker of social prestige.

As the medieval sources show, this bedouinization of speech was not a simple result of migratory movements. Late medieval authors who discuss the /g/ pronunciation have nothing to say about migrations of individual tribes, or about any migrations at all. Instead, they emphasize the significance of *qāf al-ʿArab* as a marker of supra-regional "Arab" identity, an acquired rather than innate feature of speech. Late medieval Arab clansmen had come to consider this vocalization a part of the "original language of Muḍar," a rural antithesis to the normative pronunciation of the urban scholars. It may or may not have been the Prophetic pronunciation of q*, but this is beside the point. What matters is that this Arab vocalization became socially significant as a distinct marker of identity only since the end of the eleventh century, and it is most attested as such in the Ayyubid and Mamluk eras.

By and large, this spread of the *qāf* of the Arabs coincided with the spread of Arab village clans from the twelfth to the fifteenth centuries, as described in the previous chapters. It was most likely part of the same process. In the same way villagers took on Arab lineages in search of social prestige, they also adopted what they considered to be the Arab manner of speech. The /g/ articulation appears to have been widespread in the Arabian Peninsula, and pilgrims like Ibn al-ʿArabī encountered it in the holy cities of the Hijaz. Ḥayṣa Bayṣa in Baghdad and Ibn al-ʿAdīm in Aleppo heard it spoken by migrants arriving in their cities from marginal areas on the edge of the desert. The Hawwāra Berbers west of Alexandria imitated the Arabic spoken by the Sulaym Arabs who lived in their vicinity. A variety of new dialects formed in these interactions, but these new rural, "Bedouin" dialects all shared the distinctive articulation of /g/ as a social marker. In modern contexts, this realization of q* is perceived as the most important expression of social identity, more so than any other isoglosses of Bedouin dialects.[41] This is a legacy of the Middle Ages, for it was in this postclassical period that *qāf al-ʿArab* became the shibboleth of Arab identity.

In the modern period, the Arab or Bedouin /g/ sometimes serves as a tool for religious differentiation between Muslims and non-Muslims, and this might have been also the case in the late medieval centuries. Sociolinguistic studies in Baghdad, Bahrain, and in North African towns show the Bedouin dialect as an identity marker that distinguishes Muslims from Christians and Jews.[42] By the eleventh century, the non-Muslims inhabitants of the Middle East were already speaking Arabic, as we know from documentary and literary evidence. Viewed in the wider context of the spread of Arab identities in the countryside, the bedouinization and de-creolization of language appear to have been mostly endogenous. The /g/ pronunciation carried a covert prestige for rural speakers, a signal of precedence in Islam and attachment to the Arabian Peninsula.[43] One could see how an intentional bedouinization of speech carried additional benefits for medieval converts to Islam; your /g/ would erase the traces of your non-Muslim past and distinguish you from your former co-religionists.

Lithām and *Taḥnīk*: The Arab Headgear

Sultan al-Nāṣir Aḥmad, "the Prince who favored the desert," grew up in Karak in Transjordan. When he was called to Cairo to take the throne in 741/1341, he appeared in the company of a small group of Karaki intimates, clad in the dress of the ʿurbān, the Arab auxiliary units (*zayy al-ʿurbān*).[44] The following year, the young sultan dramatically left Cairo back for Karak, accompanied again by Karaki riders on royal camels. He took off his state garments and put on luxurious Arab dress (*wa-labisa lubus al-ʿarab kawāmil mufarraja*) and "draped himself in a double *lithām* (*wa-ḍaraba lahu lithāmayn*)."[45] The change of dress indicated transformation of identity. When al-Nāṣir drew the double *lithām*, a face-veil, or perhaps an underchin strap made with the loose ends of the turban, the sartorial political statement was sealed.

Sultan Aḥmad was following a tradition of thirteenth-century and fourteenth-century rulers who adopted Arab clothes. The Ayyubid sultans al-Malik al-Qāhir, son of al-Malik al-Muʿaẓẓam, and his nephew Shādhī, are both said to have taken on Arab attire (*malābis al-ʿarab*) and adopt Arab costumes.[46] Aḥmad's own father, al-Nāṣir Muḥammad, adopted Arab dress in 713/1313, when he returned to Damascus from pilgrimage. He rode around the city on a she-camel, wearing a *busht* woolen overcoat and a *lithām*, and holding a lance.[47] The *busht*, a Persianate word that came into use only in the Mamluk period, was a short undyed robe worn by peasants in Greater Syria while performing agricultural work.[48] The overlap between Arab clothes and peasant clothes is also apparent in another sartorial choice by Aḥmad, who wore local *zarbūl* boots in his public outings in Karak.[49] The *zarbūl* (or *zaryūl*) were heavy boots with pointed tips and metal heels, later associated with the Egyptian peasantry.[50] Both the *busht* and the *zarbūl* were non-Arabic words used for clothes worn by peasants, not by desert nomads. Thus, the Arab clothes chosen by Mamluk rulers to convey Arab identity included rustic robes and shoes, and, above all, the characteristic *lithām*.

Like dialect, clothes conveyed a visible Arab identity when they were taken on, and they indicated the removal of this identity when they were taken off. As examples from late medieval texts show, non-Arab men could easily disguise themselves as Arabs, and Arab men could become non-Arab by changing their clothes. The narrative sources are nearly unanimous about the lack of physical differences between Arabs and non-Arabs: once you dressed as an Arab, you could pass as one. From the thirteenth century onward, the key item of clothing required for such sartorial transformation was the *lithām*. Originally, the *lithām* meant a veil worn by men over their mouth and nose, but in the Mamluk period it was linked with *taḥnīk*, the practice of tucking the loose ends of the turban under the chin. In the illustrations accompanying late medieval copies of the *maqāmāt*, this strip of cloth tucked under the chin is used as the primary and often the only way of distinguishing Arab men from other figures.

The convention of representing Arab identity through the manner of headgear, whether a *lithām* or a strap under the chin, emerged in the later Middle Ages. Like the contemporaneous progression of the distinctly Arab vocalization of the letter *qāf*, neither the *lithām* headgear nor the under-the-chin tucking of the turban's loose ends indicated Arab identity before the eleventh century. In the early centuries of Islam, the Arab conquerors distinguished themselves from non-Arabs through the wearing of other pieces of clothing, especially the *izār*. But in subsequent centuries the *izār* became fashionable throughout the urban milieu and was worn by Muslims and non-Muslims alike.[51] At that early Islamic period, the *lithām* was mainly worn by women as a type of veil and by men as means of protection from dust. This was true as late as the eleventh century. The *Maqāmāt* of al-Ḥarīrī (d. 1122) refer to a *lithām* used by Abū Zayd to disguise his identity, without attaching to it any particular social or religious meaning.[52] In North Africa the *lithām* was associated with Saharan tribes, and it acquired its political importance in the twelfth century, when it famously marked the members of the Ṣanhāja tribal confederacy who formed the backbone of the Almoravid dynasty.[53] It might have been used only in military contexts, in order to attach the turban in place while riding at speed.[54]

The practice of attaching the turban with a piece of cloth under the chin was known in medieval Arabic sources as *taḥnīk*, *taḥannuk*, or *iltiḥā'*, and it was recommended as the correct Muslim way of wearing the turban by Mālik b. Anas (d. 179/795).[55] From the eleventh century onward, however, Mālikī jurists had begun to identify *taḥnīk* as a specifically Arab practice, one that distinguished them from non-Arabs or non-Muslims. Abū Muḥammad ʿAbd al-Wahhāb (d. 422/1031), a Mālikī jurist of Baghdad, wrote that *taḥnīk* is distinctive of Arab dress, while a turban without it is non-Arab (*ʿajam*).[56] The Andalusian Ibn Rushd (d. 1198) stated that *iltiḥāʾ* is required in mosques and public places because it is proper Arab dress (*al-shakl al-ʿarabī al-mustaḥsan*).[57] In Egypt and Syria, the identification of *taḥnīk* as an Arab practice is found in the writings of thirteenth-century jurists of all schools. These Ayyubid- and Mamluk-era scholars state that *taḥnīk* is the Arab manner of wearing the turban and that it is used to distinguish them from non-Arabs or non-Muslims.[58] It was linked with the wearing of the *lithām* over the face, as the thirteenth-century jurist al-Qarāfī explains that *taḥannuk* means attaching the *lithām* under one's palate (*ḥanak*).[59] His wording suggests that the same piece of cloth could be used to cover the face, or to be lowered under the chin. The fact that he had to explain the term *taḥannuk* to his readers implies it was not widely used; indeed, the word and its variants are used in legal texts but are practically absent from late medieval chronicles.[60]

In the visual language of late medieval manuscript illustration, the wrapping of the headgear underneath the chin was the primary indication of Arab identity. The tradition of *maqāmāt* illustration, starting in early-thirteenth-century Iraq, had ample opportunities to represent Arab types, either in connection with the twenty-seventh *maqāma* (al-Wabariyya) that involves "horse stealing and camel rustling" in a desert context, or in other travel settings of caravans and campsites.[61] Overall, the Arabs are generally represented like other Muslim males—bearded, robed, and turbaned. The only consistent indication of their separate identity is the strap of cloth tucked under the chin.[62] Early examples include an illustration of Abū Zayd and two Arab men in BN Arabe 3929, titled "The Arab posing a question to Abū Zayd." Here the two Arab men are indicated through the strap underneath their chin and by the unusually long swords hung across their shoulders (figure 6.1). In a camp scene from a Baghdadi manuscript made circa 1230, two Arab men are conversing in the background, their identity indicated by the way they wrap pieces of cloth under their chins. One of them also has a red round cap, often associated with Arab attire in other illustrations, and may reflect the official attire of the ʿurbān.[63] As mentioned above, the text of the *maqāmāt* refers to a *lithām* used by Abū Zayd to disguise his identity when fraudulently selling his son in the slave market. The illustration in the thirteenth-century manuscript visualizes the *lithām* as a face-veil worn over his mouth and nose.[64]

Illustrated copies of the *maqāmāt* made in Mamluk Egypt and Syria, up to 1350, generally follow the same pattern of Arab representation as the Iraqi ones.[65] In BL Add. 22114, probably made in Syria circa 1300, Arab men appear in a series

FIGURE 6.1. An Arab man posing a question to Abū Zayd, in *Maqāmāt of al-Ḥarīrī*, BN Arabe 3929, second quarter of the 7th/13th century, fol. 85a. By permission of Bibliothèque nationale de France.

of caravan scenes. In one example, a camel-riding man is leading the group; he wears a *ṭirāz* band on his arm, a blue robe with yellow decorations, and a thin strap of cloth under his chin.[66] In another illustration, two Banū Tamīm figures are identified by the wrap under their chin. They also have round red caps showing through their headgear.[67] A lovely scene of this manuscript depicts Abū Zayd and other guests enjoying hospitality on a winter's night. A guest warming his hands next to the fire has a white strip of cloth under his chin and a red conical hat.[68] One example from Egypt has an Arab figure marked out not only by his headgear but also by his dark skin; he is one of the few black African figures in the illustrations of this manuscript.[69] Yet this association of Arab identity and dark skin is an outlier. An illustration that accompanies the twenty-seventh *maqāma* in MS Marsh 458, copied in Egypt in 738/1337, perfectly encapsulates the stereotypical Arab of the *maqāmāt*. The Arab riding the camel has a strap of the turban under his chin, but he is not otherwise physically or sartorially distinguishable from other figures.[70] It is the illustration used for the cover of this book.

Narrative sources of the Ayyubid and Mamluk period are replete with references to distinctive Arab dress taken on and off, not only by sultans. This was possible because observers noted no physical difference between Arabs and non-Arabs. As Burchard wrote in 1280, "The children of Esau in the Hawran differ from other people only in their way of wearing their hair and their clothes."[71] An early example of taking on Arab dress comes from Ḥayṣa Bayṣa, the twelfth-century Baghdadi poet who willfully adopted the /g/ pronunciation: he also dressed liked an Arab and carried two swords around his body.[72] In the thirteenth century, defeated Arab rebels in Upper Egypt hid themselves and changed their clothes.[73] A Syrian Arab disguised himself (*tanakkara*) in order to travel to Cairo incognito, and he was then able to converse with jailed companions through the prison's window.[74] The famous thirteenth-century delta saint Aḥmad al-Badawī (d. 675/1276) acquired his name by wearing the *lithām*.[75] Like the Ayyubid and Mamluk rulers of this period, al-Badawī made the Arab attire part of his public persona; constantly wearing the distinct *lithām* made him a Bedouin. A century later, Ibn Ḥijjī was able to escape Tīmūr's troops by stealing the clothes of one of the Arabs who had attached themselves to Tīmūr's forces, then riding out in disguise.[76] The topos of dressing up as Arab also crops up in literature. Ibn Sa'īd (d. 1286) relates a popular romantic tale set in the Fatimid era, in which the caliph al-Āmir, inflicted with passion for Arab women, decides to dress up in the clothes of the Bedouin (*budāt al-a'rāb*) so that he could travel among their camps and search for the most beautiful of their womenfolk.[77]

The 'urbān, the Arab auxiliary troops at the service of the Ayyubid and Mamluk states, wore official uniforms. Up to the end of the thirteenth century, these are described as made of inferior *musammaṭ* and *kanjī* silk varieties, alongside red *ṭarṭūr* caps.[78] European travelers of the time also note red felt hats, red cloaks, and a large loose-fitting shirt.[79] An account by a Mamluk bureaucrat, written circa 1300, describes a procession of Syrian Arab troops in Damascus. They were wearing red *mi'danī* satin jackets under their armor, white headgear, and each soldier was armed with both a sword and a lance. The procession was accompanied by their dancing slaves and a female chanteuse, who was performing a tribal war song evoking the names of the great Arab confederacies.[80] These ʿurbān troops not only wore their identity but performed it through a spectacle of music and dance.[81]

The official dress of the Syrian ʿurbān changed over the course of the fourteenth century, when tribal leaders received from Sultan al-Nāṣir Muḥammad a wide range of high-quality textiles.[82] A late-fourteenth-century account refers to the chemises of the ʿurbān as having wide sleeves, although not as extravagantly wide-sleeved as those sported by the women of Cairo.[83] This is confirmed by Bertrandon de la Brocquière, visiting Palestine in 1432–33. The Arab knights he saw on the road to Tiberias had robes with sleeves a foot and a half wide hanging down from their arms. Instead of a cap they had a round hat covered by a crimson wool strap that fell down on each side.[84] This is likely to have been an official uniform. Another official sartorial policy of this period was the use of green as the distinctive color of the *ashrāf*, the recognized descendants of the Prophet. The association of green with the *ashrāf* was promulgated through a royal edict of 773/1381.[85]

In other contexts, Arab clothing, also termed "Bedouin," was conceived as the epitome of simplicity. Al-Maqrīzī has the Arab tribesmen of the Syrian desert disingenuously complain to Sultan al-Nāṣir Muḥammad that he was spoiling their women: "Did you ever hear of a Bedouin woman (*badawiyya*) wearing anything but a cotton robe (*thawb*), a dyed veil (*burquʿ*), and anything more than a metal bracelet on her hand?"[86] Arab tribal leaders could also decide to dress down, like an amir of the Sulaym in Alexandria in the 770s/1370s, who dressed as a Sufi by carrying an ewer (*ibrīq*) and using a cane (*ʿukkāz*).[87] As noted by Ibn Khaldūn, the simplicity of clothing was the norm in the countryside, where people covered themselves in large pieces of cloth.[88] Clothes considered "Arab" distinguished rural Muslims from urban folk. A fifteenth-century Cairene merchant who used to dress in Arab clothing (*libās al-ʿarab*), like his ancestors before him, clearly stood out.[89] In the Ottoman period, the Arab leading amirs of the delta indicated their attachment to their Arab identity by wearing a *lithām*, also described as a cap (*shāsh*) with straps covering their neck, the ends thrown over one shoulder. They also wore simple woolen outer robes (*iḥrām*). The sixteenth-century chronicler al-Jazīrī noted that these wealthy and powerful amirs also rode on ornamented saddles in Ottoman fashion and had their slaves wear fancy Ottoman clothes.[90]

European travelers mostly remarked on the simple clothes worn by Arabs, whether peasants or nomads.[91] The Arabs of Sinai were repeatedly described as half naked,[92] while the peasant boys and girls in the villages of the Nile Delta were said to walk around in the nude.[93] Jean de Joinville, in his thirteenth-century chronicle of the seventh crusade, describes the Bedouin as covering themselves in long simple cloaks made of sheepskin, as well as wrapping their headgear underneath their chin. He states that the long sheepskin cloaks were cured with alum, covering the whole body of the person, down to the feet. These sheepskins could be dried quickly, even after a night's rain. He then adds that "nearly all of them wear tunics like the surplices that priests wear. Their heads are swathed in cloths which come down underneath the chin and make them hideous and repulsive to look at."[94] For de Joinville, as for the illustrators of the *maqāmāt*, the wrapping of the turban under the chin was a distinctive sign of Arab identity. He also notes that their hair and beards were very black - a rare reference in our sources to any physical difference between Arabs and non-Arabs.

The peasants of the Mamluk era did not have a sartorial identity of their own, but rather morphed into that of others. There are few textual references to distinctive peasant clothes.[95] Instead, we hear of peasants who take on clothes of other social groups in order to appear above their rank. In the *Villages of the Fayyum*, al-Nābulusī mocks the fallāḥūn of the non-Arab orchard village of Akhṣāṣ al-Ḥallāq, who have begun wearing *ṭaylasān*s and "are being called jurists and judges, without possessing either jurisprudence or judgment."[96] Elsewhere, peasants attempted to dress like Arabs. Al-Qalqashandī, writing in the early fifteenth century, noted "people of plough and sowing" who inhabited the eastern bank of the Nile in the region of Ḥulwān, south of Cairo, and who adorn themselves as Arabs.[97] There is a touch of hypocrisy in this comment by a man born in a delta village who himself claimed to come from the Banū Badr. A Florentine-Mamluk treaty of 902/1497 gives permission to European itinerant merchants traveling in the countryside to dress either as Turks or as Arabs (*turkī aw ʿarabī*), so that they do not stand out. Dressing like a fallāḥ was not an option.[98]

Likewise, the *maqāmāt* illustrations have a visual iconography for Arabs, but none for peasants. The figures in village scenes do not wear Arab clothes but neither do they wear distinctive peasant attire.[99] One exception shows a man in a short robe driving oxen around a waterwheel; in the *maqāmāt* tradition, short robes are generally reserved for slaves and servants.[100] The best representations of peasant clothing are found in illustrations accompanying *Kitāb al-Diryāq*, produced in Mosul in 1199. In a scene showing six peasants performing typical agricultural labor, they wear only *sirwāl* trousers, or very short robes that barely cover their groins. The same is true for gardeners represented in a palace scene of the same manuscript.[101] Ploughmen shown on metalwork produced in Mosul in the early thirteenth century and in a Mamluk copy of *Kalīla wa-Dimna* have generic clothing.[102]

Clothes, like the identities they represented, could be taken on and off. A peasant driving his oxen or hoeing the land would not wear distinctive Arab clothes but rather a short robe for agricultural labor. Yet the same person could adorn Arab attire for political, military, and social purposes. The iconographic conventions of the *maqāmāt* showed the Arab type as leading a caravan, going to market, or staying in an inn, but never tending to the land. This was so because different clothes were used for different social contexts. Arab rebels could become non-Arabs by taking off their dress and merging into the mass of the peasantry. It is worth recalling that the Arab attire of the "desert" sultans al-Nāṣir Muḥammad and his son Aḥmad consisted not only of a *lithām*, but also a peasant's short robe and heavy boots.

The convention of representing Arab identity through the manner of headgear, whether a *lithām* or a strap under the chin (*taḥnīk*), emerged in the later Middle Ages. While these sartorial choices were known since the earliest Islamic period, it was only from the eleventh century onward that they became markers of Arab identity, coinciding with the spread of Arab village clans. This is most visible to us in the illustrations accompanying thirteenth- and fourteenth-century copies of the *maqāmāt*, whether made in Iraq or in Mamluk lands, where Arab types are usually distinguished only by their underchin strap. Literary sources report a range of other markers of Arab dress: red conical hats and wide sleeves for the auxiliary ʿurbān, simple long robes or cloaks, green for descendants of the Prophet. Rural people who wanted to pass as Arabs had a sartorial repertoire to choose from. On the other hand, we hear very little of the peasant mode of dress, suggesting that—like the peasant identity as a whole—it became subsumed under the more socially desirable Arab figure, whose clothes indicated freedom from the subjection of agricultural work.

Painted Handmade Wares in Greater Syria

Alongside the spread of distinct Arab speech and dress, the proliferation of Arab village clans coincided with a striking change in village pottery throughout Palestine, Transjordan, and Syria. In rural contexts of the twelfth and thirteenth centuries, plain and painted handmade wares dominate the assemblage and are usually much more numerous than the fine-bodied and glazed wheel-thrown wares that had been the most common ceramics in the same rural sites since Late Antiquity. Attested in over two hundred rural sites in Greater Syria, this was a key transition in material culture, a shift that must have reflected "the advent of a new sociocultural reality."[103] There is little evidence of handmade wares of this type in Greater Syria at any earlier period, save for plain wares used for specific functions, such as large storage jars. They are first attested in southern Transjordan during the eleventh century, and perhaps even the late tenth century, but they became frequent in rural sites throughout Transjordan, Palestine, and other parts of Greater Syria from the twelfth century onward.

By the mid-thirteenth century, plain and painted handmade wares come to be represented in nearly all rural contexts known to us in Greater Syria; they became the main tableware of villagers throughout the region for the rest of the medieval period. They were formed by hand over a cloth bag filled with soil, and then finished over a slow kick wheel. In the Mamluk era, especially in the fourteenth century, the production became more professional and abundant. Many of these handmade wares were decorated with distinctive geometric patterns slip-painted in shades of red-brown or black, and they are therefore called HMGPW, shorthand for Handmade Geometrically Painted Wares. Handmade wares are in fact so distinctive of the late medieval period as to be often used as a key indicator of stratification.[104]

Until recently, the omnipresent assemblages of handmade pottery received attention only from archaeologists; they are practically unknown to historians. It is only in the last few decades that they have been subject to scientific analysis and to preliminary exploration of their social and cultural significance.[105] Our knowledge of the distribution and development of these vessels has many gaps. Archaeologists tended to neglect handmade wares in excavation reports, and painted handmade wares received more attention than the common plain ones. Because of long-term continuities in form, the dating of handmade wares is difficult and must rely on stratigraphic evidence; it is usually possible to say when these wares first appear in each context, but it is far harder to capture how they develop in the same site over time. Moreover, excavations of rural sites in modern Syria and Lebanon have been sporadic.[106] Nonetheless, handmade wares have been abundantly collected in the Galilee, in the hinterland of Jerusalem, and in central and northern Transjordan. These extensive ceramic finds allow us to draw a rough outline of their emergence as the mainstay of material culture in late medieval villages.

Our earliest evidence of a tradition of coarse handmade wares comes from several Abbasid- and Fatimid-era sites in southern Palestine and Transjordan, all located on the edge of the desert. The number and quality of finds of this type are limited, and the chronology is still a subject of debate among archaeologists. In the Yotvata oasis in the Araba, home to an early Islamic agricultural estate, handmade wares are the second most common group of ceramics in the

FIGURE 6.2. Handmade household jar, Safed, 13th or 14th century. Photograph by Smadar Gabrieli.

assemblage from the ninth century—the simplicity of the eating utensils contrasting with the elite status of the inhabitants. The Yotvata pottery may be related to a regional group of similar handmade vessels produced in the tenth or eleventh centuries, nicknamed the ʿAqaba Tupperware and found in several sites in the deserts of Transjordan.[107] The site of Gharandal in southern Jordan, some one hundred kilometers northeast of Yotvata, yielded small handmade basins, store jars, and bowls that have been dated to the tenth or eleventh centuries and that have also been considered as possible predecessors for the HMGP.[108] These handmade wares of the Abbasid and the Fatimid periods come solely from peripheral sites, and it is not yet clear whether they were related to the HMGP common in rural assemblages from the twelfth century onward, as there are differences in the consistency of the clay and the shape of the vessels.[109] Another matter of debate is whether the tradition of handmade pottery arrived at these sites in southern Jordan and Palestine from other regions of the Middle East. From a purely geographical perspective, the Arabian Peninsula would be a likely candidate, but the state of excavations in the Hijaz and northwest Arabia do not allow us at this stage to establish the chronology of handmade pottery there, so such a trajectory is purely speculative.[110]

During the twelfth century, crude handmade pottery spread rapidly to more central areas of Transjordan, Palestine, and Greater Syria, marking a stark shift in the ceramic record. Findings of handmade wares of this period are concentrated in sites of the western Galilee and the hinterland of Jerusalem—both areas under crusader control at the time—as well as in northern Syria. Because sites in and around Jerusalem were so heavily excavated, the pottery found in the city's hinterland allows us to follow the change from wheel-thrown to handmade wares in some detail.[111] When the crusaders arrived in 1099, they still encountered the well-established manufacturing of wheel-thrown wares in the rural areas that came under their control. Then, plain and painted handmade vessels first appeared in crusader and Ayyubid contexts during the twelfth century, with decoration traditions showing regional variation. At the site of Khirbat Kaʿkul, for example, the HMGP wares were initially quite coarse, with simple linear painted decorations rendered in a light or pale red color on the exterior upper body of the vessel.[112] In handmade wares from Ayyubid Jerusalem, the decoration covered the whole of the vessel, rendered in a light-reddish brown color.[113] Handmade wares form a significant amount of the ceramic assemblage of Ayyubid and Mamluk Jerusalem, but the evidence collected so far suggests that urban kilns produced wheel-thrown pottery and that the handmade vessels were produced in the rural hinterland of the city.

By the thirteenth century, crude handmade vessels, mostly painted with geometric decorations, became common in all village communities, but especially in those farther away from markets or industry.[114] They were clearly associated with rural contexts and with nonstate actors, even if many of these vessels found their way to cities and towns. Handmade pottery finds are usually substantial in Ayyubid- and Mamluk-era sites in the Galilee, averaging about 30 to 40 percent. They dominate in rural sites in Transjordan, such as Umm al-Jimāl in the Hawran (59 percent) and in the rural hinterland of Karak (86 percent).[115] On the other hand, handmade wares are far less common at urban sites on the coasts of Palestine and Lebanon, at the sites of military power such as the castle of Karak in

Transjordan, and at sites of sugar production.[116] This new rural pottery was handmade, but not simple or autarkic. A study of Mamluk-era pottery from the Galilee found regional networks of production that bypassed the towns. Villagers produced handmade pottery for other villages in the vicinity, and the geometric decoration tended to follow regional patterns.[117] A study of pottery from Mamluk-era rural sites in Transjordan found that handmade wares production was mostly local using different clay fabrics, but also evidence for exchange with different workshop centers across the southern Levant.[118]

In terms of function, detailed studies of sites in the Galilee show that handmade wares were first made as open bowls for eating, while handmade cooking jars replaced glazed wheel-thrown wares at a later stage, probably during the Mamluk period.[119] The new handmade cooking vessels had novel distinctive forms: these were deep, globular cooking pots with characteristic handles in the shape of a horseshoe or an elephant ear, which may have been associated with a new dining culture. They were quite heavy to lift and were ideal for the slow cooking of large quantities of meat stew to be shared among a large group. Analysis of cookpots found in a kitchen in Tall Hisban shows that they were used for both stews and for porridge dishes, with or without meat.[120] Some of the handmade tableware were also of new types: the bowls were bigger, and jugs acquired spouts for group use, also suggesting a shift to communal dining.[121]

These changes to the pottery record have puzzled archaeologists for a few decades. The technology of producing wheel-thrown jars was not lost, and it remained in use at elite sites, such as the Karak citadel, or at market villages in Palestine.[122] Wheel-thrown unglazed jars were also used as containers in Mamluk-era sites of sugar production.[123] On the very same site there can be spatial distinction between areas of handmade wares associated with local peasants and rooms of higher quality pottery associated with military or bureaucratic elites.[124] The spread of handmade wares should also be seen within the context of the abovementioned expansion of agriculture in Greater Syria, characterized by systematic reoccupation of sites abandoned in previous centuries and the reuse of building material.[125] The shift to handmade wares in the crusader and Ayyubid periods is somewhat counterintuitive: twelfth- and thirteenth-century rural communities experienced demographic expansion and were very familiar with wheel-thrown technology, yet they mostly chose to produce and consume simpler handmade wares that marked a break from the local ceramic traditions of previous centuries.

Today, most archaeologists attribute the sudden spread of the HMGP wares in Greater Syria to the decentralization and ruralization of pottery production from the twelfth century onward. In the well-studied example of central Transjordan, handmade pottery came to be produced in a variety of smaller workshops in towns and villages, replacing the pre-crusader center of production of fine wheel-thrown wares in the city of Jerash. The network of local workshops, often in rural sites, mainly produced handmade wares but also a variety of simple wheel-thrown wares, especially the creamware type. In this context, archaeologists view the shift to handmade wares as a corollary of rural production, although the link between the two phenomena is not usually spelled out. In his groundbreaking essay, Jeremy Johns suggested that the villagers of Greater Syria experienced impoverishment that pushed them toward these cheaper vessels, which did not require high-temperature kilns and had low transport costs: handmade wares spread as "the town grew richer and the village grew poorer."[126] This explanation, however, seems to exaggerate the costs of producing wheel-thrown wares and to underestimate the specialization of the workshops that produced handmade wares, which we now know were traded across provincial networks. Moreover, the argument for the impoverishment of the countryside in an age of demographic expansion is somewhat counterintuitive. Those who view handmade wares as a sign of material poverty also speculate on a possible impact of taxes on production and a supposed scarcity of wood, without much evidence.[127] Alternatively, archaeologists have advanced the hypothesis of a migration of itinerant specialized potters, presumably from southern Transjordan to other regions of Greater Syria. However, such migration—even if it did occur—doesn't account for the shift in the preferences of the villagers who paid for these pots to be made.[128]

What is lacking in these explanations for the sudden spread of the HMGP is the social significance of these vessels. As production became decentralized, villagers actively chose to purchase and use handmade wares, and they imbued them with cultural meanings that went beyond the material aspects of production. Edna Stern had already suggested a link between pottery and identity when comparing the crusader-Ayyubid assemblages of two villages of the western Galilee, one with an indigenous population and one with Frankish inhabitants. In the indigenous settlement, handmade wares amount to 44 percent of the assemblage, while the assemblage of the Frankish village has only 11 percent handmade wares. Likewise, excavations at Burj al-Aḥmar in Palestine show that handmade vessels came into circulation only after the end of the crusader phase.[129] The differences between the Frankish and non-Frankish villages suggest that the use of handmade wares was not determined by economic or technological considerations, but rather by cultural choices on the part of the local population.

The cultural choice involved in the production and consumption of handmade wares overlapped with and corresponded to the simultaneous formation of Arab village clans in the same areas. The decorated handmade wares became widespread in the villages of Greater Syria since the thirteenth century, in rural communities now mainly consisting of Arab village clans. While the narrative sources do not explicitly tell us that that the spread of handmade wares indicated Arab identity, the quick spread of plain and painted handmade wares in late Crusader Palestine coincided with the appearance of *beduini* groups in Latin charters. For the Mamluk era, the dominance of handmade wares is attested in the same areas of the Jerusalem highlands where we find textual evidence for Arab village clans in the early fourteenth century (see chapter 4). Viewed more broadly, the shift from wheel-thrown to handmade pottery in the villages of Greater Syria furnishes us with tangible proof of the transformation of the countryside in the twelfth and thirteenth centuries.

The decentralization and diversity of ceramics production corresponded to the diversity of clans and tribes, each fiercely proud of its distinct kinship group yet all part of the same Arab cultural milieu and notional genealogical tree. The handmade pottery of the Ayyubid and Mamluk periods has been described as having "intense regional characteristics."[130] In each village site, wares share certain decorative features but also show diversity, while each region had a radically different tradition. Like the division of the late medieval Arab villagers into tribes and clans, the handmade pottery that was produced in their villages exemplifies diversity within a unity of form, limitless variation on the same type of object. Ethnography has shown that ceramics can carry social meanings through microstyles of decoration, distinguishing kinship communities within a larger ethnic group. It has also been noted that these decorative microstyles often correspond to clusters of villages, below the level of the province. The overlap between the boundaries of the ceramic style and the kinship group is never clear-cut: while rural consumers prefer pots made by potters of their own group with distinctive decoration or marks, they could also use them to claim attachment to a new group.[131]

The material remains of late medieval villages also speak to a quest for simplicity, communal cooking, and a deep transformation that fits with other expressions of Arabness in this period. And though narrative sources do not mention distinctly Arab wares, they do mention distinctly Arab dishes. The Āl Faḍl of the Syrian desert stereotypically refused to eat anything but camel's milk and a round flat loaf of bread made over hot coals.[132] In the sixteenth century, the delta amirs of the Banū ʿAwna would feed their guests *bāzin*, a barley-based version of the *'aṣīda* stew, associated today with Arab cuisine.[133] A shift to handmade pottery, alongside the consumption of "Arab" food, was a statement about links with the Arabian Peninsula and a signal of wider appreciation of Arab values. Like Arab identity, handmade wares separated the rural from the urban, simplicity from luxury, the communal from the individual.

The shift from wheel-thrown to handmade wares was limited to Greater Syria. It did not take place, as far as we know, in the Egyptian countryside. It should be noted, however, that we are still awaiting systematic study of any Mamluk-era village site in Egypt. Intriguingly, however, the assemblages of Ayyubid and Mamluk Cairo contain an unprecedented large number of coarse handmade and unglazed wares of a new type, which constitute as many as 30 percent of the pottery found in these late medieval urban contexts. It is currently assumed that these coarse handmade bowls were used as containers for takeaway food by Cairenes, who rarely cooked at home. But we also know that these coarse wares—small, low-fired, silt bowls—were not produced in Cairo itself but were brought from the rural hinterland of the city.[134] Despite the difference in function, the sudden visibility of this type of pottery in thirteenth-century Cairo parallels the appearance of handmade rural pottery in assemblages from Ayyubid Jerusalem and is therefore suggestive of Egyptian rural production of a new type of simple pottery, mirroring the simplicity of the handmade wares of late medieval Syrian and Palestinian villages.

Novel Articulations of Arab Culture

Distinctive Arab headgear and distinctive Arab pronunciation were novel means of projecting Arab cultural identity, accompanying and propping up the proliferation of Arab village clans of Egypt and Syria since the twelfth century. The q* = /g/ articulation was in use before the twelfth century, and the *lithām* was worn as a face-veil by men and women in the early Islamic period. But it was only in the later medieval period that these manners of speech and dress became identity markers and thus a means of expressing one's Arabness. These expressions of Arab cultural identity were required by the growing mass of sedentary villagers who wished to pass as Arab. The adoption of the Arab pronunciation of /g/ was easy and widely accessible, so much so that it had penetrated most rural communities. It was also relatively easy to express an Arab identity through Arab clothing, especially by tying the loose ends of one's turban under the chin or applying a *lithām* face-veil. Additional headgear items, such as distinctive red conical hats, were only available to official 'urbān troops. Since the late fourteenth century, the use of the color green was restricted to the officially recognized descendants of the Prophet.

In the villages of Ayyubid and Mamluk Greater Syria, another major cultural change pertained to the use of handmade painted cooking and eating utensils, replacing a very old tradition of wheel-thrown wares in the same rural sites. This change is known to us only from the archaeological record, and the association with the shift to Arab village clans is not as explicit as the *qāf al-ʿArab* and the Arab dress. But the shift to handmade wares overlapped precisely with the emergence of Arab village clans. As peasants turned Arab, they obtained simpler utensils that came from rural centers of production that bypassed the cities. Yet they chose to invest in a pottery tradition that was not indigenous to the rural areas of Greater Syria that they inhabited, but instead to one that in their eyes was probably associated with other regions of the Middle East. The shape and size of the new type of handmade pottery was appropriate for communal dining and perhaps complemented the distinctively Arab dishes that marked the culinary culture of the village clans. The change in the material culture has so far been identified only in the rural contexts of Greater Syria, but parallel changes in pottery production may have been taking place in the Egyptian countryside, too.

Speech, dress, food, and household utensils expressed what villagers considered to be an authentic Arab identity. These cultural markers were brought from outside the region of Egypt and Syria: the *qāf* pronunciation had roots in twelfth-century Iraq, the tradition of handmade pottery might have come from the edge of the Arabian deserts, and the use of the *lithām* as a marker of identity possibly traveled eastward from North Africa. The foreign quality of these traditions allowed rural people in Egypt and Syria to appropriate them as key constituents of their Arab cultural identity. Yet these cultural markers were not enough. At a deeper level, the task of reinventing themselves required the villagers of Egypt and Syria to comprehensively reimagine their historical memory. It was then that the grand Arab popular epics came into being, the perfect oral vehicle to teach illiterate communities what it truly means to be Arab.

7

Popular Epics and Arab Identity

THE LATER MIDDLE AGES saw the emergence of the new genre of Arabic popular epics (*siyar*, sing. *sīra*). These long narratives, made up of repetitive cyclic episodes that could be recited periodically, tell the adventures of a hero and his band of companions and were composed in varying proportions of prose, rhymed prose, and poetry. They existed in both oral and written forms, and in a synthesis of classical Arabic and of dialect.[1] At their heart, the *siyar* are concerned with a retelling of communal history. It is this aspect that makes them "epic"—they deal "with issues of sociocultural identity . . . through the discussion and exploration of social tensions both within society and between social groups."[2] The Arabic popular epics were still performed well into the modern era, and even today they retain their place in Arabic popular culture. Writing about these modern performances, Bridget Connelly identified the *siyar* genre as "being fundamentally concerned with the anxieties of the social unit and that unit's struggle to maintain its integrity. The fear of strangers and fear of the out-group, anxiety about the unknown, are very real in the oral traditional cultures which maintain and generate the *sīra* tradition."[3]

The first direct evidence for the existence of the Arabic popular epics comes from twelfth-century Iraq and the Jazīra. They were circulating in Egypt and Syria by the following century and became very popular in Mamluk lands by the fourteenth and fifteenth centuries, when the first manuscripts are attested. The two earliest epics mentioned in the sources are the Sīra of ʿAntar ibn Shaddād, whose eponymous hero is a warrior-poet of the pre-Islamic Arabian Peninsula; and the Sīrat Dhāt al-Himma and al-Baṭṭāl, telling the adventures of Arab warriors fighting the Byzantines in the Umayyad and Abbasid periods. Another Arab epic cycle was Sīrat Banū Hilāl, recounting the migration of the eponymous tribe from Najd to North Africa in Islamic times. Epics set in urban or non-Arab settings emerged at a later stage: Sīrat Baybars, weaving an alternative narrative of the first Mamluk sultan and his establishment of just rule; Sīrat Sayf b. Dhī Yazan, an Egyptian foundation myth of an Arab king who defeats black Africans at the source of the Nile; and Sīrat ʿAlī al-Zaybaq, an urban epic about policemen and thieves in Cairo and Baghdad.[4] The Arabian Nights, which also achieved unprecedented status in the Mamluk period, deploy similar structure and linguistic register but do not share the epic aspects of the *siyar* cycles.

The appearance and spread of the Arabic popular epics in the late medieval Middle East are now recognized to be a major watershed in the history of Arabic literature. Their epic framework was a significant departure from existing genres, even if the raw materials were taken from motifs present in the canon of elite literature and historiography established in the Abbasid period. In terms of language, the surviving manuscripts demonstrate the emergence of middle Arabic as the linguistic medium for popular literature, midway between the classical Arabic of elite literature and the spoken dialects.[5] The epics also contained an alternative depository of historical memory. As Peter Heath argued, the epics "offer a version of Islamic history that in general was probably more prevalent and more widely believed than that found in specialized studies of elite historians."[6]

Historians have so far suggested two main explanations for the emergence of the Arabic popular epics and their astounding popularity in the late medieval Middle East. In his *The Written Word in the Medieval Arabic Lands*, Konrad Hirschler saw the epics as an example of textualization and popularization of reading practices in the Ayyubid and Mamluk periods.[7] On the one hand, the epics allowed non-elite groups to go beyond passive participation in reading sessions organized by the scholarly elite. On the other hand, the circulation of epics challenged scholarly production and dissemination of knowledge and was met with a barrage of criticism. Hirschler argues that the scholars didn't mind the purely oral circulation of popular romances, nor did they find the content of the works to be objectionable, for the epics did not challenge political structures or Islamic tenets and in fact incorporated elements of elite historiography. The problem was that the epics could be seen as history—that "the reading of these epics and their written circulation . . . challenged—or was perceived to challenge—scholarly authority over the textual transmission of the past."[8]

Thomas Herzog, who studied the epics in both their Mamluk and in their early modern contexts, links the appearance of the epics to the rise of new social groups in the urban milieu. Herzog points to the rise of craftsmen to positions of political power and scholarly authority in the fifteenth century, and he suggests that the economic rise of these artisan groups led to the emergence of this intermediate level of literature, between the classical form and the dialect. Like Hirschler,

Herzog emphasizes the role of the epics as an alternative history. Herzog compares the epics with medieval scholarly historiography, finding that they use similar strategies of personalization and dramatization for narrating the past. Based on this overlap between epics and elite historiography, he argues that premodern audiences did not perceive the epics as works of imagination but as an actual history of the Islamic community.[9]

These interpretations are accurate and insightful, but they tell the story from the perspective of those who opposed the emergence of the *siyar*. There were two sides to the debate over the epics, with some scholars credulous and supportive. In that aspect, the debate over the epics resembled the Mamluk-era debates about the visitation of tombs and the veneration of saints.[10] Hirschler and Herzog also do not adequately highlight the centrality of the twin Arab epics of Dhāt al-Himma and of ʿAntar to these late medieval debates. Nearly all the scathing criticism by fourteenth-century scholars was directed at these two cycles.[11] Above all, these explanations miss out on the defining characteristic of any epic, which is its capacity to generate and negotiate identities. Epics in all cultures shape the identity of their listeners by giving them examples on which to model themselves, reinforced by the repetitive cycles that lead to "partial assimilation of identity by a process of conditioned recognition."[12] The narrators always hope that the reader or listener will imitate the heroic and admirable qualities of the hero of the epic.[13] As Herzog himself puts it, an epic provides grounding in a primordial past and creates and consolidates communal identities.[14]

In this chapter, I make the following series of arguments. First, I contend that the audience of the epics was rural as much as it was urban. I will present here a range of fourteenth-century texts to suggest that the epics held particular sway outside the cities; in fact, it may have been the first major genre of Arabic literature capable of reaching out into the villages. Recitation and copying of the *siyar* in Cairo and in Damascus were merely the tip of a countryside iceberg. Second, I see the Arab cycles of ʿAntar and al-Baṭṭāl as the archetypical cycles. They were the first epics to circulate, most probably in the Jazīra or Iraq, and they preceded chronologically and in order of importance the epic cycles that became popular in the cities, such as Sīrat Baybars. Third, based on a close examination of fifteenth-century manuscript copies of Sīrat ʿAntar, I will show how the ʿAntar epic supplied the materials required for creating Arab selves: an origin myth for the Arabs, a pride in the place of Arabs within Islam, and rules of conduct within a clan-based social milieu. Fourth, I note the precise chronological and spatial overlap between the spread of Arab village clans and the emergence of the Arab epic cycles. Like Arab dialects and Arab headgear, knowledge of the Arab epics became a marker of Arab identity; moreover, the epics were crucial for the process of creating this identity and disseminating it across the land.

The Emergence of Arab Popular Epic

The two earliest mentions of the popular epics come from twelfth-century Iraq and al-Jazīra and refer to written versions of the cycles of 'Antar and of al-Baṭṭāl. The first is included in the autobiography of the Jewish physician Samaw'al al-Maghribī, composed following his public conversion to Islam in Marāgha in 558/1163. In this conversion narrative, Samaw'al recounts that as a young man in Baghdad he began to read the collection of the stories (*dīwān*, *akhbār*) of 'Antar, Dhū al-Himma and al-Baṭṭāl, and the stories of Alexander. After reading these stories, Samaw'al realized that they were primarily derived from scholarly works, and he began to read more academic chronicles, such as those by Miskawayh and al-Ṭabarī.[15] A second twelfth-century reference to the epics is found in Ibn Abī Uṣaybi'a's biography of Abū al-Mu'ayyad Ibn al-Ṣā'igh (d. circa 560/1164), a physician and litterateur from northern Syria. He was also known as al-'Antarī, since in his youth he used to write down the stories (*aḥādīth*) of 'Antar al-'Absī.[16] In both cases, the epics were consumed by young men, as texts. These twelfth-century textual versions may have not matured to the full epic format known to us from later centuries, as the term *sīra* is not yet used. Samaw'al lumps the stories of 'Antar and al-Baṭṭāl with the stories of Alexander, which transformed into an epic only in later centuries.[17]

The epics of 'Antar and of al-Baṭṭāl arrived in Egypt and Syria by the early thirteenth century. Public performance of the al-Baṭṭāl epic in Cairo is attested in al-Jawbarī's thirteenth-century book on tricksters, *al-Mukhtār fī Kashf al-Asrār wa-Hatk al-Asrār*. A rich anecdote tells of a Hawrani migrant to Ayyubid Cairo, who set up stall in Bayn al-Qaṣrayn and pretended to be a mouth doctor selling his customers an ointment made of turd. The man then started to make a living by reciting the epic (*sīra*) of al-Baṭṭāl, telling the audience stories about al-Baṭṭāl in which the epic hero is tricking fools into rubbing their mouth with filth and paying for it.[18] While Egyptians were making fun of Syrian immigrants, calling them "Syrian cattle" (*baqar al-Sha'm*), the Hawrani migrant had the last laugh. Here, a rural trickster was telling his urban audience the story of the fictional trickster al-Baṭṭāl, and both are pulling the same trick.[19]

The full popularization of the epics occurred in the Mamluk period, when the epics were regularly performed in Cairo's public spaces. In an anecdote recounted by 'Alā' al-Dīn Mughulṭāy (1290–1361), a storyteller was reciting a martyrdom section from al-Baṭṭāl when an old Maghribi in the audience responded by declaring his wish to die as a martyr too, then dropping dead on the spot.[20] This anecdote drives home the capacity of oral performance to blur the lines between the audience and the heroes of the epic. The exact location of the performance is not mentioned here. The likely place would have been again the market of Bayn al-Qaṣrayn, where, according to al-Maqrīzī, performances of the popular epics took place since the Ayyubid era.[21]

Alongside public performances, the epics circulated in Cairo in written copies, as attested in the moralist treatises of Ibn al-Ḥājj (d. 737/1336) and Tāj al-Dīn al-Subkī (d. 769/1368). Ibn al-Ḥājj warns professional copyists from the lies of the story (*qiṣṣa*) of al-Baṭṭāl, the story of ʿAntara and their like.[22] Similar advice is given to paper-sellers, who should not sell papers for those who will use it for reproducing the fabricated stories of al-Baṭṭāl and ʿAntara.[23] The moralist treatise of Tāj al-Dīn al-Subkī, an Egyptian who spent much of his life in Damascus, has similar advice. Booksellers should not sell books of innovations, astrology, or fabrications, such as the epic of ʿAntar; it is a waste of time and of no religious merit.[24] Tāj al-Dīn lumps them together with books of sexual mockery (*mujūn*), wine-themed books, and erotica.[25] Notably, the epics that attracted the attention of Ibn al-Ḥājj and al-Subkī are the two Arab epics of ʿAntar and al-Baṭṭāl, apparently the only major epics circulating as texts in Cairo.

In fourteenth-century Syria the moralist objection to the epics was championed, as to be expected, by Taqī al-Dīn Ibn Taymiyya (d. 728/1328). Ibn Taymiyya's extensive writings are a particularly rich source on the circulation of the epics, most probably in Damascus, where he spent most of his life. In response to public readings of the epics, Ibn Taymiyya forbade following in prayer "anyone who makes his living solely from reading out the epics of ʿAntara and al-Baṭṭāl and their like."[26] In his anti-Shiʿa treatise *Minhāj al-Sunna al-nabawiyya*, composed in Damascus in the 1310s,[27] he mocks his Shiʿa interlocutor for taking evidence from reading books of epics and of *maghāzī* (expeditions and raids of the early Muslims) made up by liars and street charlatans (*ṭuruqiyya*).[28] Fabrications about Islamic history included al-Bakrī's *Tanaqqulāt al-Anwār*, a pseudo-biography of the Prophet that greatly exercised Ibn Taymiyya, as well as the epics of Dalhama (Dhāt al-Himma) and al-Baṭṭāl, of ʿAntara b. Shaddād, and the stories (*ḥikāyāt*) about men-of-wiles such as Aḥmad al-Danif and the Egyptian Zaybaq. Here and elsewhere, Ibn Taymiyya emphasizes that ʿAntara was indeed a pre-Islamic poet and knight, and al-Baṭṭāl was an amir in the Umayyad army.[29] But these historical figures have now become surrounded by layer upon layer of fabrications made up by *ṭuruqiyya* street charlatans.[30]

Ibn Taymiyya's position regarding the epics of 'Antar and al-Baṭṭāl was repeated by a number of his fourteenth-century Syrian disciples. Al-Dhahabī described the epic of al-Baṭṭāl as an accumulation of lies.[31] Al-Ṣafadī states that the historical figure of al-Baṭṭāl is known, but the epic about him contains legends and impossible things.[32] Ibn Kathīr blasts the epic of al-Baṭṭāl as fabrication and deceit that has currency only among the ignorant and the imbecile. The same was true of the epics of 'Antara al-'Absī and of Ahmad al-Danif.[33] Ibn Rajab recalls how Ibn Taymiyya's brother mocked an adversary by telling him he would not know the difference between material from the canonical collections of Hadith and from the epic of 'Antar.[34] A prohibition on reading the *siyar* is found in an endowment deed for a Cairene madrasa founded in 811/1408.[35] As Hirschler argued, traditionalist authors were keen to distinguish the epics from proper history that could be authenticated through reliable chains of scholarship.

The Epics in the Late Medieval Countryside

The popular epics offered an alternative view of history, leading to deleterious attitudes from puritans and traditionalists. But in order to explain why the epics were so popular in the first place, we have to look beyond the city walls. A series of fourteenth-century texts strongly suggest that the popular epics were widely consumed and appropriated by rural communities. This was so in the Mahgreb, where Ibn Khaldūn demonstrated how the epic of the Banū Hilāl formed the historical memory of the eponymous tribal confederacy. The same was true for Ayyubid and Mamluk lands. In the Syrian countryside, the epic of Dhāt al-Himma and al-Baṭṭāl was the most popular; even when the epic of al-Baṭṭāl was recited in Cairo, the storyteller is identified as a migrant from the rural Hawran. In Egypt, it was above all the epic of 'Antar that circulated in rural contexts, providing villagers like al-Qalqashandī a historical framework of identity.

According to Ibn Khaldūn, the Banū Hilāl epic was circulating among contemporary, fourteenth-century Hilālī tribesmen. He states that the "Banū Hilāl have fantastic and strange tales to tell regarding their entry into North Africa."[36] Urban scholars did not approve of these stories, partly because the linguistic register did not conform to the case endings of classical Arabic, and partly because the stories did not stand up to the criteria of academic reliability. Nonetheless, for the Hilālīs themselves the epic of Banū Hilāl was an absolute historical truth:

> They (the Hilalīs) are all in agreement in believing the truth of the tale of al-Jāziya and the Sharīf, as it comes down from father to son, and from one

generation to another. They would dismiss as utter lunatic and a complete fool anyone casting any doubt or expressing any disbelief in the story, because of its overwhelming popularity among them.[37]

Ibn Khaldūn makes plain that the Banū Hilāl used the epic for the purpose of constructing their communal identity. His account suggests that the *sīra* emerged among the Banū Hilāl themselves and, in his day, continued to circulate primarily among this tribal group and their North African milieu. Today, the North African cycle of the Banū Hilāl typically ends with the killing of the Berber king by the Arab hero Dhiyāb, and Michael Brett has reasonably argued that epic was a means of glorifying and legitimizing the triumph of the Arabs.[38] As the Banū Hilāl epic is not mentioned in any source coming from the Mamluk lands of Egypt and Syria, it is likely that in the late medieval period it was limited to the regions of North Africa and used by the local Arab Hilālī elites in these regions to tell the story of their conquest and the historical reasons for their dominance.[39]

Ibn Khaldūn heard the epic of Banū Hilāl performed in a poetic form. To this day, the Banū Hilāl cycle is in verse, chanted and accompanied by musical instruments.[40] By extension, Ibn Khaldūn equated any form of rural poetry with the popular epics, anticipating the present-day identification of vernacular rural poetry as Hilālī. According to Ibn Khaldūn, North Africans called rural poetry *al-Aṣmaʿiyyāt*, after the Abbasid philologist who specialized in the speech of the Arabs.[41] Al-Aṣmaʿī commonly appears to be the putative narrator of the Arab epics, especially in Sīrat ʿAntar. Ibn Khaldūn adds that in the central lands of the Middle East, the Arabs call this style of poetry Qaysī, Badawī, or sometimes Ḥawrānī, with the latter term referring to the style of chanting of the poems. To exemplify the tribal poetry from Egypt and Syria, Ibn Khaldūn reproduced six pieces attributed to a Qaysī woman from the Hawran, and another ten from an Egyptian man of the Halbā of Judhām.[42] As shown by Saʿd Sowayan, the diction, themes, rhyming system, and meters of the Middle Arabic lines quoted by Ibn Khaldūn resemble modern vernacular poetry in Najd, a genre known either as *nabaṭī* or as Hilālī.[43]

While the Banū Hilāl epic was popular in North Africa, the epic of Ḥamza was popular among the Turcomans, the Turkish-speaking clans who at the time inhabited northern Syria and eastern Anatolia.[44] Ibn Taymiyya states that "Sīrat Ḥamza is transmitted by some Turks, and even their elders, and is circulated among them. In this *sīra* they mention his wars and sieges and so forth."[45] Elsewhere, he compares the Shiʿa claims about ʿAlī to the legendary claims found in the epic of Ḥamza that circulates among Turkish groups, or Turcoman.[46] His association of the Ḥamza epic with the Turks suggests a tribal and rural audience, especially given his reference to their "elders" (*shuyūkh*). The Anatolian author Ahmad of Niğde, writing in the 1330s, stated that the "invented fables" attached to Ḥamza and ʿAlī were popular in his hometown. But he warned the local lord that "were he to deny the truth of a single line of these lies before the ordinary people, the ignorant ones would consider trying to kill him licit."[47] Ahmad's account of the hold of the epic of Ḥamza on the people of Niğde, a town in southern Anatolia, is remarkably similar to Ibn Khaldūn's account of the status of Sīrat Banū Hilāl in North Africa.[48]

In the hinterland of Aleppo, the epic of Dhāt al-Himma and al-Baṭṭāl was associated with the Banū Kilāb who inhabited the border areas of southeastern Anatolia. Al-ʿUmarī, when discussing the Turkish-speaking Banū Kilāb in his genealogical treatise, says that "the epic of Dalhama and al-Baṭṭāl was composed about them," because of their military qualities and frequent raids into Byzantine lands.[49] The link between the epic and Arab groups is reinforced by the report that some of the Banū Marwān claim al-Baṭṭāl as their ancestor. His own judgment of the epic is that it contains beautiful stories, but that they are mostly fabricated (*mulaḥ al-ḥadīth wa-lumaḥ al-abāṭīl wa'l-kadhib fīhā yaghlibu al-ṣaḥīḥ*). Al-ʿUmarī notes that the historical al-Baṭṭāl lived under the Umayyads while the setting of the epic cycle is Abbasid, and that Dhāt al-Himma is not mentioned at all in any trustworthy historical source. In al-ʿUmarī's mind, this epic was a work of fiction, erroneously set in the Abbasid period, but one that emerged in reference to the actual frontier milieu of southeast Anatolia.

Another reference to the circulation of the popular epics in the Syrian countryside comes from al-Dhahabī's anti-Shiʿa *Kitāb al-Muntaqā min minhāj al-iʿtidāl*. Like other traditionalists, he blames the *ṭuruqiyya* charlatans for the spread of fabricated historical accounts through the epics of ʿAntara and of al-Baṭṭāl.[50] Much of the *ṭuruqiyya*'s audience was based in the countryside: "Those who believe the fabrications and calumny of the Shiʿa are those most ignorant in recognizing authentic traditions and who are most likely to transmit impossible, self-contradictory lies, which only circulate among the beasts among men. This is the same as the circulation of the stories told by the *ṭuruqiyya* charlatans to commoners, and to the people of villages, mountains, and the steppe."[51] The image that emerges from al-Dhahabī's diatribe is of itinerant storytellers who move easily between the circles of urban commoners and the rustics of the countryside—in the villages, in the mountains, and in the campsites of the desert.

So far we have seen the hold and reach of the epics in the North African and Syrian countryside. We have even more specific evidence for the circulation and significance of the popular epics in the Egyptian Delta. First, the sixteenth-century chronicler al-Jazīrī provides us with an account of oral narratives circulating among the leading clan of Banū ʿAwna in al-Buḥayra. According to al-Jazīrī, the Banū ʿAwna say that they originally arrived and settled in al-Buḥayra from North Africa and that they are related by kinship to other clans who arrived with them, including the rival leading delta clan of the Banū Baghdād. The Banū ʿAwna transmitted among themselves a popular story in rhymed prose, cited by al-Jazīrī, about the origin of their name and their superiority over other clans. In this story, set in the agricultural lands of the delta, the clan was hired by the poorer Lawāta and Mazāta to repair a dike, and one of their women raised her skirts and removed her veil to facilitate her manual labor. When the woman was blamed for her failure to protect her people's honor, she challenged the masculinity of her clan, saying that she had uncovered herself in front of her own people because they were all women. The clan then proceeded to make war on their neighbors, expelling them from al-Buḥayra. Their battle cry was "To their aid, men! (*ʿAwna yā rijāl*)," hence the name Banū ʿAwna. Like the epic cycle of the Banū Hilāl, this smaller oral narrative in rhymed prose has all the ingredients of an origin myth.[52]

While the clan of the Banū ʿAwna in al-Buḥayra had their own narrative cycle, it was the epic cycle of ʿAntar that most prevailed in the delta of the Mamluk era, with two prominent authors of rural backgrounds uncritically endorsing the epic as historical truth. The first is Ibn al-Dawādārī, who incorporated segments from the ʿAntar epic into his universal history completed around 736/1335–36. Ibn al-Dawādārī's favorable attitude toward the epics has already been noted, as he likened the bravery of his Mamluk colleagues to the bravery of the epic heroes of Dhāt al-Himma and al-Baṭṭāl.[53] His direct reliance on the ʿAntar epic, however, has so far gone unnoticed.[54] The relevant segments are found in the second volume of Ibn al-Dawādārī's multivolume work, titled *al-Durra al-yatīma fī akhbār al-umam al-qadīma*. They include a distinctive epic version of the battle-day of Dāḥis and al-Ghabrāʾ, named after the race between two eponymous horses that triggered a forty-year tribal war in pre-Islamic Arabia.[55] The segments are unmistakably lifted from the epic, as they are narrated in the familiar rhymed prose, and they introduce the figure of Shaybūb, ʿAntar's wily half-brother. Shaybūb appears only in the epic versions of *sīrat* ʿAntar and not in the Abbasid-era renderings of the narrative.[56] Furthermore, these segments offer a verbatim match of the earliest extant manuscripts of the ʿAntar cycle, dating to the fifteenth century. For example, the rhymed prose describing the preparation for the race has: *wa-atat sādāt Banī Dhubyān/ wa-shujʿān Banī Ghaṭafān/ li-annahum al-jamīʿ fī arḍ wāḥida/ wa-fīhum ansāb muttaṣila* ("Then came the nobles of Banū

Dhubyān / and the heroes of Banū Ghaṭafān / for they all in one land are found / and their lineages are intertwined").[57] These exact lines are also found in the corresponding section of Sīrat ʿAntar in MS Arabe 3798, copied in 848/1444–45.[58] Most of the poetry is also preserved verbatim.[59]

All in all, it is evident that Ibn al-Dawādārī had direct access to a mature version of the ʿAntar epic, perhaps in a written form, and is the only Mamluk author to incorporate long sections of Sīrat ʿAntar into his chronicle. This feature is almost certainly related to his close familiarity with the Arab clansmen of the delta province of al-Sharqiyya. Ibn al-Dawādārī's father served as *kāshif al-ʿurbān* in the province in 699/1299–1300, after having acquired some experience with the Arabs of Barqa. Upon assuming this position, he moved to the provincial capital of Bilbays, where he spent eleven years. He was then promoted to the office of the *mihmindār* in Damascus, again dealing with local Arab tribesmen. Overall, Ibn al-Dawādārī's father made his career out of his expertise in Arab affairs.[60] Ibn al-Dawādārī himself not only shows unrivaled familiarity with the military and administrative aspects of relations with the Arab clans, but also with Arab culture and literature. In a personal anecdote, he reminisces about traveling with his father back from a military operation in Sinai accompanied by Arab guides. To pass the time, Ibn al-Dawādārī's father asked the *naqīb al-ʿurbān*—an officer of the Arab regiment, although the term is not otherwise attested—to recite a familiar poem. The *naqīb* complied, melodiously chanting from memory lines of poetry on the theme of separation from the beloved all the way to Bilbays. He did so in what Ibn al-Dawādārī describes as the Qubaysī (?) meter.[61] The anecdote shows that both Ibn al-Dawādārī and his father were familiar with the etiquette and the performance of Arab poetry, further suggesting that Ibn al-Dawādārī became familiar with Sīrat ʿAntar through his long formative period among the Arabs of al-Sharqiyya.

Al-Qalqashandī's Autobiography (Sīrat ʿAntar and the Village Clan)

The most important and direct evidence for the role popular epics played in forming Arab clan identity comes from the pen of another author of the Egyptian Delta, the well-known Mamluk bureaucrat Shihāb al-Dīn Aḥmad al-Qalqashandī. Al-Qalqashandī was born in 1355 in the village of Qalqashanda (present-day Qarqashanda) in al-Qalyūbiyya, at the agricultural hinterland of Cairo. In an autobiographical notice placed within his genealogical treatise, "The Ultimate Ambition in the Knowledge of the Lineages of the Arabs" (*Nihāyat al-arab fī ma'rifat ansāb al-'arab*), al-Qalqashandī recounts the association of his native village with the Banū Badr clan of the Fazāra confederacy:

> Banū Badr, of the Fazāra, of the Qays 'Aylān. We will discuss the lineage of the Fazāra in their own entry. [Ibn Khaldūn] said in his [*Kitāb*] *al-'Ibar* that the Banū Badr were the leaders of the Fazāra during the pre-Islamic Jāhiliyya. They were leaders of the entire Ghaṭafān, while Qays and their brothers the Banū Tha'laba bin 'Adī obeyed their judgments (*tadīnū la-hum*). One of their members was Ḥudhayfa b. Badr b. 'Umar b. Ḥarba b. Lūdhān b. Tha'laba b. 'Adī b. Fazāra, owner of the horse known as al-Ghabrā', which raced the horse known as Dāḥis. That was the cause of the war known as [the Day of] Dāḥis between 'Abs and Ghaṭafān, as is recounted in the books of the *siyar* (the popular epics).
>
> I say: Those Banū Badr are our tribe (*qabīlatunā*), in which we take pride (*na'tazī*) and from which we claim lineage (*nantasibu*). They are the most noble among the Arabs of the Qalyūbiyya province in Egypt. Their neighbors in Qalyūbiyya are their paternal cousins, the Banū Māzin of the Fazāra. Each of the Banū Badr and the Banū Māzin have their own villages (*bilād*). The two are in a constant state of enmity and bad blood, but the Banū Badr have the leadership and the upper hand. The people of our village (*balda*) of Qalqashanda belong to one of the two groups (*firqatayn*), either the Banū Badr or the Banū Māzin.[62]

Al-Qalqashandī's entry for the Banū Badr begins with the pre-Islamic Arabian Peninsula. He cites Ibn Khaldūn on the elevated status of Banū Badr within the Fazāra confederacy in the Jāhiliyya, and then he reminds his readers of the heroics of Ḥudhayfa al-Badrī, familiar from the popular Arabic epics. Al-Qalqashandī then sharply shifts from the mythical and the heroic to the mundane and autobiographical. The Banū Badr of Qalqashanda, like their pre-Islamic kinsmen, successfully prevail over the neighboring clan of the Banū Māzin, also of the Fazāra. The epic battles of pre-Islamic Arabia are played out in the provincial backwaters of the late medieval Egyptian Delta.

Al-Qalqashandī wrote two other texts on the history of the Arab clans of his age, and his personal identification with the Banū Badr is highlighted in both. The genealogical section of *Ṣubḥ al-A'shā*, completed in 814/1412, has the same account of the Banū Badr, minus the triumphalist tone toward the Banū Māzin.[63] In another genealogical treatise, *Qalā'id al-jumān fī al-ta'rīf bi-qabā'il 'arab al-zamān* (The abundant necklaces regarding the knowledge of the Arab tribes of our time), written in 819/1416, he locates the Banū Māzin in the neighboring villages of Zufaytā and Sindibīs rather than in Qalqashanda itself. He also engages in a more detailed account of Ḥudhayfa's race against Qays al-ʿAbsī, referencing the twin authority of books of history (*taʾrīkh*) and the popular epics (*siyar*).[64] In all these texts, written in the 1410s, his fellow villagers in Qalqashanda claimed to be the descendants of the Banū Badr of the pre-Islamic Arabian Peninsula and heirs to their superior social status.[65]

What is remarkable here is how al-Qalqashandī used the materials of the ʿAntar epic to construct the identity of his own village clan. In the entry for the Banū Badr in his *Qalāʾid*, al-Qalqashandī draws support from the epics to back up his portrayal of Ḥudhayfa, the pre-Islamic leader of the Banū Badr and a key protagonist in Sīrat ʿAntar. He explicitly refers to the "books of the *siyar*" for information on his own Badr clan. Al-Qalqashandī was growing up with the epic of ʿAntar as the backdrop for the collective memory of the villagers of Qalqashanda, who identified themselves as the Banū Badr of the Fazāra.[66] The inhabitants of Qalqashanda had an obvious motivation to reproduce the ʿAntar epic, as it supplied the single most important link to their treasured pre-Islamic Arabian past. Al-Qalqashandī's credulous attitude to Sīrat ʿAntar certainly seems to replicate the attitude of the contemporary Hilālī tribesmen, who, according to Ibn Khaldūn, deemed the epic version of their history to be beyond doubt.

Al-Qalqashandī put his faith in the epics. In his commentary on the genealogical writings of al-ʿUmarī, the leading bureaucrat of the previous generation, he is keen to remove doubts about the historicity of the content of the epic cycles. Al-ʿUmarī, as we have seen, dismissed the Dhāt al-Himma and al-Baṭṭāl epic as a work of fiction woven around a minor historical figure from the Umayyad period. Yet al-Qalqashandī turns this assessment into an endorsement: "The author of *Masālik al-Abṣār* [i.e., al-ʿUmarī] says: informants told me that the Banū Kilāb trace their lineage to the ʿAbd al-Wahhāb mentioned in Sīrat al-Baṭṭāl. [Al-ʿUmarī] found that this ʿAbd al-Wahhāb is mentioned in other sources and not just in the epic, and therefore concluded that his [real] name was ʿAbd al-Wahhāb ibn Nawbakht."[67] Al-Qalqashandī is here forcefully reconciling the popular epics with the high historiographical tradition.

Al-Qalqashandī was not an exception among Egyptian scholars of his generation. The Egyptian Ḥanafī jurist Kamāl ibn Humām (1388–1457) cites a line of poetry commonly attributed to ʿAntar in his legal compendium *Fatḥ al-Qadīr*. In this line, which is derived from the classical Abbasid-era collections, the name of ʿAntar's brother is given as Jundub, but Ibn Humām refutes this attribution, arguing that anyone who has read (*iṭṭalaʿa*) the story (*qiṣṣa*) of ʿAntar knows that his only brother was Shaybūb.[68] As noted above, the character of Shaybūb is entirely a creature of the epic cycles and doesn't appear in classical literature, so Ibn Humām was granting the ʿAntar epic a higher truth-value than the early Islamic corpus.

The importance of the epics for al-Qalqashandī's formation of Arab identity is further shown by a section on pre-Islamic culture appended to one of his genealogical treatises, the *Nihāyat al-Arab*. This section covers *Jāhilī* religious beliefs and idols, as well as distinctively Arab sciences, such as physiognomy, dream interpretation, observation of lunar mansions, and genealogy. It concludes with a list of the battles of the pre-Islamic Arabs (*ayyām al-ʿarab*) and a long anecdote about a poetry competition involving al-Qalqashandī's ancestor Ḥudhayfa.[69] Al-Qalqashandī attempted here to create a link between antiquarian pre-Islamic practices, as reported by Abbasid litterateurs, and the Arab clansmen of his time. These pre-Islamic sciences had no direct relevance to the milieu of al-Qalqashandī's village clans, and none are reported in the entries he devoted to them. Rather, this is a deliberate attempt to construct an identity based on recourse to literary traditions, not a reflection of reality.

As we have seen throughout our discussion, the twin Arab tribal epics of ʿAntar ibn Shaddād and of Dhāt al-Himma and al-Baṭṭāl dominate the references to the *siyar* in Mamluk sources. The dominance of the ʿAntar and al-Baṭṭāl epics extends also to the manuscript record, as the preserved copies of epic segments produced in Egypt or Syria in the fifteenth century are only of these two Arab cycles.[70] The references to Sīrat Baybars and Sīrat Sayf b. Dhī Yazan, two major epics that emerged during the fifteenth century, are few and come very late in the Mamluk period.[71] Unlike Sīrat Banū Hilāl, Sīrat ʿAntar and Sīrat al-Baṭṭāl were not the exclusive preserve of one tribal group. ʿAntar's clan, the ʿAbs, were not a major group in Mamluk Egypt, and no author claims that Sīrat ʿAntar was used as the origin myth of the contemporary ʿAbs.[72] In the epic's account, the ancestor of al-Qalqashandī's clan, Ḥudhayfa, wins the horse race by cheating. His cowardly behavior causes the eventual bloodshed. But al-Qalqashandī doesn't seem to mind, since, for the purpose of identity construction, the sprawling epic had sufficient raw materials to provide Arab ancestors for everyone. The ʿAntar epic went beyond individual tribe; it offered a history of the Arab nation.

The ʿAntar Epic and Arab Identity

In this section, I would like to suggest that Sīrat ʿAntar became so popular in Mamluk lands because it offered a shared Arab identity through the elaboration of historical memories and codes of behavior, and it asserted of the prime role of the Arabs within the framework of Islamic history. As we have seen with al-Qalqashandī, the epic of ʿAntar was used by villagers for the purpose of fostering layers of identity that reached out of the village unit, both in time (linking the villagers to a pre-Islamic past) and in space (linking them to all other Arab clansmen). Moreover, although set in the deserts of the pre-Islamic Arabian Peninsula, the themes of the ʿAntar epic were attuned to the concerns and the conflicts of village clans in late medieval Syria and Egypt. Indeed, the ʿAntar epic repeatedly refers to the collective of Arab tribesmen as ʿurbān, the late medieval neologism describing the armed Arab elites of the largely sedentary countryside. Thus, Sīrat ʿAntar was the epic of the Arabs, their destiny as the first nation of Islam and the keepers of its most sacred site—but addressed to the late medieval ʿurbān and their village clans.

In order to securely locate the messages of the epics in their medieval context, this analysis will be based on reading sections of Sīrat ʿAntar from the earliest available manuscripts, copied in the fifteenth century. Specifically, I will be using four copies that are securely dated to the first half of the fifteenth century and copied in Mamluk lands.[73] Each of these copies provides only a small portion of the full cycle. But they happen to contain some key segments, such as the opening sequence and the account of the race of Dāḥis and al-Ghabrā'. The progression of the narrative in these copies is very much in line with the broad outlines of the modern edition of Sīrat ʿAntar, as summarized by Peter Heath.[74] However, for our purposes here, modern editions will be referenced only to clarify and complete key elements missing from the medieval copies. I have chosen ʿAntar over Sīrat Dhāt al-Himma and al-Baṭṭāl, for which we have only one manuscript dating to the fifteenth century.[75] The greater visibility of Sīrat ʿAntar in manuscript collections is partly down to the manner in which it was consumed: Sīrat al-Baṭṭāl was performed by storytellers, while Sīrat ʿAntar appears to have been read out of a manuscript.[76]

It is important to emphasize that the fifteenth-century manuscript copies studied here were read by—or read to—provincial commoners and artisans. We know this from readers' notations made on an early-fifteenth-century copy of a segment of Sīrat ʿAntar, probably made in Mamluk Syria. Twelve different readers had their names written on this copy of the epic, with four of them dating their notes to the first half of the fifteenth century.[77] The notes follow a standard formula: each person says that he read (*ṭālaʿa*) the epic or inspected (*naẓara*) it. Among the readers we find a skinner from Irbīl who read the work on the first day of Ramadan 835 (May 2, 1432); a storekeeper (*khazzān*) called Aḥmad b. Ibrahim b. al-Kawḥalī (?) from Hama; and Shaʿbān b. Aqʿā al-ʿUmarī al-Sayfī

Bashtāk (?) al-Nāṣirī, whose *nisba* suggests he belonged to the military elite. Other members of the military who consumed the text were two stablemen, Muḥammad and Aḥmad, of the Ūjākiyya (Turkish Ocakiyya) regiment.[78] The collective profile of these men is that of nonscholars who were either artisans or low-ranking members of the army. While it seems unlikely that they read it in a village, the range of professions—skinner, storekeeper, and a pair of stablemen—is never far from the countryside.

From the very beginning, the extant copies of Sīrat ʿAntar set out to tell the origin myth of the Arabs. The opening section of these late medieval manuscripts, as well as of later copies, begins with the division of the Arab lands among the four sons of Nizār: Muḍar in the Hijaz, whose descendants are the Banū ʿAdnān, the Qaḥṭān in the Yemen, Rabīʿa in Iraq, and Ghassān in Syria. It then lists the four great wars of pre-Islamic Arabia, including that of Dāḥis and al-Ghabrāʾ. In the late medieval versions, and in some later copies, we then find the story of Abraham, his struggle against the despot Nimrod, and the eventual building of the Kaʿba.[79] The inclusion of the Abrahamic story has been somewhat marginalized in modern scholarship and excluded in most modern editions.[80] But the Abrahamic sequence is central to the framing of the epic as a whole, as it creates a genealogical link between the Arabs and Abrahamic monotheism and is a prerequisite for the sanctity of the House of God in Mecca.

The repeated and pervasive references to the Kaʿba demonstrate the link between the coming of Islam and the Arab tribes. The opening segments include the building of the House of God by Abraham and Ishmael, followed by a segment in which the ʿAbsī leader Zuhayr wishes to build a new Kaʿba in his own lands, but his plans are destined to be foiled.[81] The Kaʿba is then invoked through the numerous oaths taken by all protagonists: "in the name of the Ancient House and its Pillars" (*wa-ḥaqq al-bayt al-ʿatīq wa'l-arkān*), "in the name of the Scared House, Zamzan and Abraham's standing-place" (*bi'l-bayt al-ḥarām wa-zamzam wa'l-maqām*), "in the name of the Pillar and the Stone" (*wa-ḥaqq al-rukn wa'l-ḥajar*), and "in the name of the Kaʿba."[82] One is never allowed to forget the special link of the Arabs with the holiest Islamic sanctuary.

Sīrat ʿAntar is set in the Jāhiliyya, before the coming of Islam, yet the religious beliefs of ʿAntar and other protagonists are occasionally monotheistic. ʿAntar beseeches Qays "in the name of Moses and Abraham" not to stand in the way of two lovers.[83] Elsewhere he appeals to the ancient Lord, the Lord of Moses and Abraham.[84] This is the Lord "who causes the sun to rise and who knows the inner soul"[85] and the one "who can count the locust when it spreads and created the sun and the moon."[86] In one of his pieces of poetry, however, he swears in the

الجزء السادس عشر من سيره
عنتر ابن شداد العبسي
غفر الله لكاتبه ولمالكه ولوالديهم
ولجميع المسلمين امين امين يا رب العالمين

FIGURE 7.1. Reading notes on a manuscript containing the sixteenth section of Sīrat ʿAntar b. Shaddād al-ʿAbsī, copied circa 805/1402–3. From the British Library Collection: MS Add 7387, fol. 2a.

name of "heavenly sphere, al-Lāt and al-ʿUzza, all our idols and our creator."[87] This stray into paganism is, I believe, intentional: it is important that ʿAntar is not yet a Muslim and that the Arabs are still on their journey toward Islam.

The Jāhiliyya Arabs exhibit some flagrantly pagan or un-Islamic customs that serve as "strategies of distinction," a term borrowed here from scholarship on medieval European narratives of origin. As Walter Pohl argued, when medieval European groups recounted their own prehistory, they emphasized unique cultural traits that characterized the groups before Christianity and settlement.[88] In the context of the ʿAntar epic, which serves as the origin narrative of the Arabs, pagan customs make the eventual conversion to Islam meaningful, and they distinguish the Arabs from other groups that came to embrace Islam. For the pre-Islamic customs of the Arabs, the epic chiefly draws on the *Ayyām al-ʿArab* material compiled in the Abbasid period.[89] When ʿAntar goes on a raid to find wine (his host has run out), the narrator explains that "in the time of the Jāhiliyya," wine merchants advertised their goods by setting flags at the opening of the tent, and the knights would come and buy, as is mentioned in the famous Hanging poem by ʿAntar.[90] Here the epic links an un-Islamic practice (selling wine) with the pre-Islamic poetry feted by the Abbasid-era litterateurs. A particularly dramatic example comes in the segment in which Shaddād captures and rapes ʿAntar's mother Zabība "out of the ignorance of the pre-Islamic ʿurbān."[91] In another fifteenth-century copy, Zabība is taken first by Shaddād, but then shockingly also by his ten companions, all on the same night.[92] Modern printed editions mitigate the severity of the crimes by having Shaddād make a promise of marriage to Zabība, a retrospective attempt to give an aura of Islamic legality to the rape.[93] But the fifteenth-century copies intentionally set up this key scene as embodying pre-Islamic customs of excessive hospitality, raiding, and rape. These "categories of distinction" fill pre-Islamic Arab identity with specific and identifiable cultural content.

Sīrat ʿAntar, like a few other major Arabic popular epics, is framed as a story of conversion, made apparent through the repeated references to the coming of the Prophet.[94] The opening Abrahamic story is the first building block in the epic's conversion narrative. The *sīra* ends with a recounting of Muḥammad's Meccan biography followed by the conversion of ʿAntar's tribe, now led by his daughter ʿUnaytira. As Remke Kruk pointed out, the ʿAntar epic is unique in offering a narrative sequence in which the Prophet actually appears as a protagonist, and not through supernatural interventions. Kruk argued that the Prophet is used here to proffer Islamic legitimacy on an un-Islamic hero, eliminating a sense of discomfort from enjoying supposedly pagan tales.[95] But in fact the journey toward

Islam is tightly woven into the fabric of the epic. Again and again, the actions of adversaries and allies are led by their certain knowledge that a Prophet from ʿAdnān will soon bring a new religion.[96] The protagonists are not yet Muslim, but they are fully aware that they or their descendants will become ones.

Thus, the epic begins with the origin of the Arabs and ends with their conversion to Islam. In this larger context, as Heath put it, "ʿAntar has a cosmic role to play."[97] The opening pages of the narrative, as found in medieval and later copies, explain that ʿAntar was chosen by God to pave the way for the appearance of Muḥammad:

> This is the story of the brave knights of the Jāhiliyya, who worshipped idols and venerated statues; they were deceived by Satan, who allured them to evil and privation. Their sole desire was to defeat each other, each wishing to overpower all other heroes on the face of the Earth. They did not fear God or honor him. So when God saw their haughtiness and their ignorance, he humiliated and overpowered them through the lowliest and humblest of his creatures—and that is easy for him—and this man was ʿAntar ibn Shaddād.[98]

In this framing of the story, ʿAntar is chosen by God to bring an end to paganism by showing the heroes of the Jāhiliyya the vanity of their ambitions. The evil of the Jāhiliyya is not the tribal system and its hierarchies, but rather the unchecked powers of the pre-Islamic mythical heroes, who all act only in their self-interest. ʿAntar is singled out for his status as a black slave, and not for his moral character or for his proto-Islamic religion. He is a sign from God; his sheer military successes, despite his servile status, help the pre-Islamic Arab tribesmen realize the error of their ways and prepare them for the coming of the true message.

Unlike other epic heroes associated with conversion, ʿAntar does not carry a universal mission. The focus on the Arabian Peninsula declares Islam to be the religion of the Arabs, a fundamentally Arab religion. There is no equivalence between Arabs and non-Arabs, and—at least in the extant medieval segments—no engagement with the spread of Islam beyond the boundaries of Arabia.[99] The superiority of the Arabs is evident through their courage and noble character. This message of the ʿAntar epic sharply differs from that of Sīrat Sayf b. Dhī Yazan, which tells the story of a Yemenite king who conquers and converts to Islam all the peoples he meets. He is destined to fulfill the divine decree of subjugating the black people of Ethiopia and the Sudan and diverting the Nile toward Egypt.[100] Sīrat Sayf is thus an epic of the Egyptians, with many characters carrying the names of Egyptian cities or provinces.[101] As Aboubakr Chraïbi insightfully pointed out, it neutralizes the bad reputation that Egyptians have in monotheistic contexts.[102] In the epic of Sayf b. Dhī Yazan, Islam arrived in Egypt from Arabia before the Muslim conquest, thus making the Egyptian audiences of the epic the descendants of primordial Muslims. Sīrat 'Antar, on the other hand, represents the Arab claim for superiority. The Arabs descended from Abraham, and the pre-Islamic Arabs revered the House of God. 'Antar is the harbinger of the Prophet, who would emerge from 'Adnān, the confederacy to which 'Antar belonged.[103] For late medieval Arab villagers, this version of history awarded them pride of place above all other social groups.

Sīrat 'Antar not only celebrates Arab primacy in Islam, but also the second constituent element of Arab identity in the later Middle Ages: the social world of clans and tribal confederacies, of feud and conflict resolution. Herzog argued that the epic carried an antitribal message, an opposition between "a tribal, collective society and a more individual conception of society which probably appealed much more to the sedentary and urban audience addressed by the Sirat 'Antar."[104] In my view, this dichotomy is based on the supposition of an entirely urban audience. While 'Antar's struggle to overcome the impediments of his birth certainly drives the plot forward, he is also the incarnation of Arab chivalry and values: brave and generous, able to compose magnificent poetry, protecting the needy and prioritizing collective solidarity over his own interests.[105] His triumphs are the triumphs of his clan and of the ideals of Arabness. His struggles against the tribal elites reflect tensions inherent to the social organization based on lineage, shaped in concentric circles of clans and confederacies. Yet his aim is to be accepted, not to overthrow social hierarchies and do away with tribes.

In the 'Antar epic, social relations are expressed through the language of lineage, yet genealogy is often determined by physical proximity. Clans that reside next to each other are tied by kinship and form larger confederacies. The sister clans that neighbor the 'Abs, such as the 'Āmir and the Fazāra, are related to them through blood. They are also their bitter rivals. These neighboring tribes all belong to the 'Adnān confederacy, which is the second major focus of identity for 'Antar (his battle cry, also used when having sex, is "Yā 'Abs, yā 'Adnān").[106] The distinction between 'Adnān and Qaḥṭān, or Qays and Yaman, is crucial for the political world of the 'Antar epic. The Yaman tribes are enemies by definition. As Heath points out, 'Antar fights other 'Adnān Arabs when necessary, but the Yaman Arabs are always fair game for his raiding.[107] This political grammar of clan, tribe, and confederacy resonated with the village clans of Mamluk lands. Al-Qalqashandī evoked the same rivalry between neighboring clans when describing his Banū Badr's relationship with their Banū Māzin cousins in the villages of al-Qalyūbiyya. As we shall see, at times of civil war, the villagers of fourteenth-century Syria organized themselves into regional alliances of Qays and Yaman, mortal enemies by definition.

In Sīrat ʿAntar, the protagonists are driven by culturally specific principles of feud and honor, "the taking of revenge and the removal of shame" (*akhdh al-thaʾr wa'l-kashf ʿan al-ʿār*).[108] These are explicitly attached to masculinity: when the despicable ʿAmāra dressed as a woman and shat in his pants, his humiliation by ʿAntar is not seen as a cause for a feud.[109] At the same time, much of the extant manuscript segments is taken up with conflict resolution based on appeals to shared ancestors.[110] The collective leadership of tribal groups, the *sādāt* and *mashāyikh*, keep trying to avert the shedding of blood by appealing to shared blood lines (*ṣilat al-nasab*). The different clans are "cousins and relatives who share the same land."[111] They also invoke the peace by dramatically carrying on their backs the idols of the Jāhiliyya. As the narrator explains, "In our own days," the idols are replaced by the message of the Prophet Muḥammad.[112] In the face of the feuding impulse, social peace is guaranteed by the twin pillars of clan and Islam.

ʿAntar's clan is sharply divided between those who have noble Arab lineage, the *sādāt al-qabīla*, and the half-caste *muwallad* slaves, often black Africans, who occupy the lower occupations. ʿAntar, who was born to the latter but aspires to be recognized among the former, embodies the tension between merit and social order.[113] For our purpose here, it is significant that the *muwallad* class is everywhere in the extant segments of the epic. Female *muwalladāt* are singers and entertainers or do menial work such as fetching water.[114] The male slaves are responsible for the herds or are sent as messengers and spies to the desert.[115] They can raid, but they receive a quarter of the share of a free person.[116] The omnipresence of slavery in the epic mirrors the visibility of slavery in the sources relating to the Arabs of Upper Egypt in the fourteenth century. The term *muwallad* is also attested as a derogatory term. As we saw in chapter 2, it was used by the monks of St. Catherine for the ʿĀʾidh tribesmen who were sent to rule over them at the beginning of the Ayyubid period. In the context of the dramatic shift of identity that engulfed the Middle Eastern countryside in the later Middle Ages, one could read ʿAntar's struggle as emblematic of rural men and women's effort to be accepted as truly Arab.

As noted by many a reader of ʿAntar, the epic is set firmly in the desert but contains very little on nomadic life. The location and the natural environment are reduced to very little, and there is hardly anything on the everyday practicalities of transhumant lifestyle.[117] The protagonists invariably live in tents clustered in a camp, but this camp is often pitched by a pool, where women and girls stroll in the evening. Valleys of running water and flowers are never far away.[118] A typical bride-price includes only proper Arab goods, such as small cattle, dates, and honey.[119] But a lovely sequence describes Shaybūb's purchase of wheat and its meticulous preparation in advance of a feast.[120] Migrations, which happen often, are not a result of a search for pasture, but of the incessant conflicts among the clans. The mobility of the clans reflects their relationship to the land: each clan can establish a territory (*diyār*), but the concept of land ownership is absent.

There are no peasants in Sīrat ʿAntar. This is mostly true of the genre as whole, except for the urban cycle of Sīrat Baybars.[121] This is part of a wider phenomenon, as peasants are almost wholly invisible in Arabic literature of the Ayyubid and Mamluk eras. While Abbasid-era literature refers to the *nabaṭī* farmer as the country bumpkin, this category practically disappears later on. As noted by both Joseph Sadan and Sarah Binay, it is the figure of the Arab who comes to typify all the rural characters that in other cultures are personified by peasants.[122] In the popular literary collection by al-Ibshīhī (d. after 850/1446) there are no fallāḥs, even though the author grew up in a delta village. Al-Ibshīhī does offer, on the other hand, a long section on the Arabs: on their hospitality and simplicity, as well as lack of familiarity with religious practices and texts, and their tendency to fart uncontrollably.[123] The absence of the peasant from Sīrat ʿAntar, as well as from other genres of late medieval Arabic literature, was a direct result of the desire of villagers to pass as Arabs. The tenant farmers who listened to the epic didn't want to hear that their ancestors were peasants, too.

The most obvious link between the medieval manuscripts of Sīrat ʿAntar and Mamluk-era village clans comes through the repeated use of the term ʿurbān. As we have seen, the neologism ʿurbān emerged in the twelfth century in reference to auxiliary troops of the Fatimid state, and in later centuries it became the common term for any armed Arab groups living under Mamluk rule. In the fifteenth-century manuscript copies of the epic, the term ʿurbān refers to the collective of the Arab tribesmen who live in the pre-Islamic Arabian Peninsula. Thus, one's tribal community are addressed either as *yā al-ʿarab* or *yā maʿāshir al-ʿurbān*. Dāḥis, the horse at the center of race segment of the epic, is said to be the best horse "among the ʿurbān," while the ʿurbān tribesmen are spread throughout the land.[124] The collective ʿurbān were bound to respect the protection given to the ʿAbs by King Nuʿmān.[125] The word of certain tribal leaders, such as Durayd or Zuhayr, is respected among all the ʿurbān.[126] There are frequent references to the *mashāyikh*, who here act as the elders, the keepers of the collective wisdom who give counsel on a variety of topics, but they are not the political leaders.[127] Even though the epic cycle is squarely set in the Arabian desert, the ʿurbān are never called *badw*. In fact, when someone appears from the desert, he is called *aʿrābī*, reflecting the prevailing linguistic practice of Mamluk chronicles.[128] The ʿurbān who obeyed Zuhayr are said to be both *bādiya* and *ḥāḍira*, those of the steppe and those of settled lands.[129] An additional link between the ʿurbān of the epic and the ʿurbān of Mamluk Egypt and Syria is their susceptibility to a range of taxes paid to distant kings: *khafāra* protection payment, *ʿidād* levy on flocks, and *kharāj* land tax.[130]

The late medieval manuscripts of Sīrat ʿAntar create an explicit link between their audience and Arab identity. Since the texts were recited in public, sequences are commonly preceded by calling out for the attention of the present listeners: "*Yā sāda, yā kirām*" (Oh you notables, oh you honorable men), sometimes in red ink. The *sāda* in the audience could be easily confused with *sādat al-ʿarab* or *sādat al-qabīla*, the notables who inhabit the epic itself.[131] This blurring of the line between the epic heroes and the audience seems to have been a typical feature of medieval public recitations. We have seen how one member of the Cairene audience listening to the recitation of al-Baṭṭāl imitated its epic heroes by dropping dead as a martyr. In the rural milieu of modern Egypt the intentional confounding of heroes and audience is one of the hallmarks of the epic performance, as beautifully shown by Dwight Reynolds.[132]

Peter Heath wrote that the stories of Sīrat ʿAntar "stretch out from the past to shape and stir the expectations and imaginations of their audiences about possibilities of action in the present and in the future."[133] The late medieval manuscripts of ʿAntar are remarkably didactic. A man of *nakhwa* and *ḥumayya* never chooses lies and trickery.[134] A father tells his son to act responsibly, to think of the implications of his actions, and not to rush.[135] Another moral is to never be jealous of anyone.[136] After being betrayed, the tragic figure of al-Rabīʿ tells his comrades that he has learned his lesson: whoever leaves his family (*ahl*) and seeks refuge with strangers will suffer. He then takes his solidarity group, his *ʿashīra*, and goes back to the ʿAbs.[137] As we are told, the person who listens to the epic (*al-mustamiʿ*) should learn the story of the Arabs and the conduct of knights of merit and nobility.[138] Sīrat ʿAntar places the Arabs as the primary nation of Islam and examines the tensions inherent in segmentary clan society. It offered "a vestige of a memory, lexicon, and set of virtues that belonged to an imagined but very intimate past."[139] It also tells you how to be an Arab even if you were not born to an Arab line; it turns you into one.

The Arab Epics and Village Clans

Our journey with the epic of 'Antar began in twelfth-century Baghdad, when the young Jewish Samaw'al al-Maghribī read it alongside the stories of al-Baṭṭāl and of Alexander. By the early thirteenth century, we found al-Baṭṭāl recited by a Hawrani immigrant in Cairo. Then came an explosion of references to the circulation of the epics in Cairo and Damascus in the first half of the fourteenth century, and the incorporation of segments of the text of Sīrat 'Antar into Ibn al-Dawādārī's universal history. The earliest extant stand-alone manuscripts of both 'Antar and al-Baṭṭāl date from the first half of the fifteenth century, and it was in this period that al-Qalqashandī adopted the epic of 'Antar as a source of historical knowledge about his own identity. The twin Arab epics of 'Antar and of al-Baṭṭāl were by far the dominant cycles in the genre, and they appear to have been developed earlier than others. Other epics, such as Sīrat Baybars and Sīrat Sayf, appeared toward the end of the Mamluk period, when the corpus of the epics became normalized, part of the cultural heritage of Mamluk society.

This medieval history of the epic, from its first appearance in twelfth-century Iraq to the its rapid spread in Mamluk Egypt and Syria, corresponds to the historical development of other cultural markers of Arab identity, such as the Arab pronunciation of the letter *qāf* and the Arab *lithām* headgear. The Arab *qāf* and the *lithām*, although not unknown practices in earlier centuries, became distinctive expressions of Arabness only in the eleventh or twelfth centuries. One could add to this repertoire of Arab cultural markers the simple handmade pottery that spread in Greater Syria during the second half of the twelfth century. Similarly, the popular epic, while grounded in the Abbasid-era literary collections, turned the classical 'Antara to 'Antar, a popular symbol of Arab values and of Arab pride of place in the Islamic community.

The Arab epic of 'Antar was not merely a marker of Arab identity—it also had the power to generate it. The epics gave rural communities a historical memory of Arabness, model rules of conduct, and even perhaps the names by which they identified themselves. For example, the term 'urbān is used in the earliest copies of the epic to fit the rhymed prose—it is a convenient counterpoint to *shuj'ān* (brave men), *fursān* (knights) and age (*zamān*), as well as to important names of tribes, such as Ghaṭafān and 'Adnān.[140] This use of the neologism 'urbān in the epics, seemingly demanded by the rhyme, is possibly behind the rather sudden appearance of the term 'urbān as a collective name for the Arab armed units that formed in the Egyptian and Syrian countrysides in the twelfth century. It is perhaps not far-fetched to speculate that the new Arab social groups adopted for themselves the language of the ʿAntar cycle, naming themselves after their epic ancestors. At a local level, the names chosen for village clans in the Mamluk countryside also resonated with the tribal groups that dominated the epics: Fazāra, ʿĀmir, ʿAbs.[141]

The form of the epics, tailor-made for periodical public recitations, meant that no other form of Arabic literature was as influential and popular in the countryside. ʿAntar and al-Baṭṭāl were well known in the cities but had a rural reach that was beyond other genres. In that sense, one could think of the Arab epics as taking hold in the landscape alongside the growing number of tombs of saints and village mosques that mushroomed in the Ayyubid and Mamluk countryside. The tombs of saints were the form of Islamic religiosity most suited for the medieval village. Similarly, the epics were the form of literature that made Arab and Islamic history accessible and digestible to a rural audience. The connection between tomb visitation and the spread of the popular epic is illustrated by an anecdote about a fifteenth-century Cairene miller who placed fictive tombstones in the Qarāfa cemetery to attract gullible pilgrims, inscribing names he plucked from the ʿAntar and al-Baṭṭāl epics.[142] Both the epics and the practice of tomb visitation involved imaginative recreation of the past for popular consumption.

The later Middle Ages saw the proliferation of epics and the consolidation of Arab clan identity, not only in Egypt and Syria but also in the broader Middle East. For North Africa, we have Ibn Khaldūn's account of the hold of the epic of Banū Hilāl within the historical memory of the group. Later in the early modern period, the Hilālī heroes of the cycle became the champions of the rural masses, whether against tribal lords or state officials.[143] The role of the Baṭṭāl cycle in promoting Turkish identity in Anatolia was suggested by Köprülü nearly a century ago. Even if his argument was couched in overly nationalist terms, the spread of the Baṭṭāl-name in Anatolia did overlap with conversion to Islam and with a shift to Turkish as a literary medium. The earliest extant Turkish manuscript copy of the Baṭṭāl cycle dates to 840/1436–37, cotemporaneous with the first Arabic copies of the ʿAntar epic made in Mamluk Egypt and Syria.[144]

Finally, the Arabic epics pulled into their orbits men who did not see themselves as Arabs. In an inscription on a Khānaqāh established by Sultan Barsbāy in 1431 or 1432, just east of Cairo, he described himself as having *ḥamalāt ʿAntariyya*, or "ʿAntar-like military campaigns."[145] There was a failed attempt to read from the epic of Baybars in the literary salon of Sultan al-Ghawrī (r. 1501–16).[146] And, of course, the earliest record of Sīrat ʿAntar comes from the conversion narrative of Samaw'al al-Maghribī, a Jewish man who read it as a young man and who described the epic as a step on the way toward the light of Islam. His autobiographical text attracted much attention in thirteenth-century Anatolia, where conversion to Islam was apace.[147] We know that Jews continued to read 'Antar in later centuries, and a nearly complete codex of Sīrat 'Antar was found in the Cairo Geniza.[148] To a degree, then, the epic cycles formed a shared Middle Eastern culture that crossed religious boundaries; or, looked at another way, a further bridge of Islamization.

PART IV

Village Clans and Rural Revolts

8

The Syrian Blood Feuds of Qays and Yaman

IN THE world of the ʿAntar epic, as popularized in Ayyubid and Mamluk lands, clans are either northern Arabs or southern Arabs, ʿAdnān or Qaḥṭān, Qays or Yaman. This division is central to the social landscape of the heroes: it marks the boundary between self and other, between potential allies and eternal foes. Fiction then found its way into social realities. By the early fourteenth century, the Arab villagers of Syria have found these categories of Qays and Yaman to be useful markers of identity, which they used to explain conflicts among peasant groups. As already noted by Robert Irwin, the division between Qays and Yaman had been important in Umayyad and early Abbasid Syria until the ninth century, but it is absent from the abundant narrative sources for Syria and Palestine in the Fatimid, crusader, and Ayyubid periods. The categories of Qays and Yaman only resurfaced five centuries later, in the early decades of the fourteenth century, in connection with feuding among villagers-turned-Arab, providing them with a "social map of whom it was appropriate to raid and feud with."[1]

The reemergence of the Qays and Yaman rivalry was linked to social groups called ʿashīr (sometimes *ʿushrān*), a term that came to designate the Arab villagers of Greater Syria at around the same time. The ʿashīr first appear in relation to the inhabitants of the high plateaus of Transjordan, but over the course of the fourteenth century they came to describe the rural communities of the hills of Palestine, the valleys around Damascus, and the villages of the Beqaa. City-dwelling observers viewed the ʿashīr as clan-based, armed, and engaged in constant infighting. The division into notional Qays and Yaman factions was considered one of their defining features; it represented a moral code of blood feuds, which for many outsiders represented a Jāhilī, pre-Islamic, or non-Islamic value system.

Narrative and administrative sources generally distinguished the ʿashīr of Greater Syria from the ʿurbān of the same regions, with the latter term reserved for the Arab auxiliary troops and provincial security. In fourteenth-century Syria, the ʿurbān units were led by the families of Banū Mahdī in the Balqa, Āl Mīrā in the Hawran, and the Āl Faḍl in the Syrian desert. The commanders of these ʿurbān tribal troops received iqṭāʿ in return for their military support and were very much part of the official structure of the state.[2] The ʿashīr, on the other hand, were not usually rewarded with state pensions or iqṭāʿ grants. Unlike the ʿurbān, they were the subjects of state control, not its officers.

The ʿashīr and the associated Qays and Yaman categories were characteristic of the countryside of Greater Syria and absent from sources regarding the Arabs of Egypt.[3] Jean-Claude Garcin used the Qays-Yaman rivalry to explain tribal conflicts in Upper Egypt, with a geographical division between Qays tribes (Banū Hilāl and Awlād al-Kanz) in the south and Yaman tribes (Juhayna, ʿArak, Baliyy) farther north. According to Garcin, the Mamluks generally allied themselves with the Qays groups against the Yaman.[4] It is important to note, however, that Qays and Yaman categories are never mentioned with regard to medieval Upper Egypt. The ʿashīr are also mentioned in relation to Greater Syria, including Palestine, but not in the Egyptian context.

This chapter examines the Qays and Yaman categories as political expressions of the Arab turn in Mamluk Syria. The first section follows the sudden proliferation of the term ʿashīr and of Qays and Yaman allegiances in legal and narrative sources of the fourteenth century, and a short-lived Mamluk attempt to enlist Syrian villagers into an auxiliary force called the *Jabaliyya*. The second section contrasts the ʿashīr peasantry with the ʿurbān, the auxiliary Arab troops of the Syrian desert since the beginning of the thirteenth century, led by a state official known as *Amir al-ʿArab*. The outbreak of the Black Death in the middle of the fourteenth century altered the balance of power in all these rural regions. The third section's focus is the salience of the Qays-Yaman coalitions during the major civil war of 791/1389 to 795/1394 between Sultan Barqūq and Minṭāsh, a conflict that stands out for its mass non-elite participation in and around Damascus. Subsequently, Arab leaders and clans in fifteenth-century Syria were able to gain control of the grain harvests and wrest some of the powers previously reserved for the Mamluk provincial governors, a process discussed in the fourth section. This increase in the power of Arab clans in the countryside of Syria and Palestine and the incorporation of leading families into provincial administration mirrored similar developments in fifteenth-century Egypt, which will be discussed in the following chapters.

"Blood Feuds of the Jāhiliyya"

Writing in the early fourteenth century, the Damascene jurist Ibn Taymiyya is our earliest Mamluk-era witness to the prevalence of the Qays and Yaman categories in the Syrian countryside. For Ibn Taymiyya, the Qays-Yaman rivalry in the surrounding rural society was a throwback to an age of Jāhiliyya, where Islamic laws and the authority of the state were set aside in favor of a culture of blood feuds and vain glory. Allegiance to Qays and Yaman was for Ibn Taymiyya a form of blind solidarity (*ʿaṣabiyya*) that goes against the values of Islam: "All those who profess *ʿaṣabiyya* to tribes (*qabāʾil*) or groups other than tribes, such as Qays, Yaman, Hilāl, Asad, and so on." Those who kill each other because of these allegiances, will all go to Hell, both the victim and murderer. Similarly, rallying for the cause of these groups, such as by calling "*yā li-Qays, yā li-Yaman, yā li-Hilāl, yā li-Asad*," is a Jāhilī practice.[5] Those who fight in the causes of Qays and Yaman are chasing worldly kingship and hollow desires.[6] In his writings, Ibn Taymiyya draws comparisons between the blind *ʿaṣabiyya* solidarity of Qays and Yaman and the *ʿaṣabiyya* of a legal school or a Sufi order. This comparison suggests that Ibn Taymiyya did not view Qays and Yaman as ethnic markers; professing allegiance to Qays and Yaman was an active and ideological choice.

Ibn Taymiyya's most extensive treatment of the topic is found in a legal response to a question about the Qays and Yaman *ʿashīra*—here in the singular, but referring to a clan-based society.[7] According to the question sent to him, ʿashīra clans engage in constant blood feuds, and they deceitfully prevent the authorities from ending the violence and bringing the culprits to justice. When any murder committed within the clan is brought to the attention of the state authorities, the ʿashīra send someone other than the murderer to confess to the murder. They also send a relative of the victim to give up any claim to blood money. This, according to the questioner, is the way the clan-based society of Qays and Yaman perpetuates the blood feud and avoids proper Islamic justice. Ibn Taymiyya is then asked whether the governor can stop this cycle of violence by imposing the blood money on the murderer's kinship group, for example, through an Islamic legal instrument of collective liability, the *qasāma*. Ibn Taymiyya responds that collective liability does not offer a solution to the question at hand, nor should governors resort to fines, which only cause further corruption (*fasād*). Instead, he suggests the governors should arrest those known for this behavior, deport them, or apply discretionary corporal punishment (*taʿzīr*).

In fact, we do know that Arab villagers brought their murder cases before the courts, as is shown in the Haram corpus from Mamluk Jerusalem. One document, also mentioned in chapter 2, records a settlement in which three Rabaʿī (i.e., of the Banū Rabīʿa) brothers from Dūrā claimed blood money from the murderers of a fourth brother. The perpetrators were identified as members of another Arab clan and residents of the nearby village of Idhnā. They admitted to the murder and agreed to pay compensation. The settlement was confirmed by the *qāḍī* of Hebron in 706/1306.[8] We do not know whether this blood-money settlement brought an end to bloodshed between the two neighboring villages; Ibn Taymiyya's contemporary discussion of blood feuds raises the possibility that this was a charade intended to avert intervention by the authorities.

In the chronicles, a steady stream of references to Qays and Yaman clans begins around the turn of the fourteenth century, focusing first on the agricultural plains south of Damascus. Following the Ilkhanid occupation in 700/1300, al-Maqrīzī reports that the leaders (*mashāyikh*) of Qays and Yaman were forced to return goods that they picked up from the soldiers and dignitaries who fled to Cairo. They were identified as both ʿashīr and ʿurbān; the context suggests that these Qays and Yaman groups lived south of Damascus, probably in the Hawran.[9] In Shawwāl 707/April 1308, fighting broke out between Qays and Yaman villagers near al-Suwaydāʾ, leading to one thousand fatalities. Ibn Kathīr reports that the Yaman were victorious and the Qaysīs were forced to flee to Damascus, where they arrived in a poor state. As a result, "the villages remained empty, and the fields abandoned (*wa-baqiyat al-qurā khāliya wa'l-zurūʿ sāʾiba*)."[10] A biographical entry for a Mamluk governor in southern Syria around the same period reports that the ʿashīr came to dominate over the state officials in these regions, and villages were deserted.[11]

By 1350, clashes between Qays and Yaman ʿashīr groups were reported around Karak. Al-Maqrīzī depicts these clashes in a manner reminiscent of Ibn Taymiyya's moralistic tone. In the anarchy that followed the outbreak of the plague, he says, "the ʿashīr and the Arabs of Karak" rose up in arms and blocked the roads. He identified these groups as Banū Rabīʿa and Banū Numayr, who went on to defeat the Mamluk governor of Karak, killing ten of his men. Al-Maqrīzī then explains to his readers that the ʿashīr of Syria were either Qays or Yaman, constantly fighting each other and causing many fatalities. Under normal circumstances the sultan was able to quell the cycles of feuds by sending gifts, but the authorities were too preoccupied with the plague to take notice.[12]

Factional fighting in the Hawran continued in the second half of the fourteenth century, with alignments also called Hilāl and Asad rather than Qays and Yaman. In 759/1358, a major battle between Banū Asad and Banū Hilāl took place in the village of ʿAqīl, leading to hundreds of casualties and the annihilation of the Banū Asad faction. The entire region of northern Hawran came to be known as Jabal Banu Hilāl.[13] In the same year, Ibn Qāḍī Shuhba reports fighting between two clans in the Hawran, one called Banū Humām and the other Banū Daraqa. This led to the murder of a villager from Zura', a man of means who held an iqṭā'.[14] Further infighting among the *'ushrān* of the Hawran took place in 791/1389, with the village of Zura' again a focal point for several killings.[15]

Communities of 'ashīr were also attested in Palestine and in the Beqaa throughout the fourteenth century. Al-Maqrīzī reports that the 'ashīr raided the lands of Hebron, Jerusalem, and Nablus in 750/1349–50, but they were eventually suppressed by the governor of Gaza.[16] Ibn Qāḍī Shuhba identifies the perpetrators of this unrest not as 'ashīr but as *a'rāb*, the common term for nomadic Arabs, and states that the Mamluk expeditionary force wrongfully took their women and children as slaves, as if they were infidels.[17] Al-'Umarī, writing in the 1340s, states that the hinterland of Gaza was inhabited by "sedentary people who are *'ushran*, and who have enmity toward each other. Were it not for the fear of the government, the fire of battle would not abate there."[18] A mutiny of the 'ashīr of Wādī al-Taym in the eastern Beqaa was suppressed in 745/1344–45, and they were accused of being Shi'ī heretics, possibly Nusayris.[19] Armed conflict among the 'ashīr of Wādī Baradā, the agricultural valley north of Damascus, is reported in Muḥarram 759/1357–58.[20]

In response to the rise of Qays-Yaman violence, the Mamluk authorities made a short-lived attempt to create auxiliary troops known as the *Jabaliyya*, which operated in the region of Karak in the middle of the fourteenth century. The composition of this force was linked to the Qays and Yaman identities of the local population, and its establishment coincided with the rise of Karak as an alternative seat of power for Mamluk sultans-in-waiting during the first half of the fourteenth century. According to al-'Umarī's administrative manual of the 1340s, *muqaddam al-Jabaliyya* was given the responsibility of reconciling the Qays and Yaman factions and bringing them over from the era of the Jāhiliyya into Islam.[21] A model appointment decree states that the *muqaddam* should bring to the role a familiarity with both factions, and the support he enjoyed among the people of the plains and the people of the hills. He should reconcile them to each other and settle their mutual claims and blood feuds, so that the two tribes (*qabīlatayn*) should become like the sons of the same father. He should forbid them the claims of the Jāhiliyya (*da'awā al-jāhiliyya*), and remind the two groups of the Prophetic age, when their ancestors, the *muhājirūn* and the *anṣār*, came together in holy war for the glory of Islam.

The Jabaliyya troops, commanded by their *muqaddam*, are mentioned in the 1340s as part of the forces defending Karak during successive sieges.[22] In 745/1344–45, a group of the Jabaliyya attacked al-Zabadānī, some thirty kilometers northwest of Damascus, and most of the inhabitants had to flee to the capital city.[23] In 750/1350, the governor of Damascus sent the *muqaddam* of the Jabaliyya to suppress the disturbances of Qays and Yaman ʿashīr and the Arabs of Karak, triggered by the shortages created by the outbreak of the Black Death.[24] Thus, the official Arab Jabaliyya troops were deployed against the ʿashīr—the Arab village clans of the same regions of Transjordan. The last reference to the Jabaliyya troops dates to 769/1367–68, when a group of Jabaliyya were accused of a series of crimes against prostitutes and other women in Damascus.[25]

One of the commanders of the Jabaliyya, Bāligh b. Yūsuf of the Ṭayy, is known to us from both documentary and narrative sources. An iqṭāʿ grant, which happened to survive on scrap paper reused by al-Maqrīzī, contains a decree in favor of Bāligh b. Yūsuf, who appears to serve as the *muqaddam* of the Jabaliyya in Karak.[26] Narrative sources report that he defended the besieged Sultan al-Nāṣir Aḥmad from forces sent by his brother al-Ṣāliḥ Ismaʿīl in 741/1342.[27] When he decided to switch allegiances, he received a large iqṭāʿ worth 450,000 dirhams as a reward and the honorific title of *zayn al-qabāʾil* (ornament of the tribes). Another *muqaddam* of the Jabaliyya mentioned by al-Maqrīzī is Aḥmad b. ʿAlī b. Ṣubḥ, a former irrigation official in Lower Egypt who was also known as al-Kurdī—suggesting that not all the Jabaliyya troops were Arab.[28] The eventual fate of the Jabaliyya and their commanders is unknown, and their official existence as a military unit is only attested for the 1340s and 1350s.

The ʿashīr become visible to us in regions where Arab village clans had already become pervasive in the previous century. Latin charters refer to a *beduini* class of landless cultivators in Transjordan and Palestine in the second half of the twelfth century (chapter 2). The Haram documentary corpus shows that Muslim-majority villages in the hinterland of Jerusalem were invariably inhabited by Arab clans in the first decade of the fourteenth century (chapter 4). Al-ʿUmarī's administrative manual and entries in biographical dictionaries show the proliferation of Arab village clans throughout the rural hinterland of Damascus, Transjordan, and the Palestinian highlands in the Ayyubid and early Mamluk periods (chapter 5). The villages occupied by the ʿashīr experienced a remarkable shift to handmade wares in the first half of the thirteenth century (chapter 6).

The eruptions of ʿashīr violence, from 1300 onward, manifested the military and political dimension of the same process. Unlike the Egyptian auxiliary ʿurbān recruited from the village clans of Ayyubid Fayyum, the Syrian ʿashīr emerged from within village communities, not remunerated by iqṭāʿ nor sent to fight in royal campaigns. While the Mamluk regime attempted to control the ʿashīr by recruiting the Jabaliyya rural corps in Transjordan, this was a response to an already established political system that was not directly dependent on the state. The ʿashīr fought not for a sultan, but for political goals defined by a rural logic of a Qays-Yaman dichotomy, through a culture of blood feud and autonomy, forming alliances that effectively channeled peasant mass mobilization.

The Auxiliary *ʿUrbān* of Transjordan and the Syrian Desert

The ʿashīr villagers of the of Transjordan and Syria existed alongside an official elite of Arab auxiliary troops, called ʿurbān by the Syrian chroniclers, whose leadership was based in the Syrian deserts to the east of the main agricultural lands. We have evidence for recruitment of ʿurbān troops in Zangid Syria during the twelfth century (see chapter 2), but the formalization of Arab auxiliary forces in the Syrian deserts took place under the Ayyubids, when Sultan al-ʿĀdil (r. 1200–18) first appointed a Syrian Amīr al-ʿArab. This state official was given military responsibility for the strategic buffer zone between Damascus-Homs-Hama in the west and the Euphrates in the east. Since 1260, recurrent Mongol invasions greatly increased the importance of Arab auxiliaries to the defense of Mamluk territories in Syria. This gave the Arab leaders of the Syrian desert room for leverage, occasionally switching their allegiances to the Ilkhanid Mongol rulers of Baghdad.[29] They reached the apogee of their power and wealth during the third reign of Sultan al-Nāṣir Muḥammad (1310–41), as reflected in the praise heaped on them by al-ʿUmarī in the 1340s (see chapter 5).

Since the inauguration of the office in the Ayyubid period, the Amīr al-ʿArab was always chosen from among the Āl Faḍl family, a transhumant, mobile group that operated across large areas and charged with protecting merchants and pilgrims as well as raising troops for royal campaigns. The Āl Faḍl claimed descent from Āl Jarrāḥ, the Arab clan that dominated Palestine in the eleventh century, showing the long-term legacy of that period of Arab domination, at least in terms of prestige. Al-ʿUmarī relates that their territory extended from Homs in the west to al-Raḥba on the Euphrates, and in the south from al-Washm to Basra. During the fourteenth century the Āl Faḍl were involved in campaigns near the Euphrates, in Tadmur, and in Aleppo. By the second half of the fourteenth century they established their headquarters in Salamiyya, to the east of Hama and Homs, which was given to them as iqṭāʿ.[30] They wintered in the Marj of Damascus although this led to conflicts with the local governor.[31] The fertile regions of Marj east of Damascus were claimed as the territory of the Āl ʿAlī, a clan of the Āl Faḍl, at least since the second half of the thirteenth century.[32] Ibn Khaldūn reports that once the Āl Faḍl managed to capture these high-quality pasture areas, they rarely traveled to the desert, remaining within the boundaries of the agricultural lands of Syria.[33]

The northern parts of the Syrian desert, bordering on Anatolia, were the lands of the Turcomans, whose amirs were similarly called up for royal campaigns.[34] Some Turcomans were pastoralists. In 780/1378–79, the Turcomans of Sīs in Cilicia reached an agreement with the Mamluk sultans about safeguarding the roads and providing *ʿidād* tax on their flocks.[35] The explicitly mobile lifestyle of the Turcomans is emphasized in the Syrian sources of the period. When attacked, the Turcomans defended themselves by surrounding themselves with their small and large cattle, to prevent the horses of their enemies from reaching them.[36] Ibn Ṣaṣrā witnessed "Turcomans and peasants" arrive in Damascus from the north with their flocks of large and small cattle, camels and tents, because of a draught that limited their grazing areas.[37]

The Syrian official ʿurbān were responsible for protecting the pilgrimage route from Damascus, responsibility which was divided between the Āl Faḍl of the Syrian desert, the Āl Mīrā of the Hawran and Banū Mahdī of the Balqa.[38] Each of these groups had official recognition and duties. During a siege of Karak in the 1340s, the amirs of Āl Faḍl and Āl Mīrā were given formal instructions to guard the roads leading to the region.[39] As we have seen, in the 1340s security in Karak in the Balqa region was handed over to the Jabaliyya corps. Leaders of the Banū Mahdī were repeatedly appointed as amirs throughout the Mamluk period.[40] As part of the local administration, Banū Mahdī were the official hosts of Sultan Barqūq when he visited Ḥisbān in the late fourteenth century.[41] Around that time, the Haram corpus also refers to an amir of the ʿurbān of Karak who came to the Jerusalem court to retrieve a lost camel identified by its brand marks.[42]

Thus, some of the official ʿurbān were based in sedentary communities. The Āl Mīrā territory was in the agricultural areas of the Hawran, from al-Zarqāʾ to the Jawlān (Golan). Only some members seasonally traveled south into the Hijaz.[43] The responsibilities of the amir of the Āl Mīrā, as laid out in an appointment decree of 1333, were central to the administration of the Hawran.[44] First, he was required to ensure that the Arabs associated with him stayed put in their territories (*manāzil*) and did not migrate from their lands. Second, he was to participate in the protection of Syria and form a metaphorical ditch around its expansive lands. Third, the amir was to get hold of high-quality horses, worthy of being presented to the sultan. Finally, the responsibility for administering the

Sharīʿa is repeated several times. That included making sure that marriages were performed properly and that inheritances were divided according to Islamic law. Overall, the amir of the Āl Mīrā appears to have held power over his people (or his territory) in the manner of a provincial governor.

By the middle of the fourteenth century, the frequent award of iqṭāʿ to ʿurbān leaders led to the establishment of a Syrian department dealing with sixty villages that had been given over to the Arabs.[45] Writing at around the same time, Tāj al-Dīn al-Subkī states that the amirs of the transhumant Arabs (*alladhīna yaẓʿanūna wa-yanzilūna*) were awarded generous revenues and iqṭāʿ grants so they do not harm the Muslims; when they are deprived of these grants, they resort to highway robbery.[46] The degree to which the leaders of the ʿurbān were dependent on official recognition comes across in an account by Bertrando de Mignanelli, an Italian resident of Damascus who established a friendship with Nuʿayr, Amīr al-ʿArab and leader of the Āl Faḍl in the final decades of the fourteenth century. Mignanelli recounts how Nuʿayr stopped him and his companions in an out-of-the-way part of the desert and that the two then struck a cordial relationship. Nuʿayr is here described in terms that could have come from the epic of ʿAntar: successful in battle despite his advanced age, short and handsome, and generous in his gifts. Mignanelli also talks affectionately about the bravery displayed by Nuʿayr's sons, with whom he became especially close.[47] In terms of the support of the Mamluk state, Mignanelli reports that Nuʿayr received fifty thousand ducats a year from the sultan in return for protecting desert travelers, specifically spice merchants.[48] Yet the sultan was also capable of depriving Nuʿayr of these privileges and awarding them to another member of the leading family. When that happened, Nuʿayr would go on rebellion and use the factionalism within the Mamluk elite to his favor. The peak of his power and intrigue came during the civil war between Sultan Barqūq and Minṭāsh, the governor of Damascus, a conflict that ravaged the Syrian countryside in the early 1390s.

The Qays-Yaman Civil War

The salience of Qays and Yaman allegiances as an organizing framework for political conflict in Syria became most evident in the 1390s, during the brutal civil war between Sultan Barqūq and the pretender amir Minṭāsh. This war was a culmination of the prolonged political and economic crisis that engulfed the sultanate in the second half of the fourteenth century, in the aftermath of the outbreak of the Black Death. It was also unprecedented in terms of the heavy dependence of both sides on non-elite urban and rural groups, blurring the lines between the Mamluk military elite and the civilian population.[49] The rural groups involved in the conflict included ʿurbān units such as Āl Faḍl and Āl Mīrā, who mostly sided with Minṭāsh, as well as organized groups of ʿashīr peasants led by their own *muqaddam* officers.[50] The conflict between the two claimants to the throne of the sultanate came to be drawn along Qays and Yaman lines, with Sultan Barqūq heading the Qays faction and his opponent Minṭāsh allied with the Yaman faction. It is remarkable that in this moment of political breakdown, the group identities that emerged from within the countryside imposed themselves on the Mamluk political elites.

The civil war began in 791/1388, when Barqūq emerged from a yearlong imprisonment in the castle of Karak.[51] Barqūq recovered the throne in 792/1390, but the amir Minṭāsh, whose real name was Timurbughā al-Ashrafī, held out in Damascus as the head of an anti-Barqūq coalition. In the countryside, Minṭāsh's chief allies were the major amirs of the ʿurbān troops of the Syrian desert and the Hawran: Nuʿayr, the amir of the Āl Faḍl, who was also Minṭāsh's father-in-law, and ʿAnqā, the amir of the Āl Mīrā.[52] Barqūq, for his part, set out to Karak to recruit an Arab army made up of rural armed groups loyal to him. His troops from among the ʿurbān and the peasants (fallāḥūn) tried to take hold of the grain harvest of the Balqa, and the sultan had to restore order.[53] As he pushed north toward Damascus, he received obeisance from the *ʿashrānāt* (plural form of *ʿushrān*), the ʿurbān, and the Turcomans of Adhriʿāt.[54] The ʿashīr and the ʿurbān in his army then looted the Ghuta fertile region surrounding Damascus.[55]

The chronicle of Ibn Ṣaṣrā, an otherwise unknown Damascene scholar who was besieged in the city loyal to Minṭāsh, provides a well-informed eye-witness account.[56] According to Ibn Ṣaṣrā, the people of Damascus viewed Barqūq's forces with contempt because those forces consisted only of peasants and Arabs; they were not considered to be a match to the regular Mamluk army based in Damascus.[57] The governor of the city offered the commoners a reward of a gold coin for anyone capturing a member of the ʿashīr who joined Barqūq.[58] When the suburb of al-Ṣāliḥiyya was abandoned by Minṭāsh's supporters, it was looted by ʿashīr from the village of Talfītā, some twenty kilometers north of Damascus.[59] The rural nature of Barqūq's army is confirmed by Mignanelli. He reports that Barqūq "gathered together the peasantry" and gave "his peasants" their order for battle.[60] Minṭāsh sent a raiding force to the village of Baʿqūbā. There, his troops rounded up forty peasants who were hiding in a cave with much booty that they had looted, and Minṭāsh ordered their mass execution.[61] Minṭāsh was supported by the official ʿurbān, and Ibn Ṣaṣrā reports parades of Arab troops inside the besieged city, often commenting on the spectacle. The amir of the Ḥāritha Arabs presented himself with one thousand iron-clad riders, their appearance resembling that of "the jinn."[62] The amir 'Anqā' also arrived with one thousand riders.[63] In a battle near Homs, 'Anqā's Arabs fought like devils (*shayāṭīn*) and emerged victorious.[64]

The following two years saw the agricultural areas west of Damascus drawn into a bloody cycle of fighting between armed groups of 'ashīr, almost certainly peasants, sponsored by opposing elements of the Mamluk regime. Barqūq recruited 'ashīr aligned with Qays in the Beqaa, while the villagers of al-Zabadānī in the Wādī Baradā region north of Damascus identified as Yaman and supported Minṭāsh.[65] Minṭāsh's forces also included 'ashīr villagers from the agricultural valley of Wādī al-Taym west of Damascus. They paraded in the city with their swords drawn out and attracted local crowds with their "jinn-like" entrance to the city.[66] As the violence escalated, the warring camps translated their conflict into the categories of Qays and Yaman. Ibn Ṣaṣrā notes that during an early lull in the fighting, there was one day in which "no one talked anymore of Barqūq or Minṭāsh, of Qays or of Yaman."[67]

The 'ashīr were involved in raids on opposition villages and in attempts to control the water supply to Damascus. The diversion of water away from the city was the responsibility of a Qays group led by a *muqaddam* called Ibn al-Jāmūs (Son of the Water Buffalo), who was active in Wādī Baradā and the suburb of al-Mizza. Minṭāsh's army relieved the city by taking Ibn al-Jāmūs's home village of Ya'fūr, some twenty kilometers west of Damascus.[68] The Qays of the Beqaa, led by a *muqaddam* called Ibn al-Ḥanash, attacked the suburb village of Kafrsūsya, burned the mosque, and caused the flight of the villagers.[69] The neighboring 'ashīr of al-Zabadānī, led by a certain Ibn Hilāl al-Dawla, sided with Minṭāsh. Ibn Hilāl al-Dawla was *muqaddam* of the Yaman; according to Ibn Qāḍī Shuhba, he was obliged to fight against Barqūq and his Qays allies by virtue of his Yamanī affiliation. When the civil war ended with Barqūq's victory, Ibn Hilāl al-Dawla returned to his rural region (*bilād*) and there traveled from village to village until he was caught in the Beqaa and executed.[70]

The Beqaa was the site of particularly heavy fighting, as Ibn al-Ḥanash took control of the regional capital Baalbek on Barqūq's behalf, supported by the Mamluk commander of the local citadel. A campaign of looting and rape followed against a resistant city population.[71] Ibn al-Ḥanash and his 'ashīr held out in Baalbek for a few months but were then overwhelmed by the 'ashīr of Ibn Hilāl al-Dawla of al-Zabadānī. Ibn Ṣaṣrā reports that more than a thousand peasants (fallāḥīn) were killed, and their swords and shields were taken.[72] Ibn al-Ḥanash himself was captured and subjected to a gruesome parade in Damascus, along with over one hundred of his Qaysī followers. According to one account by Ibn Ṣaṣrā, the parade ended up in the public square of Taḥta al-Qalʿa, where Ibn al-Ḥanash and 120 of his followers were quartered, their bodies hanged from the wall of Yalbughā's Mosque.[73]

In a variant version also reported by Ibn Ṣaṣrā, Ibn al-Ḥanash and the Beqaa Qays were given over to the Yaman forces of Ibn Hilāl al-Dawla. The brutal mass execution that followed shocked Ibn Ṣaṣrā, who regarded it as the manifestation of a godless blood-feud culture:

> What do you say about someone who passes judgment (*yataḥakkam*) over his enemy without having a religion to restrain him? For they have a blood-feud claim (*tha'r*) over them. So the Yaman stripped the Qays of their clothes and their swords, and surrounded them with swords, and started killing them off one by one, naked as they were, and their hearts were not softened—may God curse them, for they are so loathsome, and ignorant, and with little religion. The public square was filled with bodies, and the Yaman then carried the corpses and threw them over to Nahr al-Khandaq.[74]

Ibn Ṣaṣrā, like Ibn Taymiyya earlier in the fourteenth century, viewed the Qays-Yaman rivalry as an expression of deeply un-Islamic values. These groups of armed villagers adopted a blood-feud culture, perceived as harking back to the days of the Jāhiliyya and opposed to the scholarly and urban version of Islam.

Barqūq and Minṭāsh not only sponsored and exploited Qays and Yaman allegiances, they also took an interest in attaching themselves to Arab lineages. Minṭāsh married a daughter of Nuʿayr, the leader of the Āl Faḍl, although this marriage alliance didn't prevent Nuʿayr from betraying his son-in-law in 795/1393 and handing him over for execution.[75] As for Barqūq, Ibn Khaldūn mentions that he and other Circassians claimed lineage from the Arab Banū Ghassān. According to Ibn Khaldūn, a migration of Banū Ghassān to the lands of the Circassians at the time of the Arab Conquests makes this claim unlikely but still legitimate.[76] This note by Ibn Khaldūn anticipates attempts by fifteenth-century Circassian sultans to claim for themselves a noble Arab genealogy.[77]

Ultimately, the Qays villagers ended up on the winning side of the civil war, proving victorious over the coalition of ʿurbān troops who were the mainstay of Minṭāsh's Yamanī coalition. The leaders of Āl Faḍl and Āl Mīrā, who sided with Minṭāsh through the war, eventually had to transfer their allegiance to Barqūq. As Mignanelli attests, the ʿashīr were enjoying the fruits of their success: "Barqūq spent some time distributing the spoils of victory. He gave everything to the peasants, praised them for being faithful, and celebrated with them as with his own family. The peasants rejoiced in their master's familiarity, but especially in their spoils."[78]

The Fifteenth Century: Rebellion and Co-optation

The civil war between Sultan Barqūq and the pretender Minṭāsh highlighted Qays and Yaman as powerful categories of mass peasant mobilization in the Hawran, the Beqaa, and the hinterland of Damascus. In the decades that followed and throughout the fifteenth century, the Qays and Yaman labels continued to hold political meaning, with Yaman an umbrella name for loyalist urbanites and villagers, while those opposed to the regime appear to rally under the banner of Qays. More importantly, however, the salience of the Qays-Yaman rivalry was overshadowed by local revolts against tax collection and its officials, sometimes spilling over into the provincial towns. Over the fifteenth century, occasional attempts by local governors and iqṭāʿ holders to check the power of the clans proved ineffective. By the end of the Mamluk period, as evidenced also in the abundant European pilgrimage accounts from this period, a breakdown of law and order in the Palestinian and Syrian countryside led to power drifting away from the provincial governors toward the headmen of the village clans and the *muqaddams* of Arab troops.

The end of the civil war in the early 1390s led to a realignment of the Qays-Yaman rivalry. In Transjordan, Qays were those opposed to the local representatives of the regime, while the loyalists assumed a Yamanī identity. In the provincial capital of Karak, a Qays group led by the local *qāḍī* and supported by the surrounding *ʿushrān* fought against Yamanīs led by the Mamluk governor in 802/1399. The skirmishes ended with six fatalities, dozens of wounded, and the execution of the *qāḍī* and a few of his associates.[79] When a new governor tried to align himself with the Qays faction, he was locked out of the town by the Yamanīs.[80] Karak was the "ultimate symbol of Jordanian tribalism,"[81] and Qays-Yaman divisions in the city were an extension of the Arab identities of the surrounding village clans.

Rural groups loyal to the state were considered Yamanī. This is spelled out in an appointment decree for the amir of the Zabīd Arabs, a group that inhabited villages in the Hawran. The decree is cited by al-Qalqashandī and probably dates to the turn of the fifteenth century.[82] The decree extols the virtue of the Syrian Zabīd and idealizes their eternal struggle against Qays: "They are Yamanīs through and through; they drench in blood the red flag [of Qays]; their riders tighten the shackles (*kariba*) over Maʿdīkarib [an ancestor of the Qays]." The Zabīd are then told to protect the Hawran and the Ghuta of Damascus "like doves on tree branches." The *muqaddam* of the Zabīd is to exert his authority over both the mobile and sedentary elements of his people, those who live in the desert and those who live "behind fences."[83] The emphasis on Yaman identity as part of loyalty to the Mamluk court is not found in earlier appointment decrees and shows official celebration of the Qays-Yaman feud culture. This also marked a promotion in the status of the Zabīd. The fourteenth-century bureaucrats al-ʿUmarī and Ibn Nāẓir al-Jaysh were rather disparaging, describing the Zabīd Arabs of the Hawran and the Ghuta as villagers of unconfirmed lineage.[84]

By the end of the fourteenth century, Mamluk provincial officials and iqṭāʿ holders had limited ability to impose law and order in the Syrian and Palestinian countryside. A record of a faltering murder inquiry in the Haram corpus of the 1390s has villagers from Quṣūr repeatedly complaining to the governor of Jerusalem about the murder of a local leader or a headman, but nothing was done to apprehend the perpetrators. After six months the Quṣūr villagers took matters into their own hands and killed two men from a neighboring village.[85] The impression is that late-fourteenth-century Mamluk provincial administrators were not able to stop blood feuds. Ibn Ṣaṣrā has a lively anecdote about a Mamluk officer called Iyās al-Jarkasī (d. 796/1394), who was unwilling to uphold law and justice in the village he held as iqṭāʿ. When brothers of a murder victim brought the perpetrator before his court (*ḥukūma*), Iyās refused to execute him, saying that he had already lost one peasant, and it was not his intention to lose another one. Instead, he ordered the beating and imprisonment of the victim's family.[86] The context here is that of a diminished peasantry in the wake of the Black Death. In the second half of the fourteenth century, iqṭāʿ holders in the Syrian countryside attempted to force absconding villagers to return to their lands.[87]

Infighting among the village clans of Syria continued throughout the fifteenth century, with or without references to Qays and Yaman. In the 1410s, a group of *ʿushrān* recruited by the governor of Safed were involved in a brutal attack on another group of *ʿushrān* during a wedding ceremony. Both groups are described by Ibn Ḥijjī as Shiʿī, possibly Druze, and the wedding was spread over several days "as is their custom."[88] Another example of infighting comes from the abovementioned autobiography of Burhān al-Dīn al-Biqāʿī from Khirbat Rūḥā in the Beqaa, whose father and other members of his family were murdered in a raid from another village in 821/1418. The Qays-Yaman allegiances continued to provide a framework of armed conflict and competition throughout the remainder of the Mamluk period. Ibn Ṭūlūn, writing at the end of the fifteenth century, ascribes fighting in Damascus and its environs to Jāhilī claims of Qays and Yaman (*bi- sabab Qays wa-Yaman daʿwā jāhiliyya*).[89]

At the same time, much of the Arab violence came to be directed against the state and the collection of agricultural taxes. In 795/1392–93, in the immediate aftermath of the Barqūq-Minṭāsh conflict, the Arabs of the agricultural regions south of Damascus hampered the collection of the grain revenues. The governor of Damascus had to camp in the steppe (*birr*) in order to secure the harvest, and Ibn Ṣaṣrā blamed the Arabs for causing the peasants to flee their villages.[90] With Damascus occupied by Tamerlane in 803/1400–1, the harvest of the villages in the city's hinterland was taken over by people Ibn Ḥijjī identified as nomads (*aʿrāb*). In the Hawran, the amirs of the Āl Mīrā managed to "divide the land," that is, to collect the grain revenues. Mamluk amirs were sent to the Balqa, Hawran, Nablus in Palestine, and the Jordan Valley to deter the Arabs from seizing the harvests. The governor of Damascus went out to the Marj plains east of the city.[91] The following year, a Mamluk expeditionary force raided the residences of Āl Mīrā in al-Suwaydāʾ and confiscated several thousand camels.[92] Similarly, the amir of the Ḥāritha Arabs collected the grain revenues in the region of Safed. Bloody clashes with the local governor led to the deaths of some dozen Mamluk soldiers. The sultan appeased the Ḥāritha amir with a robe of honor then captured him by deceit the following year.[93] Also in 804/1401–2, the governor of Damascus campaigned against a band of highway robbers composed of both Arabs (*ʿarab, aʿrāb*) and peasants.[94] Several local *kāshifs*—a new type of officer responsible for enforcing agricultural tax collection—were killed in clashes with Arab groups in Jabal Banī Hilāl in the Hawran, in ʿAjlūn in the Balqa, and in Nablus between 795/1392–93 and 804/1401–2.[95] Fear of Arab control over the harvest is also attested in an undated edict of the period, which prohibits ʿurbān from entering Syrian villages (*bilād*) until the completion of the harvest (*ilā an yushāl al-zarʿ ʿalā al-ʿāda*). The order is addressed to all ranks of the ʿurbān, whether senior or junior, noble or lowly, on pain of severe albeit unspecified punishments.[96]

The military power of armed Arab groups in fifteenth-century Palestine and Syria is repeatedly attested in literary sources of the period. In 842/1439, hundreds of rural ʿashīr who arrived in Damascus to support the royal armies against a local rebellion were massacred by a city mob who accused them of being Shiʿa.[97] In Hebron, a Dārī faction—i.e., those who claimed descent from Tamīm al-Dārī—enlisted the support of ʿashīr clansmen from the surrounding area, who then entered the town and looted it.[98] A few years later the Arab ʿashīr of Banū Zayd attacked Jerusalem as retaliation for the killing of members of their group by the governor.[99] Late-fifteenth-century examples of Arab power in the Palestinian countryside abound in the pilgrimage literature. Felix Fabri, twice stopped for toll payments on the short trip from Bethlehem to Jerusalem, quotes the Arabs as saying that "they are the lords of the wilderness, and of all the places which are not enclosed by walls, covered by roofs, or fenced by ditches, and so forth."[100] Therefore "they take no heed of safe-conducts, but extort toll from all those who pass through the desert."[101] He ends his account by comparing them to Schwabian nobles who would not admit any townsmen to their tournaments.[102]

Rural Arab elites amassed power, resisted tax collection, and often ended up being co-opted into provincial administration. A detailed example comes from ʿAjlūn, where in 807/1404 the governor attempted to impose his authority over the clan of Banū al-Ghazāwī (or al-Maghrāwī). This clan, we are told, became the strongmen (*jabābira*) of the region. They were supported by an iqṭāʿ that dated back to the end of the Barqūq-Minṭāsh war. When the governor of Damascus arrived in their territory (*diyār*), the Banū al-Ghazāwī made themselves absent, but the governor punished them by destroying their houses (*dūr*) and taking over livestock and grains. He then forced "each section (*ṭāʾifa*) of Arabs" to contribute a quota of camels for the transport of the confiscated grains to the government warehouses in al-Adhriʿāt (present-day Daraa).[103] But this suppression was quickly followed by reconciliation and promises of safe conduct. Within a few years, the Banū al-Ghazāwī came to receive the visiting sultan in the town of Buṣrā; they are described as ʿurbān and *ʿushrān*.[104]

The Ghazāwīs were now the de facto power in this region of the Hawran, and it was in their interest to subdue local revolts. In 816/1413, a minor uprising broke out in ʿAjlūn, led by a certain Ibn Thaqāla claiming lineage from the Rabīʿa. Ibn Thaqāla was a Damascene jurist who traveled to the countryside of ʿAjlūn and claimed that he was the Sufyānī, a reference to Umayyad messianism. He established a base in the village of Jaydūr, assigned iqṭāʿ grants, and took for himself a royal title. Rural people, including "Arabs, Turcoman, and ʿashīr" rallied to his support, and he was able to enter the town of ʿAjlūn at the head of an army of several hundred men. His first announcement was that the harvests of the current year will be tax-free, and those of the next year will only be subject to the tithe, not the *kharāj* land tax. But Ibn Thaqāla was quickly defeated by Ghānim al-Ghazāwī, apparently the leader of the Ghazāwī clan, who killed him in the Friday Mosque of ʿAjlūn and handed over his main supporters to the Mamluk governor in Safed. As noted by Jo van Steenbergen, this minor uprising was subdued locally, without intervention from the representatives of the imperial center.[105] This was symptomatic of the weakening of the power of the Mamluk provincial governors in the Syrian countryside all through the fifteenth century.

The fifteenth century saw increasing co-optation of leading Arab families and armed peasants into Syrian provincial administration. Al-Qalqashandī's manual, completed in the 1410s, attests to official acceptance of semiautonomous Arab governors. In his account, the administration of the Syrian countryside is divided into areas ruled by local governors and those handed over to Arab officers ('urbān). Such division is not found in earlier administrative sources.[106] As an example, al-Qalqashandī notes that the governorship of Shayzar was abolished in the aftermath of the Barqūq-Minṭāsh war and was now subject to a *muqaddam* from among the 'urbān.[107] The Syrian army that was camped in Safed in 822/1419–20 included the *muqaddam* of the Ḥāritha Arabs as well as 'ashīr and Turcomans led by the "shaykh" of the mountains of Nablus.[108] Recruitment of 'ashīr from the mountains of Jerusalem is also reported.[109] Descendants of Ibn al-Ḥanash, the Qaysī leader in the Barqūq-Minṭāsh war, continued to dominate the Beqaa region during the fifteenth century. By the early sixteenth century, Arab Ḥanash amirs were both *muqaddams* of the Beqaa and governors of the coastal town of Sidon.[110]

Fifteenth-century sources also allow us to view peasants devising their own mechanisms to settle their disagreements about the allocation of water resources, perhaps because of the retreat of state officials. The chronicler Ibn Ḥijjī reports how he acted as arbiter in a dispute about the water quota between two villages in the region of al-Mizza, on the western outskirts of Damascus. In the event, he found that the water divisors were tampered with and fixed them in an equitable manner. He was accompanied by the official collective leader of the Arabs in Damascus, *naqīb al-ashrāf*, as well as by a Mamluk bailiff, indicating some official support.[111] Another Damascene notary was unofficially known as the *qāḍī* of the peasants, because they always consulted him on matters of cultivation.[112] The preacher of the Kafrsūsya agricultural suburb of Damascus, a personal acquaintance of Ibn Ḥijjī, was the village authority regarding the internal division of water.[113]

Documentary and literary evidence attests that Palestinian and Syrian villages continued to be collectively led by groups of headmen. A couple of documents from the Mamluk court of Jerusalem, dating to the 1390s, are addressed to the headmen (*ru'asā'*) of the village of Quṣūr (present-day Qusra), inquiring about unpaid taxes.[114] In 803/1400–1, Tamerlane collected taxation from village headmen in the Ghuta of Damascus.[115] In 830/1426, the taxes of the village of Jisreen in the hinterland of Damascus were collectively levied on the clan of the Banū Ḥāfiẓ.[116] An edict dated 1447, preserved in the Mt. Sion Monastery in Jerusalem, is addressed to the headmen and shaykhs of the village of Bethlehem, and it orders them to prevent the peasants (fallāḥīn) from harassing the monks.[117] Pilgrimage narratives of the fifteenth century also acknowledged that the Arabs they met were often part of the sedentary peasantry. In 1432, Bertrandon de La Brocquière states that the fertile Beqaa is peopled by Arabs, and so are the low hills above the coastal route from Tyre to Acre, and in the region between Homs to Hama.[118] In 1470, Jenin was inhabited by Arabs, led by a certain Tarabe. Adorno also mentions a derelict church there, and encampments of tent-dwelling Arabs who subsist on raid and extortion.[119] He adds that "one should not think that all the Arabs move from one place to another and don't have a fixed habitation."[120]

Overall, the fifteenth century saw increasing Arab control in the Syrian countryside, with Mamluk governors lacking either the resources or the will to impose their authority. This process was described in the middle of the fifteenth century by the Egyptian Muḥammad b. Muḥammad al-Asadī in his treatise calling for reform of provincial administration.[121] The main focus of his *al-Taysīr wa'l-i'tibār wa'l-taḥrīr wa'l-ikhtibār* was the decline of Egyptian agriculture, on which more will be said in chapter 10. But al-Asadī also devotes a short section to the deterioration the Syrian countryside and to the "spread of enmity and fighting between Qays and Yaman."[122] Al-Asadī explains that the maltreatment and oppression of the peasantry (fallāḥīn) and the lack of response to their concerns led many tax-paying cultivators to rebel, disobey, and to flee from their lands. These lands and villages have been taken over by 'urbān and *'ushrān*, followed by bloodshed, looting, and internal strife between the tribes (*qabā'il*, *'ashā'ir*). Many villages were deserted, while power has been given to the commanders (*muqaddams*) of the peasants and the headmen (*ru'asā'*) of the *'ushrān*. They receive official appointments (*tashārīf*) from the amirs and the sultans, and they have supporters, horses, iqṭā', and clerks (*dīwān*) in the village (*balad*) or region under their control. They profess obedience to the sultan but inwardly harbor disobedience and rebellion, extract money by injustice and oppression, and use this money to bribe state officials. Thus, according to al-Asadī, official neglect had led to the spread of tribal blood-feud culture and to the rise of local elites of 'urbān and *'ushrān*, *muqaddams* and headmen, who are supported by imperial resources but are inherently disloyal to the court. Power in the countryside now belonged to them.

Qays and Yaman Reborn

What did Qays and Yaman categories signify for Syrian villagers? Since the first reference by Ibn Taymiyya early in the fourteenth century, the sources underscore the Qays and Yaman rivalry as the grammar of violent competition and blood feud. Qays and Yaman did not reflect real ethnic groups—they probably never did, even in the Umayyad period.[123] During the fourteenth century, the violence was primarily directed at other peasant communities. The competition between Qays and Yaman peasant factions in late medieval Syria was probably over land, water, or other resources; the reasons are not specified, obliquely blamed on an atavistic desire for vengeance. Mamluk elites were aware of the power of Qays-Yaman alliances and attempted to channel these vehicles of political mobilization for their own benefit. That included a short-term experiment with Jabaliyya troops of rural Arabs to suppress Qays-Yaman disturbances among the ʿashīr of Transjordan, active in the 1340s and 1350s. Qays and Yaman coalitions were then employed against each other during the Barqūq-Minṭāsh conflict of the 1390s, a veritable civil war where the Qays coalesced around Barqūq and the Yaman supported Minṭāsh. Later on, an appointment decree hails the amir of the Zabīd clan as a ruthless leader of Yaman.

The armed villagers of the Beqaa, Transjordan, and Palestine came to be known as ʿashīr or *ʿushrān*, a term that designated the unofficial power of clan solidarity. The ʿashīr are most visible to us in villages in the Hawran and the Balqa during a period that coincided with the growing importance of Karak as a focal point of fourteenth-century Mamluk politics, when the town became a refuge for out-of-favor claimants to the throne.[124] In the context of Syria and Transjordan, the ʿashīr were distinct from official ʿurbān auxiliary forces, especially the Āl Faḍl of the Syrian desert but also the Āl Mīrā of the Hawran and Banū Mahdī of the Balqa. The ʿurbān of the Syrian desert received royal support since the beginning of the thirteenth century, when the office of the "Amir of the Arabs" was first established under the Ayyubids. They then played a pivotal role during the drawn-out Mamluk-Mongol wars, up until the middle of the fourteenth century. The official ʿurbān were part of the pro-Minṭāsh Yaman coalition that also included segments of the ʿashīr peasantry; the pro-Barqūq coalition was primarily composed of peasants.

The salience of the Qays-Yaman rivalry gave way over the course of the fifteenth century to armed resistance to the collection of taxes and the co-optation of rural elites into provincial administration. As the power of Mamluk provincial governors waned in the Syrian and Palestinian countryside during the fifteenth century, responsibility for law and order, as well as resolving water and land disputes, was taken up by dominant clans and families. Emboldened by the retreat of the state, ʿashīr villagers occasionally overtook cities like Hebron and Jerusalem, and the leaders of tribal confederacies came to hold important roles in provincial administration. As we shall see in the following chapters, the rise of rural

Arab elites and their co-optation in provincial administration was even more marked in fifteenth-century Egypt, part of a wider weakening of sultanic control over the countryside.

The Qays and Yaman alignments emerged as the Syrian countryside was becoming Arab, and as a result as of the proliferation of village clans. Qays-Yaman rivalries allowed one village clan to identify the inhabitants of another village as their mortal enemies, as well as to establish fictive genealogical links with their allies from further afield. Such factionalism remained a common feature of the Ottoman Middle East, as Qays-Yaman feuds flared up in Syria, Lebanon, and Palestine for centuries to come, up until the modern period.[125] The use of these categories by non-Arab Kurdish clans clearly shows the functional deployment of Qays and Yaman as notional labels for rural coalitions. Division into twin opposing branches in Kurdish society is well attested in historical and ethnographic sources; the Qays and Yaman labels are sometimes replaced by references to "left and right" confederacies.[126] It was not ancestry that determined whether you were Qays or Yaman, but rather your position in the network of political alliances and rivalries.

The Qays-Yaman dichotomy and the feud were themselves expressions of identity. For example, Ibn Khaldūn reported that the Arab poetry of the Hawran was called either Qaysī or *badawī*, a typical bundling of literary motifs, fictive tribal names, and cultural identities.[127] The Qays and Yaman alignments evoked an Arabian pre-Islamic past, as remembered through the cycles of the popular Arab epics of ʿAntar and of Dhāt al-Himma. It is no wonder that Damascene scholars like Ibn Taymiyya and Ibn Ṣaṣrā viewed Qays and Yaman allegiances as a throwback to the time of the Jāhiliyya. To a degree, it didn't matter so much whether you were Qays or Yaman; taking part in this rivalry was performance of an Arab identity that harked back to the origins of Islam.

This chapter examined the political mobilization of Arab village clans in Mamluk Greater Syria in the fourteenth and fifteenth centuries. Following the available sources, the emphasis has been on the emergence of the ʿashīr armed peasantry and their Qays-Yaman feud culture. The next two chapters examine the somewhat different trajectory of the mass mobilization of Arab and Berber village clans in Mamluk Egypt, from 1250 to the end of the fifteenth century. If in Mamluk Syria the resistance of the Syrian Arab villagers to tax collection was mostly localized and fractured, Mamluk Egypt was a scene of recurrent and often coordinated mass rural revolts. The next chapter will look at the major Arab uprisings in Upper Egypt during the first Mamluk century, from 1250 to 1350, and their unprecedented brutal repression by the Mamluk regime and its iqṭāʿ-holding military officers. Chapter 10 will then take up the decline of the iqṭāʿ regime since the outbreak of the Black Death in the middle of the fourteenth century. This final chapter will show how leading Arab and Berber families were co-opted into the administration of Egyptian provinces over the course of the fifteenth century, mirroring the fifteenth-century incorporation of Arab clans into the administration of Syria and Palestine.

9

The Great Arab Rebellions, 1250–1350

BETWEEN 1250 AND 1350, Upper Egypt was the focus of a series of armed uprisings by Arab rural groups against the Mamluk regime, presenting the Mamluk sultans with their most persistent domestic challenge. The first major Arab revolt, led by the Sharīf Ḥiṣn al-Dīn Ibn Thaʿlab, was directed against the Turkish sultan al-Muʿizz Aybak (r. 648–55/1250–57). This rebellion was based in Upper Egypt but may have been coordinated with another Arab uprising in the western delta. The suppression of Ḥiṣn al-Dīn's rebellion was followed by smaller-scale conflicts, peaking in a major outburst of violence circa 1300, when government granaries were targeted and tax collection disrupted. The largest Arab rebellion of the Mamluk period followed in the aftermath of the first outbreak of the plague, led by an Upper Egyptian Arab leader called al-Aḥdab. Although al-Aḥdab's rebellion was quelled in 1354, its leader was subsequently co-opted by the Mamluk state as a regional tax collector, ushering in a new stage in the relationship between the Mamluk regime and the elites of the Arab clans of the Egyptian countryside. This was the end of the major Arab rebellions in Upper Egypt—not because the Mamluks won, but rather because they gave in to the demands of the leading Arab families.

Modern historians have offered contrasting interpretations of these revolts. In an article published in 1934, A. N. Poliak argued that they should be seen as broad-based agrarian revolts, representing a coalition of "Bedouin" and non-Bedouin cultivators. He based his argument on the repeated targeting of the land tax and the explicit involvement of settled peasantry. In his general history of the Mamluk era published in Arabic in 1965, Saʿīd ʿAbd al-Fattāḥ ʿĀshūr similarly argued that the main causes of these revolts were fiscal and economic. This Marxist-inspired interpretation was subsequently played down in later scholarship. In an influential article published in 1978, Jean-Claude Garcin viewed peasant participation in the uprisings as opportunistic and short-lived. According to Garcin, the peasants were unable to act on their own against a repressive Mamluk state and so they supported Bedouin rebellions against a common enemy. In his view, the integration of the Arab leadership into Mamluk provincial administration from the second half of the fourteenth century signaled the end of any possible alliance between Bedouin and *fallāḥūn*.[1]

As the previous chapters of this book have demonstrated, Arab village clans proliferated in Ayyubid and Mamluk Egypt, including in Upper Egypt. Consequently, this chapter will argue that the armed Arab rebellions represented broad sections of the Upper Egyptian peasantry and that Arab identities were used for mass mobilization against the state. We have seen that the notional categories of Qays and Yaman divided the Syrian peasantry and legitimized blood feuds and internal divisions. While infighting among the Egyptian peasantry is also recorded, the Qays and Yaman coalitions are not attested. The emphasis of our available sources—almost entirely narrative—is not on the culture of feuds but on Arab identity and mass mobilization. In Mamluk Egypt, from 1250–1350, ideologies of Arabness were used to unite much of the Upper Egyptian peasantry in armed struggle against the Mamluk provincial governors, the iqṭāʿ holders, and their local agents of taxation.

This overarching argument does not diminish from the individual contexts of each of the three major uprisings. The leader of first rebellion, Ḥiṣn al-Dīn Ibn Thaʿlab, was a prominent member of the ʿurbān auxiliary troops and a grandson of a wealthy and influential Ayyubid state official, with a power base in Dayrūṭ in Upper Egypt. The second major uprising, in 1301, was distinctly leaderless and has much in common with the spontaneous *jacquerie* peasant revolt of fourteenth-century France.[2] The third and largest rebellion, from 1349 to 1354, was led by the previously unknown ʿArak clan and targeted the state-affiliated ʿurbān as much as it did government officials. It seems that the leader of this uprising attempted to establish himself as an intermediary between the peasantry and the iqṭāʿ holders. His success led to the formalization of this intermediary role of the elites of the Arab clans and the eventual incorporation of leading Arab families as semi-autonomous provincial governors.

A second argument of this chapter concerns the policies of the Mamluk sultans vis-à-vis the Arab clans in this first century of Mamluk rule in Egypt. In response to the challenge posed by the Ibn Thaʿlab uprising immediately following their ascent to power, the Mamluk sultans consistently strove to disarm the Egyptian peasantry and separate them from their horses to limit the power of the provincial ʿurbān. Royal edicts instructed provincial governors to prevent Arabs and peasants—the two groups were effectively interchangeable—from purchasing or carrying arms, and biographies of individual Mamluk officials demonstrate the brutal treatment they dished out to the headmen and leaders of the Arab clans. This policy met with only limited success and was discontinued after the rebellion of al-Aḥdab. While the leading families of the ʿurbān were severely weakened, the Mamluk authorities were always in need of the collaboration of rural elites, a need that became acute in the aftermath of the plague and the depopulation of the countryside.

The Uprising of the Sharīf Ḥiṣn al-Dīn Ibn Thaʿlab, 653/1254–55

The leader of the first major Arab rebellion against Mamluk rule was an Arab of Sharifian descent, Ḥiṣn al-Dīn Ibn Thaʿlab of the Jaʿāfira, who was the grandson of a major Ayyubid state official, Fakhr al-Dīn Ismaʿīl. Acting from a base in Dayrūṭ in Upper Egypt and having control over shipments of grain, the Ibn Thaʿlab were a prominent and wealthy family that gained power as part of the rise of the provincial ʿurbān in the late Fatimid period and held on to this power during the Ayyubid era. Ḥiṣn al-Dīn's rebellion was dramatic in scale and in consequences and led to a century-long suppression of the political power of the Arab clans. With the benefit of hindsight, al-Maqrīzī interpreted Ḥiṣn al-Dīn's rebellion as a cataclysmic conflict between Arabs and Mamluks, between the legitimacy of lineage on the one hand and the power of a warrior class of military slaves on the other.

The Jaʿāfira of Upper Egypt were part of the rural Arab elites sponsored by the late Fatimids and by the Ayyubids. The name of the clan is first attested at the time of the Fatimid restoration of 1074–76.[3] During the twelfth century, the Jaʿāfira came to be one of the most important state-employed ʿurbān provincial security forces. In 1154, Usāma ibn Munqidh witnessed the *muqaddam* of the Jaʿfar Arabs take an oath of loyalty to the Fatimid vizier, alongside the *muqaddam*s of several other tribal groups.[4] After overthrowing the Fatimids, Saladin restricted the power of several ʿurbān groups, both in the delta and on the Nubian border, but he left the Jaʿāfira's power unchecked. In fact, Ayyubid rule was an era of unprecedented power and visibility for the Jaʿāfira in Upper Egypt. Ibn Khaldūn, citing earlier sources, comments that the Jaʿāfira were Sharīfs (descendants of the Prophet) and specialized in commerce.[5] By the 1190s, the leader of the Jaʿāfira, the Sharīf. Fakhr al-Dīn Ismāʿīl Ibn Thaʿlab, appears to have taken control of the transport of grains coming from Upper Egypt. Al-Maqrīzī reports that during the famine of 593/1196–97, the boats of Ibn Thaʿlab were the only ones to provide Cairo with wheat, and the royal household depended on him for their bread and meat provisions. In return, the Sharīf was rewarded with an iqṭāʿ grant (*khubz*) worth sixty thousand dinars per annum, and an amiral title of kettle-drum (*kūs*) and flag.[6] In the following year, Fakhr al-Dīn Ibn Thaʿlab was given the honor of leading the pilgrimage caravan from Cairo, and the title of Amīr al-Ḥajj.[7]

Fakhr al-Dīn's power base was in Upper Egypt, and he established his headquarters at the strategic village of Dharwat Sarabām, present-day Dayrūṭ, near the head of the al-Manhā Canal. Yāqūt, writing in Aleppo in the 1220s, reports that Ibn Thaʿlab established there a congregational mosque, at the confluence of the Nile and the canal.[8] He also had residential quarters and palaces there, and the village came to be known as Dharwat al-Sharīf.[9] This village lay in the midst of the lands considered the territory of the Jaʿāfira, extending through fertile lands or meadows (*al-mutamarriʿ*) from Manfalūṭ to Samalūṭ, on both banks of the Nile.[10] At the same time, Ibn Thaʿlab used his wealth to purchase prime properties in Cairo. These included two bathhouses, a substantial orchard of fifty-five feddans, and a commercial warehouse (*qayṣariyya*) worth nearly one hundred thousand dinars.[11] By 612/1215–16, Fakhr al-Dīn Ibn Thaʿlab joined the ranks of the Ayyubid elite by founding his own madrasa in Cairo. The event was attended by several Cairene scholars, who gave their blessings and attested to Fakhr al-Dīn's genuine Prophetic lineage. He died a year later, in Rajab 613/November 1216.[12]

Fakhr al-Dīn's madrasa was built in a prestigious sector of the al-Qarāfa Cemetery, and its main hall (*īwān*) still survives.[13] Its extant elements are a testimony to his political eminence, and to the salience of his lineage, which is listed both on an impressive wooden panel (now in the Victoria and Albert Museum), and on his tombstone (figure 9.1).[14] The epitaph accords him a series of lavish titles and honorifics connected to his service to the state, including *al-amīr al-ajall*, *ʿimād al-mulūk wa'l-salāṭīn*, and *Amīr al-Ḥājj wa'l-Ḥaramayn*. The inscription also emphasizes his Prophetic origin: he is called Sharīf and a blood relation of the caliph (*nasīb amīr al-mu'minīn*), and identified by the name of his clan, al-Jaʿfarī al-Zaynabī. The inscription also traces five generations of Fakhr al-Dīn's ancestors. Such level of detail about genealogical claims is rare in tombstones from the Ayyubid and Mamluk eras and can be explained by the location of the grave in Cairo's central cemetery, as it is likely that the Arab lineage claims were a message intended for urban visitors. Fakhr al-Dīn had established himself as a member of the Ayyubid elite of Cairo, and his Prophetic lineage played a significant role in legitimizing this status.

FIGURE 9.1. Tombstone of Fakhr al-Dīn Ismaʿīl b. Ḥiṣn al-Dīn Thaʿlab, 613/1216–17, Qarāfa Cemetery, Cairo. © Creswell Archive, Ashmolean Museum, neg. EA.CA.2577.

After Fakhr al-Dīn's death in 1216–17, the Ibn Thaʿlab clan continued to exert power in Upper Egypt and in Cairo, with leadership of the family eventually falling to Ḥiṣn al-Dīn, one of Fakhr al-Dīn's grandsons. Al-Maqrīzī, probably citing the thirteenth-century author al-Ḥamdānī, is able to provide a nearly complete family tree, listing the names of Fakhr al-Dīn's sons, brothers, and nephews.[15] This Sharifian family was probably part of the provincial security forces in Upper Egypt, since a force of two thousand *ashrāf al-ʿarab* was deployed to quell a rebellion of the Turkish garrison of Qūṣ in the winter of 1242–43.[16] Ḥiṣn al-Dīn himself is first mentioned in the Coptic *History of the Patriarchs*, where he is—rather surprisingly for this Christian source—described as a valiant Arab knight who fought off a Frankish raid in Sinai in the early 1240s. He and his brothers were called back to Cairo from Gaza, where they were stationed as commanders of ʿurbān units, and encountered the Frankish force en route.[17] Ḥiṣn al-Dīn is also mentioned as selling his grandfather's Cairene orchard to Sultan al-Ṣāliḥ Ayyub for three thousand dinars—an indication of the family's wealth, as well as of his status as head of the family.[18]

Following the death of the last Ayyubid sultan, Ḥiṣn al-Dīn Ibn Thaʿlab decided to rise in revolt against his Turkish successor, al-Muʿizz Aybak, in 652/1254–55. The conflict is briefly mentioned in the annals of Baybars al-Manṣūrī (d. 725/1325), but the earliest substantial account of it comes from the pen of the Upper Egyptian bureaucrat al-Nuwayrī (d. 733/1333).[19] According to al-Nuwayrī, the ʿurbān of Upper Egypt took to looting and rape and dominated over the land, exploiting the shift of power in Cairo from al-Ṣāliḥ Ayyub to the Turkish al-Muʿizz Aybak. Al-Nuwayrī reports that the leader was Ḥiṣn al-Dīn al-Jaʿfarī, and that the rebels numbered twelve thousand horsemen and sixty thousand infantry troops. The size of these troops, even if exaggerated, strongly suggests that the rebelling Arabs represented a major section of village communities in Upper Egypt. Ḥiṣn al-Dīn appointed a vizier chosen from among the cadres of local provincial administrators, and it seems clear that he intended to establish his own state. But al-Nuwayrī also states that Ḥiṣn al-Dīn's control over his forces was minimal and that he failed in his attempts to rein in their unruly behavior.[20]

The suppression of the rebellion was achieved through the superior training of the Mamluk army and their effective archery skills. The provincial governor, Fāris al-Dīn Aqṭāy, set out with two thousand riders to confront the ʿurbān in al-Ṣalʿā, near Sūhāj, some 150 kilometers south of Dayrūṭ. Despite their numerical advantage, the ʿurbān could not cope with the salvos of arrows directed at them by the Mamluk troops and were quickly defeated. Al-Nuwayrī reports that the fleeing ʿurbān hid themselves or changed their clothes, suggesting that their Arab identity could be easily put on and taken off (on the sartorial aspect of Arab identity see chapter 6). Ḥiṣn al-Dīn himself fled farther south, accompanied by a concubine.[21] He then allied himself with the Turkish governor of Qūṣ, and the two took control of the local taxes in Ikhmīm and Asyut. Another expeditionary force was then sent from Cairo, and this force managed to capture Ḥiṣn al-Dīn. He was imprisoned in Alexandria and executed ten years later.[22]

Al-Maqrīzī's account of the rebellion, written two centuries later, confirms the basic outlines of the events but couches it in ideological terms that are not found in the earlier accounts. According to the *Sulūk* chronicle, the rebellion attracted

ʿurbān from Upper Egypt and from the delta provinces of al-Buḥayra, Giza, and the Fayyum. They numbered twelve thousand horsemen, and innumerable foot soldiers. In al-Maqrīzī's version, the battle with the force sent by al-Muʿizz Aybak (five thousand horsemen in this version) took place in Dharwat Sarabām itself, and at its end the Turkish forces captured women and children as well as horses, camels, and cattle. The defeated Ḥiṣn al-Dīn was then tricked by al-Muʿizz, who promised to reincorporate him into the Mamluk army, only to capture him and his troops when they arrived in Bilbays in the eastern delta.[23] The account in the *Bayān*, al-Maqrīzī's genealogical treatise, adds the Ibn Thaʿlab family tree and provides the names of several cousins of Ḥiṣn al-Dīn who also took part in the rebellion and were executed in Cairo after its suppression.[24]

Al-Maqrīzī framed Ḥiṣn al-Dīn's rebellion as an ideological opposition to Mamluk rule based on twin pillars: Arab claims to superiority within Islam and the Arabs' deep roots in the Egyptian countryside. While al-Nuwayrī viewed the rebellion as an opportunistic disturbance by the ʿurbān, al-Maqrīzī has Ḥiṣn al-Dīn declare that "we are the masters of the land," and "we are more befitting of kingship than the Mamluks; it is enough that we served Banū Ayyūb, who were foreigners (?, *khawārij*), for these *mamlūks* are their slaves (*ʿabīd*)."[25] In the *Bayān*, al-Maqrīzī explains that "the Arabs (ʿurbān) of Egypt disdained [al-Mu ʿizz Aybak's] rule over them, for he was a member of the Baḥriyya corps of military slaves, and was stained by bondage."[26] The phrase "stained by bondage (*massa-hu al-riqq*)" is unique to al-Maqrīzī and may indicate a later interpolation. Moreover, according to al-Maqrīzī's account, the battle between Mamluks and ʿurbān extended to the western delta, where the Mamluk army defeated a related rebellion of the tribes (*qabīlatay*) of Sinbis and Lawāta—events not reported by earlier sources.

In al-Maqrīzī's retrospective interpretation, the rebellion was a conflict between two ideal forms of political legitimacy (Sharifian kinship versus military slaves), and Ḥiṣn al-Dīn's defeat led the way to the consolidation of Mamluk rule. Therefore, the Ibn Thaʿlab rebellion was a watershed: "After [this revolt] the Arabs of Egypt scattered (*tabaddada*) and their spark extinguished," and "they weakened and their numbers decreased, until they became what they are in our days."[27] His narrative about an Arab ethnic uprising was likely to be a projection of fifteenth-century attitudes. We find a similar dichotomy between Turks and Arabs in the contemporary account of the merchant Emmanuel Piloti, a resident of Alexandria, who was writing circa 1420.[28] Piloti viewed the Arabs as the main force opposing the Mamluks, with the conflict between Arab clansmen and Turks comparable to the conflict between Guelfs and Ghibellines.[29] Like his contemporary al-Maqrīzī, Piloti also framed Arab resistance to the Mamluk regime in ideological terms: the Arabs viewed the Mamluks as illegitimate former slaves, while the Arabs themselves were the nation of the Prophet.

Viewed it its own thirteenth-century context, and not through al-Maqrīzī's retrospective lenses, Ḥiṣn al-Dīn's revolt can be best explained through the spread of Arab village clans as recorded by al-Nābulusī's 1245 register of the Fayyum (see chapter 3). In nearly all villages of the Fayyum, al-Nābulusī identified the local inhabitants with a named Arab or a Berber clan, usually one per village. Each of these villages was led by a group of headmen (*mashāyikh*) who were responsible for the payment of the collective land-tax imposed on their villages. The multivillage clans also provided a levy of riders for the Ayyubid ʿurbān auxiliary units, and in turn they were the constituent elements of larger territorial tribal confederacies, which between them carved the entire agricultural territory of the Fayyum. As we have seen, a similar blanket of Arab and Berber village clans covered all Upper Egypt and the delta by the time of the Sharifian revolt. The support given to Ḥiṣn al-Dīn by tens of thousands of men suggests that he must have had a significant following in the villages of Upper Egypt; the ʿurbān who fought for him were villagers in the same way the ʿurbān in al-Nābulusī's near-contemporary register were recruited from the villages of the Fayyum. At the same time, Ḥiṣn al-Dīn was a scion of a leading ʿurbān family that rose to prominence during the twelfth century, and he was the grandson of the most successful Egyptian Arab leader under the Ayyubids, the Sharīf Fakhr al-Dīn, who controlled strategic grain provisions from his power base in Upper Egypt. Our earliest source for the revolt, al-Nuwayrī, points to an incongruity between the semiofficial figure of the Sharīf and his unruly rural troops. Ultimately, he was a member of the Ayyubid elite, mobilizing his Arab identity to ride a wave of peasant resistance.

The Suppression of the *ʿUrbān*, 1250–1350

In the century that followed, from 1253 to the onset of the plague in 1349, Mamluk sultans attempted to assert direct control over village communities in the Nile Valley and the delta and substantially limit the power of rural ʿurbān. This was a consequence of the lessons learnt from the scale of the uprising and the efforts required to suppress it, as well as part of a wider pattern of centralization under Sultan Baybars and his successors. The first Mamluk century was the heyday of the iqṭāʿ fiscal regime, where a central bureaucracy awarded Mamluk military officers rights to nearly all agricultural revenues in the Egyptian countryside. The peak of this centralized iqṭāʿ land management was reached with a series of land surveys, most notably that of Sultan al-Nāṣir Muḥammad in 715/1315.[30] For the

Egyptian peasantry, the height of the iqṭāʿ regime coincided with a policy of unprecedented repression. The clearest manifestation of this policy was novel restrictions on the rights of rural men—whether called Arabs, peasants or Bedouin—to carry arms and to ride horses in the main agricultural provinces of the Nile Valley and the delta. During this period, Arab leaders in Egypt appear to be deprived of iqṭāʿ and were not appointed as *muqaddams*, with exceptions made for the marginal delta provinces of al-Buḥayra and al-Sharqiyya. The Jaʿāfira disappear from our view, and so do most of the ʿurbān confederacies that dominated the Egyptian countryside in the late Fatimid period.

The Mamluk policy of disarming the ʿurbān is laid out in a set of instructions, also known as the "memorandum of Qalāwūn," composed by the royal chancery during the reign of Qalāwūn (r. 1279–90). The aim of the memorandum was to guide the crown prince in the ruler's absence.[31] On the matter of the rural Arabs, the explicit counsel is to guard against the ʿurbān of the countryside (*bilād*) and to take securities from them. The provincial governors are specifically instructed to prevent any of the ʿurbān from carrying a sword, a lance, or any other weapon and that they should not be allowed to buy these weapons in Cairo. Whoever contravened this and carried a weapon traveling from one place to another should be subject to disciplinary punishment (*ta'dīb*) and his weapon should be confiscated.

The memorandum also instructs provincial governors to extract written security undertakings from these headmen and village protectors, reminiscent of the undertakings of upholding the peace made by Palestinian headmen in the same period (see chapter 4). The headmen were told to put out tents (*buyūt shiʿr*) for the village protectors, whose responsibilities were to safeguard the roads, respond to cries for help, and catch out evildoers and absconders (*idrāk al-hārib*). A variant of this document has the governors directly appoint protectors who should set up tents on the roads in between villages. These protectors are responsible for the *darak* for the road, meaning that they are obliged to pay for any losses incurred by travelers.[32] In both variants, the governors are to prohibit any travel by night, with nocturnal travelers held accountable for their losses.[33] The ban on night travel suggests limited faith in this very localized, village-based form of rural security.

Circumscribing the power of the ʿurbān in the agricultural Egyptian provinces meant that the regime had to interact directly with village communities to ensure the safety of roads for travelers and merchants and to uphold justice in the countryside. The dossier of documents originating with the amir Jamāl al-Dīn al-Azkā, who was active in al-Ashmūnayn circa 1300, sheds lights on the responsibilities of village headmen for law and order.[34] In the decrees issued by al-Azkā, most probably in his capacity as the local governor, he called upon the *mashāyikh* headmen to hand over villagers accused of crimes, such as unlawfully seizing property. The al-Azkā dossier doesn't feature any intermediaries between provincial governors and village headmen.

The memorandum's general ban on arming the Egyptian ʿurbān makes exceptions for the eastern province of al-Sharqiyya, which included the Sinai desert, and for the western province of al-Buḥayra. The memorandum instructs the *muqaddams* of the ʿĀʾidh to keep watch over the inner desert road from Suez to ʿAqaba and not to miss any of the pigeons sent from the pigeon-tower in Suez. This official role of the ʿĀʾidh Arabs for security in central Sinai was an Ayyubid legacy, as evidenced in the St. Catherine documents (see chapter 2).[35] Our knowledge of the ʿurbān of al-Sharqiyya in this period is exceptionally detailed thanks to the account of Ibn al-Dawādārī, whose father was sent to al-Sharqiyya in 703/1303–4. Ibn al-Dawādārī reports that the local ʿurbān included the Thaʿlaba, Judhām, and ʿĀʾidh, who together contributed 1,700 riders to the royal army and 1,000 camels for heavy transport. He confirms that the ʿĀʾidh were responsible for the inner desert road, while the Thaʿlaba and the Judhām had responsibilities for the main coastal route between Egypt and Syria and were required to provide ten horses for each of the fifteen postal stations along the route to Rafah. Each Arab rider in al-Sharqiyya received an iqṭāʿ (also known as *khubz*, lit. "bread") worth between thirty and five hundred army dinars (notional units of account for calculating the value of an iqṭāʿ), while regular officers of the Mamluk army received a minimum allocation of one thousand army dinars. Ibn al-Dawādārī adds that Arab leading families in al-Sharqiyya were able to pass the iqṭāʿ on to their members, but the new holder of the iqṭāʿ had to pay an entry fee (*rasm*) to the Bureau of the ʿUrbān (Dīwān al-ʿUrbān) before being confirmed in his position; this is our only reference to the existence of such a dedicated bureau.[36]

The Arabs of al-Buḥayra in the western delta were also endowed with significant authority. Al-ʿUmarī, who dismisses the meek sedentary Arabs of the Egyptian countryside, says that the most noble among them are the amirs of the Arabs of al-Buḥayra who travel as far west as Gabes and al-Qayrawan and have the quality of Arabness.[37] In the regions west of Alexandria, where economic production was predominantly focused on animal husbandry, Sultan Baybars awarded collection of the tax on cattle to leaders of the Hawwāra and the Banū Sulaym, who were expected to provide an annual payment of fifty horses in return. The tax in cattle was called *zakāt al-aghnām* (alms tax on small cattle) or *ʿidād*, a term also used for the tax imposed on Turcoman groups near Aleppo.[38]

But even in al-Buḥayra, tax collection had been by the 1340s handed over to a Mamluk officer, who used brute force and was faced with stiff resistance.[39] In addition to the Arabs of Sinai and the western desert, the Mamluk sultans of this period employed Egyptian ʿurbān troops in their campaigns into Nubia in the south.[40] Egyptian ʿurbān troops are not otherwise mentioned in the context of royal campaigns in this period.

The first century of Mamluk rule, from 1250 to 1350, was a period of unprecedented repression of the Egyptian peasantry. Mamluk officials made earnest attempts to disarm rural men in all Egyptian provinces. Aydamur al-Qashshāsh (d. ca. 700/1300), the governor of al-Gharbiyya and al-Sharqiyya, applied state policy very strictly. We are told that "none of the peasants (fallāḥīn) in these two provinces dared to wear a black waist-wrapper (*miʾzar*), to ride a horse, to arm himself with a sword, or to carry a stick coated with iron."[41] The report implies that once a fallāḥ rode a horse, armed himself, and dressed in black, he became one of the ʿurbān clansmen.[42] When Āqūsh al-Rūmī led a major irrigation project commanding thousands of oxen in 707/1307–8, he severely disciplined all the rural officials, including the bailiffs (*mushidd*) and soldiers appointed by the amirs. But he was particularly brutal with the leaders (*mashāyikh*) of the ʿurbān, probably meaning here village headmen: he used to chain and whip them, pierce their noses, and crop their ears.[43] Sunqur al-Manṣūrī (d. 709/1309–10), governor of al-Buḥayra, suppressed the ʿurbān by taking away their weapons and cattle.[44] This was true for Upper Egypt, too. In an undated appointment decree for the governor of Upper Egypt, he is counseled to prevent "any of the ʿurbān or the peasants (fallāḥīn)" to ride a horse or to carry or purchase weapons, and to impose capital punishment for contravening the prohibition on riding horses.[45] In the context of disarming rural men, the terms fallāḥ and ʿurbān were used interchangeably.

This Mamluk policy of suppression of the rural ʿurbān didn't prevent Arab village clans from mobilizing for popular uprisings. The most significant example occurred in Upper Egypt in 701/1301–2, when the main body of the Mamluk army was preoccupied with fighting the Mongols in Syria. The uprising was briefly discussed by the contemporaries Baybars al-Manṣūrī, Ibn al-Dawādārī, and al-Nuwayrī, who describe an indistinct mass of the "Arabs of Upper Egypt" capitalizing on Mamluk weakness to show disobedience and commit highway robbery. Ibn al-Dawādārī also mentions that the ʿurbān prevented the amirs and the soldiers from collecting their iqtāʿ revenues.[46] A punitive force sent against them branched out on both banks of the Nile, as well as toward the Western Oases. The Arabs were taken by surprise, and "the subjects (*riʿāyā*) were relieved, fear has gone, and security was restored." The "subjects" these authors had in mind were probably townsmen like them, while the Arabs were the people of the villages: the booty taken from the Arabs included not only thousands of horses and camels, but also many oxen, water buffalos, and asses, animals used exclusively for intensive cultivation.[47]

Al-Maqrīzī, writing a century later but utilizing earlier sources, emphasizes the *jacquerie* aspect of the 701/1301 uprising.[48] In his report, the ʿurbān of Upper Egypt released all prisoners, prevented the payment of the land tax, and instead imposed their own poll tax on merchants and artisans. The Mamluk army retaliated by raiding the agricultural provinces of Giza and al-Aṭfīḥiyya, killing some ten thousand men, looting their properties, and capturing their women. Some loyalist Arab groups in al-Sharqiyya and in Upper Egypt assisted the Mamluk forces by blocking the desert roads before the fleeing rebels. Al-Maqrīzī states that as many as eight thousand oxen were taken as booty, a number that—if true—would have devastated cultivation in Upper Egypt. Moreover, he specifically says that the 1,600 Arab captives were all agriculturalists, "men of cultivation and sowing" (*la-hum filāḥāt wa-zurūʿ*). As a result, "the countryside became empty, and one could walk and not find anyone on the road and stop in a village (*bi'l-qarya*) and see only women, boys, and children." The Mamluk army decided to release the captives and return them in order to sustain the countryside (*li-ḥifẓ al-bilād*). Al-Maqrīzī concludes the account by saying that from now on no fallāḥ or *badawī* was allowed to ride a horse, all weapons were taken away from the fallāḥīn and the ʿurbān, and "the fallāḥīn were subjugated (*dhallat*) and handed over the land tax."

The 701/1301 uprising stands out for its bottom-up character, progressing from within the villages of Upper Egypt. This uprising was not associated with any named clan or an individual Arab leader. Instead, both al-Nuwayrī and al-Maqrīzī report an amorphous uprising of ʿurbān, who never formed an army or waged pitched battles. We only hear of anonymous leaders, who called themselves by the names of the Mamluk amirs who came to attack them, a topsy-turvy motif typical of medieval popular resistance. The absence of clear leadership was likely a result of Mamluk suppression of the Arab village clans in the preceding fifty years; the few Arab groups still on the payroll of the Mamluk state chose not to join in the uprising. In the absence of official leadership, this uprising was a typical peasant rebellion, a *jacquerie* targeting merchants, artisans, and the collection of the land tax. It was also during this rebellion that the pronunciation of *qāf* was first indicated as the hallmark of an Arab dialect (see chapter 6), creating a clear link between assumed Arab identity and resistance to taxation.

In this 1301 uprising, the rebels were fallāḥs transformed into Arabs by the mere act of rebellion. Those peasants who carried arms and who rode horses, those who dressed like Arabs, were considered ʿurbān. The resistance of the fallāḥ was by definition limited, because the term itself came to be associated with poverty and subjugation. And this was a period of oppression for the Egyptian peasantry. According to the fourteenth-century North African preacher Ibn al-Ḥājj, the Egyptian cultivator (*zāriʿ*)—also called fallāḥ—was treated as less than a human being, far worse than the peasants in his Maghribi homeland. Nonetheless, even Ibn al-Ḥājj notes that the fallāḥs could oppose an ineffective iqṭāʿ holder, for example, by taking away the fodder of his horses.[49] The conflicts between village communities and state officials took on many forms. Even if the peasantry was disarmed and the ʿurbān often denied official status, the Mamluk provincial administration found it difficult to impose its will.

The Revolt of al-Aḥdab

In 1350 Upper Egypt was the focus of a full-scale Arab uprising—the third such uprising since the establishment of the Mamluk state. This revolt was led by Muḥammad ibn Wāṣil, nicknamed al-Aḥdab (the hunchback), of the previously unknown ʿArak clan. The rebellion was quashed only in 1354 or 1355, after five years of disobedience and in the face of a large military expedition from Cairo.[50] Al-Aḥdab's rebellion coincided with the outbreak of the plague and undoubtedly exploited that moment of crisis: al-Maqrīzī pairs the plague and al-Aḥdab's rebellion as two calamities that afflicted the reign of Sultan Ḥasan.[51] The long-term consequences of this uprising for the history of Upper Egypt cannot be overstated. It represented the rise of new Arab elites at the expense of the provincial governors, iqṭāʿ holders, and the loyalist ʿurbān who dominated the area since the late Fatimid period. The rebellion also signaled the beginnings of an organic alliance at the local level between the new cadre of Arab leading families and Sufi saints. Ultimately, al-Aḥdab's rebellion was focused on establishing his authority to collect taxes on behalf of the Mamluk state. Despite his military defeat, that aim was achieved. Al-Aḥdab was granted the responsibility of maintaining order and delivering taxes in parts of Upper Egypt and was remunerated by an iqṭāʿ derived from these local tax revenues.

It has been argued that al-Aḥdab's uprising was made possible because nomadic Bedouins were more resilient to the plague and that made them relatively more numerous and powerful.[52] This demographic explanation is unfounded. First, as pointed out by Büssow-Schmitz, nomadic communities were no less impacted than other groups; in fact, both al-Buḥayra and al-Sharqiyya, two provinces with significant mobile populations, had reports of high mortalities.[53] The St. Catherine documents also show that the Sinai Arabs suffered a sustained period of dearth and shortages instigated by the plague.[54] Second, hypothesizing about Arab empowerment due to the differential demographic effects of the plague rests on an untenable equation between Arab identity and a nomadic way of life. The rebelling Arabs, during al-Aḥdab's rebellion as well as during its Upper Egyptian precursors of the earlier Mamluk period, were mostly sedentary peasants.

We owe everything we know about al-Aḥdab's rebellion to al-Maqrīzī. The brief accounts by Ibn Khaldūn and Ibn Duqmāq, while written closer to the events they describe, do little more than confirm the mere existence of the rebellion.[55] Al-Maqrīzī, on the other hand, gives us an exceptionally detailed and informative account. He first narrates the events of al-Aḥdab's rebellion as brief notices interspersed within the annals of the *hijrī* years 749–54 (1348–49 to 1353–54 CE). He then provides a long, sustained narrative of Amir Shaykhū's military expedition aimed at suppressing the rebellion, which took place between Dhū al-Qaʿda 754/December 1353 and Muḥarram 755/February 1354. This narrative begins with a lamentation about the neglect of the affairs of Upper Egypt after the death of Sultan al-Nāṣir Muḥammad. Al-Maqrīzī then expands on al-Aḥdab's increasing hold over the region of Asyut in the years leading to Shaykhū's expedition and ends with three poems composed by members of the Mamluk elite that celebrate Shaykhū's military success. Al-Maqrīzī relied on a fourteenth-century source, probably from within the military elite. There are no eye-witness accounts, and the narrative appears to be derived from the reports relayed back to Cairo at the time.[56]

Al-Maqrīzī traces the beginning of the revolt to Rajab 749/October 1348, with fighting between the state-sponsored Banū Hilāl, supported by the Mamluk *kāshif* of Upper Egypt and the ʿArak, a group not previously mentioned in any of our extant sources. This battle ended with the victory of the ʿArak, who entered the provincial capital of Asyut, and with the death of the provincial *kāshif*. Two years later the ʿArak won another major battle against the Hilāl, in which a second Mamluk *kāshif* sent from Cairo was stripped of his possessions.[57] Al-Maqrīzī also reports interclan fighting in the Middle Egyptian regions of al-Bahnasāwiyya and al-Aṭfīḥiyya, leading to the deaths of many Arabs (ʿurbān). The date of these clashes is not clear, although the leaders were executed by the Mamluks in 755/1354–55.[58] Garcin insisted that the intertribal conflict in Upper Egypt was split along Qays and Yaman lines, with the Hilālī Qays siding with the government in Cairo. But al-Maqrīzī's narrative has no trace of such divisions, nor any evidence that the ʿArak considered themselves Yaman.[59]

The ʿArak uprising exposed the weakness of the Banū Hilāl, the state-sponsored ʿurbān of Upper Egypt, who were repeatedly defeated by al-Aḥdab's forces. Only after a Mamluk force had defeated the ʿArak in Shawwāl 752 (November to December 1351), causing the men to flee to the mountains, were the Banū Hilāl invited to take revenge on the defenseless ʿArak sites. The Hilālīs captured the women and looted grains, flour, small cattle, and waterskins. The sultan was thereafter informed that "the land is sown, its ʿurbān are in obedience, and its inhabitants have settled (*al-bilād qad khuḍḍirat arāḍīhā wa-aṭāʿa ʿurbānu-hā al-ʿuṣāh wa-tawaṭṭana ahlu-hā*)."[60] The ʿArak retaliated by attacking the Hilālīs in the strategic town of Ṭimā, forcing the Mamluk authorities to establish a military presence there in the spring of 1352 to secure the harvest.[61] This seems to have convinced the Mamluk authorities that the Banū Hilāl were no longer of any value. During Amīr Shaykhū's major expedition, he summoned four hundred Hilālī cavalry under the pretext of seeking their support and then executed them, seizing their horses and weapons.[62]

A key feature of al-Aḥdab's rebellion was its explicit association with large-scale tax collection. According to al-Maqrīzī, al-Aḥdab established himself as a local potentate, displaying rudimentary regalia and ruling over the peasantry (*nafadha amru-hu fī al-fallāḥīn*).[63] This meant that taxation was subject to his approval. Whenever an iqṭāʿ holder did not receive the land tax from the village assigned to him, he would ask al-Aḥdab to write a note to the *fallāḥ* in question and to the people of his village (*balad*). Al-Aḥdab would then ensure that the soldier receive his due. Beyond his interactions with individual iqṭāʿ holders, al-Aḥdab presented himself to the provincial *kāshif* and to the governor as their local fixer, promising to sort out any problems they have. Al-Maqrīzī places this account in the annals of 755/1354–55, but it may have been an aspect of al-Aḥdab's career even before the hostilities began.[64]

By Shaʿbān/Shawwāl 754 (September to November 1353), ʿurbān associated with al-Aḥdab mounted an attack against local sugar presses owned either by the state or by senior amirs. Al-Maqrīzī reports that they attacked the presses near Mallawī, north of Asyut, and looted all its sugar produce, from candy to molasses. They also destroyed the waterwheels (used for irrigating the sugarcane) and slaughtered the oxen used to drive the presses (*wa-mālū ʿalā al-maʿāṣir wa'l-sawāqī fa-nahabū ḥawāṣila-hā min al-qunūd wa'l-sukkar wa'l-aʿsāl wa-dhabaḥū al-abqār*). This was an unusual act, and al-Maqrīzī mentions it twice in his narrative.[65] As the most lucrative rural investment in Upper Egypt, the presses were symbols of Mamluk power. In addition, they might have been diverting water away from the arable lands of nearby villages. Another attack on infrastructure targeted the dams of the province of al-Ashmūnayn.[66] Al-Maqrīzī mentions other more standard targets: highway robbery and depriving Mamluk amirs and soldiers of their land-tax revenues (*mughall*).[67]

When the ʿurbān of Upper Egypt gained knowledge of Amir Shaykhū's impending expedition in November 1353, many of al-Aḥdab's supporters fled southward to Nubia, while others hid in caves and hideouts prepared in advance. Al-Maqrīzī reports that some decided to go on pilgrimage, with the caravan to Mecca leaving around that time. Informants recognized a group of ten of them, and they were arrested and executed. Their property was confiscated and handed over to the Mamluk *amīr jandār*, "since they were his fallāḥs (*li-anna kānū fallāḥī-hi*)." Nicola Ziyāda, the modern editor of the *Sulūk*, correctly remarked that this anecdote demonstrates that the ʿurbān of Egypt were peasants and that their revolts were driven by economic issues and by the violence of the Mamluk iqṭāʿ regime.[68] In al-Bahnasāwiyya, the Mamluk forces tortured the women and children until they revealed the hiding places of the men. Here, too, the context is surely that of sedentary villagers.[69]

Al-Aḥdab himself headed toward Aswan, leading a coalition of several Arab groups, some identified by name (Juhayna and Kalb) and others by territory (Arabs of Manfalūṭ). Al-Aḥdab's men were accompanied by their families, their grains, and their cattle; they learnt by now not to leave them behind at the mercy of the Mamluk soldiers. Al-Maqrīzī gives the size of al-Aḥdab's army at ten thousand cavalry and many more infantry; these numbers may well be exaggerated in order to amplify Shaykhū's eventual victory. But there is no doubt that the Mamluks faced a serious challenge. The expedition force consisted of twelve senior amirs, of which the majority went to Upper Egypt (a few were sent to the delta to suppress the Arabs there, acting independently of al-Aḥdab). Once Shaykhū arrived in Asyut, the magnitude of al-Aḥdab's army made him send for reinforcements from Cairo. Five hundred cavalry were made available to him, but then Shaykhū changed his mind, worried that such a move would raise the morale of the rebels. Another indication of the size of al-Aḥdab's army is the booty Shaykhū brought back from Upper Egypt at the end of his campaign: 2,300 horses, 2,500 camels, 700 donkeys, numerous small cattle, 100 loads of spears, 80 loads of swords, and 30 loads of leather shields.[70]

The final showdown between al-Aḥdab and Shaykhū's army occurred in a place called Wādī al-Ghizlān, probably near Aswan. The account of the battle itself appears somewhat embellished. Mamluk victory is explained by the dust (*ghibār*) raised by the attacking cavalry blinding the Arab forces; this may be literary motif, as it is reminiscent of the dust that conventionally precedes battle scenes in the popular epic of Sīrat ʿAntar. Shaykhū also managed to attack the Arab infantry from the rear, where their families and goods were placed. By morning Shaykhū sent forces to collect the booty—cash and jewelry, waterskins, textiles, and cattle—and enslave the women and children, who were subsequently sold in the markets of Cairo. The Arab men who fled to the desert died of thirst or threw themselves from the mountaintops to avoid being captured. Those who sought refuge in caves suffocated from the smoke from fires lit by the Mamluk army at the entrances to their hideouts. Ibn Duqmāq reports that the amirs assembled the severed heads of executed ʿurbān into *masṭaba* platforms. Ibn Iyās, repeating the story half a century later, evokes a comparison with Hulegu's skull pyramids of Baghdad.[71] Al-Maqrīzī is slightly less dramatic, stating that the soldiers threw the bodies of the Arabs to communal pits and raised the *masṭaba* with their insignia over the corpses.[72]

Beyond the direct military confrontation, the Mamluk authorities turned the campaign into a countrywide effort to disarm village communities. In the delta provinces of al-Sharqiyya, al-Gharbiyya, and al-Buḥayra, Mamluk raids rounded up hundreds of captives and horses. It was optimistically announced that no horses were left with the ʿurbān in the delta.[73] Following the victory over al-Aḥdab, Shaykhū's forces combed for arms and horses in Upper Egypt. This led to further executions, with poles carrying the bodies of captured Arabs lining up the banks of the Nile from Ṭimā to Minyat Ibn Khaṣīb (present-day al-Minyā), some one hundred kilometers north of Asyut. Two thousand captives were taken back, although only 1,200 made it to Cairo alive, and most of those died in jail over the coming months. Such mass executions led al-Maqrīzī to declare that no *badawī* remained in Upper Egypt.[74]

The use of the term *badawī* here is significant, as it is also reflected in the language of an order sent out to all provinces, preventing any *badawī* or fallāḥ from riding a horse, with the sole exception of guards responsible for road security (*arbāb al-adrāk*). To prevent confusion, *qāḍī*s and professional witnesses of the countryside were ordered to ride mules and carthorses (*akādīsh*).[75] Headmen (*mashāyikh*) of the ʿurbān and road protectors (*arbāb al-adrāk*) were asked to identify whether those found with horses or swords were local residents; the locals were released while the rest remained in custody. At a second stage, all the confiscated horses were presented and any peasant (fallāḥ) who recognized his horse was compensated by deducting its sale price from his land tax.[76] As this account suggests, all sections of rural elites normally owned horses. The official use of the term *badawī* here was meant to distinguish fighting, mobile Arabs from the rest of the Arab peasantry.

Yet, instead of suppressing Arab power, what transpired after the rebellion was a new Mamluk-Arab modus vivendi, in which al-Aḥdab was recognized as responsible for tax collection and security in the regions of Upper Egypt under his authority. Al-Aḥdab appeared in Cairo by the end of 1354, accompanied by a Sufi saintly figure called Abū Qāsim al-Ṭaḥāwī. This Sufi interceded on al-Aḥdab's behalf with the amir Shaykhū, who was the de facto authority in Cairo at the time and the commander of the expeditionary force that defeated al-Aḥdab a year earlier. Through the mediation of al-Ṭaḥāwī, al-Aḥdab was given the responsibility for provincial security (*darak al-bilād*) and for collection of all grains and revenues (*yaltazimu bi-taḥṣīl jamīʿ ghilālihā wa-amwālihā*) in the lands under his authority. He undertook a personal guarantee for any show of disobedience in these lands and pledged to extend hospitality to governors and *kāshifs* sent by the sultan.

After this agreement, al-Aḥdab was given robes of honor and an iqṭāʿ and sent back to Upper Egypt to assume his newly confirmed duties.[77] According to Ibn Khaldūn's very brief note, al-Aḥdab received an *amān* in return for his promise that the Arabs would avoid riding horses and carrying weapons and that they would occupy themselves with cultivation (*wa-yuqbilū ʿalā al-filāḥa*).[78] Ibn Duqmāq simply says that al-Aḥdab was reinstated in his previous position.[79] Thus, after the frenzy of bloodshed against the rural population of Upper Egypt, al-Aḥdab had come back to his role as a local fixer for the Cairo government—overseeing the collection of taxes in return for a share in the local revenue.

The involvement of a Sufi shaykh as a companion of an Arab leader was a precedent that would become commonplace in the following centuries. Al-Ṭaḥāwī's saintly presence created common ground between the Mamluk amirs and the rural rebels. On the one hand, he was seen as a saint of the "Arabs," and he stayed in a Sufi lodge known as *zāwiyat al-ʿurbān* in the Qarafa cemetery (this lodge is not otherwise attested). The amīr Shaykhū then renovated the *zāwiya* so the Sufi enjoyed patronage from both sides.[80] Sufi saints spread in the Egyptian and Syrian countrysides during the twelfth and thirteenth centuries, simultaneously with the spread of Arab identities in the same regions. Now, with the co-optation of provincial elites, saints were interwoven into the structure of Arab ruling houses, forming a mutually beneficial alliance.

A Century of Arab Revolts

Al-Aḥdab's rebellion brought an end to a century of violent clashes between the Arab village clans of Upper Egypt and the Mamluk sultans. At their heart, these revolts were about the payment of land tax to the army officers who held agricultural lands as iqṭāʿ. The most common and basic aim of the revolts was to prevent the collection of the land tax and its transfer to Cairo, and to keep as much of the revenue in the hands of the local, rural elites. These uprisings pitted the countryside against the cities and the towns, farmers against soldiers, bureaucrats, and merchants. Since all our narrative sources for these revolts were written by authors who belonged to the latter group, it is no wonder they paint the rebels in a fairly negative light, as a threat to law and order. But the peasant background of the rebels filters through the biases of the texts and has been recognized as such by several modern historians.

The century of Arab revolts was accompanied by repeated bans on horses and weapons, and by unprecedented repression of the peasantry. Bans on arms and horses were issued regularly between 1250 and 1350, and they were imposed on rural groups loosely identified as peasants, Arabs, or Bedouin. Perhaps taken aback by the scale of the Sharifian revolt of the 1250s, or simply attempting to maximize their revenues, the Mamluk authorities sought to impose direct rule on the Egyptian countryside, and iqṭāʿ holders and governors engaged in unmediated interaction with village communities. A final major roundup of horses and weapons followed the quelling of al-Aḥdab's rebellion, but this was the last we hear of this policy in the narrative sources. After 1354, the Mamluks gave up. Bans on horses and weapons were discontinued, replaced by growing reliance on the armed rural elites as agents of tax collection.[81]

The princely co-optation of al-Aḥdab at the end of his rebellion ushered in a new era in the relationship between the Arab village clans of Upper Egypt and the central government in Cairo. As was the case in rural Syria, the Mamluk sultans increasingly retreated from the countryside, folding up much of the iqṭāʿ landholding regime that prevailed in the thirteenth and fourteenth centuries. The power of provincial governors and iqṭāʿ holders, who terrorized the Egyptian peasantry in the first Mamluk century, declined markedly. Instead, power shifted to a new class of leading Arab and Berber families, such as the descendants of al-Aḥdab. The next chapter will demonstrate that the delegation of taxation and security to Arab provincial leaders became the standard practice in Upper Egypt through the remainder of the late medieval era. By the beginning of the fifteenth century, the Mamluk authorities extended this practice to several delta provinces, allowing the emergence of Arab semiautonomous rule in al-Sharqiyya, al-Minūfiyya, and al-Gharbiyya. In the long run, the Arab revolts—bloody, brutally crushed, sometimes leaderless, and seemingly futile—succeeded in overturning the balance of power between Cairo and its provinces.

10

Arab Ruling Families in the Egyptian Provinces, 1350–1517

THE FIFTEENTH CENTURY was an age of Arab and Berber power in the Egyptian countryside.[1] During the final century of Mamluk rule Arab clansmen acquired power and authority in most provinces of the delta while (Arabic-speaking) Hawwāra Berbers dominated Upper Egypt, becoming more visible in chronicles and in biographical dictionaries. Arab elite families were also the beneficiaries of an increased amount of iqṭāʿ grants and acted as officials of the Mamluk state, in some places replacing the *kāshifs* or governors. Their prominence was noted by European pilgrims and merchants, who described them as the "lords of the countryside." Their status was ultimately endorsed by the Ottoman conquerors in the early sixteenth century, who formalized the key role of Arab and Berber ruling houses in provincial administration.

The prominence of provincial Arab and Berber ruling families in fifteenth-century Egypt came on the heels of the earlier major Arab revolts against Mamluk rule, discussed in the previous chapter. The co-optation of the rebel al-Aḥdab into the provincial administration in Upper Egypt was a harbinger of things to come. In the second half of the fourteenth century, and especially under the reign of Sultan al-Ẓāhir Barqūq, the descendants of al-Aḥdab gave way to the Berber Hawwāra, who would go on to assume responsibility for tax collection and local security in Upper Egypt for several centuries. Legitimized by official appointments from Mamluk sultans in return for substantial entry fees, the Hawwāra leaders were divided between two leading families, Awlād ʿUmar in the south and Banū Gharīb in al-Bahnasāwiyya. The Awlād ʿUmar, based in Jirjā (Girga), controlled much of the agricultural production in Upper Egypt and made their wealth through ownership of sugarcane presses. As their influence grew, many villagers came to see themselves as members of the Hawwāra, with some thirty clans identifying as Hawwāra by the early fifteenth century.

Similar processes were taking place in several provinces of Lower Egypt. The best-documented Arab leading family in the delta is the Awlād ʿĪsā of the ʿĀʾidh. As we have seen, the ʿĀʾidh were first attested as a state-sponsored ʿurbān force in central Sinai in the late Fatimid period (see chapter 2). By the late fourteenth century their leading family, the Awlād ʿĪsā, became the official representatives of Mamluk royal authority in al-Sharqiyya and Sinai, replacing the governors and iqṭāʿ holders who dominated the region in the previous two centuries. The St. Catherine corpus shows that as the officials responsible for local security, the Awlād ʿĪsā guaranteed the safety of travelers and monks from attacks by other ʿurbān and issued contracts for the employment of local Arab protectors. In this period, the Arab clans of al-Sharqiyya received an unprecedented amount of iqṭāʿ grants and held a share in more than half the villages of the province.

The rise in the power of the provincial Arab families should be seen against the backdrop of a fundamental restructuring of the Mamluk sultanate. The demographic and economic shocks that followed the outbreak of the Black Death in the middle of the fourteenth century led to a long period of instability, culminating in the Barqūq-Minṭāsh civil war in the 1390s (described in chapter 8) and exacerbated by Tīmūr's invasion of Syria around the turn of the century. The reign of al-Muʾayyad Shaykh (r. 815–24/1412–21), however, ushered in a new equilibrium that lasted through much of the following century. The sultanate came to increasingly rely on commercial revenues from the international spice trade that passed through Egypt and Syria, compensating for dwindling revenues from land, limited by depopulation as well as by the growing power of local elites. While the sultanate reasserted its regional hegemony over international trade arteries, it had less incentive and less resources to invest in either the Egyptian or the Syrian countryside. The shift from agricultural to commercial revenues was accompanied by integration of civilian, non-*mamlūk* elites of Egyptian administrators and scholars. The dynastic principle, which kept descendants of Sultan Qalāwūn on the throne for nearly a century, was replaced by bureaucratic and meritocratic models of transmission of power.[2]

Most relevant for the rise of the Arab provincial elites in Egypt was the overall decline of the iqṭāʿ landholding regime and the waning of the power of provincial governors and iqṭāʿ holders. The fifteenth century saw a sharp drop in the overall number of villages given out as iqṭāʿ, and a corresponding steep rise in the number of villages either endowed as waqf or handed over to the sultan's private fisc, the *Dīwān al-Mufrad*. It has been estimated that as much as 40 percent of Egyptian land was no longer state owned by the end of the fifteenth century.[3] During the heyday of the iqṭāʿ regime, between 1250 and 1350, the officers of the Mamluk army went out to the countryside to collect the land tax directly, bypassing the need for collaborative rural elites. This period was marked by brutal suppression and widespread revolts. However, in the aftermath of the Black Death and the ensuing shortage of cultivators, iqṭāʿ holders were not able to exert sufficient leverage vis-à-vis peasant communities.[4] As was the case in fifteenth-century Syria (see chapter 8), the Mamluk sultans lost much of their authority in large swaths of the Egyptian countryside. Instead, provincial powers were often devolved to Arab ruling families in an admission of royal inability to suppress rural uprisings and collect agricultural taxes. These developments were insightfully described in a treatise on administrative reform by al-Asadī, writing in 855/1451. Al-Asadī argued that most of the disobedient ʿurbān of his own time were formerly peasants who were forced off their land, and that the policy of handing iqṭāʿ and power to obedient Arab families was a result of the state's inability to quell the resistance by these peasants-turned-Arabs. Al-Asadī's treatise confirms that the elites of the Arab clans, brutally suppressed in the first century of Mamluk rule, were now indispensable for maintaining control and delivering agricultural surpluses.

This also meant that a larger portion of agricultural tax revenues was now formally diverted toward the provincial Arab leading families. A comparison of the cadastral registers of 1376 and 1480 shows that iqṭāʿ grants for Arab leaders rose across all Egyptian provinces. While in 1376 Arab rural elites held about 5 percent of all Egyptian iqṭāʿ holdings, their share doubled to 10 percent in 1480.[5] It is important to emphasize, however, that the greater amount of iqṭāʿ handed over to Arab groups was coming out of a smaller pool of iqṭāʿ grants, reflecting the general decline of the iqṭāʿ regime during the fifteenth century.

This chapter follows the rise of Arab and Berber provincial houses in Egypt from 1350 to the end of Mamluk period. Given that the documentary and literary sources for fifteenth-century Egypt are very rich, the aim here is not a comprehensive history but a sampling of case studies that offers a new framework for understanding the phenomenon of Arab power in the last century of the sultanate. The first two sections discuss the rise of the Berber Hawwāra in Upper Egypt and the Arab ʿĀʾidh of the eastern delta (al-Sharqiyya), the latter examined through the lens of the St. Catherine documentary corpus. The third section examines the Arab leading families of other delta provinces. The fourth section presents the wider political transformations of the Mamluk sultanate in the fifteenth century, including the increasing privatization and endowment of land previously handed to iqṭāʿ holders, followed by a close reading of al-Asadī's tract. The final section examines the impact of royal co-optation of Arab and Berber elites on the Arab identities of the wider peasantry.

The Hawwāra in Upper Egypt

The Hawwāra's dominance in Upper Egypt dates to 782/1380–81, when a leading family migrated from al-Buḥayra in the western delta to Jirjā in Upper Egypt. The Hawwāra were present in al-Buḥayra since 662/1263–64, when Sultan Baybars provided Hawwāra groups with written permissions (*ḥujaj*) for the cultivation of the province.[6] Ibn Khaldūn reports, probably for the middle of the fourteenth century, that the Hawwāra were one of several Berber groups cultivating lands in al-Buḥayra (*wa-yuʿmirūna arḍa-hā bi'l-suknā wa'l-falḥ*) and paying land tax on them (*wa-ʿalayhum maghārim al-falḥ*) while maintaining seasonal migration toward Barqa.[7] Their migration to Upper Egypt coincided with Barqūq's ascent to the throne. Al-Maqrīzī states that the move was initiated by the sultan, who gave Ismaʿīl ibn Māzin al-Hawwārī the right to cultivate the desolate lands of Jirjā.[8] According to al-Qalqashandī, a contemporary observer of the same events, the Hawwāra were driven out from al-Buḥayra by an Arab rebel called Badr ibn Sallām.[9]

The installation of the Hawwāra in Jirjā was part of Mamluk experimentation with provincial tax collection, whereby officials were given responsibility for delivering local taxes in return for a share of the revenue. In 781/1380, the governors of al-Gharbiyya, al-Ashmūnayn, and al-Minūfiyya were appointed only after they had committed to pay a fixed sum (*māl iltazama bi-hi*) of the provincial tax revenues. As acknowledged at the time, this was unprecedented policy.[10] A similar arrangement was offered to the Arab rebel Badr ibn Sallām in al-Buḥayra. Following his defeat at the hands of an army sent by the new sultan, al-Ẓāhir Barqūq, Badr sought reconciliation, guaranteeing the security of the province and the cultivation of the lands that had become desolate (*iltazama tadrīk al-bilād, ʿimārat mā kharaba minhā*). Badr presented himself in the provincial capital of Damanhūr and was granted safe-conduct and a robe of honor, a scenario reminiscent of the co-optation of al-Aḥdab a few decades earlier.[11] The term used to describe these novel fiscal arrangements is *iltazama*; it anticipates the frequent use of the term *iltizām* in sixteenth-century Ottoman Egypt, where it referred to the responsibility of provincial governors and Arab leaders (*şeyhülarab*) for the collection of taxes in their district.[12]

The cadastral register by Ibn Duqmāq confirms that the Hawwāra held Jirjā as their iqṭā‘ by the end of the fourteenth century.[13] After receiving the lands of Jirjā, the leaders of the Hawwāra soon became the most powerful family in Upper Egypt, profiting from their control of village lands and in particular from the production of sugar. Al-Maqrīzī states that Isma'īl ibn Māzin was already wealthy when he died in 787/1385–86.[14] By 799/1396–97, his position was taken up by his grandson Muḥammad ibn 'Umar Abū al-Sunūn, who "exceeded in the sowing of village lands and the setting up of waterwheels for sugarcane and sugar presses."[15] Whereas the rebels loyal to al-Aḥdab had previously targeted the sugar presses as the symbols of state power, less than fifty years later the Hawwāra were co-opted into provincial administration as the rightful possessors of sugar production.

Economic success was accompanied by accumulation of political power and the spread of Hawwāra identities throughout the regions under their control. The Hawwāra's capital of Jirjā replaced Qūṣ and Asyut as the most important town of Upper Egypt.[16] By the 1410s, Muḥammad Abū al-Sunūn and his brothers, known collectively as Awlād 'Umar, had control over lands from Aswan in the south to the northern edges of al-Ashmūnayn. A second Hawwāra family, that of Banū Gharīb, controlled the province of al-Bahnasāwiyya in Middle Egypt. Al-Qalqashandī, writing during that decade of swift Hawwāra ascendancy, states that "the other 'urbān of Upper Egypt bow to their will, side with them and obey them."[17] As a result, many villagers came to identify themselves as Hawwāra. Al-Qalqashandī lists the names of about thirty different Hawwāra clans in Upper Egypt and notes that al-Ḥamdānī, writing in the mid-thirteenth century, knew of only four Hawwāra clans in the same region. The more powerful the Hawwāra grew, al-Qalqashandī explains, the more numerous they became.

The fighting in Upper Egypt concentrated on the rivalry between the two leading Hawwāra families, the Awlād 'Umar and the Banū Gharīb. The Mamluk provincial governors were relegated to the background and could only exert power if they allied themselves with one of these branches. In 791/1389, the governor contrived with the Hawwāra to keep agricultural revenues in Upper Egypt.[18] The arrest of the leader of the Banū Gharīb family in al-Bahnasā in 798/1395–96 caused his supporters to rise up against the governor and kill him, and the new governor could only act with the support of the Awlād 'Umar.[19] Soon afterward, the *kāshif* of Upper Egypt required the protection of Awlād 'Umar from an alliance of Banū Gharīb with the heirs of al-Aḥdab.[20]

The early decades of the fifteenth century saw the Hawwāra monopolize power in Upper Egypt by eliminating other Arab elites, including the descendants of al-Aḥdab and the long-lasting Kanz dynasty in Aswan. The descendants of al-Aḥdab were given promises of support from Cairo, but they were defeated in 802/1399–1400 by Muḥammad Abū al-Sunūn. A government attempt to send a punitive force failed, since the amirs refused to go on campaign, underlining the degree to which the imperial center lost control over Upper Egypt.[21] The Hawwāra then annihilated the Awlād al-Kanz in Aswan in 815/1412, taking their women and children captive. The Kanz had held power over Aswan since the early eleventh century and were the last remnant of the Arab groups installed in Upper Egypt by the Fatimids. In previous centuries the Kanz had bounced back from defeats at the hands of the Ayyubids in the 1170s, and later from a Mamluk attempt to impose their own governor in Aswan in 1365.[22] But this time the Hawwāra were there to stay, and the Kanz completely disappear from our sources.

The Hawwāra's expansion effectively ended Mamluk rule in Upper Egypt. Two successive military campaigns in the harvest seasons of 821/1418 and 822/1419 no longer aimed to impose law and order, but only to extract resources. The commander of the 1418 campaign, the amir Ibn Abī al-Faraj, imposed a tribute in cash, with some villages having to pay up to two thousand dinars. This must have been in lieu of unpaid land tax. He also imposed a tribute of twenty-five thousand dinars on the leaders of the Hawwāra. The booty he brought with him included, in addition to camels and horses, six thousand oxen and two thousand *qinṭār* of sugar.[23] A subsequent campaign in the following year brought back three thousand oxen, nine thousand water buffalos, sugar (both *qind* and *ʿasal*), and a large quantity of grains. The Hawwāra troops traveled to Aswan and then to the Oases to avoid being captured.[24] As al-Maqrīzī acknowledged, this was a state-sponsored raid that crippled the economy and deprived the peasantry of their working animals. The *mamlūk* amirs brought back to Cairo thousands of male and female slaves, including many enslaved by the Mamluk troops. The mass enslavement of peasants, also seen at the end of al-Aḥdab's rebellion, was possibly triggered by the decreasing supply of slaves from the Black Sea. Given the legal prohibitions against enslavement of Muslims in general, and of subject Muslims in particular, this enslavement further underscores how much the Mamluks came to view Upper Egypt as enemy territory.[25]

Much of the Hawwāra's wealth came from sugar production and other investment in agriculture. This was complemented by local iqṭāʿ holdings of unknown amount. Ibn al-Jīʿān's cadastral survey of the 1480s shows very limited Arab iqṭāʿ holdings in Upper Egypt, and even the Hawwāra power base of Jirjā is not listed as their iqṭāʿ.[26] It is likely, however, that Ibn al-Jīʿān's data did not represent the ordinary pattern of iqṭāʿ holdings in Upper Egypt, but rather the temporary imposition of direct Mamluk rule in the 1470s by the amir Yashbak min Mahdī.[27] The Ottoman registers of the 1550s show that about 10 percent of the village fiscal units in the region of Qūṣ, 10 out of 103, were directly in the hands of the Banū ʿUmar of the Hawwāra.[28] It is reasonable to assume that this was the share of the local tax revenues to which the Hawwāra normally had rights to during the fifteenth century.

Be that as it may, it is clear that the Hawwāra received a significant share of the agricultural revenues of Upper Egypt—significant enough for Hawwāra amirs to pay entry fees of tens of thousands of dinars, and to arm tens of thousands of villagers. In 844/1440–41, the sultan appointed Ismaʿīl ibn Yūsuf as amir of the Hawwāra for a total payment of seventy thousand dinars, of which forty thousand were a down payment. Ismaʿīl also promised the obedience of the Hawwāra, which his predecessor was unable to deliver.[29] Yet, when their leaders were snubbed or arrested, the Hawwāra and their supporters targeted grain warehouses and waterwheels.[30] As reported in the final pages of al-Maqrīzī's *Sulūk*, internal fighting among the Hawwāra continued in the 1430s.[31] They were without doubt the dominant military force in Upper Egypt throughout the fifteenth century. *Zubdat Kashf al-Mamālik*, composed in 857/1453, lists the Hawwāra as mobilizing twenty-four thousand riders for royal campaigns, far more than any other Egyptian Arab or Berber group.[32]

Like al-Aḥdab before them, the Hawwāra were closely aligned with provincial Sufi or saintly figures. In 834/1430–31, the "Shaykh of the Sufis (*al-fuqarāʾ*)," a certain ʿAbd al-Dāʾim, came to intercede on behalf of Mūsā ibn ʿUmar, the leader of the Hawwāra.[33] Eight years later, a group of saints (*ṣulaḥāʾ*) accompanied leaders of the Hawwāra to a meeting with the commander of a Mamluk raid into Upper Egypt.[34] The association with Sufi shaykhs must have granted the Hawwāra an aura of legitimacy, both in the eyes of the Mamluk authorities and, perhaps more importantly, in the eyes of the local Muslim peasantry. Sufi shaykhs would go on to become an integral part of the power wielded by Arab provincial families in the sixteenth century.

The ʿĀʾidh of the Eastern Delta

Another well-attested example of an Arab provincial ruling house is the Awlād ʿĪsā of the ʿĀʾidh, who rose to dominate the eastern delta and Sinai in the second half of the fourteenth century. As we have seen, the ʿĀʾidh Arabs had been present in Sinai since the late Fatimid period, acting in the service of the local governor of al-Ṭūr and providing security to travelers on the road from al-Qulzum (present-day Suez) to Karak and ʿAqaba. In the final decades of the fourteenth century, however, the power of the shaykhs and amirs of the ʿĀ'idh grew, and they took over most functions previously held by Mamluk governors. In 787/1385, the sultan appointed Muḥammad ibn ʿĪsā al-ʿĀ'idhī as the inspector of irrigation (*kāshif al-jusūr*) of al-Sharqiyya. Seven months later the same al-ʿĀ'idhī was promoted to the governorship of the province, although he was demoted from this position within a couple of years and subsequently executed in 796/1394.[35] The appointment of an Arab leader as provincial governor was unprecedented and was part of experiments with novel models of provincial administration seen throughout the 1380s. Alongside the settlement of the Hawwāra in Jirjā in Upper Egypt, the promotion of the ʿĀ'idh represented a countrywide co-optation of Arab elites.

By the early fifteenth century, the ʿĀ'idh shaykhs of al-Sharqiyya began to act as de facto governors.[36] The shift was formally achieved in the first decade of the fifteenth century, when the Mamluk regime stopped appointing mamluk officers as governors of the province.[37] From then on, as attested in the St. Catherine corpus, sultanic edicts were regularly addressed to the ʿĀ'idh shaykhs. The first decree of this kind is dated Rajab 805 (January to February 1403); it is addressed to *mashāyikh al-ʿurbān al-ʿĪsāwiyya*, that is, the descendants of ʿĪsā al-ʿĀ'idhī.[38] In this edict, the ʿĀ'idh shaykhs were instructed to prevent subordinate, local ʿurbān from grazing their animals in the vicinity of the monastery (incidentally, this is the earliest mention of animal husbandry in the St. Catherine corpus). Progressively, the ʿĀ'idh leaders acquired the kind of lofty titles previously reserved for the Mamluk military elite. In a royal decree of 870/1466, for example, *amīr ʿurbān* al-ʿĀ'idh in Sharqiyya is given honorary titles of *al-majlis al-sāmī* and *al-amīr al-ajall*.[39]

The ʿĀ'idh in al-Sharqiyya were now responsible for the protection of the monks from other ʿurbān.[40] They did that by introducing Arab protection, or *khafāra*, as an instrument of local security. In 874/1469, following complaints against the ʿurbān of Awlād ʿAlī, the ʿurbān of al-Sharqiyya drafted a legal contract of protection with the monastery. This contract, dated January 1470, is the earliest of its type in the St. Catherine corpus. In it, two men of the Awlād ʿAlī, identified as protectors (*khufarā'*) in the region of al-Ṭūr, undertook to provide security to the monastery. The two Awlād ʿAlī protectors stood as guarantors for losses suffered by the monks and promised to reimburse the monastery for transgressions by any of their relatives. The concluding part of the document confirms that this legal obligation was undertaken at the instigation of the leader of the ʿurbān in al-Sharqiyya, presumably a shaykh of the ʿĀ'idh.[41] Whether the Awlād ʿAlī clan were viewed as part of the ʿĀ'idh confederacy is unclear. They once refer to themselves as Awlād ʿAlī of the ʿĀʾidh, but such identification is not found in the many other documents where they appear.[42] Formal contracts for protection of the monastery carried on until the end of the Mamluk period,[43] and they are also mentioned by European travelers of the last decades of the fifteenth century.[44] Arab formal protection of monasteries is known to us from the eleventh century (see chapter 1), but it disappeared from our records in the intervening period; the return of formal Arab protection in the late fifteenth century was linked to the reemergence of an Arab provincial ruling class.

The Arabs of al-Sharqiyya were supported by generous iqṭāʿ allocations, more so than any other Arab or Berber group in fifteenth-century Egypt. As recorded in Ibn al-Jīʿān's cadastral survey of 1480, Arab groups held iqṭāʿ grants in nearly half the villages of the eastern delta, 176 out of 382 villages, and they were the major landholding group in the province. They were the sole iqṭāʿ holders in about sixty villages, with a total surface area of ninety-one thousand feddans. Compared with the 1378 register, this represented a quadrupling of the number of villages held as iqṭāʿ by Arab leaders in al-Sharqiyya.[45] Ibn al-Jīʿān's register does not record the names of individual Arab families, but it seems likely that the ʿĀʾidh, acting as de facto provincial governors, were the main beneficiaries of these iqṭāʿ grants. The St. Catherine corpus shows that the co-optation of local Arab families into provincial administration coincided with the disappearance of other iqṭāʿ holders, formerly a powerful presence in the region of al-Ṭūr. The last mention of non-Arab iqṭāʿ holders in the St. Catherine corpus occurs in a decree dated 815/1413.[46]

The ʿĀʾidh dominated over a peasantry that considered itself Arab. Al-Qalqashandī notes the "Bedouin" nature of the population of al-Sharqiyya (*badāwat ghālib ahlihi*), due to the absence of orchards and the proximity of the province to marsh lands.[47] Peasants relying on cereals rather than on perennial irrigation are again seen here as more likely to adopt Arab identities. In *Zubdat kashf al-mamālik*, written in the middle of the fifteenth century, al-Ẓāhirī states that the ʿurbān of al-Sharqiyya established many settlements in marshy steppe (*bādiya*) areas that were not suitable for cultivation, and that these villages are not registered in the records of the Dīwān.[48] Nonetheless, it is evident that the Arabs of al-Sharqiyya were primarily a sedentary population.[49] Despite the statement by al-Ẓāhirī, al-Sharqiyya had hundreds of land-tax-paying villages by the end of the fifteenth century, as recorded in Ibn al-Jīʿān's cadastral survey; only eighteen of them had substandard soil completely unfit for cultivation.[50]

In return for iqṭāʿ grants, the ʿĀʾidh carried the responsibility for guarding the roads and for local security, and they were expected to ensure road safety and provisions for travelers between Egypt and Syria.[51] Al-Qalqashandī explains that the ʿurbān of al-Sharqiyya, like those of al-Buḥayra, received iqṭāʿ grants because of their role as route protectors (*arbāb al-adrāk*) and because they supplied horses for the postal stations.[52] In fact, the Mamluk postal system was no longer in use after 1400, reflecting the general withdrawal of the regime from the countryside.[53] A legal document of 921/1515 illustrates the duties that the ʿĀ'idh have by then assumed with regard to St. Catherine's Monastery: the shaykh of the ʿĀ'idh testified in a Cairo court that he is responsible for the safety of the monks and their property when they are traveling to and from the monastery, as has been customary by his predecessors who held the leadership (*mashyakha*) of the ʿurbān. He was also responsible for reimbursing the monks for stolen property out of his own pocket.[54]

In al-Sharqiyya and elsewhere in the Egyptian countryside, narrative and documentary sources highlight the role of *arbāb al-adrāk*, or route protectors, in provincial administration. Since 800/1398, edicts sent to St. Catherine routinely include the *arbāb al-adrāk* in their formal list of addressees, alongside the leaders of the ʿurbān. Late-fifteenth-century decrees identify the Banū Sulaymān as the route protectors in al-Ṭūr.[55] In other provinces the *arbāb al-adrāk* are mentioned as offering gifts to the sultan during a hunting excursion toward Upper Egypt, chasing a rebellious amir, and guarding the corpses of executed brigands in al-Gharbiyya.[56] The *arbāb al-adrāk* were invariably identified as Arabs or ʿurbān, and they are mostly viewed in positive light. When a Mamluk official killed "many leaders of the ʿurbān and *arbāb al-adrāk*" and took over their property, he "brought about the desolation of the land."[57]

Contemporary European pilgrims to Sinai confirm the policing roles of local Arabs, who were previously mentioned only as guides. Since the second half of the fourteenth century, pilgrims had to pay tolls to official and nonofficial Arab armed men on the route to Mt. Sinai and back to Gaza. In 1384, Frescobaldi encountered the "official of the Lord of the Arabs," who checked his safe-conduct documents.[58] His fellow traveler Gucci was robbed by a group of Muslims who claimed to be officials of the "grand interpreter of the Arabs."[59] A century later, Adorno met Sinai Arabs who demanded *gaphyr*, derived from Arabic *ghafāra*, protection payment.[60] According to Adorno, the Benetye (Banū Ṭayy) took no notice of sultanic protections, and they only spared those travelers who were accompanied by a member of their own tribe.[61] Bertrandon de La Brocquière, who had fallen ill on the way to St. Catherine, was taken back to Gaza by one of the Arab guides. He was shown generosity and spent the night at an Arab camp, with his money and provisions untouched.[62] European travelers continued to comment on the extreme poverty of the Sinai Arabs.[63] But the weakly, thieving, and treacherous Arabs of the twelfth and thirteenth centuries were now often replaced with powerful and sometimes honorable individuals.

Unlike the Berber Hawwāra of Upper Egypt, the Arab ʿĀ'idh in al-Sharqiyya were not expected to make significant contributions to royal campaigns. When called upon to fight against Tamerlane, the combined forces of the ʿĀ'idh ʿĪsāwiyya and of another group, the Banū Wā'il, numbered only 1,500 riders.[64] In *Zubdat Kashf al-Mamālik*, the ʿĀ'idh are said to muster only one thousand riders, compared with twenty-four thousand expected from the Hawwāra.[65] The Hawwāra were local landowners, mostly deriving revenue from investments in sugar presses and waterwheels. In the less lucrative environment of al-Sharqiyya, the ʿĀ'idh were mainly supported by iqṭāʿ and provided regional security in return; the number of troops they were able to mount appears limited, and there is little evidence of the spread of clans claiming ʿĀ'idh lineage in the eastern delta. The peasantry of al-Sharqiyya was primarily Arab, but few saw themselves as being part of the same confederacy as the dominant Awlād ʿĪsā family.

Arab Houses in Other Delta Provinces

While our evidence for the Hawwāra of Upper Egypt and the ʿĀ'idh in al-Sharqiyya is especially rich, Arab families came to dominate other provinces of the Egyptian countryside. In several delta provinces, leaders of Arab groups were given the rank of Shaykh al-ʿArab or Amīr al-ʿArab, titles that were not widely used in Egypt before the middle of the fourteenth century.[66] Al-Qalqashandī reports such positions in al-Minūfiyya and al-Gharbiyya. He adds that the amirs of al-Minūfiyya are not amirs in the ordinary sense of military commanders, but rather in the sense of leadership over Arab clans (*fī maʿnā mashyakhat al-ʿarab*).[67] Provincial Arab leaders in the delta were now important enough to earn a place in biographical dictionaries. Al-Sakhāwī provided entries for the Shaykh al-ʿArab of al-Minūfiyya, two Shaykh al-ʿArab officials in al-Gharbiyya, and one of the *mashāyikh al-ʿurbān* in al-Buḥayra.[68] By the end of the fifteenth century, Ibn Iyās reports such a position in al-Qalyūbiyya, too.[69]

The chronicle by Ibn Iyās also allows us to trace the biography of an Arab strongman called al-Juwaylī, who was active in al-Buḥayra and al-Gharbiyya in the final decades of the sultanate. His rise to power has now been studied by Adam Sabra.[70] Al-Buḥayra, which had long-standing Arab dominance, saw internal fighting among Arab groups in the middle of the fifteenth century, leading to the deaths of more than three thousand men.[71] Al-Juwaylī first appears in Ibn Iyās's chronicle in the year 891/1486.[72] In 904/1498 he worked with a certain Marʿī to dominate al-Buḥayra and al-Gharbiyya, preventing collection of the land tax by Mamluk officials.[73] By 917/1511 he was part of the Mamluk provincial administration, since he wrote to Sultan Qāniṣawh al-Ghawrī informing him that he had arrested a number of ʿurbān responsible for murdering ʿĪsā ibn Jumayl, previous Shaykh al-ʿArab in al-Gharbiyya.[74] By 918/1512 al-Juwaylī himself acquired the title of Shaykh al-ʿArab and was involved in quelling a rebellion by ʿAzzāla Arabs and other ʿurbān in al-Buḥayra accused of marching into villages and seizing the harvests.[75] In the following year he was given the title of *shaykh jihāt al-Buḥayra.*[76] By the time of his death in Dhū al-Qaʿda 919/January 1514, al-Juwaylī had asserted himself as a rural strongman who worked with the Mamluk authorities to expel troublesome ʿurbān from al-Buḥayra.[77] Al-Juwaylī attempted to pass his post to his nephew Ismāʿīl ibn ʿĀmir.[78] The later chronicler al-Jazīrī attributed al-Juwaylī's success to his ability to unite different village clans under the umbrella confederacy of the Banū ʿAwna. According to al-Jazīrī, the Banū ʿAwna were originally made up of many smaller clans (*ṭāʾifa*), each paying its own land tax (*kharāj*). By unifying the clans under his leadership, al-Juwaylī mounted an effective challenge to the Mamluk amirs and was able to secure a provincial power base.[79]

Arab houses in the central and western delta had much in common with the Hawwāra in Upper Egypt and the ʿĀʾidh in al-Sharqiyya. Like the Hawwāra, these Arab houses allied themselves with Sufi saintly figures. Shaykh al-ʿArab of al-Minūfiyya was known for his respect and generosity toward Shaykh Madyan and his *zāwiya.* Al-Sakhāwī was doubtful about his sincerity.[80] The alliance went both ways, since Sufis readily afforded their blessing to ruling Arab families.[81] Arab provincial leaders in the central and western delta also paid entry fees. The Shaykh al-ʿArab in al-Gharbiyya had to pay thirty thousand dinars in return for his appointment, suggesting that he could expect to recoup this investment through access to a significant portion of the local tax revenues.[82] The primarily financial dimension of these positions is highlighted by al-Qalqashandī, who says that the Arabs of al-Buḥayra used to boast of the bravery of their amirs, but in his time—i.e., the 1410s—they are led by a group of ʿurbān who possess enormous wealth.[83] As for iqṭāʿ, Arab clansmen held 20 percent of the villages of the western province of al-Buḥayra. This was again conceived as a reward for their role in guarding the main routes from Alexandria.[84] In the delta provinces of al-Gharbiyya, al-Minūfiyya, and al-Daqahliyya, Arabs held a share of about 10 percent of the cultivable land.[85]

While the ruling Arab houses were the most important section of the emerging provincial elites in Lower Egypt, we also find the parallel rise of civilian, non-Arab local elites of tax farmers, known as *mutadarrikūn*. As shown by Daisuke Igarashi, the *mutadarrikūn* were merchants or scholars who were awarded contracts of tens of thousands of dinars for collection of taxes from prosperous delta villages or towns. The localities known to have been handed over to *mutadarrikūn* are al-Manzala, Fāriskūr, Jawjar, and Ziftā, all found in al-Daqahliyya and al-Gharbiyya. These localities do not overlap with the villages under the control of the Arab elite families, and it seems likely that the unarmed *mutadarrikūn* were responsible for tax collection in market villages and towns, while the Arabs were responsible for delivering the taxes in smaller, grain-producing settlements.[86] *Mashāyikh al-ʿurbān* and the *mutadarrikūn* are jointly mentioned as presenting tribute to Sultan Qāʾitbāy upon his accession to the throne in 873/1469.[87] These twin branches of the rural elites were also mentioned together as present in al-Gharbiyya by the time of the Ottoman conquest.[88]

The increase in the power of Egyptian Arab elites did not go unnoticed by fifteenth-century European visitors, who were now much more likely to comment on the prestige attached to men of Arab stock. Adorno states that the Arabs are considered the most noble among Muslims since Muḥammad was one of them.[89] While crusader-era European accounts had the Arabs "turning like reeds in the wind," later authors tended to see the Arabs as a useful thorn in the side of the sultanate. Mandeville, writing circa 1350, says that the Arabs fight the sultan if they are aggrieved.[90] Ghillebert de Lannoy (ca. 1420) states that they are brave people who fight the sultan, although they tend to mostly fight each other.[91] Adorno believed that it was precisely their incessant infighting that made them pay no attention to the sultan.[92] Santo Brasca (1480) wrote that the Arabs fight the "Moors" and usually beat them through regular use of bows.[93] The use of bow and arrow by Arabs is also mentioned by Fabri and other travelers of the 1480s.[94] This departs from earlier authors who made much of the Arab exclusive reliance on spears and lances.

The most detailed fifteenth-century European account of Arab power in the Egyptian countryside is by Emmanuel Piloti, a merchant resident of Alexandria and writing in 1420.[95] Piloti divided the population of Egypt into three "nations": the *mamlūk* military elite, the local "Egyptians," and the Arabs who are the lords of the countryside. The three groups fight each other, like Guelfs and Ghibellines in Italy, as each has its own claim to hegemony over the land; the Arab claim is based on genealogy, as they "say that power and lordship should belong to them, for Muḥammad was Arab of their nation."[96] Piloti was personally familiar with the Arabs who inhabited the lands between Cairo and Alexandria, and he states that these Arabs provided Alexandria with grains and all manner of animal product while they depended on the city for textiles, oil, honey, and soap.[97] The Arabs wage wars on the sultan because they refuse to pay him tribute, and the sultan was therefore forced to campaign every few years, with the aim of capturing the Arab chiefs and demanding ransom for their release. Piloti emphasizes the ideological aspect of the Arab resistance, which he compares to the resistance of Bologna to the Church in Rome. The Arabs refuse to pay tribute because the *mamlūks* are a blameworthy nation, slaves who were bought and sold with the money taken from the Egyptian peasants, while the Arabs themselves have been in charge of the land since ancient times.[98] The Arabs publicly say that the lords of Cairo are infidel dogs, renegade Christians who had been bought as slaves.[99] Piloti then argues that "the Arab nation is the closest to the Christians out of all the pagans" and reports that certain Arabs told him how they cannot wait for the European Christians to take over Alexandria so they can join forces with them.[100] There is much wishful thinking here, but also perhaps a reflection of a genuine, simmering animosity of rural Arabs toward a Turkish ruling elite of military slaves.

Al-Asadī on Arabs and Peasants

The processes of change in the Egyptian countryside in the final century of Mamluk rule, including the co-optation of Arab elites, are the subject of an insightful account by Muḥammad ibn Muḥammad al-Asadī, part of his *al-Taysīr wa'l-I'tibār wa'l-Taḥrīr wa'l-Ikhtibār fīmā Yajibu min Ḥusn al-Tadbīr wa-al-Taṣarruf wa'l-Ikhtiyār*, written in 855/1451 for the benefit of fellow bureaucrats in Cairo.[101] Al-Asadī composed the treatise in response to what he perceived as the maladministration of the Mamluk sultanate, with particular focus on monetary reforms and on the decline of Egyptian agriculture, which he attributed to the neglect of irrigation, the oppression of the peasantry, and the ubiquity of bribes. Al-Asadī also included a shorter discourse on the decline of Syrian agriculture and the rise of rural *'ushrān* in the Syrian countryside (see chapter 8), but most of his attention is devoted to Egypt. His account of the relationship between Arab and peasant identities is directly pertinent to the arguments of this chapter and of the book as a whole and therefore deserves to be discussed in some detail.

Al-Asadī begins his analysis of the deterioration of the Egyptian economy with the transformation of peasants into 'urbān, caused by the neglect and oppression of the Mamluk authorities: "Many of those disobedient 'urbān, who are [now] steppe people of the open country, used to be tax-paying cultivators and peasants, inclined to willingly obey the rulers (*kathīrān min hādhihi al-'urbān al-'uṣāh, alladhīna hum ahl bawādī fī al-falāh, kānū ahl zarʿ wa-rafʿ wa-filāḥa maʿa al-inqiyād bi-ḥusn al-ṭāʿa li'l-wulāh)*."[102] The cause of this shift from law-abiding cultivators to disobedient ʿurbān was the neglect of irrigation works by the authorities, followed by destruction and incessant local fighting. Since the local governors took the side of those who had money and power and capacity to cultivate, the weak were forced to migrate away from the land: "Those who were afflicted with weakness and deficiency endured much harm and suffering. When this situation continued, some of them migrated from the land due to their meekness and to the predominance of harm and disturbances.[103]

Eventually, the peasants forced out from their lands were integrated into the ʿurbān who lived outside of the agricultural areas: "This has led to resentment by those who left the land (*al-rāḥilīn*), and to their disobedience; they agreed with the people of the steppe (*al-bawādī*) to rebel and disobey the community. For there is no doubt that life among the people of the steppe is tougher compared to sedentary life (*ahl al-ḥaḍar*), and the former cultivators remember the ease of civilized life (*al-ʿumrān*). Their want for sustenance for themselves, their families, and their animals is a source of constant harm for them."[104] Therefore, concludes al-Asadī, these landless migrant peasants had no choice (*lā budda*) but to gather their forces and to set out together to destroy, fight, and loot.

After explaining the motivations of the peasants-turned-ʿurbān, al-Asadī expands on the co-optation of Arab elites into the provincial administration. Faced with uprisings by those who were forced off the land, the authorities opened criminal trials against them and called up every person, both *badw* and *ḥaḍar*, to fight the rebels. The rebels were put under constant watch, and regular expeditionary forces were sent against them. But these campaigns were of limited success, because whenever the rebels felt they were beaten, they took refuge in the mountains and fortified themselves there. Failing to quell these rebellions, the state authorities then decided to appoint amirs and *mutadarrik*s (here, either tax farmers or, in the sense of *arbāb al-adrāk*, route protectors) throughout the land. The Mamluk authorities also decided to side with the ʿurbān that they found loyal and obedient, and they handed them stipends and iqṭāʿ grants in return for their obedience and for watching over and protecting the roads.[105]

As provincial power was delegated to Arab elites, says al-Asadī, Arabs and peasants parted ways. The enmity between the state-sponsored Arab elites and those who had to leave their lands (*al-rāḥilīn ʿan al-awṭān*) increased, and so did the internal fighting among the ʿurbān. He then describes the peasants who were left on the land as being stuck between a rock and a hard place: "The fallāḥs have become stuck (*qaffān*) between two opposing forces, unable to satisfy both sides simultaneously—the people of the state (*ahl al-dawla*) are in front of them, demanding what they have and what they do not; while the belligerent Arabs (*al-ʿarab al-muḥāribūn*) are to the back, right, and left." Under these conditions, many of the peasants abandoned their lands (*tasaḥḥaba*), and even those who stayed put could not practice agriculture. The final outcome, says al-Asadī, is that the countryside grows even more impoverished and depopulated.

Al-Asadī's account, written circa 1450, describes four stages of the relationship between the peasantry and the Mamluk state. First, peasants who were forced out of their lands, either because the neglect of irrigation or due to the injustice of Mamluk officials, joined the ranks of the ʿurbān who lived outside the agricultural areas. Second, these former peasants expressed their frustration by waging guerrilla warfare against provincial Mamluk institutions and provoking military responses from the regime. Third, the Mamluk authorities, realizing that they are unable to secure victory against these mobile forces, delegated provincial authority to loyal ʿurbān elites and rewarded them with generous iqṭāʿ, hoping they will be able to quell the unrest. The result, according to al-Asadī, was that the peasants who remained on the land were now subject to double pressure, both from the tax collectors sent by the state and by the Arabs.

There is much overlap between al-Asadī's analysis of Egyptian rural society and the arguments advanced throughout this book. Al-Asadī saw Arab and peasant identities as fluid and believed that Egyptian cultivators turned Arab when they lost their land. Their "Arab rebellions" were acts of desperation in opposition to excessive extraction by military landlords and to the official neglect of the irrigation system. Writing in the middle of the fifteenth century, al-Asadī is also very much aware of the current limited capacity of the imperial center to quell rural resistance. It is this inability to suppress rebellions by peasants-turned-Arab that required the sultanate to devolve authority and wealth to loyal Arab families, who now demanded their own share of the agricultural surplus. His account fits what we know of the fifteenth-century rise of the Hawwāra in Upper Egypt, the Awlād ʿĪsā in al-Sharqiyya, and the strongman al-Juwaylī in the western delta.

In al-Asadī's scheme, Arab identities were formed on the margins of the agricultural areas of the Nile Valley, and peasants turned Arab once they left their villages. As we have seen in earlier chapters of *Becoming Arab*, however, there is consistent evidence that Arab identities had developed within village communities. In eleventh-century Fayyum, Arab protectors were a resident elite of tax guarantors that supplanted the class of wealthy Christian landowners that dominated the province in previous centuries. In thirteenth-century Fayyum, Muslim villages were inhabited by Arab clans who leased their village lands from military iqṭāʿ holders sent from Cairo. Peasants had turned Arab in the twelfth and thirteenth centuries, in response to a fiscal regime that severely limited cultivators' options of landownership, and in the aftermath of mass rural conversion. What al-Asadī witnessed in the mid-fifteenth century was the tail end of a process that lasted four centuries—the final stage in which the direct suppression of rural resistance was replaced by delegation of powers to rural Arab or Berber elites.

We also have evidence that tax-paying cultivators continued to present themselves as Arab during al-Asadī's lifetime. An anecdote reported by Ibn Taghrī Birdī in his annals of 822/1419–20, when Upper Egypt was already dominated by the Hawwāra, exemplifies peasants' continued appropriation of lineage claims as a means of resistance:

> A trustworthy person from Upper Egypt told me: most of the cultivators (*muzāriʿīn*) in our village (*balad*) were *ashrāf* of ʿAlid descent, while the tax collector (*ʿāmil*) in the village was Christian. When the tax collector came, the peasants (fallaḥūn) used to come out to greet him, some of them greeting him as customary while others refraining, and some of the poor and needy, or those fearful of the landowner (*ṣāḥib*) of the village even kiss his hand and ask for easing the burden of the land tax.[106]

The distressing image of Muslim peasants prostrating before a Christian tax collector is exacerbated here by their noble Prophetic descent. By this period, Arab identities had been established in Upper Egypt for centuries, so much so that a peasant's claim to Prophetic descent has become normalized in a way unimaginable under the Abbasids or the Fatimids. The boundaries between Arabs and villagers remained fluid during the first half of the fifteenth century: in 820/1417–18, Egyptian peasants and ʿurbān were lumped together as victims of unjust exactions. A few years later, the land tax of the peasants could only be delivered after overcoming the opposition of the Arabs.[107] Violence between villages was associated with Arab armed men well into the last decades of the sultanate. In a late-fifteenth-century petition concerning looting and killing committed by individuals from two al-Sharqiyya villages against a neighboring one, a local official identifies the perpetrators as *ʿurbā*, likely mistake for ʿurbān, and asks that they be apprehended despite the protection afforded to them by their local iqṭāʿ holder.[108]

Moreover, Egyptian villages continued to be collectively led by groups of headmen, a form of social organization that marked the Arab village clans attested throughout the Ayyubid and Mamluk periods. Three edicts from the later decades of the fifteenth century address groups of headmen and peasants (*jamāʿat al-mashāyikh waʾl-fallāḥīn*) in Egyptian villages. One was sent in 875/1470 from the senior amir Khāyirbak to the headmen and peasants of the village of Ṭūbhār in the Fayyum; he orders them to cultivate the land and to prepare the land tax and customary hospitality dues.[109] Another edict from the same period was sent to the headmen and peasants of Shaybat Shaqqāra in al-Sharqiyya.[110] Arab village clans, led by groups of headmen, endured in the Egyptian countryside up to the end of the Mamluk period.

Arabs and Peasants in the Fifteenth Century

This chapter argued that the rise of Arab ruling families in the Egyptian provinces signaled a shift in the balance of power between center and periphery, mirroring similar developments in fifteenth-century Syria and Palestine. Since the 1350s, following a century of suppression and bloody revolts, the Mamluk regime loosened its grip on the Egyptian countryside. As iqṭāʿ holders were no longer able to effectively enforce tax collection in the aftermath of the Black Death, local elites stepped in. These local elites included tax-farming merchants and scholars, known as *mutadarrikūn*, as well as leading houses of the Arab village clans. The Hawwāra became the effective rulers of Upper Egypt, and the Awlād ʿĪsā of the ʿĀʾidh the de facto governors of al-Sharqiyya. The number of iqṭāʿ grants for Arab leaders increased. As European observers noted, in the last century of the sultanate the Arabs became the lords of the countryside.

In the fifteenth century, more so than in earlier periods, rural people used Arab identity as a means of distinguishing themselves from the Mamluk ruling classes. The military elite of the Mamluk state was broadly defined as "Turk," a term that signified access to state resources, specific military practices, as well as attachment to a set of Turkic languages and culture.[111] As Arab leading houses became increasingly autonomous in several Egyptian provinces, Arabness was further developed as a counter-identity, one that separated the elites of the countryside from the ruling classes of Cairo. The merchant Piloti wrote in 1420 that the Arabs of the countryside are a third nation, alongside the Mamluk former slaves and the Egyptian city folk, while his contemporary al-Maqrīzī retrospectively interpreted the Arab uprising of Ibn Thaʿlab as a symbolic conflict between the lineage-based legitimacy of the Arabs and the might of the imported *mamlūk* slave soldiers. The labels "Turks" and "Arabs" represented social, political, and cultural distinctions between the diminished ruling class of the Mamluk state on the one hand, and the ascendant rural elites on the other.

Most Egyptian villages continued to be inhabited by clans, as they have been since the beginning of the thirteenth century. But the co-optation of Arab and Berber ruling families into Mamluk provincial administration accentuated a hierarchy of dominant and subservient clans, one that reflected relations of power on the ground. As power came to be monopolized by individual houses, their name distinguished them from the weaker clans of the same confederacy. Fifteenth-century sources often speak of the Banū 'Umar of Upper Egypt, or the Awlād 'Īsā in al-Sharqiyya, to separate them from broader groups of rural people who identified as Hawwāra or 'Ā'idh. Muslim peasants in Egypt continued to share a genealogical worldview and an Arab or Berber identity but no longer shared the same lineage as the Arab families that came to rule over them.

As al-Asadī observed, the increasing power of Arab ruling families pitted them against the mass of the peasantry over which they came to dominate. Their co-optation into state administration also marked the end of the great Arab rebellions of the thirteenth and fourteenth centuries. It was now the prerogative of the Hawwāra of Upper Egypt or the 'Ā'idh of al-Sharqiyya to collect tribute and impose law and order in the villages. Fifteenth-century accounts of clashes between Arab groups and the Mamluk regime no longer refer to the participation of peasants or to attempts to loot warehouses storing the land tax.[112] By the end of the Mamluk period there are unequivocal examples of Arab clansmen attacking peasants, quite a rare occurrence throughout the Ayyubid and Mamluk periods. Ibn Iyās reports 'urbān raids in al-Sharqiyya leading to a massacre of peasants in 922/1516, immediately following the news of the Mamluk defeat to the Ottomans. The raids were led by the provincial Shaykh al-'Arab Ibn Baqar and a group of Egyptian 'ashīr, who then continued to raid the retreating Mamluk army.[113]

In the end, it was the Shaykh al-'Arab of al-Buḥayra Ḥasan ibn Mar'ī who turned over the last Mamluk sultan Ṭūmān Bāy to the Ottoman sultan Selim for execution.[114] The Ottomans formalized the role of the provincial Arab families and granted them a share of local tax revenue in return for securing tax collection.[115] The Kanunname of 1525 recognized the role of Arab shaykhs in "promoting agriculture, collecting revenues, and maintaining order in the villages under their control by not harboring rebels or runaway slaves."[116] It also allowed the Hawwāra clan of the Banū 'Umar to pass their position in Upper Egypt among the members of the clan, as long as they paid a customary accession fee. The same privileges were accorded to the leading Arab families of al-Sharqiyya (no longer the ʿĀʾidh but rather the Banū Baqar[117]), al-Gharbiyya, and al-Buḥayra. Appointments for the leadership of Arab clans in the provinces came directly from Istanbul, bypassing the governor of Egypt who had no authority to dismiss them. Thus, the Ottomans enshrined in law the semiautonomous status of Arab ruling houses over much of Upper Egypt and the western and eastern sections of the delta—a culmination of processes that started in the aftermath of the Black Death and matured over the course of the fifteenth century.

Conclusion

THIS BOOK BEGAN in a remote corner of eleventh-century Fayyum with the appearance of Arab elites as village protectors. It continued in the twelfth century, when rural Arab elites in the Egyptian and Syrian countrysides became the nucleus for armed units of peasants called ʿurbān. By the thirteenth and fourteenth centuries, Muslim peasants in Egypt and Greater Syria had invariably become members of village clans, were led by groups of village headmen, and claimed lineage from ancestors in the Arabian Peninsula. These village clans then joined up to form broader tribal coalitions, which mobilized to fight against other rural groups under the banners of Qays and Yaman, or to mount armed revolts against the Mamluk regime. After 1350, in the aftermath of the Black Death, the success of these revolts and the decline of the Mamluk iqṭāʿ landholding regime allowed leading Arab families to act as de facto provincial governors and tax collectors. The extent of these radical transformations cannot be exaggerated: the blanket of Arab village clans that covered the countryside in Egypt and Greater Syria by the end of the fifteenth century entailed political and cultural structures that were unimaginable five centuries earlier.

The twin drivers for the proliferation of Arab village clans were Islamization and iqṭāʿ. The emergence of Arab village clans closely followed the establishment of the iqṭāʿ landholding regime in Egypt and Syria from the twelfth century onward. In this new fiscal regime, arable land was no longer held as private property but rather transformed into state land, which was then leased out to groups of peasants led by headmen. When the iqṭāʿ regime peaked and dominated the countryside in the first century of Mamluk rule, from 1250 to 1350, so did village clans; the decline of iqṭāʿ in the post-plague era, on the other hand, led to rifts between a thin class of co-opted Arab elites and the mass of the peasantry. The other major factor in the formation of Arab clans was the mass rural conversion to Islam that took place around the twelfth century, visible in the mushrooming of village mosques and Sufi shrines. New rural converts to Islam sought to ground themselves within an Islamic social and political order, and they deployed claims of Arab lineage as a means of erasing Christian pasts and attaining status through the legitimizing power of genealogy.

In order to become Arab, villagers acquired cultural markers that expressed their new identity and kindled a reimagined collective memory. It was in this period that the pronunciation of the letter *qāf* as /g/ came to be established as a manner of Arab speech, and the garbing of the *lithām* as a manner of an Arab headgear. Plain and painted handmade pottery replaced wheel-thrown pottery in rural regions of Greater Syria dominated by Arab clans. These cultural markers were not common in Egypt and Syria before the twelfth century, neither were they an indicator of Arabness in earlier centuries. The Arab collective memory was produced through the novel genre of the Arabic popular epics, first attested in Iraq in the twelfth century, which became hugely popular in Egypt and Syria during the Mamluk period. The epics of ʿAntar and Dhāt al-Himma, with their pre-Islamic and early Islamic Arab heroes, inculcated Arab values, presented a lay version of Arab history, and allowed villagers to imagine themselves as descendants of migrant nomads from the Arabian Peninsula.

Some of these cultural markers of late medieval village clans overlap with the way Arab Bedouin communities perceive their identity today. The /g/ pronunciation of *qāf* is still seen as a distinctive characteristic of "Bedouin" dialects all over the Arabic-speaking world, even if many who employ this linguistic feature do not consider themselves *badw*. The *lithām* has been replaced by variants of the *kuffiya* headgear and other items of dress associated with Bedouin Arab identity, often worn by non-Bedouin. The coffee finjan, a tradition that came about in the early modern period, is now a ubiquitous marker of Arabness, at an age when handmade pots are no longer in fashion. In the Egyptian delta village visited by Dwight Reynolds four decades ago, the narrators of the Arabic epics were identified as "Arab" while their audience were peasants who took pleasure in blurring the lines between their world and that of the Banū Hilāl. Above all, modern Bedouin identity, like that of the late medieval villagers described in this book, idealizes kinship and clan as the most significant social bonds, and claims descent from nomadic groups that had emigrated from the Arabian Peninsula.

Despite this resemblance, it is important to emphasize that the Arabs of the Ayyubid and Mamluk eras were a much more expansive category than the modern Bedouin. The people who identify as Bedouin today, whether mobile or sedentary, are currently a minority of the Muslim rural population in Egypt and Greater Syria. That was not the case in the later Middle Ages, when Arab clans inhabited nearly all Muslim-majority villages known to us. Throughout the Ayyubid and Mamluk periods, Arab village clans were pervasive—more pervasive than they are today, more pervasive than they had been in the first four Islamic centuries. The prevalence of Arab village clans throughout the countryside of late medieval Egypt and Syria can be deduced from urban-based chronicles and genealogical texts, as has been recognized by an earlier generation of historians, such as A. N. Poliak and Nicola Ziyāda, as well as recent ones, such as Usāma Jumayl. But this book adduced further evidence from documents and texts that zoom in on the singular village and the individual villager, such as a fiscal register, a legal deed, or an autobiography.

The history of Arab village clans after the Ottoman conquest of Egypt and Greater Syria is beyond the scope of this study, but a few aspects of continuity and of divergence could be highlighted here. As noted above, the new Ottoman administration created distinctions between Arabs and other villagers. For Egypt, the Ottoman Kanunname of 1525 distinguished between the *fellah taifesi* on the one hand and the *ʿarab* or ʿurbān on the other, and specifically prohibited peasants, but not Arabs, from carrying arms.[1] Sixteenth-century Ottoman cadastral surveys of Greater Syria introduced similar distinctions between ordinary villages and villages inhabited by ethnic groups, such as Arabs or Kurds. The 1005/1596-7 cadastral survey of Palestine and Transjordan listed groups of ʿurbān and other kinship groups separately from territorially defined villages.[2] The taxes on these kinship groups were listed as lump sums. Overall, the people listed as ʿurbān, mostly located in relatively arid or swampy regions, formed a substantial minority, and up to a quarter in the districts of ʿAjlūn and Hawran in Transjordan.

Yet, Ottoman administrative distinctions between Arabs and other villagers didn't necessarily reflect realities on the ground, as other types of Ottoman records suggest that village clan structures persisted. In her study of sixteenth-century Palestinian peasants, Amy Singer found that "non-Arab" sedentary villages were nonetheless led by groups of headmen that represented the community before the authorities, fulfilling the same duties as those of headmen that appear in the fourteenth century Mamluk records discussed in this book. Occasionally, these sixteenth-century headmen were also identified by their clan names.[3] A sub-district of the province of Jerusalem included twenty villages collectively known as Banū Zayd, including Bayt Rīmā, Rammūn, and ʿAyn Yabrūd mentioned in the Haram documents. Other subdistricts were named after the Banū Ḥārith and the Banū ʿAmr. These clusters of villages were not only named after a kinship group, but also had some collective fiscal obligations.[4] Social boundaries between Arabs and peasants remained blurred.[5]

Under Ottoman rule, elite Arab families continued to exercise authority over much of the countryside well into the eighteenth century. The 1525 Kanunname awarded the leaders of the Egyptian ʿurbān extensive responsibilities.[6] During the sixteenth century, the Banū Baghdād in al-Minūfiyya held the right to the agricultural tax revenues of many local villages, and they were awarded complete autonomy in terms of enforcing this payment from the cultivators. The power of the Banū Baghdād comes across in the writings of the mystic al-Shaʿrānī, a Sufi who was part of their entourage and embodied the endurance of the Arab-Sufi alliance inaugurated in the second half of fourteenth century by the rebel al-Aḥdab.[7] Prominent Arab families dominated rural regions of most of southern Syria up to the end of the eighteenth century, culminating with the powerful autonomous reign of Ẓāhir al-ʿUmar al-Zaydānī (d. 1775) in the Galilee.[8] The Hawwāra maintained their primary role in the administration of Upper Egypt up to 1760. Zeynab Abu'l-Magd argued that they represented a "native regime," as they shared common descent with the Muslim peasantry under their domination.[9]

Frank Stewart plausibly asserts that in about 1800 "almost the whole rural population of the Arab world either still retained, or had to a large degree adopted, tribal values."[10] But Ottoman-era peasant communities in Egypt and Syria did not view themselves as Arab clans in the way described in this book for the Ayyubid and Mamluk periods. Crucially, Ottoman authorities awarded legal recognition to usufruct rights of tenant cultivators and even allowed them to pass these rights in inheritance, lifting them above the fragile status accorded to them within the iqṭāʿ regime.[11] In Egypt, the Arab identity of peasant cultivators was gradually eclipsed by a distinct fallāḥ cultural identity, beautifully expressed in *Hazz al-Quhūf*, a seventeenth-century satirical celebration of Egyptian rural life in which the fallāḥ takes center stage and in which the Arabs are practically absent.[12] A sense of distinction between Arabs and *fallāḥūn* comes across in most Ottoman-era sources. The eighteenth-century account of Egypt by Cezzār Pasha describes the Arabs as tent-dwelling watchmen who guard over villages.[13] In the population censuses of the nineteenth century, from 1848 and 1897, the ʿurbān were counted separately and constituted about 10 percent of the total population of Egypt. Ghislaine Alleaume's spatial analysis of the 1897 census data for the delta shows that the people listed as ʿurbān were not nomads; instead, they inhabited villages located in sandy soils that were not as regularly watered as most other delta settlements.[14] By the colonial era, constructions of ʿurbān identities began to resemble the current ideals of the Bedouin.[15]

Becoming Arab dramatically challenges traditional historiography of the Middle Eastern countryside and its people. As such, it could lead to renewed reflections on Bedouin and Arab identities today. Over the past century, the terms ʿurbān or *ashāʾir*, which were still in use by Ottoman administrators up to the end of the nineteenth century, have been substituted by, and collapsed into, the *bedū* or Bedouin, with its association of desert nomadism.[16] But the reality is that most Bedouin today are sedentary. Bedouin identity, like its precursor Arab identity in the late medieval period, is based on heritage and culture rather than on a nomadic way of life.[17] The repercussions of this erroneous narrative for modern Bedouin communities have been devastating. The stories of past migration these communities have told about themselves are now used against them by governments intent on dispossessing them. Nowhere is this more manifest than in the modern state of Israel, where the historiography of the Bedouin as nomads is relied on in courts of law to legitimize the repeatedly brutal removal of village communities from their lands. Reputed historians testify before learned judges that, since the Bedouin only recently settled and have always been nomads, they have no rights over the lands they have cultivated or inhabited for decades, sometimes centuries.[18]

Arab identity itself shifted time and again over the past century, rising and ebbing, contracting and expanding with the vicissitudes of colonial and postcolonial struggles. In the areas of the Middle East covered in this book, Arabness is today central to self-identity. It carries meanings that go beyond the mere linguistic command of the Arabic language, and it is far more expansive than the term Bedouin, encompassing most of the indigenous population of Egypt, Palestine, Lebanon, and Syria. Arab identity is simultaneously bound with Islam as well as with a secular outlook. Yet, alongside Arabness, most Egyptians, Syrians, and Palestinians recognize that their national identities are also the sum of many other cultures that have come before the Muslim conquest, layer upon layer. The pre-Muslim and pre-Arab remains are intimately visible and cherished. Against this background, Arab identity can become exclusionary, because traditional historiography tends to define Arabness racially and to equate it with foreign migrations. *Becoming Arab* has hopefully demonstrated that this traditional historiography is mostly wrong. Arab identity was adopted by local villagers; it was not inherited by blood nor was it a product of mass migration. Concrete evidence coming from late medieval villages allows us to capture and articulate the mutual coherence of land, people, and historical memory. And once we understand the past differently, the future meanings of Arab identities could change once more—inclusive and expansive, grounded in the rural landscape, and embracing the rich culture of the Islamic countryside.

ACKNOWLEDGMENTS

THE IDEAS for this book have been many years in the making. But they could only materialize thanks to a generous three-year Leverhulme Major Research Fellowship, held between September 2019 and August 2022, which allowed me to dedicate the time required for extensive research and writing. I am extremely grateful to the Leverhulme Trust for this opportunity.

I would like to thank my colleagues at Queen Mary University London for going over drafts of the Leverhulme application and supporting it: Jo Cohen, Julian Jackson, Kate Lowe, Colin Jones, Claire Trenery-Carrothers, and, above all, Miri Rubin, who offered steadfast support for my intellectual and academic development for many years. Hugh Kennedy and Chris Wickham provided crucial endorsements that allowed the application to proceed.

The journey of writing *Becoming Arab* involved dipping into a broad range of disciplines and primary sources, well beyond my comfort zone. For nearly every chapter of this book I relied on fellow scholars who pointed out relevant primary sources and commented on oral presentations and written drafts.

For the interpretation of documentary evidence from the Fayyum and from Sinai, I had the pleasure of learning from the expertise of Mathieu Tillier, Naïm Vanthieghem, and Lev Weitz, as well as from the participants in two consecutive conferences of the International Society for Arabic Papyrology. I'm grateful to Andreas Kaplony for inviting me to the conferences, and, crucially, for establishing and maintaining the Arabic Papyrology Database, an indispensable resource for the research underlying this book. Vevian Zaki guided me to the Library of Congress microfilms of the St. Catherine corpus.

For Mamluk-era documents, I was supported by the wide-ranging expertise of Daisy Livingston, who helped in locating copies of various Mamluk-era documents and insightfully discussing their interpretation. Omar Abdel-Ghaffar's enthusiasm for the rural history of the Mamluk period has been infectious and rewarding.

I have been fortunate to enjoy the jolly companionship of my Queen Mary colleague Jim Bolton (1937–2024), one of the great medieval economic historians of our generation, who helped me make sense of the *beduini* of the Latin Kingdom of Jerusalem. He will be sorely missed. Benajmin Kedar and Tom Asbridge have also given important advice from the perspective of Crusading history.

Bethany Walker has been my guide on nearly every aspect of the material evidence discussed in this book. She has supported this project from its very beginnings by endorsing the Leverhulme application, inviting me to seminars in Bonn and to the Tall Hisban excavations, introducing me to her wonderful Islamic archaeology team, and patiently reading through many drafts that showed my lack of archaeological training. We had wished for this project to genuinely bring about a synthesis of our two disciplines, rarely attempted for the late medieval Middle East. On the interpretation of the pottery, I also received valuable advice and information about unpublished material from Ben Dolinka, Allison Gascoigne, and Salama Kassem.

A complete novice to the history of Arabic dialects, I was privileged to present at the Semitic Philology Seminar at Cambridge, at the invitation of Esther-Miriam Wagner, Johan Lundberg, and Geoffrey Khan. I further benefited from the comments of Clive Holes and Adam Rapoport.

I also relied on fellow scholars in tracing the fascinating history of Arabic popular epics. I am grateful for Lara Harb and Marina Rustow for allowing me to present on this topic at a Princeton seminar, and for the comments by Rachel Schine and Helen Blatherwick.

Wissam Halawi and Élise Voguet shared my conviction that rural customary law has a history. Our intellectual exchanges and a workshop in Lausanne have been very enriching. Mariam Sheibani commented on drafts of my blog posts on the history of Islamic customary law published by the Program in Islamic Law at Harvard Law School.

Lahcen Daaïf has been my inseparable fellow traveler in the study of the genealogical treatises of the Mamluk period. His unrivaled command of Arabic, joy in deciphering Berber names, and general good disposition sustained us through the editing, translation, and study of al-Maqrīzī's *al-Bayān wa'l-i'rāb*, which we have co-published as part of the Bibliotheca Maqriziana series under the guiding hand and spirited encouragement of Frédéric Bauden.

Jo Van Steenbergen carefully read the entire draft manuscript, and his rigorous methodological outlook and his insights regarding the evolving political structures of the Mamluk sultanate greatly improved the consistency and coherence of the final product. Adam Sabra has paved the way for a fresh, radical social history of the premodern Middle East for several decades. His research repeatedly complemented and supported mine at various junctures along the way, and he helped shape the central argument of this book. Dana Sajdi, a complete historian and gifted author, was always up to reading my drafts and testing my ideas. Her comments have helped me reframe the book morally and politically.

By a stroke of luck, the Leverhulme award overlapped with the groundbreaking EgyLandscape international research project, co-led by Nicolas Michel and Albrecht Fuess. I greatly benefited from presenting at both the inaugural and the closing conferences of this project. Nicolas Michel's long-standing support alongside his unrivaled knowledge of the countryside of premodern Egypt were invaluable in sharpening my arguments. I very much appreciated the friendship and encouragement of the project coordinator Anthony Quickel, who also assisted with an online publication of my research on the genealogical writings of al-Qalqashandī.

Over the past five years, I benefited from the advice, insights, and comments of many other friends and colleagues. I would like to mention here Amenah Abdulkarim, Najwa Adra, Omar Anchassi, Arezou Azad, Tamer el-Leithy, Ian Forrest, Martyn Frampton, Yohanan Friedman, Rob Gleave, Kenneth Goudie, Timothy Greenwood, Konrad Hirschler, Daisuke Igarashi, Wakako Kumakura, Mohamed Masharqa, Brinkley Messick and the Columbia University graduate students, Hussein Omar, Undine Ott, Carl Petry, Eyal Poleg, Ronny Razin, Majied Robinson, Marie Odile Rousset, Christian Sahner, Mohamed Saleh, Emilie Savage-Smith, Ido Shahar, Amy Singer, Frank Stewart, Malissa Taylor, Yusuf Umrethwala, Daniel Varisco, and the one and only Koby Yosef. Hamada Abuqamar reminded me of the value of having land and tending to it.

Dialogue with my students at Queen Mary has shaped this book in many subtle ways. More directly, our former MA students Mohammed Abdisalam Abdillahi, Lorenzo Bukhari, Saarah Ahmed, and Razeenah Ramtally provided targeted research assistance. Şahin Baykal assisted with compiling the bibliography.

Fred Appel, my editor at Princeton University Press, has been a constant source of tremendous support. I appreciated his detailed input regarding the arguments of the book and its place in the world. Shane Kelly produced the accessible maps, drawing also on earlier work by Andrew Satchell. This book wouldn't have been possible without the Shamela digital platform of medieval Arabic texts, twice as essential at times of plague.

Sections of this book have been published before in other formats. Chapter 3 contains a paraphrased summary of my *Rural Economy and Tribal Society in Islamic Egypt* (2018). I thank Guy Carney at Brepols for his continued support. An earlier version of chapter 10 and part of chapter 9 were published in *Mamlūk*

Studies Review as “The Rise of Provincial Arab Ruling Families in Mamluk Egypt, 1350–1517,” with the text much refined by Marlis Saleh and the editorial team of *MSR*.

The exceptionally smart Noga Levy-Rapoport helped me clarify my arguments, sharpen my introduction, and organize my thoughts. I’m immensely proud of her. Amir and Naomi patiently endured the slow progress of *Becoming Arab* and repeatedly raised my spirits in these dark times. Gilat’s love and sound counsel engulfed me and put me on firm ground: summer, this summer, is the season of watermelons.

August 2024

NOTES

Introduction

1. Mohamed Saleh, "On the Road to Heaven."

2. El-Leithy, "Coptic Culture and Conversion in Medieval Cairo." El-Leithy's argument draws on David Nirenberg's study of Jewish converts to Christianity in late medieval Spain, who constantly tried to purify their lineages (Nirenberg, "Mass Conversion and Genealogical Mentalities").

3. Chris Wickham, "The Power of Property." See also Bondioli, "Peasants, Merchants, and Caliphs: Capital and Empire in Fatimid Egypt, 900–1200 CE."

4. Nicolas Michel, "Devoirs Fiscaux." Michel argues that the fallāḥūn were the group of solvent tenants who were personally responsible for the collective payments of the village. See also Johansen, *The Islamic Law on Land Tax and Rent*; Yehoshua Frenkel, "Agriculture, Land-Tenure and Peasants in Palestine during the Mamluk Period."

5. For examples of ancient DNA studies that argue for population continuity in Egypt and Greater Syria, see Haber et al., "A Genetic History of the Near East from an ADNA Time Course"; Schuenemann et al., "Ancient Egyptian Mummy Genomes."

6. See the insightful remarks by Leder, "Nomads and Sedentary People: A Misleading Dichotomy?," 407.

7. Wickham, *The Donkey and the Boat*, 662–88; Wickham, "How Did the Feudal Economy Work?" See also Faith, *The Moral Economy of the Countryside.*

8. Much of the evidence for the values of the moral economy of the medieval English countryside comes from dispute settlement among the peasantry (Faith, *The Moral Economy of the Countryside*, 8).

9. On village clans in general, see the articles in Fabietti and Salzman, *The Anthropology of Tribal and Peasant Pastoral Societies.* For Moroccan village clans, see Eickelman, *The Middle East and Central Asia: An Anthropological Approach*, 126ff; for the Euphrates Valley, see Batatu, *Syria's Peasantry*, 10–22. Court documents and travel accounts from nineteenth-century southern Palestine show that people identified as Bedouin were often farmers, cultivating wheat and barley between Gaza and Hebron (Amara, "Beyond Stereotypes of Bedouins as 'Nomads' and 'Savages'").

10. Adra, "Decolonizing"; Varisco, "Yemen's Tribal Idiom."

11. Fried, *The Notion of Tribe.*

12. On other examples of a tribal confederacy as a response to state agents, see Tapper, *The Conflict of Tribe and State in Iran and Afghanistan*; Özoğlu, "State-Tribe Relations."

13. Nora Barakat, *Bedouin Bureaucrats*, 23–25, 147–49.

14. Barth, *Ethnic Groups and Boundaries.*

15. Lancaster, *The Rwala Bedouin*, 35.

16. Shryock, *Nationalism and the Genealogical Imagination.*

17. For African examples, see Brennan and Barnes, "Political Genealogy, Race and Territory in Eastern Africa," 401–4; Robinson, *Muslim Societies in African History*, 51–53. For the wider argument, see Szombathy, *The Roots of Arabic Genealogy*, 173–94.

18. Szombathy, *The Roots of Arabic Genealogy*; Szombathy, "Genealogy in Medieval Muslim Societies."

19. Webb, *Imagining the Arabs*. See also the editors' introduction in Ibn Qutaybah, *The Excellence of the Arabs*, trans. Sarah Bowen Savant and Peter Webb.

20. Rouighi, *Inventing the Berbers*. The quote is on p. 8.

21. On the attachment of Berber genealogies to the Arab genealogical tree, see also de Felipe, "Berber Leadership and Genealogical Legitimacy."

22. James, *Genèse du Kurdistan*, 145–49; James, "Arab Ethnonyms," 692–95.

23. As argued by Garcin, "Note sur les rapports entre Bédouins et fellahs à l'époque Mamluke." See also Garcin, *Un Centre Musulman De La Haute-Egypte Médiévale*; Büssow-Schmitz, "Rules of Communication." An earlier, underappreciated interpretation is that of Poliak, "Les revoltes populaires en Égypte à l'époque des Mameloukes."

24. Borsch, *The Black Death in Egypt and England*, 51–53.

25. Büssow-Schmitz, *Die Beduinen Der Mamluken*. For earlier general works, see Shwartz, "The Bedouin in Egypt during the Mamluk period"; Krawulsky, "al-Badw fī Miṣr wa'l-Shām"; Saleh, "Quelques remarques sur les Bédouins d'Égypte au Moyen Âge"; Saleh, "Les relations entre les Mamluks et les Bédouins d'Égypte."

26. See the comments in Büssow-Schmitz, *Die Beduinen Der Mamluken*, 31ff; and Elbendary, *Crowds and Sultans*, 51–54.

27. Jumayl, *al-Nashāṭ al-Iqtiṣādī*, esp. 83–95.

28. Stewart, "Tribalism."

29. On the gap between the terms used in the medieval sources and those used by modern scholarship see Leder, "Toward a Historical Semantic of the Bedouin"; Büssow-Schmitz, *Die Beduinen Der Mamluken*, 4.

30. On recent translations of Ibn Khaldūn, see Picard, "Les élites rurales," referring to the work of Abdesselam Cheddadi and Gabriel Martinez Gros. On the *bādiya* as lying outside of the law of the cities, see also Voguet, *Le monde rural du Maghreb central*.

31. Rapoport, *Rural Economy*; al-Nābulusī, *Villages of the Fayyum*; Rapoport, "Invisible Peasants."

32. On Ibn Khaldūn's functional purposes of genealogy, see Szombathy, "Genealogy in Medieval Muslim Societies," 23–26. For relevant critical readings of Ibn Khaldūn on the Bedouin, see Leder, "The Arabs of Ibn Khaldun"; Rouighi, *Inventing the Berbers*, 99–104; Irwin, *Ibn Khaldun*; Brett, "The Way of the Nomad."

33. Brett, "The Way of the Nomad," 267–68, citing Ibn Khaldūn, *Muqaddima*, trans. Rosenthal, 1:299–300; 3:342.

34. Ibn Khaldūn, *Tārīkh Ibn Khaldūn*, 6:3–27.

35. Ibn Khaldūn, *Tārīkh Ibn Khaldūn*, 6:7–8.

36. Ibn Khaldūn, *Tārīkh Ibn Khaldūn*, 6:10. The Berber tribes that inhabited al-Buḥayra cultivated its lands (*falḥ*) while also wintering in the western areas of al-ʿAqaba al-Kabīra.

37. Ibn Khaldūn, *Tārīkh Ibn Khaldūn*, 6:10.

38. Ibn Khaldūn, *Tārīkh Ibn Khaldūn*, 6:10. Other examples include the Ḥāritha of Syria, who were sedentary and never crossed to the desert (6:13). The Banū Hilāl in the region of Ṣarkhad made their living from tilling the land (6:24). Even the Āl Faḍl, presented as the rulers of the Syrian steppe, confined their seasonal migrations to the borders of Syria, close to the villages, and rarely traveled to the desert (6:12).

39. Barakat, *Bedouin Bureaucrats*, 10–12, 120, 133–39.

40. Hütteroth and Abdulfattah, *Historical Geography*.

41. James, *Genèse du Kurdistan*, 194–97.

42. Assi, "The Original Arabs."

43. Burton, *Genetic Crossroads.*

44. Davis, *Resurrecting the Granary of Rome.* The scientific account for the desertification of North Africa by nomads—or, indeed, by any other human group—has turned out to be baseless. The same is true for the Levant: there is no palaeoecological evidence for long-term degradation of marginal lands by overgrazing, at least in the last three millennia. See Davis, "Scorched Earth."

45. Shryock, *Nationalism and the Genealogical Imagination*; Shryock, "Bedouin in Suburbia." The quote is from Ibn Khaldūn, *The Muqaddimah* (1967), 118.

46. For the Ayyubid and Mamluk periods, see Hiyari, "The Origins and Development of the Amīrate of the Arabs"; Drory, "The Role of Banū Faḍl in Fourteenth Century Northern Syria." See also Franz, "The Bedouin in History or Bedouin History?"

47. Büssow-Schmitz, *Die Beduinen Der Mamluken*, 78–82.

48. On Mamluk historians and their agendas, see Van Steenbergen and Termonia, eds., *New Readings in Arabic Historiography.*

49. On the formation of the documentary trail available to us, see Rustow, *The Lost Archive*; Daisy Livingston, "Managing Paperwork in Mamluk Egypt."

50. On the documentary evidence from eleventh-century Fayyum, see Gaubert and Mouton, *Hommes et Villages du Fayyoum.*

51. The key publications on the St. Catherine corpus are Atiya, *Hand-list of the Arabic Manuscripts and Scrolls*; Ernst, *Die Mamlukischen Sultansurkunden des Sinai-Klosters*; Stern, *Fāṭimid Decrees*; Richards, "St. Catherine's Monastery and the Bedouin"; Richards, *Mamluk Administrative Documents from St. Catherine's Monastery.* Microfilms of the documents are available from Library of Congress (https://www.loc.gov) under the heading "Arabic Firmans," where the numbering of the documents follows Atiya's *Hand-list.*

52. Müller, *Der Kadi und Seine Zeugen.* The rural subset of documents is discussed on pp. 160–62.

53. See a summary in Walker, "Southern Syria."

54. Avni, *The Byzantine-Islamic Transition in Palestine.*

55. Johns, "The Rise of Middle Islamic Hand-made Geometrically-Painted Ware."

56. Karamustafa, "Who were the Türkmen."

57. Al-Qalqashandī, *Nihāyat al-Arab*, 408–10.

58. Ibn Taymiyya, *Iqtiḍā'*, 1:418; Berriah, "Arabic Language's Status and Merits in Ibn Taymiyya."

59. Sneath, *The Headless State.* Sneath also suggests a revision of medieval European history, arguing that the Germanic tribes were not discrete bodies of kinsmen tracing common descent, but rather the political entourages of noble families (159).

60. Sneath, "Tribe."

61. See Adra, "Decolonizing," 492, on the need to continue using the term "tribe" for groups with segmentary organization in the Middle East while suppressing social evolutionary assumptions about stages of development.

62. Halawi, *Les Druzes aux marges de l'Islam.*

63. A comprehensive study of the premodern development of Middle Eastern tribal or customary laws remains a major desideratum, both for our understanding of rural societies and for our knowledge of Islamic law outside the urban centers. For preliminary results, see my series of blogs on the Islamic Law Blog, run by the Program in Islamic Law at Harvard Law School, published in March 2020: Rapoport, "Problematizing Custom and Customary Laws"; "Whose Custom Is It?"; "On the Disinheritance of Women"; "Burying the Hatchet, Bedouin Style." Links at https://islamiclaw.blog/2020/04/03/thank-you-yossef-rapoport/.

1. Protection, Tax Collection, and Rural Elites, 960–1070

1. P.Transmission 8. Also discussed by Wickham, "The Power of Property," 96. The reading "Kalb" is probable but could also be "Kilāb."

2. For previous discussions of the evidence regarding the Arab protectors of eleventh-century Fayyum, see Gaubert and Mouton, *Hommes et Villages*, 251–59; Rapoport, *Rural Economy*, 46–47, 241–44; Wickham, "The Power of Property," 95–97; Weitz, "Fayyum Tribesmen and Country Lawyers," 348–49.

3. Al-Kindī, *Wulāt Miṣr*, 234–35.

4. Ibn Ḥawqal, *Kitāb Sūrat al-Arḍ*, 1:137.

5. Bouderbala, "*Murtaba*."

6. Bouderbala, "*Murtaba*"; al-Maqrīzī, *The Book of Clear Arabic Expression*, secs. 128–32.

7. An exception is the Upper Egyptian jurist al-Ṭaḥāwī (d. 321/933), who was known as al-Azdī, with reference to the Azd tribe (Ibn Khallikān, *Wafayāt*, 1:71–72).

8. E. Scheerlinck, "Procedures of Protection."

9. P.RagibQalamun 2, 3, 4, 7.

10. Weitz, "Fayyum Tribesmen and Country Lawyers."

11. Weitz, "Fayyum Tribesmen and Country Lawyers," 343.

12. P.Fay.Villages 39.

13. P.Fay.Villages 38.

14. P.Fay.Villages 40.

15. P.RagibQalamun VIII. Undatable document. The reading *khafārat mulk* is likely, but only partly legible. The name of the village is missing: Rāghib reads it as Ahansiya, but the word in question is likely to be *al-musammāh* ("called") with the name itself missing in a lacuna. The price, partly legible, is between three and ten dinars. The plot of land exchanged here bordered on that of another member of the Banū Rabīʿa.

16. P.Chrest.Khoury II 20, Shaʿbān 456/August 1064. Two other ʿĀmirīs were among the witnesses to these acts, and another ʿĀmirī used to own some of neighboring plots. See also M. J. Shomali, "Arabic Legal Documents from the Fatimid Period," no. 9 = P.Lond.inv. Or. 4684 (10), dated Shawwāl 456. In this document ʿUqayl b. Ḥudayj sells two feddans from the land he holds as *khafāra* (in the edition wrongly transcribed as *Ḥiyāza*). In another example of commercial relations between the Arab protectors and the local Coptic elites, Ḥassān ibn Janāḥ, one of the protectors of the village of Minyat Shushhā, bought half a foal from a Copt called Barmūda ibn Zakariyā al-Sharqāwī. The foal was shared between Barmūda, a man with a distinct Coptic name, and his brother Abū Bakr b. Zakariyā (P.Vente 27, dated 459/1067).

17. P.Chrest.Khoury II 19. In this deed, dated 417/1026, Qashshāsh b. Shabīb al-ʿĀmirī of Uqlūl bought two feddans of arable land designated as *mulk fī ḍamān* in a nearby village for the standard price of four dinars per feddan. The seller is named as Salām b. ʿAṭiya.

18. P.Vind.Arab. III 47. The published edition has the erroneous reading *bāriḥa* instead of *bādiya*. Also discussed in Wickham, "The Power of Property," 96n55.

19. Tillier and Vanthieghem, *Buljusūq* (forthcoming). Confusingly, the price of four dinars per feddan is given as the standard price for annual lease in Buljusūq and as the standard sale price of arable land in other villages of the Fayyum during the same period. I have no good explanation for this, but it certainly suggests a blurring of the boundaries between private property and tenancy, and also between tax and rent. It seems therefore that the differences between the annual tenancy lease in Buljusūq and the permanent sale of land in other villages, such as Damūya, were primarily differences in legal formulae. One possible way of resolving this would be to suggest that the sale deeds in Damūya were also for one year, perhaps because the feddan that was contracted existed as a unit of cultivation only in that year.

20. Tillier and Vanthieghem, *Buljusūq*. See P. Hamb. Ar. Inv. 77 for the list of village payments guaranteed by the three *ḍāmins*.

21. Bondioli, "Peasants, Merchants and Caliphs," 83–84, 245–46.

22. Wickham, "The Power of Property"; Bondioli, "Peasants, Merchants and Caliphs."

23. Tillier and Vanthieghem, *Buljusūq*.

24. P.Berl.Arab I 10 a, dated 406/1015. The seller, called Sha'bān ibn Hilāl, was a Muslim member of the Fatimid army, acting on behalf of his Coptic mother. See discussion in Gaubert and Mouton, *Hommes et villages*, 255n; Wickham doubts the reading *khafīr* (protector), but it is legible (see "The Power of Property," 97n58).

25. P.Chrest.Khoury II 3 (456/1064), P.Chrest.Khoury II 4 (470/1078).

26. The evidence for the use of Muslim and Coptic names is discussed in Weitz, "Islamic Law on the Provincial Margins," 9 and appendix. See also Mouton, "l'Islamisation"; Livingston, "Fāṭimid Subjects in Light of Documentary Sources," 27; Gaubert and Mouton, *Hommes et villages*, 239ff.

27. Staats- und Universitätsbibliothek Hamburg, P. Hamb. Ar. Inv. 77, discussed in Tillier and Vanthieghem, *Buljusūq*.

28. Richter, "Importance"; Björnesjö, "Toponymie de Tebtunis"; Bagnall and Rathbone, *Egypt*, 151.

29. Bagnall and Rathbone, *Egypt*, 153–54; Van der Vliet, "Reconstructing," 82.

30. See summary of the narrative sources in Lev, "Coptic Rebellions and the Islamization of Medieval Egypt," 336–37.

31. P.Transmission 2.

32. P.Chrest.Khoury I 88. Gaubert and Mouton also argue that the protectors had taken control over transactions in the villages, acquiring some seigneurial rights and limiting the freedom of the villagers (Gaubert and Mouton, *Hommes et villages*, 258).

33. Tillier and Vanthieghem, "La rançon du sermen." For discussion of the term *muslimānī*, see pp. 62–63.

34. P.RagibQalamun I, VI.

35. Naïm Vanthieghem and Lev Weitz, draft edition of Dayr al-Naqlūn doc. Nd.05.107 = inv. N.05.08. This is a fragment found in excavations at the site of Dayr al-Naqlūn. I am very grateful to Lev and Naïm for providing me with a draft edition and discussion of this document in August 2024.

36. Assuming that a peasant household could work three to five feddans, it could produce thirty to fifty irdabbs of grains annually. Since up to 50 percent would be paid as tax, we expect an individual cultivator household to pay on average fifteen to twenty-five irdabb in land tax per year. The list includes four Muslim individuals with Arab names, as well as the Banū Ḥanẓala kinship group, who deliver quantities of grains within that range of fifteen to twenty-five irdabb, suggesting that they might have been working the land directly. But their contributions amount to only 5 percent of the total amount of grains mentioned in the account.

37. P.RagibQalamun V.

38. Lev, "Army, Regime, and Society in Fatimid Egypt"; Brett, *Fatimid Empire*, 153, 170.

39. Van Nieuwenhuyse, "The Uprising of Abū Rakwa"; Brett, *Fatimid Empire*, 135ff.

40. Al-Musabbiḥī, *Akhbār*, 61/247b. Other participants in the procession were identified as Turks, Kutāma, Qayṣariyya, the *'abīd* (black African slaves), the Bāṭiliyya, and the Daylam.

41. Al-Musabbiḥī, *Akhbār*, 21/143a; reproduced in al-Maqrīzī, *Itti'āẓ*, 2:137, 415.

42. Al-Musabbiḥī, *Akhbār*, 82/264a.

43. Al-Musabbiḥī, *Akhbār*, 83/264b. The Fatimid official awarded the protection of the region is named as Ibn Abī al-Nahār.

44. Al-Musabbiḥī, *Akhbār*, 4–6, fols. 133b–134a. The edict in discussed in Bianquis, *Damas*, 2:415.

45. See Bramoullé, "l'émirat," for a synthesis of Geniza documents and narrative sources.

46. Al-Musabbiḥī, *Akhbār*, 85, 266a, and in a slightly different version on 111, 288a.

47. As reported by the contemporary al-Anṭākī, *Ta'rīkh*, 298–99.

48. Rapoport and Savage-Smith, *Eleventh-Century Guide to the Cosmos*, 32, 442, 492.

49. Al-Maqrīzī, *Itti'āẓ*, 2:218–20 (443/1051–52).

50. Ibn Ḥawqal, *Kitāb Ṣūrat al-Arḍ*, 1:133, 1:153ff.

51. Al-Maqrīzī, *Itti'āẓ*, 2:218–20. Bramoullé, "l'émirate," also cites the accounts of Ibn Muyassar and al-Nuwayrī, who say the revolt started because the Fatimids appointed unpopular men as leaders of the Banū Qurra. Bramoullé suggests that the trigger for the revolt was the decision of Jabbāra, the amir of Barqa, to shift allegiance away from the Fatimids.

52. Al-Maqrīzī, *Itti'āẓ*, 2:218–20. See also al-Maqrīzī's shorter version in his *Bayān* (*Book of Clear Arabic Expression*, secs. 15–17).

53. Al-Maqrīzī, *Itti'āẓ*, 1:254.

54. Al-Maqrīzī, *Itti'āẓ*, 2:216.

55. Al-Maqrīzī, *Book of Clear Arabic Expression*, secs. 60–61.

56. Brett, *Fatimid Empire*, 186.

57. Brett, *Fatimid Empire*, 185–86.

58. New York, Jewish Theological Seminary, ENA NS 19.29.

59. Cambridge University Library, Taylor-Schechter Collection, T-S Ar.18(1).183. It seems that the camels of the owners of the presses and of the Arabs were uprooting crops (*qā'ita*,?). S. D. Goitein read this letter as referring to the damage caused by "rapacious Bedouins," but a close reading of the letter doesn't bear this out (*Mediterranean Society*, 1:118, 426n117).

60. Cambridge University Library, Taylor-Schechter Collection, T-S 10J12.3.

61. Kennedy, *Age of the Caliphate*, 265.

62. Franz, "The Bedouin in History," 30ff. See also Kennedy, "'Uqaylids"; Bianquis, "Waththāb b. Sābiq al-Numayrī"; Heidemann, "Numayrid Ar-Raqqa"; Heidemann and Kool, "A Bedouin Amir in Fatimid Tabariyya."

63. Important studies of the rise of the Arab dynasties include Franz, "The Bedouin in History or Bedouin History?"; Franz, *Vom Beutezug zur Territorialherrschaft*; Krawczyk, "The Relationship between Pastoral Nomadism and Agriculture"; Bianquis, *Damas*, 2:664–70; Heidemann, "Arab Nomads and the Seljuq Military."

64. Franz, *Vom Beutezug zur Territorialherrschaft*.

65. Ibn Ḥawqal, *Kitāb Ṣūrat al-Arḍ*, 1:227–28.

66. Franz, "The Bedouin in History," 28. Franz also discusses the possibility that these migrations were a result of the Qarmāṭī revolt.

67. Ibn Ḥawqal, *Kitāb Ṣūrat al-Arḍ*, 1:228.

68. Ibn Ḥawqal, *Kitāb Ṣūrat al-Arḍ*, 1:211.

69. Ibn Ḥawqal, *Kitāb Ṣūrat al-Arḍ*, 1:220.

70. Ibn Ḥawqal, *Kitāb Ṣūrat al-Arḍ*, 1:221.

71. J. Paul, "Ḥimāya Revisited." Paul is revising the conclusion offered by Cahen, "Ḥimāya."

72. Arabic: *i'tamada-hu bi-ḥimāyat al-ṭuruq wa'l-manāfidh, wa-ḥirāsat al-rufaq wa'l-qawāfil, wa-khafārat al-ḍiyā' wa'l-mazāri'*. See *Rasā'il* of Ibn Abbād, 61–62; discussed also in Cahen, "Notes pour l'histoire de la *ḥimāya*," 296. The decree orders the amir to protect the holders of iqṭā' from brigand Kurds, but also to act with restraint and not to exceed in the demands of *khafāra* protection and other financial levies and not to burden the people of these areas with residing in their villages (*al-tanazzul 'alā qurāhim*). See also the discussion of the letters in Maurice Pomerantz, *Licit Magic*, 145–47, 184ff, where local leaders are given the authority to guard the roads (*ḥimāyat al-subul wa-ḥirāsat al-ṭuruq*) but warned not to harm villages and peasants (*basṭ al-yad 'alā al-ḍiyā' wa'l-akara*).

73. Paul, "Ḥimāya Revisited," 95.

74. Ibn Ḥawqal, *Kitāb Ṣūrat al-Arḍ*, 1:213.

75. Ibn Ḥawqal, *Kitāb Ṣūrat al-Arḍ*, 1:215.

76. Bowen, "Nāṣir al-Dawla"; Sato, *State and Rural Society*, 18–41.

77. The position of the village headmen (*raʾīs*) may also date from this period of Buyid rule. See Sato, "The *Iqṭāʿ* System of Iraq under the Buwayhids," 94, with references to the studies by ʿAbd al-ʿAzīz Dūrī and Ann Lambton. In Iran, however, as in Egypt and the Levant, village headmen are only attested since the end of the twelfth century (Paul, "Local Lords or Rural Notables?").

78. Ibn al-Qalānisī, *Taʾrīkh Dimashq*, 41 (for 369/979–80).

79. For a biography of Qassām al-Ḥārithī, see al-Dhahabī, *Taʾrīkh al-Islām*, ed. Tadmurī, 26:596.

80. Al-Maqrīzī, *Ittiʿāẓ*, 1:250, 1:253, 1:257 (370 H), 2:31; see also Bianquis, *Damas*, 2:132–39.

81. On the arrival of the Kalb and Āl Jarrāḥ to Syria and Palestine, see Bianquis, "Sayf al-Dawla" and "Mirdās." Based on Canard's analysis of poems by al-Mutanabbī, Bianquis argues that both groups were pastoralists, driven to the area after rebelling against the rule of Sayf al-Dawla in Aleppo in 344/955.

82. Gil, *Palestine*, 343, 349.

83. Gil, *Palestine*, 358.

84. Al-Anṭākī, *Taʾrīkh*, 291.

85. Gil, *Palestine*, 385–89; citing al-Musabbiḥī, *Akhbār*, 47–51, 57ff.

86. Al-Musabbiḥī, *Akhbār*, 68/253a.

87. Brett, *Fatimid Empire*, 163. Brett argues that the tripartite coalition sought to replace the centralized Fatimid administration in Damacus and Ramla with "government by protection, *ḥimāya*" over the cities and the sedentary population.

88. Al-Musabbiḥī, *Akhbār*, 55–6/241b-242a. See a later report by al-Nuwayrī, *Nihāyat al-Arab*, 28:205 (for 415/1024–25). The fourteenth-century author al-Nuwayrī introduces the term ʿurbān, which is not found in the Fatimid chronicle.

89. New York, Jewish Theological Seminary, ENA 4020.42, published by Gil, *Erets-Yiśraʾel ba-teḳufa ha-Muslemit ha-rishona (634–1099)*, vol. 2, no. 050; see also Gil, *Palestine*, 392–93.

90. Cambridge University Library, Taylor-Schechter Collection, T-S 13J26.13. See translation and summary by Outhwaite, "Letter (T-S 13J26.13)."

91. Al-Muqaddasī, *Aḥsan al-Taqāsīm*, 1:146.

92. Gil, *Palestine*, 166, 175, 300; al-Yaʿqūbī, *Kitāb al-Buldān*, 165; al-Hamdānī, *Ṣifat Jazīrat al-ʿArab*, 129–30. Al-Ḥamdānī gives a rich account of tribal territories of Judhām and ʿĀmila between Tiberias and Acre, but his information needs to be taken with a grain of salt, as he never traveled outside of Yemen.

93. Gil, *Palestine*, 302, 333.

94. On the limited material evidence for Muslim presence in the countryside of Palestine in the pre-crusader period, see Avni, *Byzantine-Islamic Transition*, 8–9, 31; Taxel, "Early Islamic Palestine," 161–62; Petersen, *Bones of Contention*, 16; Carlson, "Contours of Conversion."

95. Avni, *Byzantine-Islamic Transition*, 154ff. Taking as a case study the eighth-century site of Khirbet Abu Suwwana, seven kilometers east of Jerusalem, Avni argues that the dense network of residential units and open animal pens, arranged in clusters around open courtyards, is what one would expect from nomads moving into a sedentary existence. Yet no other sites of this type are known from the central highlands, as the prevalent structure and architecture in the rural hinterland of Jerusalem largely remained the same in the first centuries of Muslim rule. Avni refutes Ellenblum's argument about abandonment of Samaritan sites around Nablus and the immigration of Muslim nomadic tribes to the area (Ellenblum, *Frankish Rural Settlement in the Latin Kingdom of Jerusalem*, 253–72).

96. Avni, *Byzantine-Islamic Transition*, 247–56.

97. Gutfeld and Haber, "A Guide to Beit Loya (Lehi)," 38–40. The 2023 excavation season codirected by Gutfeld and Walker confirmed the existence of the small mosque and the date of the repurposing of the Byzantine church into a cemetery (Bethany Walker, personal communication, July 2024).

98. Tendler, "Horbat Zecharya." See also Glausiusz, "Hundreds of Israel's Archaeological Sites."

99. Rustow, *Lost Archive*, 173–93.

100. Bondioli, "Peasants, Merchants and Caliphs," 130–40. The evidence is a late-fourth/tenth century inscription from Deir al-Balah, southern Palestine, that attests that it was part of the iqṭāʿ of the Fatimid vizier Ibn Killis, and an Egyptian petition preserved in the Geniza, dated 1031 (P.GenizahCambridge 70). As we have seen above, the leader of the Āl Jarrāḥ held an iqṭāʿ in Beit Jibrīn in Palestine by 1021.

101. Cahen, "Ḥimāya"; Cahen, "Notes pour l'histoire de la *ḥimāya*," 298; Sato, "Buyid *iqṭā*ʿ," 96. For examples of the overlap between iqṭāʿ and *khafāra* in Buyid Iraq, see Miskawayh, *Tajārib al-Umam*, 6:309 (in 359/969–70, the Kurdish leader Ḥasanawayh received iqṭāʿ and *aʿmāl* for his services, but he continued to demand *khafāra* from villagers/landowners [*aṣḥāb al-ḍiyāʿ and arbāb al-niʿam*] in the mountains); Hilāl al-Ṣābī, *Taʾrīkh* (in the annals for 390/999–1000, Qarrād b. al-Ladīd would take the *khafāra* and *ḥimāya* in an inflated exchange rate of 150 dirham to dinar, and this was a burden on the iqṭāʿ holders and the peasants [*akara*]).

102. The narrative evidence for this is presented in Franz, *Vom Beutezug zur Territorialherrschaft*, 106–18.

103. Kennedy, *Age of Caliphates*, 290; Franz, *Vom Beutezug zur Territorialherrschaft*, 103–6.

104. P.MariageSeparation, no. 14.

105. P.MariageSeparation, nos. 1, 11b, 11c.

106. Ibn Ḥawqal, *Kitāb Ṣūrat al-Arḍ*, 1:146, 1:215.

107. Ceremonial tents were always appreciated as gifts, "and it would be wrong to associate them exclusively with nomadic culture" (Behrens-Abouseif, *Practising Diplomacy*, 124).

108. Ellenblum, *The Collapse of the Eastern Mediterranean*. See also Avni, *Byzantine-Islamic Transition*, 314–23, 353; Shoshan, "Fatimid Grain Policy"; Bianquis, "Une crise frumentaire dans l'Egypte fatimide."

2. The Rural Arabs of the Twelfth Century: *Urban* and *Beduini*

1. Ibn al-Muqaffaʿ [attributed], *History of the Patriarchs*, vol. 2, pt. 3, 314–15/Arabic, 203–4. According to al-Maqrīzī, the Lawāta had their base in Abyār in the delta (*Ittiʿāẓ*, 2:295).

2. Goitein, *Mediterranean Society*, 4:242; Gil, *Kingdom*, vol. 4, no. 619; Cambridge University Library Or.1080 J71 (Arabic: *wa-jawārī katīr qad harabū maʿa al-ʿarab*).

3. Al-Maqrīzī, *Ittiʿāẓ*, 2:316; al-Nuwayrī, *Nihāyat al-Arab*, 28:237; Brett, *Fatimid Empire*, 206.

4. Al-Maqrīzī, *Ittiʿāẓ*, 2:156 (in 415/1024–5, the ʿurbān take over the countryside around Damascus); 2:201 (in 440/1048–49, the tribes (*qabāʾil*) of the ʿurbān in Syria join the army); 2:215 (in 443/1051–52, in reference to the Banū Hilāl); 2:304 (in 462/1069–70, reporting that the Fatimid expenses on the ʿurbān reached sixty thousand dinar); 2:330 (in 487/1094–95, the suppression of unjust practices among the iqṭāʿ holders, whether regular army officers or ʿurbān); 3:35 (in 498/1104–5, al-Afḍal sends large numbers of ʿurbān to accompany the main army on campaign against the forces of the First Crusade).

5. Ibn al-ʿAdīm, *Bughyat al-Ṭalab*, ed. Zakkār, 6:549.

6. Ḥassān b. Mismār, who built a citadel in Ṣarkhad in the Hawran in 466/1073–74, inscribed his title as *muqaddam al-ʿarab* alongside a dedication to the Fatimid caliph (Ibn Taghrī Birdī, *al-Nujūm al-Zāhira*, 5:95).

7. ʿAbd al-Ḥamīd Ṣāliḥ Ḥamdān argued that the term ʿurbān was first used in Egypt in the Ayyubid era and became very common in the Mamluk era. See his *Taʾrīkh al-Qabāʾil al-ʿArabiyya fī Miṣr* (Cairo, 2009), cited in Jumayl, *al-Nashāṭ al-Iqtiṣādī*, 10.

8. Al-Maqrīzī, *Ittiʿāẓ*, 3:83; al-Maqrīzī, *Book of Clear Arabic Expression*, sec. 42; Richards, "S͟hāwar."

9. Al-Maqrīzī, *Ittiʿāẓ*, 3:98 (*qaṭīʿat al-ʿurbān*).

10. Al-Qalqashandī, *Ṣubḥ*, 7:114.

11. Brett, *Fatimid Empire*, 270; al-Maqrīzī, *Ittiʿāẓ*, 3:159; al-Iṣfahānī, *al-Bustān al-Jāmiʿ*, 1:350–51 (533/1138–39).

12. Ibn Munqidh, *al-Iʿtibār*, 1:8.

13. Al-Nuwayrī, *Nihāyat al-Arab*, 28:311; al-Maqrīzī, *Ittiʿāẓ*, 3:197; Brett, *Fatimid Empire*, 281.

14. Ibn Munqidh, *al-Iʿtibār*, 1:24; same in al-Maqrīzī, *Ittiʿāẓ*, 3:217.

15. Ibn al-Muqaffaʿ [attributed], *History of the Patriarchs*, vol. 3, pt. 1, 76.

16. Al-Maqrīzī, *Ittiʿāẓ*, 3:97–98.

17. Al-Maqrīzī, *Ittiʿāẓ*, 3:186; Brett, *Fatimid Empire*, 277.

18. Al-Idrīsī has similar negative views regarding the Arab and Berber tribes of Ifrīqiya and the coastal region between Gabes and Tripoli. See Hiatt, "Geography at the Crossroads," 129.

19. Brett, *Fatimid Empire*, 287ff; Ibn al-Muqaffaʿ [attributed], *History of the Patriarchs*, vol. 3, pt. 1, 80–81/Arabic 48–49; al-Maqrīzī, *Ittiʿāẓ*, 3:258–59.

20. Ibn al-Muqaffaʿ [attributed], *History of the Patriarchs*, vol. 3, pt. 1, 88.

21. Al-Maqrīzī, *Book of Clear Arabic Expression*, sec. 45.

22. Mouton, "Saladin," 199–201, 220; al-Maqrīzī, *Sulūk*, ed. ʿAṭāʾ, 1:185. Ibn Shaddād describes the Bedouin as *mufsidūn* who betray the Muslims for money, spy for the crusaders and guide them in their campaigns, and who betrayed Saladin in Sinai (Mouton, "Saladin," 198).

23. Al-Maqrīzī, *al-Ḍahab al-Masbūk*, sec. 120. Although the treatise covers narratives of royal pilgrimages from the beginning of Islam, the term ʿurbān is used only for late medieval accounts, from the twelfth century onward.

24. Ibn al-Qalānisī, *Taʾrīkh Dimashq*, 479. Arabic: *ahl Ḥawrān waʾl-ʿurbān.* It is possible to read here al-ʿArabān, a name of a town in the Khābūr region of Mesopotamia (Streck, "ʿArbān"). Modern editors have preferred to read ʿurbān (al-Dhahabī, *Taʾrīkh al-Islām*, ed. Tadmurī, 37:24)

25. Halawi, *Druzes*, 251–52, 562, 578.

26. Al-Makhzūmī, *Kitāb al-Minhāj*, 69, fol. 189v (*wa-ḍamān al-muqaddam al-darak ʿanhum fīhi*).

27. Ibn al-Ṭuwayr is cited in Ibn al-Furāt, *Taʾrīkh*, vol. 4, pt. 1, 147–48. See similar accounts of the lower value of the iqṭāʿ allocations for ʿurbān units in al-Makhzūmī, *Kitāb al-Minhāj*, fol. 190r: al-Qalqashandī, *Ṣubḥ*, 3:489.

28. On the meaning of iqṭāʿ in this period, see Bondioli, "Peasants, Merchants and Caliphs," 88ff.

29. Bondioli, "Peasants, Merchants and Caliphs," 88–91. In a report quoted by al-Maqrīzī, in connection with a reform of the nascent iqṭāʿ system of 501/1106–7, a group of major iqṭāʿ holders complained that they had already developed their own iqṭāʿ lands (by cultivating orchards and constructing presses) and that therefore they should keep their holdings on a permanent basis (al-Maqrīzī, *al-Mawāʿiẓ*, 1:157). A similar complaint on a surviving petition, dated between 1149 and 1154, has iqṭāʿ holders complain about an iqṭāʿ of 1,100 feddans that is not as productive as promised because they had not been able to establish a new market (P.GenizahCambridge 81).

30. According to a deed relating to an endowment by Ṭalā'iʿ ibn Ruzzīk, as preserved in a Mamluk-era copy, the village of Balqas was held partly as iqṭāʿ by soldiers and partly as *ḍamān* between 1102 and 1159 (Bondioli, "Peasants, Merchants, and Caliphs," 81; Cahen, Rāgib, and Taher, "L'achat et le waqf.") Ibn al-Ṭuwayr, the author of a late Fatimid administrative manual, also reports that land could be either be subject to *ḍamān* or to iqṭāʿ (cited in Ibn al-Furāt, *Ta'rīkh*, vol. 4, pt. 1, 147–48). On *ḍamān* for the taxes of a village called Qabīl, see P.GenizahCambr. 63. In 1155 or 1156, the Copt Basṭiyya b. Marqūra contracted the *ḍamān* of the lands of the village of Dayqūf in al-Bahnasā, owned at the time by a widow of the deceased caliph al-Āmir. The sum was to be paid in grains (P.GenizahCambr. 135r).

31. Bodleian Library, MS Heb. d. 66/8. Discussed in Goitein, *Mediterranean Society*, 2:361–62, 2:606. Arabic: *ʿalā an idhā khalla ʿalayhum ʿāriḍ wa-man ḥaḍar yaʿtariḍuhum bādiya saʿadat-hum bi-kull mā ajidu ilayhi al-sabīl.*

32. Ibn al-Muqaffaʿ [attributed], *History of the Patriarchs*, vol. 3, pt. 2, Arabic section, 49; (Sinbis in al-Gharbiyya), Arabic section, p. 66 (the *muqaddam* of the Arabs in Aṭfīḥ).

33. P.GenizahCambr. 58. A man called Nabhān al-Qarīṭī was appointed as leader of the Banū Kalb near Damascus in the mid-eleventh century (al-Maqrīzī, *Ittiʿāẓ*, 2:229).

34. P.Cair.Arab II 105–12. For the interpretation of this set of documents, see Tillier and Vanthieghem, *Buljusūq*.

35. P.Cair.Arab II 111; P.Chrest.Khoury I 36. Corrected and verified by Lahcen Daaïf in CALD (Corpus of Arabic Legal Documents, https://cald.irht.cnrs.fr, CaiNt_1799, accessed September 11, 2019). See also discussion in Tillier and Vanthieghem, *Buljusūq*.

36. Ibn Khallikān, *Wafayāt*, ed. Wüstenfeld, 2:443.

37. Al-Dhahabī, *Ta'rīkh al-Islām*, ed. Bashshār, 45:110.

38. Al-Dhahabī, *Ta'rīkh al-Islām*, ed. Bashshār, 46:221 (Murhif b. Ṣārim Abū al-Muhannad al-Judhāmī al-Manẓūrī [a clan of Judhām] al-Safṭī, born circa 548/1153–54); al-Dhahabī, *Ta'rīkh al-Islām*, ed. Bashshār, 49:83 (ʿAlī b. Shujāʿ Kamāl al-Dīn b. Abī al-Fawāris al-Hāshimī al-ʿAbbāsī, whose lineage is listed all the way to ʿAbdallāh b. ʿAbbās, born 572/1176–77).

39. Karamustafa, "Who Were the Türkmen."

40. The key publications are Atiya, *A Hand-list*; Ernst, *Die Mamlukischen Sultansurkunden des Sinai-Klosters*; Stern, *Fāṭimid Decrees*; D. S. Richards, "St. Catherine's Monastery and the *Bedouin*"; D. S. Richards, *Mamluk Administrative Documents from St. Catherine's Monastery.* The edited documents are available through the APD website. Microfilms of the documents are available from the Library of Congress (https://www.loc.gov) under the heading "Arabic Firmans," where the numbering of the documents follows Atiya's *Hand-list*. I am grateful to Vevian Zaki for introducing me to the full richness of this corpus.

41. P.AtiyaHandList 8, 9, 10 = P.Fatimid 5, 7, 8.

42. P.Fatimid 3 = P.AtiyaHandList 962 and P.Fatimid.4.

43. Ibn Ḥawqal states that the Arabs are not present in central Sinai (*Tīh*), since the land is too barren for grazing animals there (Ibn Ḥawqal, *Kitāb Ṣūrat al-Arḍ*, 1:19).

44. Saʿīd b. Biṭrīq, also known as Eutychius (877–940), Melkite patriarch of Alexandria, related that the servants of the monks converted under the Umayyads and came to call themselves the Banū Ṣāliḥ. See Tannous, *The Making of the Medieval Middle East*, 393.

45. Al-Anṭākī, *Ta'rīkh*, 298–99. Al-Anṭākī reports that the churches of al-Qulzum and the monastery of Tur Sinai (St. Catherine) were given as iqṭāʿ to an Arab man called Ibn Ghiyāth. Al-Ḥākim commanded him to destroy the monastery of St. Catherine and build a mosque instead. But then a *kātib* called Sulaymān b. Ibrāhīm, who took the habit in the monastery, convinced this Arab man that it would be too costly for him to destroy the monastery and gave him some money instead.

46. P.Fatimid 10.

47. P.AtiyaHandlistSinai 118. Published and translated in P.RichardsFatimidPetition 1.

48. Chalmeta and Heinrichs, "Muwallad."

49. Mouton, "Saladin."

50. Mouton et al., *Ṣadr, une forteresse de Saladin au Sinaï.*

51. P.AtiyaHandlistSinai 11 = P.SternAyyubidDecrees 1.

52. P.AtiyaHandList 14 = P.SternAyyubidDecrees 2.

53. P.AtiyaHandList 13, 15 = P.SternAyyubidDecrees 3.

54. P.AtiyaHandList no. 1063.

55. Ibn Wāṣil, *Mufarrij al-Kurūb*, 5:157, 5:635. According to this account, Sultan al-Kāmil was informed of the theft of some *bisāṭ* textiles in the desert area. He then summoned the Arabs who were guarding the road (*yakhfarūna al-ṭarīq*) and ordered them to reclaim the stolen goods as well as the thief. They wanted to offer compensation, but he refused until they relented.

56. Pringle, *Pilgrimage to Jerusalem and the Holy Land*, 121–22 (Thietmar); Chareyron, *Pilgrims to Jerusalem*, 128.

57. Ibn al-Dawādārī, *Kanz*, 9:115.

58. Al-ʿAbdarī, *al-Riḥla*, 153.

59. For recent discussions of the land regime under the Latin Kingdom, see MacEvitt, *Rough Tolerance*, 137–50; Rubin, "The Debate on Twelfth-Century Frankish Feudalism."

60. William of Tyre, *History of Deeds Done beyond the Sea*, 2:255; William of Tyre, *Chronique*, 18.11. For other examples of William of Tyre's use of the term *Arabes*, see Ann E. Zimo, "Us and Them," 7–8n36.

61. Kedar, "Tractatus," 131. I thank Professor B. Z. Kedar for bringing this work to my attention and explaining the Latin text.

62. Pringle, *Pilgrimage to Jerusalem*, 132.

63. Albert of Aacchen, *Albert of Aachen's History of the Journey to Jerusalem*, trans. Edgington, 874–75, 12:31–32. See also Jochen Schenk, "Nomadic Violence in the First Latin Kingdom of Jerusalem and the Military Orders," 45 (A small Latin raiding party that set out from Tiberias was decimated by the guards who looked over the huge flocks of cattle. Eventually the Arabs decided to pay off the Latin king to ensure the safety of their seasonal grazing).

64. William of Tyre, *History of Deeds Done beyond the Sea*, 2:255; William of Tyre, *Chronique*, 8.11; Pringle, *Pilgrimage to Jerusalem*, 100 (Thietmar).

65. William of Tyre, *History of Deeds Done beyond the Sea*, 2:508; William of Tyre, *Chronique*, 23.1.

66. Pringle, *Pilgrimage to Jerusalem*, 124.

67. Pringle, *Pilgrimage to Jerusalem*, 215; E. J. Mylod, "Latin Christian Pilgrimage in the Holy Land, 1187–1291," 112–13.

68. Delaville Le Roulx, *Cartulaire General des hospitaliers*, 1:362, no. 530; also published as Röhricht, *Regesta Regni Hierosolymitani, 1097–1291*, 1:557. See also Hans Eberhard Mayer, *Die Urkunden der lateinischen Konige von Jerusalem*, 2:687, no. 404.

69. Röhricht, *Regesta Regni Hierosolymitani*, vol. 1, no. 562. An English translation has been uploaded at http://crusades-regesta.com/regesta-past-present.

70. Delaville Le Roulx, *Cartulaire General des hospitaliers*, 1:363, no. 531.

71. Delaville Le Roulx, *Cartulaire General des hospitaliers*, 1:372, no. 550; republished in Mayer, *Urkunden*, 2:688–90, no. 405.

72. The price is subject to different readings, summarized by Mayer, *Urkunden*, 2:688. Delaville Le Roulx read here 2,500. Ellenblum, *Frankish Rural Settlement*, 245, has the Benekarkas sold for 3,500 besants, and the village for an additional 2,000. Sidelko has the total price as 5,500, and the price of the village of Seleth as 2,800; he adduces the price of the Bedouin to be 2,700 besants (Sidelko, "Acquisition," 126).

73. Prawer, *Crusader Institutions*, 214 (note that the chapter is called "Serfs, Slaves and Bedouin," 201–14). See also Schenck, "Nomadic Violence," 46.

74. Sidelko, "Acquisition," 56; Ellenblum, *Frankish Settlement*, 245.

75. Pringle, *Pilgrimage to Jerusalem*, 132.

76. Al-Dhahabī, *Ta'rīkh al-Islām*, ed. Tadmurī, 46:118; 47:102.

77. Al-Dhahabī, *Ta'rīkh al-Islām*, ed. Tadmurī, 47:278.

78. Delaville Le Roulx, *Cartulaire General des hospitaliers*, 1:216, no. 296. See also Schenk, "Nomadic Violence." In the deed, Baldwin specifies that the *beduini* should "have never served me or my predecessors and who right up to this point have not been ours," a phrasing that qualifies Prawer's claim that all Bedouin were the property of the king.

79. Delaville Le Roulx, *Cartulaire General des hospitaliers*, 1:395, no. 582; Prawer, *Crusader Institutions*, 214; Schenk, "Nomadic Violence." See also Sinibaldi, "Settlement in Crusader Transjordan (1100–1189)."

80. Prawer, *Crusader Institutions*, 184ff; Kedar, "Subjected Muslims," 148, estimates the rural population of the Kingdom of Jerusalem at fifty thousand Muslim and Oriental Christians during the demographic zenith in the 1180s.

81. See discussions of the migration of the Ḥanbalī peasants in Kedar, "Subjected Muslims," 138, 149, 168, and passim. See also Kedar and Hajjuj, "Muslim Villagers of the Frankish Kingdom of Jerusalem"; Talmon-Heller, "The Shaykh and the Community."

82. On Frankish lords forcing villagers to remain on the land, see also Prawer, *Crusader Institutions*, 203ff; Kedar, "Subjected Muslims," 165. In a charter of 1186 (Delaville Le Roulx, *Cartulaire General*, 495, no. 783), Bohemond grants possessions to the Hospitallers, but sets down that any Saracens fleeing from his possessions to those of the Hospitallers must be returned, whereas the oriental Christian fugitives may stay there if compensation is agreed.

83. Röhricht, *Regesta Regni Hierosolymitani*, no. 524. English translation uploaded at http://crusades-regesta.com/regesta-past-present.

84. Ellenblum, *Frankish Rural Settlement*, 235–42.

85. Sidelko, "Acquisition," 54–55.

86. Pringle, *Churches of the Crusader Kingdom*, 2:179–80, citing Geneviève Bresc-Bautier, *Le Cartulaire du chapitre du Saint-Sépulcre de Jérusalem*, nos. 36, 40, 43; Röhricht, Regesta Regni Hierosolymitani, nos. 278, 353.

87. Sidelko, "Acquisition," 53–54.

88. Röhricht, *Regesta Regni Hierosolymitani*, no. 174. The summary by Schenk, "Nomadic Violence," states that the deed grants the Hospitallers the right to collect tribute from Bedouin tribes grazing their livestock. This is an interpolation.

89. Strehlke, *Tabulae Ordinis Theutonici*, no. 3, pp. 3–4; Sinibaldi, "Settlement in Crusader Transjordan," 200.

90. Delaville Le Roulx, *Cartulaire General des hospitaliers*, no. 558. Discussed in Prawer, *Crusader Institutions*, 214.

91. Dyer, *Making a Living in the Middle Ages*, 97

92. Dyer, *Making a Living in the Middle Ages*, 140–41, 178, 183. On medieval European peasant migrations in search of land and freedom from servitude, see Bartlett, *Making of Europe, 950–1350*.

93. Chareyron, *Pilgrims to Jerusalem*, 112. Pilgrims to Jerusalem distinguished between urban areas on the one hand, inhabited by "Saracens," and rural areas and the desert on the other, "the haunt of nomads."

94. Jean de Joinville, "The Life of Saint Louis," 209.

95. Pringle, *Pilgrimage to Jerusalem and the Holy Land*, 315 (Burchard).

3. Village Clans in the Fayyum, 1245

1. Al-Nābulusī, *Villages of the Fayyum*, ed. and trans. Rapoport and Shahar. On al-Nābulusī, see al-Nābulusī, *Sword of Ambition*, trans. Yarbrough.

2. Rapoport, *Rural Economy*, 176–80.

3. On the Banū Qayṣar, see al-Nābulusī, *Villages of the Fayyum*, 43, 160, 174, 176, 181.

4. On *ajlāf*, see al-Nābulusī, *Villages of the Fayyum*, 80. On *ajlāf* as a derogatory term in relation to the Arabs/Bedouin, see Leder, "Towards a Historical Semantic of the Bedouin," 113.

5. On the term *muzāri'ūn*, see also Michel, "Devoirs fiscaux," 526–27. Note, however, that in the eleventh century the members of the Banū Bifām family were also called *muzāri'ūn* even though they held plots of arable land in private ownership (Gaubert and Mouton, *Hommes et villages*, 207).

6. Al-Nābulusī, *Villages of the Fayyum*, 109.

7. As demonstrated by Michel, the term fallāḥ was rarely used prior to the sixth/twelfth century, and its increasing use in the Mamluk period seems to be linked to the consolidation of the iqṭā' landholding regime. It also acquired clear pejorative connotations (Michel, "Devoirs fiscaux," 528). For examples of the use of the term fallāḥ from the Ayyubid and early Mamluk periods, see Sato, *State and Rural Society*, 185, 253; Ibn Mammātī, *Qawānīn al-Dawāwīn*, 232, 343; al-Nuwayrī, *Nihāyat al-Arab*, 8:248–49. In the Geniza, the term appears infrequently, only in a couple of undated fragments (Goitein, *Mediterranean Society*, 1:118, 425–26).

8. Al-Nābulusī, *Villages of the Fayyum*, 42.

9. For example, in Akhṣāṣ al-'Ajamiyyīn and Jarfis, the alms tax is divided into a portion due on camels seeking pasture (*muntaji'ūn*) and another portion due on local, established (*qarāriyya*) small cattle. See also entries for Umm al-Sibā' and al-Mahīmsī. In the tiny village of Ṭimā the entire alms tax was paid on the livestock that came to it seeking pasture (*al-muntaji'ūn ilayhā*).

10. Rapoport, *Rural Economy*, 181–82. Al-Qalqashandī indicates that *munājaza* lease contracts were found wherever the level of inundation was relatively stable (*Ṣubḥ*, 3:458).

11. Rapoport, *Rural Economy*, 183–92.

12. The history of *rizaq* allowances in Mamluk-era Egyptian villages has been the topic of two exemplary studies by Nicolas Michel, mostly based on the Ottoman archives but also utilizing al-Nābulusī's *Villages of the Fayyum*. See Michel, "Les Rizaq Iḥbāsiyya," 108–11; Michel, "Les services communaux." See also Sato, *State and Rural Society*, 185–88.

13. Al-Nābulusī, *Villages of the Fayyum*, 57.

14. Al-Nābulusī, *Villages of the Fayyum*, 215.

15. Rapoport, *Rural Economy*, 159; al-Nābulusī, *Luma'*, 64.

16. Rapoport, *Rural Economy*, 187. See also Michel, "Les services communaux," 30n.

17. The state collected a modest protection fee (*rasm al-khafāra*) from most villages in the Fayyum, at a fixed value of 15 dirhams, 0.375 dinar. But this minimal and uniform tax appears to be a blanket policing fee. See Rapoport, *Rural Economy*, 86, 189.

18. Livingston, "Managing Paperwork."

19. Diem, P.Vind.Arab. III 59. Other documents that form the al-Azkā dossier are Diem, P.Vind.Arab. III 50, 51, 53, 56, 58, 60, 61, 63; and possibly also 34 and 49.

20. Rapoport, *Rural Economy*, 196–98.

21. For a more detailed discussion, see Rapoport and Shahar, "Irrigation in Medieval Islamic Fayyum."

22. For examples of allocation of water to orchards in private ownership: the orchard of Zayn al-Dīn ibn Abī Sulaymān in Shisfa was assigned one *qabḍa* unit (measuring the width

of the feeder channel), while the village as a whole was allocated 3½ units; the lands leased by a certain ʿIzz al-Dīn ibn Ḥiṣn in the village of Minyat Shushhā also received separate water allocation. In Sinnūris, water rights were allocated to the local holders of allowances, including the headmen, guardsmen, the Friday preachers, and the monastery (Rapoport, *Rural Economy*, 190–92).

23. The "dredging fee" was broadly related to the size of the village. On average, villages described as large paid just under one hundred dirhams per village; "medium-sized" villages paid about fifty dirhams per village; and "small" villages paid an average of twenty dirhams. See Rapoport, *Rural Economy*, 196.

24. Derda, "From *Ptolemaic* Ἀρσινοΐτης νομός to Three Arsinoite Merides."

25. Rapoport, *Rural Economy*, 198–201.

26. Rapoport, *Rural Economy*, 199.

27. Al-Nābulusī, *Villages of the Fayyum*, 243. For a summary table, see Rapoport, *Rural Economy*, 199.

28. The Samālūs were overrepresented in this levy, possibly because they were considered more skilled in military arts; their villages lay in the grazing areas of the marshes south of the lake. The Samālūs are also the only ones that continued as a focus of local identity into the modern period (Awad, "The Assimilation of Nomads in Egypt," 246).

29. Al-Nābulusī, *The Sword of Ambition*, 133.

30. Ibn al-Muqaffaʿ [attributed], *History of the Patriarchs*, vol. 4, 192–93, 94 (Arabic).

31. Camels and tents are mentioned in the account of the siege of Damietta (Ibn al-Muqaffaʿ [attributed], *History of the Patriarchs*, vol. 4, 46). Another reference to the tents of Arab tribesmen is in an account of a rebellion in al-Gharbiyya (vol. 4, 111/p. 66 [Arabic]).

32. Ibn al-Muqaffaʿ [attributed], *History of the Patriarchs*, vol. 4, 46.

33. Ibn al-Muqaffaʿ [attributed], *History of the Patriarchs*, vol. 4, 236–37, 115 (Arabic).

34. Ibn al-Muqaffaʿ [attributed], *History of the Patriarchs*, vol. 4, 188–89.

35. Ibn al-Muqaffaʿ [attributed], *History of the Patriarchs*, vol. 4, 166 (Arabic).

36. On the calculation of the rural population of the Fayyum at the time of the 1245 register, see Rapoport, *Rural Economy*, 68–74.

37. In the 1170s, the city had a Melkite church alongside three Coptic churches (Abū al-Makārim, *Churches and Monasteries of Egypt*, 206). The work has been wrongly attributed to Abu Sāliḥ the Armenian, but more recent scholarship has shown it was composed by Abū al-Makārim ibn Jirjis. The history of the debate on the authorship of this work is summarized by Werthmuller, *Coptic Identity*, 24.

38. Cf. Abū al-Makārim, *Churches and Monasteries of Egypt*, 206–10. See also Rapoport, *Rural Economy*, 207, 211.

39. The bulk of the tax on textile production was levied on weavers in Madīnat al-Fayyūm, amounting to 484 dinars. Given the correpondence between taxes on weaving and Christian communities, it is plausible that many of the urban weavers were Christian, too. See Rapoport, *Rural Economy*, 208–10.

40. Al-Nābulusī, *Villages of the Fayyum*, 153. The identification of the village with the Hawwāra would be confirmed by the early Ottoman period, when the village was renamed Hawwārat ʿAdlān (Gaubert and Mouton, *Hommes et villages*, 2014, 12).

41. Rapoport, *Rural Economy*, 219–24.

42. Unregistered mosques are reported in Sidmant, Shisfa, and Dimashqīn al-Baṣal (a mixed Christian-Muslim village); and the hamlets of Burjtūt, Sanhūr, Munsha'at Awlād Zaydān, and Munsha'at Minyat Karbīs.

43. Al-Nābulusī, *Villages of the Fayyum*, 241. In a deed published by Abbott and dated 336/947, a Coptic woman called Tūsāna grants real estate to the two monasteries known as Naqlūn and Shallā. See P.Fay.Monast.3.

44. Saleh, "On the Road to Heaven." Saleh brings together documentary evidence from the early Islamic period (seventh to eleventh centuries), the lists of village churches and rural monasteries by Abū al-Makārim, information from al-Maqrīzī, and the Egyptian census data of 1848–68.

45. Rapoport, *Rural Economy*, 143–70.

46. Michel, "Devoirs fiscaux."

47. Al-Nābulusī, *Villages of the Fayyum*, 80. As we know from administrative manuals, it was the registration of land allocation that ensured the right of cultivation (Sato, *State and Rural Society*, 194ff).

48. For *athar* as "the use of the land in the previous year or season," within a crop rotation system, see Michel, "Devoirs fiscaux," 563. In early Ottoman Upper Egypt, the term is mentioned with the sense of continuous cultivation. By the eighteenth century, it acquired the meaning of peasants' right of ownership over their land, legally recognized by Islamic courts (Cuno, *The Pasha's Peasants*, 64).

49. Al-Nābulusī, *Villages of the Fayyum*, 45. On the attempts of Fakhr al-Dīn to increase the flow of water in the Baḥr Yūsuf, the arm of the Nile which feeds the Fayyum, see Rapoport and Shahar, "Irrigation"; Rapoport, *Rural Society*, 64–66.

50. Al-Nābulusī, *Villages of the Fayyum*, 47.

51. Villages with Arabic names are al-Istinbāṭ, al-Qubarā', Akhṣāṣ al-'Ajamiyyīn, Umm al-Sibā', al-A'lām, Thalāth, Dhāt al-Ṣafā', 'Anz, Minyat al-Usquf (a Christian village), Masjid 'Ā'isha, Ḥaddāda, Khawr al-Rammād, and Kharāb Jundī.

52. Of the total 239 place-names mentioned, 92 (38 percent) are distinct Arabic, but the vast majority of these Arabic place-names are of smaller, recently established satellite settlements, whose names began with the prefix Munsha'a. See Omaima al-Mahdī, "Taṭawwur asmā' al-amākin al-miṣriyya," 233–45.

53. The only two hamlets identified by the names of the clans which occupied them were Banū Majnūn, a hamlet of Minyat al-Dīk, and Baḥr Banī Qurīṭ, a hamlet of Muṭūl.

54. Björnesjö, "Quelques reflexions", 38.

55. Gaubert and Mouton, *Hommes et villages*, 12

56. Jean de Joinville, "The Life of Saint Louis," 208–9. See similar description of the Bedouin or Arab as nomads by Burchard (Pringle, *Pilgrimage to Jerusalem*, 315).

57. Zaborowski, *The Coptic Martyrdom*.

58. See P.GenizahCambr. 49 (654/1256), P.GenizahCambr. 93 (fifth/eleventh century). On claiming Khaybarī lineage, see also Miriam Frenkel, "Adaptive Tactics"; Marina Rustow, "Formal and Informal Patronage," 353; Fred Astren, "The Gibeonite Gambit: Ḥarrānians, Karaites, and Khaybarī Jews on the Margins of Medieval Islamic Society."

59. Al-Nābulusī, *Sword of Ambition*.

60. David Nirenberg, "Mass Conversion and Genealogical Mentalities."

61. El-Leithy, "Coptic Culture and Conversion in Medieval Cairo."

4. The Village Clans of the Palestinian Highlands

1. Livingston, "Managing Paperwork."

2. Müller, *Der Kadi Und Seine Zeugen*.

3. Müller, *Der Kadi Und Seine Zeugen*, 160–62.

4. Livingston, "Managing Paperwork," 140; Müller, *Der Kadi Und Seine Zeugen*, 161.

5. Richards, "The Qasāma in Mamlūk Society"; al-'Asalī, *Wathā'iq Maqdisiyya Tārīkhiyya*; Müller, "Crimes without Criminals?"

6. Richards, "The Qasāma in Mamlūk Society."

7. Müller, *Der Kadi Und Seine Zeugen*, 160–62.

8. In addition, four documents relate to the village of al-Ghāziya, modern Ghazieh, just south of Sidon, which was at that time endowed for the benefit of the Haram in Medina.

9. Hütteroth and Abdulfattah, *Historical Geography of Palestine*; Singer, *Palestinian Peasants and Ottoman Officials.*

10. P.HaramCat. 320.

11. Al-Nuwayrī states that in some Syrian villages cash-crops were guaranteed by their owners (*muḍammana*) for a fixed price taken from them once the harvest took place. This *ḍamān*, or surety, was conceived as a payment for the future harvest and was comparable to rental contracts (*muta'ajjirāt*) in Egypt. Al-Nuwayrī intriguingly adds that these villages are known as *mafṣūla*, from the Frankish word *faṣal* (i.e., vassal), a "term which is still used in the coastal regions taken from the Crusaders." See al-Nuwayrī, *Nihāyat al-Arab*, 8:260–61. This passage is lucidly explained by Aḥmad al-Zayn, the modern editor of this volume of al-Nuwayrī's text.

12. P.HaramCat. 19.

13. The price of grains in Mamluk Syria ranged between 50 and 150 dirhams for a *ghirāra*, under normal conditions (Ashtor, *Histoire des Prix Et des Salaires*, 392ff). The *ghirāra* of Damascus was equal to 265 liters of wheat (204.5 kilograms), about three times the Egyptian irdabb. According to al-'Umarī the price of grains in Syria in the 1340s was comparable to that in Egypt (cited in al-Qalqashandī, *Ṣubḥ*, 4:182). In the Ottoman survey of 1596, Bayt Ūniya paid 60 percent of its taxes on grains and only 30 percent on olives (Hütteroth and Abdulfattah, *Historical Geography*, no. Z339).

14. P.HaramCat.265 = P.RichardsQasama VIII.

15. P.HaramCat.691 = P.RichardsQasama II.

16. We do have at least one reference to another Ṣubāḥī man in central Palestine at the time. In Rabī' I 708/September 1308, a certain Zā'id b. Sulaymān al-Ṣubāḥī, a resident of the town of Ramla, acknowledged receipt of nintey-five dirhams from the waqf of Hebron for the sale of almonds and other fruits (P.HaramCat. 116). While this man lived in Ramla, the nature of his transaction with the waqf of Hebron suggests he had his roots in the countryside.

17. P.Haram.Cat. 202 = P.Haram II 32.

18. P.HaramCat. 223= RichardsQasama XI. On the pre-Islamic and Islamic history of this village, see Khader Salameh, *Qaryat Zakariyā.*

19. P.HaramCat. 341. Neither of the headmen can be identified with the guarantor from Ḥalḥūl listed in P.Haram.Cat. 712.

20. P.HaramCat. 346 = P.Haram II 33.

21. P.HaramCat. 697, discussed in detail below.

22. The amount of oil on sale, four *qinṭār*s or two hundred kilograms, could have been extracted from about thirty olive trees. This estimate is based on modern conditions, where a mature olive tree will produce fifteen to twenty kilograms of olives each year, and it takes about five kilograms of olives to make a liter of oil, or 2.2 kilograms.

23. There are four documents relating to al-Ghāziya in the Ḥaram corpus (P.HaramCat. 293, 332, 361, 763). The identification of the village as belonging to the endowment in Medina is found at the beginning of P.HaramCat. 763. I owe this information to Undine Ott. The name of the Turcoman individual from the village appears as Muḥammad b. Maḥmūd al-Du'ārī. See Sara Nur Yıldız, "Döger (Ghuzz)."

24. William of Tyre, *Deeds Done beyond the Sea*, 1:410 (translated as "petty chiefs"). See Riley-Smith, "Some Lesser Officials," 9.

25. MacEvitt, *Rough Tolerance*, 150–51.

26. Ibn Jubayr, *Riḥla*, trans. Broadhurst, 317.

27. Riley-Smith, "Some Lesser Officials," 10–11, 14.

28. Riley-Smith, "Some Lesser Officials," 11. For the Hospitaller documents, see Delaville le Roulx, *Cartulaire General*, no. 2915 (dated 1259), no. 2747 (dated 1255); no. 2693 (Kafr Kanna, dated 1254).

29. Amitai, "Gaza," 16; citing 'Izz al-Dīn Ibn Shaddād, *Tārīkh al-Malik al-Ẓāhir*, 293.

30. P.HaramCat. 697r = RichardsQasama IX. In Yāqūt's early thirteenth-century text, only half of the village of 'Ayn Yabrūd belonged to the waqf of the Haram, while the other half belonged to a waqf of a madrasa (Yāqūt, *Mu'jam al-Buldān* [Beirut, 1995], 5:427).

31. Hütteroth and Abdulfattah, *Historical Geography*, 121.

32. Ṣāliḥ b. Muḥammad (also could be read as Shiḥāda), the leader of this third group, is the same person as Ṣāliḥ b. Muḥammad/Shiḥāda b. Durayd al-'Āmirī, who received the payment for the olive oil in P.HaramCat. 346 discussed in note 20 of this chapter. Mūsā, brother of Zar'a b. Qāsim, is almost certainly the same person as Mūsā b. Qāsim b. Isma'īl, also mentioned as one of the headmen in that document. Here Mūsā has an inferior position as part of Ṣāliḥ's group, or *jamā'a*, and is even listed after his own brother. The third individual in P.HaramCat. 346, 'Īsā b. Fāris b. Jarīr, does not appear to be listed here, but may have been the son of Fāris b. Jarīr b. Fāris, the leader of the first grouping.

33. Singer, *Palestinian Peasants*, 40ff.

34. In sixteenth-century Abū Dīs the headmen were divided in two groups, with each of the two groups obliged to pay 50 percent of the grain taxes due to the waqf. In the village of Rammūn each of three leaders was responsible for paying a third of the village's taxes on olive oil. In the case of olive oil, at least, Singer found examples of leaders acknowledging payments on "their" olive trees, and the olive trees of their "relations" or "group" (Singer, *Palestinian Peasants*, 41).

35. Nicolas Michel, *L'Égypte des Villages*, 232–37.

36. Michel argues that even if the exact number of feddans to be cultivated by each group is given, the number represents a notional calculation of the share in the tax burden, not physical plots of land. Michel also found that peasant groupings appeared in sixteenth-century Ottoman court records. In a case concerning a village in Giza, dating from 1586, a list of twelve *ḥiṣṣa* shares is provided, as well as the individuals responsible for each *ḥiṣṣa*. The *ḥiṣṣa* shares were identified by a name, such as *al-sulṭān*, *al-fuqahā'*, or the Christians, or by reference to a clan (*ḥiṣṣat awlād* X). The village was divided up into two equal halves of six shares, each responsible for its own taxes. Several *ḥiṣṣas* were led by the same individual, and the *ḥiṣṣa* of the Christians was indeed led by a man with an apparently Coptic name (Michel, *L'Égypte des Villages*, 295). Singer also found examples of Christian headmen in the Palestinian villages she has studied (*Palestinian Peasants*, 40).

37. Michel, *L'Égypte des Villages*, 291.

38. Michel, *L'Égypte des Villages*, 300–1. In the Egyptian lists he studied, individuals are rarely identified by clan names or patronym. The *ḥiṣṣa* group could be constructed through ad hoc associations or based on family solidarities.

39. P.HaramCat. 75 = P.MuellerCrimes 2.

40. The clan's name is indicated in the final word of line 6. Müller read this word as *al-ḥallāqīn*, i.e., "the barbers," but this is unlikely (P.MuellerCrimes 2).

41. P.HaramCat. 280.

42. Adler, *Jewish Travellers*, 136, 141.

43. Frenkel, "Contribution of European Travel Literature," 715, citing Burchard, *A Description of the Holy Land* (1896), 35.

44. P.HaramCat. 712r = RichardsQasama I.

45. Richards read as *Bayt Fāsīn*. On Burj Beit Nasif, see Pringle, *Secular Buildings*, 42 (no. 72). Bayt Nāṣif appears deserted on the Palestine Exploration Fund map of 1870 but is known to have been occupied in the crusader period.

46. On the crusader remains of Beit Einun, an important settlement in the medieval period, see Pringle, *Secular Buildings*, 26 (no. 27).

47. P.HaramCat. 703 = RichardsQasama IV (27 Rajab 707/22 January 1308).

48. P.HaramCat. 596 (15 Shawwāl 707/18 April 1308). The village, located twelve kilometers northeast of Ramallah, is considered today as the only all-Christian community in the region. Pringle, *Secular Buildings*, 2:339, for the Christian and crusader history of the village.

49. A Saʿdī man, called Ibrāhīm b. Aḥmad b. Fallāḥ, was resident of Khān Banī Saʿd on the outskirts of Jerusalem (*ẓāhir al-Quds*). He died at a ripe old age in Rajab 815/1412 (al-ʿUlaymī, *Uns al-Jalīl*, 2:167). The village of Khān Banī Saʿd is also known from later Ottoman sources. See Aḥmad Ḥusayn al-Jabbūrī, *al-Quds fī al-ʿAhd al-ʿUthmānī*, 374; Cytryn-Silverman, "Khān al-Ẓāhir."

50. Al-ʿUlaymī, *Uns al-Jalīl*, 2:52.

51. P.HaramCat. 718. I am grateful to Omar Abd al-Ghaffar for bringing this document to my attention.

52. Al-Maqrīzī, *al-Ḏahab al-Masbūk*, secs. 120, 171, 191, 195, 197, 198.

53. Amitai, "Gaza," 8, citing Ibn ʿAbd al-Ẓāhir, *al-Rawḍ al-Zāhir fī Sīrat al-Malik al-Ẓāhir*, 149.

54. For the power of the Jarm amirs in the late Mamluk period, see al-ʿUlaymī, *Uns al-Jalīl*, 2:208, 2:346–7, 2:370, 2:374–7.

55. P.HaramCat. 348.

56. P.HaramCat. 459 = P.Haram II 31. The year could be read as either 707 or 708; Al-ʿAsalī (P.Haram II 31) reads 708.

57. P.HaramCat. 194. The numbers in this document are written in *siyāqa* shorthand. The three headmen here are ʿAbdallāh b. Muḥammad. b. Shaʿbān (?), Mufliḥ b. Yaḥyā, Muḥammad b. Aḥmad b. Ḥasan. The reading of the date by Little is doubtful.

58. P.HaramCat. 48 (13 Ṣafar 708/9 August 1308). Witnesses include Naṣṣār b. ʿAmāra, Muḥammad b. Ghanām, ʿAnān b. Mālik b. ʿAnān, and Naṣr b. ʿAbd Allāh.

59. P.HaramCat. 110 (Rabīʿ I 707 H).

60. Hütteroth and Abdulfattah, *Historical Geography*, 16ff (Z227, Z338 Z345).

61. The twelve peasants from Ramallah are named as ʿAbdallāh b. Hārūn (?); Ibrahīm b. Khalīl b. Ṣalāḥ; Sayf b. Qinā (?) b. Faḍl; Dāʾūd b. ʿAmr b. Rizq; Muḥammad b. ʿAbdallāh b. Khalīfa; Ṣalāḥ b. Khalīl b. Ṣalāḥ; Saʿīd b. Ḥassān; Salām b. ʿAbd al-Wāḥid; Rizqallāh b. Ruzayq, D . . . b. Muḥiyy (?); Ṣāliḥ b. Fāris.

62. P.HaramCat. 98. Such detailed description of the physical features of non-Muslim individuals is also found in legal documents from the Geniza (P.GenizahCambr. 45 and P.GenizahCambr. 37).

63. Amitai, "Islamization in the Southern Levant after the End of Frankish Rule."

64. Milka Levy-Rubin, "New Evidence Relating to the Process of Islamization in Palestine in the Early Muslim Period"; Ellenblum, *Frankish Rural Settlement*, 263–69.

65. Ellenblum, *Frankish Rural Settlement*, 235. See also discussion in Pringle, *Churches*, 2:179–80 (al-Rām). The main Latin document is found in G. Bresc-Bautier, *Le Cartulaire du Chapitre du Saint-Sépulcre de Jérusalem*, 103–4.

66. Ellenblum, *Frankish Rural Settlement*, 222. In these regions, Ellenblum identified the Frankish establishment of administrative centers of seigneurial estates and parish churches, dozens of farmhouses, and a construction of a new road.

67. Pringle, *Secular Buildings*, 29.

68. Pringle, *Secular Buildings*, 1–2. For the foundation inscription of a rural mosque in Beit Hanun, dated to 1239, see Sharon, *Corpus Inscriptionum Arabicarum Palaestinae*, 2:98–104.

69. Walker, "Jordan's Northern Highlands."

70. Walker, "Tall Hisban."

71. McPhillips and Walmsley, "Faḥl during the Early Mamluk Period." In late-Mamluk and Ottoman-era rural cemeteries, graves often lacked external markers except for a small rectangular structure for a shrine, leading archaeologists to suggest that they were employed by "Bedouin" rather than by settled villagers. See Milwright, *Introduction to Islamic Archaeology*, 133–35.

72. Brown, "Faunal Distribution."

73. Corbino, "Animal husbandry," 172. The consumption of parrotfish was likely related to days of meat abstinence in the Christian calendar.

74. On Islamization of the landscape in late medieval Syria, see Petersen, *Bones of Contention*; Talmon-Heller, *Islamic Piety in Medieval Syria*, 179–209; Talmon-Heller, "Graves, Relics and Sanctuaries"; Meri, *The Cult of Saints*, 257–61.

75. Al-Harawī, *A Lonely Wayfarer's Guide.*

76. Dana Sajdi, "From Diyārāt to Ziyārāt: Transmutations of the Sacred Landscape in Syria."

77. Meri, *The Cult of Saints*. See also Petersen, *Bones of Contention*, 96; Luz, "Aspects of Islamization."

78. The evidence for the reoccupation of sites is summarized in Bethany Walker, "Searching for a Home" and "The Northern Jordan Project."

79. Walker, "From Ceramics to Social Theory," 22.

80. Walker et al., "Did the Mamluks Have an Environmental Sense?" 198.

81. Brown, "Faunal Distribution"; Walker et al., "Did the Mamluks Have an Environmental Sense?" 240–41; Corbino, "Animal Husbandry," 173. In some sites, as in Umm al-Jimāl, Mamluk-era animal pens of crude walls dotted open and unbuilt spaces (Pini, "Walls of Identities," 304–5).

82. Finkelstein et al., *Highlands of Many Cultures*, 346–47; Magen and Finkelstein, *Seker Arkhe'ologi Bĕ-Erets Binyamin*, 70. In Latin sources, the village is known as Beitiumen or Urniet and was granted to the Holy Sepulchre by Godfrey of Bouillon. See Pringle, *Secular Buildings*, 29 (no. 40).

83. Finkelstein et al., *Highlands of Many Cultures*, 563.

84. Yāqūt, *Mu'jam al-Buldān*, 5:427.

85. K. Franz, "The Bedouin in History," 20. Unlike the shifting names of more ephemeral settlements in the desert, names of sedentary villages remained remarkably stable, often up to the modern period. Franz contrasts this continuity with the relatively short lifespan of names of desert localities, a characteristic that fits in with quick turnover of mobile populations. An exception would be the region of Aleppo, where a significant number of villages were known by Arab clan names already in the thirteenth century. Ibn al-'Adīm identifies several settlements by the names of clans, such as al-Tha'labiyya, al-Kilābiyya, and al-Buḥturiyya, as well as Nuqrat Banī Asad, named after the sedentary Banū Asad who occupied that plain (Eddé, *La principauté ayyoubide d'Alep*, 505, 508).

86. Based on searches on the Shamela database, the name Marj Banī 'Āmir is first mentioned by al-Ṣafadī, *A'yān al-'Aṣr* (1:716, 1:621, 3:610). The early-thirteenth-century Yāqūt does not mention this name.

87. See al-Maqrīzī, *Ḍaw' al-Sārī li-Ma'rifat Khabar Tamīm al-Dārī.*

88. Al-Maqrīzī, *Ḍaw' al-Sārī li-Ma'rifat Khabar Tamīm al-Dārī*, 246–47.

89. In addition, when vocalized as al-Ṣabāḥī, it refers to a clan of the Sahm and was also used for the Isma'ili followers of al-Hasan al-Ṣabāḥ. See Ibn al-Athīr, *al-Lubāb fī Tahdhīb al-Ansāb*, 2:48–49. The lacunae in that edition can be filled in by consulting al-Suyūṭī, *Lubb al-Lubāb fī Taḥrīr al-Ansāb*, 2:68.

90. Al-Qalqashandī, *Nihāyat al-Arab*, 288 (nos. 1126, 1127).

91. Paul, "Local Lords or Rural Notables?"

5. Administrative Categories and Self-Identity

1. Al-Maqrīzī's genealogical treatise has now been subject to a separate study. See Al-Maqrīzī, *The Book of Clear Arabic Expression.*

2. Webb, *Imagining the Arabs*; Szombathy, *The Roots of Arabic Genealogy*; Szombathy, "Genealogy in Medieval Muslim Societies."

3. Morimoto, "The Formation and Development of the Science of Talibid Genealogies."

4. Al-Malik al-Ashraf ʿUmar b. Yūsuf, *Ṭurfat al-Aṣḥāb fī Maʿrifat al-Ansāb.* I thank Dan Varisco for this reference.

5. İlker Evrim Binbaş, "Structure and Function of the Genealogical Tree in Islamic Historiography, 1200–1500."

6. Al-Maqrīzī provides a biography of al-Jawwānī, citing eighteen different titles, mostly on the lineage of the *ashrāf* and on Cairo (al-Maqrīzī, *al-Muqaffā*, 5:167–69, no. 1893). Al-Qifṭī met him personally and claimed that al-Jawwānī wrote "so much on genealogy, one even suspects that he tended to lie" (*al-shuʿarā*, 147–48). Al-Jawwānī's preserved works that have been published are *Fī al-Farq bayna man Ismu Abīh Sallām wa-Salām* and *al-Jawhar al-Maknūn fī Maʿrifat al-Qabāʾil waʾl-Buṭūn*, or *al-Muqaddima al-Fāḍila.*

7. Ibn al-ʿAdīm, *Bughyat al-Ṭalab*, ed. Zakkār, 1:527–68. See discussion in Eddé, *La principauté ayyoubide d'Alep*, 505; Eddé, "Ibn al-ʿAdīm."

8. Al-Qalqashandī, *Ṣubḥ*, 3:488; 4:22. See also A. Saleh, "Mihmindār."

9. Al-Ḥamdānī's firsthand accounts of receiving delegations of Arab amirs: he claims to first encounter an amir of the Āl Rabīʿa in the days of Sultan al-Kāmil (r. 615–635/1218–38). He later saw a group of Rabīʿa amirs attending the courts of the first Mamluk sultans in Cairo. He also reports spending thirty-six thousand dinars on the entertainment of the Arab amir Faraj b. Ḥayya when the latter visited al-Muʿizz Aybak (r. 1250–57). See al-ʿUmarī, *Qabāʾil al-ʿArab*, 139–40. See also a delegation of Khafāja from Iraq to Baybars (al-ʿUmarī, *Qabāʾil al-ʿArab*, 148, al-Qalqashandī, *Qalāʾid*, 123); delegations of the Rabīʿa (al-Qalqashandī, *Nihāyat al-Arab*, no. 271; al-Qalqashandī, *Qalāʾid*, 74–75); delegations of the Ghazaya (al-Qalqashandī, *Nihāyat al-Arab*, no. 269; al-Qalqashandī, *Qalāʾid*, 88); delegation from al-Baḥrayn, visiting Baybars (al-Qalqashandī, *Nihāyat al-Arab*, no. 281), delegation from the Banū Ṣakhr in Karak to al-Muʿizz Aybak (al-Qalqashandī, *Nihāyat al-Arab*, no. 1638).

10. The earliest biographies of al-Ḥamdānī are from the pen of the fourteenth-century Syrian historians al-Ṣafadī, *al-Wāfī biʾl-Wafayāt*, 29:96–97, and al-Kutubī, *Fawāt al-Wafayāt*, 4:349. They quote the poetry that al-Ḥamdānī recited to Athīr al-Dīn Abū Ḥayyān (1256–1344 CE) and Fatḥ al-Dīn Sayyid al-Nās (1273–1334 CE).

11. Al-ʿUmarī, *Qabāʾil al-ʿArab*, 157.

12. Al-Maqrīzī, *Book of Clear Arabic Expression*, sec. 118; al-ʿUmarī, *Qabāʾil al-ʿArab*, 167–68; al-Qalqashandī, *Qalāʾid*, 69.

13. For a spatial visualization of the villages listed by Ibn al-Mammātī, see the interactive map of the villages of Mamluk and Ottoman Egypt, constructed under the aegis of the EGY-Landscape project, https://egylandscape.mmsh.fr/map.html.

14. Al-Maqrīzī, *Book of Clear Arabic Expression*, secs. 57, 60–61; al-ʿUmarī, *Qabāʾil al-ʿArab*, 158. A variant version in al-Qalqashandī, *Qalāʾid*, 44; al-Qalqashandī, *Nihāyat al-Arab*, nos. 602 and 741.

15. Al-Maqrīzī, *Book of Clear Arabic Expression*, sec. 84; al-ʿUmarī, *Qabāʾil al-ʿArab*, 162.

16. Al-Maqrīzī, *Book of Clear Arabic Expression*, secs. 41, 53; al-ʿUmarī, *Qabāʾil al-ʿArab*, 174; al-Qalqashandī, *Qalāʾid*, 63; al-Qalqashandī, *Nihāyat al-Arab*, no. 1035.

17. Al-Maqrīzī, *Book of Clear Arabic Expression*, sec. 125; al-ʿUmarī, *Qabāʾil al-ʿArab*, 178; al-Qalqashandī, *Nihāyat al-Arab*, no. 771.

18. Al-Maqrīzī, *Book of Clear Arabic Expression*, sec. 6 (Thaʿlaba); sec. 16 (Sinbis); sec. 21 (Banū ʿAdī); sec. 29 (Ṭarīf b. Maknūn, a *muqaddam* of the Suwayd of the Judhām, under the Fatimids); sec. 30 (Banū Kumayl of Judhām).

19. Under Saladin, each army *ṭulb* was led by an amir with *ʿalam maʿqūd* and *būq maḍrūb* ("raised flag and blown trumpet"), commanding seventy to two hundred horsemen (al-Maqrīzī, *Ittiʿāẓ*, 3:372; see also the comments by Dorothea Krawulsky in al-ʿUmarī, *Qabāʾil al-ʿArab*, 16n2). The source for references to the Trumpet and Flag Amirs is al-Ḥamdānī; see the direct attribution to al-Ḥamdānī in al-Qalqashandī, *Nihāyat al-Arab*, no. 463 (al-ʿUlaymiyyūn), no. 1623 (Halbā Suwayd).

20. Al-Maqrīzī, *Book of Clear Arabic Expression*, secs. 6, 29, 47, 50.

21. Al-Maqrīzī, *Book of Clear Arabic Expression*, sec. 46; al-ʿUmarī, *Qabāʾil al-ʿArab*, 169.

22. Al-Qalqashandī, *Qalāʾid*, 161.

23. Al-ʿUmarī, *Qabāʾil al-ʿArab*, 109.

24. Al-ʿUmarī, *Qabāʾil al-ʿArab*, 115–16. For more examples of clans whose full lineages are not traced, see al-Qalqashandī, *Nihāyat al-Arab*, nos. 258, 264, 296, 278, 318, 397, 412, 547, 438, 1104.

25. Al-Maqrīzī, *Book of Clear Arabic Expression*, sec. 85; al-ʿUmarī, *Qabāʾil al-ʿArab*, 163.

26. Al-Maqrīzī, *Book of Clear Arabic Expression*, secs. 12, 14, 41, 94; al-ʿUmarī, *Qabāʾil al-ʿArab*, 108, 156, 164, 174.

27. For example, Awlād Baqar b. Najm was the leading household among the Banū Halbā of Baʿja (Al-Maqrīzī, *Book of Clear Arabic Expression*, sec. 34; al-ʿUmarī, *Qabāʾil al-ʿArab*, 172).

28. Al-Maqrīzī, *Book of Clear Arabic Expression*, secs. 29, 51; al-ʿUmarī, *Qabāʾil al-ʿArab*, 170, 172.

29. Al-ʿUmarī, *Qabāʾil al-ʿArab*, 141.

30. Al-ʿUmarī, *Qabāʾil al-ʿArab*, 176; al-Qalqashandī, *Qalāʾid*, 86.

31. According to al-Ḥamdānī, the clans of the Fayyum belong to the Banū Kilāb, Banū ʿAwf, and the Banū Sulaym. See al-Qalqashandī, *Qalāʾid*, 117 (Kilāb); 126 (ʿAwf); 124 (Sulaym). According to al-Nābulusī, the clans in the Fayyum belonged to the Banū Kilāb, Banū ʿAjlān, and the Lawāta.

32. Al-ʿUmarī, *al-Taʿrīf*.

33. Al-ʿUmarī, *Qabāʾil al-ʿArab*, 70. Al-ʿUmarī identifies him as Badr al-Dīn Abū al-Maḥāsin Yūsuf Ibn Abī al-Maʿālī ibn Zammāḥ, known as Ibn Sayf al-Dawla al-Ḥamdānī al-mihmindār.

34. Al-ʿUmarī, *Qabāʾil al-ʿArab*, 69ff.

35. Al-ʿUmarī, *Qabāʾil al-ʿArab*, 106ff.

36. Al-ʿUmarī, *Qabāʾil al-ʿArab*, 156. See also al-Qalqashandī, *Ṣubḥ*, 1:353–54.

37. See editor's comments in al-ʿUmarī, *Mukhtaṣar Qalāʾid al-ʿIqyān*, 9–10. The work was said to consist of four volumes (*mujalladāt*). See also Ibn Ḥajar al-ʿAsqalānī, *Durar*, 1:194.

38. Al-ʿUmarī, *Qabāʾil al-ʿArab*, 69

39. Al-ʿUmarī, *Qabāʾil al-ʿArab*, 112.

40. Al-ʿUmarī, *Qabāʾil al-ʿArab*, 118.

41. Al-ʿUmarī, *Qabāʾil al-ʿArab*, 70.

42. Al-ʿUmarī, *Qabāʾil al-ʿArab*, 112. Also cited by al-Qalqashandī, *Qalāʾid*, 73–74; al-Qalqashandī, *Ṣubḥ*, 1:324–25. See also the discussion of this advice by Szombathy, "Genealogy in Medieval Muslim Societies."

43. Al-ʿUmarī, *Qabāʾil al-ʿArab*, 143. See al-Qalqashandī, *Ṣubḥ*, 1:355.

44. Muslim sources claim that the city of al-Raḥba, a town on the right bank of the Euphrates (modern-day al-Miyādīn) was founded by Mālik b. Ṭawḳ b. ʿAttāb al-Tag̱hlibī during the caliphate of al-Maʾmūn (198–218/813–33). See Bianquis, "al-Raḥba."

45. Al-ʿUmarī, *Qabāʾil al-ʿArab*, 154–55; al-ʿUmarī, *Masālik al-Abṣār*, 4:358–59.

46. Al-ʿUmarī, *Taʿrīf*, 76.

47. Al-Qalqashandī, *Nihāyat al-Arab*, no. 579; al-Qalqashandī, *Nihāyat al-Arab*, BN MS Arabe 2049, fol. 63b; al-Qalqashandī, *Ṣubḥ*, 1:345; al-Qalqashandī, *Qalāʾid*, 114.

48. Al-Qalqashandī, *Qalāʾid*, 1–2.

49. Possibly inspired by the introduction to Ibn Ḥazm's eleventh-century genealogical treatise. See Ibn Ḥazm, *Jamharat Ansāb al-ʿArab*, 2.

50. Al-Qalqashandī, *Nihāyat al-Arab*, 7; al-Qalqashandī, *Qalāʾid*, 7–8.

51. On the *ʿāqila*, see Nurit Tsafrir, *Collective Liability in Islam*.

52. Al-Qalqashandī, *Nihāyat al-Arab*, no. 1427.

53. Al-Qalqashandī, *Qalāʾid*, 135–36.

54. Al-Qalqashandī, *Qalāʾid*, 136–37. For the biography of this scholar, born in the Egyptian village of Nashāʾ, see Ibn Ḥajar al-ʿAsqalānī, *Durar*, 1:4.

55. Al-Qalqashandī, *Qalāʾid*, 12; al-Qalqashandī, *Ṣubḥ*, 1:307.

56. Al-Qalqashandī, *Nihāyat al-Arab*, 15–20.

57. Al-Qalqashandī, *Nihāyat al-Arab*, 24ff.

58. Al-Qalqashandī, *Qalāʾid*, 12; al-Qalqashandī, *Nihāyat al-Arab*, 11; al-Qalqashandī, *Ṣubḥ*, 1:307.

59. Al-ʿUmarī, *Qabāʾil al-ʿArab*, 143; cited in al-Qalqashandī, *Qalāʾid*, 116; Al-Qalqashandī, *Ṣubḥ*, 1:340.

60. Al-Qalqashandī, *Nihāyat al-Arab*, no. 1163. A camel appears in an anecdote that explains the etymology of a name of a tribe.

61. Al-Qalqashandī, *Qalāʾid*, 71.

62. Al-Qalqashandī, *Qalāʾid*, 63.

63. Ibn Khaldūn, *Dīwān al-Mubtadaʾ waʾl-Khabar* [= *Kitāb al-ʿIbar*], 6:7.

64. Al-Qalqashandī, *Nihāyat al-Arab*, no. 482

65. See examples in al-Qalqashandī, *Nihāyat al-Arab*, nos. 1115, 1336, 1596, 1447.

66. Björnesjö, "Quelques reflexions."

67. Björnesjö, "Quelques reflexions." Michel, "Devoirs fiscaux," 229, noted the low frequency of village names based on Arab clan names in Upper Egypt. In his quantitative analysis of village names in Fayyum and al-Ashmūnayn, he finds the same ratio of 30 percent in the fourteenth-century Mamluk survey and the early Ottoman survey of 1528. He notes a rise in Arabic place-names in the region between Manfalūṭ and Asyut, where, by 1528, eleven of seventeen villages on the eastern bank had Arab clan names (Michel, *L'Égypte des villages*, 346–47).

68. Al-Sakhāwī, *al-Ḍawʾ al-Lāmiʿ*, 2:138–39, no. 393.

69. See the biographical entry of al-Busāṭī in Ibn Taghrī Birdī, *al-Manhal al-Ṣāfī*, 6:26.

70. Al-Ṣafadī, *al-Wāfī biʾl-Wafayāt*, 8:14 (as part of an entry for a Mamluk bureaucrat called Shihāb al-Dīn Ibn Ghānim al-Jaʿfarī, who died in 737 H).

71. Al-Maqrīzī, *Tamīm al-Dārī*, 296–97.

72. Ibn Ḥajar, *Durar*, 5:284, no. 1436. Ibn Ḥajar refutes the claim to lineage by citing his Shaykh Ibn al-Mulaqqin.

73. Murat Sarıcık, *Niqābat al-Ashrāf fī al-Dawla al-ʿUthmāniyya*, 85–88.

74. Koby Yosef, "Language and Style in Mamluk Historiography," 127. Yosef used al-Ṣafadī's *Aʿyān al-Aṣr*; Ibn Ḥajar's *al-Durar al-Kāmina*; Ibn Taghrī Birdī's *al-Manhal al-Ṣāfī*; Ibn Qādī Shuhba's *Ṭabaqāt*; Ibn Kathīr's *Ṭabaqāt*; and the *Ṭabaqāt* work of Tāj al-Dīn al-Subkī. In most of these Mamluk-era works Yosef found that 40 percent of Shāfiʿī scholars had a *nisba* that tied

them to an Arab clan or tribe. The exceptions were the work by al-Subkī (only 25 percent, probably because the clan of the Subkīs themselves isn't mentioned) and the biographical dictionary by al-Isnāwī (d. 772/1370), who mentions clan affiliation rarely.

75. Yosef, "Language and Style," 129–31.

76. Yosef, "Language and Style," 128. Yosef found that 40 percent of the Ḥanafī scholars had a non-Arab ethnic *nisba* or a geographical *nisba* suggesting an origin in the eastern Islamic world or Anatolia. Among Shāfiʿīs, on the other hand, only 10–15 percent have non-Arab ethnic/geographic *nisba*. Arab clan names were also less common among Ḥanbalī scholars. This lower ratio may indeed be ascribed to to the more urban milieu of Ḥanbalī scholars—villagers of the Mamluk period were predominantly Shāfiʿīs, as was true in later periods.

77. Al-Sakhāwī, *Jawāhir wa'l-Durar*, 1:103.

78. Ibn Taghrī Birdī, *al-Manhal*, 1:171.

79. The Banū al-Bārizī's claim to Juhayna lineage is found already in a biography of Sharaf al-Dīn ibn al-Bārizī by Abū al-Fidā, *Mukhtaṣar*, 4:124. It is repeated in most later sources.

80. Garcin, *Qūṣ*, xi; Evan Metzger, "Historical Representation as Resurrection."

81. The largest group represented in al-Udfūwī's biographical dictionary are the Quraysh (18 mentions), followed by Thaʿlab (9), Rabīʿa (6), Kinda (5), Ḥimyar (5), Makhzūm (4), Khazraj (4), Kināna (3), Tayyim (3), Tanūkh (2), Tamīm (2), Judhām (1), ʿĀmir (1), ʿAbs (1). Most of these men hailed from the towns of Upper Egypt—such as Qūṣ, Edfu, Esna, and Armant—and not from named villages. Garcin estimated that 20 percent of the individuals in al-Udfūwī's dictionary had names that affiliated them with Arab clans and tribes (Garcin, *Qūṣ*, 364).

82. Al-Udfūwī, *al-Ṭāliʿ al-Saʿīd*, 490.

83. See Elias Muhanna, *A World in a Book*, 73.

84. Al-Udfūwī, *al-Ṭāliʿ al-Saʿīd*, 499.

85. Jumayl, *al-Nashāṭ al-Iqtiṣādī*, 99.

86. Al-Udfūwī, *al-Ṭāliʿ al-Saʿīd*, 679.

87. Al-Udfūwī, *al-Ṭāliʿ al-Saʿīd*, 236, 490.

88. In the same entry, we also find an "Arab" man asking a saint for a doorstep to place in the house he has built. Al-Udfūwī, *al-Ṭāliʿ al-Saʿīd*, 342

89. Al-Udfūwī, *al-Ṭāliʿ al-Saʿīd*, 711. The poem is reproduced in al-Ṣafadī, *Aʿyān al-ʿAṣr*, 5:527.

90. P.Vind.Arab. III 63 verso = (descr.) PERF 1382.3. This document and the following one form part of the al-Azkā cluster discussed above (see Livingston, "Paperwork of a Mamluk *Muqṭa*").

91. P.Vind.Arab. III 58. The petitioner, the deceased wife's daughter, claimed that knowledge of this domestic murder is widespread, and she asks that the culprit be summoned before the provincial governor.

92. P.MuhlisAqda; P.MahirUqud; P.AbdarraziqMariagedesEsclaves.

93. Al-Ṣafadī, *Aʿyān al-ʿAṣr*, 3:403 (ʿAlī b. ʿAbd Allāh b. Rayyān b. Ḥanṭala al-Sīnānī).

94. Al-Ṣafadī, *Aʿyān al-ʿAṣr*, 3:25; Ibn Ḥajar al-ʿAsqalānī, *Durar*, no. 2294

95. Ibn Kathīr, *al-Bidāya wa'l-Nihāya*, ed. Turkī, 18:373 (Majd al-Dīn Ḥaramiyy b. Qāsim al-ʿĀmirī al-Fāqūsī, d. 734 H).

96. Ibn Ḥajar al-ʿAsqalānī, *Durar*, 1:265. Cf. his biography in Tāj al-Dīn al-Subkī, *Ṭabaqāt al-Shāfiʿiyya*, 9:19, where the tribe's name is not mentioned.

97. Tāj al-Dīn al-Subkī, *Ṭabaqāt al-Shāfiʿiyya*, 10:91. Tāj al-Dīn writes, "I saw in the handwriting of the grandfather that our *nisba*—i.e, that of the *maʿāshir* of al-Subkiyya—is that of the *anṣār*." See also Yosef, "Language and Style in Mamluk Historiography," 127n.

98. Al-Dhahabī, *Ta'rīkh al-Islām*, 47:278. In the edition, his village is named as *bsr*, probably a miscopying.

99. Al- Dhahabī, *Ta'rīkh al-Islām*, 50:247. The biography has Muhyī al-Dīn al-Nawawī claim, on the authority of one of his grandfathers, a lineage to Ḥizām, the father of Ḥakīm b. Ḥizām, but this claim is refuted, either by al-Nawawī himself or by his biographer.

100. On his lineage, see Sabraa, "Ibn Qāḍī Shuhba," in *New Readings*. The first attested member of the family was his great-grandfather, Jamāl al-Dīn, who was appointed as a judge in Shuhba sometime in the thirteenth century. His son died circa 687/1288–89 (al-Jazarī, *Ta'rīkh*, 2:244). The lineage was confirmed by al-Ṣafadī, who inquired with one of Ibn Qāḍī Shuhba's older relatives, who worked in the chancery of Damascus (Sabraa, "Ibn Qāḍī Shuhba," 230–31).

101. Ibn Qāḍī Shuhba, *Ta'rīkh*, ed. Darwīsh, 2:14.

102. Al-'Ulaymī, *Uns al-Jalīl*, 2:174 (Kināna); al-Sakhāwī, *al-Ḍaw' al-Lāmi'*, 1:282, gives both possibilities of Kināna and Nu'ayr and adds that his father was a textile trader.

103. Al-'Ulaymī, *Uns al-Jalīl*, 2:221. Ibn Taghrī Birdī, *Manhal*, 15:124, and al-Maqrīzī, *Sulūk*, ed. 'Aṭā, 7:106, state that al-Dayrī was born in Jerusalem in 744/1344.

104. Ibn Abī al-Wafā', *al-Jawāhir al-Muḍiyya fi Ṭabaqāt al-Ḥanafiyya*, 2:2.

105. Al-Ṣafadī, *A'yān al-'Aṣr*, 5:495.

106. Ibn Ḥijjī, *Tārīkh*, 17 (for an *ijāza* in his handwriting discovered by Ziriklī). The *nisba* Sa'dī was common among people from Ḥisbān.

107. Al-Dhahabī, *Ta'rīkh al-Islām*, 40:116 (Abū al-'Abbās al-Rabā'ī, a textile merchant and a scholar born in the village of Ḍamīr near Damascus in 486/1093–94); al-Dhahabī, *Ta'rīkh al-Islām*, 48:297 (Muwaffaq al-Dīn al-Tha'labī, born in the village of Arzūnā in 589/1193–94); al-Dhahabī, *Ta'rīkh al-Islām*, 47:191 (Nūr al-Din al-Numayrī, Qāḍī of Kafrbaṭnā who died in 643/1245–46 was the leader of the village and its most respected person, *kabīr al-qarya wa-muḥtashamu-hā*); al-Ṣafadī, *al-Wāfī bi'l-Wafayāt*, 13:301 (Khaṭīb Bayt al-Ābār al-Zabīdī, born in Bayt al-Ābār in the Ghuta of Damascus in 586/1190–91).

108. For his biography and intellectual career, see Walid Saleh, "al-Biqā'ī."

109. Kenneth Goudie, "How to Make It in Cairo"; and Goudie, "Al-Biqā'ī's Self-Reflection." The autobiographical texts are in al-Biqā'ī, *'Unwān*, 1:66–67, 2:61, 2:85, 4:116–18. He pronounced ḍamma instead of kasra because the speech of the people in the village was ungrammatical, *laḥn al-'awwām* (*'Unwān*, 1:66; Goudie, "How to Make It in Cairo," 226).

110. Al-Biqā'ī, *'Unwān*, 2:61–62; Goudie, "How to Make It in Cairo," 207–9.

111. Goudie, "Al-Biqā'ī's Self-Reflection."

112. Al-Biqā'ī, *'Unwān*, 2:61.

113. Al-Biqā'ī, *'Unwān*, 61–62.

114. A copy of a late-fifteenth-century lineage document concerning the ancestors of the Bakrī family, witnessed before the *qāḍī* of Damanhūr, is now part of a private collection. I thank Hussein Omar for providing me with a copy.

115. Goudie, "Al-Biqā'ī's Self-Reflection," using the analytical framework of Szombathy.

116. Al-Biqā'ī, *'Unwān*, 4:116–18.

117. Walker, "Searching for a Home"; Walker, "Khirba."

6. Arab Speech, Arab Dress, and Handmade Wares

1. Versteegh, *The Arabic Language*, 184–89; Holes, "Introduction," 20–22; J. Rosenhouse, "Bedouin Arabic"; Bahloul, "Linguistic Diversity"; Behnstedt and Woidich, "The Formation of the Egyptian Arabic Dialect Area."

2. Behnstedt and Woidich, *Wortatlas der arabischen Dialekte*; Behnstedt and Woidich, *Die ägyptisch-arabischen Dialekte*; Behnstedt, *Sprachatlas von Syrien*.

3. Holes, "Introduction," 22; Behnstedt and Woidich, "The Formation of the Egyptian Dialect Area"; Prochazka, "Northern Fertile Crescent," 260–63 (dates the "bedouinization" process to the thirteenth century). See also Abu-haidar, "Bedouinization."

4. Versteegh, *The Arabic Language*, 185. Holes disputes the claim that Bedouin dialects are more conservative because they retain classical features lost elsewhere ("Introduction," 20–22).

5. See Versteegh, "pidginization," in *Approaches to Arabic Dialects.*

6. Versteegh, *The Arabic Language*, 185.

7. Versteegh, *The Arabic Language*, 149–50, 187.

8. A detailed, recent example is Behnstedt and Woidich, "The Formation of the Egyptian Dialect Area."

9. Most medieval references have been compiled and discussed by ʿAbd al-Razzāq al-Ṣāʿidī, "Waqafāt maʿa al-Duktūr." The focus here is on establishing the "Prophetic" vocalization.

10. Al-Ṣāʿidī, "Waqafāt maʿa al-Duktūr."

11. Mahmud Fahmi Hijazi, *Kitāb ʿIlm al-Lugha al-ʿArabiyya*, 301; Versteegh, *The Arabic Language*, 120.

12. On Qāf al-Tamīmiyya, see Holes, "Introduction," 16. On the Arabic of Tamīm as the spoken Arabic of the second/eighth century, see Larcher, "Parlers arabes nomades et sédentaires."

13. Jāḥiẓ, *al-Bayān*, 1:51; repeated in the fourteenth century by al-Nuwayrī, who describes it as a *nabaṭī* pronunciation (*Nihāyat al-Arab*, 3:384), and al-Waṭwāṭ (*Ghurar*, 217). On Makḥūl's pronunciation, see al-Dhahabī, *Tadhkirat al-Ḥuffāẓ*, 1:82.

14. On the quest of Abbasid-era philologists to capture the pure language of the desert Arabs as part of a purposeful reconstruction of tradition, see Szombathy, "Fieldwork and Preconceptions."

15. Larcher, "Parlers arabes nomades et sédentaires."

16. Ibn Jinnī refers to "sedentary people who abandoned the language of those who are attached (*yantasib*) to the eloquent or correct form of Arabic." The verb *yantasib* has obvious genealogical connotations (Larcher, "Parlers arabes nomades et sédentaires," 371).

17. Al-Rūyānī, *Baḥr al-Madhhab*, 2:260: *law kāna mimman lā yuṣarriḥu bi'l-ḥarf fa-yatakallamu bi'l-ḥarf bayna ḥarfayn ka'l-ʿarabī alladhī lā yajʿalu al-qāf kāfān bal yukhriju-hā bayna al-ḥarafayn lā kāfān wa-lā qāfān.* This seems to be the earliest reference to a distinctive Arab pronunciation. I haven't found any reference to it in the early legal discussions on dialect pronunciations explored by Zadeh, *Vernacular Qur'an*, 93–98.

18. Al-Isnawī, *Kawkab al-Durrī*, 429. Naṣr b. Ibrāhīm al-Maqdisī or al-Muqaddasī taught in Jerusalem, Tyre, and Damascus. He made his living from a small piece of land he owned in the Nablus area, his native land. See Drory, "Ḥanbalīs of the Nablus Region in the Eleventh and Twelfth Centuries," 101–2.

19. J. W. Fück, "Ḥayṣa Bayṣa"; Orfali, "Ḥayṣa Bayṣa." The biographers give instances of the affected style of his private letters that made them nearly unintelligible to the addressee.

20. Ibn al-Shaʿʿār al-Mawṣilī (d. 1256), *Qalā'id al-Jummān*, 2:84–85.

21. Ibn al-Fūṭī, *Majmaʿ al-Ādāb*, 6:400.

22. Ibn al-Fūṭī, *Majmaʿ al-Ādāb*, 6:638. See al-Ṣāʿidī, "Waqafāt maʿa al-Duktūr Bahā' ʿAbd al-Raḥmān fī Mas'alat al-Qīf." Arabic: *kāna yaʿqidu al-qāf kāfān.*

23. Al-Irbilī, *Tārīkh Irbil*, 1:141. Arabic: *yaʿqidu al-qāf idhā takallama.*

24. Ibn al-ʿAdīm, *Bughyat al-Ṭalab*, ed. Rawāḍiyya, 9:285. Parallel to the references to the /g/ vocalization of q*, we also find twelfth- and thirteenth-century examples of the pronunciation of *q as a glottal stop, another nonnormative vocalization. Ibn ʿUnayn (Damascus, d. 1233) wrote a poem full of *qāfs* to his nephew who *yalthaghu bi'l-qāf wa-yukhriju-hā hamzatan*; the traveler al-ʿAbdarī mentions, for 688/1289, a man in Cairo who used to pronounce *qāf* and *kāf* as *hamza* (*yajʿal al-qāf wa'l-kāf hamzatan*); a Frankish toponymy of Lebanon has Cafrahael for Kafr Qāhil and Bahaelin for Baʿaqlīn. See Lentin, "The Levant," 178–80. This glottal vocalization did not seem to acquire any social significance.

25. Ibn al-ʿArabī, *al-Futūḥāt al-Makiyya*, 2:675 (chapter 295).

26. Ibn al-ʿArabī's definition of the tongue-tied *qāf*, at least as it appears in the Būlāq edition, is somewhat confusing. He states that the non-*maʿqūda qāf* is in between the *kāf* and the tongue-tied *qāf*, and it is neither a pure *qāf* nor a pure *kāf*, and for this reason is rejected by linguists. But in the next line he refers to the tongue-tied *qāf* of the Banū Fahm, and to the rejection of this pronunciation by Quran readers in North Africa and al-Andalus. Ibn al-ʿArabī clearly means that the /g/ vocalization is the *maʿqūda* tongue-tied pronunciation, as defined by all other medieval authors (Ibn al-ʿArabī, *al-Futūḥāt al-Makiyya*, 2:675). See also remarks by al-Ṣāʿidī, "Waqafāt maʿa al-Duktūr."

27. Abū Ḥayyān, *Irtishāf al- Ḍarab min Lisān al-ʿArab*, 16.

28. Abū Ḥayyān told al-Ṣafadī that "there is no one in these lands who *yaʿqidu* the letter *qāf*" (al-Ṣafadī, *Aʿyān al-ʿAṣr*, 5:332). The reference to "those lands" is probably to al-Andalus. A copyist mistake is possible here, as we would expect Abū Ḥayyān to state that all Andalusis *do* speak with tongue-tied *qāf*. In a biography of an Andalusi poet born in Murcia in 633H, we learn that he used the tongue-tied *qāf* in his conversation (al-Ṣafadī, *Aʿyān al-ʿAṣr*, 2:203).

29. Ibn Khaldūn's views on the history of the Arabic language are discussed by Versteegh, *The Arabic Language*, 173; Heinrichs, "Ibn Khaldūn as a Historical Linguist"; Larcher "Sociolinguistique et histoire de l'arabe selon la Muqaddima d'Ibn Ḫaldun (VIIIe/XIVe siècle)."

30. Until here, also translated in Versteegh, *The Arabic Language*, 174.

31. Ibn Khaldūn, *al-Muqaddima*, ed. Wāfī, 1:768 (Arabic); Ibn Khaldūn, *Muqaddimah*, trans. Rosenthal, 3:348–49 (adapted).

32. Ibn Khaldūn, *Dīwān al-Mubtada' wa'l-khabar* [= *Kitāb al-ʿIbar*], 6:186.

33. Larcher "Sociolinguistique et histoire de l'arabe selon la Muqaddima d'Ibn Ḫaldun (VIIIe/XIVe siècle)," 429–31.

34. Ibn al-Dawādārī, *Kanz al-Durar*, 9:63.

35. Al-Maqrīzī, *Sulūk*, ed. Ziyāda, 2:346–47.

36. Al-Sakhāwī, *al-Ḍaw' al-Lāmiʿ*, 3:238. Zuhayr was born in 826 H in Bāb al-Qarāfa.

37. Al-Sakhāwī, *al-Ḍaw' al-Lāmiʿ*, 3:211.

38. Ibn al-Rifʿa, *Kifāyat al-Nabīh*, 4:37; al-Isnawī, *al-Kawkab al-Durrī*, 429; al-Suyūṭī, *al-Ḥāwī*, 1:253. Shāfiʿī jurists were more concerned about nonnormative pronunciations than other schools, possibly because of doctrinal insistence on formularies.

39. Ibn Ḥajar al-Haythamī, *Tuḥfat al-Muḥtāj fī Sharḥ al-Minhāj*, 2:37. In the seventeenth century, too, al-Shirbīnī has the stereotypical Egyptian peasant speak with a /g/ when pronouncing the word *qāḍī* (*Kitāb Hazz al-Quḥūf bi-Sharḥ Qaṣīd Abī Shādūf*, 207).

40. The /g/ articulation was also common in fifteenth-century Yemen. Ibn Ḥajar al-ʿAsqalānī made fun of the Yemeni pronunciation of *qāf maʿqūda*, after a group of Yemeni scholars made fun of his Egyptian Arabic during his visit to the Yemen (al-Sakhāwī, *al-Jawāhir wa'l-Durar*, 1:150).

41. Versteegh, *The Arabic Language*, 176–77.

42. Versteegh, *The Arabic Language*, 150. On Baghdad, see Khan, "Judaeo-Arabic"; Ḥeikki Palva ("From qəltu to gələt: Diachronic Notes on Linguistic Adaptation in Muslim Baghdad Arabic") oscillates between migration and strategic use of dialect in explaining the differences between the dialects of religious communities in Baghdad.

43. I owe the use of the terms "overt" and "covert" prestige to comments by professor Clive Holes.

44. Drory, "The Prince who Favored the Desert," 24, citing al-Maqrīzī, *Sulūk*, ed. Ziyāda, 2:601.

45. Al-Shujāʿī, *Beiträge*, ed. Schafer, 101; Ibn Qāḍī Shuhba, *Ta'rīkh*, 2:247. For the events of his reign, see Drory, "The Prince."

46. Al-Yūnīnī, *Dhayl*, 3:272, 4:172. See also al-Nuwayrī, *Nihāyat al-Arab*, 30:382.

47. Büssow-Schmitz, *Beduinen*, 94, citing al-Maqrīzī, *Sulūk*, ed. Ziyāda, 2:122–23.

48. Ibrāhīm, *al-Mu'jam al-'Arabī li-Asmā' al-Malābis*, 65.

49. Al-Shujaʿī, *Ta'rīkh*, 69; Ibn Qāḍī Shuhba, *Ta'rīkh*, 1:421. See also Walker, "Tribal dimension," 93.

50. Ibrāhīm, *al-Mu'jam al-'Arabī li-Asmā' al-Malābis*, 206: Zaryūl or Zarbūl. It appears in a version of the Arabian Nights as an inferior footwear of slaves, but by the nineteenth century the word *zarbūl* was used for red boots with pointed tips worn by village headmen (Dozy, *Supplément*, 1:584).

51. Stillman, "Libās."

52. On the term *lithām* in medieval Arabic literature and poetry, see Björkman, "Li̱tẖām"; Stillman, *Arab Dress*, 20.

53. De la Véronne, "Ṣanhāḏja"; García Sanjuán, "Ibn 'Abdūn."

54. The military explanation for the *lithām* is offered by Ibn Taymiyya, *Majmūʿ Fatāwā*, 1:320–21, 21:187. See also the summary of Mālikī positions in Ibn al-Ḥajj, *al-Madkhal*, 1:140–43. Both these fourteenth-century authors rule that wearing a turban without *taḥnīk* is permitted and is not reprehensible; they were probably responding to the prevailing fashion in Cairo and Damascus.

55. I owe the ideas of this paragraph to comments by Mathieu Tillier.

56. Abū Muḥammad 'Abd al-Wahhāb, *Kitāb al-Ma'ūna 'alā 'Ālim Ahl al-Madīna Mālik b. Anas*, 3:1723.

57. Ibn Rushd, *Kitāb al-Bayān wa'l-taḥṣīl*, 19:17.

58. Ibn Shāsh (d. 616/1219–20), *'Aqd al-Jawāhir al-Thamīna fī Madhhab 'Ālim al-Madīna*, 1291; al-Qarāfī, *al-Dhakhīra*, 264 (turban without *taḥnīk*/*iltiḥā'* is not the Arab manner of dressing, *zayy al-'arab*); Ibn Qudāma, *al-Mughnī*, ed. Turkī, 1:381 ("The turbans of the Arabs mean *taḥnīk*"); Ibn Daqīq al-'Īd, *Sharḥ al-Ilmām bi-Aḥādīth al-Aḥkām*, 4:378 (*taḥnīk* is the custom of the Arabs).

59. Al-Qarāfī, *Anwār al-Burūq fī Anwa' al-Furūq*, 2:110.

60. The only reference I was able to find concerns a Damascene litterateur of the late twelfth century, Abū al-Fatḥ al-Balīṭī, who used to wear his *ṭaylasān* without *taḥnīk* (al-Dhahabī, *Ta'rīkh al-Islām*, ed. Tadmurī, 42:396).

61. Al-Ḥarīrī, *Impostures*, 239.

62. Grabar, "The Illustrated *Maqamat* of the Thirteenth Century," 180.

63. MS St. Petersburg (Oriental Institute, Academy of Science), S 23 fol. 288. Reproduced in James, *Masterpiece of Arab Painting*, 189; Ettinghausen, *Arab Painting*, 109.

64. MS St. Petersburg S 23, fol. 231 (caption reads: Abū Zayd disguised with a *lithām* brings the slave-boy to al-Ḥārith in the slave market). Reproduced in James, *Masterpiece of Arab Painting*, 186.

65. On the Mamluk-era copies of the *maqāmāt*, see Haldane, *Mamluk Painting*, 27–31.

66. BL Add. 22114, fol. 29r, (12th *maqāma*). Reproduced in Haldane, *Mamluk Painting*, plate 24.

67. BL Add. 22114, 47r (18th *maqāma*).

68. BL Add. 22114, fol. 149r reproduced in Haldane, *Mamluk Painting*, plate 30. The same tent scene, with seated figures wearing a strip under their chin, is depicted in BN 5847, fols. 139b–140a (44th *maqāma*).

69. Vienna A.F.9, fol. 165r; reproduced in Haldane, *Mamluk Painting*, plate 72 (Abu Zayd's departure while the others are sleeping). About half of the illustrations of this manuscript are reproduced in Holter, *Les principaux manuscrits à peintures de la Bibliothèque Nationale de Vienne*, 15–33. For other black African figures in this manuscript, see fol. 105r (Holter, *Principaux manuscrits*, abb. 24); fol. 126r (drinking scene); fol. 42v.

70. Bodleian Marsh 458, 45a (reproduced in http://warfare.6te.net/14/Bodleian-Ms-Marsh-458-45a.htm). The illustration accompanies the 27th *maqāma* (al-Wabariyya). The scene

depicts the moment in which al-Ḥārith faces the Arab who took his camel and Abū Zayd, himself guilty of having stolen the horse he is riding.

71. Frenkel, "Contribution of European Travel Literature," 715, citing Burchard, *A Description of the Holy Land*, 35.

72. Ibn Khallikān, *Wafayāt*, 2:365.

73. Al-Nuwayrī, *Nihāyat al-Arab*, 29:427–29.

74. Al-ʿUmarī, *Qabāʾil al-ʿArab*, 120 (the anecdote is dated to the reign of al-Ashraf Khalīl).

75. Al-Badawī's place of origin and identity were a matter of dispute. His earliest biographer, Ibn al-Mulaqqin (d. 804/1401), has him a member of otherwise unknown tribe of Syria, while later sources claim that he was born in Fez. See Mayeur-Jaouen, "al-Badawī, al-Sayyid"; Vollers and Littmann, "Aḥmad al-Badawī."

76. Jacques, "Murder," 162.

77. Cited by al-Maqrīzī, *al-Mawāʿiẓ*, 2:427.

78. Al-Maqrīzī, *Sulūk*, ed. Ziyāda, 2:528–29.

79. Thietmar: The Bedouin are "ugly and very poorly dressed . . . [t]hey wear red felt hats on their heads a cubit high and a cloth bound around the hat" (Pringle, *Pilgrimage to Jerusalem*, 132). Burchard: "wearing only a red pelisse with a large loose-fitting shirt over it and covering their heads with no more than a piece of cloth" (Pringle, *Pilgrimage to Jerusalem*, 315).

80. This is an account by Shihāb al-Dīn Abū al-Thanāʾ Maḥmud al-Ḥalabī, chief administrator under Sultans Kitbughā and Lājīn (al-Qalqashandī, *Ṣubḥ*, 4:209; al-ʿUmarī, *Taʿrīf*, 86).

81. In the fifteenth century, musical bands of Arab singers (*maghānī*) accompanied provincial Mamluk officers in Upper Egypt (al-Sakhāwī, *Ḍaw'*, 10:272).

82. Al-Maqrīzī, *Sulūk*, ed. Ziyāda, 2:528–29.

83. The wide sleeves of Arab riders are reported in connection with an attempt to limit the width of sleeves worn by Cairene women in 792/1390. See Ibn Taghrī Birdī, *Nujūm*, 12:30; see also Mayer, *Mamluk Costume*, 69.

84. Brocquière, *A Mission*, trans. Irwin, 151.

85. Sarıcık, *Niqābat al-Ashrāf*, 87. The edict dates to 773/1381. See al-Maqrīzī, *Sulūk*, ed. Ziyāda, 3:199.

86. According to the narrative by al-Maqrīzī, the womenfolk of the Arab amirs received from the sultan gold necklaces, tall *shanābir* headgear worn above their *ʿiṣāba*, bracelets inlaid with pearls, and gilded veils. See al-Maqrīzī, *Sulūk*, ed. Ziyāda, 2:527–29.

87. Al-Qalqashandī, *Qalāʾid*, 125. See also al-Qalqashandī, *Nihāyat al-Arab*, no. 1053.

88. Stillman, *Arab Dress*, 8

89. Al-Sakhāwī, *Ḍaw'*, 10:159

90. Al-Jazīrī, *al-Durar al-Farāʾid*, 2:477, 2:479. I owe this reference to Adam Sabra.

91. Pringle, *Pilgrimage to Jerusalem*, 123.

92. Frescobaldi, *Visit to the Holy Places*, 56; Felix Fabri, *Wanderings*, 9:477–84.

93. Frescobaldi, *Visit to the Holy Places*, 44 (while sailing from Alexandria to Cairo).

94. Joinville, "The Life of Saint Louis," 208–9.

95. In Mamluk-era textual sources, I have found only one reference to the clothes of peasants. It concerns a fifteenth-century Mālikī *qāḍī* in Palestine, nicknamed al-Fallāḥ, because he used to reside in the villages and wore the clothes of the peasants (al-ʿUlaymī, *Uns al-Jalīl*, 2:249).

96. Al-Nābulusī, *Villages of the Fayyum*, 78. Al-Nābulusī also repeatedly refers to the use of the *ṭaylasān* by converts and upstarts in his *Sword of Ambition* (165–67).

97. Al-Qalqashandī, *Qalāʾid*, 71. See also note 61 for chap. 5.

98. P.WansbroughCommercialPrivileges.2.

99. See the famous village scene in BN 5847, fol. 138a (43rd *maqāma*). For village scenes in Mamluk copies of the *maqāmāt*, see Vienna A.f.9 159v; BL Add 22114 147v (old 153v, 43rd *maqāma*, meeting a youth with a red cap).

100. Grabar, "The Illustrated *Maqamat* of the Thirteenth Century," 178–80; Haldane, *Mamluk Painting*, 29. For the oxen illustration, see Stillman, *Arab Dress*, 50n.

101. K. al-Diryāq, copied 1199 in Mosul, BN Arabe 2964. Discussed in Eddé, *La principauté ayyoubide d'Alep*, 504; Ettinghausen, *Arab Painting*, 84–85, 90. See also Stillman, *Arab Dress*, 50–51.

102. Eddé, *La principauté ayyoubide d'Alep*, 505; D. S. Rice, "Inlaid Brasses from the Workshop of the Aḥmad al-Dhakī al-Mawṣilī." See also Haldane, *Mamluk Painting*, plate 2 (a man ploughs on a cart pulled by oxen, from Cambridge, Corpus Christi, Ms 578, fol. 29r).

103. Piotr Makowski, "Towards a Better Understanding," 124. See the introduction and visual examples in Sinibaldi et al., *The Levantine Ceramics Project*.

104. The seminal study is Johns, "The Rise of Middle Islamic," published in 1998. See also Gabrieli and Walker, "Production and Distribution"; Milwright, *Introduction to Islamic Archaeology*, 61–63, 155ff. See the most recent summary of the ceramics evidence for Transjordan in Haron and Clark, eds., *The Pottery of Jordan*, 108–22.

105. Makowski, "Towards a Better Understanding."

106. Makowski, "Towards a Better Understanding," 121–23.

107. Taxel et al., "Early Islamic Crude Handmade Ware."

108. Walker, "The Middle Islamic Period (Fatimid, Ayyubid and Mamluk)," in Haron and Clark, eds., *The Pottery of Jordan*, 112–13.

109. Makowski, "Towards a Better Understanding," 125–28, 141.

110. On handmade pottery in Islamic Arabia, see Johns, "Rise of Middle Islamic", 76–77 (focusing on the Gulf). Makowski suggests that the tradition of handmade pottery may have spread simultaneously to Greater Syria and to the Hijaz ("Towards a Better Understanding," 122n). For a study of an Abbasid pottery workshop in al-Yamama in central Arabia, see Lesguer and Schiettecatte, "A Ninth- to Tenth-Century Pottery Workshop at al-Yamāmah." For a comparison of the painted pottery traditions of pre-Islamic northwest Arabia and the southern Levant, see Juan Manuel Tebes, "Investigating."

111. Ben Dolinka, personal communication, July 15, 2022. Dolinka was the onsite ceramic processor in several excavations over the past twenty years. The findings have mostly not been published.

112. See Adrian Boas, "The Medieval Ceramics from Khirbat Ka'kul," 76–83, and figs. 3:14, 4:25 (handmade cooking vessels).

113. This is based on four sealed strata from the Ayyubid period revealed during the Beit Strauss excavations in the Western Wall Plaza, conducted between 2014 and 2016. Ben Dolinka, personal communication, July 15, 2022.

114. Kletter and Stern, "A Mamluk-Period Site at Khirbat Burin in the Eastern Sharon."

115. Makowski, "Towards a Better Understanding," 135.

116. Makowski, "Towards a Better Understanding," 132, 134.

117. Gabrieli and Walker, "Production and Distribution."

118. Kassem, "Social and Economic Networks in Late Medieval Rural Southern Syria."

119. Makowski, "Towards a Better Understanding," 134.

120. Walker et al., "Did the Mamluks Have an Environmental Sense?" 228; Walker, "The Middle Islamic Period," 116. The analysis of the cookpots is included in a forthcoming publication by Bethany Walker et al. (Walker, personal communication, July 2024).

121. Walker, "From Ceramics to Social Theory," 18 (based on sites excavated in Israel-Palestine).

122. Milwright, *Fortress of the Raven*, 149ff.

123. McPhillips and Walmsley, "Faḥl during the Early Mamluk Period."

124. Walker and Dolinka, "Khirbet Beit Mazmil."

125. The evidence for the reoccupation of sites is summarized in Walker, "Searching for a Home" and "The Northern Jordan Project."

126. Johns, "The Rise of Middle Islamic," 81.

127. See a summary of current explanations in Makowski, "Towards a Better Understanding," 124.

128. Milwright, *Introduction to Islamic Archaeology*, 156. Ethnography shows that handmade vessels are often made by women; in traditional societies, these female potters are sometimes stigmatized.

129. E. Stern, "Pottery and Identity in the Latin Kingdom of Jerusalem"; Makowski, "Towards a Better Understanding," 134.

130. Sinibaldi, "The Crusader Period," 108.

131. Andrea Polcaro, "Sociology and Economics of Ceramics," in *The Pottery of Jordan*, eds. Haron and Clark, 19–22.

132. Al-Maqrīzī, *Sulūk*, ed. Ziyāda, 2:374, in connection with Muhannā; see Büssow-Schmitz, *Beduinen*, 57. Research on the cuisine of Mamluk Cairo has not yet identified dishes identified as distinctly "Arab." See Lewicka, *Food and Foodways of Medieval Cairenes.*

133. Al-Jazīrī, *al-Durar al-Farā'id*, 2:474, 2:479. I owe this reference to Adam Sabra.

134. Gascoigne and Sheehan, "Sherds and the City"; Gascoigne, "Providing Pots for Cairo." The evidence for the Mamluk-era Cairene pottery is presented in Julie Monchamp, *Céramiques des Murailles du Cairo.*

7. Popular Epics and Arab Identity

1. For introductions to the popular epics in the later Middle Ages, see Helen Blatherwick, "And the Light in His Eyes Grew Dark"; Herzog: "Composition and Worldview of Some Bourgeois and Petit-Bourgeois Mamluk Adab-Encyclopedias," 105–6; Doufikar-Aerts, "Sīrat al-Iskandar"; Reynolds, *Heroic Poets*, 4–8.

2. Blatherwick, *Prophets, Gods and Kings*, 14.

3. Bridget Connelly, *Arab Folk Epic and Identity*, 225, cited in Blatherwick, *Prophets, Gods and Kings*, 11n.

4. For a survey of the key epics, see Lyons, *The Arabian Epic*, vol. 1.

5. Heath, *Thirsty Sword*, 58.

6. Heath, "Antar Hangs His Mu'allaqa," 10.

7. Hirschler, *The Written Word*, chap. 5 ("Popular Reading Practices"), 164–85.

8. Hirschler, *The Written Word*, 167.

9. Herzog, "'What They Saw with Their Own Eyes . . .'"

10. Sabra, "Hirschler, *The Written Word.*"

11. Hirschler argued that these two epics posed a challenge to scholars' authority over the past, because they are more believable, lacking the fantastical and magical components of Sīrat Sayf Dhī b. Yazan (Hirschler, *The Written Word*, 181–84).

12. Lyons, *The Arabian Epic*, 1:140.

13. Driss Cherkaoui, "Historical Elements," 422, following Heath.

14. Herzog, "Orality and the Tradition of Arabic Epic Storytelling."

15. Samaw'al al-Maghribī, *Ifḥām al-Yahūd*, 100–1 (Arabic). See also Firestone, "Samaw'al b. Yaḥyā al-Maghribī." This reference to a written text of the cycle of Dhāt al-Himma and al-Baṭṭāl led Claudia Ott to pinpoint the origins of that epic in the first half of the sixth/twelfth century, in connection with the Muslim push into Byzantine Anatolia. See Claudia Ott, *Metamorphosen des Epos*; Melanie Magidow, "Epic of the Commander Dhat al-Himma."

16. Ibn Abī Uṣaybiʿa, *A Literary History of Medicine* (2020), 10.69. Herzog states that Ibn al-Ṣāʾigh earned his living by copying *aḥādīth* of ʿAntar (Herzog, "Orality," 640). But the text doesn't explicitly state whether he copied the stories of ʿAntar as a form of employment or out of curiosity.

17. Doufikar-Aerts, "Sīrat al-Iskandar," 516.

18. Al-Jawbarī, *al-Mukhtār fī Kashf al-Asrār wa-Hatk al-Asrār*, 187–88.

19. This is reminiscent of the performances within performances discussed by Dwight Reynolds in his ethnographic study, where a poet recounts to his Egyptian audience the story of a poet recounting a story to his Egyptian audience. See Reynolds, *Heroic Poets*, 72–73.

20. Reported by Da'ud al-Anṭākī (d. 1008/1600), *Tazyīn al-Aswāq*, 24.

21. Al-Maqrīzī, *al-Mawāʿiẓ*, 3:53 (in the section on Khaṭṭ Bayn al-Qasrayn). Cited in Herzog, "Orality," 637. Al-Maqrīzī is here describing the activities that took place in Bayn al-Qaṣrayn until its decline in the early fifteenth century; he is not necessarily attesting to the circulation of the epics in late Fatimid Cairo.

22. Like other puritans, he prefers to use the classical form ʿAntara and not the form that is actually used in the epics. Ibn al-Ḥajj, *Madkhal*, 4:83–84.

23. Ibn al-Ḥajj, *Madkhal*, 4:79–80.

24. Al-Subkī, *Muʿīd* (1908), 205; Al-Subkī, *Muʿīd* (1986), 1:110.

25. Al-Subkī, *Muʿīd* (1986),1:101. Translated in Herzog, "Orality," 644n71.

26. Ibn Taymiyya, *Majmūʿ Fatāwā*, 3:115. He explains that both ʿAntara and al-Baṭṭāl were historical figures, yet "the lies surrounding them have become innumerable."

27. On the date of the composition of the *Minhāj*, see Hoover, *Ibn Taymiyya*, 32.

28. The term *ṭuruqiyya* was used in the Mamluk era for all sorts of charlatans who put up stalls on the road, such as astrologers, makers of charms, and quack doctors. Al-Nuwayrī states that the *ṭuruqiyya* trained cats and mice (*Nihāyat al-Arab*, 1:284). A *muḥtasib* was instructed to prevent tricksters (*mutaḥayyalīn*) from committing fraud, including the *ṭuruqiyya* and the astrologers (al-Qalqashandī, *Ṣubḥ*, 11:96). The *ṭuruqiyya* were sometimes identified with the Banū Sāsān. See Richardson, *Roma in the Medieval Islamic World.*

29. Ibn Taymiyya, *Majmūʿ Fatāwā*, 8:92, and 18:351–53 (where the vizier is identified as Jaʿfar).

30. Ibn Taymiyya, *Majmūʿ Fatāwā*, 8:116 (*Minhāj al-Sunna*). See also Ibn Taymiyya, *Majmūʿ Fatāwā*, 7:46, 22:362.

31. Al-Dhahabī, *al-ʿIbar*, 1:107.

32. Al-Ṣafadī, *al-Wāfī bi'l-Wafayāt*, 17:371.

33. Ibn Kathīr, *al-Bidāya wa'l-Nihāya*, ed. Iḥyāʾ al-Turāth, 9:365. See translation of this passage in Frenkel, "Volksroman," 6.

34. Ibn Rajab, *Dhayl Ṭabaqāt al-Ḥanābila*, 3:35.

35. Hirschler, *The Written Word*, 170.

36. Ibn Khaldūn, *Dīwān al-Mubtada' wa'l-Khabar* [= *Kitāb al-ʿIbar*], 6:25. According to his autobiography, Ibn Khaldūn was sent to the Banū Hilāl on a diplomatic mission in 774/1372–73. It therefore seems that his account is based on his firsthand encounter with the Hilālīs.

37. Ibn Khaldūn, *Dīwān al-Mubtada' wa'l-Khabar* [= *Kitāb al-ʿIbar*], 6:25–26. Also discussed in Sowayan, "The Hilali Poetry in the Muqaddimah," 281–82.

38. Brett, "The Way of the Nomad," 262–63.

39. Hirschler suggested that Sīrat Banī Hilāl didn't attract the attention of scholarly elites because it only circulated in oral form (Hirschler, *The Written Word*, 183–84).

40. Reynolds, *Heroic Poets.*

41. Ibn Khaldūn, *Dīwān al-Mubtada' wa'l-Khabar* [= *Kitāb al-ʿIbar*], 1:805–6; Sowayan, "The Hilali Poetry in the Muqaddimah," 284.

42. Sowayan notes that this Egyptian poem does not appear in all early manuscripts of Ibn Khaldūn's *ʿIbar*, but only in the Bursa manuscript Celebi 793, copied on 8 Shaʿbān 806/28

February 1404 by Ibrāhīm b. Khalīl al-Saʿdī al-Shāfiʿī al-Miṣrī (Sowayan, "The Hilali Poetry in the Muqaddimah," 283).

43. Sowayan, "The Hilali Poetry in the Muqaddimah," 286.

44. On the history of Sīrat Ḥamza, see Marzolph, "Ḥamza." The oldest extant version is in Persian and dates from the Safavid period.

45. Ibn Taymiyya, *Majmūʿ Fatāwā*, 6:194.

46. Ibn Taymiyya, *Majmūʿ Fatāwā*, 4:12 (*Minhaj al-Sunna*). Arabic: *yaẓunna ṭāʾifa min al-turkmān anna Ḥamza la-hu maghāzin ʿaẓīma wa-yanqulūnuhā baynahum.*

47. Peacock, *Mongol Anatolia*, 208.

48. On the emergence of a seventeenth-century epic celebrating Turcoman tribal identities as opposed to Ottoman and Safavid powers, see Karamustafa, "Who Were the Türkmen."

49. Al-ʿUmarī, *Qabāʾil al-ʿArab*, 143; paraphrased in al-Qalqashandī, *Qalāʾid*, 116; idem., *Ṣubḥ*, 1:34.

50. Al-Dhahabī, *Kitāb al-Muntaqā min Minhāj al-Iʿtidāl*, 517.

51. Al-Dhahabī, *Kitāb al-Muntaqā min Minhāj al-Iʿtidāl*, 374.

52. Al-Jazīrī, *al-Durar al-Farāʾid*, 2:475–76. I owe this reference to Adam Sabra.

53. Ibn al-Dawādārī, *Kanz al-Durar*, 9:276. Ibn al-Dawādārī also had a couple of references to the Sīra of al-Ḥākim (6:312 and 8:122). See Braun, "Equipped with Shovels," 94, citing Antje Lenora, "Der gefalschte Kalif," PhD diss., University of Halle (2011).

54. Edward Badeen, the editor of this volume of Ibn al-Dawādārī's universal chronicle, notes in his introduction that the style of writing has similarities with popular literature (*adab shaʿbī*), but that he was unable to identify the source (Ibn al-Dawādārī, *Kanz al-Durar*, 2:21).

55. Ibn al-Dawādārī, *Kanz al-Durar*, 2:395–413.

56. See summary of the narrative of the Sīra in Cherkaoui, "Historical Elements." Cherkaoui states that historians know of Shaybūb's existence but do not involve him in the race. The figure of Shaybūb is indeed central to the ʿAntar epic, as he is the man-of-wiles companion to the main hero. As shown by Lyons, the man-of-wiles character is an essential component of each of the Arab folk epics (Lyons, *Man of Wiles*; see Doufikar-Aerts, "Sīrat al-Iskandar").

57. Ibn al-Dawādārī, *Kanz al-Durar*, 2:401–2.

58. BN MS arabe 3798, Fol. 29b.

59. See the following comparisons: Ibn al-Dawādārī, *Kanz al-Durar*, 2:403 = BN MS arabe 3798, fols. 32b—33a (Qays and Ḥudhayfa); *Kanz al-Durar*, 2:404 = MS arabe 3798, fols. 33b (Shaybūb's poem); *Kanz al-Durar*, 2:408 = MS arabe 3798, 42a (a poem by a shaykh of Ḥudhayfa's clan to prevent bloodshed); *Kanz al-Durar*, 2:410 = MS arabe 3798, 62b (Ḥudhayfa's wife desires revenge). *Kanz al-Durar*, 2:410–11 = MS arabe 3798, fol. 63b (long poem by Ḥudhayfa's wife, demanding revenge). None of these poems appear in earlier accounts of the Dāḥis battle day. See the account of Dāḥis in the thirteenth-century chronicle of Ibn al-Athīr, the most prominent author on the subject of the Battle Days of Arabs in the preceding generation (Ibn al-Athīr, *al-Kāmil*, 1:509–22). In Ibn al-Athīr's version, following Ibn Qutayba, Qays acquires both Dāḥis and al-Ghabrā.

60. Büssow-Schmitz, *Beduinen*, 74–77.

61. Ibn al-Dawādārī, *Kanz al-Durar*, 9:204–5.

62. Al-Qalqashandī, *Nihāyat al-Arab*, no. 579; al-Qalqashandī, *Nihāyat al-Arab fī Maʿrifat Ansāb al-ʿArab*, BN MS Arabe 2049, fol. 63b.

63. Al-Qalqashandī, *Ṣubḥ*, 1:345. Here there is no explicit mention of the popular epics (*siyar*) as a source for the biography of Ḥudhayfa.

64. Al-Qalqashandī, *Qalāʾid*, 114.

65. Al-Qalqashandī's claims for status have proved enduringly powerful. As late as the 1970s, Garcin cited this autobiographical note to dispute any suspicion that al-Qalqashandī had Coptic origins (Garcin, *Qūṣ*, 362).

66. Al-Qalqashandī may have encountered the epic in his native village, either through public readings or through written copies. In the early nineteenth century the ʿAntar epic was given to village children to copy out and thus acquire the habit of speaking elegantly (Heath, *Thirsty Sword*, 7).

67. Al-Qalqashandī, *Qalāʾid*, 116.

68. Ibn Humām, *Fath al-Qadīr*, 4:32.

69. Al-Qalqashandī, *Nihāyat al-Arab*, 408–10.

70. The catalogue of the library of the Ashrafiyya Madrasa, dated to around 1270, has entries for the story (*qiṣṣa*) of Dalīla the Crafty, which later became of part of the Arabian Nights, and for the *sīra* of Alexander, which may be the Syriac version and not the mature epic. These are the only two titles that appear related to the epic genre (Hirschler, *Plurality and Diversity in an Arabic Library*).

71. On Sīrat Baybars, see Herzog, "The First Layer of the Sirat Baybars," where he argues for a late-thirteenth-century origin, and Herzog, "'What They Saw with Their Own Eyes . . . ,'" 32. The earliest mention of Sīrat Baybars is in Ibn Iyās, *Badāʾiʿ*, 1:341. For the dating of Sīrat Sayf to the late Mamluk period, see Andrea Crudu, "The Sudanese Elements in the Sīrat Sayf b. Ḏī Yazan"; Giovanni Canova, "Sayf b. Dhī Yazan: History and Saga." Finally, we hear nothing of the circulation of the Alexander epic in Mamluk lands, despite two earlier references to a *sīra* or a *dīwān* of Alexander. Doufikar-Aerts, "Sīrat al-Iskandar," 516.

72. In Egypt, the ʿAbs are mentioned as a clan of the Lakhm in Middle Egypt (Al-Maqrīzī, *Book of Clear Arabic Expression*, sec. 118; al-ʿUmarī, *Qabāʾil al-ʿArab*, 168).

73. The fifteenth-century manuscripts of Sīrat ʿAntar studied here are:

I. BN MS arabe 3798, 99 folios, containing the fifteenth section (*juzʾ*) of Sīrat ʿAntar b. Shaddād. Copied by Nāṣir al-Dīn Muḥammad b. Sūdūn al-Murādī in Ramaḍān 848/December 1444. The content concerns the beginning of the Dāḥis and al-Ghabrāʾ war, and corresponds to Heath, *Thirsty Sword*, secs. 21 and 22.

II. BL MS Add 7387, containing the sixteenth section of Sīrat ʿAntar b. Shaddād al-ʿAbsī. The content corresponds to Heath, *Thirsty Sword*, secs. 27.4–28. In the final folio a certain Muḥammad b. Muḥammad b. ʿAbd al-Qādir testifies that he went on the pilgrimage to Mecca in 805/1402–3.

III. BN MS arabe 3790, containing the opening segments of the cycle. Purchased 24.1.1876 and dated to the fifteenth century on the basis of the handwriting.

IV. BL Add 24,949. Copied Monday, 22 Rabīʿ I 841/1 October 1437. No copyist's name. Contains the first section of *Qiṣṣat ʿAntar fī al-Tawārīkh*, including the story of Ismaʿīl, the building of the sacred house, the children of Nizār, marriage of Zuhayr and Tamāṭur, and the birth and childhood of ʿAntar.

74. A detailed comparison of the late medieval copies with modern editions is beyond the remit of this study. But on the relative stability of the ʿAntar cycles, see Heath, "Antar Hangs His Muʿallaqa," 21–22.

75. The first manuscript of Dhāt al-Himma is dated 1430 (BN MS arabe 3890 and Gotha, Landes- und Forschungsbibliotek, MS orient A 2545, 2546 and 2556). See Ott, *Metamorphosen des Epos*. The colophon with the date, according to Ott, is given in BN MS arabe 3890, f. 88b.

76. This would be in line with the way Sīrat ʿAntar was performed in nineteenth-century Cairo, as reported by Lane (Lyons, *Arabian Epic*, 1:2; Reynolds, "Epic and History in the Arabic Tradition").

77. BL MS Add 7387. The earliest note is from 23 Ṣafar 805 (22 September 1402), and the latest from 8 Shaʿbān 837 (20 March 1434).

78. See also the reader note in BL Add 24,949, fol. 105b. The readers often call the story *sīra ʿajība*, "a wonderful (or curios) tale."

79. Heath, *Thirsty Sword*, 157–58.

80. Kruk, "Sīrat ʿAntar ibn Shaddād," 305.

81. BN MS arabe 3790, fol. 63a; BL Add 24,949, fol. 20b (Cf. Heath, *Thirsty Sword*, 4.4). In one version he is advised against relocating the Kaʿba by the nobles and heroes of his tribe (*sādāt qawmi-hi and abṭāl ʿashīrati-hi*). In another version, Satan plants the idea in his head, but a wise old man steeped in monotheism explains to him why he shouldn't take this step.

82. For examples of oaths taken in the name of the Kaʿba, out of many, see BN MS arabe 3798, fols. 10b, 32a, 36a, 62b; BL Add 24,949, fol. 108b (*al-rukn wa'l-ḥajar wa'l-bayt al-muṭahhar*).

83. BN MS arabe 3798, fol. 59a.

84. BL MS Add 7387, fol. 32a.

85. BL MS Add 7387, fol. 44b

86. BL MS Add 7387, fol. 6b.

87. BL MS Add 7387, fol. 69b.

88. See Pohl, "Narratives of Origin and Migration in Early Medieval Europe"; Pohl and Reimitz, eds., *Strategies of Distinction.*

89. On the compilation of the Ayyām al-Arab material in the Abbasid period, see Alan Jones, "Ayyām al-ʿArab"; Webb, *Imagining the Arabs.*

90. BL MS Add 7387, fol. 61a.

91. BN MS arabe 3790, fol. 73a.

92. BL Add 24,949, fols. 37a–37b.

93. Herzog, "Wild Ancestors," 59n45.

94. Lyons, *Arabian Epic*, 1:47–48; Blatherwick, "And the Light in His Eyes Grew Dark"; Leeuwen, "Conversion as a (Meta-)Historical Concept in the Epic Stories of the Thousand and One Nights."

95. Kruk, "Role of the Prophet in Popular Epics," 72; Kruk, "Sīrat ʿAntar ibn Shaddād," 297.

96. Heath, *Thirsty Sword*, 159.

97. Heath, *Thirsty Sword*, 158–59.

98. BN MS arabe 3790, fol. 3a. This passage has also been translated by Herzog, "Orality," 636.

99. ʿAntar's excursions beyond the Arabian Peninsula—to Rome, India, and Africa—are found in the final sections of modern editions but are not found in the extant fifteenth-century segments, although that may well be a matter of chance.

100. *The Adventures of Sayf Dhi Ben Yazan*, 8 (as explained by an Ethiopian vizier).

101. Blatherwick, *Prophets, Gods and Kings.*

102. Aboubakr Chraïbi, "Le roman de Sayf Ibn ḏî Yazan," 134.

103. Another example comes from Sīrat Dhāt al-Himma. Here the simple Bedouin Ẓālim doesn't believe that Caliph Harun al-Rashid could be descended of the Prophet, as the caliph is a "townsman" and the Prophet was of Muḍar (Lyons, *Arabian Epic*, 1:29).

104. Herzog, "Wild Ancestors," 64. Herzog, however, qualifies Renan's depiction of ʿAntar as the embodiment of individual freedom.

105. Herzog, "Wild Ancestors," 58ff.

106. BL MS Add 7387, fol. 8b (one example out of many).

107. Heath, *Thirsty Sword*, 156–57. See examples from BL Add 24,949: a raid on Banu Qaḥṭān, because ʿAntar's group didn't want to raid their own lands, for they have relations of *ḥasab wa-nasab* (fol. 35a); when they go on raid, they leave the camps (*aḥyāʾ*) of Adnān and enter the lands of their enemies, the Qaḥṭān (fol. 111a). In BL MS Add 7387, fol. 5a, 8b, the enemies are the devils of al-Yaman, and ʿAntar's friends disguise themselves as people (*qawm*) from Yaman.

108. BN MS arabe 3798, fol.68a, 74a, 88a; BN MS arabe 3790, 62a.

109. BN MS arabe 3798, fol. 95a–95b.

110. See Ana Luengo, "Conflict Resolution in the Sīrat Baybars."

111. BN MS arabe 3798, fol. 33b.

112. BN MS arabe 3798, fols. 49a–52b. Another example in fols. 38b–39a.

113. Herzog, "Wild Ancestors," 62n, quoting BN MS arabe 3790, fol. 100b: ʿAbla's father says: "He is a slave, son of his mother, he has no might and no value, no ruse (and no resort), no *ḥasab* and no *nasab* and no father among the noble Arabs (*sādāt al-ʿarab*)." On blacks and slavery in the epic genre, see Rachel Schine, "Conceiving the Black-Arab Hero."

114. BN MS Arabe 3798: *muwalladāt* and *mughaniyyāt* are a separate group to ordinary female slaves (fol. 40a); *muwalladāt* play the tambourines (fol. 61a); Qays sends a *muwallada* to spy on al-Rabīʿ and his wife (fol. 78b). There is a separate tent (*maḍrab*) for *muwalladāt* where ʿAmāra is able to dress as a woman (fol. 91a); the *muwalladāt* are dancing to entertain the other women (fol. 92a). BL Add 24,949: *muwalldāt* play music at a wedding (fol. 26a); *muwalladāt* play tambourine at a party (fol. 52b); one of the *muwalladāt* chants to celebrate the coming of spring (fol. 59b).

115. On shepherds, see BL Add 24,949, fols. 40b–41a; BL MS Add 7387, fol. 20b ("I know my worth, and I know that I started as shepherd for camels and small cattle, and have been wearing wool"), fol. 55a (herds). On slaves sent on reconnaissance mission, see BL MS Add 7387, fol. 33a.

116. BL Add 24,949, fol. 110a (described as the *sunna* of the Arabs).

117. Chraïbi, "Genre et narration," 555; Heath, *Thirsty Sword*, 161; Herzog, "Wild Ancestors," 53.

118. Lyons, *The Arabian Epic*, 1:67. See, for example, BL MS Add 7387, fol. 76b (the party reach a beautiful valley, with flowers and running water in its midst); BL Add 24,949, fol. 59b (description of the land in spring, when the land is dotted with colorful flowers, birds are singing, and the lilies are blooming).

119. BN MS Arabe 3798, fol. 59b: a bride-price includes small cattle, tents, dates, and honey.

120. BN MS Arabe 3798, fol. 39b.

121. On peasants in the genre as a whole and in Sīrat Baynars, see Lyons, *The Arabian Epic*, 1:31–32, 106.

122. Binay, *Die Figur des Beduinen in der arabischen Literatur*; Joseph Sadan, "An Admirable and Ridiculous Hero." See also Van Gelder, *Dishes*, 30, 103.

123. Al-Ibshīhī, *Mustaṭraf*, 471–73 (chapter on *nawādir al-ʿarab*). On al-Ibshīhī, see Kelly Tuttle, "al-Ibshīhī, Bahāʾ al-Dīn"; Herzog, "Composition and Worldview."

124. BN MS Arabe 3798, fols. 28b–29a.

125. BL MS Add 7387, fol. 26b.

126. BL MS Add 7387, fol. 59b; BN MS arabe 3790, fol. 60b.

127. BN MS Arabe 3798, fols. 38b–39a; BL MS Add 7387, fol. 97b; BN MS arabe 3790, fol. 50b. (*mashāyikh*).

128. BN MS Arabe 3798, fol. 51b; fol. 14b (*aʿrābī*).

129. BN MS arabe 3790, fol. 60b.

130. BN MS arabe 3790, fols. 55b, 58a, 59b. The fiscal categories of *kharāj*, *ʿidād*, and *khafāra* were established in the Islamic era, and their use in the ʿAntar epic set in pre-Islamic Arabia is, of course, anachronistic.

131. Examples of *sādat al-ʿarab* in BL MS Add 7387, fol. 95b, and passim. 24949, 7b, 32b, and passim.

132. Reynolds, *Heroic Poets*, 72–73.

133. Heath, *Thirsty Sword*, 164.

134. BL MS Add 7387, fol. 44b.

135. BL MS Add 7387, fol. 118b.

136. BL Add 24,949, fol. 97a.

137. BN MS Arabe 3798, fol. 76a.

138. BL MS Add 7387, fol. 79a.

139. This phrase comes from a personal communication by Omar Abd al-Ghaffar, October 12, 2020.

140. For one example among many, see BL MS Add 7387, fol. 59b: the word of the tribal leader Durayd was obeyed among all the tribes and ʿurbān, and he was respected among the *fursān*.

141. For a seventeenth-century Yemeni epic that was later woven into tribal genealogies, see Marieke Brandt, "Heroic History, Disruptive Genealogy," 130.

142. Nūr al-Dīn ʿAlī b. Aḥmad al-Sakhāwī, *Tuḥfat al-Aḥbāb*, 180–81. My understanding of this passage differs somewhat from the readings by Herzog, "Orality," 640; and Shoshan, "On Popular Literature in Medieval Cairo."

143. Brett, "The Way of the Nomad," 263.

144. Peacock, *Mongol Anatolia*, 151–53. One could also refer here to the Danishmend-name, an epic on the exploits of the founder of the Danishmend dynasty that ruled central Anatolia in the twelfth century. A sixteenth-century author claimed that the text was composed in 642/1244–45 in Persian. For a contextual reading of the ideological message of the Turkish epics, see Gottfried Hagen, "Heroes and Saints."

145. Rizq, *Khānqāwāt al-Ṣūfiyya fī Miṣr*, 2:637–38; reproduced on Thesaurus d'Épigraphie Islamique, http://www.epigraphie-islamique.org/epi/consultation.php, no. 42783.

146. Mauder, "Salon," in *New Readings*, 415. The attempt to read from Sīrat Baybars met with opposition, partly because it was too long, partly because it was inappropriate for a Ramadan session, and partly because it might have invited unflattering comparison with the reigning al-Ghawrī.

147. Peacock, *Mongol Anatolia*, 66. Quṭb al-Dīn al-Shīrāzī, a *qāḍī* in several cities in Anatolia as well as an astronomer and philosopher, copied *Ifḥām al-Yahūd* in 1286, and attached Samawʾal's reply to a person who accused him of insincere conversion.

148. Baker, "Judaeo-Arabic Material in the Cambridge Genizah Collections," 453; Oded Zinger, "Meanderings in the Arabic Literary Genizot." T-S Ar.13.3, which is the longest Geniza fragment of any of the epics, contains 120 leaves of Sīrat ʿAntar.

8. The Syrian Blood Feuds of Qays and Yaman

1. Robert Irwin, "Tribal Feuding and Mamluk Factions in Medieval Syria," 253. See also Baer and Hoexter, "Ḳays and Yaman in the Ottoman Period."

2. Walker, "Tribal Dimension," 86–87; Irwin, "Tribal Feuding," 255.

3. A. N. Poliak was the first Western-language historian to point out that *ʿashir* and *ʿushran* were terms used to designate the great agricultural tribes of Syria (Poliak, "Les révoltes populaires en Égypte à l'époque des Mameloukes et leurs causes économiques," 264).

4. Garcin, "Note sur les rapports entre Bédouins et fellahs," 152. Garcin accepted that Qays and Yaman were "onomastic emblems," following the anthropologist J. Berque.

5. Ibn Taymiyya, *Majmūʿ Fatāwā*, 28:422.

6. Ibn Taymiyya, *al-Jawāb al-Ṣaḥīḥ*, 3:176; Ibn Taymiyya, *al-Siyāsa al-Sharʿiyya*, 77; Ibn Taymiyya, *Majmūʿ Fatāwā*, 28:487; 28:327.

7. Ibn Taymiyya, *Majmūʿ Fatāwā*, 34:146–47.

8. P.HaramCat. 75 = P.MuellerCrimes 2.

9. Al-Maqrīzī, *Sulūk*, ed. ʿAṭāʾ, 2: 330.

10. Ibn Kathīr, *al-Bidāya wa'l-Nihāya*, 18:95.

11. Al-Ṣafadī says the villages resembled the ruins (*aṭlāl*) of al-Khūla. The amir, Jamāl al-Dīn Aqūsh al-Sharīfī, died in 700/1300–1 (*Aʿyān al-ʿAṣr*, 1:559)

12. Al-Maqrīzī, *Sulūk*, ed. ʿAṭāʾ, 4:102.

13. Ibn Qāḍī Shuhba, *Taʾrīkh*, 2:130–31; the report is cited on the authority of Ibn Kathīr.

14. Ibn Qāḍī Shuhba, *Ta'rīkh*, 2:129. The victim's name was Shihāb al-Dīn Ibn al-Basiriyya. His iqṭā' was of the *ḥalqa* auxiliary troops.

15. Ibn Qāḍī Shuhba, *Ta'rīkh*, 3: 274.

16. Al-Maqrīzī, *Sulūk*, ed. 'Aṭā', 4:102.

17. Ibn Qāḍī Shuhba, *Ta'rīkh*, 1:670, 673. He also notes that their camels were taken as booty.

18. Al-'Umarī, *Masālik al-Abṣār*, ed. Sayyid, 142–43; discussed in Amitai, "Gaza," 18.

19. Ibn Qāḍī Shuhba, *Ta'rīkh*, 1:410.

20. Ibn Qāḍī Shuhba, *Ta'rīkh*, 2:129.

21. Al-'Umarī, *Ta'rīf*, 113–14.

22. Ibn Qāḍī Shuhba, *Ta'rīkh*, 1:220, 1:354. The term *Jabaliyyūn* (literally, men of the hills) may have been used as an alternative to *'ashīr* already in the thirteenth century (Irwin, "Tribal Feuding," 255, quoting Etienne Quatremère based on the *Tashrīf al-Ayyām wa'l-'Uṣūr* of Ibn 'Abd al-Zāhir [d. 692/1292)]. I have not been able to locate this reference in the modern edition of Ibn 'Abd al-Ẓāhir's work).

23. Ibn Qāḍī Shuhba, *Ta'rīkh*, 1:412.

24. Al-Maqrīzī, *Sulūk*, ed. 'Aṭā', 4:102.

25. Ibn Qāḍī Shuhba, *Ta'rīkh*, 2:314.

26. Bauden, "The Recovery of Mamluk Chancery Documents in an Unsuspected Place."

27. Al-Shujā'ī, *Beiträge*, 258, 264. Bāligh fought alongside the Jabaliyya and another *muqaddam* by the name of Mas'ūd.

28. Al-Maqrīzī, *Sulūk*, ed. 'Aṭā', 4:102 (mentioned as Ibn Ṣubḥ). For his biography, which doesn't include a reference to his role as commander of the al-Jabaliyya, see Ibn Ḥajar al-'Asqalānī, *al-Durar al-Kāmina*, 1:243. I thank Jo Van Steenbergen for this information.

29. On the Amīr al-'Arab, see Hiyari, "The Origins and Development of the Amīrate of the Arabs"; Drory, "Role of Banū Faḍl"; Franz, "Bedouin and States"; Bakhīt, "Muhannā, Banū"; Tekindağ, "'Īsā b. Muhannā."

30. Ibn Qāḍī Shuhba, *Ta'rīkh*, 2:160 (751/1350–51); 2:220 (764/1362–63, the *a'rāb* attack Tadmur); 2:350 (770/1368–69, coalition of Āl Faḍl and Kilāb defeat the governor of Aleppo); 3:17 (781/1379–80, the amir of Āl Faḍl buried in Salamiyya); 3:676 (800/1397–98, the amir of Āl Faḍl killed near Raḥba).

31. Ibn Ṣaṣrā, *Chronicle*, 31 (782/1380–81).

32. Al-'Umarī, *Ta'rīf*, 79; al-Qalqashandī, *Ṣubḥ*, 4:210.

33. Ibn Khaldūn, *Dīwān al-Mubtada' wa'l-Khabar* [= *Kitāb al-'Ibar*], 5:498–99, 6:9. According to the information that was available to Ibn Khaldūn, the Āl Faḍl used to inhabit the agricultural areas of the Hawran but were driven out of there by the Āl Mirā. It was only then that they attached themselves to Ayyubid sultans and were awarded authority over the other Arab clans (*aḥyā'*). This edition has Āl Murād instead of Āl Mirā.

34. See, for example, Ibn Nāẓir al-Jaysh, *Tathqīf*, 73ff, 131.

35. Al-Maqrīzī, *Sulūk*, ed. 'Aṭā', 5:58–59. Al-Maqrīzī describes the attack on the Turcomans as foolish, as they had been loyal until then.

36. Ibn Ṣaṣrā, *Chronicle*, 132 (795/1392–93).

37. Ibn Ṣaṣrā, *Chronicle*, 165–66 (797/1394–95).

38. Al-Maqrīzī, *al-Ḏahab al-Masbūk*, sec. 195. This paragraph also mentions the Banū Lām of the Hawran. Al-'Umarī, who was on good personal terms with the leaders of the Āl Faḍl, says that the 'urbān of Syria are the pride of the Arabs, led by Āl Faḍl, Āl Mirā, and Āl 'Alī (Al-'Umarī, *Ta'rīf*, 79).

39. The amir of Āl Faḍl, Sulaymān b. Muhannā, employed over a thousand men of the countryside (or Beqaa, Arabic: *al-biqā'*) to guard the roads (Ibn Qāḍī Shuhba, *Ta'rīkh*, 2:220). In 743/1342–43, the amir of the Shaṭṭī Arabs in Karak blocked all roads to the city, using his 'urbān (Ibn Qāḍī Shuhba, *Ta'rīkh*, 1:313).

40. Al-ʿUmarī, *Taʿrīf*, 80. Al-Ḥamdānī lists some twenty sections, and he names localities in the Balqa with which the Banū Mahdī were associated (cited in al-Qalqashandī, *Ṣubḥ*, 4:212–13). For appointment decrees for amirs of the Banū Mahdī, detailing the responsibilities of the Banū Mahdī, see al-Qalqashandī, *Ṣubḥ*, 12:135, 12:136, 12:422, 7:130 (four named individuals, each holding a quarter of the emirate). According to al-Ẓāhirī, writing in the mid-fifteenth century but probably relying on earlier sources, at times of royal campaigns the Banū Mahdī were expected to raise one thousand riders, jointly with the Banū ʿUqba (al-Ẓāhirī, *Zubdat Kashf al-Mamālik*, 174).

41. Walker, "Tribal Dimension," 97; Ibn Qāḍī Shuhba, *Taʾrīkh*, 3:294.

42. P.HaramCat. 718.

43. Al-ʿUmarī, *Taʿrīf*, 80; al-Qalqashandī, *Ṣubḥ*, 4:207–8.

44. Al-Qalqashandī, *Ṣubḥ*, 12:132–35.

45. Ibn Qāḍī Shuhba, *Taʾrīkh*, 1:450 (746 H, *Dīwān al-Murtajaʿ min Akhbāz al-ʿArab*).

46. Al-Subkī, *Muʿīd* (Beirut, 1986), 74–75, sec. 35.

47. Fischel, "*Ascensus Baroch*," 164.

48. Fischel, "*Ascensus Baroch*," 153, 163.

49. See the discussion in Onimus, *Les Maîtres du jeu*, 326–27 (with focus on the urban gangs of *zuʿar*).

50. Irwin, "Tribal Feuding," 257

51. For a brief account of the events of the war, see Onimus, *Les Maîtres du jeu*, 23.

52. Franz, "Nuʿayr Muḥammad b. Ḥiyār." See also Schultz, "Barqūq, al-Malik al-Ẓāhir."

53. Ibn Ṣaṣrā, *Chronicle*, 25 (791/1389).

54. Ibn Ṣaṣrā, *Chronicle*, 26 (791/1389 and 792/1390).

55. Ibn Ṣaṣrā, *Chronicle*, 30.

56. These events have also been discussed by Walker, "Tribal Dimension," 101–4; Irwin, "Tribal Feuding," 262–63. See also discussion of the chronicle of Ibn Ṣaṣrā in Onimus, *Les Maîtres du jeu*, 56.

57. Ibn Ṣaṣrā, *Chronicle*, 27.

58. Ibn Ṣaṣrā, *Chronicle*, 34.

59. Ibn Ṣaṣrā, *Chronicle*, 90 (793/1390–91).

60. Fischel, "*Ascensus Barcoch*," 155–56.

61. Ibn Ṣaṣrā, *Chronicle*, 60.

62. Ibn Ṣaṣrā, *Chronicle*, 64 (Rajab 792/June 1390).

63. Ibn Ṣaṣrā, *Chronicle*, 89.

64. Ibn Ṣaṣrā, *Chronicle*, 65–66.

65. Ibn Ṣaṣrā, *Chronicle*, 64; Ibn Qāḍī Shuhba, *Taʾrīkh*, 3:265 (791/1389).

66. Ibn Ṣaṣrā, *Chronicle*, 5 (791/1389).

67. Ibn Ṣaṣrā, *Chronicle*, 63.

68. Ibn Qāḍī Shuhba, *Taʾrīkh*, 3:333 (792/1390).

69. Ibn Qāḍī Shuhba, *Taʾrīkh*, 3:300 (791/1389).

70. Ibn Qāḍī Shuhba, *Taʾrīkh*, 3:452–53 (794/1392).

71. Ibn Qāḍī Shuhba, *Taʾrīkh*, 3:303; Ibn Ṣaṣrā, *Chronicle*, 7, 28. See discussion in Irwin, "Tribal Feuding"; al-Bakhīt, "The Role of the Ḥanash Family," 258–60.

72. Ibn Ṣaṣrā, *Chronicle*, 80.

73. Ibn Ṣaṣrā, *Chronicle*, 57–58.

74. Ibn Ṣaṣrā, *Chronicle*, 81.

75. Franz, "Nuʿayr"; Onimus, *Les Maîtres du jeu*, 105.

76. Ibn Khaldūn, *Dīwān al-Mubtadaʾ waʾl-Khabar* [= *Kitāb al-ʿIbar*], 5:536; cited in Irwin, "Tribal Feuding," 265. See also Onimus, *Les Maîtres du jeu*, 146, where the emphasis is on the

need to respond to Tamerlane's anti-Mamluk propaganda, which highlighted their slave origins.

77. Julien Loiseau, "Tribal Genealogy, Ethnic Nobility"; Christian Mauder, "The Quraysh of the Unbelievers."

78. Fischel, "*Ascensus Barcoch*," 156.

79. Ibn Qāḍī Shuhba, *Ta'rīkh*, 4:81. Walker, "Tribal Dimension," 99.

80. Ibn Qāḍī Shuhba, *Ta'rīkh*, 4:107; see also Ibn Ḥijjī, *Ta'rīkh*, 443 (801/1398–99); and a slightly different version in al-Maqrīzī, *Sulūk*, ed. 'Aṭā', 6:18.

81. Walker, "Tribal Dimension," 89.

82. Al-Qalqashandī, *Ṣubḥ*, 12:137. This is likely to be an early-fifteenth-century decree as it is not attributed by al-Qalqashandī to earlier sources and is not found in al-'Umarī's works.

83. Al-Qalqashandī, *Ṣubḥ*, 12:138–39.

84. Al-'Umarī, *Ta'rīf*, 80; Ibn Nāẓir al-Jaysh, *Tathqīf*, 130, 144.

85. Müller, "Crimes without Criminals?" based on P.Haram.Cat. 75, P.Haram.Cat. 30 and Haram.Cat. 373v. In another case, dated 796/1394, an injured man from the village of Taqū' came to Jerusalem accompanied by fellow villagers to accuse a group of Christian men from the village of attacking him the previous night. This man, Nuṣayr b. Naṣr Allāh b. Muḥammad, seems to have had faith in the Mamluk judicial process. See P.Haram.Cat. 642 (= P.Haram I 27 = P.MuellerCrimes 6).

86. Ibn Sasrā, *Chronicle*, 192–93 (796/1393–94). See also Ibn Qāḍī Shuhba, *Ta'rīkh*, 3:630–31 (799/1396); Walker, "Tribal Dimension," 91.

87. Subkī, *Mu'īd*, 48.

88. Ibn Ḥijjī, *Ta'rīkh*, 912 (810/1407–8); 1001 (815/1412–13).

89. Ibn Ṭūlūn, *Mufākahat al-Khilān*, 1:29 (885/180–81).

90. Ibn Sasrā, *Chronicle*, 161 (795/1392–93).

91. Ibn Ḥijjī, *Ta'rīkh*, 502 (803/1400–1); 540 (804/1401–2). See also Ibn Qāḍī Shuhba, *Ta'rīkh*, 4:190 (803/1400–1, the *a'rāb* coveted and took over the *ghilāl* grains of the villages; 4:266, 4:313).

92. Ibn Ḥijjī, *Ta'rīkh*, 635 (806/1404); Ibn Qāḍī Shuhba, *Ta'rīkh*, 4:395 (807/1404–5).

93. Ibn Qāḍī Shuhba, *Ta'rīkh*, 4:189 (803/1400–1).

94. Ibn Ḥijjī, *Ta'rīkh*, 523, 525.

95. Ibn Qāḍī Shuhba, *Ta'rīkh*, 3:469 (795/1392–93, a *kāshif* called Sūdūn al-Nawrūzī was killed in Bilād Banī Hilāl fighting the Arabs of Sa'd and Mudlij); 3:589 (798/1395–96, the governor of Damascus, accompanied by the amir of Āl Mirā, quells Arabs of Sa'īda and Farīr in Jabal Banī Hilāl, and then continues to Ṣarkhad. They flee to the steppe, and their camels and cattle are taken); Ibn Ḥijjī, *Ta'rīkh*, 545 (*kāshif* of Nablus killed, apparently by the Arabs); Ibn Ḥijjī, *Ta'rīkh*, 549 (Banū Ṣakhr Arabs kill the *kāshif* of the villages in the southern part of the province).

96. Al-Qalqashandī, *Ṣubḥ*, 7: 203–4. The edict is undated but is not found in the earlier fourteenth-century administrative collections.

97. Al-Maqrīzī, *Sulūk*, ed. Ziyāda, 4:1138–39. I owe this reference to Mustafa Banister.

98. Al-'Ulaymī, *Uns al-Jalīl*, 2:298–99. The Dārīs were fighting a Kurdish faction.

99. Al-'Ulaymī, *Uns al-Jalīl*, 2:364.

100. Fabri, *Wanderings*, 9:479.

101. Fabri, *Wanderings*, 9:64. See also Chareyron, *Pilgrims*, 124; Yehoshua Frenkel, "The Contribution of European Travel Literature," 712.

102. Fabri, *Wanderings*, 9:483. But Fabri also compares the Arabs to gypsies and says that they come out of the wilderness to commit theft, sometimes forming troops, and to raid a village or a town, or to "pitch their tents in green pastures, build themselves huts, and dwell there harming the people of the region by stealing all the cattle that comes their way" (9:482–83).

103. Ibn Ḥijjī, *Ta'rīkh*, 642 (807/1404–5); Ibn Qāḍī Shuhba, *Ta'rīkh*, 4:397.

104. Ibn Ḥijjī, *Ta'rīkh*, 881.

105. Al-Maqrīzī, *Sulūk*, ed. 'Aṭā', 6:351; Steenbergen, "Revisiting the Mamlūk Empire," 83.

106. Al-Qalqashandī, *Ṣubḥ*, 4:197; 4:203.

107. Al-Qalqashandī, *Ṣubḥ*, 4:227.

108. Al-Maqrīzī, *Sulūk*, ed. 'Aṭā', 6:247.

109. Al-'Ulaymī, *Uns al-Jalīl*, 2:332.

110. Al-Bakhīt, "The Role of the Ḥanash Family," 261–62.

111. Ibn Ḥijjī, *Ta'rīkh*, 161 (798/1395–96).

112. Ibn Ḥijjī, *Ta'rīkh*, 343 (801/1398–99).

113. Ibn Ḥijjī, *Ta'rīkh*, 663.

114. P.Haram.Cat. 847 = RichardsQasama VI and P.Haram.Cat. 679a.

115. Ibn Qāḍī Shuhba, *Ta'rīkh*, 4:173 (803/1400–1): Tīmūr's army takes hold of the village headman (*ra'īs al-balad*) so that he will present the peasants (fallāḥīn).

116. Ibn Tulun, *Quḍāt Dimashq*, 154; cited in Jacques, "Murder."

117. P.RiscianiSultani 23 a = (descr.) P.TerraSanta 51. Another edict of 1466 is addressed only to the fallāḥīn (P.RiscianiSultani 26 = (descr.) P.TerraSanta 6).

118. Brocquière, *A Mission to the Medieval Middle East*, 135 (Beqaa); 146 (Tyre to Acre); 175 (Homs to Hama). He also describes Turcoman and Arab pastoralists in Antioch (181) and around Mt. Tabor, near Nazareth (149).

119. Adorno, *Itinéraire*, 309–11.

120. Adorno, *Itinéraire*, 97. He describes small communities of one hundred to two hundred tents, as well as larger ones of four hundred to two thousand tents.

121. Al-Asadī, *al-Taysīr wa'l-I'tibār*. Al-Asadī's text has been studied by John L. Meloy, "The Privatization of Protection," focusing on al-Asadī's description of *ḥimāya*, and by Abdul Azim Islahi, "Al-Asadi and His Work al-Taysir," focusing on al-Asadī's suggestions for monetary reforms. I am grateful to Daisuke Igarashi for bringing this passage to my attention.

122. Al-Asadī, *al-Taysīr*, 91–92.

123. For the function of Qays and Yaman as broad coalitions in the Umayyad period, see Patricia Crone, "Were the Umayyad Qays and Yaman of the Umayyad Period Political Parties?"

124. Walker, "Tribal Dimension," 89ff; Drory, "The Prince Who Favored the Desert."

125. Baer and Hoexter, "Ḳays and Yaman in the Ottoman Period."

126. James, *Genèse du Kurdistan*, 189.

127. See Sowayan, "The Hilali Poetry in the Muqaddimah," 283; and chap. 7 of this book.

9. The Great Arab Rebellions, 1250–1350

1. Garcin, "Note sur les rapports," 162; Garcin, *Qūṣ*, 407ff; Poliak, "Les revoltes populaires"; 'Āshūr, *al-'Aṣr al-Mamālīkī*, 327–29. See also Rapoport, "Invisible Peasants"; Büssow-Schmitz, *Beduinen*.

2. See Firnhaber-Baker, *The Jacquerie of 1358*.

3. Al-Maqrīzī, *Itti'āẓ*, 2:316; al-Nuwayrī, *Nihāyat al-Arab*, 28:237; Brett, *Fatimid Empire*, 206.

4. Ibn Munqidh, *al-I'tibār*, 1:24. Similar in al-Maqrīzī, *Itti'āẓ*, 3:217.

5. Ibn Khaldūn was writing at the end of the fourteenth century, but his report has no mention of the thirteenth-century revolt. It is possibly based on early-thirteenth-century sources. He reports that the Banū Ja'far used to live between Aswan and Qūṣ, but they were driven from there by Banū al-Ḥasan. He adds that they are known as the Sharīfs of the Ja'āfira and make their living out of commerce. See Ibn Khaldūn, *Tārīkh Ibn Khaldūn*, 6:10.

6. Al-Maqrīzī, *Sulūk*, ed. 'Aṭā', 1:244.

7. Al-Maqrīzī, *Sulūk*, ed. 'Aṭā', 1:245, 248–49.

8. Yāqūt, *Mu'jam al-buldān*, ed. Wüstenfeld, 2:570–71.

9. Al-'Umarī, *Ta'rīf*, 243.

10. Al-'Umarī, *Masālik al-Abṣār*, 4:367–68 (on the authority of al-Ḥamdānī).

11. Al-Maqrīzī, *al-Mawā'iẓ*, 3:159 (on the authority of Ibn 'Abd al-Ẓāhir); 3:212–13 (orchard); 3:146 (bathhouses).

12. Al-Maqrīzī, *al-Mawā'iẓ*, 4:216; Ibn Abd al-Ẓāhir, *al-Rawḍa*, ed. al-Sayyid, 91–92.

13. Galila El Kadi and Alain Bonnami, *Architecture for the Dead*, 53, 59.

14. The panel is now held in the Victoria and Albert Museum. See Thesaurus d'Épigraphie Islamique (http://www.epigraphie-islamique.org), no. 3054, 1216–17 (wooden panel); no. 3055, 1216–17 (tombstone). The panel is also reproduced in Barry Wood, "Panel from a Cenotaph."

15. Al-Maqrīzī, *Book of Clear Arabic Expression*, secs. 65–79.

16. Ibn al-Muqaffa' [attributed], *History of the Patriarchs*, vol. 4, 236–37, 115 (Arabic). For this report, see also chap. 3 of this book.

17. Ibn al-Muqaffa' [attributed], *Tārīkh Misr*, 774–76.

18. Al-Maqrīzī, *al-Mawā'iẓ*, 3:212–13.

19. Al-Nuwayrī, *Nihāyat al-Arab*, 29:427–29. Baybars al-Manṣūrī has a brief note on the capture of the Sharīf Ḥiṣn al-Dīn Ibn Tha'lab with a group of Upper Egyptian 'urbān by Aqṭāy (*Zubdat al-Fikra*, 12). See also Garcin, *Qūṣ*, 375.

20. Al-Ṣafadī, *al-Wāfī bi'l-Wafayāt*, 2:180 (biography of Ibn Bashā'ir al-Qūṣī).

21. Al-Nuwayrī, *Nihāyat al-Arab*, 29:429.

22. Al-Nuwayrī, *Nihāyat al-Arab*, 30:126. See also al-'Umarī, *Masālik al-Abṣār*, 4:367–68; al-Yūnīnī, *Dhayl*, 2:323.

23. Al-Maqrīzī, *Sulūk*, ed. 'Aṭā', 1:479–81.

24. Al-Maqrīzī, *Book of Clear Arabic Expression*, secs. 73, 76.

25. Al-Maqrīzī, *Sulūk*, ed. 'Aṭā', 1:479.

26. Al-Maqrīzī, *Book of Clear Arabic Expression*, sec. 18.

27. Al-Maqrīzī, *Sulūk*, ed. 'Aṭā', 1:481. See also al-Maqrīzī, *Book of Clear Arabic Expression*, sec. 18, on decline of the Sinbis in al-Gharbiyya because of the failure of the rebellion.

28. Piloti, *L'Égypte au commencement du quinzième siècle*, 11–20. See Büssow-Schmitz, *Beduinen*, 1–2.

29. A similar comparison is made by Frescobaldi in 1384: "These are rural folk who have no abode, and who do no work, and who have among them captains who lay certain small taxes on the cities of Egypt as is the custom with companies in Italy." (Frescobaldi, *Visit to the Holy Places*, 56).

30. Steenbergen, Wing, and D'hulster, "Mamlukization," 553.

31. Shāfi' ibn 'Alī, *Biography of the Mamluk Sultan Qalāwūn*, 336ff. A variant of this memorandum, attributed to Kitbughā, is in Ibn al-Furāt, *Ta'rīkh*, 7:199. See also Fernandes, "On Conducting the Affairs of State."

32. Ibn al-Furāt, *Ta'rīkh*, 7:198. Arabic: *wa-ayy man 'adima lahu shay'un yalzimu-hu daraku-hu*.

33. Shāfi' ibn 'Alī, *Biography of the Mamluk Sultan Qalāwūn*, 340.

34. Livingston, "Paperwork." See also chap. 3 of this book.

35. Shāfi' ibn 'Alī, *Biography of the Mamluk Sultan Qalāwūn*, 341–42. The inner desert road was known as al-Badriyya. It was a smuggler route, traversed by merchants who wished to avoid paying duty in the custom station of Qaṭyā. See Silverstein, *Postal Systems*, 174ff.

36. Ibn Dawādārī, *Kanz*, 9:114–18. On grants of iqṭā' to Arab amirs during the first Mamluk century (1250–1350), see also al-'Umarī, *Qabā'il al-'Arab*, 76–77; al-'Umarī, *Ta'rīf*, 175. On the contributions of the Arab tribes of Sinai to the stations of postal service between Egypt and Syria, see Silverstein, *Postal Systems*, 174.

37. Al-ʿUmarī, *Taʿrīf*, 76.

38. See al-Nuwayrī, *Nihāyat al-Arab*, 30:107, cited in al-Maqrīzī, *Sulūk*, ed. ʿAṭā', 2:13; Ibn al-Dawādārī, *Kanz al-Durar*, 8:173 (for 672/1273–74). On these taxes in heads of cattle, see Büssow-Schmitz, *Beduinen*, 27.

39. Al-ʿUmarī records information on the agricultural potential of the region of Barqa west of Egypt. This information was passed on to him by the Arab iqṭāʿ holder of the region, the amir Fā'id (or Qā'id) b. Miqdam al-Sulamī (al-ʿUmarī, *Masālik al-Abṣār*, 3:502–3).

40. For an example of a raid into Nubia using Arab auxiliary forces, see al-Nuwayrī, *Nihāyat al-Arab*, 31:39, and Ibn al-Furāt, *Ta'rīkh*, 8:52. The troops sent to Nubia in 686/1287–88 included the ʿurbān of the region, Awlād Banī Bakr, Awlād ʿUmar, Awlād Sharīf, Awlād Shaybān, Awlād al-Kanz, Banū Hilāl, and a band (*jamāʿa*) of the ʿurbān of al-Burullusiyya.

41. Al-Maqrīzī, *Sulūk*, ed. ʿAṭā', 2:366.

42. Ibn Taghrī Birdī adds, perhaps for clarification, that under Aydamur even the road protectors, *arbāb al-adrāk*, went unarmed (Ibn Taghrī Birdī, *al-Nujūm al-Zāhira*, 8:205).

43. Al-Maqrīzī, *Sulūk*, ed. ʿAṭā', 2:426.

44. Ibn Ḥajar, *al-Durar al-Kāmina*, 2:327.

45. Al-Qalqashandī, *Ṣubḥ*, 11:430, 11:433.

46. Ibn al-Dawādārī, *Kanz*, 9:63.

47. Al-Nuwayrī, *Nihāyat al-Arab*, 32:16. The booty also included one hundred thousand small cattle and swords and lances. Baybars al-Manṣūrī describes the uprising as a mere instance of highway robbery (*Zubdat al-Fikra*, 363–64). See also Garcin, *Qūṣ*, 402.

48. Al-Maqrīzī, *Sulūk*, ed. ʿAṭā', 2:340; 2:346–47; Al-Maqrīzī, *Sulūk*, ed. Ziyāda, 1:914.

49. Ibn al-Ḥajj, *al-Madkhal*, 4:237–38.

50. See narrative of the events in Jean-Claude Garcin, "Al-Aḥdab, Muḥammad b. Wāṣil"; Garcin, *Qūṣ*, 381–85; Büssow-Schmitz, "Rules of Communication."

51. Al-Maqrīzī, *Sulūk*, ed. Ziyāda, 2:843. The late 1340s saw other ʿurbān disturbances in Upper Egypt, only briefly reported by al-Maqrīzī. See *Sulūk*, ed. Ziyāda, 2:731 (highway robbery by ʿurbān in Upper Egypt and the Fayyum); 2:752 (royal expedition fails to capture the culprits, who had fled to the desert, and instead loots and kills the agriculturalists [*aṣḥāb al-zurūʿ*] left behind). See also Büssow-Schmitz, "Rules of Communication," 75–80.

52. Conrad, "Die Pest und ihr soziales Umfeld im Nahen Osten des frühen Mittelalters"; Borsch, *Black Death*, 53; Raymond Ruhaak, "An Analysis of What Fostered Resilience of the Irish Sea Gaels."

53. Büssow-Schmitz, *Beduinen*, 14–17.

54. The years 1347–53 show an unprecedented wave of harassing by local Arabs, pressing the monks for petty provisions. See P.AtiyaHandlistSinai 35 (= P.St.Catherine I 12); P.AtiyaHandlistSinai 37 (= P.St.Catherine I 13 A; reedited and translated in P.SternMamlukPetitions 2 verso); P.AtiyaHandlistSinai 36 (= P.St.Catherine I 14); P.AtiyaHandlistSinai 30 (= P.St.Catherine I 15, reedited and translated in P.SternMamlukPetitions).

55. Ibn Khaldūn, *Tārīkh Ibn Khaldūn*, 5:968; Ibn Duqmāq, *al-Nafḥa al-Miskiyya*, 173; Ibn Iyās, *Badā'iʿ* 1/1, 550–51.

56. The long narrative account is found in al-Maqrīzī, *Sulūk*, ed. Ziyāda, 2:911–15; idem, *Sulūk*, ed. ʿAṭā, 4:191–96.

57. Al-Maqrīzī, *Sulūk*, ed. ʿAṭā, 4:79, 4:21.

58. Al-Maqrīzī, *Sulūk*, ed. ʿAṭā, 4:191 (on the clashes); 4:195 (executions). Al-Maqrīzī compares the eruption of these clashes with the successful policies of al-Nāṣir Muḥammad, who used to plough the lands of disobedient Arabs with oxen and kill them.

59. Garcin, *Qūṣ*, 363, 372ff; Garcin, "al-Aḥdab"; Büssow-Schmitz, "Rules of Communication," 74.

60. Al-Maqrīzī, *Sulūk*, ed. ʿAṭā, 4:149 (for Shawwāl 752/November–December 1351); ed. Ziyāda, 2:855.

61. Al-Maqrīzī, *Sulūk*, ed. ʿAṭā, 4:153 (for 753/1352–53). In later decades, al-Aḥdab's son Abū Bakr (d. 1397) established a commercial *qayṣariyya* in Ṭimā, demonstrating its economic importance (Büssow-Schmitz, *Beduinen*, 49).

62. Al-Maqrīzī, *Sulūk*, ed. ʿAṭā, 4:193.

63. Al-Maqrīzī, *Sulūk*, ed. ʿAṭā, 4:191 (for 755/1354–55). See also Büssow-Schmitz, "Rules of Communication," 76ff.

64. Al-Aḥdab was not the first Arab leader to offer iqṭāʿ holders tax-collection services. A certain Miqdām ibn Shammās al-Badawī operated in a similar fashion in Upper Egypt in the first decades of the fourteenth century. He was captured by Sultan al-Nāṣir Muḥammad and then told to settle on new lands reclaimed from the desert through the Alexandria Canal. Miqdām brought these lands under cultivation and established waterwheels for permanent irrigation (Ibn Ḥajar, *al-Durar al-Kāmina*, 4:356–57). Ibn Ḥajar emphasizes his wealth and his extraordinary number of slaves and progeny, as well as his control of agricultural lands. Miqdām was identified as a *badawī*, one of the ʿurbān of Upper Egypt. Yet his specific clan affiliation is not mentioned, suggesting that he did not belong to any existing elites. This is another similarity between Miqdām and al-Aḥdab, who also emerged among the previously undistinguished ʿArak.

65. Al-Maqrīzī, *Sulūk*, ed. Ziyāda, 2/3:896, 2/3:911.

66. Al-Maqrīzī, *Sulūk*, ed. Ziyāda, 2/3:896.

67. Al-Maqrīzī, *Sulūk*, ed. ʿAṭā, 4:191.

68. Al-Maqrīzī, *Sulūk*, ed. Ziyāda, 2/3:899 and note; *Sulūk*, ed. ʿAṭā, 4:183.

69. Al-Maqrīzī, *Sulūk*, ed. ʿAṭā, 4:193.

70. Al-Maqrīzī, *Sulūk*, ed. ʿAṭā, 4:195. Ibn Duqmāq reports the same figures for the loads of arms, and somewhat lower figures for the booty of riding animals: 1,700 horses, 500 camels, 700 donkeys (*al-Nafḥa al-Miskiyya*, 173)

71. Büssow-Schmitz, *Die Beduinen*, 86–88; Ibn Duqmāq, *al-Nafḥa al-Miskiyya*, 173. Ibn Iyās reported that the Mamluks "cut off the heads of the ʿurbān and the peasants (fallāḥīn) of the villages of Upper Egypt, using their skulls to build *maṣṭaba* monuments and minarets on the bank of the Nile like those built by Hulegu in Baghdad (*fa-lā zāla yuqṭāʿ min ruʾūs al-ʿurbān waʾl-fallāḥīn alldhīna bi-ḍiyāʿ al-ṣaʿīd ḥattā banā min ruʾūsihim maṣāṭib wa-maʾādhin ʿalā shāṭiʾ baḥr al-nīl ka-mā faʿala Hūlākū bi-baghdād*)." See Ibn Iyās, *Badāʾiʿ*, 1/1:550.

72. Al-Maqrīzī, *Sulūk*, ed. ʿAṭā, 4:193–94.

73. Al-Maqrīzī, *Sulūk*, ed. ʿAṭā, 4:193.

74. Al-Maqrīzī, *Sulūk*, ed. ʿAṭā, 4:195.

75. Al-Maqrīzī, *Sulūk*, ed. ʿAṭā, 4:195.

76. Al-Maqrīzī, *Sulūk*, ed. ʿAṭā, 4:192, 195. According to the shorter account of Ibn Duqmāq, the decree specified that no fallāḥ should be riding a horse or purchase one (*al-Nafḥa al-Miskiyya*, 173). Tadmurī, the modern editor of the *Nafḥa*, read here *lā yarkibu faras wa-lā yashtarī qimāsh* ("not to ride horses or purchase textiles"), but the variant *wa-lā yashtarī farasān*, which is found in Ibn Duqmāq's *al-Jawhar al-Thamīn*, 2:204, makes more sense in this context. See Büssow-Schmitz, *Beduinen*, 65; Büssow-Schmitz, "Rules of Communication," 93.

77. Al-Maqrīzī, *Sulūk*, ed. ʿAṭā, 4:197.

78. Ibn Khaldūn, *Tārīkh Ibn Khaldūn*, 5:968.

79. Ibn Duqmāq, *al-Nafḥa al-Miskiyya*, 173.

80. Al-Maqrīzī, *Sulūk*, ed. ʿAṭā, 4:197; Büssow-Schmitz, "Rules of Communication," 89.

81. Usāma Jumayl provides a useful list of the number of horses taken from the ʿurbān in Mamluk campaigns and raids, before and after al-Aḥdab's revolt. While raids and confiscations of horses belonging to the ʿurbān continued after 755/1354, the number of horses taken each time is much smaller. After 755/1354, there are also several examples of taxes levied on the horses of the ʿurbān, demonstrating that the Mamluk authorities no longer restricted horse ownership (Jumayl, *al-Nashāṭ al-Iqtiṣādī*, 206–18).

10. Arab Ruling Families in the Egyptian Provinces, 1350–1517

1. See Elbendary, *Crowds and Sultans*, 48–51; Garcin, "The Regime of the Circassian Mamluks"; Borsch, *The Black Death*, 51–53. On the Ottoman endorsement of Arab and Berber provincial power, see Michel, *L'Égypte des villages*, 45ff.

2. Steenbergen, "Mamlūk Sultanate"; Apellániz Ruiz de Galarreta, *Pouvoir et finance*; Steenbergen, Wing, and D'hulster, "Mamlukization," 561–64.

3. On this process, see Igarashi, *Land Tenure, Fiscal Policy and Imperial Power in medieval Syro-Egypt*; Sabra, "The Rise of a New Class?"

4. Stuart Borsch argued that the Mamluk military class responded by closing ranks against the villagers. As for the rise of the Arab tribes, he argued that these were nomads who benefited from more pasturage areas is areas that were no longer fit for cultivation. Part of the problem with this argument is that in Egypt, unlike in Europe, unirrigated lands do not provide good pasture, certainly not for horses and camels. See Borsch, "Thirty Years after Lopez, Miskimin, and Udovitch"; Borsch, "Plague Depopulation and Irrigation Decay in Medieval Egypt."

5. For these estimates, see the calculations in Blaydes, "Mamluks." For a list of all the villages allocated as iqṭāʿ to Arab rural elites, see Jumayl, *al-Nashāṭ al-Iqtiṣādī*, 128–51. Jumayl notes that the survey rarely records tribal affiliation of the Arab groups to whom the iqṭāʿ was awarded. He also observes that villages named after Arab groups are rarely given out as iqṭāʿ (156). As shown by Lisa Blaydes, the villages held as iqṭāʿ by the Arabs were smaller (on average less than one thousand feddans) and of lesser value than the typical Egyptian village handed over to Cairo-based mamlūk military officers (Blaydes, "Mamluks"). See also Jumayl, *al-Nashāṭ al-Iqtiṣādī*, 156ff, 246, who argues that these lower-quality lands were handed out to Arab groups in the hope that they would put them into cultivation.

6. Al-Nuwayrī, *Nihāyat al-Arab*, 30:107; cited in al-Maqrīzī, *Sulūk*, ed. ʿAṭā, 2:13. Baybars also sent a *muqaddam* of the Hawwāra to compel the Arabs of Barqa, farther west, to pay taxes on their cattle and fields. In 672/1273–74, a force led by Muḥammad al-Hawwārī defeated the Arabs of Barqa and compelled them to pay taxes (Ibn al-Dawādārī, *Kanz al-Durar*, 8:173). Prior to the Mamluk period, groups of the Hawwāra are attested in Jabal Nafūsa (al-Maqrīzī, *Sulūk*, ed. ʿAṭā, 1:186, for 574/1178–79) and in the Fayyum (Rapoport, *Rural Economy*, for 643/1245).

7. Ibn Khaldūn, *al-ʿIbar* (Beirut, 1959), 6:10. The other groups mentioned are Muzāta, Zunāra, and a clan (*baṭn*) of Lawāta.

8. Al-Maqrīzī, *Book of Clear Arabic Expression*, sec. 117. Al-Maqrīzī's account of the settlement of the Hawwāra in Upper Egypt is found in a short insert, in al-Maqrīzī's handwriting, added to the copy of the *Bayān in* Leiden Or. 560, a collection of opuscules by al-Maqrīzī copied by a scribe at al-Maqrīzī's request in 841/1438.

9. Al-Qalqashandī reports that the Hawwāra came to dwell in Jirjā and its surroundings during the days of Barqūq, after the Zanāra wrested al-Buḥayra away from them (*Nihāyat al-arab*, no. 1635; al-Qalqashandī, *Ṣubḥ*, 1:364).

10. Garcin, *Qūṣ*, 406; al-Maqrīzī, *Sulūk*, ed. Ziyāda, 3:371–72. Al-Maqrīzī laments the inefficiencies of the system: when a new governor is appointed, all the property of the previous governor must be confiscated.

11. Ibn Ḥajar al-ʿAsqalānī, *Inbāʾ al-Ghumr*, 1:176–77, 1:213–14; al-Maqrīzī, *Sulūk*, ed. ʿAṭā, 5:53, 5:88–90. He was then accused of supporting a failed coup led by the caliph. Badr was executed in 789/1387–88, after escaping from jail in Alexandria (Ibn Ḥajar, *Inbāʾ*, 1:333; al-Maqrīzī, *Sulūk*, ed. ʿAṭā, 5:201). On his identification as a member of the Zunāra, see al-Qalqashandī, *Ṣubḥ*, 1:420.

12. On *iltizām* in sixteenth-century Egypt, see Michel, *L'Égypte des villages*, 308ff.

13. See Halm, *Ägypten nach den mamlukischen Lehensregistern*, 1:80, with reference to Ibn Duqmāq, *Kitāb al-Intiṣār*, 27, and Ibn al-Jīʿān, *al-Tuḥfa al-Sanīya*, 189.

14. Al-Maqrīzī, *Sulūk*, ed. ʿAṭā, 5:202; see also Ibn Taghrī Birdī, *al-Manhal al-Ṣāfī*, 2:460, where he is called shaykh and amir of the ʿurbān in Upper Egypt.

15. Al-Maqrīzī, *Book of Clear Arabic Expression*, sec. 117. For biographies of these leaders of the Hawwāra, see *Sulūk*, ed. ʿAṭā, 5:397, 5:403; Ibn Taghrī Birdī, *al-Nujūm al-Zāhira*, 12:156; Ibn Ḥajar, *Inbāʾ al-Ghumr*, 1:526.

16. See discussion of the rise of the Hawwāra in Garcin, *Qūṣ*, 468–77.

17. Al-Qalqashandī, *Ṣubḥ*, 4:69 (also on the territorial division between Awlād ʿUmar and Awlād Gharīb).

18. Al-Maqrīzī, *Sulūk*, ed. ʿAṭā, 5:258; Ibn Taghrī Birdī, *Nujūm*, 11:353.

19. Al-Maqrīzī, *Sulūk*, ed. ʿAṭā, 5:384, 388; Ibn Ḥajar, *Inbāʾ al-Ghumr*, 1:512–13.

20. Al-Maqrīzī, *Sulūk*, ed. ʿAṭā, 5:435.

21. Al-Maqrīzī, *Sulūk*, ed. ʿAṭā, 6:19–20; Ibn Taghrī Birdī, *Nujūm*, 12:198. Previously, the leaders of Banū al-Aḥdab and the Hawwāra came before the sultan to seek a state-approved settlement for Upper Egypt (al-Maqrīzī, *Sulūk*, ed. ʿAṭā, 5:439).

22. Al-Maqrīzī summarizes the history of the Banū Kanz in his *al-Mawāʿiẓ*, 1:366–67. He states that they regained complete control of Aswan after 790/1388–89 and that no Mamluk governors were appointed there after 806/1403–4. On the Mamluk deposition of the Kanz in 1365, see al-Maqrīzī, *Sulūk*, ed. ʿAṭā, 4:294. See also Holt, "Kanz, Banu 'l"; Büssow-Schmitz, *Die Beduinen*, 100–5.

23. Al-Maqrīzī, *Sulūk*, ed. ʿAṭā, 6:435.

24. Al-Maqrīzī, *Sulūk*, ed. ʿAṭā, 6:466, 6:470, 6:491; Ibn Ḥajar, *Inbāʾ al-Ghumr*, 3:161, 167, 191. See also discussion in Elbendary, *Crowds and Sultans*, 51–54.

25. On the decreasing supply of Black Sea slaves in this period, see Barker, *That Most Precious Merchandise*. For another example of Mamluks enslaving free people in Upper Egypt, see Ibn Ḥajar, *Inbāʾ al-Ghumr*, 3:271 (annals of 825/1422–23, following infighting among the Hawwāra).

26. Ibn al-Jīʿān, *Tuḥfa*, 149.

27. Dated inscriptions on the Friday Mosque of Qūṣ refer to the imposition of direct Mamluk rule as well as to the preparation of a cadastral survey. See Garcin, *Qūṣ*, 493.

28. Michel, "Les rizaq iḥbāsiyya," 159. The numbers refer to villages in the provinces of al-Qūṣiyya, al-Asyūṭiyya, and al-Ikhmīmiyya.

29. Al-Maqrīzī, *Sulūk*, ed. ʿAṭā, 7:460, 469. See Garcin, *Qūṣ*, 488.

30. See Ibn Ḥajar, *Inbāʾ al-Ghumr*, 3:459–60 (834/1430–31); al-Maqrīzī, *Sulūk*, ed. ʿAṭā, 7:408 (842/1438–39).

31. Al-Maqrīzī, *Sulūk*, ed. ʿAṭā, 7:282–83 (838/1434–35), 7:408, 7:413.

32. Al-Ẓāhirī, *Zoubdat kachf el-Mamâlik* (Paris, 1894), 103–6; Al-Ẓāhirī, *La zubda kachf al-Mamālik* (Beirut, 1950), 174.

33. Ibn Ḥajar, *Inbāʾ al-Ghumr*, 3:459–60. The agreement was overseen by Badr al-Dīn al-ʿAynī.

34. Al-Maqrīzī, *Sulūk*, ed. ʿAṭā, 7:408; Ibn Taghrī Birdī, *Nujūm*, 15:308.

35. Al-Maqrīzī, *Sulūk*, ed. ʿAṭā, 5:185, 5:212, 5:215. For his execution, see Ibn Qāḍī Shuhba, *Taʾrīkh*, 3:509, 511, 537; Büssow-Schmitz, *Beduinen*, 108. Onimus, *Maîtres du jeu*, 459, has Muḥammad b. ʿĪsā al-ʿĀʾidhī as governor of al-Sharqiyya for two weeks only, from 22 December 1388 to 4 January 1389.

36. On the allocation of iqṭāʿ to Arabs of al-Sharqiyya, see also Elbendary, *Crowds and Sultans*, 49–50.

37. Wakako Kumakura, personal communication, June 2022. Professor Kumakura is currently finalizing a research paper on Arab provincial administration in fifteenth-century Egypt, titled "Irrigation and Tax Collection in Mamluk Egypt: Arab Tribes, Peasants and Sultans" (in Japanese). In a list of governors of al-Sharqiyya compiled by Clément Onimus, non-Arab governors are appointed regularly until 802/1400, but not in the following decade.

Onimus does list a non-Arab governor for al-Sharqiyya appointed in 811/1409, as well as three *kāshifs* mentioned for the period 811/1409 to 814/1412 (*Maîtres du jeu*, 460).

38. P.AtiyaHandlistSinai 47 = P.St.Catherine I 23. This edict also addresses government officials (*shādd* and *mutaṣṣarifūn*) on the coast of al-Ṭūr.

39. See royal decree by Sultan Khushqadam in P.St.Catherine I 29. Stern's reading "al-Raqqa" had been corrected to "al-Sharqiyya" by Richards. See Richards, "St. Catherine's Monastery and the Bedouin," 151.

40. Other decrees from the turn of the century protect the monks from transgressions by generic Arabs, or from troops known as *rāmika* (P.AtiyaHandlist 29, 45 = P.St.Catherine I 21, 46 = P.St.Catherine I 22).

41. P.AtiyaHandlist 79 = P.St.Catherine I 37, and P.AtiyaHandlist 188 = P.RichardsBedouin 3.

42. The explicit identification of Awlād ʿAlī as part of the ʿĀʾidh occurs in P.AtiyaHandlist 189 = P.RichardsBedouin 5, dated 901/1496. But this was twenty-five years after the Awlād ʿAlī had been first mentioned in the decrees and petitions from St. Catherine. During that period, they were mentioned seven times without ever being identified as a clan of the ʿĀʾidh (P.AtiyaHandlist 79 = P.St.Catherine I 37, 874/1469; P.AtiyaHandlist 58 = P.St.Catherine I 38, 875/1471; P.AtiyaHandlist 59 = P.St.Catherine I 40, 877/1472; P.AtiyaHandlist 67 = P.St.Catherine I 46, 891/1486; P.AtiyaHandlist 304 = P.RichardsBedouin 4, 891/1486; P.AtiyaHandlist 76, P.St. Catherine I 44, 898/1492. See also the unpublished Library of Congress, Microfilm 5014, Scroll 16, firmans 316, dated 902/1497).

43. See example in P.AtiyaHandlist 79 = P.St.Catherine I 37. On *darak* and *khafāra* in the early Ottoman period, see Michel, *L'Égypte des villages*, 149, 271. Two sixteenth-century documents refer to *khufarāʾ* in connection with *arbāb al-adrāk* (P. Vind.Arab. III 35, P. Vind. Arab. III 7).

44. According to Adorno, the Bedouin took it upon themselves not to destroy the monastery and to defend it from other Arabs, in return for bread that was given to them through a high-gated window (Chareyron, *Pilgrims to Jerusalem in the Middle Ages*, 149–50). Obadia Da Bertinoro (1487–90) reported that the Bedouin did not harm the monks because they had an arrangement with them and with the sultan (Adler, *Jewish Travellers in the Middle Ages*, 225).

45. As much as 65–75 percent of Arab iqṭāʿ holdings in Egypt were concentrated in al-Sharqiyya. See Garcin, "Note sur les rapports," 156n. In the late-fourteenth-century cadastral survey, where admittedly information is often incomplete, Arab iqṭāʿ holdings are mentioned in only forty-seven villages of al-Sharqiyya.

46. A major inspection was conducted by a certain Sayf al-Dīn al-Radādī, the iqṭāʿ holder in al-Tūr, in 700/1301 (P.AtiyaHandlist 933 = P.St.Catherine II 4 and 934 = P.St.Catherine II 56–58). For the last document in which iqṭāʿ holders are mentioned, see P.AtiyaHandlist 49 = P.St.Catherine I 24.

47. Al-Qalqashandī, *Ṣubḥ*, 3:404.

48. Al-Ẓāhirī, *La Zubda* (1950), 52; al-Ẓāhirī, *Zoubdat kachf el-Mamâlik* (1894), 34.

49. Borsch, "Plague Depopulation"; Büssow-Schmitz, *Beduinen*, 43.

50. Büssow-Schmitz, *Beduinen*, 31.

51. According to Ibn Khaldūn, the ʿĀʾidh of Judhām guarded the travelers between the Egyptian capital and ʿAqaba (*ʿIbar*, 6:8). On the services provided by the ʿĀʾidh in this period, see Ibn Ḥajar, *Inbāʾ al-Ghumr*, 1:367; al-Maqrīzī, *Sulūk*, ed. ʿAṭā, 5:226; Ibn Taghrī Birdī, *Nujūm*, 11:277 (Muḥammad al-ʿĀʾidhī as responsible for the provisions of a military campaign toward Syria, delivering fourteen thousand irdabbs of barley, eight thousand loads of hay, and two hundred loads of timber); al-Maqrīzī, *Sulūk*, ed. ʿAṭā, 6:273 (in 813/1410–11, Shaʿbān ibn Muḥammad ibn ʿĪsā al-ʿĀʾidhī guided the soon-to-be Sultan al-Muʾayyad Shaykh from

Upper Egypt toward Suez, al-Ṭūr, and through the desert road to Karak). See also al-Maqrīzī, *Sulūk*, ed. ʿAṭā, 5:282, 5:353 (imprisonment of ʿĀʾidh leaders).

52. Al-Qalqashandī, *Ṣubḥ*, 3:457–58.

53. Silverstein, *Postal Systems*, 184.

54. P.AtiyaHandlist 94 (= P.St.Catherine II 13). This document was issued after the Awlād ʿAlī were accused of murdering one of the monks. See also P.St.Catherine II 12 C = P.AtiyaHandlistSinai 935; P.St.Catherine II 15 = P.AtiyaHandlistSinai 96; and P.St.Catherine I 63 = (descr.) P.AtiyaHandlistSinai 95.

55. P.AtiyaHandlist 45 = P.St.Catherine I 21 (800/1398); P.AtiyaHandlist 49 = P.St.Catherine I 24 (815/1413); P.AtiyaHandlist 50 and 114 = P.St.Catherine I 25 (850/1446); P.AtiyaHandlist 69 = P.St.Catherine I 36 (873/1468); P.AtiyaHandlist 67 = P.St.Catherine I 46 (891/1486); P.AtiyaHandlist 72 = P.St.Catherine I 52 (895/1490). The ones addressed to Banū Sulaymān are P.AtiyaHandlist 76 = P.St.Catherine I 54 (898/1492); P.AtiyaHandlist 109 = P.St.Catherine II 9 (898/1492).

56. See al-Maqrīzī, *Sulūk*, ed. ʿAṭā, 4:339 (hunting excursion in the direction of Upper Egypt, 771/1369–70); Ibn Taghrī Birdī, *Nujūm*, 14:170, and al-Sakhāwī, *Ḍawʾ*, 10:167 (follow a rebellious amir from Siryāqūs to Ṭīna, 824/1421–22); al-Maqrīzī, *Sulūk*, ed. ʿAṭā, 7:119 (guarding corpses in al-Gharbiyya, 828/1424–25); Ibn Taghrī Birdī, *Nujūm*, 15:185 (preventing rebels from reaching Qaṭyā, 837/1433–34). On the positive role of the *arbāb al-adrāk* of Juhayna on the pilgrimage route, see al-Maqrīzī, *Sulūk*, ed. ʿAṭā, 7:291 (838/1434–35). On *arbāb al-adrāk* in the direction of Nubia, see al-Qalqashandī, *Ṣubḥ*, 8:5 (referring to the 1360s).

57. Ibn Taghrī Birdī, *Nujūm*, 13:175 (812/1409–10).

58. Frescobaldi, *Visit to the Holy Places*, 65.

59. Frescobaldi, *Visit to the Holy Places*, 121.

60. Adorno, *Itinéraire*, 239–43.

61. Adorno, *Itinéraire*, 215.

62. Brocquière, *A Mission to the Medieval Middle East*, 124, 129. Brocquière explains that the interpreter in Gaza negotiates safe passage with the Arabs, who enjoy the right of conducting the pilgrims. They were not always obedient to the sultan, and one must use their camels.

63. In 1290, the Maghribi traveler al-ʿAbdarī wrote that the Sinai Arabs are wretched people (*ṣaʿālīk*), pastoralists who subsist on plundering lonely travelers (*Riḥlat al-ʿAbdarī*, 153). In 1384, Frescobaldi described them as "almost nude and without arms," living with their animals in low tents or caves, and always asking for bread or biscuits (Frescobaldi, *Visit to the Holy Places*, 56–57, 59). Fabri described an armed but starving Bedouin standing at the gate to the monastery (Chareyron, *Pilgrims*, 149). See also Adorno, *Itinéraire*, 211–13; Chareyron, *Pilgrims*, 121–22.

64. Ibn Taghrī Birdī, *Nujūm*, 12:251.

65. Al-Ẓāhirī, *Zoubdat kachf el-Mamâlik* (1894), 103–6; al-Ẓāhirī, *La Zubda* (1950), 174.

66. See Büssow-Schmitz, *Beduinen*, 135–37.

67. Al-Qalqashandī, *Ṣubḥ*, 4:71.

68. Al-Sakhāwī, *Ḍawʾ*, 6:161 (Ibn Nuṣayr al-Dīn from al-Minūfiyya, d. 866/1462); 3:78 (Jamīl ibn Aḥmad ibn Yūsuf, Shaykh al-ʿArab in villages of al-Gharbiyya, d. 865/1461); 2:34 (Aḥmad ibn ʿAlī ibn al-Sābiq, Shaykh al-ʿArab in villages of al-Gharbiyya); 2:34 (Ismaʿīl ibn Zāyid, one of the shaykhs of the ʿurbān in al-Buḥayra, executed 853/1449–50).

69. For the identification of leading regional families in the fifteenth-century delta, based on the chronicle of Ibn Iyās, see Garcin, "Note sur les rapports," 157. These include Banū Abū al-Shawārib in al-Qalyūbiyya; Banū Baghdād in al-Gharbiyya; and Banu Ṣaqr of the Hilāl in al-Buḥayra, whose capital was in al-Busāt, near Tarūja. See also Ibn Iyās, *Badāʾiʿ*, 4:121, 5:453.

70. I owe the references to Juwaylī to Adam Sabra, who kindly shared with me a draft of his forthcoming paper, "Local Power in an Imperial Context: The Rise and Fall of an Arab Shaykh in Sixteenth-Century Egypt."

71. Al-Ẓāhirī, *Zoubdat Kachf el-Mamâlik* (1894), 35–36.

72. Ibn Iyās, *Badāʾiʿ al-Zuhūr*, 3:232.

73. Ibn Iyās, *Badāʾiʿ al-Zuhūr*, 3:398.

74. Ibn Iyās, *Badāʾiʿ al-Zuhūr*, 4:214.

75. Ibn Iyās, *Badāʾiʿ al-Zuhūr*, 4:256.

76. Ibn Iyās, *Badāʾiʿ al-Zuhūr*, 4:258.

77. Ibn Iyās, *Badāʾiʿ al-Zuhūr*, 4:353.

78. Ibn Iyās, *Badāʾiʿ al-Zuhūr*, 4:359.

79. Al-Jazīrī, *al-Durar al-Farāʾid*, 2:476–78.

80. Al-Sakhāwī, *Ḍaw'*, 6:161.

81. Al-Sakhāwī, *Ḍaw'*, 2:114. (A biography of a Sufi scholar who afforded hospitality to one of shaykhs of the Arabs.)

82. Al-Sakhāwī, *Ḍaw'*, 2:34. (Aḥmad ibn ʿAlī ibn al-Sābiq. His year of death is left blank in the text. He was replaced by his half-brother Ibrāhīm ibn ʿUmar, to whom al-Sakhāwī dedicated a separate entry.)

83. Al-Qalqashandī, *Ṣubḥ*, 4:71, 7:161.

84. Al-Qalqashandī, *Ṣubḥ*, 3:457.

85. See Garcin, "Note sur les rapports," 156–57n; Blaydes, "Mamluks." Michel's study of the 1528 Ottoman register surprisingly shows that, alongside the eastern delta, the iqṭāʿ of the ʿurbān was concentrated in Upper Egypt (*L'Égypte des villages*, 149).

86. Igarashi, "Rural Administration, Tax-Farming, and the *Mutadarriks*." Here the key text is al-Ẓāhirī, *Zoubdat kachf el-Mamâlik* (1894), 130, listing localities and prices of tax-farming contracts. For biographies of individual *mutadarriks*, see al-Sakhāwī, *Ḍaw'*, 11:93–94 (tax-farming of al-Manzala); 10:29 (Ziftā); Ibn Ḥajar, *Inbāʾ al-Ghumr*, 3:96 (Jawjar). For campaigns to extract money from *mutadarriks*, see al-Maqrīzī, *Sulūk*, ed. ʿAṭā, 7:75 (825/1422–23, in al-Buḥayra and al-Gharbiyya).

87. Ibn Iyās, *Badāʾiʿ*, 3:33.

88. Ibn Iyās, *Badāʾiʿ*, 5:437.

89. On the Arab lineage of Muḥammad as a source of ethnic pride, see also the thirteenth-century account by Thietmar (Pringle, *Pilgrimage to Jerusalem*, 130); and the fifteenth-century accounts by Adorno (*Itinéraire*, 95) and by Fabri (*Wanderings*, 9:484).

90. Chareyron, *Pilgrims*, 122.

91. Chareyron, *Pilgrims*, 124.

92. Adorno, *Itinéraire*, 95 (the context is the Arabs of Ifriqya).

93. Chareyron, *Pilgrims*, 123.

94. Chareyron, *Pilgrims*, 106; Fabri, *Wanderings*, 7:449–51.

95. Piloti, *L'Égypte*, 56–61, fols. 11–20. This important text by Piloti is discussed in Büssow-Schmitz, *Beduinen*, 1–2.

96. Piloti, *L'Égypte*, 33, 11v. On the Arabs as lords (seigneurs) of the countryside and of large villages, 56, 18r.

97. Piloti, *L'Égypte*, 58–59.

98. Piloti, *L'Égypte*, 57.

99. Piloti, *L'Égypte*, 58.

100. Piloti, *L'Égypte*, 59.

101. Al-Asadī, *al-Taysīr wa'l-Iʿtibār*. As noted previously, al-Asadī's text has been studied by John L. Meloy, "The Privatization of Protection," focusing on al-Asadī's description of *ḥimāya*,

and by Abdul Azim Islahi, "Al-Asadi and His Work al-Taysir," focusing on al-Asadī's suggestions for monetary reforms.

102. Al-Asadī, *Taysīr*, 93. The term *rafʿ* here means bringing crops to the threshing floor, and more generally delivering agricultural taxes.

103. Arabic: *ʿalā man ḥaṣala fī ḥālihi ḍuʿf wa-ikhtilāl, wa-kathura iḥtimāl al-ḍayim wa'l-ṣabr wa'l-iḥtimāl, wa-tamādā ʿalā hadhā al-ḥāl, ilā an raḥala man raḥala min ḍuʿf al-quwwa wa-tasalluṭ al-adhā wa-dukhūl al-khalal.* Al-Asadī, *Taysīr*, 93.

104. Al-Asadī, *Taysīr*, 93–94.

105. Arabic: *fa-lam yasaʿ ahl al-tadbīr fī al-dawla illā an aqāmū umarāʾ wa-mutadarrikīn fī kull makān wa-mālū maʿa ahl al-ṭāʿa min al-ʿurbān wa-jaʿalū la-hum ʿalā qiyāmihim bi'l-ṭāʿa wājib al-idrāk wa'l-khafr al-arzāq wa'l-iqṭāʿāt fī al-dīwān.* Al-Asadī, *Taysīr*, 94.

106. Ibn Taghrī Birdī adds that "when al-Malik al-Mu'ayyad [Shaykh] prevented the employment of Christians in tax collection, all of this ceased" (*Nujūm*, 14:83). This change in policy was part of the transformation of the fiscal system of the sultanate under al-Mu'ayyad Shaykh's reign.

107. Al-Maqrīzī, *Sulūk*, ed. ʿAṭā, 6:432 (820/1417–18); Ibn Ḥajar, *Inbāʾ al-Ghumr*, 3:239 (824/1421–22).

108. P.CahenFaitDivers.

109. P.Vind.Arab. III, no. 1.

110. P.Vind.Arab. III, no. 2, sent from Yashbak al-Muḥammadī *al-dawādār*. P.Vind.Arab. III, no. 3, sent from the same senior amir to the headmen and peasants in a village called al-Jummayza, informs them that he now holds the iqṭāʿ of the village.

111. For a recent assessment of the Turkish identity of the Mamluk elite, see Kristof d'Hulster, *Browsing through the Sultan's Bookshelves*.

112. Garcin, "Note sur les rapports," 147–63.

113. Garcin, "Note sur les rapports," 162, citing Ibn Iyās, *Badāʾiʿ*, 5:82.

114. Winter, *Egyptian Society*, 80.

115. On this, see Michel, *L'Égypte des villages*, 45ff; Sabra, "Sufism and Practice of Politics."

116. Sabra, "Sufism and Practice of Politics," 476, based on Akgündüz, ed., *Osmanlı Kanunnâmeleri ve Hukuk Tahlilleri*, 6:113–15.

117. On the Banū Baqar in al-Sharqiyya, see Sabra, "Sufism and Practice of Politics," 475–76; Garcin, "Note sur les rapports," 159. They were based in Minyat Ghamr and are first mentioned in 1472. They fought the ʿĀ'idh in 1506.

Conclusion

1. Michel, *L'Égypte des villages*, 72.

2. Hütteroth and Abdulfattah, *Historical Geography*, esp. 27–28. I thank Razeenah Ramtally and Saarah Ahmed for their research project on the quantitative data of the 1005/1596–97 Ottoman cadastral survey, conducted as part of their MA in History, Queen Mary University London, November–December 2022.

3. Singer, *Palestinian Peasants*, 32, 114.

4. Singer, *Palestinian Peasants*, 35, 76–77.

5. Singer, *Palestinian Peasants*, 113.

6. Michel, *L'Égypte des villages*, 202.

7. Sabra, "Sufism and Practice of Politics."

8. Yazbak, "The Politics of Trade and Power"; Philipp, *Acre*.

9. Abul-Magd, *Imagined Empires*, 17–19.

10. Stewart, "Tribalism."

11. Taylor, *Land and Legal Texts in the Early Modern Ottoman Empire.*

12. Al-Shirbīnī, *Hazz al-Quḥūf.*

13. Cezzâr Paşa, *The Nizâmnâme-i Misir*, 26.

14. Alleaume, "Water Management, Land Use, and Population in the Low Lands of Northern Delta 16th–19th C."

15. Barakat, *Bedouin Bureaucrats.*

16. Amara, "Beyond Stereotypes," 73.

17. See, for example, the influential article by Cole, "Where Have the Bedouin Gone?"

18. The story of the dispossession of the Negev Bedouin is told in Kedar, Amara, and Yiftachel, *Emptied Lands: A Legal Geography of Bedouin Rights in the Negev.*

BIBLIOGRAPHY

A. Documents and manuscripts

Editions of Arabic Documents

The following abbreviations are used in the Arabic Papyrology Database (https://www.apd.gwi.uni-muenchen.de/apd/project.jsp), where the editions are available online.

P.Abdarraziq MariagedesEsclaves	ʿAbd ar-Rāziq, Aḥmad. "Un document concernant le marriage des esclaves au temps des Mamlūks." *Journal of the Economic and Social History of the Orient* 13 (1970): 309–14.
P.AtiyaHandList	Atiya, Aziz Suryal. *The Arabic Manuscripts of Mount Sinai: A Handlist of Arabic Manuscripts and Scrolls Microfilmed at the Library of the Monastery of St. Catherine, Mount Sinai.* Publications of the American Foundation for the Study of Man, volume 1. Baltimore, MD: Johns Hopkins Press, 1955.
P.Berl.Arab	Abel, Ludwig. *Ägyptische urkunden aus den königlichen museen zu Berlin: Arabische urkunden.* Berlin: Weidmannsche Buchhandlung, 1896–1900.
P.CahenFaitDivers	Cahen, Claude. "Un fait divers au temps des Mamluks." *Arabica: Journal of Arabic and Islamic Studies* 25, no. 2 (1978): 198–202.
P.Cair.Arab	Grohmann, Adolf. *Arabic Papyri in the Egyptian Library.* 5 vols. Cairo: Egyptian Library Press, 1934–62.
P.Chrest.Khoury I	Grohmann, Adolf, and Raif Georges Khoury. *Chrestomathie de papyrologie arabe: Documents relatifs à la vie privée, sociale et administrative dans les premiers siècles islamiques.* Handbook of Oriental Studies, Section 1: Near and Middle East, supplementary volume 2.2. Leiden: Brill.
P.Chrest.Khoury II	Grohmann, Adolf, and Raif Georges Khoury. *Papyrologische studien: Zum privaten und gesellschaftlichen leben in den ersten islamischen jahrhunderten.* Codices Arabici Antiqui, Bd. 5. Wiesbaden: Harrassowitz, 1995.

P.Fay.Villages Gaubert, Christian, and Jean-Michel Mouton. *Hommes et villages du Fayyoum dans la documentation papyrologique arabe (Xe–XIe siècles): Avec une introduction archéologique de Włodzmierz Godlewski.* Hautes études orientales. Moyen et Proche-Orient, volume 52. Genève: Droz, 2014.

P.Fay.Monast Abbott, Nabia. *The Monasteries of the Fayyūm.* Chicago: University of Chicago Press, 1937.

P.GenizahCambridge Khan, Geoffrey. *Arabic Legal and Administrative Documents in the Cambridge Genizah Collections.* Cambridge Library Genizah Series, volume 10. Cambridge, UK: Cambridge University Press, 1993.

P.HaramCat Little, Donald P. *A Catalogue of the Islamic Documents from Al-Ḥaram Aš-Šarif in Jerusalem.* Beirut: Universitäts- und Landesbibliothek Sachsen-Anhalt; Orient-Inst. der Deutschen Morgenländischen Gesellschaft. Wiesbaden: Steiner in Komm, 1984.

P.Haram II A-ʿAsalī, Kāmil Jamīl. *Wathāʾiq Maqdisiyya Tārīkhiyya: Maʿa Muqaddima ḥawla Baʿḍ al-Maṣādir al-Awwaliyya li-Tārīkh al-Quds.* 3 vols. Vol. 2. Amman: al-Jāmiʿa al-Urdunniyya, 1983.

P.MahirUqud Māhir, Suʿād. "ʿUqūd al-Zawāj ʿalā l-Mansūjāt al-Āthāriyya." In *Al-Kitāb al-Dhahabī li'l-Iḥtifāl al-Khamsīnī bil-Dirāsāt al-Āthāriyya bi-Jāmiʿat al-Qāhira,* 39–54. Cairo: Al-Jihāz al-Markazī li'l-Kutub al-Jāmiʿiyya wa'l-Madrasiyya wa'l-Wasāʾil al-Taʿlīmiyya, wa-Jāmiʿat al-Qāhira, 1978.

P.MariageSeparation Mouton, Jean-Michel, Dominique Sourdel, and Janine Sourdel-Thomine. *Mariage et séparation à Damas au Moyen Âge: Un corpus de 62 documents juridiques inédits entre 337/948 et 698/1299,* Documents relatifs à l'histoire des Croisades, 21. Paris: Geuthner, 2013.

P.MuellerCrime Müller, Christian. "Crimes without Criminals? Legal Documents on Fourteenth-Century Injury and Homicide from the Haram Collection in Jerusalem." In *Legal Documents as Sources for the History of Muslim Societies: Studies in Honour of Rudolph Peters,* edited by Maaike van Berkel, Léon Buskens, and Petra Sijpesteijn, 129–79. Leiden: Brill, 2017.

P.MuhlisAqda Mukhliṣ, ʿAbd Allāh. "ʿAqdā Nikāḥ Kutibā fī Awāsiṭ al-Qarn al-Thāmin." *Majallat al-Majmaʿ al-ʿIlmī al-ʿArabī (Dimashq)* 21, no. 9–10 (1946): 419–26.

P.RagibQalamun Rāġib, Yūsuf. "Les archives d'un gardien du monastère de Qalamun." *Annales Islamologiques* 29 (1995): 25–57.

P.RichardsBedouin Richards, Donald S. "St. Catherine's Monastery and the Bedouin: Archival Documents of the Fifteenth and Sixteenth Centuries." In *Le Sinaï de la conquête arabe à nos jours*, edited by Jean-Michel Mouton, 149–81. *Cahier des Annales islamologiques* 21. Cairo: Institut Français d'Archéologie Orientale, 2001.

P.RichardsFatimidPetition Richards, Donald S. "A Fāṭimid Petition and 'Small Decree' from Sinai," *Israel Oriental Studies (IOS)* 3, no. 1 (1973): 140–58.

P.RichardsQasama Richards, Donald S. "The Qasāma in Mamluk Society: Some Documents from the Ḥaram Collection in Jerusalem." *Annales Islamologiques (AnnIs)* 25 (1991): 245–84.

P.RiscianiSultani Risciani, Norberto, and Eutimio Castellani. *Documenti e firmani dei sultani che occuparono il trono d'rgitto, dal 1363–1496*. Jerusalem, 1931.

P.St.Catherine Ernst, Hans, *Die mamlukischen sultansurkunden des sinai-klosters*. Wiesbaden: Harrassowitz, 1960.

P.SternMamluk Petitions Stern, Samuel Miklos. "Petitions from the Mamlūk Period (Notes on the Mamlūk Documents From Sinai)." *Bulletin of the School of Oriental and African Studies (BSOAS)* 29, no. 2 (1966): 233–76.

P.TerraSanta Castellani, Eutimio. *Catalogo dei firmani ed altri documenti legali emanati in lingua araba e turca concernenti i Santuari, le proprietà, i dritti della Custodia di Terra Santa conservati nell'Archivio della stessa Custodia di Gerusalemme*. Jerusalem, 1922.

P.Transmission Rāġib, Yūsuf. *Transmission de biens, mariage et répudiation à Uqlūl, village du Fayyoum au Ve/XIe siècle. Cahiers des Annales Islamologiques* 33. Cairo: Institut Français d'Archéologie Orientale, 2016.

P.Vente Rāġib, Yūsuf. *Actes de vente d'esclaves et d'animaux d'Égypte médiévale/1. Cahier des Annales islamologiques* 23. Cairo: Institut Français d'Archéologie Orientale, 2001.

P.Vind.Arab. I Diem, Werner. *Arabische Geschäftsbriefe des 10. bis 14. Jahrhunderts aus der Österreichischen Nationalbibliothek in Wien*. Documenta Arabica antiqua (DAA), volume 1. Wiesbaden: Harrassowitz, 1995.

P.Vind.Arab. III Diem, Werner. *Arabische amtliche Briefe des 10. bis 16. Jahrhunderts aus der Österreichischen Nationalbibliothek in Wien*. Documenta Arabica antiqua (DAA), volume 3. Wiesbaden: Harrassowitz, 1996.

P.WansbroughCommercial Privileges Wansbrough, John. "Venice and Florence in the Mamluk Commercial Privileges." *Bulletin of the School of Oriental and African Studies (BSOAS)* 28, no. 3 (1965): 483–523.

Cairo Geniza Judeo-Arabic documents

BODLEIAN LIBRARY

Bodl. MS Heb. d. 66/8

CAMBRIDGE UNIVERSITY LIBRARY

CUL Or.1080 J71

CAMBRIDGE UNIVERSITY LIBRARY, TAYLOR-SCHECHTER COLLECTION

T-S 10J12.3
T-S 13J26.13
T-S Ar.13.3
T-S Ar.18(1).183

NEW YORK, JEWISH THEOLOGICAL SEMINARY

ENA NS 19.29
ENA 4020.42

Sīrat ʿAntar Manuscripts

British Library MS Add 7387, containing the sixteenth section of Sīrat ʿAntar b. Shaddād al-ʿAbsī. In the final folio Muḥammad b. Muḥammad b. ʿAbd al-Qādir testifies that he went on the pilgrimage to Mecca in 805/1402–3.

British Library MS Add 24,949. Copied Monday, 22nd Rabīʿ al-Awwal 841/1 October 1437.

Bibliothèque nationale de France (BnF), BN MS arabe 3790, containing the opening segments of Sīrat ʿAntar b. Shaddād. Dated to the fifteenth century.

Bibliothèque nationale de France (BnF), BN MS Arabe 3798, containing the fifteenth section (*juzʾ*) of Sīrat ʿAntar b. Shaddād. Copied by Nāṣir al-Dīn Muḥammad b. Sūdūn al-Murādī in Ramaḍān 848/December 1444.

Illustrated Manuscripts of al-Ḥarīrī's Maqāmāt

British Library MS BL Add. 22114
Bibliothèque nationale de France (BnF), MS BN 5847
Österreichische Nationalbibliothek Vienna, MS Vienna A.F.9
Bodleian Library (Oxford), MS Marsh 458

B. Medieval Narrative and Literary Sources

ʿAbd al-Wahhāb al-Baghdādī, Abū Muḥammad. *Kitāb al-Maʿūna ʿalā ʿĀlim Ahl al-Madīna Mālik b. Anas.* Edited by Ḥamīsh ʿAbd al-Ḥaqq. 3 vols. Mecca: al-Maktaba al-Tījāriyya, n.d..

Abū al-Fidāʾ, Ismāʿīl ibn ʿAlī (1273–1331). *Al-Mukhtaṣar fī Akhbār al-Bashar.* 4 vols. Cairo: Maṭbaʿat al-Ḥusayniyya al-Miṣriyya, 1907.

Abū al-Makārim [aka Abū Ṣāliḥ al-Armanī]. *The Churches and Monasteries of Egypt and Some Neighbouring Countries.* Translated by B.T.A. Evetts and A. J. Butler. Oxford: Clarendon Press, 1969.

Abū Ḥayyān al-Andalusī, Muḥammad ibn Yūsuf al-Gharnāṭī (1256–1344). *Irtishāf al-Ḍarb min Lisān al-ʿArab.* Edited by Rajab ʿUthmān Muḥammad. 3 vols. Cairo: Maṭbaʿat al-Khānjī, 1418/1998.

Abū Shāma, Shihāb al-Dīn, *Tarājim Rijāl al-Qarnayn al-Sādis wa'l-Sābi' al-Ma'rūf bi'l-Dhayl 'alā al-Rawḍatayn*. Edited by Muḥammad al-Kawtharī. Cairo: Maktab Nashr al-Thaqāfa al-Islamiyya, 1947.

Adler, Elkan Nathan. *Jewish Travellers*. Reprint. London: Routledge Curzon, 2005.

Adorno, Anselme. *Itinéraire d'Anselme Adorno en Terre sainte, 1470–1471*. Edited by Jacques Heers and Georgette de Groer. Paris: 1978.

Al-'Abdarī. *Riḥlat al-'Abdarī al-Musammāh al-Riḥla al-Maghribiyya*. Edited by Muḥammad al-Fāsī. Rabbat: 1968.

Al-Anṭākī, Da'ud ibn 'Umar (d. 1008/1600). *Tazyīn al-Aswāq fī Akhbār al-'Ushshāq*. Beirut: Dār wa-Maktabat al-Hilāl, 1984.

Al-Anṭākī, Yaḥyā ibn Sa'īd. *Tārīkh al-Anṭākī*. Edited by 'Umar 'Abd al-Salām al-Tadmurī. Tripoli, Lebanon: Jarrūs Press, 1990.

Al-Asadī. *Al-Taysīr wa'l-I'tibār wa'l-Taḥrīr wa'l-Ikhtibār fīmā Yajib min Ḥusn al-Tadbīr wa'l-Taṣarruf wa'l-Ikhtiyār*. Edited by 'Abd al-Qādir Aḥmad Ṭulaymāt. Cairo: 1968.

Albert of Aachen. *Albert of Aachen's History of the Journey to Jerusalem*. Translated by Sue Edgington. Crusade Texts in Translation 24, 25. Burlington, VT: Ashgate, 2013.

Al-Biqā'ī, Burhān al-Dīn Ibrāhīm ibn 'Umar. *'Unwān al-Zamān bi-Tarājim al-Shuyūkh wa'l-Aqrān*. Edited by Ḥasan Ḥabashī. 5 vols. Cairo: Dār al-Kutub wa'l-Wathā'iq al-Qawmiyya, Markaz Taḥqīq al-Turāth, 2001.

Al-Dhahabī, Shams al-Dīn Muḥammad ibn Aḥmad (1274–1348). *Al-'Ibar fī Khabar man Ghabar*. Edited by Abū Hājar Muḥammad al-Sa'īd ibn Basyūnī Zaghlūl. 4 vols. Beirut: Dār al-Kutub al-'Ilmiyya, 1985.

———. *Al-Muntaqā min Minhāj al-I'tidāl fī Naqḍ Kalām Ahl al-Rafḍ wa'l-I'tizāl, wa-huwa Mukhtaṣar Minhāj al-Sunna*. Edited by Muḥibb al-Dīn al-Khaṭīb. Riyadh: Dār 'Ālam al-Kutub, 1996.

———. *Ta'rīkh al-Islām wa-Wafayāt al-Mashāhīr wa'l-A'lām*. Edited by 'Abd al-Salām al-Tadmurī. 52 vols. Beirut: Dār al-Kitāb al-'Arabī, 1987–99.

———. *Ta'rīkh al-Islām wa-Wafayāt al-Mashāhīr wa'l- A'lām*. Edited by Bashshār 'Awwāḍ Ma'rūf. 17 vols. Beirut: Dār al-Gharb al-Islāmī, 1424/2003.

———. *Kitāb Tadhkirat al-Ḥuffāẓ*. Edited by Zakariyā 'Umayrāt. 5 vols. Beirut: Dār al-Kutub al-'Ilmiyya, 1998.

Al-Hamdānī, al-Ḥasan b. Aḥmad. *Ṣifat Jazīrat al-'Arab*. Edited by David Heinrich Müller. Leiden: Brill, 1884.

Al-Harawī, 'Alī ibn Abī Bakr. *A Lonely Wayfarer's Guide to Pilgrimage: 'Alī Ibn Abī Bakr al-Harawī's Kitāb al-Ishārāt Ilā Ma'rifat al-Ziyārāt*. Edited and translated by Josef W. Meri. Princeton, NJ: Darwin Press, 2004.

Al-Ḥarīrī. *Impostures*. Translated by Michael Cooperson; foreword by Abdelfattah Kilito. New York: New York University Press, 2020.

Al-Ibshīhī, Abū al-Fatḥ Muḥammad ibn Aḥmad. *Al-Mustaṭraf fī Kull Fann Mustaẓraf*. Edited by Sa'īd Muḥammad al-Laḥḥām. Beirut: 'Ālam al-Kutub, 1419/1998.

Al-Idrīsī, Muḥammad ibn Muḥammad. *Opus Geographicum*. Edited by Enrico Cerulli. 9 fasc. Napoli: Istituto Universitario Orientale, 1970.

Al-Irbilī, Sharaf al-Dīn Abū al-Barakāt Ibn al-Mustawfī. *Tārīkh Irbil: Al-Musammā Nabāhat al-Balad al-Khāmil bi-man Waradahu min al-Amāthil*. Edited by Sāmī ibn al-Sayyid Khammās Ṣaqqār. Baghdād: Dār al-Rashīd li'l-Nashr, 1980.

Al-Iṣfahānī, 'Imād al-Dīn. *Al-Bustān al-Jāmi' li-Jamī' Tawārīkh Ahl al-Zamān*. Edited by 'Umar 'Abd al-Salam Tadmurī. Beirut: al-Maktaba al-'Aṣriyya li'l-Ṭibā'a wa'l-Nashr, 1423/2002.

Al-Isnawī, 'Abd al-Raḥīm ibn al-Ḥasan (1305–1370). *Al-Kawkab al-Durrī fī-Mā Yatakharraj 'alā al-Uṣūl al-Naḥwiyya min al-Furū' al-Fiqhiyya*. Edited by Muḥammad Ḥasan 'Awwād. Amman: Dār 'Ammār li'l-Nashr wa'l-Tawzī', 1985.

Al-Jawbarī, 'Abd al-Raḥmān ibn 'Umar. *Al-Mukhtār fī Kashf al-Asrār wa-Hatk al-Astār*. Edited by Mundhir Ḥāyik. Damascus: Dār Ṣafaḥāt li'l-Nashr wa'l-Tawzī', 2014.

Al-Jawwānī, Muḥammad b. As'ad. *Al-Jawhar al-Maknūn fī Ma'rifat al-Qabā'il wa'l-Buṭūn*, or *al-Muqaddima al-Fāḍila*. Saudi Arabia: 2006.

———. *Fī al-Farq Bayna man Ismu Abīh Sallām wa-Salām*. Damascus: Al-Majma' al-'Ilmī al-'Arabī, 1962.

Al-Jazarī, Shams al-Dīn Muḥammad ibn Ibrāhīm ibn Abū Bakr. *Tārīkh Ḥawādith al-Zamān wa-Anbā'ih wa-Wafayāt al-Akābir wa'l-A'yān min Abnā'ih al-Ma'rūf bi-Tārīkh Ibn al-Jazarī: Juz' fīh (min Wafayāt Sanat 689 ḥattā Ḥawādith Sanat 699 H.)*. Edited by 'Umar 'Abd al-Salām Tadmurī. 3 vols. Sidon and Beirut: al-Maktaba al-'Aṣriyya, 1998.

Al-Jazīrī, 'Abd al-Qādir ibn Muḥammad al-Anṣārī al-Ḥanbalī (1520–68). *Durar al-Fawā'id al-Munaẓẓama fī Akhbār al-Ḥājj wa-Ṭarīq Makka al-Mu'aẓẓama*. Edited by Muḥammad Ḥasan Ismā'īl. Beirut: Dār al-Kutub al-'Ilmiyya, 2002.

Al-Kindī, Muḥammad ibn Yūsuf. *Wulāt Miṣr*. Edited by Ḥusayn Naṣṣār. Beirut: Dār Bayrūt, 1959.

Al-Kutubī, Muḥammad b. Shākir. *Fawāt al-Wafayāt*. Edited by Iḥsān 'Abbās. 5 vols. Beirut: Dār Ṣādir, 1974.

Al-Makhzūmī, Abū al-Ḥasan 'Alī b. 'Uthmān al-Makhzūmī (d. 585/1189–90). *Al-Muntaqā min Kitāb al-Minhāj fī 'ilm kharāj Misr*. Edited by Claude Cahen and Yūsuf Rāghib. Cairo: Institut français d'archéologie orientale, 1986.

Al-Malik al-Ashraf 'Umar b. Yūsuf, *Ṭurfat al-Aṣḥāb fī Ma'rifat al-Ansāb*. Edited by K. V. (Karl Vilhelm) Zetterstéen and Ṣalāḥ al-Dīn al-Munajjid. Damascus: Maṭba'at al-Taraqqī, 1949.

Al-Maqrīzī, Aḥmad b. 'Alī (d. 845/1442). *Kitāb al-Muqaffā al-Kabīr*. Edited by Muḥammad al-Ya'lāwī. 8 vols. Beirut: Dār al-Gharb al-Islāmī, 1991.

———. *Al-Mawā'iẓ wa'l-I'tibār bi-Dhikr al-Khiṭaṭ wa'l-āthār*. 4 vols. Beirut: Dār al-Kutub al-'Ilmiyya, 1418/1997.

———. *Ḍaw' al-Sārī li-Ma'rifat Khabar Tamīm al-Dārī* (On Tamim Al-Dari and His Waqf in Hebron). Critical edition, annotated translation, and introduction by Y. Frenkel. Bibliotheca Maqriziana vol. 2. Leiden: Brill, 2014.

———. *Durar al-'Uqūd al-Farīda fī Tarājim al-A'yān al-Mufīda*. Edited by Maḥmūd al-Jalīlī. 4 vols. Beirut: Dār al-Gharb al-Islāmī, 1423/2002,

———. *Itti'āẓ al-Ḥunafā' bi-Akhbār al-A'imma al-Fāṭimiyyīn al-Khulafā'*. Edited by Jamāl al-Dīn Muḥammad Shayyāl and Muḥammad Ḥilmī Muḥammad Aḥmad. 3 vols. Cairo: Lajnat Iḥyā' al-Turāth, 1967–73.

———. *Kitāb al-Sulūk li-Ma'rifat Duwal al-Mulūk*. Edited by Muḥammad 'Abd al-Qādir 'Aṭā. 8 vols. Cairo and Beirut: Dār al-Kutub al-'Ilmiyya, 1418/1997.

———. *Kitāb al-Sulūk li-Ma'rifat Duwal al-Mulūk*. Edited by Muḥammad Muṣṭafā Ziyāda. 4 vols. Cairo: Dār al-Kutub, 1934–72.

———. [aka *al-Ḍahab al-Masbūk*] *Caliphate and Kingship in a Fifteenth-Century Literary History of Muslim Leadership and Pilgrimage*. Edited and translated by Jo van Steenbergen. Bibliotheca Maqriziana, vol. 4. Leiden, Boston: Brill, 2017.

———. *The Book of Clear Arabic Expression regarding the Arab Tribes of Egypt. An Edition, Translation and Study of al-Maqrīzī's* al-Bayān wa'l-i'rāb 'ammā bi-arḍ Miṣr min al-A'rāb. Edited by Lahcen Daaïf and Yossef Rapoport. Leiden: Brill, 2024.

Al-Muqaddasī, Abū 'Abdallāh Muḥammad. *Aḥsan al-Taqāsīm fī Ma'rifat al-Aqālīm. Descripto Imperii Moslemici*. Edited by Michael Jan de Goeje. Bibliotheca Geographorum Arabicorum. 2 vols. Leiden: Brill, 1877.

Al-Musabbiḥī, 'Izz al-Mulk Muḥammad b. 'Ubayd Allāh b. Aḥmad. *Al-Juz' al-Arba'ūn min Akhbār Miṣr*. Edited by Ayman Fu'ād Sayyid, Th. Bianquis, and Ḥusayn Naṣṣār. Cairo: Institut français d'archéologie orientale, 1978.

Al-Nābulusī, ʿUthmān ibn Ibrāhīm. *Kitāb Lumaʿ al-Qawānīn al-Muḍiyya fī Dawāwīn al-Diyār al-Miṣriyya.* Édition préparée par C. Becker et mise au point par C. Cahen. *Bulletin d'études Orientales* 16 (1960): 119–34; 1–78.

———. *The Sword of Ambition: Bureaucratic Rivalry in Medieval Egypt.* Translated by Luke B. Yarbrough. New York: New York University Press, 2016.

———. *The Villages of the Fayyum: A Thirteenth-Century Register of Rural, Islamic Egypt.* Edited and translated by Yossef Rapoport and Ido Shahar. The Medieval Countryside, vol. 18. Turnhout, Belgium: Brepols, 2018.

Al-Nuwayrī, Shihāb al-Dīn Aḥmad b. ʿAbd al-Wahhāb al-Nuwayrī. *Nihāyat al-Arab fī Funūn al-Adab.* 33 vols. Cairo: Dār al-Kutub al-Miṣriyya, 1923–90.

Al-Qalqashandī, Aḥmad b. ʿAbd Allāh. *Nihāyat al-Arab fī Maʿrifat Ansāb al-ʿArab.* Edited by Ibrāhīm al-Abyārī. Baghdad: Maṭbaʿat al-Najāḥ, 1958.

———. *Qalāʾid al-Jumān fī al-Taʿrīf bi-Qabāʾil ʿArab al-Zamān.* Edited by Ibrāhīm al-Abyārī. Cairo: Dār al-Kutub al-Ḥadītha, 1962.

———. *Nihāyat al-Arab fī Maʿrifat Ansāb al-ʿArab.* BnF MS Arabe 2049.

———. *Ṣubḥ al-Aʿshā fī Ṣināʿat al-Inshāʾ.* 14 vols. Cairo, 1913–18.

Al-Qarāfī, Shihāb al-Dīn Aḥmad ibn Idrīs (d. 1285). *Al-Dhakhīra.* Edited by Muḥammad Ḥijjī, Saʿīd Aʿrāb, and Muḥammad Abū Khabza. 14 vols. Beirut: Dār al-Gharb al-Islāmī, 1994.

———. *Al-Furūq aw Anwār al-Burūq fī Anwāʾ al-Furūq.* Edited by Khalīl al-Manṣūr. 4 vols. Beirut: Dār al-Kutub al-ʿIlmiyya, 1998.

Al-Qifṭī, Jamāl al-Dīn ʿAlī b. Yūsuf (d. 646/1248). *Al-Muḥammadūn min al-Shuʿarāʾ.* Edited by Ḥasan al-Muʿammirī. 2 vols. Riyadh: Dār al-Yamāma, 1970.

Al-Rūyānī, Abū al-Maḥāsin ʿAbd al-Wāḥid b. Ismaʿīl. *Baḥr al-Madhhab.* Edited by Ṭāriq Fatḥī al-Sayyid. 14 vols. Beirut: Dār al-Kutub al-ʿIlimyya, 2009.

Al-Ṣafadī, Khalīl b. Aybak. *Kitāb al-Wāfī biʾl-Wafayāt.* Edited by Aḥmad Arnāʾūṭ and Turkī Muṣṭafā. 29 vols. Beirut: Dār Iḥyāʾ al-Turāth al-ʿArabī, 2000.

———. *Aʿyān al-ʿAṣr wa-Aʿwān Al-Naṣr.* Edited by Fāliḥ Aḥmad Bakkūr. 4 vols. Beirut: Dār al-Fikr, 1998.

Al-Sakhāwī, Nūr al-Dīn ʿAlī b. Aḥmad b. ʿUmar al-Ḥanafī. *Tuḥfat al-Aḥbāb wa-Bughyat al-Ṭullāb fī al-Khiṭaṭ waʾl-Mazārāt, waʾl-Tarājim waʾl-Biqāʿ al-Mubārakāt.* Edited by Maḥmūd Rabīʿ and Ḥasan Qāsim. Cairo: Maṭbaʿat al-ʿUlūm waʾl-Ādāb, 1937.

Al-Sakhāwī, Shams al-Dīn Muḥammad b. ʿAbd al-Raḥmān. *Al-Ḍawʾ al-Lāmiʿ li-Ahl al-Qarn al-Tāsiʿ.* 12 vols. Cairo: Maktabat al-Qudsī, 1353–55/1934–36.

Al-Shirbīnī, Yūsuf ibn Muḥammad. *Kitāb Hazz al-Quḥūf bi-Sharḥ Qaṣīd Abī Shādūf* (Brains confounded by the ode of Abū Shādūf expounded). Edited by Humphrey Davies. 3 vols. Leuven: Peeters, 2004.

Al-Shujāʿī, Shams al-Dīn. *Beiträge zur mamlukischen Historiographie nach dem Tode al-Malik an-Nāṣirs, mit einer Teiledition der Chronik Šams ad-Dīn as-Šuǧāʿīs.* Edited and translated Barbara Schäfer. Freiburg: Klaus Schwarz Verlag, 1971.

Al-Subkī, Tāj al-Dīn. *Kitāb Muʿīd an-Niʿam wa-Mubīd an-Niqam* (The restorer of favours and the restrainer of chastisements). Edited by David W. Myhrman. London: Luzac and Co., 1908.

———. *Kitāb Muʿīd an-Niʿam wa-Mubīd an-Niqam.* Beirut: Muʾassasat al-Kutub al-Thaqafiyya, 1986.

———. *Ṭabaqāt al-Shāfiʿiyya al-Kubrā.* Ed. Maḥmūd Muḥammad al-Ṭanāḥī and ʿAbd al-Fattāḥ Muḥammad al-Ḥilū. 10 vols. Cairo: Maṭbaʿat ʿĪsā al-Bābī al-Ḥalabī wa-Shurakāhi, 1964.

Al-Suyūṭī, Jalāl al-Dīn (1445–1505). *Al-Ḥāwī liʾl-Fatāwā fī al-Fiqh wa-ʿUlūm al-Tafsīr waʾl-Ḥadīth waʾl-Uṣūl waʾl-Naḥw waʾl-Iʿrāb wa-Sāʾir al-Funūn.* Edited by ʿAbd al-Laṭīf Ḥasan ʿAbd al-Raḥmān. 2 vols. Beirut: Dār al-Kutub al-ʿIlmiyya, 2000.

———. *Lubb al-Lubāb fī Taḥrīr al-Ansāb.* Beirut: Dār al-Kutub al-ʿIlmiyya, 1991.

Al-Udfūwī, Ja'far b. Tha'lab a (d. 748/1347–8). *Al-Ṭāli' al-Sa'īd al-Jāmi' Asmā' Nujabā' al-Ṣa'īd*. Edited by Sa'd Muḥammad Ḥasan and Muḥammad Ṭāhā Hājirī. Cairo: al-Dār al-Miṣriyya li'l-Ta'līf wa'l-Tarjama, 1966.

Al-'Ulaymī, Mujīr al-Dīn. *Al-Uns al-Jalīl bi-Ta'rīkh al-Quds wa'l-Khalīl*. 2 vols. Amman: Maktabat al-Muḥtasib, 1973.

Al-'Umarī, Aḥmad b. Yaḥyā Ibn Faḍl Allāh (d. 749/1349). *Al-Durar al-Farā'id min Ghurar al-Qalā'id al-Musammā Mukhtaṣar Qalā'id al-'Iqyān*. Beirut: Dār al-Kutub al-'Ilmiyya, 2017.

———. *Al-Ta'rīf bi'l-Muṣṭalaḥ al-Sharīf*. Cairo: 1894.

———. *Masālik al-Absār fī Mamālik al-Amṣār*. Edited by Muḥammad 'Abd al-Qādir Khuraysāt, 'Iṣām Muṣṭafā Hazāyima, and Yūsuf Aḥmad Banī Yāsīn. 29 vols. Abu Dhabi: al-Majma' al-Thaqāfī, 2001–4.

———. *Masālik al-Abṣār fī Mamālik al-Amṣār: L'Égypte, le Ḥiğāz et le Yémen*. Edited by Ayman Fu'ād Sayyid. Cairo: Institut français d'archéologie orientale, 1985.

———. *Masālik al-Absār fī Mamālik al-Amsār: Qabā'il al-'Arab fī al-Qarnayn al-Sābi' wa'l-thāmin al-hijriyyayn* [= *Qabā'il al-'arab*]. Edited by Dorothea Krawulsky. Beirut: Al-Markaz al-Islāmī li'l-Buḥūth, 1985.

Al-Waṭwāṭ, Muḥammad ibn Ibrāhīm (1235–1318). *Ghurar al-Khaṣā'iṣ al-Wāḍiḥa wa-'Urar al-Naqā'iṣ al-Fāḍiḥa: Al-sakhā' wa'l-Bukhl wa'l-Shajā'a wa'l-Jubn*. Edited by Ibrāhīm Shams al-Dīn. Beirut: Dār al-Kutub al-'Ilmiyya, 2008.

Al-Ya'qūbī, Aḥmad b. Ja'far. *Kitāb al-Buldān*. Edited by M. J. de Goeje. Leiden: Brill, 1892.

Al-Yūnīnī, Mūsā ibn Muḥammad. *Dhayl Mir'āt al-Zamān*. 4 vols. Cairo: Dār al-Kutub al-Islāmiyya, 1413/1992.

Al-Ẓāhirī, Ghars al-Din Khalīl ibn Shāhīn (d. 1467/1468). *Zoubdat kachf el-Mamâlik; tableau politique et administratif de l'Égypte, de la Syrie et du Ḥidjâz sous la domination des sultans mamloûks du XIIIe au XVe siècle*. Edited by Paul Ravaisse. Paris: Ernest Leroux, 1894.

———. *La zubda kachf al-Mamālik de Khalīl az-Zāhirī*. Edited by Jean Gaulmier. Beirut: Institut français de Damas, 1950.

Anon. *The Adventures of Sayf Dhi Ben Yazan: An Arab folk epic*. Translated by Lena Jayyusi. Introduction by Harry Norris. Bloomington, IN: Indiana University Press, 1999.

Baybars al-Manṣūrī (ca. 1245–1325). *Zubdat al-Fikra fī Tārīkh al-Hijra*. Edited by Donald Sidney Richards. Beirut: al-Ma'had al-Almānī li'l-Abḥāth al-Sharqiyya; Berlin: al-Kitāb al-'Arabī, 1998.

Brocquière, Bertrandon De La. *A Mission to the Medieval Middle East: The Travels of Bertrandon de la Brocquière to Jerusalem and Constantinople*. Edited by Robert Irwin. London: 2019.

Burchard, of Mount Sion. *A Description of the Holy Land*. Translated by Aubrey Stewart, with geographical notes by Lt. Col. C. R. Conder. London: 1896.

Cezzâr Paşa, Ahmed. *Ottoman Egypt in the Eighteenth Century: The Nizâmnâme-i Misir of Cezzâr Ahmed Pasha*. Edited and translated by Stanford J. Shaw. Cambridge, MA: Harvard University Press, 1962.

Fabri, Felix. *The Wanderings of Felix Fabri*. Translated by Aubrey Stewart. The Library of the Palestine Pilgrims' Text Society, vols. 7–10. London: 1897.

Frescobaldi, Leonardo di. "Pilgrimage of Lionardo di Niccolò Frescobaldi to the Holy Land." In *Visit to the Holy Places of Egypt, Sinai, Palestine and Syria in 1384*, translated by Theophilus Bellorini, Eugene Hoade, and Bellarmino Bagatti. Jerusalem: 1948.

Hilāl al-Ṣābī', Abū al-Ḥasan. *Tuḥfat al-Umarā' fī Tārīkh al-Wuzarā'* [= *Ta'rīkh*]. Edited by 'Abd al-Sattār Aḥmad Farrāj. Cairo: Dār Iḥyā' al-Kutub al-'Arabiyya, 1958.

Ibn 'Abbād, Ṣāḥib al-Ṭālqānī Abū al-Qāsim Ismā'īl. *Rasā'il al-Ṣāḥib ibn 'Abbād*. Edited by 'Abd al-Wahhāb 'Azzām and Shawqī Ḍayf. Cairo: Dār al-Fikr al-'Arabī, 1947.

Ibn ʿAbd al-Ẓāhir, Muḥyī al-Dīn. *Al-Rawḍ al-Zāhir fī Sīrat al-Malik al-Ẓāhir*. Edited by ʿAbd al-ʿAzīz b. ʿAbd Allāh Khuwayṭir. Riyadh: 1976.

———. *Al-Rawḍa al-Bahiyya al-Zāhira fī Khiṭaṭ al-Muʿizziyya al-Qāhira*. Edited by Ayman Fuʾād Sayyid. Cairo: Maktabat al-Dār al-ʿArabiyya liʾl-Kitāb, 1996.

Ibn Abī al-Wafāʾ al-Qurashī, ʿAbd al-Qādir ibn Muḥammad (1297–1373). *Al-Jawāhir al-Muḍiyya fī Ṭabaqāt al-Ḥanafiyya*. 2 vols. Hyderabad: Maṭbaʿat Majlis Dāʾirat al-Maʿārif al-Niẓāmiyya, 1332/1914.

Ibn Abī Uṣaybiʿa. *A Literary History of Medicine: The Uyūn al-Anbā Fī Ṭabaqāt al-Aṭibbāʾ*. Edited by Emilie Savage-Smith et al., 5 vols. Leiden: Brill, 2020.

Ibn al-ʿAdīm, Kamāl al-Dīn ʿUmar ibn Aḥmad (1192–1262). *Bughyat al-Ṭalab fī Taʾrīkh Ḥalab* (History of Aleppo). Edited by Suhayl Zakkār. 11 vols. Damascus: Maṭābiʿ Dār al-Baʿth, 1988–89.

———. *Bughyat al-Ṭalab fī Tārīkh Ḥalab* (History of Aleppo). Edited by Al-Mahdī ʿĪd al-Rawāḍiyya. 12 vols. London: Muʾassasat al-Furqān lil-Turāth al-Islāmī, Markaz Dirāsāt al-Makhṭūṭāt al-Islāmiyya, 2016.

Ibn al-Athīr, ʿIzz al-Dīn ʿAlī ibn Muḥammad. *Al-Lubāb fī Tahdhīb al-Ansāb*. 3 vols. Cairo: Maktabat al-Qudsī, 1938.

———. *Al-Kāmil fī all-Tārīkh*. Edited by ʿUmar ʿAbd al-Salām Tadmurī. 10 vols. Beirut: Dār al-Kitāb al-ʿArabī, 1997.

———. *The Chronicle of Ibn al-Athir for the Crusading Period from* al-Kamil fiʾl-Taʾrikh. *Part 2, The Years 541–589/1146–1193: The Age of Nur al-Din and Saladin*. Translated by D. S. Richards. Aldershot: Ashgate, 2006.

Ibn al-Dawādārī, Abū Bakr ibn ʿAbd ʿAllāh ibn Aybak. *Kanz al-Durar wa-Jāmiʿ al-Ghurar*. 9 vols. Cairo: Deutsches Archäologisches Institut, 1960–92.

Ibn al-Furāt, Muḥammad ibn ʿAbd al-Raḥīm. *Tārīkh Ibn al-Furāt* (The history of Ibn al-Furāt). Edited by Constantin Zurayq and Nejla Izzedin. Vols. 7–9. Beirut: American University of Beirut Press, 1936–42.

Ibn al-Fūṭī, Kamāl al-Dīn Abū al-Faḍl. *Majmaʿ al-Ādāb fī Mʿujam al-Alqāb*. Edited by Muḥammad al-Kāẓim. 6 vols. Tehran: Muʾassasat al-Ṭibāʿa waʾl-Nashr, Wizārat al-Thaqāfa waʾl-Irshād al-Islāmī, 1416.

Ibn al-Ḥājj, Muḥammad ibn Muḥammad. *Al-Madkhal Ilá Tanmiyat al-Aʿmāl bi-Taḥsīn al-Nīyāt*. Edited by Tawfīq Ḥamdān, 4 vols. Beirut: Dār al-Kutub al-ʿIlmīya, 1995.

Ibn al-Jīʿān. *Al-Tuḥfa al-Sanīya bi-Asmāʾ al-Bilād al-Miṣrīya*. Edited by B. Moritz. Cairo: Al-Maṭbaʿa al-Ahliyya, 1898.

Ibn al-Muqaffaʿ, Severus [attributed]. *History of the Patriarchs of the Egyptian Church: Known As the History of the Holy Church*. Translated by Yassā ʿAbd al-Masīḥ, O.H.E. Burmester, Antoine Khater, and Aziz S. Atiya. 4 vols. Cairo: Société d'Archéologie Copte, 1943.

Ibn al-Muqaffaʿ, Severus [attributed]. *Tārīkh Misṛ: Min Bidāyat al-Qarn al-Awwal al-Mīlādī ḥattā Nihāyat al-Qarn al-ʿIshrīn min khilāl Makhṭūṭāt Tārīkh al-Baṭārika li-Sāwīrus Ibn al-Muqaffaʿ*. Edited by ʿAbd al-ʿAzīz Jamāl al-Dīn. Cairo: Maktabat al-Madbūlī, 2006.

Ibn al-Qalānisī, Ḥamza ibn Asad. *Tārīkh Dimashq: 360–555 H*. Edited by Suhayl Zakkār. Damascus: Dār Ḥassān, 1983.

Ibn al-Rifʿa, Najm al-Dīn Aḥmad b. Muḥammad. *Kifāyat al-Nabīh Sharḥ al-Tanbīh*. Edited by Majdī Muḥammad Surūr Bāsallūm. 21 vols. Beirut: Dār al-Kutub al-ʿIlmiyya, 2009.

Ibn al-Shaʿʿār, Kamāl al-Dīn al-Mawṣilī. *Qalāʾid al-Jumān fī Farāʾid Shuʿarāʾ Ahl al-Zamān*. Edited by Kāmil Salmān al-Jabbūrī. 9 vols. Beirut: Dār al-Kutub al-ʿIlmiyya.

Ibn ʿArabī. *Al-Futūḥāt al-Makiyya*. 4 vols. Būlāq: Dār al-Ṭibāʿa, 1293/1876.

Ibn Daqīq al-ʿĪd, Taqī al-Dīn Abū al-Fatḥ Muḥammad. *Sharḥ al-Ilmām bi-Aḥādīth al-Aḥkām*. Edited by Muḥammad Khalūf al-ʿAbdallāh. 5 vols. Syria: Dār al-Nawādir, 1430/2009.

Ibn Duqmāq. *Al-Jawhar al-Thamīn fī Siyar al-Mulūk wa'l-Salāṭīn*. Edited by Muḥammad Kamāl al-Dīn 'Izz al-Dīn 'Alī. Beirut, 1985.

———. *Al-Nafḥa al-Miskiyya fī al-Dawla al-Turkiyya: Min Kitāb al-Jawhar al-Thamīn fī Siyar al-Khulafā' wa'l-Mulūk wa'l-Salāṭīn (min Sanat 637 ḥattā Sanat 805 H.)*. Edited by 'Umar 'Abd al-Salām Tadmurī. Beirut: 1999.

———. *Kitāb al-Intiṣār li-Wāsiṭat 'Iqd al-Amṣār*. Edited by Karl Vollers. Le Caire: Impr. nationale 1893.

Ibn Ḥajar al-'Asqalānī. *Inbā' al-Ghumr bi-Anbā' al-'Umr*. 4 vols. Edited by Ḥasan Ḥabashī. Cairo: 1969.

———. *Al-Durar al-Kāmina fī A'yān al-Mi'a al-Thāmina*. 4 vols. Edited by Sālim al-Karnūkī. Hayderabad: Maṭba'at Majlis Dā'irat al-Ma'ārif, 1929–31.

Ibn Ḥajar al-Haythamī. *Tuḥfat al-Muḥtāj fī sharḥ al-Minhāj*. 10 vols. Cairo: al-Maktaba al-Tijāriyya al-Kubrā, 1358/1983.

Ibn Ḥawqal, Abū al-Qāsim Muḥammad. *Kitāb Ṣūrat al-Arḍ*. 2 vols. Edited by J. H. Kramers. Leiden: Brill, 1938.

Ibn Ḥazm. *Jamharat Ansāb al-'Arab*. Beirut: Dār al-Kutub al-'Ilmiyya, 1983.

Ibn Ḥijjī, Shihāb al-Dīn Abū al-'Abbās Aḥmad (1350/51 to 1413/14). *Tārīkh Ibn Ḥijjī*. 2 vols. Edited by Abū Yaḥyā 'Abd Allāh al-Kundarī. Beirut: Dār Ibn Ḥazm, 2003.

Ibn al-Humām, Muḥammad ibn 'Abd al-Wāḥid (1388–1459/ 60). *Sharḥ Fatḥ al-Qadīr 'alā al-Hidāyah: Sharḥ Bidāyat al-Mubtadī*. 10 vols. Cairo: Sharikat Maktabat wa-Maṭba'at Muṣṭafā al-Bābī al-Ḥalabī wa-Awlādih, 1970.

Ibn Iyās. *Badā'i' al-Zuhūr fī Waqā'i' al-Duhūr*. 5 vols. Edited by Muḥammad Muṣṭafā. Wiesbaden: Franz Steiner Verlag, 1960–75.

Ibn Jubayr. *The Travels of Ibn Jubayr* [= *Riḥla*]. Translated by R.J.C. Broadhurst. London: Jonathan Cape, 1952.

Ibn Kathīr, Abū al-Fidā' Ismā'īl ibn 'Umar. *Al-Bidāya wa'l-Nihāya*. 14 vols. Edited by 'Alī Shīrī. 14 vols. Beirut: Dār Iḥyā' al-Turāth al-'Arabī, 1408/1988.

———. *Al-Bidāya wa'l-Nihāya*. 21 vols. Edited by 'Abdallāh b. 'Abd al-Muḥsin Turkī. Dār Hajar li'l-Ṭibā'a wa'l-Nashr wa'l-Tawzī' wa'l-I'lān: 1418/1997.

Ibn Khaldūn, 'Abd al-Raḥmān b. Muḥammad. *Tārīkh Ibn Khaldūn* [= *Kitāb al-'Ibar*]. 6 vols. Beirut: Dār al-Kitāb al-Lubnānī, 1956–60.

———. *Dīwān al-Mubtada' wa'l-Khabar fī Tārīkh al-'Arab wa'l-Barbar wa-man 'Āṣara-hum min al-Sha'n al-Akbar* [= *Kitāb al-'Ibar*]. 8 vols. Edited by Khalīl Shiḥāda and Suhayl Zakkār. Beirut: Dār al-Fikr, 1981.

———. *The Muqaddimah: An Introduction to History*. 2nd ed., 3 vols. Edited and translated by F. Rosenthal. Princeton, NJ: Princeton University Press, 1967.

———. *The Muqaddimah. (An Introduction to History.)* Translated by Franz Rosenthal. Abridged and Edited by N. J. Dawood. London: Routledge & Kegan Paul in association with Secker & Warburg, 1967.

———. *The Muqaddimah: An Introduction to History*. Princeton, NJ: Princeton University Press, 2015.

———. *Muqaddimat Ibn Khaldūn*. 4 vols. Edited by 'Alī 'Abd al-Wāḥid Wāfī. Cairo: Lajnat al-Bayān al-'Arabī, 1957–62.

Ibn Khallikān, Aḥmad ibn Muḥammad. 8 vols. *Wafayāt al-A'yān wa-Anbā' Abnā' al-Zamān*. Edited by Iḥsān 'Abbās. Beirut: Dār al-Thaqāfa, 1968–72.

———. *Ibn Challikani Vitae illustrium virorum* [= *Wafayāt*]. 2 vols. Edited by Ferdinand Wüstenfeld. Gottingae: Deuerlich, 1835.

Ibn Mammātī, As'ad ibn al-Khaṭīr. *Qawānīn al-Dawāwīn*. Edited by Aziz S. Atiya. Cairo: Royal Agricultural Society, 1943.

Ibn Munqidh, Usāma. *Usāmah's Memoirs, Entitled Kitāb al-I'tibār* [= *al-I'tibār*]. Arabic text edited by Philip K. Hitti. Princeton, NJ: Princeton University Press, 1930.

Ibn Nāẓir al-Jaysh, Taqī al-Dīn ʿAbd al-Raḥmān. *Kitāb Tathqīf al-Taʿrīf biʾl-Muṣṭalaḥ al-Šarīf par Taqī al-Dīn ʿAbd al-Raḥmān b. Muḥibb al-Dīn Muḥammad al-Taymī al-Ḥalabī appelé Ibn Nāẓir al-Ǧayš*. Edited by Rudolf Veselý. Cairo: Institut français d'archéologie orientale, 1987.

Ibn Qāḍī Shuhba. *Taʾrīkh Ibn Qāḍī Shuhba*. 4 vols. Edited by ʿAdnān Darwīsh. Damascus, 1994.

Ibn Qudāma, Muwaffaq al-Dīn. *Al-Mughnī*. 15 vols. Edited by ʿAbd Allāh ʿAbd al-Muḥsin al-Turkī and ʿAbd al-Fattāḥ al-Ḥilū. Riyadh: Dār ʿĀlam al-Kutub, 1417/1997.

Ibn Qutaybah, ʿAbd Allāh ibn Muslim. *The Excellence of the Arabs*. Translated by Sarah Bowen Savant and Peter Webb. New York: New York University Press, 2019.

Ibn Rajab, ʿAbd al-Raḥmān ibn Aḥmad. *Dhayl ʿalā Ṭabaqāt al-Ḥanābila*. 5 vols. Edited by ʿAbd al-Raḥmān ibn Sulaymān al-ʿUthaymin. Riyadh: Maktabat al-ʿUbaykān, 2005.

Ibn Rushd, Abū al-Walīd Muḥammad. *Kitāb al-Bayān waʾl-Taḥṣīl waʾl-Sharḥ waʾl-Tawjīh li-Masāʾil al-Mustakhraja*. 20 vols. Edited by Muḥammad al-Ḥijjī et al. Beirut: Dār al-Gharb al-Islāmī, 1988.

Ibn Ṣaṣrā, Muḥammad ibn Muḥammad. *A Chronicle of Damascus 1389–1397*. 2 vols. Translated, edited, and annotated by William M. Brinner. Berkeley and Los Angeles: University of California Press, 1963.

Ibn Shāsh, Abū Muḥammad ʿAbd Allāh ibn Najm Jalāl al-Dīn (d. 616/1219–20). *ʿIqd al-Jawāhir al-Thamīna fī Madhhab ʿĀlim al-Madīna*. Edited by Ḥāmid Laḥmar. 3 vols. Bayrūt: Dār al-Gharb al-Islāmī, 2003.

Ibn Taghrī Birdī, Jamāl al-Dīn Yūsuf. *Al-Nujūm al-Zāhira fī Mulūk Miṣr waʾl-Qāhira*. 16 vols. Cairo: Dār al-Kutub al-Miṣriyya, 1929–1938.

———. *Al-Manhal al-Ṣāfī waʾl-Mustawfā baʿd al-Wāfī*. 7 vols. Edited by M. M. Amīn and ʿAbd al-Fattāḥ ʿĀshūr. Cairo: al-Hayʾa al-ʿĀmma liʾl-Kitāb, 1984–90.

Ibn Taymiyya, Aḥmad ibn ʿAbd al-Ḥalīm. *Al-Siyāsa al-Sharʿiyya fī Iṣlāḥ al-Raʿī waʾl-Raʿiya*. Beirut: 1981.

———. *Majmūʿ Fatāwá Shaykh al-Islām Aḥmad Ibn Taymiyya*. 37 vols. Edited by ʿAbd al-Raḥmān ibn Muḥammad Ibn Qāsim and Muḥammad ibn ʿAbd al-Raḥmān Ibn Qāsim. Riyadh: 1961–97.

———. *Al-Jawāb al-Ṣaḥīḥ li-man Baddala Dīn al-Maṣīḥ*. 7 vols. Edited by ʿAlī ibn Ḥasan ibn Nāṣir, ʿAbd al-ʿAzīz ibn Ibrāhīm al-ʿAskar, and Ḥamdān ibn Muḥammad al-Ḥamdān. Riyadh: Dār al-ʿĀṣima liʾl-Nashr waʾl-Tawzīʿ, 1999.

———. *Iqtiḍāʾ al-Ṣirāṭ al-Mustaqīm li-Mukhālafat Aṣḥāb al-Jaḥīm*. 2 vols. Edited by Nāṣir al-Dīn ʿAbd al-Karīm ʿAql. Beirut: Dār ʿĀlam al-Kutub, 1999.

Ibn Ṭūlūn, Shams al-Dīn Muḥammad ibn ʿAlī. *Mufākahat al-Khillān fī Ḥawādith al-Zamān*. Edited by Khalīl al-Manṣūr. Beirut: Dār al-Kutub al-ʿIlmiyya, 1998.

———. *Quḍāt Dimashq: Al-Thaghr al-Bassām fī Dhikr Man Wulliya Qaḍāʾ al-Shām*. Edited by Ṣalāḥ al-Dīn al-Munajjid. Damascus: al-Majmaʿ al-ʿIlmī al-ʿArabī, 1956.

Ibn Wāṣil, Jamāl al-Dīn Muḥammad ibn Sālim. *Mufarrij al-Kurūb fī Akhbār Banī Ayyūb*. Vols. 4–5. Edited by Ḥasanayn Muḥammad Rabīʿ and Saʿīd ʿAbd al-Fattāḥ ʿĀshūr. Cairo: Maṭbaʿat Dār al-Kutub, 1972–1977.

Ibn Shaddād, ʿIzz al-Dīn Muḥammad ibn ʿAlī. *Taʾrīkh al-Malik al-Ẓāhir*. Edited by Aḥmad Ḥuṭayṭ. Wiesbaden: Franz Steiner Verlag, 1983.

Jāḥiẓ, ʿAmr b. Baḥr. *Al-Bayān waʾl-Tabyīn*. 3 vols. Beirut: Dār al-Hilāl, 1423/2002.

Joinville, Jean de. "The Life of Saint Louis." In *Chronicles of the Crusades*, edited by Caroline Smith. London: Penguin Books, 2008.

Miskawayh, Aḥmad b. Muḥammad. *Tajārib al-Umam wa-Taʿāqub al-Himam*. 8 vols. Edited by Abū al-Qāsim al-Imāmī. Tehran: Dār Sorūsh liʾl-Ṭibāʿa waʾl-Nashr, 2000–2.

Piloti, Emmanuel. *L'Égypte au commencement du quinzième siècle: d'après le traité d'Emmanuel Piloti de Crète, incipit 1420*. Edited and translated by P. H. Dopp. Cairo: Imp. Université Fouad 1er, 1950.

Samaw'al al-Maghribī. *Ifḥām al-Yahūd*. Edited and translated by Moshe Perlmann. *Proceedings of the American Academy for Jewish Research* 32 (1964): 5–93.

Shāfi' Ibn 'Alī. *Shāfi' Ibn 'Alī's Biography of the Mamluk Sultan Qalāwūn*. Edited by Paulina B. Lewicka. Orientalia polona 2. Warsaw: Academic Publishing House, 2000.

William of Tyre. *Chronique*. Edited by R.B.C. Huygens. Turnhout: Brepols, 1986.

———. *A History of Deeds Done beyond the Sea*. 2 vols. Edited and translated by Emily Atwater Babcock and August C. Krey. New York: Columbia University Press, 1943.

Yāqūt al-Ḥamawī. *Mu'jam al-Buldān*. 6 vols. Edited by F. Wüstenfeld. Leipzig: Brockhaus, 1866–73.

———. *Mu'jam al-Buldān*. 7 vols. Beirut: Dār Ṣādir, 1995.

C. Modern Studies

Abu-haidar, Farida. "Bedouinization." In *Encyclopedia of Arabic Language and Linguistics*, edited by Kees Versteegh et al., 269–74. Leiden: Brill, 2006.

Abul-Magd, Zeinab. *Imagined Empires: A History of Revolt in Egypt*. Berkeley: University of California Press, 2013.

Adra, Najwa. "Decolonizing Tribal 'Genealogies' in the Middle East and North Africa." *International Journal of Middle East Studies* 53, no. 3 (August 2021): 492–96.

Akgündüz, Ahmed, ed. *Osmanlı Kanunnâmeleri ve Hukuk Tahlilleri*. Istanbul: Fey Vakfı, 1990.

Al-'Asalī, Kāmil Jamīl. *Wathā'iq Maqdisiyya Tārīkhiyya: Ma'a Muqaddima ḥawla Ba'ḍ al-Maṣādir al-Awwaliyya li-Tārīkh al-Quds*. 3 vols. Amman: al-Jāmi'a al-Urdunniyya, 1983.

Al-Bakhīt, Muḥammad 'Adnān. "The Role of the Ḥanash Family and the Tasks Assigned to It in the Countryside of Dimashq al-Shām, 790/1388–976/1568: A Documentary Study." In *Land Tenure and Social Transformation in the Middle East*, edited by Tarif Khalidi, 257–89. Beirut: American University, 1984.

Al-Jabbūrī, Aḥmad Ḥusayn. *Al-Quds fī al-'Ahd al-'Uthmānī, 1516–1640 Mīlādī*. Amman: Dār al-Ḥāmid li'l-Nashr wa'l-Tawzī', 2010.

Alleaume, Ghislaine. "Water Management, Land Use, and Population in the Low Lands of Northern Delta 16th–19th C." Paper presented at the Egyplandscape Closing Conference, September 6–8, 2022, MMSH, Aix-en-Provence.

Al-Mahdī, Omaima Hasan. "Taṭawwur asmā' al-amākin al-miṣriyya fī al-'uṣūr al-wusṭā (al-Fayyūm numūdhajan)." In *Décrire, imaginer, construire l'espace: toponymie égyptienne de l'Antiquité au Moyen-Âge*, edited by Sylvain Dhennin and Claire Somaglino, 233–45. Cairo: Institut Français d'Archéologie Orientale, 2016.

Al-Ṣā'idī, 'Abd al-Razzāq. "Waqafāt ma'a al-Duktūr Bahā' 'Abd al-Raḥmān fī Mas'alat al-Qīf." *Majma' al-Lugha al-'Arabiyya al-Iftirāḍī*, August 12, 2014, http://almajma3.blogspot.com/2014/08/blog-post_12.html.

Amara, Ahmad. "Beyond Stereotypes of Bedouins as 'Nomads' and 'Savages': Rethinking the Bedouin in Ottoman Southern Palestine, 1875–1900." *Journal of Holy Land and Palestine Studies* 15, no. 1 (May 2016): 59–77.

Amitai, Reuven. "The Development of a Muslim City in Palestine: Gaza under the Mamluks." Annemarie Schimmel Kolleg Working Paper 28 (2017). Republished in *History and Society during the Mamluk Period: Studies of the Annemarie Schimmel Institute for Advanced Studies III*, edited by Bethany J. Walker, 163–96. Göttingen: V&R Unipress, 2021.

———. "Islamization in the Southern Levant after the End of Frankish Rule: Some General Considerations and a Short Case Study." In *Islamisation: Comparative Perspectives From History*, edited by A. C. S. Peacock, 156–86. Edinburgh: Edinburgh University Press, 2017.

Apellániz Ruiz de Galarreta, Francisco Javier. *Pouvoir et finance en Mediterranee pre-moderne: le deuxieme Etat mamelouk et le commerce des épices (1382–1517)*. Madrid: Consejo Superior de Investigaciones Cientificas, 2009.

Ashtor, Eliyahu. *Histoire des Prix et des Salaires dans L'Orient Médiéval.* Paris: Touzot, 1969.
'Āshūr, Sa'īd 'Abd al-Fattāḥ. *Al-'Aṣr al-Mamālīkī fī Miṣr wa'l-Shām.* Cairo: Dār al-Nahḍa al-'Arabiyya, 1965.
Assi, Seraj. "The Original Arabs: The Invention of the 'Bedouin Race' in Ottoman Palestine." *International Journal of Middle East Studies* 50, no. 2 (May 2018): 213–32.
Astren, Fred. "The Gibeonite Gambit: Ḥarrānians, Karaites, and Khaybarī Jews on the Margins of Medieval Islamic Society." *Journal of Medieval Worlds* 1, no. 2 (June 2019): 3–26.
Avni, Gideon. *The Byzantine-Islamic Transition in Palestine: An Archaeological Approach.* Oxford: Oxford University Press, 2014.
Awad, Mohamed. "The Assimilation of Nomads in Egypt." *Geographical Review* 44, no. 2 (April 1954): 240–52.
Baer G., and M. Hoexter. "Ḳays and Yaman in the Ottoman Period." Online entry in EI-2, Encyclopaedia of Islam.
Bagnall, Roger S., and Dominic W. Rathbone, eds. *Egypt: From Alexander to the Copts: An archaeological and historical guide.* London: British Museum Press, 2004.
Bahloul, Maher. "Linguistic Diversity: The Qaaf across Arabic dialects." In *Perspectives on Arabic Linguistics XIX: Papers from the Nineteenth Annual Symposium on Arabic Linguistics, Urbana, Illinois, April 2005*, edited by Elabbas Benmamoun, 247–67. Amsterdam: John Benjamins, 2007.
Baker, Colin. "Judaeo-Arabic Material in the Cambridge Genizah Collections." *Bulletin of the School of Oriental and African Studies* 58, no. 3 (1995): 445–54.
Bakhīt, M. A. "Muhannā, Banū." Online entry in EI-2, Encyclopaedia of Islam.
Banister, Mustafa. *The Abbasid Caliphate of Cairo, 1261–1517.* Edinburgh: Edinburgh University Press, 2021.
Barakat, Nora. *Bedouin Bureaucrats: Mobility and Property in the Ottoman Empire.* Stanford, CA: Stanford University Press, 2023.
Barker, Hannah. *That Most Precious Merchandise: The Mediterranean Trade in Black Sea Slaves, 1260–1500.* Philadelphia: University of Pennsylvania Press, 2019.
Barth, Frederik, ed. *Ethnic Groups and Boundaries: The Social Organization of Culture Difference.* Bergen and London: Universitetsforlaget; Allen & Unwin, 1969.
Bartlett, Robert. *The Making of Europe: Conquest, Colonization and Cultural Change; 950–1350.* London: Penguin Books, 1994.
Batatu, Hanna. *Syria's Peasantry, the Descendants of its Lesser Rural Notables, and their Politics.* Princeton, NJ: Princeton University Press, 1999.
Bauden, Frédéric, "The Recovery of Mamluk Chancery Documents in an Unsuspected Place." In *The Mamluks in Egyptian and Syrian Politics and Society*, edited by Amalia Levanoni and Michael Winter, 59–76. Leiden: Brill, 2004.
Behnstedt, Peter. *Sprachatlas von Syrien.* Wiesbaden: Harrassowitz, 1997.
Behnstedt, Peter, and Manfred Woidich. *Die ägyptisch-arabischen Dialekte.* Wiesbaden: L. Reichert, 1985.
———. "The Formation of the Egyptian Arabic Dialect Area." In *Arabic Historical Dialectology: Linguistic and Sociolinguistic Approaches*, edited by Clive Holes, 64–95. Oxford: Oxford University Press, 2018.
———. *Wortatlas der arabischen Dialekte.* Leiden: Brill, 2011.
Behrens-Abouseif, Doris. *Practising Diplomacy in the Mamluk Sultanate: Gifts and Material Culture in the Medieval Islamic World.* Revised paperback ed. London: I. B. Tauris, 2016.
Berriah, Mehdi. "Arabic Language's Status and Merits in Ibn Taymiyya." Paper presented at the Ninth Conference of the School of Mamluk Studies, Brown University in Providence, RI, June 8–10, 2023.
Bianquis, Thierry. *Damas et la Syrie sous la domination Fatimide (359–468/969–1076).* 2 vols. Damas: Institut français de Damas, 1986–89.

Bianquis, Thierry. "Mirdās." Online entry in EI-2, Encyclopaedia of Islam.

———. "Sayf al-Dawla." Online entry in EI-2, Encyclopaedia of Islam.

———. "Waththāb b. Sābiq al-Numayrī." Online entry in EI-2, Encyclopaedia of Islam.

———."Une crise frumentaire dans l'Égypte Fatimide." *Journal of the Economic and Social History of the Orient* 23, no. 1/2 (April 1980): 67–101.

Binay, Sara. *Die figur des Beduinen in der arabischen Literatur: 9.-12. Jahrhundert.* Wiesbaden: Reichert, 2006.

Binbaş, İlker Evrim. "Structure and Function of the Genealogical Tree in Islamic Historiography, 1200–1500." In *Horizons of the World: Festschrift for İsenbike Togan* (Hudûdü'l-âlem: İsenbike Togan'a Armağan), edited by Kılıç-Schubel, Binbaş, and Togan, 465–544. Istanbul: İthaki, 2011.

Björkman, W. "Lithām." Online entry in EI-2, Encyclopaedia of Islam.

Björnesjö, Sophia. "Quelques reflexions sur l'apport de l'arabe dans la toponymie égyptienne." *Annales Islamogiques* 30 (1996): 21–40.

———. "Toponyme de Tebtynis à l'époque islamique." *Annales Islamogiques* 27 (1993): 233–43.

Blatherwick, Helen. "'And the Light in His Eyes Grew Dark': The Representation of Anger in Arabic Popular Epic." *Cultural History* 8, no. 2 (2019): 226–47.

———. *Prophets, Gods and Kings in Sīrat Sayf Ibn Dhī Yazan: An Intertextual Reading of an Egyptian Popular Epic.* Leiden: Brill, 2016.

Blaydes, Lisa. "Mamluks, Property Rights and Economic Development: Lessons from Medieval Egypt." *Politics and Society*, 47 no. 3 (2019).

Boas, Adrian. "The Medieval Ceramics from Khirbat Ka'kul." *'Atiqot* 54 (2006): 75–104.

Bondioli, Lorenzo. "Peasants, Merchants, and Caliphs: Capital and Empire in Fatimid Egypt, 900–1200 CE." PhD diss., Princeton, 2021.

Borsch, Stuart J. *The Black Death in Egypt and England: A Comparative Study.* Austin: University of Texas Press, 2005.

———. "Plague Depopulation and Irrigation Decay in Medieval Egypt." *Medieval Globe* 1, no. 1 (2014): 125–56.

———. "Thirty Years after Lopez, Miskimin, and Udovitch." *Mamlūk Studies Review* 8, no. 2 (2004): 191–201.

Bouderbala, Sobhi. "*Murtaba' al-Jund wa Manzil al Qabā'il*: Pénétration militaire et installation tribale dans la campagne égyptienne au premier siècle de l'Islam." In *Authority and Control in the Countryside: From Antiquity to Islam in the Mediterranean and Near East (Sixth–Tenth Century)*, edited by Alain Delattre, Marie Legendre, and Petra Sijpesteijn. 367–91. Leiden: Brill, 2019.

Bowen, H. "Nāṣir al-Dawla." Online entry in EI-2, Encyclopaedia of Islam.

Bramoullé, David. "L'émirat de Barqa et les Fatimides: les enjeux de la navigation en Méditerranée centrale au XIe siècle." *Revue des mondes musulmans et de la Méditerranée* 139 (2016): 73–92.

Brandt, Marieke. "Heroic History, Disruptive Genealogy: Al-Hasan al-Hamdānī and the Historical Formation of the Shākir Tribe (Wā'ilah and Dahm) in al-Jawf, Yemen." *Medieval Worlds* 3 (2016): 116–45.

Braun, Christopher. "Equipped with Shovels, Pickaxes, and Books: Treasure Hunters and Grave Robbers in Medieval Egypt." In *Living with Nature and Things: Contributions to a New Social History of the Middle Islamic Period*, edited by Bethany J. Walker and Abdelkader Al Ghouz, 79–99. Göttingen: V & R Unipress, 2020.

Brennan, James R., and Cedric Barnes. "Political Genealogy, Race and Territory in Eastern Africa." *Social Identities* 12, no. 4 (July 2006): 401–4.

Bresc-Bautier, Geneviève. *Le Cartulaire du chapitre du Saint-Sépulcre de Jérusalem.* Paris, 1984.

Brett, Michael. *The Fatimid Empire*. Edinburgh: Edinburgh University Press, 2017.

———. "The Way of the Nomad." *Bulletin of the School of Oriental and African Studies* 58, no. 2 (June 1995): 251–69.

Brown, Robin M. "Faunal Distributions from the Southern Highlands of Transjordan: Regional and Historical Perspectives on the Representations and Roles of Animals in the Middle Islamic Period." *In Landscapes of the Islamic World: Archaeology, History, and Ethnography*, edited by Stephen McPhillips and Paul D. Wordsworth, 71–93. Philadelphia: University of Pennsylvania Press, 2016.

Burton, Elise K. *Genetic Crossroads: The Middle East and the Science of Human Heredity*. Stanford, CA: Stanford University Press, 2021.

Büssow-Schmitz, Sarah. *Die Beduinen Der Mamluken: Beduinen Im Politischen Leben Ägyptens Im 8./14. Jahrhundert*. Nomaden Und Sesshafte, Band 19. Wiesbaden: Dr. Ludwig Reichert Verlag, 2016.

———. "Rules of Communication and Politics between Bedouin and Mamluk Elites in Egypt: The Case Of The Al-Aḥdab Revolt, c. 1353." *Eurasian Studies* 9 no. 1–2 (2011): 67–104.

Cahen, Claude. "Ḥimāya." Online entry in EI-2, Encyclopaedia of Islam.

———. "Notes pour l'histoire de la *ḥimāya*." In *Mélanges Louis Massignon*, 287–303. Damascus: Institut Français de Damas, 1956.

Cahen, Cl., Y. Rāġib, and M. A. Taher. "L'achat et le waqf d'un grand domaine égyptien par le vizir fatimide Ṭalāiʿ b. Ruzzīq." *Annales islamologiques* 14 (1978): 59–126.

Canova, Giovanni. "Sayf b. Dhī Yazan: History and Saga." In *Fictionalizing the Past: Historical Characters in Arabic Popular Epic*, a workshop held at the Netherlands-Flemish Institute in Cairo, November 28–29, 2007, In Honor of Remke Kruk, 95–105. Leuven: Peeters, 2012.

Carlson, Thomas A. "Contours of Conversion: The Geography of Islamization in Syria, 600–1500." *Journal of the American Oriental Society* 135, no. 4 (December 2021).

Chalmeta, P., and W. F. Heinrichs. "Muwallad." Online entry in EI-2, Encyclopaedia of Islam.

Chareyron, Nicole. *Pilgrims to Jerusalem in the Middle Ages*. New York: Columbia University Press, 2005.

Cherkaoui, Driss. "Historical Elements in the 'Sīrat ʿAntar.'" *Oriente Moderno* 22, no. 2 (2003): 407–24.

Chraïbi, Aboubakr. "Le roman de Sayf Ibn ḏî Yazan." *Studia Islamica* 84 (1996): 113–34.

Cole, Donald P. "Where Have the Bedouin Gone?" *Anthropological Quarterly* 76, no. 2 (2003): 235–67.

Connelly, Bridget. *Arab Folk Epic and Identity*. Berkeley: University of California Press, 1986.

Conrad, Lawrence I. "Die Pest und ihr soziales Umfeld im Nahen Osten des frühen Mittelalters." *Der Islam* 73, no. 1 (1996): 81–112.

Corbino, Chiara. "Animal Husbandry." In *Living with Nature*, edited by Bethany J. Walker and Abdelkader Al Ghouz, 159–77. Göttingen: V&R Unipress, 2020.

Crone, Patricia. "Were the Umayyad Qays and Yaman of the Umayyad Period Political Parties?" *Der Islam* 71 (1994): 1–57.

Crudu, Andrea. "The Sudanese Elements in the Sīrat Sayf b. Ḏī Yazan." *Arabica* 61, no. 3/4 (2014): 309–38.

Cuno, Kenneth M. *The Pasha's Peasants: Land, Society, and Economy in Lower Egypt, 1740–1858*. Cambridge: Cambridge University Press, 1992.

Cytryn-Silverman, Katia. "Khān al-Ẓāhir: Bi-Ẓāhir al-Quds!" *Journal of the Royal Asiatic Society* 19, no. 2 (2009): 149–71.

D'Hulster, Kristof. *Browsing through the Sultan's Bookshelves: Towards a Reconstruction of the Library of the Mamluk Sultan Qanisawh al-Ghawri (r. 906–922/1501–1516)*. Göttingen: V&R Unipress, 2021.

David, James. *A Masterpiece of Arab Painting: The "Schefer" Maqamat Manuscript in Context.* London: East & West Publishing Ltd., 2013.

Davis, Diana K. *Resurrecting the Granary of Rome: Environmental History and French Colonial Expansion in North Africa.* Athens: Ohio University Press, 2007.

———. "Scorched Earth: The Problematic Environmental History that Defines the Middle East." In *Is There a Middle East?: The Evolution of a Geopolitical Concept,* edited by Michael E. Bonine, Abbas Amanat, and Michael Ezekiel Gasper. Stanford, CA: Stanford University Press, 2012.

De Felipe, Helena. "Berber Leadership and Genealogical Legitimacy: The Almoravid Case." In *Genealogy and Knowledge in Muslim Societies,* edited by Sarah Bowen Savant and Helena de Felipe, 55–70. Edinburgh: Edinburgh University Press, 2014.

De la Véronne, Ch. "Ṣanhāḏja." Online entry in EI-2, Encyclopaedia of Islam.

Delaville le Roulx, Joseph Marie Antoine. *Cartulaire général de l'Ordre des Hospitaliers de S. Jean de Jérusalem, 1100–1310.* Paris: 1894.

Derda, Tomasz. "Arsinoitēs Nomos: Administration of the Fayum under Roman Rule." *Journal of Juristic Papyrology.* Supplement 7. Warsaw: Faculty of Law and Administration of Warsaw University, 2006.

Doufikar-Aerts, Faustina C. W. "Sīrat al-Iskandar: An Arabic Popular Romance of Alexander." *Oriente Moderno* 22 (2003): 505–20.

Dozy, Reinhart Pieter Anne. *Supplément aux dictionnaires Arabes.* Leiden: Brill, 1881.

Drory, Joseph. "Ḥanbalīs of the Nablus Region in the Eleventh and Twelfth Centuries." *Asian and African Studies* 22 (1988): 93–112.

———. "The Prince Who Favored the Desert: Fragmentary Biography of al-Nasir Ahmad (d. 745/1344)." In *Mamluks and Ottomans: Studies in Honour of Michael Winter,* edited by David Wasserstein and Ami Ayalon, 19–33. London and New York: Routledge, 2006.

———. "The Role of Banū Faḍl in Fourteenth Century Northern Syria." In *Egypt and Syria in the Fatimid, Ayyubid and Mamluk Eras V,* proceedings of the 11th, 12th, and 13th International Colloquium, edited by Urbain Vermeulen and Kristof D'Hulster, 471–85. Katholieke Universiteit Leuven, May 2002, 2003 and 2004. Leuven: Uitgeverij Peeters, 2007.

Dyer, Christopher. *Making a Living in the Middle Ages: The People of Britain 850–1520.* New Haven, CT: Yale University Press, 2002.

Eddé, Anne-Marie. "Ibn al-ʿAdīm." Online entry in EI-3, the Encyclopaedia of Islam.

———. *La Principauté Ayyoubide d'Alep, (579/1183-658/1260).* Freiburger Islamstudien, Bd. 21. Stuttgart: Steiner, 1999.

Eickelman, Dale F. *The Middle East and Central Asia: An Anthropological Approach.* 4th ed. Upper Saddle River, NJ: Prentice Hall, 2001.

El Kadi, Galila, and Alain Bonnami. *Architecture for the Dead: Cairo's Medieval Necropolis.* Cairo: American University in Cairo Press, 2007.

Elbendary, Amina. *Crowds and Sultans: Urban Protest in Late Medieval Egypt and Syria.* Cairo: American University in Cairo Press, 2015

El-Leithy, Tamer. "Coptic Culture and Conversion in Medieval Cairo, 1293–1524 A.D." PhD diss., Princeton University, 2004.

Ellenblum, Ronnie. *The Collapse of the Eastern Mediterranean: Climate Change and the Decline of the East, 950–1072.* Cambridge, UK: Cambridge University Press, 2013.

———. *Frankish Rural Settlement in the Latin Kingdom of Jerusalem.* Cambridge, UK: Cambridge University Press, 1998.

Ernst, Hans. *Die Mamlukischen Sultansurkunden des Sinai-Klosters.* Wiesbaden: O. Harrassowitz, 1960.

Ettinghausen, Richard. *Arab Painting.* New York: Rizzoli, 1977.

Fabietti, Ugo, and Philip Carl Salzman, eds. *Antropologia Delle Società Pastorali Tribali e Contadine: La Dialettica Della Coesione e Della Frammentazione Sociale* (The Anthropology of Tribal and Peasant Pastoral Societies: The Dialectics of Social Cohesion and Fragmentation). Como: Collegio Ghislieri, Ibis, 1996.

Faith, Rosamond. *The Moral Economy of the Countryside: Anglo-Saxon to Anglo-Norman England.* Cambridge, UK: Cambridge University Press, 2020.

Fernandes, L. "On Conducting the Affairs of State: A Guideline of the 14th Century." *Annales Islamologiques* 24 (1988): 81–91.

Finkelstein, Israel, Zvi Lederman, Shelomoh Bunimovits, and Ran Barkai, *Highlands of Many Cultures: The Southern Samaria Survey: The Sites.* Tel Aviv: Institute of Archaeology of Tel Aviv University Publications Section, 1997.

Firestone, Y. "Samaw'al b. Yaḥyā al-Maghribī." Online entry in EI-2, Encyclopaedia of Islam.

Firnhaber-Baker, Justine. *The Jacquerie of 1358: A French Peasants' Revolt.* Oxford: Oxford University Press, 2021.

Fischel, W. J. "*Ascensus Baroch*: A Latin Biography of the Mamluk Sultan Barqùq of Egypt (d. 1399) Written by Bertrando de Mignanelli in 1416." *Arabica* 6 (1959): 57–74; 152–72.

Franz, Kurt. "The Bedouin in History or Bedouin History?" *Nomadic Peoples* 15, no. 1 (November 2011): 11–53.

———. "Bedouin and States: Framing the Mongol-Mamlūk Wars in Long-term History." In *Nomad Military Power in Iran and Adjacent Areas in the Islamic Period*, edited by Kurt Franz and Wolfgang Holzwarth, 29–105. Wiesbaden: Dr. Ludwig Reichert Verlag, 2015.

———. "Nuʿayr Muḥammad b. Ḥiyār." Online entry in EI-3, Encyclopaedia of Islam.

———. *Vom Beutezug Zur Territorialherrschaft: Das Lange Jahrhundert Des Aufstiegs von Nomaden Zur Vormacht in Syrien Und Mesopotamien 286-420/899-1029.* Nomaden Und Sesshafte, Bd. 5. Wiesbaden: Reichert Verlag, 2007.

Frenkel, Miriam. "Adaptive Tactics: The Jewish Communities Facing New Reality." *Medieval Encounters* 21, no. 4–5 (December 2015): 364–89.

Frenkel, Yehoshua. "Agriculture, Land-Tenure and Peasants in Palestine during the Mamluk Period." In *Egypt and Syria in the Fatimid, Ayyubid and Mamluk Eras III*, proceedings of the 6th, 7th, and 8th International Colloquium, edited by Urbain Vermeulen and Jo Van Steenbergen, 193–208. Katholieke Universiteit Leuven, May 1997, 1998, and 1999. Leuven: Uitgeverij Peeters, 2001.

———. "The Contribution of European Travel Literature to the Study of the Environmental History of the Levant (13th–15th Centuries)." In *Living with Nature and Things*, edited by Bethany J. Walker and Abdelkader Al Ghouz, 705–24. Göttingen: V&R Unipress, 2020.

———. "Volksroman under the Mamluks: The Case of the Tamīm ad-Dārī Popular Sīra." In *History and Society during the Mamluk Period (1250–1517)*, edited by Stephan Conermann, 21–36. Bonn: Bonn University, 2014.

Fried, Morton H. *The Notion of Tribe.* Menlo Park, CA: Cummings Pub. Co., 1975.

Fück, J. W. "Ḥayṣa Bayṣa." Online entry in EI-2, Encyclopaedia of Islam.

Gabrieli, R. Smadar, David Ben-Shlomo, and Bethany J. Walker. "Production and Distribution of Hand-Made Geometric-Painted (HMGP) and Plain Hand-Made Wares of the Mamluk Period: A Case Study from Northern Israel, Jerusalem and Tall Hisban." *Journal of Islamic Archaeology* 1, no. 2 (February 2015): 193–229.

García Sanjuán, Alejandro. "Ibn ʿAbdūn." Online entry in EI-3, Encyclopaedia of Islam.

Garcin, Jean-Claude. "Al-Aḥdab, Muḥammad b. Wāṣil." Online entry in EI-3, Encyclopaedia of Islam.

———. *Un Centre Musulman de La Haute-Egypte Médiévale: Qûs.* Cairo: Institut Français d'Archéologie Orientale Du Caire, 1976.

Garcin, Jean-Claude. "Note sur les rapports entre bédouins et fellahs à l'époque mamluke." *Annales islamologiques* 14, no. 1 (1978): 147–63.

———. "The Regime of the Circassian Mamluks." In *The Cambridge History of Egypt*, vol. 1, edited by Carl F. Petry, 290–317. Cambridge, UK: Cambridge University Press, 1998.

Gascoigne, A. L., and Sheehan, P. D. "Sherds and the City: Pottery Production, Society, and the Changing Urban Fabric of Fustat, Egypt." *Journal of Field Archaeology* (2024): 1–20.

Gascoigne, Alison. "Providing Pots for Cairo: Urban and Rural Resourcing of Medieval Ceramics Industries." EGYLandscape Closing Conference, September 6–8, 2022, MMSH, Aix-en-Provence.

Gaubert, Christian, and Jean-Michel Mouton. *Hommes et villages du Fayyoum dans la documentation papyrologique arabe (Xe-XIe siècles)*. Hautes études orientales 52. Genève: Librairie Droz, 2014.

Gelder, G.J.H. van. *Of Dishes and Discourse: Classical Arabic Literary Representations of Food*. Richmond: Curzon, 2000.

Gil, Moshe. *Be-malkhut Yishma'el bi-tekufat ha-ge'onim* [= Gil, *Kingdom*]. 4 vols. Tel Aviv: 1997.

———. *A History of Palestine, 634–1099* [= Gil, *Palestine*]. Cambridge, UK: Cambridge University Press, 1997.

———. *Erets-Yiśra'el ba-tekufa ha-Muslemit ha-rishona (634–1099)*. 3 vols. Tel Aviv: 1983.

Glausiusz, Josie. "Hundreds of Israel's Archaeological Sites Are Vanishing under Concrete." *Nature* 582, no. 7813 (June 2020): 474–77.

Goitein, S. D. *A Mediterranean Society: The Jewish Communities of the Arab World as Portrayed in the Documents of the Cairo Geniza*. 5 vols. Berkeley: University of California Press, 1967–85.

Goudie, Kenneth. "Al-Biqāʿī's Self-Reflection: A Preliminary Study of the Autobiographical in His Unwān al-Zamān." In *New Readings in Arabic Historiography from Late Medieval Egypt and Syria*, edited by Jo van Steenbergen and Maya Termonia, 377–400. Leiden: Brill, 2021.

———. "How to Make It in Cairo: The Early Career of Burhān al-Dīn al-Biqāʿī." *Mamlūk Studies Review* 23 (2020): 203–30.

Grabar, Oleg. "The Illustrated *Maqamat* of the Thirteenth Century: The Bourgeoisie and the Arts." In *Islamic Visual Culture, 1100–1800*, vol. 2, 167–186. Hampshire: Ashgate Publishing Limited, 2006. First published in *The Islamic City*, edited A. Hourani, 207–22 (Oxford, 1970).

Gutfeld, Oren, and Michael Haber. "A Guide to Beit Loya (Lehi): An Archaeological Site in the Judean Lowland." Beit Lehi Foundation. Jerusalem: Old City Press, 2009.

Haber, Marc, Joyce Nassar, Mohamed A. Almarri, Tina Saupe, Lehti Saag, Samuel J. Griffith, Claude Doumet-Serhal, et al. "A Genetic History of the Near East from an ADNA Time Course Sampling Eight Points in the Past 4,000 Years." *American Journal of Human Genetics* 107, no. 1 (July 2020): 149–57.

Hagen, Gottfried. "Heroes and Saints in Anatolian Turkish Literature." *Oriente Moderno* 89, 2 (2009): 349–61.

Halawi, Wissam H. *Les Druzes aux marges de l'Islam: Ésotérisme et normativité en milieu rural, XIVe–XVIe siècle*. Paris: Les éditions du Cerf, 2021.

Haldane, Duncan. *Mamluk Painting*. Warminster: Aris and Phillips, 1978.

Halm, Heinz. *Ägypten nach den mamlukischen Lehensregistern*. 2 vols. Wiesbaden: L. Reichert, 1979–82.

Haron, Jehad, and Douglas R. Clark, eds. *The Pottery of Jordan: A Manual*. Amman: American Center of Research & Madaba Regional Archaeological Museum Project, 2022.

Heath, Peter. "'Antar Hangs His Muʿallaqa: History, Fiction, and Textual Conservatism in Sirat 'Antar Ibn Shaddād." In *Fictionalizing the Past: Historical Characters in Arabic Popular Epic*, edited by Sabine Dorpmueller. Leuven–Paris–Walpole MA: Uitgeverij Peeters en Department Oosterse Studies, 2012.

———. *The Thirsty Sword: Sīrat ʿAntar and the Arabic Popular Epic*. Salt Lake City: University of Utah Press, 1996.

Heidemann, Stefan. "Arab Nomads and the Seljuq Military." In *Shifts and Drifts in Nomad-Sedentary Relations*, edited by Stefan Leder and Bernhard Streck. Wiesbaden: L. Reichert, 2005.

———. "Numayrid Ar-Raqqa. Archaelogical and Historical Evidence for a 'Dimorphic State' in the Bedouin Dominated Fringes of the Fatimid Empire." In *Egypt and Syria in the Fatimid, Ayyubid and Mamluk Eras IV: Proceedings of the 9th and 10th International Colloquium Organized at the Katholieke Universiteit Leuven in May 2000 and May 2001*, edited by Urbain Vermeulen and J. van Steenbergen, 85–110. Leuven: Peeters, 2005.

Heidemann, Stefan, and Robert Kool. "A Bedouin Amir in Fatimid Tabariyya: The Earliest Numayrid Coin Excavated in Tiberias." *Israel Numismatic Research* 10 (2015): 207–14.

Heinrichs, Wolfhart. "Ibn Khaldūn as a Historical Linguist with an Excursus on the Question of Ancient Gāf." In *Wolfhart Heinrichs' Essays and Articles on Arabic Literature: Authors, Semitic Studies, and Islamic Jurisprudence*, edited by H. Biesterfeldt and A. Giese. London: Routledge, 2024.

Herzog, Thomas. "Composition and Worldview of Some Bourgeois and Petit-Bourgeois Mamluk Adab-Encyclopedias." *Mamlūk Studies Review* 17 (2013): 100–29.

———. "The First Layer of the Sirat Baybars: Popular Romance and Political Propaganda." *Mamlūk Studies Review* 7 (2003): 137–48.

———. "Orality and the Tradition of Arabic Epic Storytelling." In *Medieval Oral Literature*, edited by K. Reichl, 627–49. Berlin: De Gruyter, 2012.

———. "'What They Saw with Their Own Eyes . . .': Fictionalisation and 'Narrativisation' of History in Arab Popular Epics and Learned Historiography." In *Fictionalizing the Past*, edited by Sabine Dorpmüller, 25–43. Cairo: American University of Cairo Press, 2012.

———. "Wild Ancestors: Bedouins in Medieval Arabic Popular Literature." In *Shifts and Drifts in Nomad-Sedentary Relations*, edited by Stefan Leder and Bernhard Streck, 421–42. Wiesbaden: L. Reichert, 2005.

Hiatt, Alfred. "Geography at the Crossroads: The *Nuzhat al-Mushtāq fī Ikhtirāq al-Āfāq* of al-Idrīsī." In *Cartography between Christian Europe and the Arabic-Islamic World, 1100–1500: Divergent Traditions*, edited by Alfred Hiatt, 113–36. Leiden: Brill, 2021.

Ḥijāzī, Maḥmūd Fahmī. *ʿIlm al-Lugha al-ʿArabiyya: Madkhal Tārīkhī Muqāran fī Ḍaw' al-Turāth wa'l-Lughāt al- Sāmiyya*. Cairo: Dār al-Thaqāfa li'l-Nashr wa'l- Tawzī', 1992.

Hirschler, Konrad. *Medieval Damascus: Plurality and Diversity in an Arabic Library: The Ashrafiya Library Catalogue*. Edinburgh: Edinburgh University Press, 2016.

———. *The Written Word in the Medieval Arabic Lands: A Social and Cultural History of Reading Practices*. Edinburgh: Edinburgh University Press, 2012.

Hiyari, M. A. "The Origins and Development of the Amīrate of the Arabs during the Seventh/Thirteenth and Eighth/Fourteenth Centuries." *Bulletin of the School of Oriental and African Studies* 38 (1975): 509–24.

Hofer, Nathan. *The Popularisation of Sufism in Ayyubid and Mamluk Egypt, 1173–1325*. Edinburgh: Edinburgh University Press, 2015.

Holes, Clive. "Introduction." In *Arabic Historical Dialectology: Linguistic and Sociolinguistic Approaches*, edited by Clive Holes. Oxford: Oxford University Press, 2018.

Holt, P. M. "Kanz, Banu'l." Online entry in EI-2, Encyclopaedia of Islam.

Hoover, Jon. *Ibn Taymiyya*. London: Oneworld Academic, 2019.

Hütteroth, Wolf-Dieter, and Kamal Abdulfattah. *Historical Geography of Palestine, Transjordan and Southern Syria in the Late 16th [Sixteenth] Century.* Erlangen: Fränkische Geographische Ges; Palm und Enke [in Komm.], 1977.

Ibrāhīm, Rajab 'Abd al-Jawwād. *Al-Mu'jam al-'Arabī li-Asmā' al-Malābis: Fī ḍaw' al-Ma'ājim wa-al-Nuṣūṣ al-Muwaththaqa min al-Jāhiliyya ḥattā al-'Aṣr al-Ḥadīth.* Cairo: Dār al-Āfāq al-'Arabiyya, 2002.

Igarashi, Daisuke. "Rural Administration, Tax-Farming, and the *Mutadarriks* in Egypt from the Late 14th to the Early 16th Centuries." *Journal of the Economic and Social History of the Orient* 66, no. 5–6 (2023): 628–55.

Igarashi, Daisuke. *Land Tenure, Fiscal Policy and Imperial Power in Medieval Syro-Egypt.* Chicago: Middle East Documentation Center, 2015.

Irwin, Robert. *Ibn Khaldun: An Intellectual Biography.* Princeton, NJ: Princeton University Press, 2018.

———. "Tribal Feuding and Mamluk Factions in Medieval Syria." In *Texts, Documents and Artefacts: Islamic Studies in Honour of D. S. Richards*, edited by Chase F. Robinson, 251–64. Leiden: Brill, 2003.

Islahi, Abdul Azim. "Al-Asadi and His Work al-Taysir: A Study of His Socio-economic Ideas." MPRA Paper No. 80122, posted July 11, 2017. https://mpra.ub.uni-muenchen.de/80122.

Jacques, Kevin R. "Murder in Damascus: The Consequences of Competition among Medieval Muslim Religious Elites." *Mamlūk Studies Review* 18 (2014–15): 149–85.

James, Boris. "Arab Ethnonyms ('Ajam,' Arab, Badū and Turk): The Kurdish Case as a Paradigm for Thinking about Differences in the Middle Ages." *Iranian Studies* 47, no. 5 (2014): 683–712.

———. *Genèse du Kurdistan: les Kurdes dans l'Orient mamelouk et mongol (1250–1340).* Paris: Éditions de la Sorbonne, 2021.

Johansen, Baber. *The Islamic Law on Land Tax and Rent: The Peasants' Loss of Property Rights as Interpreted in the Hanafite Legal Literature of the Mamluk and Ottoman Periods.* London: Routledge, 2018.

Johns, Jeremy. "The Rise of Middle Islamic Hand-made Geometrically-Painted Ware in Bilād al-Shām (11th–13th centuries A.D.)." In *Colloque internationale d'archéologie islamique. IFAO, Le Caire, 3–7 février 1993*, edited by R. P. Gayraud, vol. 36, pp. 65–93. Cairo: Institut français d'archéologie orientale, 1997.

Jones, Alan. "Ayyām al-'Arab." Online entry in EI-3, Encyclopaedia of Islam.

Jumayl, Usāma al-Sa'dūnī. *Al-Nashāṭ al-Iqtiṣādī li'l-Qabā'il al-'Arabīya fī Miṣr fī 'Aṣr al-Mamālīk (648–923 H)-(1250–1517 M).* Cairo: Tārīkh al-Miṣrīyīn, 2019.

Karamustafa, Ali. "Who Were the Türkmen of Ottoman and Safavid Lands? An Overlooked Early Modern Identity." *Der Islam* 97, no. 2 (October 2020): 476–99.

Kassem, Salama. "Social and Economic Networks in Late Medieval Rural Southern Syria: An Archaeometrical Study of Mamluk Pottery, 13th–16th century." PhD diss., University of Bonn (forthcoming).

Kedar, Alexandre, Ahmad Amara, and Oren Yiftachel. *Emptied Lands: A Legal Geography of Bedouin Rights in the Negev.* Stanford: Stanford University Press, 2018.

Kedar, B. Z. "The Subjected Muslims of the Frankish Levant." In *Muslims under Latin Rule, 1100–1300*, edited by J. M. Powell, 135–74. Princeton, NJ: Princeton University Press, 1990.

———. "The *Tractatus de locis et statu sancte terre ierosolimitane.*" In *The Crusades and Their Sources: Essays Presented to Bernard Hamilton*, edited by J. France and W. G. Zajac, 111–33. Aldershot: 1998.

Kedar B. Z., and M. Hajjuj. "Muslim Villagers of the Frankish Kingdom of Jerusalem: Some Demographic and Onomastic Data." In *Itinéraires d'Orient: Hommages à Claude Cahen*

[=*Res Orientales*, vol. 6], edited by E. Curiel and R. Gyselen, 145–56. Bures-sur-Yvette: Groupe pour l'Étude de la Civilisation du Moyen-Orient, 1994.

Kennedy, Hugh. "The 'Uqaylids of Mosul: the origins and structure of a nomad dynasty." In Kennedy, *The Byzantine and Early Islamic Near East*. Aldershot: Ashgate Variorum, 2006.

———. *The Prophet and the Age of the Caliphates: The Islamic Near East from the Sixth to the Eleventh Century* [= *Age of the Caliphate*]. New York: Routledge, Taylor & Francis Group, 2016.

Khan, Geoffrey. "Judaeo-Arabic." In *Arabic Historical Dialectology: Linguistic and Sociolinguistic Approaches*, edited by Clive Holes. Oxford: Oxford University Press, 2018.

Kletter, Raz, and Edna J. Stern. "A Mamluk-Period Site at Khirbat Burin in the Eastern Sharon." *'Atiqot* 51 (2006): 173–214.

Krawczyk, Jean-Luc. "The Relationship between Pastoral Nomadism and Agriculture: Northern Syria and the Jazira in the Eleventh Century." *Jusūr* 1 (1985): 1–22.

Krawulsky, Dorothea. "Al-Badw fī Miṣr wa'l-Shām fī al-Qarnayn al-Sābi' wa'l-Thāmin al-Hijrīayn 'inda al-'Umarī fī Masālik al-Abṣār." *Al-Ijtihād* 4, no. 17 (1992/1413): 35–72.

Kruk, Remke. "Role of the Prophet in Arabic Popular Epic." In *A Life with the Prophet? Examining hadith, Sira and Qur'an*, edited by Albrecht Fuess and Stefan Weninger, 69–84. Berlin: EB-Verlag Dr. Brandt. 2017

———. "Sīrat 'Antar ibn Shaddād." In *Arabic Literature in the Post-Classical Period*, edited by Roger Allen and D. S. Richards. Cambridge: Cambridge University Press, 2006.

Lancaster, William. *The Rwala Bedouin Today*. New York: Cambridge University Press, 1981.

Larcher, Pierre. "Parlers arabes nomades et sédentaires et diglossie chez Ibn Ǧinnī (IVe/Xe siècle). Sociolinguistique et histoire de la langue vs discours épilinguistique." *Al-Qanṭara* 39, no. 2: 359–89.

———. "Sociolinguistique et histoire de l'arabe selon la Muqaddima d'Ibn Ḫaldun (VIIIe/XIVe siècle)." In *Linguistic and Oriental Studies in Honour of Fabrizio A. Pennacchietti*, edited by Pier Giorgio Borbone, Alessandro Mengozzi, amd Mauro Tosco, 425–35. Wiesbaden: Harrassowitz, 2006.

Leder, Stefan. "The Arabs of Ibn Khaldun." *Al-Abḥāth* 57 (2009): 47–64.

———. "Nomads and Sedentary People: A Misleading Dichotomy? Bedouin and Bedouinism in the Arab Past." In *Shifts and Drifts in Nomad-Sedentary Relations*, edited by S. Leder and Bernhard Streck, 401–19. Wiesbaden: 2005.

———. "Towards a Historical Semantic of the Bedouin, Seventh to Fifteenth Centuries: A Survey." *Der Islam* 92, no. 1 (January 2015): 85–123.

Leeuwen, Richard van. "Conversion as a (Meta-)Historical Concept in the Epic Stories of the Thousand and One Nights." In *Fictionalizing the Past: Historical Characters in Arabic Popular Epic*, edited by Sabine Dorpmüller, 125–37. Workshop Held at the Netherlands-Flemish Institute in Cairo, November 28–29, 2007. Leuven: Peeters, 2012.

Lentin, Jérôme. "The Levant." In *Arabic Historical Dialectology: Linguistic and Sociolinguistic Approaches*, edited by Clive Holes, 170–205. Oxford: Oxford University Press, 2018.

Lesguer, F., and J. Schiettecatte. "A Ninth- to Tenth-Century Pottery Workshop at al-Yamāmah, Central Arabia." *Proceedings of the Seminar for Arabian Studies* 50 (2020): 203–24.

Lev, Yaacov. "Army, Regime, and Society in Fatimid Egypt, 358–487/968–1094." *International Journal of Middle East Studies* 19, no. 3 (1987): 337–65.

———. "Coptic Rebellions and the Islamization of Medieval Egypt (8th–10th Century): Medieval and Modern Perceptions." *Jerusalem Studies in Arabic and Islam* 39 (2012): 303–44.

Levy-Rubin, Milka. "New Evidence Relating to the Process of Islamization in Palestine in the Early Muslim Period: The Case of Samaria." *Journal of the Economic and Social History of the Orient* 43, no. 3 (2000): 257–76.

Lewicka, Paulina B. *Food and Foodways of Medieval Cairenes: Aspects of Life in an Islamic Metropolis of the Eastern Mediterranean.* Leiden: Brill, 2011.

Little, Donald P. A. *Catalogue of the Islamic Documents from Al-Ḥaram Ash-Sharīf in Jerusalem.* Beiruter Texte Und Studien, Bd. 29. Beirut and Wiesbaden: Orient-Institut der Deutschen Morgenländischen Gesellschaft, 1984.

Livingston, Daisy. "Managing Paperwork in Mamluk Egypt (c. 1250–1517): A Documentary Approach to Archival Practices." PhD diss., School of Oriental and African Studies, University of London, 2018.

———. "The Paperwork of a Mamluk Muqṭaʿ: Documentary Life Cycles, Archival Spaces, and the Importance of Documents Lying Around." *Al-ʿUṣūr al-Wusṭā (The Journal of Middle East Medievalists)* 28, 1 (2020): 346–75.

Loiseau, Julien. "Tribal Genealogy, Ethnic Nobility: Al-ʿAynī and the Glorious Circassian Ancestry of Sultan al-Mu'ayyad Shaykh." Paper presented at the Ninth Conference of the School of Mamluk Studies, Brown University, June 10, 2023.

Luengo, Ana. "Conflict Resolution in the 'Sīrat Baybars.' A Peace Research Project." *Oriente Moderno* 22, no. 2 (2003): 465–84.

Luz, Nimrod. "Aspects of Islamization of Space and Society in Mamluk Jerusalem and its Hinterland." *Mamlūk Studies Review* 6 (2002): 133–54.

Lyons, Malcolm Cameron. *The Arabian Epic: Heroic and Oral Story-Telling.* Cambridge, UK: Cambridge University Press, 1995.

———. *The Man of Wiles in Popular Arabic Literature: A Study of a Medieval Arab Hero.* Edinburgh: Edinburgh University Press, 2012.

Magen, Yitsḥaq, and Israel Finkelstein. *Seker Arkhe'ologi Bĕ-Erets Binyamin.* Jerusalem: Rashut ha-ʿatiḳot, ha-Minhal ha-ezraḥi bi-Yehuda uva-Shomron, 1993.

Magidow, Melanie. "Epic of the Commander Dhat al-Himma." *Medieval Feminist Forum* 6 (2019): 3–5.

Makowski, Piotr. "Towards a Better Understanding of the Chronological and Geographical Distribution Patterns of Plain and Painted Handmade Wares in Bilād al-Shām." *Bulletin of the American Society of Overseas Research* 389 (May 2023): 121–63.

Marzolph, Ulrich. "Ḥamza, Romance of." Online entry in EI-3, Encyclopaedia of Islam.

Mauder, Christian. "'And They Read in That Night Books of History': Consuming, Discussing, and Producing Texts about the Past in al-Ghawrī's Majālis as Social Practices." In *New Readings in Arabic Historiography from Late Medieval Egypt and Syria,* edited by Jo van Steenbergen and Maya Termonia, 401–28. Leiden: Brill, 2021.

———. "The Quraysh of the Unbelievers: Constructing Circassian Ethnicity in the Court of Sultan Qāniṣawh al-Ghawrī." Paper presented at the Ninth Conference of the School of Mamluk Studies, Brown University, June 10, 2023.

Mayer, Leo Ary. *Mamluk Costume, a Survey.* Genève: Albert Kundig, 1952.

Mayer, Hans Eberhard. *Die Urkunden der lateinischen Könige von Jerusalem.* 4 vols. Hannover: Hahnsche Buchhandlung 2010.

Mayeur-Jaouen, Catherine. "al-Badawī, al-Sayyid." Online entry in EI-3, Encyclopaedia of Islam.

McPhillips, Stephen, and Alan Walmsley. "Faḥl during the Early Mamluk Period: Archaeological Perspectives." *Mamlūk Studies Review* 11, no. 1 (2007): 119–56.

Meloy, John L. "The Privatization of Protection: Extortion and the State in the Circassian Mamluk Period." *Journal of the Economic and Social History of the Orient* 47, no. 2 (2004): 195–212.

Meri, Josef W. *The Cult of Saints among Muslims and Jews in Medieval Syria*. Oxford: Oxford University Press, 2002.

Metzger, Evan. "Historical Representation as Resurrection: Al-Udfūwī and the Imitation of Allah." In *New Readings in Arabic Historiography from Late Medieval Egypt and Syria*, edited by Jo van Steenbergen and Maya Termonia, 429–65. Leiden: Brill, 2021.

Michel, Nicolas. "Devoirs Fiscaux et Droits Fonciers: La Condition Des Fellahs Égyptiens (13e—16e Siècles)." *Journal of the Economic and Social History of the Orient* 43, no. 4 (2000): 521–78.

———. *L'Égypte Des Villages Autour Du Seizième Siècle*. Collection Turcica, vol. 23. Bristol, CT: Peeters, 2018.

———. "Les rizaq iḥbāsiyya, terres agricoles en mainmorte dans l'Égypte mamelouke et ottoman: Étude sur les Dafātir al-Aḥbās ottomans." *Annales Islamologiques* 30 (1996): 105–98.

———. "Les services communaux dans les campagnes égyptiennes au début de l'époque ottomane." In *Sociétés rurales ottomanes/Ottoman Rural Societies*, edited by N. Michel, M. Afifi, R. Chih, B. Marino, and I. Tamdogan, 19–46. Cairo: Ifao, 2005.

Milwright, Marcus. *The Fortress of the Raven: Karak in the Middle Islamic Period (1100–1650)*. Leiden: Brill, 2008.

———. *An Introduction to Islamic Archaeology*. Edinburgh: Edinburgh University Press, 2022.

Monchamp, Julie. *Céramiques des Murailles du Caire: fin Xe-début XVIe siècle*. Cairo: Institut français d'archéologie orientale, 2018.

Morimoto, Kazuo. "The Formation and Development of the Science of Talibid Genealogies in the 10th & 11th Century Middle East." *Oriente Moderno* 79, no. 2 (August 1999): 541–70.

Mouton, Jean-Michel. "L'islamisation de l'Égypte au Moyen âge." In *Chrétiens du monde arabe*, edited by B. Heyberger, 110–26. Paris: Autrement, 2003.

———. "Saladin et les Bédouins du Sinaï." In *Le Sinaï: De la conquête arabe à nos jours*, edited by Jean-Michel Mouton, 197–206. Cairo: Institut français d'archéologie orientale, 2001.

Mouton, Jean-Michel, and Jean Olivier Guilhot. *Ṣadr, Une Forteresse de Saladin Au Sinaï: Histoire Et Archéologie*. Paris: Académie Des Inscriptions et Belles-lettres: Diff. De Boccard, 2010.

Muhanna, Elias. *The World in a Book: Al-Nuwayri and the Islamic Encyclopedic Tradition*. Princeton, NJ: Princeton University Press, 2018.

Müller, Christian. "Crimes without Criminals? Legal Documents on Fourteenth-Century Injury and Homicide from the Haram Collection in Jerusalem." In *Legal Documents as Sources for the History of Muslim Societies: Studies in Honour of Rudolph Peters*, edited by Maaike van Berkel, Léon Buskens, and Petra Sijpesteijn, 129–79. Leiden: Brill, 2017.

———. *Der Kadi Und Seine Zeugen: Studie Der Mamlukischen Ḥaram-Dokumente Aus Jerusalem*. Abhandlungen Für Die Kunde Des Morgenlandes, Bd. 85. Wiesbaden: Harrassowitz, 2013.

Mylod, Elizabeth J. "Latin Christian Pilgrimage in the Holy Land, 1187–1291." PhD diss., University of Leeds, 2013.

Nieuwenhuyse, S. Van. "The Uprising of Abū Rakwa and the Bedouins against the Fāṭimids." *Acta Orientalia Belgica* 17 (2003): 245–64.

Nirenberg, David. "Mass Conversion and Genealogical Mentalities: Jews and Christians in Fifteenth-Century Spain." *Past & Present* 174, no. 1 (February 2002): 3–41.

Oettinger, Karl. *Les Principaux manuscrits à peintures de la Bibliothèque Nationale de Vienne. [Described by Ernst Trenkler, Curt Holter and Carl Oettinger. With plates.]*. Paris: n.p., 1937.

Onimus, Clément. *Les maîtres du jeu: Pouvoir et violence politique à l'aube du sultanat mamlouk circassien (784–815/1382–1412)*. Paris: Éditions de la Sorbonne, 2019.

Orfali, Bilal. "Ḥayṣa Bayṣa." Online entry in EI-3, Encyclopaedia of Islam.

Ott, Claudia. *Metamorphosen des Epos: Sīrat al-Muǧāhidīn (Sīrat al-Amīra Dāt al-Himma) zwischen Mündlichkeit und Schriftlichkeit*. Leiden: Leiden University, Research School CNWS, 2003.

Outhwaite, Ben. "Letter (T-S 13J26.13)." Cambridge Digital Library. https://cudl.lib.cam.ac.uk/view/MS-TS-00013-J-00026-00013/1.

Özoğlu, Hakan. "State-Tribe Relations: Kurdish Tribalism in the 16th- and 17th-Century Ottoman Empire." *British Journal of Middle Eastern Studies* 23, no. 1 (1996): 5–27.

Palva, Heikki. "From qəltu to gələt: Diachronic Notes on Linguistic Adaptation in Muslim Baghdad Arabic." In *Arabic Historical Dialectology: Linguistic and Sociolinguistic Approaches*, edited by Clive Holes. Oxford: Oxford University Press, 2018.

Paul, Jürgen. "Ḥimāya Revisited." *Annales Islamologiques*, no. 54 (October 2020): 83–106.

———. "Local Lords or Rural Notables? Some Remarks on the Raʾīs in Twelfth-Century Eastern Iran." In *Medieval Central Asia and the Persianate World: Iranian Tradition and Islamic Civilisation*, edited by A.C.S Peacock and D. G. Tor, 174–209. London: I. B. Tauris & Co. Ltd., 2015.

Peacock, A.C.S. *Islam, Literature and Society in Mongol Anatolia*. Cambridge, UK: Cambridge University Press, 2019.

Petersen, Andrew. *Bones of Contention: Muslim Shrines in Palestine*. Singapore: Palgrave Macmillan, 2018.

Philipp, Thomas. *Acre. The Rise and Fall of a Palestinian City, 1730–1831*. New York: Columbia University Press, 2001.

Picard, Christophe. "Les élites rurales du monde Musulman Méditerranéen: les enjeux historiographiques." *Mélanges de l'École Française de Rome. Moyen Âge*, no. 124 (December 2012).

Pini, Nicolò. "Walls of Identities. Built Environment as a Social Marker." In *Living with Nature and Things: Contributions to a New Social History of the Middle Islamic Period*, edited by Bethany J. Walker and Abdelkader Al Ghouz, 375–400. Göttingen: V&R Unipress, 2020.

Pohl, Walter, and Helmut Reimitz. *Strategies of Distinction: The Construction of Ethnic Communities, 300–800*. Leiden: Brill, 1998.

Pohl, Walter. "Narratives of Origin and Migration in Early Medieval Europe: Problems of Interpretation." *Medieval History Journal* 21, no. 2 (2018): 192–221.

Poliak, A. "Les révoltes populaires en Égypte à l'époque des mamelouks et leurs causes économiques." *Revue des Études Islamiques* 8 (1934): 251–73.

Pomerantz, Maurice A. *Licit Magic: The Life and Letters of al-Ṣāḥib b. ʿAbbād (d. 385/995)*. Boston: Brill, 2018.

Prawer, Joshua. *Crusader Institutions*. Oxford: Oxford University Press, 1980.

Pringle, Denys. *The Churches of the Crusader Kingdom of Jerusalem: A Corpus*. Cambridge, UK: Cambridge University Press, 1993.

———. *Pilgrimage to Jerusalem and the Holy Land, 1187–1291*. London: Routledge, 2016.

———. *Secular Buildings in the Crusader Kingdom of Jerusalem: An Archaeological Gazetteer*. Cambridge, UK: Cambridge University Press, 2009.

Prochazka, Stephan. "Northern Fertile Crescent." In *Arabic Historical Dialectology: Linguistic and Sociolinguistic Approaches*, edited by Clive Holes, 64–95. Oxford: Oxford University Press, 2018.

Rapoport, Yossef, and Ido Shahar. "Irrigation in the Medieval Islamic Fayyum: Local Control in a Large-Scale Hydraulic System." *Journal of the Economic and Social History of the Orient* 55, no. 1 (2012): 1–31.

Rapoport, Yossef. "Invisible Peasants, Marauding Nomads: Taxation, Tribalism, and Rebellion in Mamluk Egypt." *Mamlūk Studies Review* 8, no. 2 (2004): 1–22.

———. "Problematizing Custom and Customary Laws"; "Whose Custom Is It?"; "On the Disinheritance of Women"; "Burying the Hatchet, Bedouin style," with links at Islamic Law Blog, https://islamiclaw.blog/2020/04/03/thank-you-yossef-rapoport/. Blog run by the Program in Islamic Law at Harvard Law School, published in March 2020.

———. "The Rise of Provincial Arab Ruling Families in Mamluk Egypt, 1350–1517." *Mamlūk Studies Review* 25 (2023): 127–60.

———. *Rural Economy and Tribal Society in Islamic Egypt: A Study of al-Nābulusī's Villages of the Fayyum*. The Medieval Countryside, volume 19. Turnhout: Brepols, 2018.

Reynolds, Dwight Fletcher. "Epic and History in the Arabic Tradition." In *Epic and History*, edited by David Konstan and Kurt A Raaflaub, 392–410. Oxford: Wiley-Blackwell, 2010.

———. *Heroic Poets, Poetic Heroes: The Ethnography of Performance in an Arabic Oral Epic Tradition*. Ithaca, NY: Cornell University Press, 1995.

Rice, D. S. "Inlaid Brasses from the Workshop of the Aḥmad al-Dhakī al-Mawṣilī." *Ars Orientalis* 2 (1957): 283–326.

Richards, D. S. *Mamluk Administrative Documents from St. Catherine's Monastery*. A.P.H.A. Memoires, no 5. Leuven; Walpole, MA: Peeters, 2011.

———. "The Qasāma in Mamlūk Society: Some Documents from the Ḥaram Collection in Jerusalem." *Annales islamologiques* 25 (1990): 245–84.

———. "Shāwar." Online entry in EI-2, Encyclopaedia of Islam.

———. "St. Catherine's Monastery and the Bedouin: Archival Documents of the Fifteenth and Sixteenth Centuries." In *Le Sinaï: De la conquête arabe à nos jours*, edited by Jean-Michel Mouton. Cairo: Institut français d'archéologie orientale, 2001.

Richardson, Kristina L. *Roma in the Medieval Islamic World: Literacy, Culture, and Migration*. London: I. B. Tauris, 2022.

Richter, Sigfried. "Importance of the Fayoum for Coptic Studies." In *Christianity and Monasticism in the Fayoum Oasis: Essays From the 2004 International Symposium of the Saint Mark Foundation and the Saint Shenouda the Archimandrite Coptic Society in Honor of Martin Krause*, edited by Gawdat Gabra, 1–9. Cairo: American University in Cairo Press, 2005.

Riley-Smith, Jonathan. "Some Lesser Officials in Latin Syria." *English Historical Review* 87, no. 342 (1972): 1–26.

Rizq, ʿĀṣim Muḥammad. *Khānqāwāt al-Ṣūfiyya fī Miṣr*. 2 vols. Cairo: Maktabat Madbūlī, 1997.

Robinson, David. *Muslim Societies in African History*. Cambridge, UK: Cambridge University Press, 2004.

Röhricht, Reinhold. *Regesta Regni Hierosolymitani, 1097–1291. Edidit R. Röhricht. (Additamentum.)*. Oeniponti [Innsbruck]: Libraria Academica Wageriana, 1893.

Rosenhouse, J. "Bedouin Arabic." In *Encyclopedia of Arabic Language and Linguistics*, edited by C.H.M. Versteegh and Mushira Eid, vol. 1, 259–69. Leiden: Brill, 2006.

Rouighi, Ramzi. *Inventing the Berbers: History and Ideology in the Maghrib*. Philadelphia: University of Pennsylvania Press, 2019.

Rubin, Jonathan. "The Debate on Twelfth-Century Frankish Feudalism: Additional Evidence from William of Tyre's Chronicon." *Crusades* 8 (2009): 53–62.

Ruhaak, Raymond. "An Analysis of What Fostered Resilience of the Irish Sea Gaels and the Bedouin of the Mamluk Frontier Leading up to the Black Death." In *Living with Nature and Things: Contributions to a New Social History of the Middle Islamic Periods*, edited by Bethany J. Walker and Abdelkader Al Ghouz, 221–58. Göttingen: Bonn University Press, 2020.

Rustow, Marina. "Formal and Informal Patronage among Jews in the Islamic East: Evidence from the Cairo Geniza." *Al-Qanṭara* 29, no. 2 (December 2008): 341–82.

———. *The Lost Archive*. Princeton, NJ: Princeton University Press, 2019.

Sabra, Adam. "Book Review: Hirschler, *The Written Word*." *Journal of Islamic Studies* 27, no. 1 (2016): 70–73.

———. "Local Power in an Imperial Context: The Rise and Fall of an Arab Shaykh in Sixteenth-Century Egypt." Forthcoming.

———. "The Rise of a New Class? Land Tenure in Fifteenth-Century Egypt: A Review Article." *Mamlūk Studies Review* 8, no. 2 (2004): 203–10.

———. "Sufism and Practice of Politics in Early Ottoman Egypt." In *The Mamluk-Ottoman Transition: Continuity and Change in Egypt and Bilād al-Shām in the Sixteenth Century*, edited by Stephan Conermann and Gül Şen, 471–88. Göttingen: V&R Unipress and Bonn University Press, 2022.

Sabraa, Tarek. "Ibn Qāḍī Shuhba (1377–1448): His Life and Historical Work." In *New Readings in Arabic Historiography from Late Medieval Egypt and Syria*, edited by Jo van Steenbergen and Maya Termonia, 189–234. Leiden: Brill, 2021.

Sadan, Joseph. "An Admirable and Ridiculous Hero: Some Notes on the Bedouin in Medieval Arabic Belles Lettres, on a Chapter of Adab by al-Râghib al-Iṣfahânî, and on a Literary Model in Which Admiration and Mockery Coexist." *Poetics Today* 10, no. 3 (1989): 471–92.

Sajdi, Dana. "From Diyārāt to Ziyārāt: Transmutations of the Sacred Landscape in Syria." *Journal of Arabic Literature* 53 (2022): 216–45.

Salameh, Khader Ibrahim. *Qaryat Zakariyā*. Ramallah: 2013.

Saleh, Abdel Hamid [= Ṣāliḥ, ʿAbd al-Ḥamīd]. "Mihmindār." Online entry in EI-2, Encyclopaedia of Islam.

———. "Quelques remarques sur les Bédouins d'Égypte au Moyen Âge." *Studia Islamica* 48 (1978): 45–70.

———. "Les relations entre les Mamluks et les Bédouins d'Égypte." *Annali Istituto Orientale di Napoli* 30, no. 40 (1980): 365–93.

———. *Taʾrīkh al-Qabāʾil al-ʿArabiyya fī Miṣr*. Cairo: 2009.

Saleh, Mohamed. "On the Road to Heaven: Taxation, Conversions, and the Coptic-Muslim Socioeconomic Gap in Medieval Egypt." *Journal of Economic History* 78, no. 2 (June 2018): 394–434.

Saleh, Walid. "Al-Biqāʿī." Online entry in EI-3, Encyclopaedia of Islam.

Sarıcık, Murat. *Niqābat al-Ashrāf fī al-Dawla al-ʿUthmāniyya*. Cairo: 2007.

Sato, Tsugitaka. "The *Iqṭāʿ* System of Iraq under the Buwayhids." *Oriens* 18 (1982): 83–106.

———. *State and Rural Society in Medieval Islam: Sultans, Muqtaʿs, and Fallahun*. Leiden: Brill, 1997.

Savage-Smith, Emilie, and Yossef Rapoport, eds. *An Eleventh-Century Egyptian Guide to the Universe:* The Book of Curiosities. Leiden: Brill, 2014.

Sharon, Moshe. *Corpus Inscriptionum Arabicarum Palaestinae*. 7 vols. Leiden: Brill, 2007.

Scheerlinck, Eline. "Procedures of Protection: Coptic Protection Letters and Village Life." *Annales Islamologiques*, no. 54 (October 2020): 15–30.

Schenk, Jochen G. "Nomadic Violence in the First Latin Kingdom of Jerusalem and the Military Orders." *Reading Medieval Studies* 36 (2010): 39–55.

Schine, Rachel. "Conceiving the Pre-Modern Black-Arab Hero: On the Gendered Production of Racial Difference in *Sīrat al-Amīrah Dhāt al-Himmah*." *Journal of Arabic Literature* 48, no. 3 (2017): 298–326.

Schuenemann, Verena J., Alexander Peltzer, Beatrix Welte, W. Paul van Pelt, Martyna Molak, Chuan-Chao Wang, Anja Furtwängler, et al. "Ancient Egyptian Mummy Genomes Suggest an Increase of Sub-Saharan African Ancestry in Post-Roman Periods." *Nature Communications* 8, no. 1 (May 2017): 15694.

Schultz, Warren C., "Barqūq, al-Malik al-Ẓāhir." Online entry in EI-3, Encyclopaedia of Islam.

Shomali, Mohammad Javad. "Arabic Legal Documents from the Fatimid Period and Their Historical Background." PhD diss., University of Cambridge, 2020.

Shoshan, Boaz. "Fāṭimid Grain Policy and the Post of the Muḥtasib." *International Journal of Middle East Studies* 13, no. 2 (May 1981): 181–89.

———. "On Popular Literature in Medieval Cairo." *Poetics Today* 14, no. 2, (1993): 349–65.

Shryock, Andrew. "Bedouin in Suburbia: Redrawing the Boundaries of Urbanity and Tribalism in Amman, Jordan." *Arab Studies Journal* 5, no. 1 (1997): 40–56.

———. *Nationalism and the Genealogical Imagination: Oral History and Textual Authority in Tribal Jordan.* Berkeley: University of California Press, 1997.

Shwartz, Ygal. "The Bedouin in Egypt during the Mamluk Period" [in Hebrew]. PhD diss., Tel Aviv University, 1987.

Sidelko, Paul L. "The Acquisition of the Landed Estates of the Hospitallers in the Latin East, 1099–1291." PhD diss., University of Toronto, 1998.

Silverstein, Adam J. *Postal Systems in the Pre-Modern Islamic World.* Cambridge, UK: Cambridge University Press, 2007.

Singer, Amy. *Palestinian Peasants and Ottoman Officials: Rural Administration around Sixteenth-Century Jerusalem.* Cambridge, UK: Cambridge University Press, 1994.

Sinibaldi, Micaela. "Settlement in Crusader Transjordan (1100–1189): A Historical and Archaeological Study." PhD diss., University of Cardiff, 2014.

Sinibaldi, Micaela, Ian Jones, Edna J. Stern, and Smadar Gabrieli. The Levantine Ceramics Project. https://www.levantineceramics.org/wares/491-medieval-modern-levantine-handmade-geometric-painted-ware-hmgp.

Sneath, David. "Tribe." In *Cambridge Encyclopedia of Anthropology*, edited by Felix Stein, Matei Candea, Hildegard Diemberger, Sian Lazar, Joel Robbins, Andrew Sanchez, and Rupert Stasch. Cambridge: Division of Social Anthropology, University of Cambridge, 2016.

———. *The Headless State: Aristocratic Orders, Kinship Society, and Misrepresentations of Nomadic Inner Asia.* New York: Columbia University Press, 2007.

Sowayan, Saad. "The Hilali Poetry in the Muqaddimah: Its Links to Nabati Poetry." *Oriente Moderno* 22, no. 2 (2003): 277–306.

Steenbergen, Jo van. "Mamlūk Sultanate." Online entry from EI-3, Encyclopaedia of Islam.

———. "Revisiting the Mamlūk Empire: Political Action, Relationships of Power, Entangled Networks, and the Sultanate of Cairo in Late Medieval Syro-Egypt." In *The Mamluk Sultanate from the Perspective of Regional and World History: Economic, Social and Cultural Development in an Era of Increasing International Interaction and Competition*, edited by Reuven Amitai and Stephan Conermann, vol. 17, pp. 77–108. Göttingen: Bonn University Press and V&R Unipress, 2019.

Steenbergen, Jo van, and Maya Termonia, eds. *New Readings in Arabic Historiography from Late Medieval Egypt and Syria: Proceedings of the Themed Day of the Fifth Conference of the School of Mamluk Studies.* Boston: Brill, 2021.

Steenbergen, Jo van, Patrick Wing, and Kristof D'hulster. "The Mamlukization of the Mamluk Sultanate? State Formation and the History of Fifteenth-Century Egypt and Syria, Part II: Comparative Solutions and a New Eesearch Agenda." *History Compass* 14, no. 11 (2016): 560–69.

Stern, Edna. "Pottery and Identity in the Latin Kingdom of Jerusalem: A Case Study of Acre and Western Galilee." In *Medieval and Post-Medieval Ceramics: Fact and Fiction. Proceedings of the First International Conference on Byzantine and Ottoman archaeology, Amsterdam, 21–23 October 2011*, edited by J. Vroom, 287–317. Ruenhout: Brepols, 2015.

Stern, Samuel Miklos. *Faṭimid Decrees: Original Documents from the Fatimid Chancery.* London: Faber & Faber, 1964.

Stewart, Frank H. "Tribalism." In *The Princeton Encyclopedia of Islamic Political Thought*, edited by Gerhard Böwering et al., 563–67. Princeton, NJ: Princeton University Press, 2013.

Stillman, Yedida Kalfon, and Norman Stillman. *Arab Dress: A Short History, from the Dawn of Islam to Modern Times*. Leiden: Brill, 2000.

Stillman, Yedida Kalfon. "Libās, Part I - In the Central and Eastern Arab Lands." Online entry in EI-2, Encyclopaedia of Islam.

Streck, M. "ʿArbān." Online entry in EI-2, Encyclopaedia of Islam.

Strehlke, Ernst Gottfried Wilhelm. *Tabulae Ordinis Theutonici*. Berlin, 1869.

Szombathy, Zoltán. "Fieldwork and Preconceptions: The Role of the Bedouin as Informants in Mediaeval Muslim Scholarly Culture (Second-Third/Eighth-Ninth Centuries." *Der Islam* 92/1 (2015): 124–47.

———. "Genealogy in Medieval Muslim Societies." *Studia Islamica*, no. 95 (2002): 5–35.

———. *The Roots of Arabic Genealogy: A Study in Historical Anthropology*. Piliscsaba: The Avicenna Institute of Middle Eastern Studies, 2003.

Talmon-Heller, Daniella. "Graves, Relics and Sanctuaries." *ARAM Periodical* 18–19 (2006–7): 601–20.

———. *Islamic Piety in Medieval Syria: Mosques, Cemeteries and Sermons under the Zangids and Ayyūbids (1146–1260)*. Vol. 7. Boston: Brill, 2007.

———. "The Shaykh and the Community: Popular Hanbalite Islam in 12th–13th Century Jabal Nablus and Jabal Qasyun." *Studia Islamica*, no. 79 (1994): 103–20.

Tannous, Jack Boulos Victor. *The Making of the Medieval Middle East: Religion, Society, and Simple Believers*. Princeton, NJ: Princeton University Press, 2018.

Tapper, Richard. "Tribe and State in Iran and Afghanistan: An Update." *Études Rurales*, no. 184 (1996): 33–46.

———. *The Conflict of Tribe and State in Iran and Afghanistan*. London: Croom Helm, 1983.

Taxel, Itamar. "Early Islamic Palestine: Toward a More Fine-Tuned Recognition of Settlement Patterns and Land Uses in Town and Country." *Journal of Islamic Archaeology* 5, no. 2 (January 2019): 153–80.

Taxel, Itamar, Orit Shamir, Paula Waiman-Barak, Willie Ondricek, and Etan Ayalon. "Early Islamic Crude Handmade Ware: New Insights on the Typology, Chronology and Provenance of a Southern Levantine Handmade Pottery." *Oxford Journal of Archaeology*, 41 (2022).

Taylor, Malissa. *Land and Legal Texts in the Early Modern Ottoman Empire: Harmonization, Property Rights and Sovereignty*. London: I. B. Tauris, 2023.

Tebes, Juan Manuel. "Investigating the Painted Pottery Traditions of the First Millennium BC Northwestern Arabia and Southern Levant: Contexts of Discovery and Painted Decorative Motives." *ARAM* 27, no. 2 (2015): 255–82.

Tekindağ, M. C. Şehabeddin. "ʿĪsā b. Muhannā." Online entry in EI-2, Encyclopaedia of Islam.

Tendler, Avraham S. "Horbat Zecharya: Preliminary Report, 14/11/2021." *Hadashot Arkheologiyot, Excavations and Surveys in Israel* 133 (2021).

Thesaurus d'Épigraphie Islamique, https://www.epigraphie-islamique.uliege.be/Thesaurus/, Fondation Max van Berchem Genève, 1998–2024.

Tillier, M., and Naïm Vanthieghem. *Bulǧusūq. Un village du Fayoum sous les Fatimides (IVe–Ve/Xe–XIe siècles)*. Leuven: Peeters, forthcoming 2026.

———. "La rançon du serment: un accord d'amiable au tribunal fatimide de Ṭalīt." *Revue des mondes musulmans et de la Méditerranée* 140 (2016): 53–72.

Tsafrir, Nurit. *Collective Liability in Islam: The ʿĀqila and Blood-Money Payments*. Cambridge, UK: Cambridge University Press, 2020.

Tuttle, Kelly. "Al-Ibshīhī, Bahāʾ al-Dīn." Online entry in EI-3, Encyclopaedia of Islam.

Van der Vliet, Jacques. "Reconstructing the Landscape: Epigraphic Sources for the Christian Fayoum." In *Christianity and Monasticism in the Fayoum Oasis*, edited by Gawdat Gabra, 79–89. Cairo: American University in Cairo Press, 2005.

Varisco, Daniel Martin. "Yemen's Tribal Idiom: An Ethno-Historical Survey of Genealogical Models." *Journal of Semitic Studies* 62, no. 1 (2017): 217–41.

Versteegh, C.H.M. *The Arabic Language*. 2nd ed. Edinburgh: Edinburgh University Press, 2014.

———. "Pidginization and Creolization Revisited: The Case of Arabic." In *Approaches to Arabic Dialects: A Collection of Articles Presented to Manfred Woidich on the Occasion of His Sixtieth Birthday*, edited by Martine Haak, 343–57. Leiden: Brill, 2003.

Voguet, Élise. *Le monde rural du Maghreb central: (XIVe–XVe siècles): Réalités sociales et constructions juridiques d'après les Nawāzil māzūna*. Bibliothèque historique des pays d'Islam 5. Paris: Publ. de la Sorbonne, 2014.

Vollers, K., and E. Littmann. "Aḥmad al-Badawī." Online entry in EI-2, Encyclopaedia of Islam.

Walker, Bethany J. "From Ceramics to Social Theory: Reflections on Mamluk Archaeology Today." *Mamlūk Studies Review* 14 (2010): 109–57.

———. "Jordan's Northern Highlands in the Later Islamic Periods: Rural Prosperity Beyond the Decapolis." In *Drawing the Threads Together: Studies on Archaeology in Honour of Karin Bartl*, edited by Alexander Ahrens, Dörte Rokitta-Krumnow, Franziska Bloch, and Claudia Bührig, 143–64. Münster: Zaphon, 2020.

———. "Khirba." Online entry in EI-3, Encyclopaedia of Islam.

———. "The Northern Jordan Project and the 'Liquid Landscapes' of Late Islamic Bilad al-Sham." In *Landscapes of the Islamic World: Archaeology, History, and Ethnography*, edited by Stephen McPhillips and Paul D. Wordsworth, 184–99. Philadelphia: University of Pennsylvania Press, 2016.

———. "Searching for a Home in Long-Abandoned Places: The Resettlement of Late Medieval Syria." In *Humanistische Anthropologie. Ethnologische Begegnungen in einer globalisierten Welt. Festschrift fur Christoph Antweiler zu seinem fünfundsechzigsten Geburtstag von seinem Freundinnen und Kolleginnen*, edited by Trang-Dai Vu, Oliver Pye, Hans Dieter Olschleger, and Günther Distelrath, 451–72. Bonn: V&R Press, 2021.

———. "Southern Syria." In *The Oxford Handbook of Islamic Archaeology*, edited by Bethany J. Walker, Corisande Fenwick, and Timothy Insoll. NY: Oxford University Press, 2020.

———. "Tall Hisban." *Archaeology in Jordan* 3 (2022), 35–37.

———. "The Tribal Dimension in Mamluk-Jordanian Relations." *Mamlūk Studies Review* 13, 1 (2009): 83–106.

Walker, Bethany, and Ben Dolinka. "Khirbet Beit Mazmil, Investigations of Medieval Jerusalem's Hinterland: Preliminary Report on the 2015 and 2017 Seasons." *Zeitschrift der Deutschen Palaestina-Verein* 136, no. 1 (2020).

Walker, Bethany, Sofia Laparidou, Annette Hansen, and Chiara Corbino. "Did the Mamluks Have an Environmental Sense? Natural Resource Management in Syrian Villages." *Mamlūk Studies Review* 20 (2017): 167–245.

Webb, Peter A. *Imagining the Arabs: Arab Identity and the Rise of Islam*. Edinburgh: Edinburgh University Press, 2017.

Weitz, Lev. "Fayyum Tribesmen and Country Lawyers: A 5th/11th-Century Arabic Sale of Guardianship Rights Concerning Ṭalīt." *Chronique d'Égypte* 98, no. 195–96 (2023): 337–56.

———. "Islamic Law on the Provincial Margins: Christian Patrons and Muslim Notaries in Upper Egypt, 2nd–5th/8th–11th Centuries." *Islamic Law and Society* 27, no. 1–2 (February 2020): 5–52.

Werthmuller, Kurt J. *Coptic Identity and Ayyubid Politics in Egypt, 1218–1250*. Cairo: American University in Cairo Press, 2010.

Wickham, Chris. *The Donkey and the Boat: Reinterpreting the Mediterranean Economy, 950–1180*. Oxford: Oxford University Press, 2023.

———. "How Did the Feudal Economy Work? The Economic Logic of Medieval Societies." *Past & Present* 251, no. 1 (May 2021): 3–40.

———. "The Power of Property: Land Tenure in Fāṭimid Egypt." *Journal of the Economic and Social History of the Orient* 62, no. 1 (December 2019): 67–107.

Williams, Greg. "Medieval Ceramics from Aswan." *Bulletin de liaison de céramique égyptienne* 28 (2019): 297–306.

Winter, Michael. *Egyptian Society under Ottoman Rule, 1517–1798*. London: Routledge, 1992.

Wood, Barry. "Panel from a Cenotaph." In *Discover Islamic Art*. Museum With No Frontiers, 2023. https://islamicart.museumwnf.org/database_item.php?id=object;ISL;uk;Mus02;49;fr.

Yazbak, Mahmoud. "The Politics of Trade and Power: Dahir al-ʿUmar and the Making of Early Modern Palestine." *Journal of the Economic and Social History of the Orient* 56, no. 4–5 (2013): 696–736.

Yıldız, Sara Nur. "Döger (Ghuzz)." Online entry in EI-3, Encyclopaedia of Islam.

Yosef, Koby. "Language and Style in Mamluk Historiography." In *New Readings in Arabic Historiography from Late Medieval Egypt and Syria*, edited by Jo van Steenbergen and Maya Termonia, 33–111. Leiden: Brill, 2021.

Zaborowski, Jason R., ed. *The Coptic Martyrdom of John of Phanijōit: Assimilation and Conversion to Islam in Thirteenth-Century Egypt*. Boston: Brill, 2005.

Zadeh, Travis E. *The Vernacular Qur'an: Translation and the Rise of Persian Exegesis*. Oxford: Oxford University Press, 2012.

Zimo, Ann E. "Us and Them: Identity in William of Tyre's Chronicon." *Crusades* 18 (2019): 1–19.

Zinger, Oded. "Meanderings in the Arabic Literary Genizot." *Intellectual History of the Islamicate World* 8, no. 2–3 (2020): 188–223.

INDEX